Forgotten SKILLS of Cooking

Darina Allen

Forgotten SKILLS of Cooking

Darina Allen

Kyle Books

Photography by Peter Cassidy

For all of my grandchildren

Joshua, Lucca, Willow, India,
Amelia, and Scarlet Lily...

Kyle Books
An imprint of Kyle Cathie Ltd
www.kylebooks.com
Distributed by National Book Network
(800) 462-6420

First published in Great Britain in 2009 by
Kyle Cathie Limited

ISBN 978-1-906868-06-2

Project editor **Jenny Wheatley**
Designers **Lucy Gowans** and **Carl Hodson**
Photographer **Peter Cassidy**
Illustrations **Lydia Hugh-Jones**
Home economist **Linda Tubby**
Stylists **Róisín Nield** and **Cynthia Inions**
Copy editors **Susan Rossi-Crean** and **Stephanie Evans**
Editorial Assistance **Catharine Robertson** and **Laura Wheatley**
Index **Alex Corrin**
Production **Gemma John**

A Cataloguing in Publication record for this title is available from Library of Congress.

Printed in Singapore by TWP.

Important note to readers
The information contained in this book is intended as a general guide and is not specific to
individuals or their particular circumstances. Many plants, herbs, seaweeds, funghi, and shellfish,
whether used externally or internally, can cause an allergic reaction in some people. Before trying
any remedies, herbal or otherwise, the reader is recommended to sample a small quantity first to
establish if there is an adverse reaction. Always seek medical advice if any symptoms persist. The
reader is further advised not to attempt self-treatment for serious or long-term problems without
consulting a qualified doctor. Neither the author nor the publisher can be held responsible for any
adverse reactions to the recipes, recommendations or instructions contained herein, and the use of
any remedy or herbal derivative is entirely at the reader's own risk.

Contents

Introduction 6

Foraging 14 · Fish 74 · Game 120 · Beef 150

Dairy 190 · Eggs and Poultry 234 · Pig 288

Lamb 330 · Vegetables, Herbs, and Salad 358

Preserving 420 · Desserts 490 · Cakes and Cookies 518

Bread 554 · Household Tips 582

Resources 584 · Index 586 · Acknowledgements 600

Introduction

I was fortunate to catch the end of an era. In my early childhood I used to go on holidays to my great aunt and uncle's farm in County Tipperary. Even in the 50s, Aunt Lil was still cooking over an open fire and baked a daily loaf of soda bread (which she called cake bread) in a bastible on the hearth. The cream was churned into butter twice or three times a week; I loved watching the butter pats being made and eagerly learned to roll them using wooden butter bats that were far too large for my tiny hands. Aunt Lil and Uncle Bob also killed a pig on the farm several times a year. Even though I was only nine or ten, I was delighted to be part of this ritual and wasn't at all squeamish; I just accepted it as everyday life. I was perfectly happy to stir the pig's blood so it didn't coagulate and wash out the intestines under the fresh spring water from the pump in the yard. I helped to salt the bacon and was fascinated by the sight of the hams hanging high up in the enormous chimney, to smoke slowly over the turf fire. Even then, this sort of work was unfamiliar to many of my friends, whose families had already abandoned these "old-fashioned" ways. But for me, these experiences were magical, and now, more than ever, I realize how lucky I was.

At home in County Laois, even though we were relatively self-sufficient, we weren't doing things as esoteric as killing pigs. We did, however, have a kitchen garden, a house cow, a flock of hens, and regularly fattened chickens for the table. There was always cooking going on in our house. With nine children, by the time we had finished clearing up after one meal it was almost time to start preparing for the next. Mummy baked brown soda bread every day, there was constantly something bubbling on the stove, and during summer and autumn I remember regular jam- and chutney-making sessions. The table was nicely laid for every meal. It was never a question of grab, gobble, and go – we all sat down and ate together around the kitchen table – we loved Mummy's food. It was rare at that time for people to discuss food – they just ate it. But Daddy would always remark on how good something was, and encourage us all to hug the cook. Looking back, I now realize that at a very early age I absorbed the universal truth that the way to everyone's heart is through their tummy!

I came to Ballymaloe after hotel school in Dublin and there I met Myrtle Allen, who is now my mother-in-law. I feel deeply fortunate that our paths crossed in life. I was inspired by her philosophy and I soaked up everything she said like a sponge. Along with my own mother, she has been the other great influence in my life and my cooking. Even in the late 1960s, when I arrived at Ballymaloe House, Myrtle held an unshakeable belief in and appreciation of the quality of our local ingredients at a time when many were convinced that Italian or French or Californian food had to be better than what we had here at home. Both women had a strong ethic of "waste not want not," as did many of their generation, something I continue to feel strongly about and which is reflected throughout this book.

During the 25 years I've been running the Ballymaloe Cookery School, I've noticed an alarming loss of skills in many students. The art of thrifty housekeeping has gradually petered out and became strangely unfashionable. Our mothers and grandmothers knew how to eke out a small budget to feed a family, and how to make a delicious meal from meager leftovers. Given a chicken or a fish, they would have simply rolled up their sleeves and got on with eviscerating or filleting it. It mightn't have been perfect but they just did it in their pragmatic way. The loss of these and other such skills over subsequent generations is partly a consequence of the availability of convenience foods. Every time we go to the supermarket, an increasing number of items are oven-ready or ready-to-eat: cheese is grated, mushrooms sliced, fruit segmented – I swear if they sold toast we'd buy it.

The actual incident that prompted me to start the Forgotten Skills courses happened in the Cookery School about seven or eight years ago when I came across a student who was just about to dump her over-whipped cream into the hens' bucket. She was totally unaware that she had inadvertently made butter. I rescued it just in time and in a matter of minutes made it into butter pats, much to the delight of the class, most of whom didn't realize that butter is made from cream. This reinforced my belief that even many country dwellers have lost the connection with how their food is produced. This is also apparent when lovely, bright inquisitive children come on school tours to visit the farm and gardens. They are always excited by the hens and pigs and cows and all the vegetables, but it's obvious that many are no longer able to identify even fairly common plants like rhubarb, spinach, or elderflowers – and they are longing to learn.

Forgotten Skills courses

Foraging has been a passion and a pastime of mine ever since I was a child – it was part of the natural rhythm of the year and something that we all took completely for granted. Yet in later years, I found that when I came back from a walk with some berries or a bunch of wild greens, students would be intrigued and curious. I realized that the skill of identifying food in the wild, something that I had grown up with, was no longer common knowledge. In the early 1990s I decided to put a foraging course on our schedule called "A Walk on the Wild Side with Darina Allen" and people have been flocking to it ever since.

I started the other Forgotten Skills courses much later, in 2005, in response to the "butter incident" and to questions like, "Can you show me how to skin a rabbit or pluck a pheasant?" These questions came not from "old grannies" like me, but from hip young students, and I realized there was a deep craving among the younger generation to reconnect with these forgotten skills. The series of courses now includes "How to Keep a Few Chickens in the Garden," "How to Make Butter, Yogurt, and Simple Cheese" and "Growing your own Organic Vegetables." I make what is hopefully a convincing argument in the vegetables chapter for the benefits of growing your own food, but let me just say here that urban dwellers can still enjoy the pleasures of the country. Even if you live on the 10th floor, don't deny yourself the thrill of growing something. To tend, harvest, and finally eat a crop you've planted is a delight to that frustrated farmer in all of us, and you'll be amazed by the proud glow you get when you survey your shelf of jam or pickles.

Another course that's caused great excitement from the outset is "How to Keep a Few Chickens in the Garden." I always used to say that you could drive the length and breadth of Ireland and scarcely see a hen, unlike in France, Spain, and Italy where, in many rural areas, people still cultivate a kitchen garden and keep a few hens and often rear a few plump rabbits for the table as well. Happily, in a few short years, thousands of people have rediscovered the joy of keeping hens and recycling their food scraps to produce the kind of eggs that are, for many, almost a forgotten flavor.

I remember the day we butchered one of our own organic pigs and used every scrap of it in the time-honored way – it was one of the most

thrilling experiences I've had at the Cookery School. And as we worked I was delving deep into my store of childhood memories of the process on my great uncle's farm in County Tipperary. I also remember how intimidated yet excited I felt as we tentatively experimented with salami and chorizo for the first time – we couldn't wait to taste it – and I could hardly believe how good it was and how easy it had been to make. Our first dry-cured ham was even more tantalizing because we had to wait for a whole year to find out whether it had worked or not. When the big moment came, it was a mixture of relief and sheer delight to discover how delicious and flavorful the slivers of our very own prosciutto were. We continue to experiment and enjoy passing on the skills to others on our "How to Cure a Pig in a Day" course.

As the courses developed, we began linking traditional skills and recipes with new ingredients, or new machinery or gadgets that often make the old skills far easier. New ingredients have lifted many of the old recipes into a fresh arena of flavor, which makes them all the more exciting. Tradition grows and changes, but of course we need to start with the tried-and-tested, the wisdom and knowledge that have survived through generations.

Eating good food in season

It's not easy for young people who are accustomed to finding all manner of fruits and vegetables in their supermarkets year-round to know when things are in season. I remember vividly a student asking me a few years ago, "How exactly do you tell when something is in season?" It was a perfectly logical question from her point of view but I was stunned. It hadn't occurred to me until then how difficult it is to work it out, particularly for those living in urban areas who are even further removed from the reality of the agricultural year. But when you grow your own or shop at farmers' markets you will quickly become familiar with the seasons. The fact is that fruit and vegetables out of season always disappoint and are invariably much more expensive. For example, I rarely use tomatoes in the colder months as they are hard and disappointing. I will replace them with something else – I make a salad with winter vegetables instead of tomatoes, while in cooked dishes I might use canned tomatoes or tomato paste made with tomatoes preserved in the summer. I have a gut feeling that the foods that are in season are the foods our bodies need at that particular time of year. What can be better, for example, than good, strong, iron-rich kale in winter time? And you'll discover the excitement of tasting the first stalks of rhubarb, fava beans, or tart green gooseberries of the year.

At home in Ballymaloe, we often sit down to a plate of food where absolutely everything on the plate, including the butter and cream, is produced on the farm or by our neighbors, so we feel much blessed. It's rare nowadays to say grace before a meal but I always loved the Quaker concept of silently giving thanks for your food before you eat, and I like to continue that tradition.

There's no reason why every meal shouldn't be a celebration. When my mother died, a neighbor came up to me with one of her fond memories. "Your mother could never understand people who could sit down at the table with the milk bottle and a pound of butter, still in its wrapper," she said. "She always laid the table properly, with a little vase of flowers, as if the Queen of England was coming to dine!"

Thrifty cooking

I remember life before electricity – I was nine when electricity came to our village in the Irish countryside. There were no fridges or freezers, and for that matter, no "best-before" or "sell-by" dates either. People bought foods little and often, and used their common sense to judge whether food was fresh or spoiled. The introduction of best-before dates on packaging started out as a good idea, but in reality this system has served to de-skill us, as it has undermined our confidence and ability to judge for ourselves when food is safe to eat. In the process, we have inadvertently handed over the power to make such decisions to multinationals and food manufacturers who, out of necessity, have to be conservative in their judgement. Consequently, over 30 percent of the food we buy is thrown into the garbage and a high percentage of that is still perfectly safe to eat.

Trust your senses. Look at food. Smell it. Taste it – if in doubt, just have a small taste. A piece of meat that smells a little high might just need a wash. A piece of cheese with mold on it might just need to be trimmed. When I was young, if we came across some mold in a pot of jam we were told to just stir it in – "It's penicillin, it'll do you good!" I don't know if that was true or not, but we survived to tell the tale.

Nowadays, provided the fruit was organic, I wouldn't throw out the jam, I would just scrape the mold off and carry on. But if the fruit was of questionable provenance, I might be a bit more drastic.

Strange as it may sound, it can be beneficial to challenge your body with bacteria that will strengthen your immune system. Constantly eating sterile food tends to weaken your resistance, so when you eat something naturally produced with an enhanced bacteria level, it may make you ill.

I'd also like to dispel the idea that food made from leftovers is of lesser value and ought to be served up with an apology. It can give a cook enormous satisfaction to create another appetizing meal from the remains of the last. Throughout the book, I've included many ideas for using up leftovers in a delicious way.

The other gratifying skill worth reviving is that of knowing how to identify and cook with cheaper cuts of meat. This often involves slow cooking, which may sound impossibly time-consuming but remember, it takes time, but not *your* time. The flavor and melting texture, not to mention the money saved, certainly make the effort worthwhile. I've included several recipes to whet your appetite.

A recurring theme throughout this book is the art of cooking from scratch, the value of which can be hard to convince people about these days. When you bake your own bread or make yogurt, there's a wonderful feeling of satisfaction which is quite unlike the buzz you get from snipping off the top of a packet and reheating something in the microwave.

Reconnecting with the older generation

I've been writing this book on and off for several years and one day, when I was scribbling away at the kitchen table, my youngest daughter Emily breezed in and remarked, "Mum, don't you think some of those skills may have been forgotten for a very good reason?" She may have a point, but now that I'm a grandmother many times over, I'm more aware than ever of the importance of passing on cooking skills to future generations.

There's a Mother's Day and a Father's Day, but grandparents are so often taken for granted and don't feel as though their skills are relevant any longer. I felt this was such a waste that I started to campaign for a

Grandmother's Day in Ireland. Slow Food suggested that it be an international Grandmother's Day in April. There are still some old-timers out there, collecting carrageen moss or growing traditional varieties of fruit or whisking up their sponge cakes by hand, and we should seek them out before they disappear. The Irish Countrywoman's Association, for instance, has for years acted as custodian of these traditions, with women sharing favorite recipes, tips for good cultivation and their best cake recipes. Like the Women's Institute, this organization has been at the forefront of preserving and handing on the traditional ways. The newer Slow Food movement, which originated in Italy but is now worldwide, also works on preserving and developing forgotten skills.

So many of our happiest childhood memories are connected to food. Picnics by the sea, afternoon tea with Granny, Mammy's lamb stew, or treacle pudding around the kitchen table. How many times have I heard, "I remember Aunt Margie used to make a wonderful apple pie. I wish I'd asked her for the recipe." So don't leave it until it's too late. Maybe even start a little booklet of favorite family recipes and add to it from time to time. It'll make a terrific and worthwhile present for your youngsters when they eventually leave home.

In the past 20–30 years, many people have concentrated on careers and a certain set of academic skills. The subliminal message coming through our educational system, and in many cases from parents as well, was that cooking and gardening were skills that one shouldn't be bothered with and would never need to know. But the path of life doesn't always run smoothly and so many confident young people who were riding the crest of a wave are suddenly forced to face the reality that they are virtually helpless in a changed situation. So part of the mission of this book is to urge parents and grandparents not to allow any more of our young people to leave home without the life skills they need, not only to survive, but also to enhance the quality of their lives. With oil supplies diminishing and energy prices rising, we are likely to need these skills even more in the future.

The other reason for writing this book was to provide a resource for the growing number of farmers and food producers with excellent raw materials who are interested in adding value to their produce. There is also a new generation whose interest in artisan food production has taken them to careers in small-scale cheese making, meat curing, or beer brewing. If we want to keep them alive, we need to support them too. I hope this book will be a valuable resource for them all.

Foraging

When I was a child, foraging was a way of life, a part of every year – I just didn't know back then that it was called foraging. Every spring we used to go down to the chapel meadows outside our village to pick fresh watercress. Come autumn, we'd pick blackberries and collect damsons around the old castle in the village and go up to the top of Cullohill Mountain around Lughnasa to collect first herts (wild blueberries) and then hazelnuts in September. We picked wild mushrooms too, in August and September. Some years there were none; other years, the fields were white with mushrooms, something you rarely see nowadays because of the overuse of fertilizers and pesticides.

When I came to Ballymaloe, local children with shiny, expectant faces would tiptoe shyly up to the back door holding tin cans full of berries and sloes. Myrtle Allen would weigh them and pay the children and incorporate the fruit into her menu. It was only when I went to Canada for the first time in the 1990s and visited the Sooke Harbour House on Vancouver Island that I realized that something I'd been doing since childhood suddenly had a lot of cachet! The menu of this gourmet waterside hotel included phrases like "Salad of wild greens foraged by so-and-so" and boasted its own in-house forager who would collect wild food from the woods and fields.

Since then, we've incorporated foraging into our curriculum and now offer a one-day course called "A Walk on the Wild Side." Going for walks gets a lot more interesting once you can identify edible plants that previously just looked like weeds. The course is always filled with people who are thrilled to learn about all the things they never dreamed could be so delicious to eat: nettles, wild garlic, burdock, and much more.

People normally connect foraging with autumn, "the season of mellow fruitfulness," but in reality you can forage all year round for things like wild sorrel, watercress, and some seaweeds and shellfish. A really important consideration is that foraging should be sustainable: take only what you need and harvest it in a way that ensures the future survival of the species.

If you're interested in foraging but don't know much about it, check local notices for tutored walks or mushroom hunts. And don't forget the obvious resource: older people for whom foraging was common practice – as it was for me.

Until recently, we in Ireland were deeply suspicious of mushrooms, restricting ourselves to field mushrooms, which come in great waves of feast or famine. Now that a few chefs and mushroom enthusiasts have sparked a wide interest in the multiplicity of available and edible species, we realize that the woodlands and forests can be treasure troves all year long.

I have a real feeling that wild foods may well contain vital minerals and trace elements that have vanished from intensively produced foods. And there may be other benefits. It is known, for example, that some wild seeds contain more fat, protein, or carbohydrates than farmed seeds. After all, they have to be naturally strong and healthy in order to survive – in the wild, "survival of the fittest" really applies. Wild foods flourish, receiving their nourishment in appropriate amounts, without chemicals and fertilizers. They grow where conditions favor them, surviving and thriving off the natural environment.

This chapter could quite easily have been a book in itself and I've just included the more common and easily accessible plants, berries, and so on. But once you get started you'll find that foraging can become addictive and you might want to invest in a good book on the subject. Check Resources (see page 584) for more information.

A WORD TO THE WISE

Undeniably, some species of mushrooms are extremely poisonous, so don't be foolhardy; it's well worth going on wild mushroom hunts with trained people before venturing out on your own. But don't let the fact that a few species happen to be poisonous keep you away from discovering the incredible variety of flavors available for the gathering. Consult a few well-illustrated books to be doubly sure. Once you find your secret caches, you might even find yourself turning into one of these people who becomes incredibly secretive and won't let anyone else come along. Be streetwise about where you forage. Avoid busy roads, where exhaust fumes may have settled on the flora. Also, I wouldn't be madly keen to forage on land that's likely to have been chemically sprayed, for example adjacent to intensively grown field crops or commercial orchards. But I would urge farming families to consider planting damsons, crabapples, hawthorn, elder, even gooseberries and red currants in the hedgerows around their farms as people did long ago, not only to enhance biodiversity but for the joy of foraging.

Wild Greens

In many cultures around the world, people know and understand the importance of incorporating wild greens into their diet – in Greece and southern Italy, for example. I have lovely memories of visits to Greece and seeing old women clad in black shawls, walking along the road with a basket, collecting roadside greens or *horta*. I remember stopping and asking the women what they were picking, even though we couldn't speak the same language. In some places I've traveled to, wild greens actually cost more to buy than meat! Although there may not be scientific research to prove it, I'm sure that there is an incredible variety of nutrients in these greens.

FORAGER'S SALAD

Make a beautiful salad with leaves and flowers that you pick on walks. Taste as you go along, so that you end up with a balanced set of flavors. Wild garlic and dandelion can be quite bitter or astringent, so go light on those.

selection of leaves (consider watercress, bitter cress, salad burnet, sorrel, dandelion, chickweed, wild garlic, pennywort, young primrose leaves, or fat hen)

edible flowers to garnish (violets, wild garlic flowers, borage, primroses, nasturtiums, or marigolds)

FOR THE DRESSING
¼ cup extra virgin olive oil
1 tablespoon balsamic or Cabernet Sauvignon red wine vinegar
pinch of sea salt and cracked pepper
1 garlic clove, crushed

Rinse and carefully dry the leaves. Mix the olive oil, balsamic vinegar, and crushed garlic. Season with salt and pepper to achieve a tasty dressing. Mix the greens in a large bowl and toss with enough dressing to make the leaves glisten. Scatter the flowers over the top and enjoy!

FORAGER'S SOUP

Here's the formula that we use to make a soup from foraged greens. The flavor is a surprise every time, depending on the combination. Don't overdo the very bitter herbs, like dandelion · SERVES 6

4 tablespoons butter
1 cup diced onion
1 medium potato, peeled and diced
2 cups Chicken Stock (see page 262), Vegetable Stock (see page 390), or hot water
1½–2 cups creamy milk (use ¼ heavy cream and ¾ whole milk), brought to boiling point
9oz chopped wild greens (nettles, wild sorrel, young dandelions, wild garlic, borage, wild arugula, nasturtium leaves, poppy leaves, watercress)
extra virgin olive oil
3oz chorizo or bacon, chopped
wild garlic flowers, if available

Melt the butter in a heavy-bottomed saucepan. When it foams, add the diced onion and potatoes and stir until well coated. Sprinkle with salt and freshly ground pepper. Cover with a piece of parchment paper (to trap the steam) and the saucepan lid, and cook over low heat for 10 minutes until the vegetables are almost soft but not colored. Discard the paper lid and add the hot stock and boiling milk. Return to a boil and cook until the potatoes and onions are fully cooked. Add the greens and boil uncovered for about 2–3 minutes until the greens are just cooked. Do not overcook or the soup will lose its fresh green color. Purée the soup in a blender. Taste and correct seasoning.

Heat a little oil in a frying pan. Add the diced chorizo or bacon, cook over medium heat until the fat starts to run and the bacon is crisp. Remove the pieces and drain on paper towels. Sprinkle over the soup, drizzle with the chorizo oil, and serve, scattered with a few wild garlic flowers, if available.

Opposite: *Forager's Soup.*

My Foraging Year

I've put sorrel first because it is one of the wild greens that can be found just about all year round. The rest of the greens are in order of seasonal appearance.

Sorrel *(Rumex acetosa)*

PARTS TO USE: leaves

WHEN TO PICK: early spring–late autumn

Sorrel is one of the most widely available wild plants, so it's perfect for foraging. You'll find it on grassland, along banks, dunes, and cliffs, especially in iron-rich soil. It resembles spinach – you will recognize it by its pointy leaves on stems that sprout from the base of the plant. Some of the most common varieties are common sorrel, lambs' tongue or sheep sorrel (gorgeous in salads), buckler leaf sorrel (use them whole), and wood sorrel (high in oxalic acid). It has a lovely lemony taste that wakes you up: a sudden little electric shock in a salad. A few leaves of wild sorrel are delicious added to homemade lemonade and it makes a wonderful soup. Sorrel is a diuretic, an antiseptic, it cools fevers, and people say you make a poultice out of it to get rid of a skin cancer. Years ago, people used wild sorrel as a substitute for apples in turnovers, using lots of brown sugar. Sorrel is in season between gooseberries and apples.

POTATO AND SORREL SOUP

Potatoes are a wonderful foil for the clean, crisp, lemon flavor of sorrel. Use the basic formula for Forager's

Above: *Sorrel.*

Soup on page 18 and add 2oz fresh sorrel leaves just before puréeing. It loses its fresh green color and goes brown on contact with heat, but still tastes delish.

PORK, SORREL, AND FRESH HERB TERRINE

This terrine tastes different every time we make it, depending on the variety of herbs used. It should be highly seasoned before it is cooked, otherwise it may taste bland when cold. Use organically produced greens, meat, egg, and herbs if possible ·
SERVES ABOUT 10

1lb pork belly
4oz pig's liver
3oz Canadian bacon or ham
3oz bacon
1 medium onion, finely chopped
1 tablespoon butter
¾ lb sorrel (add watercress and spinach if you don't have the full amount)
1 garlic clove, chopped
1 organic egg, beaten
salt, freshly ground black pepper, and grated nutmeg, to taste
3 tablespoons freshly chopped herbs (e.g. basil, marjoram, parsley, chives, and a little less of rosemary and thyme)

1 terrine or loaf pan, about 8 x 4in

Grind together all the meat. Cook the onion in the butter over low heat. Stem and rinse the leaves, then cook in the water that clings to the leaves until soft. Don't worry when the sorrel turns brown – it's meant to. Drain very well and chop. Allow to cool. Mix all the ingredients together thoroughly in a bowl, adding the seasoning and herbs to taste. Cook a little piece of the mixture in a pan, taste, and correct seasoning if necessary.

Preheat the oven to 350°F. Put the mixture into the terrine or loaf pan, cover with a lid or aluminum foil, and bake for about 1 hour in a double boiler. About 15 minutes before the end of cooking time remove the cover to allow the top to brown slightly. Serve warm or cold with crusty bread, a salad of organic leaves, and some delicious pickles and relishes. We particularly like Beet and Ginger Relish (see page 439), Onion Jam (see page 450), and Sweet Cucumber Pickle (see page 488).

Ground-elder
(Aegopodium podagraria)
PARTS TO USE: leaves
WHEN TO PICK: spring
This pernicious "weed" grows with vigor and enthusiasm in damp, shady places throughout the British Isles. The good news for all of us, including me, is you can eat it and enjoy it all the more because it is such a pest in so many gardens. Ground-elder is best harvested in spring before it flowers: the young leaves can be added to the green salad bowl and are also delicious cooked like spinach and tossed in butter or extra virgin olive oil. We also make a delicious Forager's Soup with it (see page 18). Herbalists, like John Evelyn and Nicholas Culpeper, wrote of its ability to cure gout and sciatica, hence one of its popular names, "goutweed," or "bishop's goutweed."

Burdock (Arctium minus)
PARTS TO USE: leaves, stems, and roots
WHEN TO PICK: leaves and stems in spring, roots in autumn
If you believe the herbalists, there's nothing – from baldness to acne to syphilis – that burdock won't cure. Common or lesser burdock stems are lined with red, the leaves are heart-shaped and the flower heads stick in your hair and your clothes like Velcro. Common throughout Britain, most of Europe, and America, burdock is found in woodland margins and on waste ground. The fresh, young stems can be boiled and eaten with melted butter, or eaten raw in a salad. The leaves can be cooked like spinach, and the root can be peeled and boiled in salted water, then sautéed in butter, much like Jerusalem artichokes.

Chickweed (Stellaria media)
PARTS TO USE: leaves
WHEN TO PICK: spring and autumn
Chickweed grows abundantly all over these islands, and widely throughout the world. Like ground-elder, it can become a pest, so I was thrilled to discover it was edible and I now eat it with relish. Not only that, but I was amused to see it

Above: *Ground-elder surrounded by golden marjoram.*

being sold in the Union Square Greenmarket, a farmers' market in New York City, for green salads. It is delicious in the latter (see Forager's Salad, page 18) or with a mixture of cooked greens. Harvest it in spring with a pair of scissors. It gets straggly in summer, but recovers in autumn. Heavy frost will burn it, but it often shoots again. It grows up to 13in tall and has tiny white star-like flowers.

Chickweed also makes a delicious soup. Follow the Watercress Soup recipe (page 28).

Above: *Comfrey Fritters.*

Comfrey *(Symphytum officinale)*

PARTS TO USE: leaves

WHEN TO PICK: spring, before it flowers

Comfrey is a really important plant to know about, especially from a gardener's point of view. It has tremendous healing qualities and was known as "knitbone" in the past, as it draws out infections and multiplies healing cells when bones are broken. It occurs widely in damp, shady locations. Comfrey has broad hairy leaves and white, pink, and purple bell-shaped flowers. We mostly use it to make comfrey tea as a liquid garden feed (see page 366), and we throw in the occasional comfrey plant for the pigs – they love it! Comfrey has more potassium than farmyard manure and is especially good for growing potatoes; you can lay the fresh leaves right on top of the potato trenches (avoid using the flowering stems, as they can take root).

COMFREY FRITTERS

No one should eat too much comfrey, as it can cause liver toxicity, but these fritters, made from the young leaves, are delicious and nutritious – in small doses of course! This recipe is based on one of Roger Phillips' · SERVES 4

¾ **cup all-purpose flour**
pinch of salt
1 organic egg, separated
½ **cup tepid water**
young comfrey leaves (about 16, depending on size)
cayenne pepper or freshly roasted cumin seeds, crushed
hot oil for frying

Above: *Dandelion leaves.*
Below, right: *Haws and sloes often grow side by side in our hedgerows.*

Sift the flour and salt into a bowl, make a well in the center, and drop in the egg yolk. Add the water, mixing it in gradually with a whisk. Leave to stand. Whip the egg white to stiff peaks and fold into the batter. Pick the comfrey leaves, leaving a small amount of the stem, rinse and dry well, and dip the leaves into the batter. Deep-fry in hot oil until golden brown on both sides (work in batches to avoid overcrowding the pan). Drain on paper towels and serve sprinkled with salt and cayenne or cumin.

Dandelion
(Taraxacum officinale)
PARTS TO USE: young leaves
WHEN TO PICK: early spring
Dandelions are common throughout the northern hemisphere, and the bane of those who love their lawns. The young leaves are delicious in salads and can be added sparingly to soup. Dandelion is a well-known diuretic (its French name, *pissenlit,* reflects these qualities and always used to make my children giggle) and antioxidant. The flowers can also be used to make wine (see Preserves, page 466).

Hawthorn
(Crataegus monogyna)
PARTS TO USE: Leaves, flowers, and berries
WHEN TO PICK: spring to early summer; berries in autumn
The tender, young new leaves of hawthorn make a delicious addition to a green salad. It is another plant with wonderful health benefits: it is known to improve coronary blood flow and a healthy heart. Apart from adding the leaves (and, later, the flowers and berries) to salads, you can make a hawthorn tea: put a little fistful of young leaves into a teapot, cover with boiling water and allow to infuse for 3–4 minutes.

HAWTHORN BRANDY, GIN, OR VODKA

Like many other autumn berries, hawthorns benefit from a couple of nights' frost, but you can simulate this by putting them in a freezer for a couple of hours. Put into a bottle, top up with brandy, gin, or vodka. Allow to macerate for a few months.

Above: *Horseradish.*

Horseradish
(Armoracia rusticana)

PARTS TO USE: root and young leaves
WHEN TO PICK: all year round
The perennial horseradish grows wild in many parts of Europe and North America and its foliage resembles giant dock leaves. If you can't find it growing locally, plant some in your garden. It is very prolific, so be careful where you place it, as it can quickly become a pest. The root, which you grate, can be dug up at any time of the year; you'll need a spade, because it can be over 1ft long. If you're not going to use it immediately, store the root in peat or sand. The tall, shiny leaves are easy to identify from June onward, but they go down from about November to March. The fresh, young leaves, sliced thinly, are delicious added to potato salad. Horseradish often grows on old estates, where it might have escaped from walled gardens. There is a vast difference between fresh horseradish and the store-bought stuff, so it's well worth seeking out. Scrub the root well, peel, and grate it quickly on a Microplane because the fumes can really irritate your eyes. To preserve horseradish, see page 433.

HORSERADISH SAUCE

This is a fairly mild sauce. If you want to really clear the sinuses, increase the amount of horseradish! Serve with roast beef, smoked venison, or smoked mackerel · SERVES 8–10

3–6 tablespoons freshly grated horseradish (use a Microplane)
2 teaspoons white wine vinegar
1 teaspoon freshly squeezed lemon juice
¼ teaspoon English mustard powder
¼ teaspoon salt
lots of freshly ground black pepper
1 teaspoon sugar
1 cup softly whipped cream

Put the grated horseradish into a bowl with the vinegar, lemon juice, mustard powder, salt, freshly ground pepper, and sugar. Fold in the softly whipped cream, but do not overmix or it will curdle. The sauce keeps in the fridge for 2–3 days, covered, so that it doesn't pick up other flavors.

Nettle (*Urtica dioica*)

PARTS TO USE: leaves
WHEN TO PICK: spring
Stinging nettles grow in great profusion throughout the countryside in temperate regions all round the world, particularly in nitrate-rich soil. Gather them in spring when they are young and tender and not too strongly flavored.

Local herbalist Kelli O'Halloran told me that in parts of County Cork April 30 was once known as Michaelmas night, when young lads would parade through the streets carrying large bunches of nettles with which to sting their playmates and the occasional innocent bystander. The girls would join in, of course, to sting the boys they fancied and apparently everyone enjoyed themselves!

You'll need gloves to protect your hands. If you do get stung, rub with a dock leaf to relieve the pain – happily, they usually grow side by side. With their high iron and vitamin C content, nettles were prominent in folk medicine and, like many other wild foods, they helped in some small measure to alleviate hunger during the Irish famine. Among the older generation, the tradition of eating nettles four times during the month of May to clear the blood still persists. In fact, herbalists confirm that nettles contain iron, formic acid, histamine, ammonia, silica acid, and potassium. These minerals are known to help rheumatism, sciatica, and other pains. They lower blood pressure and blood sugar levels to increase the hemoglobin in the blood, improve circulation, and purify the system, so our ancestors weren't far wrong.

In more recent times, nettles have become a much sought-after ingredient for trendy chefs. We have been delighted by the demand for organic nettles at our stall at the farmers' market in nearby Midleton. They wilt quickly, so use them fast.

Sometimes we make nettle tea in exactly the way as comfrey tea (see page 366): the garden loves it!

IRISH NETTLE SOUP

This is a particularly good version of nettle soup · **SERVES 6**

3 tablespoons butter
½ cup chopped onions
1 medium potato, peeled and
    chopped
salt and freshly ground black
    pepper
1 quart Chicken Stock (see page
    262)
5oz young nettles, washed
    and chopped
½ cup whole milk

Melt the butter in a heavy saucepan. When it foams, add the chopped onion and potato, and toss them in the butter until well coated. Sprinkle with salt and pepper. Cover with a piece of parchment paper (to trap the steam) and the saucepan lid, and cook over low heat for 10 minutes, or until the vegetables are soft but not colored. Discard the parchment paper, add the stock, and boil until the vegetables are just cooked. Add the nettle leaves and simmer uncovered for just a few minutes. Do not overcook or the vegetables will lose their flavor. Add the milk and purée in a blender. Taste and correct seasoning if necessary. Serve hot.

Above: *Young nettles.*

NETTLE CHAMP
Substitute nettles for scallions in the Champ recipe on page 383. Take 4oz of chopped young nettle leaves and simmer in the milk for about 10–15 minutes until soft. Then continue as per the recipe.

ROGER'S NETTLE BEER

My research assistant Nathalie found this recipe in Roger Phillips' book, Wild Food. *It made delicious beer – sweet, fizzy, perfect for summertime. But she bottled it before it had finished fermenting, and one night, the glass bottles exploded. Oh well, practice makes perfect!* · **MAKES 3¼ GALLONS**

100 nettle stems, with leaves
3 gallons water
3lb granulated sugar
2oz cream of tartar
½ oz fresh compressed yeast

Boil the nettles in the water for 10 minutes. Strain, and add the sugar and the cream of tartar. Heat and stir until dissolved. Remove from the heat and leave until tepid, then add the yeast and stir well. Cover with muslin and leave for several days.

Remove the scum and decant without disturbing the sediment. Bottle, cork, and tie down.

Above: *Fat hen.*

Fat Hen *(Chenopodium album)*
PARTS TO USE: young, tender leaves
WHEN TO PICK: early spring
Fat hen, a swiftly growing annual "weed," occurs very widely in the world, especially in freshly cultivated rich soils or old dung heaps. It is also called dungweed, white goosefoot, lamb's quarters, or pigweed. It is sometimes confused with common orache (*Atriplex patula)* or its closely related cousin, Good King Henry (*Chenopodium bonus-henricus)*, but be sure not to assume that fat hen is another name for henbane, *Hyoscyamus niger,* which is a deadly poison! Fat hen and orache, like many other wild plants, have been eaten since ancient times and are known to contain iron, calcium, protein, and other trace elements. The young leaves of red orache are wonderful tossed into salads. Fat hen has been used as a pot herb for centuries, cooked like

spinach, and used, obviously, to fatten hens. Gather three or four times the amount you think you'll need because, like spinach, it diminishes in cooking. These plants are best eaten when young in the spring – if we don't keep on top of the weeds in our gardens it becomes a pest, so I eat it with great pleasure. To make fat hen soup, follow the Watercress Soup recipe (page 28).

Above: *Pennywort.*

Pennywort, Navelwort *(Umbilicus rupestris)*
PARTS TO USE: leaves
WHEN TO PICK: year round
The round, indented, fleshy leaves of pennywort are what you often see growing in the cracks of old stone walls and sometimes on old trees. You'll find it in Britain, France, and parts of the Mediterranean. I love to

nibble a few when I am hill-walking. They are delicious as part of a green salad or in sandwiches, which is perhaps why some people call them "bread and butter."

Above: *Tansy.*

Tansy *(Tanacetum vulgare)*
PARTS TO USE: leaves
WHNE TO PICK: early summer
Tansy, rumored to keep flies away, has little yellow flowers popping out from thin stems and frilly leaves. It grows in hedgerows, on wastelands and roadsides in most of Europe – and in my garden. Tansy has a quite distinctive, bitter flavor and may not be to everyone's taste. There are warnings not to eat it in large quantities because it can be toxic. However, used sparingly, it's good for cutting the fat in rich dishes, which is why traditionally, a little would have been added to drisheen blood pudding. At the Arbutus

Lodge in Cork, they used to serve drisheen with a tansy sauce. You can also dry the flowers for winter flower arrangements.

TANSY SAUCE

Add 1 tablespoon finely chopped tansy to 2 cups Béchamel Sauce (see page 116). Serve with drisheen, blood sausage, baked potatoes, pasta … or with boiled bacon or ham. It's a great combination for a change.

TANSY OMLETTE

A little bit of tansy really perks up an omelette and might be just the thing to cure a Sunday morning hangover! Add 1 teaspoon finely chopped tansy leaves to a two-egg omelette (see page 248) – it's surprisingly delicious.

Watercress
(Nasturtium officinale)

PARTS TO USE: leaves

WHEN TO PICK: spring and autumn

For those who like to be on the cutting edge, you may be interested to know that watercress is the new arugula! Chefs are going crazy for it and using it in all kinds of recipes. But in reality there's not much new under the sun. There are references to watercress – the original hydroponic vegetable – in many early Irish manuscripts. It formed part of the diet of hermits and holy men who valued its special properties, which we now know include significant amounts of iron, calcium, folic acid, and vitamins A and C. Watercress is brilliant for detox – the mustard oils boost and regulate the liver's enzymes. Its beta carotene and vitamin A are good for

healthy skin and eyes, and watercress is naturally low in calories and fat. Gram for gram, watercress has more iron than spinach, more vitamin C than oranges, and more calcium than whole milk. Legend has it that it was watercress that enabled St. Brendan to live to the ripe old age of 180! And Hippocrates, the father of medicine, chose the location of his first hospital so he could use only the freshest watercress to treat his patients.

Watercress grows naturally in most of Europe and North America. When you're looking for it in the wild, make sure the watercress you pick comes from a pure water source with constantly running water. Avoid water drained from fields that are grazed, especially by

sheep, which may infest the plant with the liver fluke parasite. Look for darker leaves, which signify older plants and deliver more peppery flavor. Watercress often grows side by side with a plant called fool's watercress (*Apium nodiflorum*), which is sometimes referred to as wild celery but it isn't, even though it is part of the parsley and celery family. It has small green flowers, whereas watercress has small white flowers. With watercress, the top leaf is the biggest and they decrease in size as you go down the stem; with fool's watercress, it's the reverse. When the watercress begins to form little white flowers the leaves elongate.

Below: *Wild watercress.*

WATERCRESS SOUP

Wild watercress has more depth of flavor than farmed versions, so see if you can find some. This soup has been a favorite on the menu of Ballymaloe House since it opened in 1963 ·
SERVES 6-8

2 tablespoons butter
½ cup chopped onion
1 medium potato, peeled and chopped
salt and freshly ground pepper
2 cups Chicken or Vegetable Stock (see pages 262 and 390), or hot water
2 cups whole milk
8oz chopped watercress (remove the coarse stems first)

Melt the butter in a heavy-bottomed saucepan, when it foams, add the chopped onion and potatoes and toss them until well coated. Sprinkle with salt and freshly ground pepper. Cover with a piece of parchment paper (to trap the steam) and the saucepan lid, and sweat over low heat for 10 minutes. Meanwhile, prepare the watercress. When the vegetables are almost soft but not colored, discard the paper lid and add the hot stock. Return to a boil and cook until the potatoes and onions are tender. Add the watercress and boil uncovered for 4–5 minutes, until the watercress is just cooked. Do not overcook or the soup will lose its fresh green color. Purée the soup in a blender. Taste and correct the seasoning.

WATERCRESS SALAD WITH DUCK EGGS AND OLIVES

This is a lovely little clean, fresh-tasting salad · **SERVES 4**

4 organic duck eggs
12 large black olives
2 parts watercress
1 part wild garlic leaves
1 part lamb's lettuce (mache)

FOR THE DRESSING
¼ cup olive oil
1 tablespoon balsamic vinegar
1 garlic clove, crushed
pinch of sea salt and cracked pepper

Hard-boil the eggs for 14 minutes in boiling salted water and chill under cold running water. Peel the eggs and separate the yolks, then finely chop the whites. Mix the olive oil, balsamic vinegar, and garlic. Season with salt and pepper to achieve a tasty dressing. Pit the olives and chop finely.

To assemble the salad: mix the greens in a large bowl and coat with enough dressing to make the leaves glisten. Divide the chopped egg whites between 4 large plates.

Place a bunch of the dressed leaves on each plate. Sprinkle the chopped olives around the salads and rub the egg yolks through a sieve over the salads to create a "Mimosa" effect. Serve immediately, with a few slivers of cheese, if you like.

Above: *Wild garlic* (Allium triquetrum).

Wild Garlic and Snowbell (*Allium ursinum* and *A. triquetrum*)

PARTS TO USE: leaves, flowers, and roots, although we mostly use the first two
WHEN TO PICK: late spring
Wild garlic has been used as a condiment or as part of a relish since earliest times throughout Britain and much of Europe. In the heyday of many large estates it was apparently quite common to plant it on the edges of woodland and pasture. In late spring the garlic was thought to have a beneficial effect on cattle and sheep when they were put out to grass after the long winter indoors. That said, the milk, cream, and butter from cows that have been eating wild garlic often has a tainted flavor, so dairy farmers are less enthusiastic about the wild garlic season.

There are two types of wild garlic, the wider leafed *Allium ursinum,* which grows in shady places along the banks of streams and in undisturbed mossy woodland, and *A. triquetrum,* known as the three-cornered leek or snowbell because it resembles white bluebells. This type of wild garlic is a native of southern Europe but it occurs in California and is now naturalized in southwest England where it is found along the sides of country lanes. Wild garlic lasts a few days when gathered into a bouquet and placed in water. It's easily over-used, so be sparse. Wild garlic butter melts deliciously over a piece of pan-grilled fish or meat, a chicken breast or a spring lamb chop. The chopped leaves are delicious in Champ (see page 383), broths, and pasta sauces, and you can use the pretty flowers in salads and as a garnish. In Germany, wild garlic is used to flavor schnapps and is believed to cure all ails.

Above: *Wild garlic (*Allium ursinum).

WILD GARLIC PESTO

We make this gorgeous pesto from April to mid-May. It's also good over salad leaves, goat cheese, bruschetta, and pasta. Sprinkle the flowers over the finished dish as a garnish ·
MAKES 2 X 8OZ JARS

2oz wild garlic leaves
3 tablespoons pine nuts (taste to make sure they are not rancid)
1 garlic clove, peeled and crushed
¾–1 cup olive oil
6 tablespoons finely grated Parmesan cheese
salt and sugar to taste

Pulse the wild garlic leaves, pine nuts, garlic, and olive oil in a food processor or pound together in a pestle and mortar. Remove to a bowl and fold in the grated Parmesan. Taste and season. Store, in a sterilized, covered jar in the fridge.

Clean the top and sides of the jar each time you dip in. Cover with a layer of extra virgin olive oil and the lid of the jar. Pesto also freezes well, but for best results don't add the grated Parmesan until it has defrosted. Freeze in small jars for convenience.

Variations
ARUGULA PESTO
Replace the wild garlic with arugula leaves.

BASIL PESTO
Replace the wild garlic with 4oz fresh basil leaves.

WATERCRESS PESTO
Replace the wild garlic with watercress.

KALE PESTO
Replace the wild garlic with blanched kale.

POTATO AND WILD GARLIC SOUP

In late April, the air in the top of Wilson's Wood, near our home, is heavy with the smell of wild garlic. The pretty white flowers mix with the bluebells and primroses. Wild garlic is used in this soup and the pretty flowers are divine, sprinkled over the top of each soup bowl · **SERVES 6**

3 tablespoons butter
1 medium potato, peeled and
    chopped
½ cup chopped onion
salt and freshly ground black
    pepper
3 cups Chicken or Vegetable Stock
    (see pages 262 and 390), or hot
    water
1 cup whole milk, heated
5oz wild garlic leaves, chopped
wild garlic flowers, for garnish

Melt the butter in a heavy-bottomed saucepan. When it foams, add the onion and potatoes and stir them until well coated. Sprinkle with salt and freshly ground pepper. Cover with a piece of parchment paper (to trap the steam) and the saucepan lid, cook over low heat for 10 minutes until the vegetables are almost soft but not colored.

Discard the parchment paper and add the hot stock or water and milk. Return to a boil and cook until the potatoes and onions are tender. Add the wild garlic leaves to the soup when the potatoes and onions are fully cooked. Simmer, uncovered, for 4–5 minutes until the wild garlic is cooked. Be sure not overcook or the soup

Above: *Spaghetti with Wild Garlic and Herbs.*

will lose its fresh green color.

Purée the soup in a blender. Taste and correct seasoning. Serve sprinkled with a few wild garlic flowers.

SPAGHETTI WITH WILD GARLIC AND HERBS

This is a little gem of a recipe. You can vary the herbs and the fats, and throw in choice bits like chanterelles or periwinkles or cockles, if you have any around · **SERVES 4-6**

1lb thin spaghetti

8 tablespoons butter, or butter and
   extra virgin olive oil

2 tablespoons chopped parsley

1 tablespoon chopped mint

2 tablespoons chopped wild garlic
   (leaves and bulbs)

2 tablespoons basil or lemon balm,
   chopped

4 garlic cloves, crushed

½–1 cup finely grated cheese,
   preferably Parmigiano Reggiano

chive flowers or wild garlic (leaves
   and bulbs) in season, for garnish

Cook the spaghetti in salted boiling water until al dente – about 10 minutes. Drain and return to the pan. Melt the butter in another pan and add all the herbs and the crushed garlic. Cook gently for no more than 2 minutes. Pour over the hot spaghetti, toss, and serve with grated cheese, preferably Parmigiano Reggiano, though we often use Irish Cheddar. Sprinkle chive flowers and wild garlic over the top for extra excitement.

Variations

• Add 8oz cooked sliced wild or cultivated mushrooms to the herbs and garlic – chanterelles are great
• Add some halved cherry tomatoes to the herbs and garlic and cook for 2–3 minutes
• Add 1 teaspoon red chile flakes to the herbs and garlic
• Add 4–8oz diced chorizo to the herbs and garlic

CRAB AND WILD GARLIC TART

This tart is incredibly rich, so serve small helpings with a big salad of organic greens · **SERVES 6**

FOR THE PASTRY

2 cups all-purpose flour

pinch of salt

8 tablespoons butter, cubed

beaten organic egg or egg yolk
   and a little water

FOR THE FILLING

2 organic eggs and 1 egg yolk,
   beaten together

1 cup heavy cream

1 teaspoon freshly grated ginger

1lb brown and white crabmeat,
   mixed (see page 114)

3oz wild garlic leaves, finely
   chopped

½ cup freshly grated Parmigiano
   Reggiano

salt and freshly ground black
   pepper

10–11in tart pan with a removable
bottom

First make the pastry. Sift the flour with the salt, and rub the butter into the flour using your fingertips. Keep everything as cool as possible – if the fat is allowed to melt, the finished pastry may be tough. When the mixture looks like coarse breadcrumbs, stop. Whisk the egg or egg yolk and add some water. Take a fork or knife (whichever you feel most comfortable with), and add just enough liquid to bring the pastry together, then use your hands to collect it into a ball – this way you can judge more accurately if you need a few more drops of liquid. Although rather damp pastry is easier to handle and roll out, the resulting crust can be tough and may well shrink out of shape as the water evaporates in the oven. The drier and more difficult to handle it is, the crispier the crust.

Cover the pastry with plastic wrap and leave to rest in the fridge for a minimum of 15 minutes. This will make the pastry much less elastic and easier to roll.

Preheat the oven to 350°F.

Roll the pastry out on a lightly floured board until ⅛in thick, then fit into the pan, trimming the pastry just a little above the rim. Line the tart shell with parchment paper and fill it to the top with dried beans to hold the paper in place. Bake for 15–20 minutes, then remove from the oven. Take out the beans and paper and set aside.

Meanwhile, whisk the eggs in a bowl. Add the cream, grated ginger, crabmeat, wild garlic, and cheese. Mix gently. Taste and correct seasoning. Pour mixture into the baked tart shell and continue to cook for 20–30 minutes at 350°F.

Remove from the pan to cool on a wire rack. Serve warm with a salad of organic leaves.

Wild Flowers

Leaves, roots, and wild herbs are not the only things you can gather to eat – the flowers of many plants are edible, too. Crystallized violets, wild rose petals, and bramble flowers make irresistible decorations for cakes and puddings or to pop into a glass of Prosecco. We use elderflowers in a myriad of ways to flavor cordials, syrup, granitas, and fritters. Edible wild flowers include cowslips, violets, primroses, wild fennel flowers, wild roses, daisies (*Bellis perinnis*), gorse, sweet cicely, jasmine, chamomile, crabapple blossom, hyssop, wild garlic flowers, wild sorrel flowers, elderflowers, and comfrey flowers.

Cowslip *(Primula veris)*

WHEN TO PICK: spring
Cowslip flowers have a wonderfully delicate flavor. Only use them if they really are abundant in your area. We are lucky enough to have hundreds in our wildflower meadow – I'd recommend you plant some yourself if you can.

COWSLIP FRITTERS

A delicate and delicious little dessert ·
MAKES ABOUT 20

crêpe batter (see page 580)
about 30 cowslip flowers
Clarified Butter (see page 216)
superfine sugar

Add cowslip flowers to the batter. Melt a little clarified butter in a frying pan over medium heat. Working in batches, put tablespoons of batter in the hot pan and tilt it to thin them out. Cook on one side until golden, then flip over and cook on the other side. Sprinkle with sugar and serve.

Left: *Primroses surrounded by herb Robert and ivy leaves.*

Violet
(Viola odorata, V. riviniana)

WHEN TO PICK: early spring
Violets appear early in spring and are gone in a couple of months. They grow in hedgerows, scrub and woodlands and have kidney-shaped leaves and long-stemmed purple flowers.

A Quaker brother and sister, Wilson and Lydia Strangman, once owned Kinoith, the beautiful Regency house and farm that we now live in. They grew a large patch of fragrant violets, which they used to pick and send on the Inishfallen boat from Cork to Covent Garden in London. When I started to restore the gardens here in the early 1970s, I gathered up all the remnants of the fragrant Parma violets I could find and made a violet bed. One of the bedrooms in our Pink Cottage is called the Violet Loft, because this was where the violets were arranged into little posies surrounded by leaves for people's lapels. We do not know of a better way to remember Lydia than to crystallize the little flowers to use as edible decorations.

See also the Violet and Vinegar Prosecco on page 427.

CRYSTALLIZED VIOLETS

The art of crystallizing flowers simply takes patience and a meticulous nature – the sort of job that drives some people around the bend, but which others adore. If it appeals to you, the work will be well rewarded, as they look and taste divine. Properly done, they will last for months. We store ours in a pottery jar or a tin box interleaved with parchment paper.

freshly picked, sweet-smelling
    violets
egg white
superfine sugar

an child's unused paint brush

Your sugar needs to be absolutely
dry, so for extra protection, sift it
onto a jelly roll pan and place in the
oven at 275°F for about 30 minutes.
Break up the egg white slightly with
a fork, but don't beat it much; it
doesn't need to be fluffy. Using a
clean pastry brush, brush the egg
white very carefully and sparingly
over each petal and into every
crevice. Then gently pour some
sugar over the violet so that every
part is coated with a thin, sugary
coating. Arrange the flower carefully
on a parchment paper-lined tray,
and continue with the remaining
violets. Allow the violets to dry
overnight in a warm dry place (say
over a radiator, or in an airing
cupboard).

Variations
There are other flowers – and leaves
– to crystallize: primroses, violas,
apple blossom, rose petals, mint,
lemon balm, lemon verbena, sweet
cicely, and rose geranium leaves.

LYDIA'S LEMON CAKE WITH CRYSTALLIZED VIOLETS AND ANGELICA

*This recipe comes from Lydia
Strangman, the former occupant of our
house mentioned opposite. We often
make this delicious, rich little cake. A
tiny slice is just perfect to nibble slowly
with a demi tasse of espresso or a cup
of China tea. We decorate it with
crystallized violets and angelica and
remember Lydia every time we enjoy it.
It keeps well in an airtight tin for
ages. If you have one, a loose-bottomed
pan is handy but not essential ·*
SERVES 10

1 cup ground almonds
1 cup confectioners' sugar
zest of 1 organic (unwaxed) lemon
    and juice of ½ lemon
½ cup all-purpose flour
3 organic egg yolks
9 tablespoons butter, melted and
    cooled

FOR THE ICING
1½ cups confectioners' sugar
zest and 1½ tablespoons freshly
    squeezed juice from 1 organic
    lemon

FOR THE DECORATION
Crystallized Violets (see recipe
    above)
Candied Angelica (see recipe
    on page 458)

7in shallow-sided round pan

Preheat the oven to 350°F. Grease
the pan well with melted butter and
dust with a little flour; tap out the
excess.
    Put the ground almonds,
confectioners' sugar, lemon zest, and
flour into a bowl and mix well.
Make a well in the center and add
the egg yolks, the cooled melted
butter, and the lemon juice. Stir until
the ingredients are thoroughly
mixed.
    Spread the cake mixture evenly
in the prepared pan, make a little

Above: *Wild violets* (Viola riviniana).

hollow in the center, and tap on
the countertop to release any large
air bubbles.
    Bake in the oven for about
20 minutes. The cake should still
be moist but cooked through. Allow
to rest in the pan for 5–6 minutes
before turning out onto a wire
rack to cool.
    Sift the confectioners' sugar into
a bowl, and mix to a thickish
smooth icing with the lemon juice
and zest. Spread it gently over the
top and sides of the cake using an
offset spatula dipped in boiling
water and dried. Decorate with the
crystallized violets and little
diamonds of angelica.

Above: *Elderflowers.*

Elder *(Sambucus nigra)*

WHEN TO PICK: spring–early summer
The common or black elder grows in profusion around the Irish countryside, as well as throughout Britain and much of Europe. In fact, elder is really easy to grow – even a twig pushed into the ground will root. If you have the space, it's really worth considering. The low-growing, bushy tree with its grayish-brown bark smells musty and unappealing, but its tiny white flower heads, hanging on reddish stems, are transformed with cooking and impart a delicious Muscat-like flavor to syrups, lemonades, cordials, tarts, sorbets, compotes, and more. The fact that elderflower tastes delicious and is so versatile is reason enough to gather it, but it is also known to contain antioxidants and is commonly used in remedies for hay fever, rheumatism, and the common cold. The elder tree was traditionally known as the "village pharmacy" and people were reluctant to cut it down. The roots, bark, leaves, and berries were all used medicinally and recent studies have shown that elderflowers have the ability to inactivate viruses. We've noticed a growing demand for organic elderflowers at our local farmers' market. See also recipes for Elderflower Cordial, Elderflower Bellini, Elderflower Fizz, and Elderflower and Green Gooseberry Jam (pages 469, 471, and 444).

ELDERFLOWER VINEGAR

This vinegar works well in salads and salad dressings. When heating the vinegar, do not leave it to boil or even simmer · MAKES 1 PINT

2 cups red or white wine vinegar
5 elderflower blossoms

Put the cold vinegar into a stainless-steel saucepan with the elderflower. Warm them together gently until just hot; do not let boil. Leave the vinegar to cool. Strain the liquid and put it back into its bottle.

ELDERFLOWER FRITTERS

These are very easy to make, very crispy and once you've tasted one, you won't be able to stop! Serve them with the Gooseberry and Elderflower Compote, below · SERVES 4

1 cup all-purpose flour
pinch of salt
1 organic egg
½ cup lukewarm water
8–12 elderflower heads
superfine sugar
sunflower oil for frying

Sift the flour and salt into a bowl. Make a well in the center and drop in the egg. Using a whisk, bring in the flour gradually from the edges, slowly adding in the water at the same time. Heat the oil in a deep fryer to 350°F. Hold the flowers by the stems and dip into the batter. Fry in the hot oil until golden brown. Drain on paper towels, toss in sugar, and serve immediately with gooseberry and elderflower compote.

GREEN GOOSEBERRY AND ELDERFLOWER COMPOTE

When the elderflowers come into bloom, then I know it's time to pick green gooseberries. They feel as hard as hailstones, but for cooking it's the perfect time. Enlist the help of little ones to top and tail the gooseberries · SERVES 8–10

2lb green gooseberries
2 or 3 elderflower heads
2 cups cold water
1lb granulated sugar

First, top and tail the gooseberries. Tie the elderflower heads in a little square of muslin or cheesecloth, put the bag in a stainless-steel or enamelled saucepan, add the sugar, and cover with cold water. Bring slowly to the boil and continue to boil for 2 minutes. Add the gooseberries and simmer just until the fruits burst. Let cool completely. Serve in a pretty bowl and decorate with fresh elderflowers.

Gorse *(Ulex europaeus)*

WHEN TO PICK: flowers in profusion in early summer (but you'll find some blooms almost all year round) As the old saying goes, "When the gorse is out of bloom, kissing's out of fashion!" The ubiquity of gorse – or furze as it is called in Ireland – around the Irish landscape, meant that it was once widely used as fuel, as fodder for livestock, to make fences, hurleys, and walking sticks, for harrowing, for cleaning chimneys, to fuel bakers' ovens and limekilns. We love a few blossoms

added to salad, steeped in boiling water for tea, or dropped into a whiskey glass for a fragrant tipple. Look for the spiky bushes growing near the sea, with yellow flowers that stay in bloom nearly all year. Wear gloves to harvest the flowers, as the thorns can be very sharp.

ROGER PHILLIPS' GORSE WINE

We love this recipe – it makes a fragrant, slightly effervescent, very refreshing summer drink. It comes from Roger Phillip's Wild Food – *a book no serious forager should be without* · MAKES ABOUT 1 GALLON

8 cups (2 quarts) gorse flowers
about 1 teaspoon active dry yeast, preferably without GMO
2¼lb granulated sugar
juice and zest of 2 organic lemons
juice and zest of 2 organic oranges

Pick nice fresh flowers that have bloomed fully. Activate the yeast by stirring it into a little tepid water. Simmer the flowers in 1 gallon water for 15 minutes then dissolve the sugar, pour into a large containers, and add citrus juice and zest. Allow to cool to body temperature, add the yeast, and let it stand with a cloth over it. After 3 days, strain off the solids and pour into a large glass jar, seal airtight, and allow it to ferment until it is finished. Transfer to a clean jar, filling it up to the neck with cold boiled water. Leave for a month and then filter, or leave until completely clear then bottle in sterilized bottles.

Wild Fruit

Wild fruit harvests can be really unpredictable – that's the reality of nature. Bad weather – hailstones especially – during blossom time can affect the setting of the fruit, and consequently the yield. These days, dwindling bee populations add to the problem of pollination. Some years, you might end up with a huge crop of crabapples or damsons and then there might not be a single fruit on the tree for another couple of years. In a bountiful year, collect everything you see and use the fruit in every way possible – jams, pickles, tarts, pies, compotes, chutneys – in case next year's harvests are light. Many wild fruits also freeze well, either raw or cooked and puréed.

I don't know what it is about picking stuff in the wild, but it seems to give me twice the buzz. The experience is always enhanced if I'm with my children or grandchildren. Sometimes we'll pack a picnic and go up the hills on a bilberry-picking expedition, and it turns into a real adventure. I love passing on my foraging skills to the next generation.

Blackberry *(Rubus fruticosus)*

WHEN TO PICK: late summer
All over the countryside every year, blackberries rot on the hedgerows. Think of all the wonderful jam that

Above: *Blackberries.*

could be made – so full of vitamin C! This year, why not organize a blackberry-picking expedition and take a picnic? You'll find it's the greatest fun, and when you come home, one person could make a few scones while someone else is making the jam. The children could be kept out of mischief and gainfully employed drawing and painting homemade jam labels, with personal messages like "Amelia Peggy's Jam – keep out!," or "Grandma's

Blackberry Jam." Then you can enjoy the results of your labors with a well-earned cup of tea.

Make sure you check the berries before you pop them into your mouth – if the core is discolored rather than pale and unblemished, it usually means that the little crawly beasties have gotten there first, so it's best to discard those. If you have the time and space, it's really worth "tray freezing" (flash freezing) some of your harvest – that way all those little berries stay separate. A few small cartons close to the top of the freezer will come in handy to add to a sauce or gravy and partner with a pheasant or a grouse later in the year.

BLACKBERRY ICE CUBES
Pop a fat, juicy blackberry into each section of an ice cube tray, and add a tiny rose geranium or mint leaf if you have them on hand. Fill with cold water and freeze. Pop into a glass of dry white wine, homemade lemonade, or champagne.

WILD BLACKBERRY AND ROSE PETAL SPONGE CAKE
When the first blackberries ripen in the fall, we scatter them over the whipped cream filling in Mrs. Lamb's Layer Cake (see page 526), and top with fragrant rose petals. We sprinkle confectioners' sugar over the top and decorate with whipped cream rosettes, blackberries, and crystallized rose petals.

BLACKBERRY AND APPLE MUESLI

This fruit muesli is served for breakfast throughout the year at Ballymaloe; the fruit varies with the season. My grandchildren also love it with strawberries, raspberries, and loganberries · SERVES 2-4

4 heaping tablespoons rolled oats (old-fashioned oatmeal)
4oz fresh blackberries
4oz grated dessert apple
1 teaspoon (or more) honey
Soak the oatmeal in 6 tablespoons water for 10–15 minutes. Meanwhile, mash the blackberries coarsley with a fork then mix with the apple and the oatmeal. Sweeten to taste with honey – a scant teaspoon is usually enough, but it depends upon how sweet the fruit is. Serve with cream and brown sugar.

BLACKBERRY AND ROSE GERANIUM SORBET

Rose geranium (Pelargonium graveolens) *has a wonderful affinity with blackberries. We use rose geranium leaves to flavor lots of dishes, including this lovely sorbet* · SERVES 6

½ cup granulated sugar
½ cup water
4–6 large rose geranium leaves (depending on size), plus extra to decorate
1lb blackberries, plus extra to decorate

Put the sugar, water, and rose geranium leaves into a saucepan and slowly bring to a boil. Boil for 3–4 minutes. Allow to cool. Meanwhile, purée the blackberries in a blender, then press through a nylon sieve. When the sugar syrup is cold, mix with the blackberry purée. Try it – it ought to taste a little too sweet at this stage, but add some fresh lemon juice if it's cloying. Freeze in an ice cream maker according to the manufacturer's instructions. Alternatively, put into a freezer until almost frozen, then take it out and break up the crystals with a whisk or in a food processor. Return to the freezer and repeat once or twice more. (If you do not have an ice cream maker, you could fold half a stiffly beaten egg white into the sorbet to lighten the texture.)

Serve a scoop of sorbet on chilled white plate, and garnish with whole blackberries and rose geranium leaves.

BLACKBERRY AND ROSE GERANIUM CORDIAL

Keep a bottle of this handy to serve over ice cream, carrageen moss pudding, or panna cotta. Alternatively, dilute with hot or cold water or sparkling wine to make a delicious drink · 1½ QUARTS

6lb fresh blackberries
10–12 rose geranium leaves
2 cups water
about 2¼lb granulated sugar
juice of 1–2 organic lemons (depending on size)

Put the blackberries, rose geranium leaves, and water into a stainless-steel saucepan. Cook for 15–20 minutes or until the blackberries are completely soft and juicy. Crush with a potato masher. Strain through a jelly bag or tie in a square of muslin and allow to drip into a bowl. Measure the juice and, depending on how sweet your blackberries are, add at least 18oz and up to 2¼lb sugar to every 2 cups of juice. Add the lemon juice, stir to dissolve sugar, then pour into sterilized bottles with screw tops. Store in a cold place.

Bilberry, wild blueberry
(Vaccinium uliginosum)

WHEN TO PICK: summer and early autumn

Bilberries, whortleberries, fraughans, herts … all local names for the tiny, intensely flavored wild blueberries that grow on low-lying bushes in many parts of the British Isles, much of northern Europe and North America. They thrive in acid soil on hilltops, woodland areas, and bogs. The fruits are ripe around the beginning of August; in the Irish countryside they were traditionally picked on Fraughan Sunday around the Feast of Lughnasa, when many young couples sped to the tops of the hills to pick berries and indulge in a bit of courting, out of sight of their parents.

The flavor of the wild berries is truly intense and delicious, and compensates for the length of time it takes to pick the tiny fruit and the multiple scratches one endures trying to reach them in the scratchy undergrowth. There may be more reasons to forage for these little berries than taste: scientists at Tufts University in Boston, Massachusetts, claim that blueberries counteract the ageing process, while others believe they help short-term memory as well as balance and co-ordination.

CRUSHED FRAUGHANS (WILD BLUEBERRIES)

Rare and so precious – we feel they're best eaten crushed with sugar and cream or scattered on a sheet of tender cake with some softly whipped cream. Wild blueberries were also used to make a drink called fraochán.

fraughans or wild blueberries
superfine sugar
softly whipped cream

Crush the berries with a pestle or potato masher. Sweeten to taste with sugar. Serve with softly whipped cream. Alternatively, fold in about half their volume of whipped cream to make fraughan fool.

EMER FITZGERALD'S FRAUGHAN SCONES

One of the brilliant cooks at the school, Emer Fitzgerald, first made this with cultivated blueberries, but it's even more wonderful with wild fraughans or bilberries · **MAKES 18-20 SCONES USING A 3IN CUTTER**

2lb all-purpose flour
3 heaping teaspoons baking
    powder
¼ cup superfine sugar
pinch of salt
1½ sticks cold butter, cubed
4oz fraughans, bilberries, or
    wild blueberries
3 organic eggs
about 1¾ cups whole milk, to mix

FOR THE GLAZE
egg wash (see page 539)
granulated sugar

Preheat the oven to 475°F.

Sift all the dry ingredients together in a large, wide bowl. Toss the cubed butter in the flour mixture and rub it in. Add the bilberries. Make a well in the center. Whisk the eggs with the milk, add to the dry ingredients, and mix to a soft dough. Turn out onto a floured board.

Knead lightly, not more than a few seconds, just enough to shape into a round. Roll out the dough to about 1in thick and cut or stamp into scones. Put onto a baking sheet – no need to grease. Brush the tops with egg wash and dip each one into granulated sugar. Bake on the middle rack in the preheated oven for 10–12 minutes until golden brown on top. Cool on a wire rack. Serve split in half with butter.

BILBERRY JELLY WITH A FRESH MINT CREAM

The Bog of Allen, not far from where I grew up in the Irish Midlands, produces abundant crops of fat, juicy bilberries. They are now grown commercially with considerable success. I managed to secure this wonderful, fresh-tasting recipe from my brother, Rory O'Connell · **SERVES 9-10**

FOR THE SYRUP
1 cup water
1⅛ cups sugar
4 sprigs fresh mint

2 teaspoons myrtille liqueur,
    optional
1 tablespoon lemon juice
3 teaspoons powdered gelatin
3 tablespoons water
1lb bilberries or wild
    blueberries, slightly crushed

FRESH MINT CREAM
about 15 fresh mint leaves
1 tablespoon lemon juice
½ cup heavy cream

9–10 ramekins about 2½in diameter brushed with vegetable oil or lined with plastic wrap

To make the syrup, put the water and sugar into a saucepan with the mint sprigs. Slowly bring to a boil. Simmer for a few minutes and allow to cool. Add the myrtille liqueur and lemon juice. Meanwhile, soften the gelatin in 3 tablespoons of water, then place the bowl in a pan of simmering water until the gelatin is completely dissolved. Remove the mint leaves from the syrup, stir well, then pour the syrup onto the gelatin and then add the slightly crushed bilberries. Pour into the prepared molds. Put into the fridge, cover, and leave to set for 3–4 hours.

Meanwhile, make the fresh mint cream: crush the mint leaves in a pestle and mortar with the lemon juice, add the cream and stir (the lemon juice will thicken the cream). If the cream becomes too thick, add a little water.

Turn out onto chilled plates, and serve with a little mint cream and decorate with a sprig of fresh mint.

Crabapple *(Malus sylvestris)*

WHEN TO PICK: late summer
Crabapples grow all around the British Isles, many parts of Europe and America. They are in season in autumn and may be picked off the tree, but many grow quite high so they can be difficult to reach. However, the windfalls that lie on the ground are also worth collecting. Once the bruised bits are cut out and thrown into the compost bin, the remaining skin, seeds, and stems are fine for making jellies.

Crabapple trees grow in hedgerows all around the British Isles and many parts of Europe. We've got several wild crabapple trees in the hedges around the farm (they grow well in chalky soil and burst into white blossom in the spring) but we also planted two new varieties, "Red Sentinel" and "Yellow Hornet," which are decorative as well as useful. The latter produces an abundance of small, yellow fruit about the size of a small walnut, which last for 2–3 weeks. The fruit of "Red Sentinel," however, will remain on the tree all through the late autumn and winter, until the new leaves appear in early spring. Apart from enjoying them as a decorative feature in the fruit garden, we use clusters of the berries for Christmas garlands and wreaths. The individual berries make a delicious pickle. We serve them with glazed ham and other cold meats.

PICKLED CRABAPPLES

We use the ornamental crabapple "Red Sentinel" to make this delicious and pretty pickle. We love to serve them with a glazed ham or some cold pork or bacon · **MAKES ABOUT 10 X 13OZ JARS**

15 cloves
15 allspice berries
2 star anise
1in stick of cinnamon
1 quart white wine vinegar
1lb granulated sugar
3–4lb small crabapples

Tie the spices in a little muslin bag. Put them into a stainless-steel

Above: *Crabapples.*

saucepan with the vinegar and sugar and bring to a boil, stirring until the sugar dissolves.

Rinse the crabapples and trim their stems to ¼in. Put them into a perforated wire basket (like a deep-fry basket) and carefully lower them into the boiling vinegar. Leave for 5 minutes and remove before the skins start to crack. Put the apples into small, sterilized canning jars or jam pots.

Meanwhile, boil down the vinegar and sugar until very syrupy, then cover the apples in the jars with it and seal immediately. Leave for months before using. In time the apples will leach their red color into the liquid, which makes a pretty pickle. Serve with pork or ham.

Variation

Soft fruit, like peaches, may be pickled in the same way, but use 1lb sugar to 1 cup vinegar, and vary the spices according to the fruit.

CRABAPPLE OR COOKING APPLE JELLY

Making jellies is immensely rewarding. This is a brilliant master recipe that can be used for many combinations. A jelly bag is an advantage, but by no means essential. Years ago we strained the juice and pulp through an old cotton pillow and hung it on an upturned stool. A couple of thicknesses of muslin will also do the job. Place a stainless steel or deep pottery bowl underneath to catch the juice. Tie with kitchen string and hang from a sturdy cup-hook. If you can't get enough crabapples, use a mixture of crabapples and windfall cooking apples, or any other tart cooking apple · MAKES 6–7LB

6lb crabapples or windfall cooking apples
1½ cups water
2 organic lemons
1lb granulated sugar to every 2 cups of juice

Rinse the apples, cut into quarters, but do not remove either the peel or core. Windfalls may be used, but be sure to cut out the bruised parts. Put the apples into a large stainless-steel saucepan with the water and the thinly pared zest of the lemons and cook for about 30 minutes until reduced to a pulp.

Pour the pulp into a jelly bag and allow to drip until all the juice has been extracted, usually overnight. (The pulp can later go to the hens or compost. The jelly bag or muslin may be washed and reused over and over again.)

Measure the juice into a preserving pan and allow 1lb sugar to each 2 cups of juice. Warm the sugar in a low oven. Squeeze the lemons, strain the juice, and add to the pan. Bring to a boil and add the warm sugar. Stir over low heat until the sugar is dissolved. Increase the heat and boil rapidly without stirring for about 8–10 minutes. Skim, test, and can immediately. Flavor with rose geranium, mint, sage, or cloves as required (see below).

CRABAPPLE AND ELDERBERRY JELLY

Add a handful or two of elderberries to the apple and continue as above. Up to half the volume of elderberries can be used. A sprig or two of mint or rose geranium or a cinnamon stick further enhances the flavor.

CRABAPPLE AND SLOE JELLY

Substitute sloes for elderberries in the above recipe. You want about the same quantity by weight of crabapples and sloes.

CRABAPPLE AND SAGE JELLY

Follow the Crabapple or Cooking Apple Jelly and add 3–4 sprigs of sage to the apples as they stew. Add 2–3 tablespoons of finely chopped sage to the jelly just before it's canned.

CRABAPPLE AND ROSEMARY JELLY

Add 2 sprigs of rosemary to the apples as they stew and put a tiny sprig into each jar. Serve with lamb.

CRABAPPLE AND ROSE GERANIUM JELLY

Add 8–10 leaves to the apples initially and 5 more when boiling to set.

ROSE PETAL AND CRABAPPLE JELLY

Follow the recipe but add 4oz fresh rose petals (they must be heritage varieties or they won't be fragrant).

CRABAPPLE AND ROWANBERRY JELLY

Rowanberries (sorbus aucuparia) are the fruit of the rowan tree (also known as mountain ash) and are in season in autumn. Rowans grow in acid soil in hills, and their brilliant orangey-red berries were historically much eaten, although few people eat rowanberries any more.

crabapples or cooking apples
rowanberries
1lb granulated sugar to every 2 cups of juice

Follow the Crabapple or Cooking Apple Jelly recipe above, and for every 1¼–1lb 10oz of apples add 9–14oz rowanberries (basically you want between one-quarter and one-third rowanberries to three-quarters to two-thirds apples). Serve with game or a fine leg of mutton.

CRABAPPLE AND BLACKBERRY TART

If you don't have enough crabapples, use sour cooking apples instead. Here I economize by using shortcrust pastry underneath and the light, flaky puff pastry as the lid. It does, however, mean using two pastries, so if you're short on time, you can just pick one and use that. It's a bit of a waste to use puff pastry for the base, though, as it won't have a chance to rise · **SERVES 6-8**

8oz Sweet Shortcrust Pastry (see page 542) for the base
8-10oz Puff Pastry or Billy's Cream Pastry (see pages 218 and 209) for the lid
16-24 crabapples or 3-4 cooking apples
4oz blackberries
1¾ cups granulated sugar (or more, depending on the sweetness of the apples)
3-4 cloves
egg wash (see page 539)
superfine sugar

To Serve
brown sugar
whipped cream

10in heatproof glass or other deep ceramic pie plate

Preheat the oven to 475°F.

Roll out the shortcrust pastry and line the pie plate. Trim, but leave about ¾in of pastry over the edge. Peel and quarter the apples, cut out the core and, if using cooking apples, cut the quarters in half, although your pieces of apple should be quite chunky. Put the apples onto the tart, piling them up in the center. Put the blackberries on top, leaving a 1in border around the edge. Sprinkle with the granulated sugar and add the cloves.

Roll out the puff or flaky pastry a little thicker than the base, wet the border strip around the tart and press the pastry lid down onto it. Trim the pastry, leaving a ¼in edge again. Crimp the edges with a sharp knife, then scallop them. Make a hole in the center to allow steam to escape. Egg wash. Roll out the trimmings and cut into leaves and decorate the top of the tart; egg wash again.

Bake in the oven for 15-20 minutes, then lower the temperature to 350°F for another 40-45 minutes, depending on how firm the apples are. Test the apples with a skewer. Sprinkle with superfine sugar, serve with brown sugar and softly whipped cream.

Damson *(Prunus insititia)*

WHEN TO PICK: early autumn
Damsons, sometimes called bullaces, are wild plums. They are in season in autumn and are less tart than sloes; in fact they're deliciously bittersweet. Damsons still grow wild in many parts of Europe, usually near orchards or gardens – bullaces are the result of natural hybridization between the sloe and cherry plum. They ripen towards the end of September, depending on the weather. They are a little unpredictable – some years there's a terrific crop, others barely a damson on the tree. But we love collecting them and eat lots freshly picked. The surplus we make into damson pies, compotes, and jam (see the Preserving chapter). They also make a delicious sauce to accompany roasted pork with cracklings, and they freeze perfectly.

DAMSON OR PLUM SAUCE

This is delicious with duck breast or wild duck · **SERVES 6-8**

1lb damsons or blood plums
1 cup plus 2 tablespoons sugar
2 cloves
1in piece cinnamon stick
2 tablespoons butter
2 tablespoons Red currant Jelly (see page 451)
½ cup port wine

Put the plums into a stainless-steel saucepan with the sugar, cloves, cinnamon, 1 tablespoon water, and the butter. Cook slowly until reduced to a pulp. Push the fruit through a fine sieve and return the purée to a clean saucepan. Add the red currant jelly and port, bring to a boil, and simmer for a few minutes. The sauce may be served either hot or cold. It keeps well.

Variation

DAMSON AND APPLE SAUCE
Make a separate apple purée. Poach and purée the damsons as above, then combine with an equal volume of apple purée. Serve with pork.

COMPOTE OF DAMSONS

Poach the fruit whole – they'll taste better, but quite apart from that you'll have the fun of playing "He loves me, he loves me not" as you count the pits on your plate! (You could just fix it by making sure you use an uneven number.) Greengages are also delicious cooked in this way.

Fruit should be cooked in a stainless steel or enamel saucepan, never aluminum, as the fruit will react with it · SERVES 8

2 cups sugar, a bit less if the
    fruit are very sweet
2 cups cold water
2lb fresh damsons
whipped cream, to serve

Put the sugar and water into a stainless-steel saucepan and slowly bring to a boil. Add the fruit, cover the saucepan, and return to a boil. Simmer for 4–5 minutes until they begin to burst. Turn into a bowl and serve warm with a dollop of softly whipped cream. Divine!

Poached damsons keep very well in the fridge and are delicious for breakfast (perhaps without the cream) or dessert.

Variation
DAMSON FOOL
If you have the patience to remove the pits, the fruit can be puréed. When cold, mix with an equal quantity of whipped cream. Taste and serve with Shortbread Cookies (see page 548).

Opposite: *Compote of Damsons.*

Elderberry *(Sambucus nigra)*
WHEN TO PICK: early autumn
The fluffy white elderflowers turn into elderberries in autumn, hanging in purple clusters off their burgundy stems. The berries don't have quite the same appeal as the flowers, but they make lovely jellies and can be added to sauces and gravies to serve with game, particularly venison. My brother Rory tells me that they freeze brilliantly.

To use elderberries in cooking, see the Crabapple and Elderberry Jelly recipe (page 40), or you can substitute dried elderberries for dried fruits like raisins or currants in barmbrack and cakes. Otherwise, make an elderberry syrup and serve it with prosecco or mineral water.

Frozen elderberries
Elderberries freeze well, just pop the heads into a plastic container, separated by sheets of parchment paper. They are really easy to stem when frozen. Use for jellies and game sauces.

ELDERBERRY SYRUP

There are a ton of cures attributed to this syrup. Put a little into the bottom of a glass and fill with sparkling water, wine, or sparkling prosecco.

It also makes an excellent hot drink if you add a tablespoon or two to hot whiskey; just add boiling water and a couple of cloves · MAKES ABOUT 2 CUPS

1lb elderberries
1lb sugar to every 2 cups of juice
1 organic lemon

Strip the fruit from the stems, put into a stainless-steel saucepan, and cover with cold water. Using a swivel-bladed vegetable peeler, remove thin strips of zest from the lemon and add.

Bring to a boil and simmer for 20–30 minutes or until the elderberries are soft.

Strain through a jelly bag or piece of muslin. Measure the juice and put it back into the saucepan. Add 1lb sugar for each 2 cups of juice and the juice of the lemon. Return to a boil for about 10 minutes, allow to cool before pouring into sterilized bottles, seal with a screw cap, and store in a cool, dry place.

Below: *Elderberries.*

Rose hip *(Rosa canina)*

WHEN TO PICK: late summer–autumn
Rose hips are packed with vitamin C
– Roger Phillips claims they've got
20 times more than oranges – and
are often attributed with the ability
to prevent urinary tract infections,
as well as relieve dizziness and
headaches. Rose hips are little
fuchsia-like globes that contain
many seeds and that grow on the
dog rose found in hedges, woodland
and scrub all over Europe and in
much of North America. Rose hips
are sweetened by a touch of frost,
but these days with global warming
you might be left waiting.

Above: *Rose hips.*

ROSE HIP SYRUP

*Use either wild rose hips or the hips of
the bristly hedge rose,* Rosa rugosa.
*Serve with ice cream or use as the basis
for a drink* · MAKES 4 CUPS

1½ **cups water**
2lb **fresh rose hips**
1lb **granulated sugar**

Bring 1½ quarts (6 cups) of water to
a boil. Meanwhile chop or mince
the rose hips and, just as soon as
they are ready, add them to the
water and bring it back to a boil.
Remove from the heat and allow to
infuse for 15 minutes. Strain through
muslin. Put the pulp back into the
saucepan, add another 2–4 cups of
water and bring to a boil: infuse and
strain as before.

Pour all the juice into a clean
stainless-steel saucepan, reduce
uncovered, until 3 cups of liquid
remains. Add in the sugar, stir to
dissolve, and allow to boil for just
5 minutes. Pour the syrup into
sterilized bottles. Seal with screw
top caps.

ROSE HIP JELLY
Add a couple of handfuls of rose
hips to the Crabapple Jelly recipe
(see page 40).

Wild strawberry
(Fragaria vesca)

WHEN TO PICK: all summer
These are one of the real prizes of
summer foraging. When I was little
in Tipperary, there was a whole
double bank of wild strawberries
that lined the boreen down to the
bog. My Aunt Lil would give me a
little tin pail and tell me to go and
fill it with strawberries. For the next
hour I would have an intense
struggle – they were so bittersweet –
and I would be torn between eating
them there and then or taking them
home, because if I resisted the
temptation and took them home,
Aunt Lil would make this thin sheet
of tender sponge cake, and while it
was cooking she would go out to the
dairy and skim a thick layer of
cream off the milk and scatter the
little wild berries over the top of
the softly whipped cream with a
sprinkling of sugar. Nothing I've
tasted before or since has been
quite as delicious.

Wild strawberry plants have
trefoil-shaped leaves with white five-
petaled flowers. They grow in
woodlands and grasslands in
calcareous soils.

WILD STRAWBERRY CAKE
See page 526 for a good cake recipe
and sprinkle little wild strawberries
on top. Or arrange them on top of
little tartlets for a rare treat. My
friend Lana Pringle, who has
swathes of these wild strawberries
growing in the gravel path behind
her house, picks them and makes
the most exquisite wild strawberry
jam, given in tiny pots to a few
fortunate friends.

WILD STRAWBERRY JAM
Follow the strawberry jam recipe on
page 442 or page 447 but quarter
the ingredients and use 1lb of wild
strawberries, 1¾ cups of granulated
sugar, and the zest and juice of
½ lemon.

Sloe *(Prunus spinosa)*

WHEN TO PICK: autumn

Sloes, the fruit of the blackthorn tree, are tart little berries that resemble tiny purple plums in appearance; they grow on prickly bushes atop stone walls and are in season in early fall. Even though they look quite appetizing they are inedibly sour and mouth-puckeringly tannic. As with so many wild foods, some years there is a bumper crop and others there is scarcely enough to make a few bottles of sloe gin. We love to make Crabapple and Sloe Jelly (see page 40) which is possible even if the harvest is light.

SLOE OR DAMSON GIN

It's great fun to organize a few pals to pick sloes and have a sloe gin-making party. Sloes make a terrific beverage for Christmas presents. Either enjoy it neat or put a measure of damson or sloe gin in a glass, add ice, a slice of lemon, and top it up with tonic.

1½lb sloes or damsons
1¾ cups granulated sugar
1 quart gin

Wash and dry the fruit and prick it in several places (we use a sterilized darning needle). Put the fruit into a sterilized glass jar and cover with the sugar and gin. Seal tightly.

Shake the jar every couple of days to start with and then every now and then for 3–4 months, by which time it will be ready to strain and bottle. It will improve upon keeping so try to resist drinking it for another few months.

Above: *Freshly picked sloes.*

Variation

SLOE OR DAMSON VODKA
This slips down easily but has quite a kick! Simply substitute vodka for the gin in the recipe above.

SLOE AND BLACKBERRY CHEESE

Serve with goat cheese · MAKES
8 X 12½ OZ

2¼lb sloes
2¼lb blackberries
4½lb granulated sugar, warmed
 (see page 440)

Put the sloes and blackberries in a wide stainless-steel saucepan, add ⅓ cup of water. Cook over medium heat, stirring, for 5–6 minutes, or until the fruit begins to soften. Add the warmed sugar, stir until dissolved, bring to a boil, and continue to cook for 40–45 minutes, skimming occasionally. Working in batches, push through a nylon sieve.

Pour into sterilized jars, seal, and store in a cool dry place.

Wild Nuts

Hazelnuts are by far the most common wild nuts although you will occasionally come across a Spanish chestnut tree (*Castanea sativa)* with its prickly casings that hide the edible nut. Somehow they never seem to swell to the same size as they do in France and Spain, but they can still be sweet and delicious. Pignuts (*Conopodium majus)*, so-called even though they are a tuber, are also fun to forage in spring. You'll need a knife to root out the crunchy "nuts" that grow under slender umbelliferous plants in woods and fields. They must be peeled and scraped before eating raw.

Hazelnut *(Corylus avellana)*

WHEN TO PICK: autumn
Hazelnuts grow wild on poorer land on hillsides. Hazelnuts and cobnuts are what you find growing wild; filberts were the type chosen for commercial cultivation. The nuts ripen in autumn, usually from the end of September and October onward. Wild ones grow in clusters of two or three, depending on the variety, whereas some cultivated varieties grow individually. They are ripe when their shells harden and turn brown. It's best to gather the nuts that fall under the tree.

Nuts that adhere to the husks are normally empty inside. When they are ready to harvest, the shells turn brown and the nuts usually fall out of the husks. Store in a single layer in a warm place, like a hot press or in a boiler house, if available.

Alternatively, they can be hung in an old nylon onion bag in a warm airy place. Eat soon, as nuts do turn rancid and won't keep beyond Christmas.

There were pagan traditions and superstitions associated with the hazelnut, many now forgotten, but hazel twigs are still used by water diviners. A forked hazel twig is cut from a hazel tree and it is truly astonishing to see how the twig quivers in the water diviner's hand when there is water below the surface of the earth. The twig genuinely appears to have a life of its own. Some people have the gift, others do not; there doesn't seem to be a logical explanation, but it certainly works.

MENDIANTS

These simple little petits fours are adorable and look and taste delicious ·
MAKES 25-30

8oz semi-sweet or bittersweet chocolate, chopped
whole shelled hazelnuts and almonds, toasted
whole pistachio nuts
plump dark raisins
plump golden raisins
crystallized ginger, diced

Put the chocolate in a heatproof bowl placed over a saucepan of hot water (the bottom of the bowl should not touch the water). When the water comes to a boil, turn off

Above: *Cobnuts.*

the heat and leave until the chocolate melts.

Lay a sheet of parchment paper on a baking sheet. Fill the chocolate into a parchment piping cone, cut a tiny hole and pipe out 1in blobs. Alternatively, spoon small blobs onto the parchment paper. Shake the paper gently to spread the chocolate evenly. Sprinkle a mixture of nuts, dried fruit, and crystallized ginger on top of each one. Let set in the fridge, then peel off and enjoy.

HAZELNUT CHOCOLATE BROWNIES

Everyone has their own favorite brownie recipe and indeed we have several – this is one of the greats ·
MAKES 9 GENEROUS BROWNIES

10oz chocolate
1¼ cups butter
5 organic eggs
1⅔ cups granulated sugar
1¼ cups self-rising flour
1 cup toasted, peeled and
    chopped hazelnuts
cocoa powder, for dusting

12 x 8 x 2in baking pan

Preheat the oven to 350°F. Line the
pan with parchment paper.

Melt the chocolate and butter in
a heatproof bowl over hot but not
simmering water. Whisk the eggs
and sugar together until the mixture
becomes light. Gradually stir in the
melted chocolate mixture. Fold in
the flour. Finally, add the chopped
hazelnuts. Spoon into the prepared
pan, smooth the surface, and cook in
the preheated oven for 35–40
minutes. The center will be slightly
wobbly. Leave to sit in the pan to
cool, and cover the pan with a large
rectangular plate or tray.

When set, turn out by inverting
the pan carefully. Peel off the paper.
Place another tray on top of the
brownies to turn them right side up.
Cut into squares, dust with cocoa,
and serve.

YOGURT WITH HONEY AND TOASTED HAZELNUTS

*So simple and so good. Delicious for
either dessert or breakfast.*

best-quality thick, natural yogurt
    (see page 220 for recipe)
strongly flavored local honey
toasted hazelnuts, sliced

Above: *Hazelnut Brittle.*

Serve a portion of chilled yogurt per
person. Just before serving, drizzle
generously with honey and sprinkle
with hazelnuts.

HAZELNUT BRITTLE

*Sliced almonds are also delicious in
this recipe ·* MAKES LOTS

1 teaspoon sunflower oil
¾ cup granulated sugar
1 cup toasted, peeled and sliced
    hazelnuts

9 x 13in jelly roll pan

Brush the pan with oil. Put the sugar
and 3 tablespoons water into a
heavy-bottomed saucepan. Stir over
low heat until the sugar is dissolved.
Bring to a boil and cook without
stirring, swirling the pan
occasionally, until the sugar turns a
rich chestnut-colored caramel. Add
the nuts and stir to coat.

Pour the mixture onto the
pan. Spread into an even layer with
the back of an oiled metal spoon.
Allow to cool completely. Break into
pieces, and use as garnish for ice
cream, mousses, cakes, or to
simply nibble.

Wild Mushrooms

The mere mention of wild mushrooms sends most people, particularly country folk, into a nostalgic trip down memory lane – but in these islands we're usually talking about the common field mushroom (*Agaricus campestris*). Those of us of a certain age remember racing out at dawn with our tin cans to collect wild mushrooms in the dewy fields. Many also recall cooking them over embers on the hearth and on the cool plate of the range with nothing more than a few grains of salt for seasoning. Sometimes they were stewed in milk and occasionally, when there was a glut, in warm, humid autumn weather, we'd collect bucketfuls and make Grandpoppy's Mushroom Ketchup.

Those of us with a spark of entrepreneurial spirit threaded the bigger mushrooms on twine and sold them to passing motorists on "the main road" for a few pence a string. Nowadays the common field mushroom is scarce because of modern intensive farming, but there is a growing awareness of – and a hunger for – knowledge about the other types of mushrooms that grow in our woods and forests.

When you pick mushrooms, always use a knife. Responsible fungi hunters just cut the stem and leave the root end in the ground. Sometimes mushrooms get infested with worms. To check, break or cut the stem away from the cap.

For some reason, apart from the common mushroom we have always been scared of collecting wild mushrooms. A few inquisitive and adventurous souls have plucked up courage in recent years. Emboldened by information gleaned on mushroom hunts around the country, a growing number of chefs are eager to learn about wild fungi and to feature them on their menus. Here at the cookery school we've offered mushroom hunts led by eminent botanist Roger Goodwillie from Lavistown Centre in County Kilkenny. We have found up to 40 species on the farm and local woods. Of those, a few were edible, but most weren't worth eating. There is, however, a core group of wild mushrooms that really are worth being able to identify: field mushrooms, chanterelles, morels, ceps/porcini, and puffballs, as well as the little wood blewits.

Field or flat mushrooms
(*Agaricus campestris*)

WHEN TO PICK: end of summer

Field mushrooms are the most common of all and the ones people are most comfortable identifying. When they first pop up, usually on old pastureland, they look like little white buttons. They gradually get bigger, and by the next day, they will have opened up and begin to go flat. The longer they're there, the flatter they become. Sometimes the snails have gotten there first and gobbled a bit out of the side, but don't worry about that, you can always cut that part away – they're too precious to pass up. When they're young, the caps are white and almost downy, and the gills underneath are pale pink but they darken with age.

WILD MUSHROOM SOUP

The soup base of this recipe without the stock is a perfect way to preserve field mushrooms for another time. It freezes perfectly for several months. To reconstitute, just defrost, add stock and milk and then bring to a boil for 3–4 minutes. Taste and correct the seasoning before serving. If wild mushrooms are unavailable, flat mushrooms also make a delicious soup.

If you don't have time to chop the mushrooms very finely, just slice them and then process the cooked soup in a blender for a few seconds. Be careful not to overdo it, as the soup should be slightly chunky · SERVES 8–9

2 tablespoons butter
½ cup finely chopped onions
1lb wild mushrooms
¼ cup all-purpose flour
salt and freshly ground pepper
2 cups Chicken Stock
  (see page 262)
2 cups hot whole milk
dash of heavy cream (optional)

Opposite: *Chanterelles, Wood Blewits, and Horn of Plenty.*

Melt the butter in a saucepan over low heat. Toss the onions in it, cover, and cook until soft and completely tender. Meanwhile, chop the mushrooms very finely. Add to the saucepan and cook over a high heat for 3–4 minutes. Now stir in the flour, cook over low heat for 2–3 minutes, season with salt and freshly ground pepper, then add the boiling stock and milk gradually, stirring all the time. Increase the heat and bring to a boil. Taste and add a dash of cream, if necessary. Serve immediately or reheat later.

WILD MUSHROOMS À LA CRÈME

Mushrooms à la crème is a fantastic all-purpose recipe, and if you've got a surplus of wild mushrooms, use those instead of cultivated ones. You can even use dried mushrooms · **SERVES 8**

4 tablespoons butter
1 medium onion, finely chopped
1lb wild mushrooms (chanterelles, morels, ceps, false chanterelles, or the common field mushroom), sliced
salt and freshly ground pepper
good squeeze of lemon juice
1 cup heavy cream
freshly chopped parsley
1 tablespoon freshly chopped chives (optional)

Melt half the butter in a heavy saucepan until it foams. Add the chopped onion, cover, and cook over low heat for 5–10 minutes or until quite soft but not colored; remove the onions to a bowl. Meanwhile, cook the sliced mushrooms in a hot frying pan with the remaining butter, in batches if necessary. Season each batch with salt, freshly ground pepper, and a tiny squeeze of lemon juice. Add the mushrooms to the onions in the saucepan, then add the cream and allow to bubble for a few minutes. Taste and correct the seasoning, and add the chopped herbs.

Mushrooms à la crème keeps well in the fridge for 4–5 days and freezes perfectly.

Good things to do with Wild Mushrooms à la Crème:

· Served as a vegetable
· Filling for omelettes or savory pancakes
· Filling for vol-au-vents or pastry tartlets
· Topping for baked potatoes
· Sauce for chicken breasts, steaks, hamburgers, lamb chops, or veal
· Sauce for pasta
· Mushrooms on toast
· Posh enrichment for casseroles and stews

WILD MUSHROOM VOL-AU-VENTS

Use this method for either savory or sweet recipes · **MAKES ABOUT 24**

Puff Pastry (see page 218)
egg wash (see page 539)
Wild Mushrooms à la Crème (see above)
parsley or watercress sprigs, for garnish

Roll out the pastry to ⅛–¼in thickness depending on the size of the vol-au-vents. We use a 4in round cutter for individual helpings. Stamp out the vol-au-vents, turn upside down and put onto a damp baking sheet. Brush with egg wash. Take a 2½in cutter and press down two-thirds of the way into the pastry (this will lift out later and act as a lid). Score the edges and the center with the blunt edge of a knife – we normally do a zig zag around the edge and a criss-cross pattern in the center. Refrigerate for at least 15 minutes. Meanwhile, preheat the oven to 450°F.

Bake the vol-au-vents in the hot oven for 10 minutes and then lower the temperature to 350°F and bake for another 10–15 minutes or until completely cooked through. Remove the lids and scoop out the moist centers; return them to the oven to dry out for a few minutes if necessary. Heat the filling and spoon into the center of each and garnish with a sprig of parsley or watercress. Serve on warm plates.

WILD MUSHROOM AND POTATO GRATIN

If you have a few wild mushrooms – any kind, really – mix them with ordinary mushrooms for this dish. If all you can find are wild mushrooms, so much the better, they have much more flavor than the button variety. Either way it will still be delectable. The gratin is terrifically good with a haunch of venison, rack of lamb, or a piece of steak.

Mushrooms are one of the rare vegetables that taste better when they are a few days old. The stems taste every bit as good as the caps so don't discard. If the root end is still attached trim it off and add it to the compost bin · SERVES 8

¾lb flat or wild mushrooms
2lb potatoes, e.g. Golden Wonder
    or Kerr's Pink
2 garlic cloves, finely chopped
salt and freshly ground black
    pepper
2 tablespoons fresh thyme leaves
1½ cups light cream
4 tablespoons grated Parmesan
    (preferably Parmigiano
    Reggiano)

gratin or other baking dish
    10 x 8in

Preheat the oven to 350°F.

Slice the mushrooms (caps and stems) thinly. Peel the potatoes and cut into scant ¼in thick slices. Bring a large saucepan of water to a boil. Add the potato slices. As soon as the water returns to a boil, drain the potatoes. Refresh under cold water. Drain again and spread out on paper towels or a clean kitchen towel.

Sprinkle the chopped garlic over the base of a shallow gratin dish. Arrange half the potatoes in the bottom of the dish, season with salt and freshly ground pepper. Cover with the sliced mushrooms. Sprinkle with fresh thyme leaves. Season again and finish with a final layer of overlapping potatoes.

Bring the cream almost to the boiling point, pour over the potatoes. Sprinkle the freshly grated cheese on top and bake the gratin

for about 1 hour until the surface is crisp and golden brown with the cream bubbling up around the edges.

WILD OR FLAT MUSHROOM FRITTATA

A frittata is an Italian omelette. Persian "kuku," Middle Eastern "eggah," and Spanish "tortilla" all sound much more exciting than a flat omelette, although that's basically what they are. Unlike their soft and creamy French cousin, these omelettes are cooked slowly over a very low heat during which time you can be whipping up a delicious salad to accompany it! A frittata is cooked gently on both sides and cut into wedges like a cake. Omit the mushrooms, and you have a basic recipe, flavored with grated cheese and a generous sprinkling of herbs. Like the omelette, though, you'll occasionally want to add some tasty morsels for a change – perhaps some spinach, ruby chard, calabrese, asparagus, smoked mackerel ... the list is endless, but be careful not to use it as a dustbin; think about the combination of flavors before you empty your fridge! · SERVES 4-8

2 tablespoons olive oil
1lb mushrooms – a mixture
    of mushrooms or chanterelles:
    flat, oyster, and shiitake, rinsed
    and sliced
salt and freshly ground black pepper
8 large organic eggs
1 teaspoon salt
1 tablespoon chopped parsley
2 teaspoons thyme leaves
1 tablespoon chopped basil or
    marjoram

1 cup shredded Gruyère cheese
⅓ cup freshly grated Parmigiano
    Reggiano, Pecorino, Desmond,
    or Gabriel cheese
2 tablespoons butter

7 x 9in non stick ovenproof frying
    pan

Heat the olive oil in a hot saucepan and add the sliced mushrooms. Season with salt and freshly ground pepper and cook over high heat until just wilted, then allow to cool. Whisk the eggs in a bowl, then add the salt, more freshly ground pepper, chopped herbs, cooled mushrooms, and grated cheese.

Melt the butter in a non stick frying pan. When it starts to foam, add the eggs and turn down the heat as low as it will go; use a heat diffuser on the burner, if you have one. Leave the eggs to cook gently for 15 minutes on a heat diffuser mat, or until the bottom is set. The top should still be slightly runny.

Preheat a broiler. Pop the pan under the broiler for 1 minute to set and barely brown the surface. Slide an offset spatula under the frittata to free it from the pan. Slide onto a warm plate.

(An even a more foolproof method is to transfer the frittata to a preheated 350°F oven and bake it for 12–15 minutes.)

Serve warm or at room temperature, cut in wedges with a good green salad and perhaps a few olives.

Horse mushroom
(*Agaricus arvensis*)

WHEN TO PICK: late summer–early autumn

Horse mushrooms are a terrific find – they are a kind of field mushroom that can be found in pastures and sometimes at the edge of woods. They grow in great rings that can be up to several feet across. Each mushroom is large and fleshy and can be as big as a Portobello and so make excellent eating. Pick them carefully because if they bruise they become discolored and yellow.

HORSE MUSHROOM BURGER
Cook a large flat mushroom drizzled with olive oil on a grill pan or in the oven. Season with salt, freshly ground pepper, a little crushed garlic, and some thyme leaves. Toast a hamburger bun and spread with goat cheese and pesto or garlic butter. Top with the juicy mushroom and the other half of the bun. Serve immediately.

Wood blewit (*Lepista nuda*)

WHEN TO PICK: autumn–early winter

This is quite a common mushroom throughout Europe and North America that grows prolifically in beech woods, under hedges, and sometimes even in gardens. It shouldn't be eaten raw – it must be cooked first. You can use it in any mushroom recipe. With its purple tinge, it is very beautiful and it has a strong perfumed smell.

Opposite: *Chanterelles on Buttered Toast.*

Chanterelles
(*Cantharellus cibarius*)

WHEN TO PICK: mid-summer–early autumn

Chanterelles – *girolles* in French – are one of the easiest wild mushrooms to identify. They grow in mainly deciduous woodlands and mossy clearings and I've also collected them under rhododendron bushes. They're yellow to deep orange in color and have a trumpet-like appearance. One of the ways to ensure that what you have is a chanterelle is to look for ridges running down the stem. They dry really well: I just put them on the shelf over my oven for a day or two, and then store them in a glass jar.

CHANTERELLES ON BUTTERED TOAST

This is the simplest of all recipes and one of my favorite ways to enjoy chanterelles · SERVES 6 GREEDY PEOPLE

2–3lb chanterelles
butter
1 garlic clove, finely chopped (optional)
salt, freshly ground black pepper
chopped parsley
6 slices or more of well-buttered toast
freshly snipped parsley

Trim off the earthy part of the chanterelle stems, then rinse the caps quickly but carefully, and drain them well. Cook them in a hot frying pan in several tablespoons of sizzling butter, adding the garlic if using. Keep the heat high once the

Above: *Wood blewit mushrooms.*

mushrooms begin to exude their juice – some people drain off this liquid, and complete the cooking of the mushrooms in fresh butter. It very much depends on how wet or dry the chanterelles are, which varies with the season in which they are picked. The answer is to drain off the liquid if it doesn't evaporate before the mushrooms are cooked; they must not be allowed to stew to the point of becoming leather. Season with salt and pepper, sprinkle with parsley, and serve immediately on hot buttered toast with some snipped fresh parsley on top.

CHANTERELLES À LA CRÈME
Chanterelles sautéed quickly in a little butter, as in the above recipe make a fine vegetable to go with veal – escalopes, chops, or a roast. If they are being served with chicken, it is customary to add some heavy

cream just before serving them, 5 or 6 tablespoons should be enough, and stir it well into the pan juices so that the sauce is well amalgamated. Chanterelles à la crème also make a great filling for an omelette, or for a whole range of pastry shells. Such recipes stretch a small quantity of chanterelles in the most economical way possible.

BAKED PLAICE WITH CHANTERELLES

This can be served as a first course or as a main course, depending on the size of the fish. All flat fish are delicious cooked in this way, e.g. black sole, lemon sole, brill, turbot, dab and flounder, John Dory, and halibut. The sauce can be varied: Hollandaise, Mousseline, Beurre Blanc, Lobster, and Champagne sauces are all very good · **SERVES 4 AS A MAIN COURSE**

4 very fresh plaice on the bone
salt and freshly ground pepper
8oz fresh chanterelles
4–8 tablespoons butter
4 teaspoons finely chopped fresh
**   parsley or a mixture of parsley,**
**   chives, fennel, and lemon**
**   thyme leaves**

Preheat the oven to 350°F.

Turn each fish onto its side and remove the head. Rinse the fish and clean the slit very thoroughly. Use a sharp knife to cut through the skin right around the fish, just where the "fringe" meets the flesh. Be careful to cut neatly and to join the side cuts at the tail or it will be difficult to remove the skin later on.

Sprinkle the fish with salt and pepper and lay them in ¼in of water in a shallow baking pan. Bake in the preheated oven for 20–30 minutes according to the size of the fish. The water should have just evaporated as the flesh is cooked. Check to see if the fish is ready by lifting the flesh from the bone at the head: it should lift off easily and be quite white with no trace of pink. Keep warm while you cook the mushrooms.

Pick over the chanterelles carefully and cut off the tough end bits. Rinse quickly, drain on paper towels, and cut into pieces. Melt 1 tablespoon butter and when it foams, toss in the chanterelles and season with salt and freshly ground pepper. Cook over high heat for 3–4 minutes or until soft.

Melt the remaining butter and stir in the freshly chopped herbs and chanterelles. Just before serving, grasp the skin of the plaice down near the tail and pull off gently (the skin will tear badly if not properly cut). Lift the fish onto warm plates and spoon the herb butter and chanterelles over the top. Serve immediately.

Ceps, porcini *(Boletus edulis)*

WHEN TO PICK: summer–autumn

This is a large family of mushrooms that grows from summer to autumn. The majority are edible but avoid any specimens with red or orange spores. They are large and fleshy but they don't have gills like field mushrooms. The cap, which varies in color from dark brown to golden yellow on the outside, has a spongy texture and a thick bulbous stem. Our favorite varieties are bull boletus, penny buns, and bay boletus. Don't expect to find perfect specimens – if a snail has gotten there first you can still use it – just trim as needed. Sharing is fun!

Morels *(Morchella esculenta)*

WHEN TO PICK: spring

Morels start to appear in the woods from about St. Patrick's Day. These are the first to appear in spring, and are in season from March to May. They are really worth the effort. In fact, they are one of the most sought after of all wild fungi and people are notoriously secretive about their sources, not surprisingly. They can be found in woods in loose, sandy soil. Because of their texture, they tend to be very sandy. Shake well, then trim and discard the root end. You may want to split them in half from top to bottom. The hollow center sometimes harbors insects. Rinse well.

CHICKEN WITH MORELS

Use as many morels as you can find or afford. In this recipe 2oz will perfume the sauce deliciously – 8oz will be very good indeed · **SERVES 6**

4 tablespoons butter, at room
**   temperature**
1 free-range chicken, preferably
**   organic, about 4lb**
salt and freshly ground pepper
1½ cups Meursault or other
**   good Chardonnay wine**
6 garlic cloves, unpeeled
1 bouquet garni with a few
**   parsley stems, a sprig of**
**   thyme, a sprig of tarragon,**
**   and a bay leaf**

4oz fresh morels or 2oz dried morels
¾ cup Chicken Stock (see page 262)
1 cup light cream
Roux (see page 165)

Preheat the oven to 350°F.

Smear half the butter over the breast and legs of the chicken. Season the cavity and breast with salt and freshly ground pepper. Put into a flameproof casserole with the wine, garlic, and bouquet garni. Bring to a boil on top of the stove, cover and transfer to the oven for 1¼–1½ hours, depending on the size of the chicken.

If the morels are fresh, rinse carefully to dislodge any grit or clay. If you are using dried ones, cover with boiling chicken stock and leave to soak for 1 hour.

As soon as the chicken is cooked, transfer it to a carving board and keep warm. Skim off the fat from the juices, add the cream, bring to a boil, and simmer for 4–5 minutes, then thicken by whisking in just a little roux.

Trim the morel stems. Melt the remaining butter in a hot pan and toss the mushrooms gently for 2–3 minutes. Season with salt and freshly ground pepper. Add the morels to the sauce and the chicken stock (along with the strained soaking liquid, if you used dried mushrooms – be careful not to get any sand in). Allow to simmer gently for 5 minutes.

Meanwhile, carve the chicken and arrange on a serving dish. Taste the sauce and season if necessary, spoon over the chicken and divide the morels equally between each helping. Garnish simply and serve immediately with a few boiled potatoes. Follow with a good green salad.

Pavement mushrooms
(Agaricus bitorquis)
WHEN TO PICK: spring to late autumn

This intriguing mushroom loves compacted sandy soil in urban areas and can push up through tarmac or even lift pavement stones – I first saw some in Copenhagen in the 1970s. Unfortunately, I didn't realize they were edible because we were very poor and could have done with a little treat to embellish our simple diet. They look similar to field mushrooms but have two separate sheaths on the stem. They can be sautéed or added to mixed mushroom dishes, stews, casseroles – the possibilities are endless.

Puffball
(Langermannia gigantea)
WHEN TO PICK: summer to autumn

Almost every year we find one or two giant puffballs on our lawn under the weeping ash tree. Sometime between summer and autumn they suddenly appear. They look like misshapen white footballs and have a dense, spongy texture. The flavor is far from distinguished, but they take on other flavors well and are enhanced by interesting sauces. Young ones are best to eat, they should be white throughout. If they are beginning to turn yellow, it's best to discard them.

The best puffballs are the very white giant puffball (*Langermannia gigantea)*, the mosaic or engraved puffball (*Calvatia utriformis)* which is gray-white, warty and shaped like a pear, and the pestle or long-stemmed puffball (*Calvatia excipuliformis)*, also warty and pestle-shaped. They are all best when the flesh is firm, young, and pure white.

CRISPY PUFFBALL

Puffballs need all the help they can get in the way of extra flavorings, so feel free to experiment: add some soy sauce, fresh herbs, spices, fish sauce, or whatever, and let the puffball be the vehicle for their flavors. Serve with a lovely chutney or pickle · SERVES 6-12, DEPENDING ON THE SIZE OF MUSHROOM

firm white puffball
flour seasoned with salt, freshly ground pepper, and, if you wish, a little cayenne or smoked paprika
1 organic egg, beaten
fresh bread crumbs (see page 577)
freshly chopped herbs, e.g. parsley, chives, thyme, sage, or rosemary (optional)
Clarified Butter (optional, see page 216)

Cut the puffball into ¼in slices, dip into seasoned flour, then beaten egg, and then into fresh bread crumbs mixed, if you wish, with a few freshly chopped herbs.

Deep-fry at 350°F until golden and crispy. Alternatively, you can shallow-fry the slices in clarified butter. Serve immediately on their own or with crispy bacon or Tomato Fondue (see page 378).

Preserving Mushrooms

PICKLED MUSHROOMS

A good way to preserve a glut ·
MAKES 2-3 X 13OZ JARS

2¼lb wild mushrooms (such as
   penny buns, field mushrooms,
   or a mixture)
4 cups/1 quart best white
   vinegar or 2½ cups
   best white vinegar and 1 cup
   verjuice
4 fresh bay leaves
4 garlic cloves, peeled
4 sprigs thyme
3 teaspoons salt
extra virgin olive oil

Trim the mushrooms carefully and,
only if really necessary, rinse quickly
under cold water. Dry on paper
towels or a kitchen towel.

Put the vinegar and verjuice (if
using) into a stainless steel saucepan
with the bay leaves and garlic.

Bring to a boil, add the
mushrooms, and continue to simmer
for 4–5 minutes – lay a clean saucer
or butter plate on top of the
mushrooms to keep them immersed
in the liquid. Drain the pickling
liquid – this can be saved for
another batch. Put a little olive oil
into sterilized glass jars, divide the
mushrooms, garlic, bay leaves,
thyme, and salt between them, press
down well to remove air bubbles.
Cover with extra virgin olive oil to a
depth of ¾in. Cover and seal, store
in a cool dry place. Serve as part of
an antipasto or on crostini.

WILD MUSHROOMS IN OIL

*These are delicious added to pasta
sauces or stews or just eaten as a snack
on buttered toast ·* **MAKES 2 X 13OZ
JARS**

2¼lb wild or flat mushrooms
salt
extra virgin olive oil for sautéing
   and preserving
1 teaspoon freshly cracked black
   peppercorns
1 sprig thyme, leaves stripped

Slice the mushrooms into ¼in slices,
spread on a baking sheet in a single
layer, and sprinkle lightly with salt.
Allow to stand for 1 hour then drain.

Heat a few tablespoons of extra
virgin olive oil in a wide pan over
high heat, sauté the mushrooms until
cooked, and add lots of freshly
cracked black pepper and thyme
leaves. Pour some extra virgin olive
oil into a couple of sterilized jars,
divide the mushrooms between the
jars and press down to remove any
air bubbles. Cover with extra virgin
olive oil and screw on the lid tightly.
Store in a cool place.

GRANDPOPPY'S MUSHROOM KETCHUP

*It only makes sense to make mushroom
ketchup in the rare years when there's
a glut of wild mushrooms in the fields.
This is becoming less and less common
because of the level of pesticides used in
conventional farming. Occasionally,
though, when the weather at the end of
the summer is warm and humid, we
get a flush of mushrooms, and we can't
bear to waste any of them. We eat
them in every possible way – we make
masses and masses of the base of Wild
Mushroom Soup (see page 48), and we
make a supply of mushroom ketchup,
which keeps for years. You can add it
to game, beef, lamb, chicken stews and
casseroles, shepherd's pie, or just use it
as you would soy sauce.*

as many wild field mushrooms as
   you can gather
salt

FOR EACH 2 PINTS OF KETCHUP, USE:
1 tablespoon whole peppercorns
½oz whole fresh ginger
allspice
cloves
mace
¼ cup whiskey or, if you prefer,
   omit the whiskey and add
   1 tablespoon of best brandy
   to each bottle before sealing

Put the mushrooms into a large
bowl. Sprinkle salt between each
layer to extract juice. Steep for
24 hours, occasionally stirring and
breaking the mushrooms. Allow to
stand for another 12 hours to settle
the sediment.

Pour into another vessel, leaving
behind the sediment. Measure,
strain, and to every quart of ketchup
add the ingredients listed above.
Bottle and seal.

Mushroom ketchup keeps for
years: I have some that is over
5 years old and is still perfect. The
steeped mushrooms themselves can
be composted or fed to the hens.

Wild Coast

When you go to the beach to forage take a good look around you. See what kind of shells have accumulated on the tideline or are scattered here and there on the sand. They're an indicator of the live mollusks you'll find – after all, they haven't fallen out of the sky!

When foraging on the beach it's best to go barefoot or wear flexible-soled shoes or "sand socks." If it's cold, don your wellies (rain boots) because the sand, mud, and rock pools where you're likely to find shellfish and seaweed will be close to the water's edge.

Shellfish

You don't need any special equipment to collect mussels and periwinkles, other than a bucket to put them in, but for cockles or clams, it's good to have a scuffle or rake. For limpets, you'll need a knife to knock them off the rock (we use an old chisel).

There are rich pickings around our shores, but only take what you need, don't abuse the coastline. When foraging for bivalves, it is crucial to make sure that the water is clean and unpolluted. Call your local sea fisheries protection authority, or similar body, for information. Also, be mindful about incoming tides, particularly in areas where you can gather cockles – the waves can be stronger than you think. As with wild mushrooms, it's a very good idea to go out with someone who knows what they're doing, at least the first time. I really recommend taking a bit of time to find someone who knows the local coastline, because there's no substitute for local knowledge.

Cockles *(Cerastoderma edule)*

WHEN TO PICK: in the northern hemisphere, like all shellfish, cockles are best when there is an "R" in the month.

Of all the shellfish I collect, cockles are probably my favorite. Viewed from the front they have a heart-shaped shell, rather like scallops but convex on both sides. Sweet and briny to taste, cockles are so underrated. They're quite hard to find in shops, which makes it all the more pleasurable to go foraging for

them. You'll find them in patches of dark muddy-looking sand, soft mud and muddy gravel around the coastline and estuaries of Ireland and Britain; and they occur as far north as Norway, and around the shores of the Netherlands, France, Spain, and Portugal. Some come up to the surface; some hide underneath. Sometimes I can feel a nubbly textured shell under my welly boot so I know where to dig. We just take a rake with us, but I personally use my fingers to scoop the cockles out of the sand. Look out for spurts of water coming through the sand – another clue that there's a juicy cockle hiding below the surface.

When I forage for cockles, I put them into a woven basket with holes. When I've collected just enough for supper, I wave the basket through the sea water to clean the shells. We always throw one back for good karma. When you find a good spot, don't be greedy; take only the amount you'll use.

One of my favorite ways to eat cockles is just to steam them open in their own juices and eat them with homemade mayonnaise and fresh brown soda bread.

How to clean cockles

Once home, transfer your cockles into a bucket. Cover with fresh cold water for at least an hour so they have a chance to exude any impurities and clean themselves. Discard that water, along with any cockles that aren't tightly shut. Then cook them in the same way as you would mussels.

COCKLES, INDIAN STYLE

Not so much a forgotten skill as just a delicious way to serve cockles. I ate them this way in south India and it's become one of my favorite dishes. The great thing about this recipe is that you can also use it for other bivalves, such as mussels, clams, or palourdes ·

SERVES 6

36–48 cockles
4 tablespoons extra virgin olive oil
1 large onion, finely chopped
6 garlic cloves, crushed or grated
2 teaspoons freshly grated ginger
1–2 fresh green chiles, thinly sliced
2 teaspoons freshly ground cumin
½ teaspoon ground turmeric
½ teaspoon salt
14fl oz can of coconut milk
lots of fresh cilantro, for garnish

Check the cockles; discard any open ones which refuse to close when tapped on the countertop, or those with broken shells. Rinse well.

Put the oil in a sauté pan, add the onion, garlic, and ginger and stir. Cover and cook over low heat until soft but not colored. Add the chile, cumin, turmeric, and salt and cook for 1–2 minutes. Add the coconut milk. Stir and bring to a boil. Add the cockles and toss in the spicy liquid. Cover the sauté pan. Increase the heat and cook for 4–5 minutes or until the shells have opened.

Spoon the cockles in their shells and the spicy liquid into deep bowls. Sprinkle lots of fresh cilantro on top and serve with rice or crusty bread to soak up the delicious juices.

With all these shellfish we save the shells and use them to make shell pictures and to decorate mirrors and picture frames. I grew up in a Midlands village – about as far as it's possible to be from the sea in Ireland – and so pretty seashells remind me of precious day trips to Tramore beach on sunny summer days, where I would collect shells and bring them home in my little tin bucket. My lovely friend Blot Kerr-Wilson used my collection of shells to create the most wonderful shell-encrusted folly in our garden. Another friend has embellished the walls of her loo but it could be your garage or garden shed. Once you get started there's no knowing where you'll stop.

In the kitchen we save several types of shells, particularly Gigas oyster shells and use them as receptacles to serve sauce or flavored butters on the side of a plate. They also make pretty containers for sea salt and freshly cracked pepper or butterballs.

Failing all that, throw shells out to the hens – they will gradually break down into grit which the hens take in with their feed. The shells are full of calcium and will help to strengthen the shells of the eggs.

Variation

COCKLES OR PALOURDES PROVENÇALE

For those of you unfamiliar with the word palourdes, this is a type of clam which is native to the south and west coasts of Ireland and Britain, but it is commercially produced in many countries. Palourdes, also known as the carpet clam, are prepared in the same way as Moules Provençale (see page 64).

Above: *Limpets.*

Limpets (*Crepidula fornicata*)

WHEN TO PICK: year-round, but best after it's had "three drinks of the March water," meaning, after late-winter rains

Limpets (*bairneach* in Irish) are found on rocky shores, exposed at low tide, and look like little Vietnamese hats stuck to the rocks with a vice-like grip (hence the term "stuck like a limpet"). They were probably imported to Europe from North America in the late 19th century on the hulls of ships but they have spread, particularly around the coasts of southern Britain, Ireland, and South Wales.

They are rarely eaten nowadays, but formerly they were part of the coastal Irish diet, not only on the islands but also on the mainland, especially during Lent. Many coastal people can remember that on Holy Thursdays harbors were thronged with women filling their aprons with bairneachs for the Good Friday dinner. It's fun to forage for them with children but making a meal out of them is a bit of a last resort, as they're tough and chewy. Having said that I've found that if you cut the cooked limpets into thin slivers with a sharp knife they are delicious added to herby rice salad or a risotto.

BAIRNEACHS (LIMPETS) WITH BACON

Soak the limpets in fresh, cold water for several hours or overnight to get rid of any impurities. Discard the water. Transfer them to a saucepan and cover with more fresh, cold water. Bring slowly to a boil and simmer gently for 15–20 minutes. Drain, reserving the cooking liquid for fish soup or chowder. Remove the limpets from their shells. Then "de-horn" them, drawing out the trail, which looks like a long, thin string.

Fry a few slices of bacon in the pan until crisp on both sides, remove to a plate. Fry the bairneachs in the bacon fat for a few seconds. Serve with bread and butter.

Opposite: *Bairneachs (Limpets) with Bacon.* **Right:** *Periwinkles.*

Periwinkles *(Littorina littorea)*
WHEN TO PICK: year-round

Periwinkles can be found all along the coast of Ireland but they have also been introduced to the northwest shores of North America and are now a commmon sight in New England rock pools. Sometimes we'll find them crawling up the sea wall in the harbor, sometimes hiding under little fronds of seaweed. Down on Shanagarry strand, when the tide is out and we turn over the stones we find a whole little clutch of these edible little sea snails clinging to them. I always take the students down to collect periwinkles, to pass on this skill. Make sure they're a good size when you collect them – if you collect the tiny ones there won't be any to collect at a later stage, and there's very little in them anyway. We find that there are two types of sea snail that grow side by side. The locals call one "horse perries" and always say they're not edible. They're flatter in shape and have a mother-of-pearl inside. There are still quite a few people around the coast, particularly older people, who collect periwinkles and sell them to a dealer who exports them to Paris to become part of an *assiette de fruits de mer* served along the Champs-Elysées!

Take your children or grandchildren with you when you're foraging for periwinkles. We sometimes light a fire in a little circle of stones so we can cook our foraged feast on the beach. Our grandchildren giggle with delight as they extract the little coiled periwinkles from their shells with pins that have little bobbles on top.

There's a little black disc at the mouth of the shell called the operculum; don't eat it, just flick it off with your pin. Traditionally they were just winkled out of the shell with a pin, dipped in vinegar and eaten there and then. I also remember them being sold in little paper cornets on the pier in Lahinch, County Clare.

How to clean periwinkles
Cover with cold, fresh water and leave to soak for at least 1 hour, longer if possible. You'll need to cover the bucket because they make a valiant and determined effort to escape, which can be a bit unnerving. Discard the water and cook. They are best cooked in seawater.

PERIWINKLES WITH HOMEMADE LEMON MAYONNAISE

The world is made up of people who either take one periwinkle at a time or those who gather a little pile before they start eating – I belong to the first camp because I am too impatient to wait.

fresh live periwinkles
boiling salted water –
    4 tablespoons to every
    ½ gallon/8 cups water

FOR THE LEMON MAYONNAISE
homemade Mayonnaise (see page 252)
zest and freshly squeezed juice of 1 organic lemon

To make the lemon mayonnaise, add the lemon zest to the basic mayonnaise recipe and substitute freshly squeezed lemon juice for the vinegar.

Bring the water to a boil, add the salt and the periwinkles, then bring the water back to a boil. Cook for 3–4 minutes, strain off the water, and allow the periwinkles to get cold. Serve with homemade lemon mayonnaise. Some people love to dip them in vinegar. Either way you will need to supply a large pin for each person to extract the winkles from the shells.

Mussels *(Mytilus edulis)*

WHEN TO PICK: autumn to spring

Mussels live in cooler waters throughout the world and can be collected near the coastlines. They grow in clusters fairly low on the rocks around the coastline, where the tide will wash over them every day. Mussels, like other bivalves, constantly filter water through their bodies, so it's crucially important that the water is clean and unpolluted, otherwise you will be ill. Our closest source for wild mussels is Ballyandreen, east of Cork Harbor. For some reason, they never get very big there, but they are very sweet. You can, however, find full-grown mussels in other places; they're also cultivated in many bays up and down our coasts. You can tell the difference between wild and cultivated mussels by picking them up; wild mussels have much heavier shells, often with little barnacles attached. When you're collecting them, pick the larger ones, but do so carefully, so you don't damage the rest of them.

How to clean mussels

Rinse them in several changes of cold water to clean the shells and get rid of as much sand as possible. If you need to store them, put them into a deep bucket and cover them with some seaweed or damp paper towels and a weight; I'm not sure why we weight them down, but we always do. Keep them in a cold place, and most of them will stay alive for several days, but it's best to eat them as soon as possible, as they'll be most delicious that way.

How to check that mussels are fresh

With cockles, mussels, and oysters, the shells must be tightly shut. If they're even slightly open, they're dead. So check that every shell is totally closed. If any is open, tap the mussel on the countertop; if it does not close within a few seconds, discard. (The rule with shellfish is always: "If in doubt, throw it out.")

How to cook mussels

You may want to scrape off any barnacles from wild mussel shells, but this is not essential. Remove the beard (the little tuft of tough "hair" which attached the mussel to the rock or rope it grew on). Wash the mussels well in several changes of cold water. Then spread them in a single layer in a pan, covered with a folded kitchen towel or the lid and cook over low heat – no need to add any liquid. This usually takes 2–3 minutes; the mussels are cooked just as soon as the shells open (cockles and palourdes can be cooked in the same way). Remove them from the pan immediately or they will shrink in size and become tough.

MUSSELS WITH HOMEMADE MAYONNAISE

One of my favorite simple suppers. Just before eating, steam open the mussels, turn them out into a big bowl and serve warm with homemade Mayonnaise (see page 252) and lots of crusty Brown Soda Bread (see page 199). You don't even need cutlery – use empty mussel shells to scoop.

Opposite: *Periwinkles with Homemade Lemon Mayonnaise.*

Foraging · 63

MOULES PROVENÇALE

Don't skimp on the garlic in this recipe or the mussels will taste rather dull and "bready." Wild garlic or watercress can be substituted for parsley here, depending on the season. This recipe can also be used for cockles and oysters · **SERVES 6-8**

48 fresh mussels, about 3½-4lb

PROVENÇALE BUTTER
2 large garlic cloves
2 tablespoons finely chopped parsley
1 tablespoon olive oil
6 tablespoons butter, softened
fresh white bread crumbs (see page 577)

Cook mussels as instructed on previous page. Discard one shell from each of them. Loosen the mussel from the other shell, but leave it in the shell. Allow to get quite cold.

While the mussels cook, make the Provençale butter. Peel and crush the garlic and pound it in a mortar with the finely chopped parsley and extra virgin olive oil. Gradually beat in the butter (this may be done either in a bowl or a food processor).

Spread the soft garlic butter evenly over the mussels in the shells and dip each one into the soft, white bread crumbs. They may be prepared ahead to this point and frozen in a covered box lined with plastic wrap or aluminum foil.

Arrange in individual serving dishes. Brown under the grill and serve with crusty white bread to mop up the delicious garlicky juices.

Razor Clams *(Ensis arcuatus)*
WHEN TO GATHER: spring

Razor clams are great fun but certainly challenging to gather. They live along North America's Atlantic coast, from Canada to North Carolina, buried in intertidal sand. In late spring, just before Easter, we usually get a craving and head off to collect them on some sandy beaches we know in West Cork. We take containers of salt with us and search for the little tell-tale air-holes in the sand that indicate that a clam is hiding below. We crouch down and pour a little salt into the hole, which forces the razor clam to shoot up out of the sand. You need to have your hand over the hole, ready to grab the clam when it shoots up. You have to be quick, because in a split second the clam will have shot back down. Several times I've been left with the empty shell in my hand, the clam having disappeared back underground. The ones we get are not as small and delicate as those from the Venetian lagoons, but I still absolutely love them and keep wondering why I don't see them more often on restaurant menus or for sale in fish shops. No matter, a razor clam outing is one of the most exciting foraging expeditions.

How to clean razor clams
Put the razor clams into a bucket, cover with cold water and leave to purify for a few hours. Discard the water. Dry the razor clams.

PAN-GRILLED RAZOR CLAMS WITH WILD GARLIC BUTTER

Razor clams, unlike mussels, don't have to be tightly shut before you cook them because you will only have gathered live ones. They are delicious either cooked in a pan like mussels or opened on a grill over an open fire. Don't remove anything – you can eat every bit of the clam except the shell.

Heat a grill pan or sauté pan until it's very hot and lay the razor clams in a single layer on the surface. Reduce the heat to medium and cook the clams until they open more fully, 3–4 minutes depending on size. As they cook, turn them over so the heat is evenly distributed. Serve them in warm bowls with wild garlic butter (see page 216) melting into their juices, and some crusty bread to mop it all up.

Variation
RAZOR CLAM RISOTTO
Razor clams are delicious added to risotto. Cook them as above and when they open remove from the shell. Slice thinly across the grain and add to the risotto at the end of cooking, with lots of freshly chopped herbs. Large razor clams can be quite chewy, so this is a brilliant way to deal with them and make a few razor clams go a long way.

Sea urchin *(Echinus esculentus)*
WHEN TO EAT: late autumn to spring
Edible sea urchins are widespread along the coasts of America and north and west

Europe. They used to be plentiful on the West Coast of Ireland, but were fished nearly to extinction in the 1980s. They're now undergoing a revival as farmed seafood, which do little damage to the environment, and the net result is very good. The supply is recovering, but don't be greedy with what you take. You'll find them in rock pools, often hidden in crevices. Sea urchin can be served raw as part of a seafood platter – you just eat the five little briny pieces of roe inside. At Ballymaloe, we also serve them lightly cooked or we mix the sieved roes with a little homemade mayonnaise, as in the recipe below.

SEA URCHINS WITH HOMEMADE MAYONNAISE

Sea urchins certainly can require an act of faith to tackle for the first time. Real connoisseurs eat them raw and our Mediterranean students make all sorts of appreciative "Oo la la" noises when they find them au naturel on their plates. Lightly cooked, the corals can be sieved and mixed with a little mayonnaise. We then dip little soldiers of toast into the delicate purée and eat the rest with a spoon from the shell, just like a prickly egg! · **SERVES 6 AS A STARTER**

6 sea urchins
about 3 tablespoons homemade Mayonnaise (see page 252)

3 slices hot buttered toast, to serve

Cook the sea urchins for 3–4 minutes in boiling salted water.

Drain and allow to cool. Scrape the prickles from the top of the shell. Lever out the plug with the end of a teaspoon or the point of kitchen scissors. Cut a larger hole. Scoop out the coral, sieve it and mix with the mayonnaise. But be careful not to make it too mild – it should still taste distinctively of sea urchin! Taste and add more mayonnaise if necessary. Fill back into the shells and serve with fingers of hot toast.

Variation

SEA URCHIN WITH SCRAMBLED EGG
If you happen to have a few spare sea urchins, make a little soft scrambled egg and lay some sea urchin coral and snipped flat parsley on top. Serve immediately. The sea urchin will warm gently as you make your way to the table. Eat with hot buttered toast.

Seaweed

Like mushrooms, seaweeds are an entire world of undiscovered knowledge for many people although they have been part of the diet of coastal peoples since time immemorial. Historically, carrageen moss and dillisk have been the most widely used as foods in Ireland. Now there is a renewed interest in seaweeds, as more people realize the value of this completely natural source of minerals and trace elements: iodine, bromine, iron, zinc, and magnesium. In our family, the babies are weaned onto carrageen moss pudding and we

ourselves, and guests at Ballymaloe House and the cookery school, enjoy it at least once a week.

I'm a great believer in the value of seaweed for the soil and consequently the flavor and nutritional make-up of the food grown in it. Anyone can collect seaweed. The next time you walk on the beach, why not take along a net bag to collect some seaweed for your garden or balcony. We collect as much seaweed as we possibly can for the farm; it is then spread directly onto the fields and garden. We also add some to the compost, and our pigs and hens love it too!

Seaweed is a brilliant fertilizer. Years ago, coastal farmers collected seaweed from the local beaches several times a year. Conditions were, and still are, best after a storm – the high winds and rough seas blew the seaweed into mounds, making it easy to collect. Farmers really valued this in an era before artificial fertilizer. They marked out their patch with pitch forks, and occasionally tempers flared and a battle ensued when someone encroached on someone else's patch. Oarweed (*Laminaria digitata*) was particularly highly prized. Previous generations knew it was high in iodine and potash, and was especially good for potatoes and root vegetables like carrots and turnips. They were careful not to let the oarweed dry out or get crispy, and spread it onto the ground as soon as possible after it was collected.

Before you collect seaweed, learn how to harvest it sustainably and only take what you need.

Carrageen, Irish Moss
(Chondrus crispus)

WHEN TO PICK: at the lowest spring tides, usually in late spring, but earlier in the season is fine too

WHERE TO FIND: on both sides of the Atlantic: on western and southern shores of Britain and Ireland

Carrageen moss has moderate levels of iodine and trace elements and is full of natural gelatin. It is one of the most valuable of all wild foods as it is loaded with vitamins, minerals and trace elements, and is rich in natural gelatin. Carrageen helps the metabolism to work to its optimum, and so breaks down fats while giving us lots of strength and energy. It can be used to set liquids or give body to soups, stews, and jams. It's another example of a peasant food being rediscovered by chefs and made "cool."

The recipe for the pudding below is from my mother-in-law, Myrtle Allen. It's the best and most delicious I know for carrageen. Our guests are fascinated by the idea of a dessert made with seaweed and they just love it. The secret with carrageen is not to use too much. It is such an effective natural gelling agent that if you are over-generous the pudding will be like Indian rubber – most unappetizing.

The late Fred Dawes, who was a neighbor of ours in nearby Ballyandreen in East Cork, taught Myrtle how to forage for and harvest carrageen moss, and she, in turn, brought me down to the strand and taught me. Fred picked it off the rocks in the little cove of Ballyandreen after the spring tides (in fact, "carrageen" means "little

rock" in Irish). He then spread it out on the bouncy grass on the cliffs where it would be washed by the rain and bleached by the sun. He turned it every few days and when it was ready, he'd store it. Carrageen keeps almost indefinitely. Jockeys eat it because it gives them strength without putting on weight, and racehorse and greyhound owners have been known to feed their animals carrageen for speed. All our babes were weaned onto Carrageen Moss Pudding.

If you don't live near the sea, you may be able to find packets of dried carrageen from Caribbean stores, because it is traditionally used in the West Indies to make a spiced milk shake thought to have aphrodisiac properties.

CARRAGEEN MOSS PUDDING WITH RHUBARB AND SWEET CICELY COMPOTE

My favorite way to eat carrageen moss pudding is just with softly whipped cream and some brown sugar sprinkled over the top, but it's also lovely with a fruit compote. The fruit I use varies with the season, but I'm giving this particular recipe for Rhubarb and Sweet Cicely Compote because we use a wonderful variety of rhubarb that's been passed down through the Allen family from generation to generation; even when they moved house, they brought their rhubarb and globe artichokes with them. If there's a particularly good variety of fruit or vegetable in your family, treasure it and make sure you pass it on ·

SERVES 6

¼oz cleaned, well-dried carrageen moss (1 semi-closed handful)

3 cups whole milk

1 vanilla bean or ½ teaspoon pure vanilla extract

1 organic egg

1 tablespoon superfine sugar

TO SERVE

packed brown sugar and softly whipped cream

Rhubarb and Sweet Cicely Compote (see below)

Soak the carrageen in a little bowl of tepid water for 10 minutes. It will swell and increase in size. Strain off the water and put the carrageen into a saucepan with the milk and the vanilla bean, if using. Bring to a boil and simmer very gently, covered, for 20 minutes. At that point and not before, separate the egg, put the yolk into a bowl, add the sugar and vanilla extract, if using, and whisk together for a few seconds, then pour the milk and carrageen moss through a strainer onto the egg yolk mixture, whisking all the while. By now the carrageen remaining in the strainer will be swollen and exuding jelly. You need as much of this as possible, so press it through the strainer and whisk it into the egg and milk mixture. Test for a set in a saucer as one would with gelatin. Whisk the egg white stiffly and fold it gently into the custard; it will rise to make a fluffy top.

Serve chilled with packed brown sugar and cream, or with a compote of fruit in season, such as the poached rhubarb and sweet cicely compote below.

Above: *Off to forage for carrageen, with Ballycotton Island visible in the distance.*
Below: *Myrtle Allen teaching myself and my son-in-law, Rupert, the skill of identifying carrageen.*

RHUBARB AND SWEET CICELY COMPOTE

Follow the rhubarb compote recipe on page 494. Add 4 sprigs of sweet cicely to the cold syrup and poach the fruit in the usual way. Sweet cicely is a naturally sweet herb, a perennial that we grow in the garden but also grows in the wild in spring. It's got feathery, fern-like leaves and fluffy white flowers in late spring. We use it a lot for garnishing, but also to flavor syrups, as in this compote. You can even reduce the sugar in the compote, as the inclusion of sweet cicely will sweeten the fruit. Decorate with sweet cicely leaves and flowers.

CARRAGEEN MOSS SYRUP

Not the most palatable drink in the world, but miraculous for chest infections and coughs. Carrageen is so light that it's difficult to measure in small amounts, so a cup measure is what we use here · SERVES 1

¼ **cup carrageen**
1–2 teaspoons honey
freshly squeezed juice of 1 lemon

Soak the carrageen for 10 minutes in ¾ cup of cold water. Remove the carrageen and discard the water. Put the carrageen in 1 cup fresh, cold water and bring slowly to a boil. Strain, stir in honey and lemon juice to taste. The drink should be thick and syrupy.

Dulse *(Palmaria palmata)*

WHEN TO PICK: spring to autumn; best in autumn

WHERE TO FIND: along the shores of the north Atlantic

Dulse is a winey-brown seaweed known as dillisk in Ireland. Its leathery fronds are said to resemble the human hand, hence its Latin name. It was obviously an important food from earliest times: it is mentioned in the ancient Irish, pre-Christian, Brehon Laws, and there was a penalty for consuming another person's dulse without their permission. It continues to be popular in Ireland, Northern Ireland, Iceland, and parts of Canada. Dulse has thick stems or stipes and anchors itself to rocks by a holdfast. It can be picked at low tide; use a sharp knife and don't damage the holdfast. Traditionally it is spread out on a tin roof or on grass or shingles to dry in the sun. It was sold at fairs and markets all over the country, but is now available in health food shops and local shops close to the coast. Many people told me of sending little parcels of it to the emigrants in America who had a yearning for it. It can be eaten raw or added to fish soups or stews or soda bread. It was also mixed with potatoes for dulse champ. It is known to be rich in potassium and magnesium and iron, and adds a salty flavor to otherwise bland foods.

DILLISK SANDWICHES

In County Antrim an old man told me about dillisk sandwiches. He would simply put a good layer of raw dillisk between two slices of buttered white bread. The result was nutritious, delicious – and the saltiness is addictive!

DILLISK BREAD

Follow the White Soda Bread recipe on page 561. Soak ½–1oz dried dillisk in cold water for about 10 minutes. Drain and chop. Add to the dry ingredients of the soda bread and follow the rest of the recipe.

DILLISK CHAMP

Follow the recipe for Nettle Champ on page 25 but replace the nettles with 1–2oz pre-soaked dillisk, drained and cut into strips.

Oarweed, kelp *(Laminaria digitata)*

WHEN TO PICK: spring–autumn
WHERE TO FIND: on the North Atlantic coasts of Europe and North America and around most of Britain except parts of the east coast

This prolific seaweed is easy to recognize, light to dark brown in color, with thick, leathery wide fronds attached to a thick stipe and a root called a holdfast that attaches it firmly to the rocks.

Kelp is best harvested at low tide in spring or early summer with a billhook, machete, or a sharp knife, but much of it washes ashore, particularly after a storm. Sustainable harvesting is a really important consideration as always: be sure to cut the fronds well above the growing tip, leaving it intact and able to regenerate. Irish oarweed is tougher than Japanese kombu, although both are species of kelp. The best variety for eating found in Ireland and Scotland is the winged kelp, *Alaria esculenta*. Oarweed is high in iodine, especially in the spring, so use it sparingly; too much iodine is not good for the system.

Oarweed makes an interesting and nutritious addition to salads and can also be used as a thickener in soups, stews and casseroles. It dries excellently; it can then be ground into a powder and used as a condiment. Add a piece of kelp to the pot when you're cooking potatoes.

KELP AND SMOKED SEAFOOD SALAD

My nephew Ivan Whelan used to serve this lovely salad at his restaurant, Grapefruit Moon, in Ballycotton. If you can't find kelp then try wakame, a Japanese seaweed that can be found in health-food shops · SERVES 6–8

2oz dried kelp or wakame
5oz Cold-smoked Salmon (see page 482)
5oz smoked eel, weighed after skinning and boning
2oz pickled ginger (gari)
⅓ cup pine nuts
3 tablespoons soy sauce
3 tablespoons Asian sesame oil
1½ tablespoons rice wine vinegar
salt and freshly ground pepper
1 tablespoon freshly chopped cilantro
30 Smoked Mussels (see page 484)

Soak the seaweed in cold water for about 30 minutes to reconstitute. Drain very well in a colander and press out all the excess water. Put into a large mixing bowl.

Cut the smoked salmon and eel into small pieces and chop the ginger. Add these to the seaweed, along with the pine nuts, soy sauce, sesame oil, and rice wine vinegar,

Above: *Dried carrageen.*

cilantro, and salt and pepper to taste. Mix gently to avoid breaking up the fish. Serve mounded on a plate with smoked mussels dotted around.

Coastal Plants

These plants grow within sight and sound of the sea and have a slightly salty tang.

Alexander, horse parsley
(Smyrnium olusatrum)

PARTS TO USE: leaves, stems
WHEN TO PICK: spring
WHERE TO FIND: widespread in Europe, western Asia, and North Africa

Alexander grows in profusion along the cliffs, roadsides, and hedges near the sea in the south of Ireland and the UK. It flowers from late March to June, depending on the weather. It's a Mediterranean plant that was introduced to the British Isles by the Romans, and was originally planted as a vegetable. It can still be found growing around monasteries, abbeys, and castles. The flavor is delicate and delicious; in fact, the taste is slightly like sea kale.

Alexanders can grow up to 5ft tall, are bright green and stalky, and have umbelliferous flowers. The young leaves are good in salads and the peeled stems make a tasty vegetable. They are best harvested just before the buds burst into flower. Otherwise, like many plants, they become bitter.

COOKED ALEXANDERS

This simple way of cooking alexanders can be the basis for several other recipes
· SERVES 4–6

1½lb Alexander stems (cut close to the ground for maximum length)
4 cups/1 quart water
1 tablespoon salt
butter or extra virgin olive oil
freshly ground pepper

Cut the stems into ½–2in lengths and peel off the thin outer skin as you would with rhubarb. Cook in boiling salted water for 6–8 minutes or until a knife will pierce a stem easily. Drain well, then toss in a little melted butter or extra virgin olive oil and lots of freshly ground pepper.

Variation
Cook as above, drain, and transfer to a gratin dish. Coat with a rich Mornay Sauce (see page 119) and top with a mixture of shredded Cheddar cheese and Buttered Crumbs (see page 577).

ALEXANDER FRITTERS
Cook the Alexanders as in the recipe above. Drain well and pat dry. Dip the pieces one by one in the same kind of egg-white batter used for Fish and Chips (see page 94). Deep-fry until crisp. Toss in superfine sugar and enjoy as a snack.

Sea spinach, Sea beet
(Beta vulgaris ssp. maritima)

WHEN TO PICK: spring–early autumn
WHERE TO FIND: common around the shores of England, Wales, most of Ireland, and far west Scotland

If you live near a rocky strand, look out for sea spinach – its shiny green leaves are unmistakable. It is, in fact, the ancestor to most cultivated varieties of beets. It can

Above: *Sea spinach.*

Above: *Alexander.*

be cooked exactly like garden spinach and used in the same way, for example, try serving it in Middle Eastern-style with raisins and pine nuts and a touch of cinnamon. Not surprisingly, because sea spinach is washed by the tides, it is full of iodine, minerals, and other trace elements and it has an addictive salty tang. Sea spinach is tougher and slightly stronger in flavor than garden spinach, so it takes a little longer to cook.

SEA SPINACH SOUP

Like so many wild plants, sea spinach has a much more robust and distinctive flavor than garden spinach, and feels even more nutritious as you eat it. You can make make this soup with either · SERVES 6–8

4 tablespoons butter
½ cup chopped onion
1 medium potato, chopped
salt and freshly ground black
    pepper
2 cups Chicken Stock
    (see page 262)
2 cups whole milk
8–12oz sea spinach, stems removed,
    chopped
freshly grated nutmeg

FOR THE GARNISH
whipped cream (optional)
freshly chopped parsley

Melt the butter in a heavy-bottomed saucepan. When it foams add the onion and potato and stir them until well coated. Sprinkle with salt and freshly ground pepper. Cover and cook over low heat for 10 minutes.

Add the boiling stock and milk, return to a boil, and cook until the potatoes and onions are soft. Add the sea spinach and boil, uncovered, for about 3–5 minutes, until the sea spinach is cooked. Do not overcook or the soup will lose its fresh green color.

Purée in a blender, taste, and add some freshly grated nutmeg. Serve in warm bowls garnished with a dollop of whipped cream and some chopped parsley.

BAKED SEA OR RAINBOW TROUT WITH SEA SPINACH BUTTER SAUCE

We can sometimes get large trout that are about two years old and have wonderful flavor – much better than the smaller ones. The skill here is cooking en papillote, wrapped either in aluminum foil or parchment paper, which is a great way to cook fish because it seals in the juices. You can use this technique to cook anything from a large fish to an individual portion · SERVES 4

4–4½lb whole rainbow trout
2–4 tablespoons butter
salt and freshly ground black
    pepper
sprig of fennel

SEA SPINACH BUTTER SAUCE
3oz sea spinach leaves
½ cup heavy cream
6 tablespoons butter, cubed

aluminum foil or parchment paper

Preheat the oven to 375°F.

Gut the trout and rinse well, making sure to remove the line of blood from the inside near the backbone. Pat dry with paper towels, season inside and out with salt and freshly ground pepper. Put a blob of butter and a sprig of fennel into the cavity of the trout. Take a large sheet of aluminum foil or parchment, smear a little butter on the center, put the trout on top and fold loosely over the edges into a papillote shape. Seal and crimp well to make sure that none of the juices escape. Place on a baking sheet and bake for about 30 minutes.

Meanwhile make the sea spinach butter sauce. Remove the stems from the sea spinach, rinse and cook the leaves in 2 cups boiling water with a pinch of salt. Cook for 4–5 minutes or until soft, drain, press out all the water and chop finely.

Pour the cream into a saucepan and simmer over low heat until reduced to about 3 tablespoons or until it is in danger of burning. Then, over very low heat, whisk in the butter bit by bit, as though you were making Hollandaise sauce. Stir in the sea spinach.

When the fish is cooked, open the parcel – there will be lots of delicious juice, use some of this to thin out the sauce and further enhance its flavor. Put the parcel onto a warm serving dish and bring to the table. Skin the fish and lift the juicy pink flesh onto warm plates. Spoon the sea spinach butter sauce over the fish and serve immediately.

Sea kale *(Crambe maritima)*

WHEN TO PICK: early spring for
3–4 weeks only

WHERE TO FIND: Common on the
shores of Britain, Ireland, the North
Atlantic and Mediterranean coasts of
Europe, but rare in North America

Sea kale, known as strand
cabbage or *praiseach trá* in Gaelic,
grows on sandy, pebbly strands all
around the coast of Britain and
much of Europe. It's easy to
recognize as it resembles a rough
cabbage. Later in the year it will be
covered with white flowers which
become bobbly seed heads in
autumn. As with wild mushrooms,
people who knew where to find
patches of sea kale would guard
them secretly. The plants are
perennial, re-emerging in the same
place every year, and when the first
strands appeared, the locals would
pile up pebbles or rocks around the
crown so the shoots would grow
blanched, making them more
delicate and delicious (sea kale has a
much stronger cabbagey-kale flavor
when the growing shoots are
exposed to light).

In the 18th and 19th centuries
people found sea kale so delectable
that it was a sought-after vegetable
in country-house gardens. We grow
it in the herb garden and in the
kitchen garden. It's rarely found in
shops, so for that reason alone it's
really worth trying to find a space in
your garden or flower bed. To
protect the sea kale from late
autumn through spring, you'll need
chimney liners, plastic buckets or, in
an ideal world, terracotta sea kale
pots to block the light. When sea
kale becomes more abundant, it

makes a wonderful accompaniment
to fish, particularly poached wild
Irish salmon or sea trout.

SEA KALE WITH CHERVIL HOLLANDAISE SAUCE

*Sea kale is so delicate and precious,
you want a sauce that won't mask its
flavor. Chervil has a very light touch,
and, as such, enhances rather than
overwhelms* · SERVES 4–6

1lb young sea kale stems
salt and freshly ground pepper
Hollandaise Sauce (see page 248)
1–2 tablespoons freshly snipped
chervil

Wash the sea kale gently and trim
into manageable lengths – about 4in.
Bring about 2 cups water to a rolling
boil, and add 1 teaspoon salt. Drop
in the sea kale, cover and boil until
tender, about 5–10 minutes,
depending on thickness. Meanwhile
make the Hollandaise sauce and add
1–2 tablespoons freshly snipped
chervil. Taste and correct the
seasoning.

Just as soon as a knife will pierce
the sea kale easily, drain it and then
serve on hot buttered toast with
chervil Hollandaise.

Sea purslane *(Halimione portulacoides)*

WHEN TO PICK: early summer
WHERE TO FIND: salt marshes and
coastal dunes throughout much of
Europe

This edible species of sea
purslane grows in profusion on salt
marshes in the south and east of

Above: *Rock samphire.*

England and in pockets on the coast
of County Down in Northern
Ireland. It flowers from mid-summer
to late autumn, so pick the succulent
evergreen leaves before then. The
grey-green leaves look very similar
to sage, but are smaller. Sea purslane
is delicious raw in salads or quickly
tossed in a little butter or olive oil as
an accompaniment to fish or lamb.

Rock samphire *(Crithmum maritimum)* and Marsh samphire *(Salicornia europea)*

WHEN TO PICK: Rock samphire:
spring–early summer, before it
flowers; marsh samphire: summer.
WHERE TO FIND: Rock samphire: all
around the coast of Britain; marsh
samphire: tidal estuaries, saltmarsh
and mudflats of England, especially
Norfolk, and France

The two types of samphire that
we gather in the wild are rock
samphire and marsh samphire (also

known as glasswort or sea asparagus). They are unrelated in all but name, but you can cook both in the same way. They work beautifully with butter sauces and vinaigrettes.

Rock samphire grows in little cracks between the cliff rocks. Years ago, it was much sought after and gathered annually on the higher cliffs, along with gulls' eggs. We pick it on the lower cliffs at a local beach called Ballyandreen from April to June, before it flowers, otherwise the flavor becomes petrol-like, bitter, and nasty. Never uproot the plants. Marsh samphire, which looks a bit like a miniature cactus without the prickles, grows, as the name suggests, in salt marshes close to the sea. It's easy to gather if you don't mind the occasional scratch from surrounding bushes and getting covered in mud. Pinch off the young shoots above the root. Later in the season, marsh samphire develops a tough fibrous core, so the earlier you harvest it, the better. The fresher it is, the more vibrant the flavor, but it keeps remarkably well for 1–2 weeks. Marsh samphire is now much sought after by creative young chefs who are putting it onto their menus. We sell it at the farmers' market and people who aren't familiar with it fall in love with its salty flavor and crunchy texture.

Right: *Marsh samphire.*

ROCK OR MARSH SAMPHIRE WITH MELTED BUTTER

Serve alone on toast with fish dishes ·
SERVES 8 AS AN ACCOMPANIMENT

8oz samphire
freshly ground pepper
2–4 tablespoons butter

Cover the samphire with cold water, bring to a boil, and simmer for about 5–6 minutes or until tender. Drain off the water, season with freshly ground pepper, and toss in butter – no salt because samphire has a natural salty tang.

PICKLED SAMPHIRE
Samphire can also be pickled. Anne Kennedy from Rostrevor in County Down sent me this recipe. Gather the samphire and soak it for 3 hours in brine. Place in a pan, cover with a mixture of 3 parts white vinegar to 1 part water and a little salt. Cover, simmer for 30 minutes, leave until cold, pack into jars, and cover with the cooking liquid mixed with a little fresh white vinegar. It should retain a good green color.

Fish

Even though I grew up in a Midlands village, far from the sea, we had fish for dinner virtually every Friday. This was tradition because Friday was a fast day in the Catholic church when meat was forbidden. Our fish came on the bus that travelled daily from Dublin to Cork. As soon as it arrived, we would race down to the village shop to have first choice. There was virtually always whiting, and bright orange smoked haddock in a wooden box, but occasionally there was plaice which was a great treat. Mummy would dip it in seasoned flour and fry it in a little butter in a pan. We all loved it. Years later, when I came to Ballymaloe, which is just two miles from the sea, a local fisherman brought a bucket of fresh plaice to the kitchen door on my very first evening. Myrtle Allen showed me how to fillet it, and then she too dipped it in seasoned flour and cooked it in foaming butter, just as Mummy had done. We ate it for supper with a little green salad and some bread and butter. When I tasted it, I simply couldn't believe it was the same fish I'd had at home. It was exquisite, and I suddenly realized that I had never tasted truly fresh fish before. I now know that the fish I'd had growing up must have been at least a week old, though I didn't realize it at the time. I feel that must be the explanation for why some people can't get excited about fish.

At the Cookery School we've been doing a sustainable seafood course for the last few years, as part of the Forgotten Skills series. The whole issue of sustainability is a big one, and if we want to keep fish in the sea we have to be careful how we eat them. Many species have been seriously overfished in recent years, some virtually to the point of extinction. Years ago most fish was caught in small trawlers close to the shore but now fishermen need bigger boats that can go out further to catch enough fish to make a living. They regularly stay at sea for three to five days, so by the time the catch is landed, the reality is that the fish will be anywhere from one to five days old. The latter, even when iced down, is far from fresh by my standards.

The hardships that many fishermen have had to contend with in recent times has led some to sell directly to the public, which has delighted people in coastal areas. One day-boat fisherman in our area telephones his wife with the list of the catch on his way back to the harbor. She then calls her friends and customers – and sometimes the whole catch is sold before he even sails into the harbor. Now, that's fresh!

For decades, a much-loved local character called Tommy Sliney sold fish fresh off the boats from a donkey and cart on Ballycotton pier. He always used to tell me that he was surprised that I bought fish whole because according to him, the housewives in the modern bungalows he sold to didn't know what to do with a whole fish – and that was 30 years ago! Buying a whole fish is cheaper, and it's not rocket science to fillet one. Even if the fish fillets are not a thing of beauty the first time around, practice makes perfect – and you'll have the bones and head to make stock. Plus, when you're on holiday by the sea, wouldn't it be great to know how to deal with a fresh fish you've just caught or bought from a local fisherman?

The other forgotten skill is collecting fish in the wild. If you're going to go foraging for fish, however, be responsible and think of the future – take only enough for your own consumption. See the Foraging chapter for more on gathering shellfish such as cockles, mussels, periwinkles, and razor clams.

Whereas nowadays it may not be necessary to preserve fish for survival, salting, pickling, and curing are also skills worth mastering, purely because the flavor you can produce is so good. It also adds another dimension to your cooking repertoire, and to your diet.

Buying fresh fish

For those of us who love fish, the skill of being able to judge accurately whether fish is fresh or not is vital. The most important thing to remember when buying or sourcing fish, is that fresh fish never smells, it just has the merest scent of the sea, reminiscent of fresh seaweed. Fresh fish looks lively and stiff, and the skin glistens. By the time the eyes are sunken, the fish is a week old. Stale fish looks distinctly miserable; the gills will be dark and the skin can be gritty and dry, and it has a strong fishy smell. It doesn't matter if the fishmonger winks at you and says he caught it himself, if it smells, it's not fresh.

That's all straightforward enough, but between the time fish is really fresh and the time it is stale there are several days during which time it will be gradually deteriorating. It is during this period that it is most difficult to tell just what condition it is in, particularly if the fish has been filleted and cut into small pieces. You have to judge by the color and smell. Check that the flesh of white fish is white and not at all discolored, and that the under-skin of flat fish is quite white and not yellowing.

For those who live far from the sea, frozen fillets can be excellent. Good firms freeze their fish in prime condition within hours of being caught, so it is far preferable to buying "fresh" fish that is several days old.

HOW TO PREPARE FISH

First decide whether you need to scale the fish. Grey sea mullet has scales as large as a thumbnail and definitely needs scaling. Other fish with smaller scales, such as plaice or sea bream, need not necessarily be scaled. Some fish either have tiny scales or are completely smooth, and don't need to be scaled at all. If you're poaching the fish, there is no need to scale it as the skin will be taken off after cooking. I always leave the skin on in this case as I feel the scales help to keep more flavor in. If you're pan-grilling, however, the fish must be scaled because you'll want to eat the delicious crispy skin – and crispy scales are quite a different matter!

How to scale a fish

Remove the scales by holding the fish by the tail and pushing against the scales with the back of a knife from the tail to the head on both sides.

How to gut a fish

Flat fish are gutted in the boats as soon as they are caught because their insides deteriorate very quickly, so you just need to wash them out thoroughly. You can use the method below to gut any round fish, such as salmon, mackerel, pollock, and grey sea mullet.

It's best to gut fish close to the sink. Put a cutting board on the drainer and cover with a couple of sheets of newspaper. If you are cooking the fish whole, you don't need to remove the head. However, if you plan to fillet the fish you may find it easier to remove the head before gutting, for ease of handling.

1. REMOVE THE HEAD

Lay the fish on its side, lift up the fin below the head and using a filleting knife, cut off the head. But rather than cutting straight across, cut into a V-shape around the back of the fin so you don't waste the lovely thick piece of flesh at the back of the head. Turn the fish over and repeat on the other side. Then twist the head and detach it from the body. Discard the head or use for fish stock (in which case you'll need to remove the gills first).

2. GUT THE FISH

Insert the tip of the filleting knife into the vent at the tail end, and slit through the belly towards the head end. Then scoop out the intestines with your hand and discard. Rinse out the cavity under cold running water. Pay particular attention to the line of blood under the backbone – this can be removed using your fingertip. In larger fish like salmon, a teaspoon with a pointed end is a great help because you can just run it along the backbone. Rinse the fish well again and refrigerate until needed. When gutting herring, you'll want to save the roe, so slit the belly carefully so as not to damage the roes. Detach the roe from the intestines and discard the latter. Rinse the roe gently, refrigerate, and use as quickly as possible.

How to fillet a flat fish

Use this method for flat fish such as plaice, sole, halibut, brill, or turbot. If you are going to fillet a fish with any kind of finesse, allow yourself the luxury of a sharp filleting knife with a flexible blade.

• Place the fish on a cutting board, dark skin upwards with the head towards you. With the point of the knife, cut down the center of the fish, onto the bone, from tail to head – just left of the spine, placing the other hand flat on the fillet to steady the fish. Keeping the knife almost flat, slide it between the flesh and the bone.

• Use long, sweeping strokes from tail to head to gradually detach the fillet.

• Turn the fish around and slip the knife over the spine. This time cut from head to tail and remove the fillet in the same way.

• Turn the fish over and repeat the process on the other side.

• Use the well-rinsed bones for a fish stock (see page 80).

How to fillet a round fish

Use this method for round fish such as salmon, haddock, cod, pollock, grey sea mullet, or mackerel. Use a sharp filleting knife with a flexible blade.

• Put the gutted fish on a cutting board.

• First, using the point of the knife, cut around the base of the head (if it is still attached) down to the bone.

• With one hand flat on the fish to steady it, slit the skin from the head end to the tail, just above the backbone, using the back fin as a guide.

• Slide the knife across the bone in long, sweeping movements – keeping the blade as flat as possible – until you reach the pin bones. Then use your thumb to press the flesh back off the bones, and tease your knife under the pin bones until they're released.

• Slide the knife down under the rib cage and detach the remaining part of the fillet.

• Turn the fish over and detach the fillet from the other side in the same way.

When filleting salmon, remove the flesh all in one piece and remove the pin bones with salmon tweezers afterwards.

Above: *Scaling a sea bass.*

How to skin fish

Put the fillet of fish skinside down on the board. Cut through the flesh, down onto the skin at the tail end. Hold onto the skin then pull the tail end and, with the knife at a 45° angle, half push, half saw the flesh off the skin. If the knife is at the right angle there should be no waste. Use the skin in fish stock (see page 80).

Seasoning fish before cooking

Sprinkling a fish with salt on both sides and leaving it for even 10 minutes before cooking dramatically improves both the flavor and texture. Even if the fish is not spanking fresh, it firms up the flesh and imbues it with extra flavor. This is often common practice in Japan. It's particularly worthwhile with salmon.

Raw Fish

As far as I know, there was never a tradition of eating raw fish in the British Isles apart from a few adventurous souls, unlike countries like Japan where sushi and sashimi are a way of life. When I serve thinly sliced raw fish at a dinner party people absolutely love it, but I know now not to tell them it's raw until after they've told me it's delicious. Raw fish is wonderful, but only if you have access to really, really fresh fish.

WILD SALMON CARPACCIO

I love wild salmon served in this way. Sometimes I serve it with a plain mayonnaise, other times I use a thin dill- or fennel-flavored mayonnaise. And sometimes I sharpen it up with lemon or lime. Served with fresh soda bread, it's a fantastic appetizer. But don't dream of doing this with farmed salmon; only do it if you have a fantastically fresh, wild fish. I love to scatter a few dill flowers or fennel flowers over the top, too · **SERVES 10**

a fillet of very fresh, wild salmon, skin on
Mustard and Dill Mayonnaise (see page 105)
olive oil
fresh lemon juice
freshly ground black pepper
brown soda bread, to serve (see page 199 or 560)

Put the salmon in the freezer for about 30 minutes, until it is very firm. Cut it into the thinnest slices possible (they should be virtually see-through). Spread a little dill mayonnaise on each chilled plate. Arrange the salmon slices in a single layer on top and brush with a little olive oil. Sprinkle with some freshly squeezed lemon juice and a grind of black pepper. Serve immediately with brown soda bread.

ASIAN CEVICHE

We do several types of ceviche where the fish is "cooked" in lime juice. Antony Worrall Thompson introduced me to this Asian-inspired version of ceviche when he taught one of his hugely entertaining classes at the Cookery School · **SERVES 8**

1lb monkfish (or plaice or lemon sole), cut into ½in cubes
¼ cup cilantro leaves
2 tablespoons shredded mint
1 avocado, peeled and diced into ½in cubes
¼ cup cubes peeled and diced ½in cubes of mango
4 scallions, sliced
2–3 red chiles, seeded and thinly sliced
¼ cup diced cucumber

FOR THE MARINADE
¾ cup freshly squeezed lime juice
⅓ cup Asian fish sauce (nam pla)
½ cup superfine sugar
¾ cup well-shaken coconut milk

TO SERVE
shredded lettuce

Trim the monkfish of all skin and membrane and cut into cubes. Next, make the dressing. Whisk all the ingredients together in a large bowl. Add the monkfish and toss to coat evenly. Cover and marinate in the fridge for 30 minutes.

Meanwhile, prepare the other ingredients. Add them to the chilled monkfish and mix gently to combine.

Serve with some shredded lettuce in little bowls or glasses, or in a martini glass for extra panache.

Stock

BASIC FISH STOCK

Fish stock takes only 20 minutes to make. If you can get lots of nice fresh fish bones from your fishmonger it's well worth making two or three quantities of this recipe. It freezes perfectly and then you will have fish stock ready for any recipe that needs it · **MAKES ABOUT 3 PINTS**

2¼lb fish bones, preferably sole, turbot, or brill
1 tablespoon butter
½ medium onion, finely sliced
½–1 cup dry white wine
4 peppercorns
bouquet garni containing a sprig of thyme, 4–5 parsley stems, a small piece of celery, and a tiny piece of bay leaf
no salt!

Rinse the fish bones thoroughly under cold running water until no trace of blood remains. Chop the bones into pieces. Melt the butter in a large stainless-steel saucepan, stir in the onions, and cook over low heat until soft but not colored. Stir in the bones and cook very briefly with the onions. Add the white wine and boil until nearly all of it has evaporated. Cover the bones with cold water, add the peppercorns and the bouquet garni. Bring to a boil and simmer for 20 minutes, skimming often. Strain and leave to get cold, skim off any fat, if necessary, and refrigerate.

Variations

HOUSEHOLD FISH STOCK
Fish heads with the gills removed, fish skin, and shellfish or mollusk shells may be added to the fish stock. It will be slightly darker in color and less delicate in flavor. Cook for 30 minutes.

SHELLFISH STOCK
A selection of crustacean and mollusk shells such as prawn, shrimp, mussels, crab, or lobster may be used. Cook for 30 minutes.

DEMI-GLACE DE POISSON
Reduce the strained fish stock by half to intensify the flavor. Chill and refrigerate or freeze.

GLACE DE POISSON
Reduce the stock until it becomes thick and syrupy, then chill. It will set into a firm jelly which has a very concentrated fish flavor, and is excellent to add to fish sauces or soups to enhance the flavor.

FRESH AND SMOKED SEAFOOD CHOWDER

Chowder is a wonderfully substantial fish soup or, indeed, it could almost be classified as a stew. It is certainly a meal in itself and there are lots of variations on the theme. You may not always have the choice, but if you do, select fish with a firm texture and use new potatoes, otherwise it will disintegrate into a purée · SERVES 6

1 tablespoon extra virgin olive oil or sunflower oil
4oz slab bacon, rind removed and cut into ¼in cubes
1 medium onion, chopped
¼ cup all-purpose flour
2 cups Fish Stock (see page 80) or, as a last resort, hot water
1½ cups whole milk
bouquet garni made up of 6 parsley stems, 2 sprigs of thyme, and 1 bay leaf
6 medium-sized new potatoes, peeled and cut into ¼in cubes
salt and freshly ground black pepper
pinch of mace
pinch of cayenne pepper
18 mussels
1½lb haddock, monkfish, winter cod, or other firm, white fish (or a mixture), free of bones and skin
4oz smoked haddock, free of bones and skin
½ cup light cream
2oz cooked shrimp (see page 109)
lots of freshly chopped parsley and chives, for garnish

Heat the oil in a stainless-steel saucepan and cook the bacon until it is crisp and golden. Add the onions, cover, and cook for a few minutes over low heat. Stir in the flour and cook for a couple of minutes more. Add the fish stock or water gradually, then the milk, bouquet garni, and potatoes. Season well with salt, pepper, mace, and cayenne. Cover and simmer until the potatoes are almost cooked (5–6 minutes). The recipe may be prepared up to a day ahead at this point.

Meanwhile, rinse the mussels. Put the wet mussels in a covered saucepan over medium heat for 3–4 minutes, or until the mussels open. Allow the mussels to cool, remove the beards and discard the shells. Save the liquor.

As soon as the tip of a knife will pierce the potatoes, add the fish to the pot. Simmer gently for 3 or 4 minutes, stir in the cream, the shellfish, and any of the liquor from opening the mussels. Pour the liquid in carefully to ensure that you leave behind any grains of sand that may have accumulated in the bottom of the container.

As soon as the soup returns to a boil, remove it from the heat. Remember that the fish will continue to cook in the heat of the chowder so it should not be overcooked. Taste, correct the seasoning and sprinkle with freshly chopped parsley and chives. Crusty hot white bread or hot crackers are usually served with a chowder.

Pan-grilling

If you have a really fresh fish, pan-grilling is one of the most delicious ways to cook it. You can fillet the fish or, if you're working with a big fish like cod, cut into filleted portions. We allow 6oz fish per person for a main course, and 3oz for an appetizer, but you may serve larger portions if you wish. Pan-grilling is one of the most important of all fish cooking techniques, and one of the most difficult to perfect.

When we're teaching this at the school, it's quite difficult to get people to concentrate on the finer points because to the casual observer, it just looks really easy. But it's important to be persnickety about the little details.

So what do you need for success? A very fresh fish, for starters. When you're pan-grilling a fish, there's nothing to cover a taint. You need a heavy cast iron or other ridged grill pan. The fish must be dry, otherwise it will stick to the grill pan. For pan-grilling, keep the skin on the fish, but if it has scales, the scales must be removed before filleting.

Fillets of any small fish are delicious pan-grilled as in this next recipe. Fish under 2lb such as mackerel, herring, and brown trout can also be grilled whole in the pan. Fish over 2lb can be filleted first and then cut crosswise into portions. Large fish (4lb) can also be grilled whole. Cook them for approximately 10–15 minutes on each side, and then put in a hot oven for another 15 minutes or so to finish cooking. Grey sea mullet is worth seeking out – it has a delicious flavor, a wonderful texture, and is a fraction of the price of sea bass.

How can I tell it's cooked?
Resist the temptation to turn the fish over and over. It's ready when the edges are sizzling and turning brown. If you want an authentic criss-cross pattern, lift it up halfway through cooking, turn it 90°, and put it back down on the hot grill pan. If it's a piece of fish rather than a fillet, you can tell by looking at the cut end how far it has cooked, as the flesh will have transformed from translucent to opaque.

PAN-GRILLED FISH WITH FLAVORED BUTTER

For pan-grilling you can use either olive oil or butter, but make sure the fish is completely dry before you apply it. Be sure to rinse and dry the grill pan between batches, too · SERVES 4

8 fillets of very fresh fish with skin attached and scales removed where necessary (see page 78), such as mackerel, sea bass, grey sea mullet, or John Dory
seasoned all-purpose flour
soft butter

GARNISH
Flavored Butter (see page 216)
lemon wedges
flat-leaf parsley sprigs

First make the flavored butter of your choice.

Then grill the fish. Heat the grill pan. Just before cooking but not earlier, dip the fish fillets in flour that has been seasoned with salt and freshly ground pepper. Pat each floured fillet between the palms of your hands to shake off the excess flour and then spread a little soft butter evenly over the entire surface of the flesh side, as though you were buttering a slice of bread, and then put it flesh-side down diagonally on the pan. I prefer to put the butter on the fish rather than on the pan because otherwise all of the excess fat just burns around the edge.

When the color of the flesh has changed halfway up the fish, use an offset spatula to flip it over and cook the other side. There will be enough butter or oil on the grill pan to cook the second side. The cooked side should be nicely colored and golden. Continue to cook until it's just cooked through, erring if you must on the slightly undercooked side, as the fish will continue to cook a little more from the residual heat.

Put on a warm plate and serve immediately with a few slices of flavored butter and a wedge of lemon. The flavored butter may be served directly on the fish, or if you have a pretty oyster shell, place it at the side of the plate as a container for the butter. Garnish with a sprig of parsley.

Opposite: *Pan-grilled Fish (in this case, sea bream) with Flavored Butter.*

sides with salt and pepper, and brush liberally with clarified butter.

Broil, turning once, until cooked through – the length of time will depend on the size and thickness of the fish. Test by lifting a little of the flesh close to the head where it is thickest; it should lift easily from the bone and there should be no trace of blood.

Serve immediately on a large, warm plate with some extra butter and lemon wedge.

Variation

GRILLED WHOLE ROUND FISH ON THE BONE
You can grill one, whole round fish up to 2lb on a grill pan. Simply season the fish with salt and freshly ground pepper before cooking. Larger fish weighing about 4lb can be started on a grill pan by cooking for 8–10 minutes on each side over medium heat. Then transfer to a preheated oven (350°F) for another 10–15 minutes, or until the fish lifts easily off the bone at the top of the fillet where the flesh meets the head.

Above: *Mackerel with Almond Migas.*

GRILLED DOVER SOLE ON THE BONE

In Ireland, Dover sole is called Black sole. In the past, many restaurants had special copper pans to cook sole on the bone and the fish was served at the table from the pan with a flourish. It may be either fried in Clarified Butter (see page 216) in a pan, or cooked under a broiler as I do below · **SERVES 1**

1 Dover sole
salt and freshly ground black pepper
Clarified Butter (see page 216)
lemon wedge, to serve

Preheat the broiler.

Ask your fishmonger to skin the fish on both sides, or do it yourself (see box opposite).

About 10 minutes before cooking, sprinkle the fish on both

MACKEREL WITH ALMOND MIGAS

Migas is a Spanish way of using up bread crumbs that's really worth knowing about. They are served in lots of different ways. We love them here with mackerel · **SERVES 4 AS AN APPETIZER**

4 fresh mackerel fillets, rinsed and patted dry
extra virgin olive oil
16 cherry tomatoes, halved

FOR THE ALMOND MIGAS

1 cup coarse bread crumbs, made from about 4 slices of stale-ish sourdough bread

¾ cup chopped almonds

4 garlic cloves, peeled and finely chopped

1⅛ cups extra virgin olive oil

4 tablespoons flat-leaf parsley, chopped

First make the almond migas. Mix together the bread crumbs, almonds, and garlic. Heat half the olive oil in a frying pan, add half the bread crumb mixture and toss over medium heat for 4–5 minutes, until golden. Turn onto a plate while you do the same with the other half.

Meanwhile, heat a grill pan. Season the dry mackerel fillets, drizzle with olive oil, and pan-grill for a few minutes on each side, first on the flesh side, then on the skin side, until crisp and golden.

To serve, add the parsley to the almond migas. Divide the migas between 4 plates. Add a few halved cherry tomatoes to each plate, and serve the almond migas with a fillet of hot mackerel. Serve immediately.

Fish Baked on the Bone

My mother-in-law, Myrtle Allen, taught me how to cook fish in this way. The following "master recipe" can be used for a variety of fresh, flat fish – plaice, Dover sole, lemon sole, brill, turbot, halibut, flounder, or megrim. Depending on the size of the fish, it can be served as a starter or main course. Because the fish is cooked on the bone with the skin intact, it will have maximum flavor. It can be served with or without sauce, but for people who are on a fat-free diet, this is the best way to have fish with fantastic flavor.

BAKED FLAT FISH WITH HERB BUTTER

Baked fish can either be served as suggested here, or olive oil may be substituted for butter. Or serve it with any sauce of your choice spooned over the top, such as Hollandaise sauce, lobster sauce, or shrimp butter sauce. For a large halibut, brill, or turbot, double or triple the amounts listed below · **SERVES 4**

4 very fresh plaice, sole, or other fish on the bone

salt and freshly ground pepper

8 tablespoons butter

4 teaspoons each finely chopped fresh parsley, chives, fennel, and thyme leaves

Preheat the oven to 350°F.

Turn the fish on its side and remove the head, or leave it intact if you like. Rinse the fish and clean the slit very thoroughly. With a sharp knife, cut through the skin around the edge of the fish where the "fringe" meets the flesh. Be careful to cut neatly and to cross the side cuts at the tail or it will be difficult to remove the skin later on.

Sprinkle the skin of the fish with salt and pepper and lay them in ½in of water in a shallow baking pan or pans. Bake for 20–30 minutes,

HOW TO SKIN DOVER SOLE

Unlike other flat fish, the skin of Dover sole can be pulled off in one piece. Lay the fish on a chopping board with the dark skin facing up. With a sharp knife, cut across the skin, just below where the tail joins the body. Lift the edge of the skin and run your thumb between the skin and the flesh to loosen it. Then grasp the skin with a cloth in one hand. Use your other hand to hold down the tail end. Pull the skin towards the head and detach completely. Turn the fish over, and repeat on the other side.

according to the size of the fish. The water will be almost – but not completely – evaporated when the fish is cooked. If it dries up completely, the fish will stick to the pan. To check whether the fish is cooked, lift the flesh from the bone close to the head, where the flesh is thickest; it should lift off the bone easily and be white with no trace of pink.

Just before serving, melt the butter and stir in the chopped herbs. Grasp the skin down near the tail and pull it off gently (the skin will tear badly if not properly cut). Lift the fish onto hot plates and spoon the herb butter over them. Serve immediately with some extra butter on the side.

FISH BAKED IN A SALT CRUST

Although it may sound like a new trendy, way to cook fish, the reality is fish has been cooked in a salt crust for hundreds of years. It's a great way to seal in flavor and it's a semi-forgotten skill that is well worth mastering. It always causes a stir when you bring it to the table. The fish will be moist and delicious and needs no more in the way of embellishment than a little butter with a few fresh herbs snipped into it or maybe a light beurre blanc. A few tiny new potatoes and a salad on the side would be a delicious accompaniment · **SERVES 2–4**

1 grey sea mullet, about 5lb 8oz, or a fat trout or sea bass, about 1½lb
1 organic egg white, lightly beaten (optional)
2¼lb sea salt

1 oval ovenproof dish, preferably cast iron, large enough to hold the fish and presentable enough to bring to the table

Preheat the oven to 425°F.

Gut the fish and rinse the inside well to remove any trace of blood (I use a clean washing-up brush for this). Do not remove the head. Use strong kitchen scissors to cut away the dorsal fin. Scale the fish (see page 78).

If you want a harder crust than using salt alone, mix the egg white with the salt. Spread one-third of the salt evenly over the bottom of an oval cast-iron dish. Lay the fish on top. Cover completely with the remainder of the salt. Bake for 18–35 minutes, depending on the size of the fish.

Meanwhile, make the chosen herb butter or sauce. When the fish is cooked, bring the dish to the table, crack the hard salt crust on top. Remove the top crust to a plate and peel the skin off the fish. When serving, lift the fillets onto individual serving plates and spoon over a little herb butter.

POLLOCK BAKED IN CREAM AND BAY LEAVES

In the olden days, milk was put into skimming bowls in the cold dairy to set so there was always some rich, thick cream that could be spooned off the top to add a little extra savor to a dish such as this one. A mixture of fresh herbs (e.g. parsley, chives, fennel, and thyme leaves) may be used instead of the bay leaves, but it's particularly delicious with bay, and one of the only recipes in which you actually want the flavor of bay to predominate. We normally use pollock for this recipe, but you can also use ling, grey sea mullet, haddock, hake, or cod (provided it's not endangered in your area).

Tommy Sliney, whom I've mentioned earlier (see page 77), used to sell a lot of pollock to local people from his donkey cart on the pier in Ballycotton. One day I asked him why so many people wanted pollock. "Sure missus, isn't it how it doesn't taste of fish at all!" Fish was associated with Fridays – fast days when people weren't allowed to eat meat, so fish was looked on as penance rather than a treat. I never thought much of
pollock, but this recipe changes what to me has always been a fairly mundane fish into a feast · **SERVES 6**

2 tablespoons butter
1 tablespoon finely chopped onion
6 fish fillets, allow about 4oz filleted fish per person (pollock, ling, grey sea mullet, haddock, hake, or cod)
salt and freshly ground pepper
3 fresh bay leaves
light cream to cover the fish, about 1 cup
about 1 tablespoon Roux (see page 165)

Melt the butter in a sauté pan just wide enough to hold the fish fillets. Cook the onion gently for a few minutes until soft but not colored. Put the fish in the pan and cook on each side for 1 minute. Season with salt and freshly ground pepper. Add the bay leaves. Cover with cream and simmer, covered, for about 5 minutes, until the fish is cooked. Remove the fish to a serving dish. Bring the cooking liquid to a boil and thicken lightly with roux. Taste and correct the seasoning. Coat the fish with sauce and serve immediately.

This dish can be prepared ahead and reheated and it also freezes well. Reheat in a moderate 350°F oven, for 10–20 minutes, depending on the size of the container.

Leftover salt can be saved to add to fish poaching water at a later date.

HADDOCK WITH PEPERONATA AND BUTTERED CRUMBS

Fresh fish with a crunchy topping in a creamy sauce is always tempting. This is a kind of mother recipe for all round fish – you can do many variations, all of which are delicious. It's fun to make a big single dish, but of course you can also plate it up individually or put it in scallop shells. If you want to have a whole meal in one dish, then pipe a border of fluffy Duchesse Potatoes (see page 90) around the edge. Here we add peperonata, as the sweetness of the peppers is delicious with the fish ·
SERVES 6–8

2½lb haddock, hake, ling, grey sea
    mullet, or pollock
salt and freshly ground black
    pepper
1 tablespoon butter
Peperonata (see below)

FOR THE MORNAY SAUCE
2 cups whole milk
a few slices of carrot and onion
4 peppercorns
sprig each of thyme and parsley
4 tablespoons Roux (see page 165),
    or less, as needed
1¼ cups shredded Cheddar cheese
    or ¾ cup finely grated
    Parmesan cheese
½ teaspoon mustard (preferably
    Dijon mustard)
salt and freshly ground black
    pepper

FOR THE BUTTERED CRUMBS
2 tablespoons butter
½ cup soft white bread crumbs (see
    page 577)

First make the Mornay sauce. Put the cold milk into a saucepan with the carrot, onion, peppercorns, thyme, and parsley. Bring to a boil and simmer for 4–5 minutes. Remove from the heat and leave to infuse for about 10 minutes.

Strain out the vegetables, herbs, and peppercorns. Bring the milk back to a boil and whisk in enough roux to reach a coating consistency. Remove from the heat and allow to cool for 1 minute. Then add the mustard and two-thirds of the grated cheese, saving the remainder of the cheese for sprinkling over the top. Season with salt and freshly ground pepper, taste, and correct the seasoning if necessary.

Next make the buttered crumbs. Melt the butter in a pan and stir in the bread crumbs. Remove from the heat immediately and allow to cool.

Preheat the oven to 350°F.

Skin the fish and cut into portions: 6oz for a main course or 3oz for an appetizer. Season with salt and freshly ground pepper. Lightly butter an ovenproof dish, then spread half the peperonata over the bottom of the dish (save the remainder for another use). Lay the fish on top and coat generously with the Mornay sauce. Mix the remaining grated cheese with the buttered crumbs and sprinkle over the top.

Transfer to the oven and bake for 25–30 minutes, or until the fish is cooked through and the top is golden brown and crispy.

PEPERONATA

This is an indispensable stew that we always have on hand. We use it not only as a vegetable but also as a topping for pizzas, as a sauce for pasta, grilled fish or meat, and as a filling for omelettes and pancakes ·
SERVES 8–10

2 tablespoons olive oil
garlic clove, crushed
1 onion, sliced
2 red bell peppers
2 green bell peppers
6 large tomatoes (dark red and
    very ripe)
salt, freshly ground pepper and
    sugar
a few leaves of fresh basil

Heat the olive oil in a casserole. Add the garlic and cook for a few seconds, then add the onion, toss in the oil and allow to soften over a gentle heat, covered, while the peppers are being prepared.

Halve the peppers, remove the seeds carefully, cut into quarters and then into strips crosswise, rather than lengthwise. Alternatively, cut the pepper flesh into 1in squares. Add to the onion and toss in the oil. Then replace the lid and continue to cook.

Meanwhile, peel the tomatoes (scald in boiling water for 10 seconds, pour off the water and peel immediately). Slice the tomatoes and add to the casserole. Season with salt, freshly ground pepper, a sprinkling of sugar, and a few leaves of fresh basil. Cook uncovered until the vegetables are just soft, about 30 minutes.

SALMON COOKED IN NEWSPAPER

A fisherman from the west of Ireland told me about this great way of cooking salmon. It produces a tender, succulent result and makes magical picnic food. We use the Examiner, *our local newspaper, to wrap the salmon. It's best to cook the fish whole, but if the salmon is too large to fit on your barbecue, just use a portion of the fish*

• **SERVES 6–12 DEPENDING ON SIZE OF SALMON**

**1 fresh, wild salmon
sea salt and freshly ground pepper**

newspaper

Gut the salmon as soon as it is caught. Carefully scrape out the line of blood along the backbone, and wash out meticulously in sea or river water.

Season the cavity well with sea salt and freshly ground pepper. Wrap the salmon tightly in at least 7 or 8 sheets of newspaper, making sure the ends are well tucked in to create a neat package. Using cotton string, tie in 3 or 4 places to secure. Dip the entire parcel in sea or river water (salty water gives it a delicious flavor). Cook in the embers of an open fire or on a barbecue until the package is charred on both sides.

Cut off the charred paper with strong scissors. Lift off the skin and eat the fish warm with soda bread and butter or with any sauce or accompaniment of your choice.

Left: *Salmon Cooked in Newspaper.*

FISH IN FIG LEAVES WITH FRESH HERB BUTTER

Wrapping and cooking fish in fresh fig leaves imparts a delicious flavor. We're fortunate to have a fig tree planted by the school library wall and we use the leaves from late spring to late autumn. We use them on the cheeseboard or to wrap fish or some game birds (see page 135 for Partridge Wrapped in Vine Leaves) · **SERVES 8**

8 portions of fresh fish, such as sea bass, haddock, hake, grey sea mullet, or wild salmon, about 2½lb total
salt and freshly ground pepper
8 large fresh fig leaves (or more, if they are small)
extra virgin olive oil
Fresh Herb Butter (see page 216) or Wild Garlic Butter (see page 216) in season
flat-leaf parsley and wild garlic flowers

Preheat the oven to 400°F. Skin the fish and season it.

Rinse the fig leaves in cold water and dry gently. Dip each portion of fish in extra virgin olive oil. Wrap individually in a fig leaf, it may not be completely enclosed but that's fine.

Roast the fish on a baking sheet in the oven for 8–10 minutes, depending on the thickness. Serve on warm plates. Open the fig leaf parcels, put a slice of flavored butter on top, and serve immediately as the butter melts over the fish.

HAKE WITH TOMATOES AND SWISS CHARD

This is a delicious way to use both the stem and leaves of chard. You can use salmon or haddock in place of the hake · **SERVES 6**

6 thick hake fillets, about 1½lb total
salt and freshly ground black pepper
12oz Swiss chard stems and leaves
3 tablespoons extra virgin olive oil
1 medium onion, sliced
1 teaspoon grated fresh ginger
8 very ripe tomatoes, peeled and chopped
a little sugar
1 cup well-shaken canned coconut milk
coriander leaves, for garnish

Season the hake generously with salt and pepper on both sides. Leave to sit for no more than an hour while you prepare the vegetables. Separate the chard leaves from the stems. Cut the chard stems into ¼in slices. Shred the chard leaves into thin strips and set aside.

Choose a sauté pan wide enough to hold all the fish in a single layer, and heat the pan over medium heat. Add the oil, onions, ginger, and chard stems. Stir and cook for 4–5 minutes. Add the tomatoes. Season with salt, pepper, and sugar. Increase the heat and continue to cook for 5–6 minutes. Add the coconut milk. Bring to a boil and simmer for a minute or two.

Just before serving, reheat if necessary. Add the shredded chard leaves and stir. Lay the pieces of fish

TICKLING FISH

I had an uncle who used to be adept at what he'd call "tickling fish." He would stand in the water very still, close to the bank, and slide his hand into the water, tickle the belly of the fish and then catch it with his bare hands. This is certainly not a skill I've mastered myself.

These days, there aren't even enough trout to catch at all, let alone with your bare hands. The fish all but disappeared as farming intensified and the run-off from the fertilizers contaminated the water. Now that the EU has brought in the Nitrogen Directive, which limits the amount of nitrogen being used on farms and therefore entering our rivers, perhaps the waters will become clean enough again to support more fish.

in a single layer on top of the sauce. Spoon some of the hot liquid over the fish. Cover and simmer for 4–5 minutes, depending on the thickness of the fish.

Serve on warm plates, dividing the sauce and chard stems between each portion. Scatter with lots of fresh cilantro leaves.

CLASSIC FISH PIE

It is difficult to write a hard and fast recipe for fish pie because it all depends on what kind of fish you have access to. But make sure the fish is fresh, there is plenty of sauce, and you have lots of fluffy mashed potatoes on top. Years ago, if eggs were plentiful but fish was scarce, people used to add hard-boiled eggs to the fish pie to stretch the fish. A little smoked haddock is a nice addition to this recipe, but don't use more than 4oz unless you want the flavor to dominate
· **SERVES 6–8**

2½lb fillets of cod, haddock, ling, hake, salmon, or pollock or a mixture, skinned
salt and freshly ground pepper
18 mussels (optional)
1 small onion, chopped
1 tablespoon butter
8oz sliced mushrooms
2 cups whole milk
1 fresh bay leaf
Roux (see page 165)
a little heavy cream (optional)
1 teaspoon chopped thyme leaves
2 tablespoons chopped parsley
1 cup peas, fresh or frozen (if they're fresh, they'll first need to be blanched)
2lb fluffy Duchesse Potatoes (recipe follows)

To Serve
Parsley Butter (see page 216) or Dill Butter (see page 217), optional

1 large pie dish (1 quart) or 6–8 small ones

Cut the fish into 5oz chunks and season with salt and freshly ground pepper.

Wash the mussels, if using, and put into a shallow pan in a single layer. Cover and cook for about 3–4 minutes over medium heat, just until the shells open. Cool, pull out the beard and remove from the shells.

Cook the onion in a little melted butter over low heat until soft but not colored, remove to a plate. Increase the heat, add a little more butter, sauté the sliced mushrooms in batches in the hot pan. Season with salt and pepper and add to the onions.

Put the fish into a wide sauté pan or frying pan in a single layer, cover with the milk and add a fresh bay leaf. Season with salt and freshly ground pepper. Cover and simmer gently until the fish is just cooked, about 3–4 minutes depending on the thickness of the fish. Remove the fish to a plate with a slotted spoon, and carefully remove any bones or skin. Discard the bay leaf.

Preheat the oven to 350°F.

Bring the cooking liquid to a boil and thicken it by whisking in the roux. Add a little cream, if using, and the chopped thyme and parsley, mushrooms, onions, chunks of fish, mussels, and peas. Stir gently, taste, and correct the seasoning. Spoon into a single large or 6–8 small baking dishes and pipe duchesse potatoes on top. The pie may be prepared ahead to this point.

To finish cooking, bake in the preheated oven for 10–15 minutes if the filling and potato are warm, or for 30 minutes if reheating the dish later. Flash under the grill if necessary to brown the top. Serve with dill or parsley butter.

DUCHESSE POTATOES

If the potatoes are not peeled and mashed while hot and if the boiling milk is not added immediately, the duchesse potatoes will be lumpy and gluey. The egg in the recipe contributes to the browning of the potatoes and gives the dish an appetising look. If you have only egg whites they will be fine and will make deliciously light mashed potatoes also, but it won't be as golden when baked in the oven ·
SERVES 4

2lb unpeeled potatoes, preferably Yukon Gold
pinch of salt
1 cup whole milk
2 egg yolks or 1 whole egg and 1 egg yolk
2–4 tablespoons butter
salt and freshly ground pepper

Scrub the potatoes well. Put them into a saucepan of cold water, add a good pinch of salt, and bring to a boil. After about 15 minutes, the potatoes are half-cooked. At that point, strain off two-thirds of the water, replace the lid of the saucepan, place over low heat, and allow the potatoes to steam until they are cooked. Peel immediately by just pulling off the skins, so you have as little waste as possible, and mash while hot. (If you have a large quantity, put the potatoes into the bowl of an electric mixer and beat with the paddle attachment).

While the potatoes are being peeled, bring about the milk to a boil. Beat the eggs into the hot mashed potatoes, and add enough boiling milk to mix to a soft light consistency suitable for piping. Then beat in the butter, the amount depending on how rich you like your potatoes. Taste and season with salt and pepper.

Poaching

If you want to poach a whole salmon or sea trout with the head and tail on, then you really need to have access to a fish poacher (fish kettle), a long, narrow saucepan that will hold a fish weighing up to 9lb. It has a perforated rack on which the fish rests as it cooks, with handles on either end to lift the whole fish out of the water intact. The best poachers have a little groove at the sides that allow the two metal handles to stick up higher than the kettle, because otherwise, as I once discovered to my disadvantage, you have to plunge your fingers into the boiling water to retrieve the shelf.

Not everyone owns a fish poacher, so if you want to keep the fish whole then the best solution would be to bake it in the oven wrapped in aluminum foil (see page 92). Or you can see whether your fishmonger or even the fish section of your supermarket might have a fish poacher available to rent.

Alternatively, you could cut the salmon into three pieces, and cook them separately in the way I describe for cooking a piece of salmon (at right). Later, you could arrange the salmon on a board or serving dish, skin it, and do a cosmetic touch-up job with rosettes of mayonnaise and lots of fresh herbs.

The proportion of salt to water is very important in order to give it flavor. Follow the proportions in the recipe below.

If you're fortunate enough to live by the sea, collect a bucket of seawater and poach your fish in the seawater by exactly the same method. It'll be the best thing you've ever tasted!

Poaching a piece of fish

The secret to poaching a piece of fish is to remember that the minimum amount of water gives you the maximum flavor. Although the piece of fish must be just covered with water, the aim is to use as little as possible, so use a pan that will fit the fish exactly.

We never poach salmon fillets, because in that case one has the maximum surface exposed to the water and therefore maximum loss of flavor. Salmon fillets are best dipped in a little seasoned flour and cooked slowly in a little butter in a pan, or, alternatively, pan-grilled with a little butter. Serve with a few pats of Maître d'Hôtel Butter (see page 216) and a wedge of lemon.

POACHED PIECE OF ROUND FISH

Most cookbooks will tell you to poach salmon in a court bouillon. This is a mixture of wine and water with perhaps some sliced carrots, onion, peppercorns, and a bouquet garni including a bay leaf. But I feel strongly that a beautiful salmon is at its best poached gently in just boiling, salted water. The proportion of salt to water is extremely important. We use 1 rounded tablespoon of salt to every quart of water and measure it meticulously · SERVES 8

center-cut piece of fresh salmon or other round fish, about 3lb

salt

homemade Mayonnaise, see page 252, to serve (optional)

Choose a saucepan that will barely fit the piece of fish: an oval cast-iron saucepan is usually perfect. Half-fill the saucepan with water, add the salt and bring to a boil. Put in the piece of fish, then add enough water to cover. Return to a boil and simmer gently for 20 minutes.

Turn off the heat and let it stand for a couple of minutes if eating warm. Alternatively, let cool and serve with homemade mayonnaise.

WHOLE POACHED SALMON

Nothing could be finer than to serve a beautiful salmon as the centerpiece for a dinner party or special occasion, but salmon can easily be ruined in the cooking, so the aim here is to get it to the table in peak condition. An 8lb salmon will feed 16 people very generously and it could quite easily be enough for 20. Generally, 4½oz cooked salmon is plenty to allow per person, as salmon is very rich. Decide whether you want to serve it hot or cold and follow the relevant instructions below · **SERVES 16–20**

1 whole salmon or sea trout or any other whole, round fish
salt

fish poacher or kettle

TO SERVE HOT
sprigs of fresh parsley, lemon balm, and fennel
wedge of lemon for each person
Hollandaise Sauce (see page 248)

TO SERVE COLD
fresh, crisp lettuce leaves
sprigs of watercress, lemon balm, and fennel
fennel flower or cucumber (optional)
homemade Mayonnaise (see page 252)
lemon wedges

Clean and gut the salmon carefully; do not remove the head, tail, or scales. Carefully measure the water and half fill the fish kettle, add 1 rounded tablespoon of salt to every quart of water. Cover the pan and bring the water to a boil. Add the salmon, and, if needed, enough water to cover. Allow the water to return to a boil. Cover and simmer gently for 20 minutes. Then turn off the heat and leave the salmon in the water for 4–5 minutes to settle. Then remove from water. It will remain hot for 20–30 minutes.

To serve hot, carefully lift the whole fish out of the fish kettle and leave to drain on the rack for a few minutes. Then slide it onto a large, warm serving dish, preferably a beautiful long white china dish, but failing that, whatever it will fit on! Garnish with lots of parsley, lemon balm, and fennel, and 10–12 wedges of lemon. I don't remove the skin until I am serving it at the table, then I peel it back gradually as I serve. However, if you prefer, remove the skin just at the last second before bringing the salmon to the table. When you have served all the fish from the top, remove the bone as delicately as possible, put it aside and continue as before. Serve with Hollandaise sauce.

To serve cold, when the fish is barely cold, remove from the poacher and drain for a few minutes. Line a large board or serving dish with fresh crisp lettuce leaves, top with sprigs of watercress, lemon balm, and fennel sprigs and flowers, if available. Carefully slide the salmon onto the board. Just before serving, peel off the top skin, leaving the tail and head intact. (We don't scrape off the brown flesh in the center because it tastes good.) Pipe a line of homemade mayonnaise along the center of the salmon lengthwise, garnish with tiny sprigs of fennel and fennel flowers, or very thin twists of cucumber. Put some lemon wedges around the dish between the lettuce and herbs. Resist the temptation to use any tomato or – horror of horrors – to put a slice of pimento-stuffed green olive over the eye! The pale pink of the salmon flesh with the crisp lettuces and fresh herbs is just perfect. Serve with a bowl of homemade mayonnaise.

WHOLE FISH COOKED IN FOIL

This is the best way to cook a whole salmon, sea trout, or other round fish if you don't happen to have a fish poacher. You can use the buttery juices from the cooking process to make a Hollandaise-type sauce, too · **SERVES ABOUT 8**

1 salmon or sea trout, about 8lb
8 tablespoons butter, softened
sea salt and freshly ground pepper
sprig of fennel (optional)

GARNISH
lemon wedges and sprigs of parsley or fennel

a large sheet of heavy-duty aluminum foil

Preheat the oven to 350°F.
Clean and gut the fish if necessary, and rinse well, making sure to remove the line of blood from inside near the backbone. Dry carefully. Put the sheet of aluminum foil on a large baking sheet,

preferably with edges. Place the whole fish in the center of the foil. Smear butter on both sides of the fish and put a few lumps in the center. Season with salt and freshly ground pepper and put a sprig of fennel in the center if you have it. Be generous with the butter as it will mix with the juices to make a delicious sauce to spoon over your cooked fish.

Bring the aluminum foil together loosely and fold the edges over to seal them well. Bake for about 35–40 minutes. Remove from the oven and open the parcel, being careful of the steam. Test the fish by lifting the flesh off the backbone at the thickest point, where the flesh meets the head. The fish should lift off the bone easily and there should be no trace of blood; if there is, seal the parcel again and pop it back in the oven for another 5 or so minutes, but be careful not to overcook it.

Serve the fish hot or cold. If you are serving it hot, spoon the juices over each helping. Serve with some freshly made salads and a bowl of homemade mayonnaise (see page 252). Garnish with parsley and fennel.

WARM POACHED MACKEREL WITH SAUCE DE QUIMPER

This is a gentle poaching technique which is a terrifically good way to cook fresh mackerel, or several other fish like grey sea mullet or sea bass, for that matter. It can be served with lots of different sauces or fresh herb butters, but this combination is particularly magical, and is one of my favorite summer dishes – you can't imagine how delectable fresh mackerel is cooked in this way. Warm cooked and peeled shrimp or prawns are also totally delicious served with this sauce, which is named after a seaside town in Brittany · **SERVES 4 AS A MAIN COURSE OR 8 AS AN APPETIZER**

4 **fresh mackerel**
1 **teaspoon salt**

FOR THE SAUCE DE QUIMPER
2 **organic egg yolks**
1 **teaspoon Dijon mustard (we use Maille Verte Aux Herbs)**
2 **teaspoons white wine vinegar**
1 **tablespoon chopped chervil, chives, tarragon, and fennel**
8 **tablespoons butter**

Top and tail the mackerel. Gut and clean them but keep them whole. Be careful to remove the line of blood inside the backbone and rinse well.

Bring 1 quart of water to a boil in an oval flameproof casserole. Add the salt and the mackerel. Cover, return to a boil, and remove from the heat. After about 5–6 minutes, depending on size, check to see whether the fish are cooked. The flesh should lift off the bone and will be tender and melting.

Meanwhile, make the sauce. Put the egg yolks into a heatproof bowl, and add the mustard, wine vinegar, and the herbs. Mix well. Melt the butter and allow it to boil. Whisk the hot melted butter into the egg yolk mixture, little by little so the sauce emulsifies. Keep the sauce warm by placing the bowl over a saucepan of hot – but not boiling – water.

When the mackerel is cool enough to handle, remove it to a plate. Skin the fish, lift the flesh carefully from the bones and arrange on a serving dish. Coat with the sauce and serve while still warm with a good green salad and new potatoes.

Below: *Beautiful fresh mackerel.*

Fried Fish

Fried fish is an enduring favorite, even though it can so often be disappointing. The popularity of fried fish is incredible, given that most of the time the batter would lay on you like a third mortgage; and any accompaniments, such as the quintessential chips, are served tired and soggy. But when you have a spanking fresh fish, the batter is crisp and the frying oil is of good quality, what a feast!

Olive oil is unquestionably the best for all kinds of frying. But a good-quality sunflower oil also gives very good results. Steer well clear of the cooking oils that are sold for deep frying – the quality is usually poor, sometimes downright disgraceful, and will spoil otherwise deliciously fresh fish – and make your house smell like a chip shop. Good-quality oil can be used up to five times, but be meticulous about straining it after each cooking session. Then cook a few lettuce leaves in the strained oil to purify it, as the Spaniards do.

FISH AND CHIPS

When Brenda O'Riordan pulls into the cookery school with her lovely fresh fish just off the pier in Ballycotton and we make fish and chips with them, it's one of the lunches that barely makes it into the dining room, because the students can't resist starting to eat it in the kitchen · **SERVES 8**

8 very fresh fillets of cod, haddock, plaice, or lemon sole

8–16 well-scrubbed unpeeled all-purpose potatoes
salt

FOR THE BATTER
1⅓ cups all-purpose flour
2 tablespoons extra virgin olive oil
1 large organic egg white
sea salt

GARNISH
1 lemon

ACCOMPANIMENTS
vinegar
Tartare Sauce (see below)

First make the base for the batter. Sift the flour into a bowl and make a well in the center. Pour in the olive oil and stir. Gradually add enough water (about ¾ cup), to make a batter about the consistency of heavy cream. Cover and allow to stand while you make the chips.

Heat the oil in the deep fryer to 350°F. Cut the potatoes into chips of any size you fancy (remember, the bigger they are the longer they take to cook). Add the chips to the deep-fat fryer. Make sure they are absolutely dry, and do not cook too many together. Cook for a few minutes until they are just soft, then drain.

Whisk the egg white to stiff peaks and fold it into the batter, adding a good pinch of salt. Dip a small piece of fish in the batter and fry to test the seasoning. Allow the excess batter to drip off, then lower gently into the oil, shaking the basket at the same time. Cook until crisp and golden, then drain on paper towels. Taste, and add more salt to the batter if necessary.

Increase the heat of the deep-fat fryer to 375°F. Put the chips back in and cook for a minute or two until they are really crisp. Drain on paper towels, sprinkle with salt, and keep hot. Continue to cook the rest of the fish.

Serve the crispy fish and chips immediately, either on a plate or in a cornet of newspaper. Serve tartare sauce or vinegar as an accompaniment.

TARTARE SAUCE

This classic is great with deep-fried fish, shellfish, or fish cakes. Tartare sauce will keep for 5–6 days in a fridge, but omit the parsley and chives if you want to keep it for more than a day or two. A quick tartare sauce can be made by adding the extra ingredients into a homemade mayonnaise at the end · **SERVES 8-10**

2 hardboiled organic egg yolks
2 organic egg yolks
¼ teaspoon Dijon mustard
1 tablespoon white wine vinegar
1 cup extra virgin olive oil and ½ cup sunflower oil, mixed together
1 teaspoon chopped capers
1 teaspoon chopped gherkins
2 teaspoons chopped chives
1 tablespoon chopped parsley
salt and freshly ground pepper
lemon juice, optional

Take the hardboiled eggs and remove the yolks from the whites. Set the whites aside. Sieve the hardboiled egg yolks into a bowl and add the raw egg yolks, Dijon mustard, and vinegar. Mix well and whisk in the oil drop by drop, increasing the volume as the mixture thickens. When all the oil has been absorbed, add the capers, gherkins, chives, and parsley. Coarsley chop the reserved hardboiled egg whites and fold gently into the sauce with salt, freshly ground pepper, and a squeeze of lemon juice, if necessary.

Variation
FISH FINGERS
Cut fresh white fish into 1in-thick strips. Coat with flour, egg, and bread crumbs, then fry as above. Drain on paper towels and serve with Tartare Sauce.

CRISPY DEEP-FRIED MACKEREL WITH TARTARE SAUCE

The forgotten skill here is breading the fish. It is so easy to do yourself and uses up stale bread · SERVES 6

6 fresh mackerel
all-purpose flour, well-seasoned
egg, well-beaten
white bread crumbs (see page 257)
Tartare Sauce (see opposite)

Fillet the fish and dry them well (see page 79). Dip each fillet first in seasoned flour, pat off the excess and then dip in the egg, and finally in the bread crumbs. Make sure that each fillet is evenly coated. Heat the oil in a deep fryer to 350°F or a little less if the fillets are quite thick. Cook one at a time, until crisp and golden. Serve with tartare sauce, boiled new potatoes, ripe tomatoes, and a green salad.

FRESH FRIED EEL

If I was to be completely honest, my favorite fish of all is eel, a freshwater rather than saltwater species. Perhaps it's because we so rarely get them, two or three times a year if we are lucky. When I lived in Denmark in the early 1970s, the postman also sold fresh fish out of the back of his van, and occasionally he would have eel. We would cook them simply in butter, some of the best things I've ever eaten · SERVES 4

2lb eel, skinned
seasoned all-purpose flour
2 tablespoons butter, or as needed
1 lemon

GARNISH
chopped parsley
lemon wedges

Cut the eel into 3–4in pieces and toss in seasoned flour. Melt the butter in a wide frying pan. Cook the pieces of eel over medium heat, turning once, until just cooked through and golden. Transfer the fish to a serving dish or warm plates.

Squeeze a little lemon juice into the butter in the pan, add a little more fresh butter if necessary and spoon the bubbling mixture over the fish. Serve immediately with a sprinkling of chopped parsley and some lemon wedge.

MACKEREL

When I first came to Ballymaloe, it was summertime and we used to have our lunch on a little table outside the kitchen door. We had the same lunch virtually every day, and I never tired of it because it was so good. We'd have mackerel coated with fresh bread crumbs and fried until crisp, served with homemade tartare sauce, boiled new potatoes, and fresh tomatoes from the greenhouses, and a green salad.

Still today, fresh mackerel, even though many people consider them to be the poor relations, are my favorite sea fish. We only eat them in summer, when they come into Ballycotton Harbor in shoals. All coastal communities know that mackerel, being an oily fish, is best eaten on the same day it is caught.

Two West Cork fishing brothers, Michael and Dinny Donovan, gave me a great tip for keeping mackerel fresh. When you catch the fish, immediately gut them. Cut off the head and tail and wash in seawater. The fish bleeds and will then keep immeasurably better than when merely gutted. I store them in a plastic bag in the vegetable box of the fridge, but still use them within a day.

Mackerel freeze excellently when prepared as above, provided they are less than five hours out of the sea. They may be frozen whole or filleted.

Sprats and Whitebait

Sprats and whitebait come into Ballycotton only once or twice a year; sprats in winter, chased in by the herrings, and whitebait in late summer, when mackerel are following them. When they're in, they come in the millions and the water looks as if it is boiling with their activity. If you're fortunate enough to get word that they're in, you can scoop them up by the bucketful. Then, they disappear just as mysteriously as they arrived. We cook them in a simple way and feast on them, but they actually also freeze very well. When I worked at the Talbot Hotel in Wexford during my first season out of hotel school, they were on the menu all the time.

I also came across whitebait on a trip to New Zealand. Everywhere we went on the South Island, they were serving delicious little whitebait fritters. Possibly the most beautiful farmers' market I've ever been to in the world was the Matakana Farmers Market north of Auckland. One of the many joys of that terrific trip was cruising along in our campervan and then stopping at the farmstands along the road, that sold everything from free-range eggs to cherries, avocados, and whitebait.

FRIED MINNOWS

Some of my happiest childhood memories are of afternoons spent paddling in the cold river catching minnows with a little net. We stored them in a jam pot and fed them watercress. I had no idea then that you could eat them, so if things get really tough one can always go back to catching minnows.

minnows
seasoned all-purpose flour
lemon

Toss the minnows in seasoned flour. Shake off the excess.

Fry for a few seconds in hot oil in a deep fryer or in a pan on the stovetop.

Serve with a lemon wedge.

WHITEBAIT FRITTERS WITH A LEMON WEDGE

Often the whitebait sold at farmstands in New Zealand was already frozen in a block. We would just toss them in seasoned flour and shallow-fry them, but this was the favorite way to eat them locally · SERVES 2

1½ tablespoons all-purpose flour
2 organic eggs, lightly beaten
8oz whitebait, defrosted, washed gently and drained
1 tablespoon finely chopped parsley
salt and freshly ground pepper
Clarified Butter (see page 216)
lemon wedges, to serve

Whisk the flour and beaten eggs together. Add the whitebait and

parsley and season with salt and freshly ground pepper. Stir gently to coat.

Heat a small amount of clarified butter in a heavy frying pan over medium-high heat. Drop a tablespoon of the whitebait mixture onto the pan. Fry quickly on one side, just until the mixture sets – do not wait for the whitebait to go white or they will be overcooked. Flip the fritters onto the other side and brown quickly. Drain on paper towels.

Serve on warm plates with wedgse of lemon.

DEEP-FRIED SPRATS OR WHITEBAIT WITH AIOLI

In general, January has few highlights, apart from the arrival of the marmalade oranges in the shops – but when the sprats arrive into Ballycotton the excitement is tangible. We feast on them for a few short days – deep-fried, soused, pickled, and smoked. We eat them insides and all – and they are completely delicious! Deep-fried sprats and whitebait are just as good served simply with lemon wedges or tartare sauce · SERVES 6-8

1lb sprats or whitebait
1¼ cups well-seasoned all-purpose flour, or more if you need it
lemon wedges

FOR THE AIOLI
3 garlic cloves
salt
2 organic egg yolks
2 teaspoons white wine vinegar
½ teaspoon Dijon mustard
1 cup oil (sunflower or olive oil, or

a mixture) – we use ¾ cup sunflower oil and ¼ cup extra virgin olive oil
few drops of freshly squeezed lemon juice
2 tablespoons chopped flat-leaf parsley
freshly ground pepper

To Serve
flat-leaf parsley sprigs
oyster shells (optional)

First make the aioli. Mash the garlic with a little salt. Put the egg yolks into a glass bowl with the crushed garlic, white wine vinegar, and mustard. Whisk in the oil, drop by drop. Once the sauce has started to thicken, you can add the oil more quickly. Stir in the chopped parsley. Taste the aioli and add a few drops of lemon juice, pepper, and more salt if necessary.

Heat the oil in a deep-fat fryer to 400°F. Toss the sprats in well-seasoned flour, and cook a few at a time until crisp and golden. Drain on paper towels. Put an oyster shell on each plate to hold a generous spoonful of aioli. Serve immediately with lemon wedges and parsley sprigs as garnish.

Variation

DEEP-FRIED WHITEBAIT OR SPRATS WITH WILD GARLIC AND SAFFRON AIOLI

Prepare as above but put ¼ teaspoon saffron in a small bowl and add 1 tablespoon of warm water. Allow it to infuse and add to the egg yolks and crushed garlic. Stir in 5 tablespoons chopped wild garlic leaves instead of parsley at the end.

Above: *Deep-fried Whitebait with Aioli.*

Above: *Deep-fried Squid.*

Squid

Squid needs to be carefully cooked either for a few minutes – just long enough to change from translucent to opaque – or for at least 45–60 minutes. In between, it will have the texture of India rubber. Squid also makes delicious fish cakes.

Remove the intestines by grasping the head of the squid and gently pulling it away from the body.

The intestines will come out of the body. Cut the tentacles just above the eyes and set aside. Discard the eyes and the intestines. Pull the wings off the body and cut the wings diagonally into ¼in strips. Rinse out the body. An easy way to do this is to cut a piece off the end and run cold water through, squeezing out any remaining entrails (do not do this if you plan to stuff the body).

Insert your fingers into the top of the body cavity and remove the plastic-like quill and discard. Peel away the exterior skin (this step may be omitted if the squid are very fresh). Rinse in fresh water and drain. Keep the squid whole to stuff or cut it into rings about ¼in in width, i.e. approximately the same width as the tentacles. Keep the tentacles intact or cut the tentacles into lengths of approximately 4in.

DEEP-FRIED SQUID

Do not fry all the squid at once here, as the temperature of the oil will drop and cause sticking and the flour will absorb too much oil, making the squid greasy rather than crisp. You can add some chili powder or smoked paprika to the flour to add a bit of extra oomph · **SERVES 6–8**

4 medium-sized fresh squid
seasoned all-purpose flour
oil for frying

lemon quarters and green salad

First, prepare the squid as above.

Dredge all the pieces of squid in flour seasoned with salt and pepper, taking care to coat well. Shake off excess flour.

Heat the oil in a deep-fat fryer to about 350°F (or until a piece of bread sizzles when dropped into it). Carefully place the floured squid pieces into the oil and cook quickly, until the squid is just colored. Remove, drain, and leave aside in a warm spot on paper towels.

Repeat the frying process in batches until all the squid is cooked. Season to taste. Serve with lemon quarters, a peppery watercress salad, and tomato and chile jam.

CHARGRILLED SQUID WITH CHILE AND PARSLEY OIL AND CHORIZO

The chile and parsley oil used here will keep a week in the fridge and is also good served with pasta, shrimp, or steak · **SERVES 8 AS AN APPETIZER**

3 medium-sized squid (squid must be fresh for this recipe, frozen squid will be tough cooked in this way)
4oz chorizo
extra virgin olive oil, for grilling

FOR THE CHILE AND PARSLEY OIL
3 garlic cloves, peeled and chopped
1 large red chile, seeded and finely chopped
½ cup finely chopped flat-leaf parsley
½ cup extra virgin olive oil
sea salt and freshly ground black pepper

TO SERVE
arugula leaves (enough for 8)
extra virgin olive oil

Prepare the squid. Cut the sac and wings into pieces about 2in square and lightly score the inside of each piece with the tip of a knife. Separate the tentacles. Cover and refrigerate the squid until needed.

To make the chile and parsley oil, combine the chopped garlic, chile, and parsley and continue to chop them together until fine. Put into a bowl with the olive oil and season with salt and freshly ground pepper.

Just before serving, heat a gas or charcoal grill or a cast-iron grill pan. Cook the chorizo for a few minutes in a little olive oil. Meanwhile, toss the arugula leaves in a little olive oil. Brush the squid pieces with olive oil and put them on the very hot grill for a few seconds on each side – just long enough for them to change color and be marked by the grill. Lay on a bed of arugula leaves with the chorizo, spoon a little chile and parsley oil over each piece of squid, and serve immediately.

SQUID PROVENÇAL

Remember, squid takes only a couple of minutes to cook. It will taste sweet and tender and convert even the most ardent squid hater! If you boil it or cook it for longer, it can be extremely tough – squid needs to be cooked for just a few seconds or for ages, there is no in-between · **SERVES 4 AS A MAIN COURSE, 8 AS AN APPETIZER**

4 medium-sized squid
4 tablespoons extra virgin olive oil
2 garlic cloves, crushed
2 onions, sliced
¾ cup dry white wine
5 large ripe tomatoes, peeled, seeded, and sliced
½ teaspoon smoked paprika
salt, freshly ground pepper and sugar
1 tablespoon chopped parsley

To prepare the squid, see page 98. Cut the squid into ¼in rounds or slices.

Heat the olive oil in a wide saucepan, toss in the crushed garlic and sliced onions, cover, and cook for 5 minutes over low heat. Add the wine and reduce by half. Meanwhile, peel and slice the tomatoes and add to the onions with the smoked paprika. Season with salt, pepper, and sugar and cook, uncovered, until thickish (about 10 minutes). The recipe may be prepared ahead up to this point.

Just before serving, add the squid and chopped parsley, cover the saucepan, and cook for 2–3 minutes or until the color of the squid changes. Taste, correct the seasoning, and serve immediately.

Ray or Skate

We get several types of ray, or skate, in our waters – blond ray and thornback ray, for instance. They're graceful fish that are shaped like a kite with a tail. You just eat the two wings and discard the rest. When you're handling the latter, be careful not to get scratched by the sharp thorns on the wings and along the back.

Use a sharp knife to cut off each wing close to the body. Fishmongers tend to skin the wings before they sell them, but we generally cook them with the skin on and then remove it once cooked, which is easier.

Ray wing is still very under-used and children love its mild flavor, plus the fact that once served, it has no bones. There's flesh on both sides, although the flesh on top is thicker than the flesh beneath. The long strands of flesh lift easily off the cartilaginous bones once cooked. Ray is one of the few fish that's tough when quite fresh, so keep it for a day or two, but not more; otherwise it will smell and taste strongly of ammonia.

SKATE WITH BLACK BUTTER

This classic recipe is one of the most delicious ways of serving a beautiful piece of skate wing. Hold your nerve – the butter must go past the hazelnut stage and begin to burn, otherwise it doesn't cut the richness of the fish ·
SERVES 2–3 AS A MAIN COURSE

1 **medium skate (ray) wing weighing about 1¼lb**
1 **onion, sliced**
a few sprigs of flat-leaf parsley, plus extra for garnish
a little salt
2 **tablespoons white wine vinegar**

FOR THE BLACK BUTTER
4 **tablespoons butter**
2 **tablespoons white wine vinegar**
2 **teaspoons capers**

Choose a pan wide enough for the skate to lie flat while cooking. Put the skate in and cover completely with cold water. Add the onion, parsley, salt, and vinegar. Bring to a gentle boil, simmer for a minute, then cover and turn off the heat. Leave the skate in the water for 10–15 minutes, depending on the thickness of the fish. When the flesh lifts easily from the cartilage, the skate is cooked.

Transfer the fish to a large serving plate. Remove the dark skin from the top and starting at the outer side of the wing, use a spatula to lift the flesh off the cartilage. Transfer the flesh onto hot plates. Then flip the fish over, scrape the white skin off the underside, and lift the flesh onto hot plates. Cover and keep hot.

Next make the black butter. Melt the butter in a hot pan, allow it to foam, and as it turns a dark hazelnut brown, just before it burns, add the wine vinegar and the capers. Allow to bubble up again and then pour, sizzling, over the hot fish. Sprinkle with snipped parsley and run to the table!

Variation

WARM RAY WING WITH WILD GARLIC AND BLACK OLIVE PESTO
Follow the recipe above, skin the fish and keep hot. Then mix 2 tablespoons of Wild Garlic Pesto (see page 29) with enough extra virgin olive oil (about 4 tablespoons) to thin to a coating consistency. Add 8 pitted and coarsely chopped Kalamata olives. Spoon the dressing over the warm fish, scatter with a few chopped olives, sprinkle with wild garlic flowers, and serve immediately on warm plates. This dish is best eaten lukewarm.

Fish Roe

Fish roe is very nutritious, and inexpensive, but often forgotten. I adore smoked cod roe – once I start to slather it on hot thin toast it's hard to stop – bliss with a chilled glass of Sauvignon Blanc. To smoke your own cod roe, see the recipe on page 484.

HERRING ROE ON TOAST

I adore herring roes. There are two distinct types: the knobbly roe from the female herring, made up of thousands of little eggs, and the soft roe which is the melt of the male herring. Both are delicious and each kind has its devotees – I'm particularly partial to the female herring roe.

butter
3 **or 4 herring roes per person**

seasoned all-purpose flour
lemon
freshly made buttered toast
a sprig of parsley

When you are ready to eat, melt a little butter in a pan, toss the herring roes gently in seasoned flour and cook in the foaming butter for a few minutes on each side until just firm.

Sprinkle with a few drops of lemon juice and serve immediately on hot buttered toast. Pop a little sprig of parsley on top for garnish.

SOFT HERRING ROE PÂTÉ

This is a simple little recipe for using the soft male herring roe. The flavor is delicate but if you'd rather, add some freshly chopped herbs such as fennel, dill, thyme, or marjoram to taste · **SERVES 3–4**

4oz soft herring roe
4 tablespoons unsalted butter, softened
salt and freshly ground pepper
pinch of cayenne pepper
½ tablespoon or more freshly squeezed lemon juice

Gently sauté the roes for a couple of minutes in a little butter over low heat. Turn the roes halfway through cooking but take care because they are very delicate. Transfer to a food processor, leave to cool a little, then add the rest of the butter and blend for a minute or two, until smooth.

Season with salt and pepper and sharpen with lemon juice. Spoon into little pots or ramekins, cover and refrigerate. Serve chilled with hot buttered toast.

POACHED COD ROE WITH HERB BUTTER

You'll need a fishmonger to help you find cod roe. It's not everyone's cup of tea, but try it; it's an unusual treat · **SERVES 4**

cod roe, about 1lb
salt
1 tablespoon freshly squeezed lemon juice or wine vinegar
toast

FOR THE HERB BUTTER
4–8 tablespoons butter
4 teaspoons mixed finely chopped fresh parsley, chives, fennel sprig, and thyme leaves
salt and freshly ground black pepper

Rinse the cod roe gently and wrap it in muslin to keep it intact as it cooks. Slip it into a saucepan of hot, salted water, allowing 2 teaspoons of salt to 1 quart of water. Add freshly squeezed lemon juice and poach the roe gently until firm, about 15–20 minutes depending on size.

Just before serving, make the herb butter by melting the butter and stirring in the freshly chopped herbs.

Drain the roe, slice, and serve on hot toast with the herb butter.

Variations

ROE WITH ANCHOVY BUTTER
Follow the recipe above, but mash 4 anchovies and add to the herb butter.

SHRIMP BUTTER SAUCE
Add 4oz peeled cooked shrimp to the herb butter.

TARAMASALATA

For perfection, taramasalata should be made in a pestle and mortar, but I make a very passable version in a food processor. Many taramasalata recipes suggest using 100 percent olive oil but I find the flavor too strong, so I use a small proportion of olive oil with sunflower or peanut oil. I find the salty flavor of taramasalata addictive, it's totally unlike the scary pink stuff served in many Greek restaurants, and it's so easy to make · **SERVES 8–10 AS AN APPETIZER**

4oz Smoked Cod Roe (see page 484)
2 slices good white bread
1 organic egg yolk
1 garlic clove, peeled and crushed
½–1 cup olive oil or a mixture of sunflower or peanut oil and olive oil
freshly squeezed lemon juice

TO SERVE
Kalamata olives
crusty hot bread or hot thin toast

Remove the thin skin from the cod roe. Soak the roe in cold water for 15–30 minutes, depending on how salty it is. Drain well.

Trim the crusts off the bread and soak in a little water for a few minutes so that it can be made into a paste. (Squeeze out any excess liquid.)

Put the egg yolk into a pestle and mortar or the bowl of a food

processor. Add the crushed garlic, soggy bread, and smoked cod roe. Pound or process for a few seconds, then (with the machine running, if using) add the oil gradually as though you were making mayonnaise. Add freshly squeezed lemon juice to taste.

Serve chilled with a few Kalamata olives and crusty white bread or hot thin toast.

Smoked Fish

There was once a strong tradition of home smoking in Ireland, particularly herrings (known as kippers) and white fish, principally haddock. In later years, however, commercial smokeries tended to use a smoke dye rather than actually smoking the fish, and this gave it a bright orange hue. Consequently, when some of the artisan fish smokers offer their pale, naturally smoked products for sale, they have the added challenge of overcoming the public's perception that real smoked fish should be bright orange in color. When buying smoked fish, do not let the color fool you!

Here are a couple of recipes for using smoked fish that are available from your fishmonger, but if you want to get into smoking fish yourself, then see the Preserving chapter.

SMOKED EEL WITH LEMON AND HORSERADISH CREAM

Fresh eel is now endangered so it may be difficult to find some to smoke yourself, but you can buy it smoked. Brown soda or yeast bread is a perfect accompaniment. We sometimes serve the smoked eel on a little salad of frisée and lamb's lettuce with crispy bacon and chorizo – also delicious! ·
SERVES 6–8

a whole smoked eel
lemon wedges
Horseradish Sauce (see page 24)

To skin and slice the smoked eel, cut the eel just behind the head and gently peel off the skin down towards the tail, exposing only as much as you intend to eat. With a sharp knife, cut thin slices about 3in in length from each side. Depending on the thickness of the eel, you can sometimes get 2 or even 3 thin slices from one part of the eel by cutting down a third or halfway before sliding the blade of the knife towards the tail. Repeat on the other side.

Arrange 3–5 slices of the smoked eel on a cold plate. Serve simply with lemon wedges and perhaps a dollop of mild horseradish sauce.

PROPER BREAKFAST KIPPERS

It was a well known fact that my father-in-law, Ivan Allen, would go to the ends of the earth for a decent kipper, so little parcels of kippers regularly arrived in the post from all over the British Isles.

These days I don't have to go such extremes – our neighbors Sally Barnes of Woodcock Smokery and Frank Hederman of Belvelly Smokehouse near Cobh smoke the very best kippers I have ever tasted. I like them best cooked for breakfast by what I call the jug method. But when they are lightly smoked they can be cooked in a little foaming butter in a frying pan instead · SERVES 2

2 undyed kippers
Maître d'Hôtel Butter (see page 216)

GARNISH
2 lemon wedges
2 sprigs of parsley

Put the kippers head-down in a deep heatproof pitcher or measuring cup. Cover them with boiling water right up to their tails as though you are making tea. Leave for 2–3 minutes to heat through. Lift them out carefully by the tail and serve immediately on hot plates with a pat of maître d'hôtel butter melting on top. Garnish each with lemon wedges and a sprig of parsley.

Opposite: *Proper Breakfast Kippers.*

Preserving

If you overcome the difficulty of getting fresh fish, what do you do when you have a glut?

Before the days of refrigeration it was vital for coastal communities to know the rudiments of how to preserve the abundant catch for the lean winter months. The principal way to preserve fish in Ireland and many other countries was simply to salt it, and that tradition still exists in some areas. In the Cork market you can buy salt cod or pollock, which was originally called "battleboard." It's still much loved by older people particularly, and salt cod in white sauce with boiled potatoes was a traditional Christmas Eve supper.

PICKLED HERRING

This is one of the ways to preserve herring during the glut for the winter season · **SERVES ABOUT 12**

12 fresh herrings
2 cups distilled white vinegar
7 tablespoons sea salt
¼ cup sugar
1 tablespoon black peppercorns, crushed
1 generous teaspoon pimento or allspice berries, slightly crushed
6 bay leaves

Gut, scale, and rinse the herrings, but leave the heads on. Put the herrings into a container, pour in the vinegar, and leave them overnight.

The next day, mix the rest of the ingredients together and put a layer into the bottom of a stoneware crock. Then put in a layer of herrings. Continue to layer the herrings and salt mixture, finishing with a layer of the salt mixture. The salt will extract the moisture from the herring. Weigh everything down with a clean plate and a weight so that the herring is submerged in the liquid

Cover and keep in a cold larder or in the fridge if you have space (note, the herrings must be submerged in the liquid, more will come out of them). Keep for at least 2 or 3 days before use, but they will actually keep for ages. There are many ways to serve pickled herrings. Serve with bread, potato salad, green salad, or the accompaniment of your choice.

ROLLMOPS WITH CUCUMBER PICKLE AND MUSTARD AND DILL MAYONNAISE

In the summer, huge shoals of mackerel come into Ballycotton, so we serve them for breakfast, lunch, and dinner and in every conceivable way. The following are two ways that have been passed down through the family of preserving a glut of herring or mackerel ·

SERVES 8 AS A MAIN COURSE OR 16 AS AN APPETIZER

8 herrings or mackerel
1 onion, thinly sliced
1 teaspoon whole black peppercorns
6 cloves
1 teaspoon salt
1 teaspoon sugar
1 bay leaf
1 cup white wine vinegar

Sweet Cucumber Pickle (see page 488)
Mustard and Dill Mayonnaise (see recipe opposite)

Preheat the oven to 275°F.

Gut, rinse, and fillet the herring or mackerel, making sure there are no bones (a tall order with herring – but do your best). Roll up the fillets, skin side out, and pack tightly into a flameproof casserole. Sprinkle the thinly sliced onion, peppercorns, cloves, salt, sugar, vinegar, and bay leaf over the top. Bring to a boil on the stovetop and then pop into the oven for 30–45 minutes.

Remove the casserole and leave to cool. "Soused" herring or mackerel will keep for 7–10 days in the fridge. To serve: put one of two fillets on a plate, surround with three little mounds of sweet cucumber pickle, and create a zig zag design with mustard and dill mayonnaise. Serve with fresh crusty bread. I also love piped potato salad with soused herring.

ALICIA'S SOUSED MACKEREL

My friend Alicia Wilkinson has a cooking school in Cape Town, and has spent her life passing on skills to a generation of young people. She learned many of her skills from her mother, Leslie Fawl, an Irishwoman who emigrated to South Africa and started the first cooking school there, Silwood Kitchen. Alicia's daughter, Carianne, who was a student at the Ballymaloe Cookery School, now runs the school. This is a lovely way to use a glut and preserve mackerel for the short term ·

SERVES 4 AS A MAIN COURSE,
OR 8 AS AN APPETIZER

1½lb very fresh mackerel
½ cup olive oil
juice of 1½ lemons
2 or 3 garlic cloves
a few sprigs of parsley
salt
½ cup dry white wine

Remove the heads from the
mackerel, rinse, and gut them.
Cut into 2½in chunks.

Heat a small amount of the oil in
an earthenware dish. Place the
mackerel carefully in the dish and
squeeze the lemon juice over them.
Crush the garlic and parsley in a
mortar with a little salt and pour
over the fish, then wash the mortar
out with the wine and add that, too.
Pour in the rest of the olive oil and
give the dish a shake so that the
liquid spreads throughout the dish.

Cook over low heat on top of the
stove for about 10 minutes, or until
fish is cooked. Serve cold.

MARINATED MACKEREL

*The Japanese often salt fish to enhance
the flavor, but only the freshest fish
should be eaten raw. Mackerel
deteriorates rapidly if not handled
properly once caught. Marinating
mackerel in vinegar enhances the flavor
and also helps to preserve and firm the
flesh, making it easier to slice. It can
be prepared up to six hours in advance.
If you can't get mirin, substitute the
equivalent amount of superfine sugar.
This is another method for preserving
in the short term* · SERVES 6–8

6 fresh mackerel fillets, about
5oz each
6 tablespoons sea salt
2¼ cups rice vinegar
3 tablespoons mirin or superfine
sugar
3 teaspoons salt

Mustard and Dill Mayonnaise (see
right) or Sweet Cucumber
Pickle (see page 488)

Put the mackerel fillets onto a sheet
pan and sprinkle with salt. Gently
rub the fillets to ensure that they are
evenly covered. Lay the fillets on a
wire rack and leave to drain for
about 30 minutes or, better still, an
hour. Rinse off the salt in cold water
and dry the fillets with paper towels.

Choose a dish large enough to
hold the fish. Mix the vinegar, mirin
or sugar, and salt together. Add the
fish and allow to marinate for an
hour or so. Remove the fillets from
the pickle and pat dry with paper
towels. The flesh will look paler.
Slowly peel off the papery thin outer
skin, starting at the head end.

To serve, cut the fillets into
paper-thin slices and arrange on a
plate. Serve with a thin mustard and
dill mayo or sweet cucumber pickle.

GRAVLAX WITH MUSTARD AND DILL MAYONNAISE

*People in Nordic countries take the
basic pickling technique and create
many exciting variations. Gravlax is
flavored with beets, black pepper,
mustard, and even vodka. We are all
addicted to this pickled salmon which
keeps for up to a week* · SERVES 12–16
AS AN APPETIZER

1½lb tail piece of fresh wild salmon
1 heaping tablespoon sea salt
1 heaping tablespoon sugar
1 teaspoon freshly ground black
pepper
2 tablespoons finely chopped fresh
dill

FOR THE MUSTARD AND DILL
MAYONNAISE
1 large organic egg yolk
2 tablespoons Dijon mustard
1 tablespoon sugar
½ cup peanut or sunflower oil
1 tablespoon white wine vinegar
1 tablespoon finely chopped dill
salt and freshly ground white
pepper

Fillet the salmon and remove all the
bones with a tweezers. Mix the salt,
sugar, pepper, and dill together in a
bowl. Place the fish on a piece of
plastic wrap and scatter the mixture
over the surface of the fish.

Wrap the salmon tightly with the
plastic wrap and refrigerate for a
minimum of 24 hours.

To make the mustard and dill
mayonnaise, whisk the egg yolk with
the mustard and sugar, then drip in
the oil drop by drop, whisking all
the time, then add the vinegar, fresh
dill and seasoning.

To serve, wipe most of the dill
mixture off the salmon and slice
thinly. Arrange simply on a plate or
make a rosette shape. Fill the center
of the rosette with mustard and dill
mayonnaise. Garnish with fresh
dill and serve with brown bread
and butter.

BEET GRAVLAX

This modern Scandinavian version results in a two-tone gravlax, with a deep-red beet color on the outside, and salmon pink within · SERVES 30–40

2 **sides of wild salmon or organic farmed salmon**
2 **heaping tablespoons sea salt**
3 **heaping tablespoons sugar**
2 **teaspoons freshly ground pepper**
2 **tablespoons chopped dill,**
1 **medium (6oz) beet, peeled and grated**

Cucumber and Dill Sauce, see page 481

Prepare the salmon as in the previous gravlax recipe.

Line a long oval dish with plastic wrap. Put one fillet, skin side down, on the lined dish. Mix together the salt, sugar, pepper, dill, and freshly grated beet and spread over the surface of the salmon.

Place the other salmon fillet on top and wrap the salmon tightly with the plastic wrap. Place a weight on top (I use a cutting board). Refrigerate; turn a couple of times during the next few days. Serve with the cucumber and dill sauce.

SALT COD

Nowadays we salt to preserve fish in the short term or to enhance flavor so there's no need to use so much salt (or salt for so long) as years ago.

dairy or sea salt
thick, unskinned cod fillet or ling fillet

Sprinkle a thin layer of salt over the bottom of a lasagne dish or plastic container. Put the cod fillet on top. Cover completely with another layer of salt.

Cover and refrigerate overnight. By the next day, most of the salt will have turned into brine. Remove the cod from the brine and rinse under cold water. Cover with fresh water and leave to soak for 1 hour. Discard the water and dry the fish. It is now ready to be cooked.

Salt cod can keep for up to a month if heavily salted, but we normally lightly salt it and use it within a couple of days or a week.

BRANDADE DE MORUE WITH PIQUILLO PEPPER AND ARUGULA

Salt cod is most often eaten just on toast, but I was introduced to this recipe at a tapas restaurant in Spain. You poach the cod and process it with other ingredients to make a sort of purée to spread on toast. Variations on this can be found in France and other Mediterranean countries where salt cod is enjoyed. I love the sweetness of the piquillo pepper with the salty fish and peppery arugula leaves. The piquillo peppers make perfect little receptacles for the fish · SERVES 4–6

1lb **fresh salt cod (see recipe above), soaked overnight in cold water**
12 **thin slices of thin baguette**
½ **cup extra virgin olive oil**
2 **large garlic cloves, crushed**
¾ **cup heavy cream**
lemon juice, to taste
freshly ground black pepper
12 **piquillo peppers**

GARNISH
black olives
arugula leaves

Drain the soaked salt cod and rinse well. Put it into a saucepan with enough fresh water to cover, bring to a boil, and simmer for 4–5 minutes. Lift out with a slotted spoon, drain away the excess water and remove the skin and any bones. Transfer the cod into a food processor.

Cook the slices of baguette in a few tablespoons of the olive oil for a minute or two on either side until golden brown. Drain briefly on paper towels and keep warm in a low oven.

Put the garlic, remaining olive oil, and cream into a small pan and bring to a boil. Add to the fish in the food processor and blend together until just smooth. Season with freshly squeezed lemon juice and plenty of black pepper. Taste, it is unlikely to need salt.

Spoon the cod mixture into piquillo peppers. Serve a few slices of the fried bread alongside. Garnish with the black olives and arugula and serve warm.

SALT COD CROQUETAS WITH GARLIC AND SAFFRON AIOLI

Of all the ways of preparing salt cod, this one is always a favorite. They're an irresistible nibble or a delicious appetizer. Now that cod is becoming scarce we also salt ling and hake and use them in this recipe · **SERVES 8, MAKES ABOUT 40**

8oz skinned and boned dried salt
    cod (see opposite)
1lb medium-sized all-purpose
    potatoes, peeled
2 garlic cloves, crushed
1 tablespoon chopped parsley
freshly ground pepper
2 organic egg yolks

Garlic and Saffron Aioli
    (see page 97)

oil, for deep frying

Soak the salt cod in several changes of cold water for 12–24 hours, depending on how salty it is. Drain.

Put the potatoes into a saucepan, cover with water, and bring to a boil. Cover and simmer for 15–20 minutes or until the potatoes are cooked through. Meanwhile, cover the salt cod with cold water, bring to a boil and simmer for 5–7 minutes or until the flesh has changed from translucent to opaque.

Drain the potatoes and push through a ricer or food mill into a bowl. Remove the skin from the cod, flake the flesh, and mix with the mashed potatoes. Add the garlic, parsley, pepper, and egg yolks. Mix well. Taste and add salt if necessary.

To cook the croquetas, drop teaspoons of the mixture into hot oil. They will puff up and crisp on all sides. Drain on paper towels. Keep warm while you fry the remainder. Serve with garlic and saffron aioli or just plain aioli.

SOUSED SPRATS, HERRINGS, OR MACKEREL WITH TOMATOES AND MUSTARD SEED

The fish will keep refrigerated for up to one month · **SERVES 4**

½ cup white wine vinegar
½ cup dry white wine
½ small onion, thinly sliced
8oz ripe tomatoes, peeled and
    sliced
2 sprigs of fennel
2 small bay leaves
1 teaspoon white mustard seed
2 teaspoons sugar
1 teaspoon salt
lots of freshly ground pepper
4 fresh mackerel or herrings or
    12–16 sprats

Pour the vinegar and white wine into a stainless-steel saucepan, add the onion and tomatoes, herbs, mustard seed, sugar, and seasoning. Bring to a boil and reduce by half. Meanwhile gut and fillet the fish. Roll the fish fillets or lay flat in a flameproof casserole or sauté pan. Pour the pickling liquid over the top. Cover and bring to a boil, simmer gently for 4–5 minutes or until the fish is cooked. Serve chilled with a salad of little leaves and fresh herbs.

SALT FISH

Salting fish was once a standard way of preserving an abundance of summer fish around the coast. Peter Lawton, who works with us on the farm, explained to me how they salted fish at home in County Cork: "In August, take a timber barrel and sprinkle curing salt on the base. Layer the gutted fish on their back (not side), sprinkle with salt and rub in well, layer up the fish when you catch more and continue to salt (cod, herring, pollock, mackerel), always ending with a layer of salt. Cover with a wet sack. Store in a cold shed near the house. We used them during the winter months – they were usually eaten up by January or February. When we wanted to cook it, we'd rinse off the salt with cold water and either cook it on tongs over the open fire or in a saucepan. It would need to be covered with cold water and brought to a boil, then the cooking water would be discarded and more fresh cold water added. We'd eat it with parsley sauce and boiled potatoes."

In Kerry they gutted the fine horse mackerel along the backbone in September, then dipped both sides in coarse salt and built them up in layers in a barrel. These fed entire families throughout the winter. The mackerel were soaked in cold water overnight then drained and cooked on top of potatoes. For may years there was a big export trade to Spain but this ended in the 1930s.

Prawns and Shrimp

There is some confusion about the difference between prawns and shrimp. A Dublin Bay prawn looks for all the world like a mini lobster, with a straight body and large claws, whereas shrimp have more of a curled up shape and tiny claws. A marine biologist might dismiss me for this rather simplistic definition but I find it helps to clarify the difference in my students' minds.

Shrimp are also referred to as the common prawn (*palaemon serratus*) and there are several different types in the world, including the famous little brown shrimp (crangon crangon) from Morecambe Bay in England. Asian, or tiger prawns, are of similar shape and are actually a type of shrimp. We avoid using Asian prawns for environmental and health concerns, unless we can source organic tiger prawns that are produced sustainably.

Dublin Bay prawns are not caught in Dublin Bay as the name might suggest. The name was bestowed because the fishing boats coming into Dublin Bay often had these prawns on board, having caught them as a by-catch. They are also sometimes called langoustine or Norway lobster.

These prawns are very expensive so to get your money's worth ask the fishmonger for really fresh prawns that have not been dipped in sodium metalisulphate on the boats to prolong their shelf life. Dipped prawns may look perfect, but they don't taste nearly as good as spanking fresh undipped prawns.

How to cook prawns

The whole secret of well-flavored prawns or shrimp, or in fact any kind of shellfish, is to add enough salt to the cooking water – 1 well-heaping tablespoon of salt to quart of water. We measure this meticulously every time.

Any prawns, either whole or just the tails, can be cooked in this way. Bring ½ gallon of water to a fast, rolling boil and add 2 generous tablespoons of salt. Add the prawns to the water and as soon as it returns to a boil, test a prawn to see if it is cooked. It should be firm and white, not opaque or mushy. If cooked, remove the prawns immediately and drain on paper towels. Allow to cool in a single layer on a sheet pan, making sure each one is lying flat for better presentation. Do not cook too many prawns together, as they may overcook before the water returns to a boil.

Left: *Dublin Bay prawns.*

How to extract the meat from cooked prawns

If the cooked prawns are whole, detach the head from the tail. Hold the tail belly-side-up and tug at the fan-shaped piece at the end of the tail, clicking it back and forth so that the shell breaks in half. Then separate the shell from the flesh. I love the soft meat inside the head, so I detach a claw and use the pincers to scoop the soft meat out of the head, which I then mix with mayonnaise and eat. To get the full value from prawns, you'll need to have a claw cracker to crack the claws and get at the soft, sweet meat inside. The claws of Dublin Bay prawns are really quite big, so it's a bit of a waste not to do this. Use the shells to make shellfish stock and bisque. When there's roe, we use it to decorate dishes or to mix into the mayonnaise.

Preparing Dublin Bay prawn tails

Remove the heads of the prawns and discard or use for making Fish Stock (see page 80) or Prawn Bisque (see page 112). With the underside of the prawn uppermost, tug the little fan-shaped tail at either side and carefully draw out the trail. The trail is the intestine, so it is important to remove it before cooking. You may now either cook the prawns as above in boiling, salted water, or the shell can be removed. They can then be dipped in batter for scampi or used in other recipes that called for peeled prawns. The freshly peeled and cooked prawn tails tossed in a little butter are delicious served on a piece of toast and coated with Sauce de Quimper (see page 93).

How to cook shrimp

If you have a shrimp net you can sometimes catch shrimp around the keel of boats in a harbor. Ours are caught in shrimp pots out at sea. They are gray when alive and turn pinky-orange as they cook.

Cook shrimp in the same way as prawns. Because of their texture, they usually take a little longer than prawns to cook, even though they can be smaller. To check if they are cooked, ensure there is no trace of black on the back of the heads. When they are fully cooked, the shells turn a uniformly orangey-pink.

How to extract the meat from cooked shrimp

Shrimp shells are much softer than prawn shells. Our grandchildren adore them and can peel them easily with their little fingers. As with prawns, hold the shrimp belly uppermost. If you want to just serve the body, detach the head from the tail and then pinch the shell at the end of the tail; often the whole shell comes off in one piece, including the legs. If you want to serve the shrimp whole, just pinch the tail shell off. Use the shells to make shellfish stock or bisque (see pages 81 and 112). As with prawns, when there's roe, we use it to decorate dishes or to mix into the mayonnaise.

WHOLE BALLYCOTTON PRAWNS IN THE SHELL

I frequently serve this as an appetizer at my dinner parties because we're so fortunate to have prawns coming in so spanking fresh from the boats in Ballycotton. It's easy to prepare and fun for people to eat. Guests can enjoy every single scrap from the tail up to the claws. You'll need to provide claw crackers and finger bowls, because the guests break the shells themselves.

Serve with homemade mayonnaise made with finest extra virgin olive oil. For variation, flavor the mayonnaise with saffron, chervil, dill, or fennel ·
SERVES 4

24 large whole very fresh Dublin
  Bay prawns
4 tablespoons homemade
  Mayonnaise (see recipe on
  page 252)
wild watercress leaves
4 lemon wedges

Cook the whole prawns as described at left.

Put 6 cooked, whole prawns on each plate. Spoon a tablespoon of homemade mayonnaise into a little bowl or oyster shell on the side of the plate and pop a lemon wedge onto the plate, too. Garnish with a few sprigs of fresh wild watercress. Serve with fresh crusty brown soda bread and Irish butter.

PRAWNS OR SHRIMP ON BROWN BREAD WITH MAYONNAISE

Don't dismiss this very simple appetizer. Prawns or shrimp are wonderful served on good, fresh brown bread with a homemade mayonnaise. If using shrimp, use a little of the coral for garnish · SERVES 4

6oz prawn tails or shrimp, freshly cooked and peeled
4 slices Ballymaloe Brown Yeast Bread (see page 569) or Brown Soda Bread (see page 199), thinly sliced, crusts removed and buttered
4 leaves butter, oakleaf, or lollo rosso lettuce
3 tablespoons homemade Mayonnaise (see page 252)

GARNISH
4 lemon wedges
sprigs of watercress, flat-leaf parsley, fennel, or garden cress

Peel the fat, freshly cooked prawn tails or shrimp. Put a slice of buttered bread on a plate, arrange 1 or 2 lettuce leaves on top, and place 5–6 prawns on the lettuce. Pipe a coil of homemade mayonnaise on the prawns, just enough so the proportion of each ingredient looks right. Garnish with lemon wedges and sprigs of watercress, parsley, fennel, or garden cress.

Variation
PRAWN OR SHRIMP CANAPÉS
Tiny versions of these on rounds or squares of bread make a delicious canapé to go with drinks.

DEEP-FRIED PRAWNS WITH TARTARE SAUCE

Deep-fried prawns were the "must have" appetizer of the 60s and 70s, utterly delicious when made with fresh prawns. Sadly, nowadays it is more often a travesty made with inferior soggy, frozen prawns. To understand the magic, one must start with undipped, peeled fresh prawn tails (see page 108).

very fresh Dublin Bay prawns, peeled
Tartare Sauce (see page 94)
Batter (see Fish and Chips recipe, page 94)

TO SERVE
lemon wedges

Make and finish the batter according to the Fish and Chips recipe on page 94.

Preheat the oil to 350°F in a deep fryer.

Dip the very fresh prawns individually in the batter and deep-fry in hot oil until crisp and golden. Drain on paper towels. Serve immediately with a little bowl of tartare sauce and a lemon wedge – sublime.

POTTED PRAWNS OR SHRIMP

Traditionally, when the shrimp boats arrived into the south of England from their shrimping expeditions, the fishermen's wives would be waiting in the port to cook and peel the shrimp. Then they'd drop them into big vats of sizzling butter to preserve them in the

form of potted shrimp. Potting is a great way to make a little fish go a long way. Chopped marjoram instead of thyme also flavors potted shrimp in a delicious way · SERVES 8 AS AN APPETIZER

1 garlic clove
salt and freshly ground pepper
½ cup Clarified Butter (see page 216)
2 teaspoons thyme leaves
8oz shrimp or Dublin Bay prawns, shelled and cooked
2 teaspoons lemon juice, freshly squeezed

Crush the garlic to a paste with a little salt. Melt the clarified butter, thyme, and garlic. Add the prawns or shrimp and toss for about 30 seconds, leave to rest for a couple of minutes. Season carefully with 1–2 teaspoons of lemon juice. Pack into pots or ramekins and pour more melted butter over the top to seal, then put into the fridge and allow to set. Serve with crusty bread or hot, thin toast.

Potted shrimp will keep in the fridge for 3 or 4 days.

Variation
POTTED LOBSTER OR CRAYFISH
If you have a few delicious morsels of lobster or crayfish left over, this is a lovely way to preserve them. Replace the shrimp or prawns in the recipe above with lobster or crayfish. Serve with lots of crusty bread or hot thin toast.

Opposite: *Prawn Bisque.*

PRAWN OR LOBSTER BISQUE

Using leftovers is definitely a forgotten skill for many people, but we can't bear to waste any scrap of shellfish. Use leftover prawn or lobster shells to make this delicious bisque – then you get double value from the shellfish. It's rich, so serve it in small bowls ·

SERVES 8

12 **heads and claws of large fresh prawns or the cracked claws and body shells of 2 lobsters**
2 **tablespoons olive oil**
2 **shallots, finely chopped**
2 **garlic cloves, crushed**
1 **cup Fish Stock (see page 80)**
1lb **ripe fresh tomatoes, peeled and chopped or 1 x 14oz can of tomatoes, chopped**
2 **tablespoons finely chopped parsley**
2 **tablespoons brandy**
¾ **cup heavy cream**
salt and freshly ground pepper

GARNISH
fresh flat-leaf parsley leaves

Use a hammer to crush the prawn and lobster shells into small pieces. Heat the olive oil in a saucepan, add the shallots and garlic, and sauté for 1–2 minutes. Add the bits of prawns and lobster shells and also the fish stock. Stir and cook for 5 minutes. Add the chopped tomatoes, parsley, and brandy and cook for 5–10 minutes (the bisque should be just simmering).

Take the bisque off the heat, strain out the big bits, and purée the remainder. Then strain through a sieve. Return to the saucepan. Stir in the cream, season, and taste. If necessary, dilute with a little more fish stock. The bisque should be light and smooth in texture.

Serve in warmed bowls and garnish with a few parsley leaves.

Lobster

The best place to eat lobster is at home on the odd occasion when you can get hold of a couple of live lobsters from a local fisherman. Many restaurants keep lobster and other shellfish in tanks for days and sometimes even weeks, depending on how brisk their trade is. The idea is to keep them fresh for customers – but even though they are still alive they will have lost much of their sweetness and rarely compare to a lobster that's come straight from the sea. Lobster can be wonderful in a restaurant but for the mind-blowing experience that it ought to be, make sure they've come in straight from the lobster pots.

Buying lobster

Lobster and crab should be bought either alive or already cooked. Once dead, they deteriorate rapidly and can even become toxic – and if you buy a dead one, you have no way of knowing how long ago it expired. We once cooked a lobster that had been dead only an hour and were surprised to see how quickly the texture of the meat had changed. It had become soft and pulpy.

How to handle lobster

When handling lobster you will need to be very careful. Usually, the fisherman will have put strong rubber bands around the claws, but if the claws haven't been bound, lift the lobster by the back (up by the head). The claws are very strong and can really hurt your fingers and you won't forget about it for a long time! The only way to get them to loosen their grip at that point is to kill them.

How to extract meat from lobster

First, cook the lobster (see below). Lay it underside down on a baking sheet to cool. If necessary, put a weight on top of it to keep it flat. When it's cool enough to handle, transfer the lobster to a heavy cutting board and twist off the claws close to the body.

The way you proceed from here depends on how you wish to serve the lobster. If you plan to use just the tail meat for a lobster cocktail or lobster salad, then twist and pull to detach the tail from the head at the natural break. It will now look like a large prawn still in its shell. Tug and twist the fan end of the tail; more likely than not, half the shell will come off. Extract the meat from the inside of the shell, but keep the meat in one piece if you can. Use scissors to snip the underside of the shell if necessary. Once the meat has been extracted, slit with the blade of a knife along the belly and lift out the intestinal tract, which runs from the fleshiest part right down to the tail.

If you want collops (thin slices), insert a satay stick down the length of the tail so that it lays flat as it cools. Later, take out the stick and cut the lobster meat into slices about ¼in thick. If, however, you want to serve the lobster meat back in the shell again, for example, for lobster Thermidor, lobster Mornay, or Hot Buttered Lobster (see below), then set the whole lobster down on its belly, grip firmly at either side of the head, and put your knife at the base of the head, cutting down the length of the body through the shell to make two identical halves. Separate the two sides. Remove the tail meat from both sides and reserve for later use. Scoop out the tomalley (the soft green or fawny-colored head meat; it can even be a bit black, that just means the lobster's slightly undercooked). By law, because, like so many other fish and shellfish, lobster numbers have massively decreased, fishermen cannot land a female lobster, so you shouldn't see any roe or eggs.

Remove the stomach sac from the tip of the head, just behind the eyes, and discard. Go back to the claws. Separate the three joints of the claws. When you separate the two joints closest to the body, if you're lucky the nugget of meat inside will come out in one piece. Otherwise, use a lobster pick or the thin handle of a teaspoon to extract the juicy piece of lobster from the joints. Lay the main claw on its side. With the back of the blade of a chef's knife, tap sharply to crack the shell where the pincers meet the main part of the claw. The shell will break and you can extract the claw meat in one piece.

There is a thin piece of cartilage inside the meat in the large claw which you'll need to extract if you're going to use the meat chopped up. Don't worry about it if you're going to serve the claws whole. Repeat with the other claw. Save the shells for stock or a bisque (see pages 80 and 112).

THE HUMANE WAY TO COOK LOBSTER OR CRAYFISH

The method described here is considered by the RSPCA to be the most humane way to cook lobster and certainly results in deliciously tender and juicy flesh. When we are cooking lobster we judge by color. Lobster are a bluey-black color when alive, but change to a bright orange color when cooked. If you are uneasy about judging by color, then allow 15 minutes for the first 1lb and 10 minutes per pound after that. Crayfish, on the other hand, look more like a very large shrimp with a pinky-orange shell when raw, which deepens in color when cooked · SERVES 2-4

2 x 2lb live lobsters

FOR THE COURT-BOUILLON
1 carrot, sliced
1 onion, sliced
2 cups dry white wine
bouquet garni of parsley stems, sprig of thyme, celery ribs, and a small bay leaf
6 peppercorns
no salt!

In a stainless-steel saucepan, cover the lobsters or crayfish with lukewarm, salted water, using 6oz salt to every ½ gallon (8 cups) of water. Put the pan over low heat and slowly bring to a simmer. Lobster and crab die at about 112°F. By the time they start to simmer, the lobster will be changing color so remove them, and discard all the water.

Put the carrot and onion with the wine, 2 cups of fresh water, the bouquet garni, and peppercorns into the saucepan. Bring to a boil. Put the lobsters back into the pan and cover it with a tight-fitting lid. Steam the lobsters until they changes color to bright orange. Then remove them from the pot. Strain the cooking liquid and reserve for a sauce.

Variations

HOT BUTTERED LOBSTER
Simply toss the pieces of lobster in foaming melted butter and add a few drops of freshly squeezed lemon juice. Taste, add a little seasoning if necessary, then pile the lobster back into the half shell and enjoy immediately.

LOBSTER ON BROWN BREAD WITH MAYONNAISE
See page 110 for Prawns or Shrimp on Brown Bread with Mayonnaise recipe – also delicious with lobster.

LOBSTER COOKED IN SEAWATER
If you have access to fresh seawater, cook the lobster in it – it will be memorable.

Crab

There are many varieties of crab around the world but the most common crab in our waters is the brown crab (*cancer pagurus*). There is also the much smaller velvet swimming crab (*necora puber*), which we use for soup. Also look out for spider crabs (*maia squiado*). They are not so much forgotten as undiscovered, and tend not to be so widely available – although there are lots of them around our coast. Because they are more fiddly to prepare, choose large spider crabs to make it worth your while. They have wonderful sweet meat inside their long, spindly legs, but extracting the meat is unquestionably time-consuming.

Buying crab

Choose ones that are heavy for their size, and if you have a choice, take females rather than males because they usually have more meat in them. You can tell which is which because the female has a wider underneath flap than the male. If they feel very light, they are probably molting (about to change their shell) and have virtually no meat inside.

Be careful when handling live crabs, because they can take you unawares and are strong enough to actually break your finger. Always lift them by one of the back legs or by the shell.

Should I buy crab claws?

We are fortunate to get lots and lots of crabs from our local fishermen in Ballycotton during the season. They're actually available all year round, but the female crabs tend to have lots of orange roe in them from September to January, so we avoid them during that time. We've always had a policy at Ballymaloe not to buy crab claws, because that encourages unscrupulous fishermen to just pull off the claws, which contain the white meat and for which there is more demand. The bodies, which contain the lovely, delicious creamy – but not so popular – brown meat are discarded.

The fishermen would strongly deny that this practice happens, and it has to be said that occasionally, crabs do get tangled in the nets and inadvertently lose their claws. It's also a pity just to use the claws because you miss out on the brown meat which is so good in so many things: dressed crab, potted crab, crab soup, crab mayonnaise ...

Crab mayo

Try adding a couple of tablespoons of cooked, soft brown crabmeat to homemade mayonnaise to serve with crab or as an accompaniment to other shellfish and seafood salads.

How to cook crab

All types of crab are best cooked in seawater. Alternatively, cook in well-salted freshwater. For common crab, put the crab into a deep saucepan, cover with cold or barely lukewarm water, using 6oz of salt to every ½ gallon (8 cups) of water. This may sound like an incredible amount of salt, but try it: the crab will taste deliciously sweet.

Cover the saucepan, bring to a boil, and then simmer from there on, allowing 15 minutes for the first 1lb, and 10 minutes for the second and third (I've never come across a crab bigger than that!). We usually pour off two-thirds of the water halfway through cooking, and then cover and steam the crab for the remainder of the time. As soon as it is cooked, remove it from the saucepan and allow to get cold.

How to cook spider crabs

For spider crabs, cook in the same way but boil for just 12 minutes. Remove the pan from the heat and leave to stand for 5 minutes, then remove the crabs, and cool and pick the meat from the legs and clean and wash out the carapace. My favorite way to eat spider crab is to mix the sweet white meat with the very best extra virgin olive oil and a little freshly squeezed lemon juice to taste. I then spoon it back into the shell and enjoy it as the Italians do, with a glass of dry white wine.

How to extract crab meat

First remove the large claws. Hold the crab with the underside uppermost and lever out the center portion – I do this by catching the little lip of the projecting center shell against the edge of the table and pressing down firmly. The Dead Man's Fingers (lungs) usually come out with this central piece, but check in case some are left in the body. If so, remove and discard them.

Press your thumb down over the light shell just behind the eyes so that the shell cracks slightly, and then the sac which is underneath can be removed easily and discarded. Everything else inside the body of the crab is edible. The soft meat varies in color from cream to coffee to dark tan, and towards the end of the season it can contain quite a bit of bright orange coral which is stronger in flavor. Scoop it all out and put it into a bowl. There will also be one or two teaspoonsful of soft meat in the center portion attached to the small claws – add that to the bowl also. Scrub the large shell and keep it aside if you need it for dressed crab.

Crack the large claws with a hammer or weight and extract every bit of white meat from them. Also poke out the meat from the small claws using a lobster pick, skewer, or even the handle of a teaspoon.

Mix the brown and white meat together or use separately, depending on the recipe. Use shells for fish stock or crab soup (see pages 80 and 116).

CRAB CAKES

There are lots of different recipes for crab cakes, some use only white meat. Nam pla (Thai fish sauce) is a terrific flavor enhancer and very nutritious

· SERVES 5–15, DEPENDING ON HOW
THEY ARE TO BE SERVED

2 x quantity dressed crab (see page 118), without the buttered crumbs
2 tablespoons chopped cilantro
1 chile, finely chopped
1 tablespoon Thai fish sauce (nam pla)
¼ cup seasoned all-purpose flour
1 beaten organic egg mixed with a few tablespoons milk
½ cup white bread crumbs (see page 577)
olive or sunflower oil for deep frying

TO SERVE
sour cream
tomato salsa
fresh cilantro leaves

Mix the dressed crab with the chopped cilantro, chile, and fish sauce. Shape the mixture into crab cakes, about 2oz in weight, or smaller or larger if you please. Dip in well-seasoned flour, beaten egg, and bread crumbs.

Deep fry the crab cakes until crisp and golden in hot oil at 350°F. Drain on paper towels. Serve with sour cream, tomato salsa, and lots of fresh cilantro leaves.

POTTED CRAB WITH MELBA TOAST

This is a tasty way to make a little crab go a long way. Sealing in small pots is a good way of both preserving and stretching food, and can be done with either fish or meat. The thin layer of clarified butter poured on top will preserve this for some time, but remember, it's still fish, so eat it within 3–4 days. This can be served as an appetizer or on hot, thin toast with drinks. Or sometimes we use it as a layer in a fish or shellfish terrine ·
SERVES 8–10 AS AN APPETIZER

**8oz crab meat, freshly picked
    and cooked**
8 tablespoons softened butter
pinch of mace
**1–2 teaspoons finely chopped
    parsley**
**freshly squeezed lemon juice,
    to taste**
**English mustard powder (optional),
    to taste**
Clarified Butter (see page 216)

Mix all the ingredients together in a chilled bowl or, better still, pulse them in a food processor. Taste carefully and continue to season until you are happy with the flavor: it may need a little more lemon juice or even a little English mustard.

Press the mixture into little pots or ramekins, cover with a thin layer of clarified butter and refrigerate. Serve with Melba Toast (see page 578) or hot, thin toast. Keeps for 3 or 4 days.

BALLYMALOE CRAB SOUP

Rich and gorgeous, this soup provides a great way to use all the brown and white meat of the crab, plus the shell
· **SERVES 8**

FOR THE BÉCHAMEL SAUCE
2 cups whole milk
1 small carrot, sliced
1 small onion, sliced
1 sprig thyme
a few parsley stems
2 tablespoons Roux (see page 165)
**salt and freshly ground black
    pepper**

FOR THE SOUP BASE
1 tablespoon butter
extra virgin olive oil
1 small carrot, sliced
1 small onion, sliced
1 small celery rib, finely diced
**3 very ripe tomatoes, peeled and
    chopped**
sprig of fennel
sprig of thyme
**salt, freshly ground black pepper,
    and sugar**
1 cup Fish Stock (see page 80)
dash of heavy cream (optional)

**8oz crab meat, brown and white
    meat mixed**
**3 cups Fish Stock (see page 80),
    with some of the crab shells
    added to the stock**

GARNISH
Crisp Croutons (see page 579)
chopped parsley and chives

To make the béchamel sauce, put the milk into a saucepan and add the sliced carrot and onion with the sprig of thyme and the parsley stalks. Bring slowly to a boil and simmer for a few minutes to extract the flavor. Strain, discard the vegetables and herbs, return the milk to a boil, thicken with roux, and season with salt and freshly ground pepper. Cover and set aside while you prepare the soup base.

Melt the butter in a heavy saucepan with a dash of extra virgin olive oil; add the carrot, onion, celery, chopped tomatoes, fennel, and thyme. Season with salt, freshly ground pepper, and a pinch of sugar. Stir well, cover, and cook over low heat for 5–6 minutes. Add the 1 cup of fish stock and simmer until the vegetables are fully cooked.

Combine this mixture with the béchamel sauce, crab meat, and the 3 cups of fish stock. Purée in a blender or food processor. Return to a saucepan, bring back to a boil. Taste, correct the seasoning, add some more fish stock, if necessary, and perhaps a dash of cream.

Serve the soup in warm bowls. Garnish with crisp croutons and sprinkle with freshly chopped parsley and chives.

Opposite: *Potted Crab with Melba Toast.*

OLD-FASHIONED HOT DRESSED CRAB

This was taught to me by my father-in-law, Ivan Allen, when I first came to cook in the kitchens at Ballymaloe House. Having come from a little village called Cullohill in the midlands of County Laois, I had no idea how to either cook or extract the meat from a crab, so I found the lesson fascinating and the end result delicious. We remember him with great fondness every time we make dressed crab, which was one of his great specialities.

Note: 1lb cooked crab in the shell yields approximately 6oz crab meat, depending on the time of the year. When preparing dressed crab, be sure to save the carapaces to use as serving receptacles · **SERVES 5–6 AS A MAIN COURSE**

15oz cooked crab meat, brown and white mixed (2 or 3 crabs should yield this)
¾ cup soft white bread crumbs (see page 577)
2 teaspoons white wine vinegar
2 tablespoons tomato chutney
2 tablespoons butter
generous pinch of English mustard powder or 1 level teaspoon Dijon mustard
salt and freshly ground pepper
¾ cup Parsley Sauce (see page 315)
1 cup Buttered Crumbs (see page 577)

Preheat the oven to 350°F.

Scrub the crab shells inside and out. Mix all the ingredients except the buttered crumbs together, taste carefully and correct the seasoning.

Spoon into the shells and sprinkle the top with the buttered crumbs. The crab mixture should be a soft texture.

Bake for about 15–20 minutes, until heated through and brown on top. If necessary, flash under the broiler to crisp the crumbs.

Oysters

The native oysters (*Ostrea edulis)* in these islands are in season only when there is an "R" in the month, Gigas (*Crassostrea gigas)* oysters, on the other hand, are available all year round because they are farmed in our waters.

Oysters are fresh when their shells are tightly shut. Even if they are a little open, the oyster is dead and should not be eaten. My son-in-law Rupert taps two oysters shells together. If they sound solid, they are fine, but if they sound hollow, they should be discarded, even if they aren't open.

Opening oysters

I've seen people in desperation attempt to open oysters with vice grips, even a screwdriver, ooch – not a good idea. To open oysters, there is no getting away from the fact that you'll need an oyster knife. I prefer the ones with a strong, narrow blade rather than the short, squat version. I know it'll probably sit at the back of a kitchen drawer for most of the year but when you need it, you really need it.

You'll need to wrap your hand in a carefully folded kitchen towel.

The oysters must be tightly shut, otherwise discard them. Tuck the oyster's deep shell downwards in between the folds of the kitchen towel, with the narrow end outwards. Insert the tip of the knife into the hinge at the pointed end. Push and twist, then lever the shell open. Slide the blade underneath the top shell to detach the oyster. Be careful not to lose the precious briny juices.

Cut underneath the oyster in the bottom shell and flip over to reveal the plump mollusk. The briney flavor of fresh native Irish oysters in season is quite simply unrivalled.

OYSTERS AU NATUREL

Simply arrange 6–12 oysters on a bed of seaweed. Serve with nothing more than a wedge or two of lemon, some brown soda bread, and a glass of Irish stout.

HOT BUTTERED OYSTERS IN THE SHELL OR ON TOAST

The curvaceous deep shell of Gigas oysters tends to topple over maddeningly on the plate, so that the delicious juices escape. In the Ballymaloe House restaurant we solve this problem by piping a little blob of mashed potatoes on the plate to anchor each shell · **SERVES 4**

12–16 Pacific (Gigas) oysters
4 tablespoons butter
lemon juice
2 teaspoons finely chopped parsley

4 lemon wedges
4 slices of hot buttered toast
(optional)

Open the oysters and detach completely from their shells. Discard the top shell but keep the deep shell and reserve the oyster liquid. Put the shells into a low oven to heat through. Meanwhile, melt half the butter in a pan until it foams. Toss the oysters in the butter for about 1 minute, until hot through. Season with a few drops of lemon juice.

Put a hot oyster into each of the warmed shells. Pour the reserved oyster liquid into the pan and boil up, whisking in the remaining butter and the parsley. Spoon the hot juices over the oysters and serve immediately on warm plates with a wedge of lemon.

Alternatively, discard the shells and just serve the hot buttered oysters and juices on the toast. The toast soaks up the juices and is simply delicious.

Scallops

The best way to buy scallops (*pecten maximus*) is in the shell, when they're at their freshest. You can ask your fishmonger to take them out of the shell if you like, but as with anything else, it's good to be able to do it yourself.

How to shell scallops
Simply lay the scallop on a chopping board. Insert the tip of a knife in the little gap close to the hinge. This will break the seal. Then slide your knife along, keeping the blade of the knife flat against the top shell, so that you detach the scallop from the shell. This motion will also allow you to separate the top shell from the bottom shell.

Once you have opened the scallop shell, use a spoon to scoop the scallop with the coral and frill still attached, as well as the black vein of the stomach, out of the deep shell. With your fingers, separate the frill, the black bit and the vein from the scallop so that only the scallop nugget and its coral (orange piece) remain. Discard everything but the nugget and coral. Then trim the little pipe bit from the coral and discard. Wash, dry, and cook as desired.

Save the scallop shells to use as containers for Scallops Mornay (below) or other fish appetizers. They also make good receptacles for sauces, sea salt, and butter balls.

SCALLOPS MORNAY

This is a classic, old-fashioned French recipe for scallops, and is an excellent method of stretching a few little scallops in a delicious way. You can either spoon the mixture back into the scallop shell and pipe a little ruff of potato around the shell, or you can use the filling in vol-au-vents or cut the scallops a little smaller and use the mixture as a sauce with another fish. This mixture also makes a delicious filling for crêpes. It can be cooked ahead and reheated the next day ·
SERVES 12 AS AN APPETIZER,
6 AS A MAIN COURSE

12 plump fresh scallops
dry white wine and water to cover
1 heaping tablespoon parsley, chopped
Duchesse Potatoes (see page 90) for piping around the shells (optional)

FOR THE MORNAY SAUCE
⅓ cup chopped shallots or onion
2 tablespoons butter
6oz mushrooms, chopped
2 heaping tablespoons all-purpose flour
full-cream milk
salt and freshly ground pepper
¾ cup (3oz) shredded Cheddar cheese

Put the scallops in a small stainless-steel saucepan and cover with half white wine and half water. Poach for 3–5 minutes (be careful to simmer and not to overcook). Remove the scallops and reduce the cooking liquid to about 1⅛ –1¼ cups.

To make the mornay sauce: cook the shallots gently in butter for about 5–6 minutes, until soft. Add the mushrooms and cook for another 3–4 minutes. Stir in the flour and cook for 1 minute. Add the milk to the scallop cooking liquid to make 2 cups and add to the saucepan. Taste the sauce. Reduce it over medium-high heat until the flavor is really good. Season to taste.

Cut the scallops crosswise into 4 discs and add to the sauce with some of the cheese and the parsley. Decorate the scallop shells or serving dish with duchesse potatoes, fill the center with the scallop mixture, and sprinkle the top with the remaining grated cheese.

Game

Years ago, game and wildfowl featured much more regularly in many people's diets, particularly those living within easy reach of the countryside. There are a few understandable reasons why many people stopped eating wild meat. Some wild creatures, like rabbits, are connected in people's minds with less affluent times. Then, in 1950, when rabbits introduced to Australia had multiplied so prolifically that whole areas of farmland were devastated, the authorities developed a virus called myxomatosis to eliminate the rabbit population: one of the first instances of germ warfare. Shortly afterward, the disease was deliberately introduced to Europe, where rationing was still in force and governments needed to boost farm production. It was extraordinarily effective and killed off the bulk of European rabbit stocks – and as a result people simply stopped eating rabbit.

As we became more and more removed from the reality of nature and rural life, restaurateurs found, to their surprise, that people complained at finding stray lead pellets in their meat, apparently unaware that wild game is not slaughtered in a slaughterhouse but shot with a gun, and that the pellets lodge in the flesh. A number of restaurants were actually sued by customers, some successfully. As a result, many restaurants stopped serving game, while people's tastes for blander meat meant that they avoided anything that tasted "gamey" or well hung.

Happily, although game fell out of favor during the 70s, 80s, and early 90s, it is now experiencing a revival and has become more popular again as an increasing number of people become disillusioned with modern farming methods and look for truly organic meat. Today, there's even a restaurant in Manhattan that serves only wild game. For organic meat, you must specify wild game that is free of chemicals and antibiotics. This includes wild (but not farmed) venison, wild duck (with the exception of reared mallard), grouse, wild goose, snipe, woodcock, hare, and wild rabbit. Feeding encourages most pheasants and partridges, even wild birds, so their food is more likely to contain chemicals and additives. The same applies where lakes and ponds are specially fed to attract mallard and other wild ducks.

Today, we tend to eat beef, lamb, chicken, and pork *ad nauseam,* so varying our diet by eating wild game is doubly welcome, not just for flavor but also for the health benefits. Wild game ranges freely, so it provides us with a whole other set of precious nutrients – vitamins, minerals, and trace elements – not normally found in domestically reared meats, because no matter how freely the animals are allowed to range, they are usually fed on pasture containing a limited number of species.

I've been surprised to note how young people's attitudes to game have suddenly changed. A few years ago, students would expect to be presented with a prepared and sanitized piece of game – they wouldn't entertain the thought of plucking or gutting. But now, more and more students are interested in accompanying local sportspeople on shoots. They want to learn the forgotten skills of how to pluck and eviscerate, how to skin rabbits, and butcher venison. Somehow, it's become really cool, and it's not just the boys who are interested in learning, which really gives me hope for the future.

Many people are unsure what to do when cooking game for the first time, so they tend to overcook it. Because wild meat is very lean, it dries it out easily, which makes it dull and unappetizing and discourages people from trying again. Provided they haven't been overcooked, all wild birds are wonderfully delicious cold, but are seldom served this way today.

If you want to shoot game you'll need to check the specific dates for hunting seasons in your country or region. The season for some game is fixed, but others vary from season to season, depending on stocks.

How to tell the age of game

You can tell the age of a cock pheasant by the length of the spurs on his legs; the longer the spur, the older the bird. Pheasants from a driven shoot are usually younger, so if you come across a bird with very long spurs, chances are that it'll be a wild pheasant. In that case, it might be tough, so perhaps slow-cook it.

Some people believe they can tell the age of a duck by feeling the tip of the breast bone. If it is flexible, it's a younger bird; if it's hard, it's not.

You can tell a young rabbit by seeing whether the tip of the ear tears easily. Young game animals can be roasted, but older ones should be stewed, casseroled, or slow-roasted.

The young-bird fallacy

Many cooks go to tremendous lengths to seek out (and pay handsomely for) young birds, in the mistaken belief that they will be more tender and juicy. Grouse shoots in particular charge more than twice the price for "this year's birds." To me, this is a mistake: the problem of toughness is generally one of overcooking.

How long should I hang game?

There is often a difference of opinion about how long game should hang, but ultimately it depends on your taste. Game cooked within 12 hours of being shot will be tender, but its flavor will be less distinctive. If it is allowed to hang for a few days in a cool, airy place, enzyme action in the flesh will tenderize the meat, giving that characteristic gamey flavor.

Most people nowadays seem to prefer a more natural flavor; personally, I like my game to taste really, really gamey, otherwise, one may as well eat chicken. I love the whole house to smell of gamey pheasant when I'm roasting it, whereas this is not quite so appealing for some members of my family, who don't necessarily share my taste for pungent game.

Does the weather affect hanging time?

In warm, humid weather, game will mature much faster and needs less time hanging. When it's cold and frosty,

game can hang longer and the hanging time can even double. This is all a matter of preference. There is no hard-and-fast rule and, ultimately, everything depends on how you like your meat. The most important thing is to examine all hanging game each day to ensure it remains in peak condition.

Watch out for signs of deterioration

If you are out shooting on a warm day, do watch where you put the bag. Birds such as grouse, partridges, mallard, and wood pigeons shot in hot weather may have received unwelcome attention from flies even before you return home. This won't be a problem if you are buying from a game dealer, since they will already have weeded out any spoiled birds, but remember to examine anything you have been given carefully before hanging it.

How to examine game

Carefully part the feathers around the lower stomach and vent, and look for any signs of discoloration. If the flesh color is normal you can hang it up for a day or two. If it is discolored this does not necessarily mean it should be thrown away – but you do need to pluck and dress it immediately, and then either eat it within a day or two or freeze it for future use.

How do I hang game?

Birds are usually left to hang in their feathers, undrawn (i.e., complete with their intestines) for between one and seven days to allow the flavors to develop. The time varies according to the type of bird and the weather conditions. Feathered game should be hung by the neck, while furred game and rabbits should be hung by the hind legs. Also it is important to allow plenty of space between birds for the air to circulate. Hang them individually, otherwise they will deteriorate faster where they touch each other.

Venison is often wrongly described as being "overhung" when the real problem may be that you have bought (or been given) part of a large, tough old stag, shot at the height of the rut (mating season). Where

Above: *Sportsmen Tom Duane and Frank Mansell with their Springer spaniels, in pursuit of dinner.*

possible, you should buy whole animals and try to find very young bucks, does, or fawns.

Hanging times

Pheasant	5–7 days, longer if preferred
Grouse	3–7 days
Partridge	3–4 days
Woodcock	2–5 days
Snipe	2–5 days
Mallard and Teal	2–3 days
Wood Pigeon	2–5 days
Wild Goose	up to 2 weeks
Hare	3–7 days
Rabbit	2–3 days
Venison	2–3 weeks

Where to hang game

It is important to remember that our predecessors had specially constructed sheds or hutches for hanging game. They were intended to be cool, airy, completely safe from flies and vermin, and were designed to allow game to hang individually with the air circulating freely around it. We cannot easily reproduce this situation in our homes today and have to arrive at a reasonable compromise.

Game should hang in a cool, dry, well-ventilated, fly- and cat-proof pantry or refrigerated cold room, ideally at a temperature of 32°–41°F. If the weather turns warm and humid, deal with any game immediately, or hang it in a refrigerated cold room.

After hanging, feathered game should be plucked and gutted, while furred game should be skinned and butchered.

Freezing

If you are in the happy position where you have an overabundance of game, it may be necessary to freeze some of it. Freezing does have a slightly adverse effect on the flavor and texture, but it is safe.

Prepare game as for cooking; hanging for the minimum rather than the maximum time to ensure that it is not too strong. Use strong, thick polythylene bags and expel air before closing the bags or, better still, use a vacuum packing machine.

Label clearly with the date of freezing and the date by which it must be eaten. Six months is the maximum freezing time for good flavor. When defrosting, thaw carefully and cook immediately.

Do remember that wild game has little or no natural fat, something that only develops when there is an abundance of food sources. Pheasants from a driven shoot or game farm will have been fed wheat, to keep them in the coverts, and the same applies to game farm birds. This gives them an obvious layer of thick, dark-yellow fat, which is normally absent on wild birds unless feeding is very abundant. Mallard that feed in fallow fields in the fall may also have a layer of fat but, if this is present at other times, the bird is likely to have been specially reared and released for shooting.

Barding and larding

These are techniques to add moisture to lean meats like game that would otherwise dry out in cooking. In barding, the meat is wrapped in fat and cooked. In larding, strips of fat are sewn into the surface of the meat. In both cases, the fat bastes the lean meat as it cooks, giving a juicier, more succulent roast.

How to bard game

Wrap the piece of meat in a thin sheet of pork back fat or caul fat (see page 325). If using caul fat, rinse it, dry it, and enclose the piece of meat in it completely. Then roast the meat as directed.

If you are using a sheet of thin pork back fat, choose a piece large enough to cover the breast and legs – it should be more than ⅛in thick. Wrap around the bird and secure in one or two places with kitchen string.

How to lard game (see page 145 for venison)

You will need:
– Back fat or fatty pork
– A larding needle, available from good cookware stores

Cut the pork back fat into ¼in wide strips. Insert a strip into a barding needle, draw a lardon through the meat to make a stitch; trim the end. Repeat the stitches at 1in intervals to make horizontal rows, positioning each row about ½in away from the previous row; repeat with the remainder of the fat.

Game Birds

Buying birds from a game dealer

Game birds are usually sold unplucked for two reasons.

1. They are easily identifiable.
2. Feathers keep the bird moist during hanging.

Start by asking how long the bird has been hung. Examine the bird yourself to see where it has been shot and avoid any birds that have been peppered (hit in the body with many pellets), since this will result in a lot of waste.

Unless you wish to pluck and draw the game, buy it already dressed, but ask for the heart and gizzard (for stock) and liver (for pâté, or if you want to make a terrine).

Buying direct

If you live in the country and don't mind a bit of plucking, try to buy directly from local hunters. You will get an extraordinarily good price and you'll know exactly when the birds were shot (and that they have never been frozen or "chilled"). If you do this, check carefully for torn or badly shot birds. Some hunting clubs clean and pack birds, so you may have the option to buy plucked and dressed birds that are oven-ready.

Choosing game birds

If you are asked to choose a brace of birds after a hunt remember to take care as you make your selection. Feathers often hide damage caused by a hard-mouthed retriever or that results fro a close-range shot. If you are not given a choice and simply presented with a bird or two, then just hope for the best and examine whatever you are given carefully when you reach home.

What to do if a bird is full of shot?

If the bird is very full of shot, try to remove as many pellets as possible while preparing it. You'll see where the shot entered the body; feel for it with the tips of your fingers. If the leg or the breast is very badly shot, cut it off and discard it.

What do I do with a badly shot bird?

Birds that have been badly shot can be jointed and used in casseroles or stews, rather than roasted. You could grind them for sausages, pâté, or terrines, but do be careful. Shot is made of lead, which is a cumulative poison in the body, and it also destroys your food processor blade. Better to use badly shot birds for casseroles or stock.

Plucking

See the chapter on poultry for more explicit directions on plucking (see page 256), but there are a few game-specific things to say.

Traditionally, game birds were plucked very carefully, right out to the end of the wings, taking great care to leave the skin as intact as possible, but today some people in a rush simply pull off all of the skin, or it tears when they pluck overvigorously. I understand that this saves time, but it is a real shame, because the skin carries the flavors of the different species and adds immeasurably to the taste. Skinned pheasant is little different from skinned partridge (or skinned chicken, for that matter). So it's a trade-off: time against traditions and flavor. We always keep the skin on, except with wood pigeon (see page 128).

Pheasants have really long feathers at the tail and wing, which need to be plucked out one by one to keep from tearing the skin. I sometimes like to save a few of the most beautiful tail feathers to decorate the birds with when they are brought to the table.

Singeing and gutting

See the poultry chapter for instructions on singeing and gutting (see page 257) game birds.

Above: *A beautiful brace of pheasants, hung by the neck.*

Wood Pigeon

In Europe, wood pigeons are probably the most plentiful edible wild bird. Because they do considerable damage to crops, many farmers welcome local sportsmen coming to their farms to shoot pigeons. The wood pigeon is the only game bird that I skin before cooking: the skin really is surprisingly tough, and the legs have so little meat that preparing the whole bird is almost a waste of time when you are only going to use the breast. Wood pigeon has lots of wild gamey flavor but can be tough as old boots, so either cook for a very short time, as in the first recipe, or long and slowly, as in the second.

To skin a wood pigeon

Hold the feathered bird breastside up, with the vent toward you. Use your thumbs to puncture the skin underneath the breastbone, above the vent. Catch the skin at the tip of the breastbone and peel it backward over the breast, toward the neck. Once the skin is removed, pull the breastbone with the two breasts attached upward and bend backward toward the neck. It will break naturally at the joint close to the neck. Use a sharp knife to detach it and discard the remainder of the carcass. You now have what is called a crown, i.e., the two breasts attached to the breastbone.

How to marinate pigeon breasts ready for cooking

Skin the pigeon as described above. You can either leave the breasts attached to the breast bone or cut

Above: *Pigeon Breasts with Field Mushrooms and Tarragon.*

them off before marinating.

Pack the breasts tightly into a plastic container, cover with red wine, and add a generous helping of extra virgin olive oil. Tuck in a slice or two of onion, a sprig of thyme, and a bay leaf. Cover and leave in the refrigerator for a couple of days before using – they will keep perfectly in the refrigerator for up to a week. When you want to cook the pigeon breasts, take out the number required and slice the meat thinly. They can also be frozen in this way.

PIGEON BREASTS WITH FIELD MUSHROOMS AND TARRAGON

The great thing about this recipe is that it is so fast. If you have a box of pigeon breasts marinating in your fridge you can have this delicious little dish on the table in minutes · SERVES 4

8 marinated pigeon breasts, sliced
   (see above)
2 tablespoons butter
8oz field or flat mushrooms, sliced
salt and freshly ground pepper
8oz bacon
extra virgin olive oil
8 juniper berries, crushed
4 tablespoons brandy
½ cup Game or Chicken Stock (see
   pages 149 and 262)
¼ cup sour cream
1 tablespoon fresh French
   tarragon, chopped

Melt the butter on a hot pan. Add the mushrooms, season with salt and pepper, and toss over high heat for 3–4 minutes, or until beginning to brown at the edges. Keep aside.

Sauté a few strips of bacon in a little olive oil in a hot pan. Remove when crisp and transfer to a plate. Add a little butter, if necessary, and quickly toss the pigeon breast slices. Add a good few crushed juniper berries and flame with a generous dose of brandy. Add back in the bacon, pour in some game or chicken stock, and simmer for just a couple of minutes. Add the sautéed mushrooms, a dollop of sour cream, and the tarragon.

Once the mushrooms are cooked, none of the subsequent stages should take more than a couple of minutes; the pigeon meat should still be pink. If it overcooks, it will be incredibly tough.

Serve on very hot plates with chargrilled bread or croutons to soak up the delicious juices. Pasta or mashed potatoes sprinkled with chervil or parsley would also be a good accompaniment.

WOOD PIGEON PIE

This was a favorite dish for winter house parties at Ballymaloe. It is a bit time-consuming because first you need to make a stew and allow it to cool, but the end result is really worth it · SERVES 10–12

4–6 fresh pigeon breasts
the pigeons' weight in lean beef
half the pigeons' weight in bacon,
   rind removed
bacon fat or olive oil for frying
8 baby carrots or carrot sticks
10–12 button onions
1 garlic clove, crushed
1–2 teaspoons flour
1 cup red wine
1 cup Game or Chicken Stock (see
   pages 149 and 262)
⅔ cup homemade Tomato Paste
   (see page 376) or smaller
   quantity of canned tomato
   paste: use according to
   concentration and make up
   with extra stock
Roux (see page 165), if necessary
salt and freshly ground pepper
2 teaspoons chopped thyme and
   parsley
1 cup Wild Mushrooms à la Crème
   (see page 50)

8oz Puff Pastry or Billy's Cream
   Pastry (see pages 218 and 209)

Cut the pigeon, beef, and bacon into pieces about 1in wide. Preheat the oven to 300°F.

Heat some bacon fat or olive oil in a frying pan and fry the bacon until crisp and golden. Remove using a slotted spoon to a 2½ quart casserole dish, add the pigeon and beef a little at a time to the pan, and toss until it changes color. Add to the bacon in the casserole dish then turn the carrots, onions, and crushed garlic in the fat and add them to the meat. Stir the flour into the fat in the pan, cook for a minute or so, and then stir or whisk in the wine, stock and tomato paste. Bring to a boil, thicken with roux, if necessary. Pour over the meat and vegetables in the casserole dish. Season with salt and pepper, add the thyme and parsley, return to a boil, cover, and cook in the oven for 1–2 hours, depending on the age of the pigeons. When it is cooked, stir in the wild mushrooms à la crème. Check the seasoning.

(The pigeon stew can be eaten at this point, although it is also great if cooled overnight and reheated the next day. Serve with fluffy mashed potatoes and buttered cabbage.)

As soon as the pigeon stew is cold, or the following day, fill into 1 or 2 pie dishes, cover with puff or flaky pastry and bake for 10 minutes at 450°F, then at 375°F for another 20 minutes, or until the pastry is nicely risen and golden brown on top.

Serve with a green salad.

Pheasant

These days, it's especially important to hang pheasant well, particularly birds from a preserve hunt that may not have done as much foraging as truly wild pheasants. Otherwise, these birds can taste rather bland. The hen pheasants, although smaller, have a slightly more subtle, delicate flavor than the cock birds, as well as more meat and plumper breasts.

Traditionally, really well-dressed pheasants should also have the sinews carefully drawn – but only after they have been hung and plucked. This is seldom, if ever, done today. If your birds are ungutted, remove the crop from the neck end; wash, and dry well. Save the giblets (and the cooked carcass) for stock and the liver for pâté.

When roasting pheasant, remember to allow at least 15 minutes of resting time so that the juices can redistribute themselves evenly. This can be the time during the time in which you make the gravy.

TRADITIONAL ROAST PHEASANT WITH ALL THE TRIMMINGS

A roast pheasant makes the perfect dinner for two and you'll probably have a little left over for a tasty cold supper. This slightly unorthodox way of cooking the pheasant produces a moist, juicy bird. Guinea hen is also wonderful cooked and served in this way. The skill here is to make sure the pheasant is not overcooked ·

SERVES 2-3

1 young, plump pheasant
4 tablespoons butter

FRESH HERB STUFFING
4 tablespoons butter
⅔ cup chopped onions
½ cup soft white bread crumbs (see page 577)
1 tablespoon freshly chopped herbs, e.g., parsley, thyme, chives, marjoram
salt and freshly ground pepper

GRAVY
1 cup Game or Chicken Stock (see pages 149 and 262)

Game Chips (see page 387)
Spicy Cranberry Sauce (see page 271)
Bread Sauce (see page 271)

a square of muslin large enough to enclose the bird

Pluck and eviscerate (gut) the pheasant, if necessary (see introduction). Wash it inside and out and pat dry.

To make the stuffing, melt the butter in a heavy saucepan, add the onions, cover, and sweat until soft but not colored, then remove from the heat. Stir in the soft white bread crumbs and herbs, season with salt and pepper, and taste. Unless you are going to cook the bird right away, allow the stuffing to get cold before putting it into the bird.

Season the cavity with some salt and pepper and stuff the pheasant loosely. Sprinkle the breast also with salt and pepper.

Preheat the oven to 375°F. Melt the butter and soak the muslin in it.

Wrap the pheasant completely in the buttery muslin. (Don't worry, it won't melt or ignite in the oven. You can even wash out the muslin and use it later!)

Roast the wrapped bird in the oven for about 30–35 minutes. Test by pricking the base of the thigh at the thickest point; the juices should just run clear. Remove the muslin from the pheasant and keep the meat warm on a serving dish while you make the gravy.

Spoon off any surplus fat from the roasting pan (keep it for roasting or sautéing potatoes). Put the roasting pan on top of the stove. Deglaze the pan with game or chicken stock. Bring it to a boil, and use a whisk to dislodge the crusty caramelized juices so they can dissolve into the gravy. Season with salt and pepper, taste, and boil until you are happy with the flavor. Pour into a hot gravy boat.

Carve the pheasant and serve with the stuffing, gravy, game chips, cranberry sauce, and bread sauce – a truly wonderful feast.

SAUTÉED PHEASANT BREASTS WITH SAVOY CABBAGE

Savoy cabbage and pheasant share a season and complement each other very well. Use the pheasant legs for stock or game pie · **SERVES 4**

4 tablespoons bacon fat or clarified butter
4 pheasant breasts
1 teaspoon slightly crushed juniper berries
sprigs of thyme

½ **Savoy cabbage**
salt, freshly ground pepper, and
**   paprika**
1 cup light cream
thyme leaves and sprigs of parsley,
**   for garnish**

Heat the bacon fat or clarified butter over medium heat in a sauté pan large enough to accommodate the four breasts in a single layer. Brown the pheasant on all sides. Add the crushed juniper berries and a sprig of thyme. Cover the pan, lower the heat, and leave to stew for 10–15 minutes on both sides. Remove the pheasant to a plate.

Slice the cabbage thinly and add to the pan. Season with salt, pepper, and paprika then add the cream. Lay the pheasant breasts on top, cover again, and cook for another 8–10 minutes, or until fully cooked. Taste, and correct the seasoning. Serve strewn with lots of thyme leaves and sprigs of parsley.

Variation

If you like, you could add juniper berries to the pheasant at the start of the cooking. Then add finely sliced raw cabbage after 20 minutes, toss well, and add the cream – this way the cabbage will have a slight bite.

PHEASANT WITH CHORIZO, BACON, AND TOMATOES

The pheasant that is farm-reared from a preserve rarely has quite as much flavor as a truly wild bird. This Spanish-style recipe is good because the chorizo contributes lots of extra oomph

· **SERVES 6**

2 pheasants, each cut into 4
**   serving portions (see method)**
1 tablespoon extra virgin olive oil
6oz good-quality bacon cut into
**   ½in cubes**
2 garlic cloves
2 large onions, sliced
1lb ripe tomatoes, peeled (see
**   page 375) and chopped (or 1 x**
**   14oz can chopped tomatoes)**
salt and freshly ground pepper
2 teaspoons good-quality paprika –
**   preferably sweet Hungarian**
8oz chorizo sausage, sliced
thyme leaves and lots of parsley
**   sprigs**

Rice Pilaf, to serve (see below)

I cut the legs into two, the wings into two (assuming they are intact and not shot off as sometimes happens), and take the breasts off the bone and cut them into two or three – along the seams rather than across the grain. The carcass can then be used to make a game stock. If this is done in advance, the stock is used for cooking the rice pilaf.

Heat the olive oil in a pan over medium heat. Add the bacon and fry until the fat runs and the bacon begins to crisp around the outside. Transfer to a casserole dish. Add the pheasant pieces to the frying pan and brown lightly a few at a time. Remove, and add to the casserole.

Add the garlic and onion to the frying pan, toss, cover, and cook gently for 4–5 minutes. Remove the lid, add the chopped tomatoes and the salt, pepper, and paprika (if you're using canned tomatoes, you might need a little sugar to help the flavor). Increase the heat. Add the

chorizo. Cook briskly until the sauce thickens slightly.

Return the bacon and the pheasant pieces to the tomato sauce. Add the wings and thigh pieces first, and the breast sections a little later, because they will require less cooking. The casserole will need about 25 minutes in total. Check the seasoning. If the sauce has become too thick, stir in a little stock or water. Garnish with the thyme and flat parsley.

Serve the pheasant, surrounded by pieces of chorizo and bacon, on a bed of rice pilaf – accompanied by a good green salad.

RICE PILAF

2 tablespoons butter
2 tablespoons finely chopped
**   onion or shallot**
2 cups Basmati rice
salt and freshly ground pepper
4 cups Game Stock (see page 149)
2 tablespoons freshly chopped
**   herbs, e.g., parsley or thyme**

Melt the butter in a casserole dish, add the onion, and cook gently for 2–3 minutes. Add the rice and toss for 1–2 minutes, just long enough for the grains to change color. Season, add the chicken stock, cover, and bring to a boil. Reduce the heat to a minimum, then simmer on top of the stove or in the oven at 300°F for about 15 minutes. By then, the rice
should be just cooked and all the water absorbed. Just before serving, stir in the herbs.

PHEASANT, BACON, AND WILD MUSHROOM CASSEROLE WITH SCALLION CHAMP

This is a great recipe for pheasant. If you have a bit of partridge or grouse, you could use that instead of, or in addition to, the pheasant · SERVES 4–6

12oz unsmoked bacon, rind removed
1 plump pheasant
flour, seasoned with salt and pepper
1lb onions (baby ones are nicest)
12oz carrots, peeled and thickly sliced
sprig of thyme
¾ cups Pheasant or Chicken Stock (see page 262)
a little butter and oil for sautéing
Roux (see page 165), optional
Wild Mushrooms à la Crème (see page 50)
parsley, for garnish

Champ, to serve (see page 383)

Preheat the oven to 350°F. Cut the bacon into ¾in cubes. Blanch, if salty, in cold water, drain, and dry on paper towels.

Pluck and gut the pheasant if necessary, then wash and pat dry. Joint into 4–6 pieces and roll in well-seasoned flour. Shake off the excess. Heat a little oil in a large sauté pan and sauté the bacon until crisp, remove, and put in a casserole dish. Add the pheasant pieces to the pan and sauté until golden before transferring to the casserole dish. Controlling the heat is crucial here; the pan mustn't burn, yet it needs to be hot enough to sauté the pheasant. If it is too cool, the pheasant pieces will stew rather than sauté and, as a result, the meat may become tough. Toss the onion and carrot in the pan, adding a little butter, if necessary. Add to the casserole. Degrease the sauté pan and deglaze with stock, bring to a boil and pour over the meat and vegetables.

Season well, add a sprig of thyme, and bring to simmering point on the top of the stove, then transfer to the preheated oven, and cook for 30–45 minutes. The cooking time will depend on how long the pheasant pieces were sautéed.

While the casserole is cooking, make the wild mushrooms à la crème. If you don't have any wild mushrooms available, use flat or, better still, field mushrooms, which have much more flavor than the white button mushrooms.

When the casserole is just cooked, strain off the cooking liquid into another saucepan. Degrease and bring to a boil. Thicken with a little roux, if necessary. Add the meat, carrots, and onions back into the casserole. Stir in the wild mushrooms à la crème, bring back to a boil. Serve bubbling hot with Champ, sprinkled with parsley.

PHEASANT BRAISED WITH CORK GIN

Casserole roasting is a technique worth noting. The bird cooks in the steamy atmosphere of the tightly covered casserole dish, either on top of the stove or in the oven. This method produces lots of cooking juices, which make a delicious little sauce · SERVES 4

1 plump pheasant
salt and freshly ground pepper
2 teaspoons extra virgin olive oil
2oz bacon, diced
3 tablespoons gin (we use Cork gin) or brandy
2 juniper berries, crushed
½ cup white wine
sprigs of parsley

oval casserole dish about 10 x 3in with a volume of just over 2 quarts

Pluck and eviscerate (gut) the pheasant, if necessary (see the introduction on page 127). Wash inside and out and pat dry.

Season the pheasant with salt and freshly ground pepper. Heat the oil in an oval casserole dish just large enough to accommodate the pheasant. Toss in the diced bacon and cook for a few minutes, until it begins to crisp; remove the bacon and keep to one side.

Add the pheasant to the pan, breast side down, and allow it to brown. Turn the other way up, return the bacon to the casserole dish, pour in the gin or brandy, and flame or boil for a few minutes.

Add the crushed juniper berries. Cover the casserole dish and simmer gently for about 40 minutes on the stove or transfer to the oven and cook at 350°F for the same time. Place the pheasant in a serving dish and keep warm. Degrease the cooking juices, and add the white wine. Allow the sauce to boil up and reduce until slightly thickened.

Joint the pheasant and arrange on a hot serving plate, spoon the sauce over, and garnish with parsley sprigs.

PHEASANT BREAST WITH PAPRIKA AND PARMESAN

Although this recipe calls for pheasant breast, it is also a good recipe to use up leftover pheasant if you find yourself in that happy position · SERVES 6

2 tablespoons butter
6 pheasant breasts
salt and freshly ground black
    pepper
1 onion, sliced
8oz flat or, better still, field
    mushrooms
⅔ cup light cream
1 heaping teaspoon chopped
    rosemary
1 teaspoon paprika
6 slices best-quality cooked ham
    or bacon
finely grated Parmesan

Preheat the oven to 400°F.

Melt the butter in a pan. Season the pheasant breasts on both sides with salt and pepper. When the butter foams, add the pheasant and sauté until brown on all sides – the breasts should be almost cooked. Transfer to a plate. Add the onion to

the pan and cook for a few minutes, stirring regularly until soft and slightly colored; increase the heat, add the mushrooms, season with salt and pepper, and cook until the mushrooms are well wilted. Add the cream, rosemary, and paprika; allow to bubble for 3–4 minutes.

Wrap each pheasant breast in a thin slice of best-quality ham. Put a layer of the mushroom mixture on the base of an oven-proof serving dish. Arrange the pheasant and ham on top, and cover with the remaining mushroom mixture. Sprinkle with grated Parmesan and put into the oven for about 15 minutes, or until hot and bubbling. Serve with a good green salad.

RED CABBAGE

Some varieties of red cabbage are very tough and don't seem to soften much, even with prolonged cooking. We find that Red Drummond gives the best results · SERVES 6–8

1lb red cabbage
1lb cooking apples
1 tablespoon wine vinegar
1 level teaspoon salt
2 heaping tablespoons sugar
2 teaspoons roughly ground
    caraway seeds

Remove any damaged outer leaves from the cabbage. Cut in quarters, remove the core, and slice the cabbage finely across the grain. Put the vinegar, caraway, salt, and sugar into a cast-iron casserole dish or stainless steel saucepan with ½ cup water. Add the cabbage and bring to a boil.

Peel and core the apples and cut into quarters (no smaller). Lay them on top of the cabbage, cover, and continue to cook gently until the cabbage is tender: about 30–50 minutes. Do not overcook or the color and flavor will be ruined. Taste for seasoning and add more sugar, if necessary. Serve in a warm serving dish.

CELERIAC AND MASHED PARSNIP

The flavor of celeriac marries deliciously with many different types of game. Here I mix it with parsnips, but it also works really well with mashed potatoes or a purée of Cox's Orange Pippin apples. The latter are particularly good with wild duck or goose · SERVES 6

1lb celeriac, cut into ½in cubes
12oz parsnips, cut into ½in cubes
4 tablespoons butter
salt, freshly ground black pepper,
    and sugar
chopped parsley, for garnish

Cook the celeriac and parsnips separately in boiling salted water until soft. Strain both, mash together and add butter, salt, and freshly ground pepper.

Partridge

The Gray (English) partridges are considered to be far superior to the Red legs (French partridges), but, sadly, they are rarely encountered these days. Farmed birds are best for recipes with lots of herbs and spices, whereas wild birds are best for simple roasts. Straw potatoes (very thinly cut fries) and a bunch of watercress are all that's needed as an accompaniment. Wild roast partridge will take 15–20 minutes to cook in the oven. Cold partridge makes a superb country breakfast – the ultimate old-fashioned luxury.

Above: *Benny the labrador rewards his handler with a fine retrieve.*

ROAST PARTRIDGE

I like partridge best plain, roasted with a little gravy made from the roasting juices. Rub the breast generously with butter. Season the breast and cavity with salt and freshly ground pepper and roast in a preheated oven at 400°F for 15–20 minutes, depending on size. As ever, be very vigilant – if overcooked, it will be hopelessly dull and dry.

A little bacon wrapped over the breast bastes and flavors the bird at the same time.

PARTRIDGE WRAPPED IN VINE LEAVES WITH ELDERBERRIES

Wrapping the partridge in vine leaves imparts a delicious flavor and keeps the breasts moist. If you don't have any leaves, do bard the breasts with the bacon or caul to stop the meat from drying out. Partridge love elderberries, and the two flavors complement each other perfectly, so if you have some fresh or frozen berries, add them to the sauce at the end · **SERVES 4**

4 young partridges
salt and freshly ground black
   pepper
4 tablespoons butter
8 fresh vine leaves, if available
4 strips of bacon or caul fat
1 medium onion, chopped
½ cup dry white wine
½ cup cream
½ cup fresh or frozen elderberries
   (see page 43)

Preheat the oven to 350°F.

Pluck, singe, and eviscerate (gut) the partridges if they are not already prepared. Wash and pat dry. Season the cavities with salt and pepper. Smear the breasts with a little of the butter. Cover with one or two fresh vine leaves, if available. Wrap each bird in bacon or caul fat, and secure with kitchen string, if necessary.

Over low heat, melt the remaining butter in a casserole dish large enough to fit the birds. Add the birds, breastside down, and allow to brown gently. Remove the partridges to a plate, add the chopped onion, and toss for a minute or two to soften but not brown, then add the dry white wine and boil for 2 minutes. Return the birds and any juices to the pan, breast side up. Cover the casserole dish and transfer it to the preheated oven to cook for about 30 minutes.

When just cooked, remove the birds. Degrease the juices, if necessary, then pour in the cream and add the elderberries. Allow the sauce to bubble for a couple of minutes. Taste, and correct the seasoning.

Serve one bird per person with the elderberry sauce. An endive and watercress salad is particularly delicious with this dish.

PARTRIDGE WITH BRAISED ENDIVE

This was inspired by a recipe in Roger Vergé's Cuisine of the Sun *– one of the great classics of the nouvelle cuisine era. Just barely caramelize the endive otherwise you'll lose the delicacy, which is the charm of this delicious sauce ·*
SERVES 2

2 **partridges**
2 **heads of endive**
⅓ **cup Game or Chicken Stock (see pages 149 and 262)**
1 **tablespoon butter**
⅔ **cup cream**
salt and freshly ground pepper

Preheat the oven to 450°F.

Pluck, singe, and eviscerate (gut) the partridges if they are not already prepared. Wash and pat dry. Season the cavities with salt and pepper. Smear the breast of the partridges with butter and cook for about 10 minutes, until very rare. Carve into serving portions, cover with aluminum foil, and keep warm while you prepare the endive.

If you have not had time to prepare stock in advance, put the partridge carcasses into a saucepan with a sliced onion and a sliced carrot, cover with cold water, bring to a boil, and simmer for 30 minutes.

Slice the heads of endive in two lengthwise, arrange cutside down in the roasting pan on top of the stove. Cover with the stock and boil rapidly until all the liquid has almost disappeared. Add a generous dab of butter and fry quickly, then add the cream and any juices from the partridge. Reduce until the sauce thickens to a light coating consistency. Taste, and correct the seasoning.

Add the partridge portions to the sauce, and allow to heat through and bubble for a minute or two.

Serve the cooked partridge on top of a bed of endive, surrounded by the sauce. Fresh noodles or tiny roast potatoes are good with this dish.

Woodcock and Snipe

Woodcock and snipe are highly regarded, not only for their delicious flesh, but also for their innards. They defecate continually while in the air so they are very "clean" birds. For this reason they are traditionally roasted with their innards intact, with the exception of the gizzard, which can be removed before the birds are roasted. Few people, however, bother to remove the gizzard first; they simply do not eat it.

Woodcock and snipe are similar in appearance because they both have long, thin beaks. Woodcock, which are two or three times larger than snipe, can be served for a main course, while snipe makes a perfect little appetizer. Snipe is stronger in flavor, whereas woodcock is delicate. Traditionally, these birds are skewered with their own beak and roasted on a piece of toast on which the trail (the innards or entrails) are allowed to ooze. This produces a particularly delicious flavor, with more than a hint of anchovy.

Sportsmen love to tell you that they bagged a few snipe to prove what a good shot they are – that's because snipe zigzag in flight and are difficult to shoot. Traditionally, when a woodcock was shot, the legs were immediately broken at the joint and literally pulled from the bird to "draw the sinews" before they could harden. This made the leg and thigh far easier to eat, and much more delicate.

ROAST WOODCOCK OR SNIPE

Roasting these birds simply is one of the most delicious ways to eat them. If you're really hardcore, eat the delicious brains of the roast woodcock or snipe. Cut the heads off after roasting and then split the heads vertically down the middle, starting at the back of the head; your knife will follow the groove in the beak until the head splits into two. The edible brains, considered a real delicacy by game lovers, can then be scooped out ·
SERVES 4

2 **woodcock or 4 snipe, gizzards removed**
1 **tablespoon melted butter (more if you need it) plus extra butter for the toast**
salt and freshly ground pepper
4 **slices of bacon**
2–4 **slices of white bread large enough to fit each bird**
1 **tablespoon of brandy (optional)**
watercress, for garnish

Preheat the oven to 450°F.

First, pluck not only the body, but also the neck, right up to the head. Pull the skin off the head. Remove the gizzard from the birds by making a small insertion in the thin skin of the bird's abdomen slightly to the right of the center. Locate the gizzard using a skewer or trussing needle: it will feel like a hard lump. Remove and detach from the innards, which should remain in the bird. Trim the toes.

Cross one of the bird's thighs over the other and twist the feet together, then tuck them under toward the cavity (between the crossed thighs). Then bend the neck toward the legs and skewer the legs and body of the bird with its beak. This is the traditional way of preparing both woodcock and snipe, but squeamish people can just chop off the head; the tucked-in legs hold together very well on their own, giving the bird a neat shape.

Brush the birds with melted butter, season with salt and freshly ground pepper, and wrap in bacon. Secure with kitchen string.

Toast the bread and butter one side. Put the toast, buttered side down, on a baking sheet, and place the prepared snipe or woodcock on top.

Roast in the oven for 15–22 minutes for woodcock, depending on size, and about 7–10 minutes for snipe. They are usually cooked when the bacon is crispy! The flesh should be pinkish and moist.

Serve the woodcock or snipe on the croutons (remove the string first). Garnish with sprigs of watercress or fresh herbs and serve.

NOTE: a tablespoon of brandy may be added to the juices in the roasting pan with the mashed innards, seasoned with salt and freshly ground pepper. Warm through but don't boil. Arrange the croutons on a hot serving dish, spoon the sauce over, and sit the birds on top.

Grouse

For me, grouse is the finest game bird of them all. The meat is rich, dark, and bursting with gamey flavor. Though grouse are plentiful in some places, they are rare and scarce in Ireland, so we relish every morsel. Young birds can be distinguished by their pointed wings and rounded spurs, but even the old ones make a wonderful casserole or terrine. Grouse has very little fat so will be dry as a board if it is overcooked. I love to serve a compote of quince with a simple roast grouse or add a dice of softened quince to the juices in the roasting pan about 10 minutes before the end of cooking.

ROAST GROUSE

We seldom get enough grouse to experiment with so – as ever – I love a simply roasted grouse.

Prepare for roasting as for pheasant. Roast in an oven preheated to 425°F for 20–30 minutes, depending on size. Make a little gravy from the pan juices – I like to sauté the chopped liver in a little butter and then mash it into the pan juices.

Above: *A beautifully engraved side-by-side shotgun – the most commonly used type of gun for shooting game.*

Taste and season. Serve slathered on toast or croutons. My friend George Gossip, who knows more about game cooking than almost anybody else I know, tells me the traditional sportsman's breakfast is a cold roast grouse and a glass of good dry (but not fino) sherry: "In my experience one glass is never enough."

Above: *A two-and-a-half brace of wild Mallard; two females and three males.*

Duck

We have access to many species of wild duck: Mallard, Wigeon, Teal, Shoveler, Pintail, Pochard, Tufted Duck, and Merganser. Other species are occasional visitors, which most of us are unlikely to encounter. They are in season in the fall and through the winter, but in practice only Mallard are present in any numbers early in the season, since the other ducks are all migratory (as indeed are some Mallard), which means that they do not fly southward to us until they encounter hard weather farther north.

Wild duck can be eaten within a day of being shot, and should only be hung for two or three days. One Mallard will feed two people as a main course. It usually takes up to 30 minutes to cook in a hot oven. If wild duck have been been feeding on salt marshes during cold winter weather they can sometimes pick up a fishy taste. A potato in the cavity can help to absorb this fishy taint.

Wigeon are about two-thirds the size of a Mallard and take up to 20 minutes to cook. They can be delicious – particularly earlier in the year – but should be avoided in continuous frosty weather, since they can develop a really fishy flavor. You can serve one per person but when carved carefully, three Wigeon will feed five people or six in a pinch.

Teal are about half the size of a Mallard. They take between 12 and 16 minutes in a hot oven and are always delicious. You will need one per person.

Pintail are known as sea-pheasant and are traditionally served with red currant jelly. They are a little larger than Wigeon but are longer and more streamlined in appearance. Again, serve one per person.

Shoveler, so called because they have huge spatulate bills, are a shorter and squatter species of duck and are not much bigger than a Teal, so, once again, serve one per person. Shoveler and Pintail are less frequent visitors to our shores in recent years, largely due to milder winters. Both are very beautiful birds and for this reason many sportsmen no longer shoot them.

Merganser, because they eat fish and taste as if they do, should, in my opinion always be avoided, unless you're terribly hungry.

Wild duck is usually roasted and accompanied by apple sauce or sauce bigarade (a bitter orange sauce). It can also be roasted covered with bacon, but if you are using orange, don't use bacon, and vice versa.

Usual accompaniments are roast potatoes, roast parsnips, or other root vegetables, red cabbage, green cabbage, or – better still – kale, Jerusalem artichokes, or indeed any winter vegetables. Duck is particularly good when followed by an orange and watercress salad, with orange juice used sparingly instead of vinegar. Endive salad would also be good.

Cold wild duck is also excellent with both of these salads – always providing it has not been over-cooked in the first place.

ROAST WILD MALLARD

The skill in roasting game is always to be vigilant and not let it overcook because when it's "a point" it's tender and juicy and succulent, but cook it for too long and it becomes tough and uninteresting. Be sure to save the carcass to add to a game stock ·
SERVES 2

1 **Mallard**
salt and freshly ground pepper
3–4 **juniper berries, crushed**
1 **sprig of thyme**
1 **sprig of marjoram**
4–5 **slices thin rindless bacon**
1 **tablespoon butter**

⅔ cup Game or Chicken stock (see pages 149 and 262)
a splash of red or white wine or the juice of 1 orange

Make sure the crop has been removed. Pluck, singe, and eviscerate (gut) the Mallard if it is not already prepared. Wash and pat dry. Season the cavity with salt and freshly ground pepper, and drop in a few crushed juniper berries. Bard the bird with the bacon and truss with kitchen string, or smear the breast with butter.

Preheat the oven to 450°F. Place the duck in a roasting pan and roast for about 20 minutes if you like your meat fairly rare, or 30 minutes if you prefer it more well done. Be careful not to overcook or it will be dry. Duck that has been barded with bacon will take longer to cook by up to 10 minutes.

Just as soon as the duck is cooked, transfer it to a warm serving dish. Degrease the roasting pan and add some stock and a splash of red or white wine or the juice of an orange. Boil well, taste, correct seasoning, and strain. Carve the duck and serve the hot gravy with it.

ROAST WIGEON, PINTAIL, OR SHOVELER
Follow the preparation and oven temperature as above and roast for 13–20 minutes.

ROAST TEAL
Follow the preparation and oven temperature as above and roast for 12–15 minutes.

ROAST WILD MALLARD STUFFED WITH JERUSALEM ARTICHOKES

Jerusalem artichokes are a must-have winter vegetable. They grow underground like knobbled potatoes. I love them in soups, gratins, and stews or simply roasted, but they are also particularly delicious as a stuffing for pheasant and duck. By coincidence, Jerusalem artichokes are one of their favorite foods · SERVES 4

2 Mallard
1lb Jerusalem artichokes
4 tablespoons butter
salt and freshly ground black pepper
watercress, for garnish

GRAVY
1 cup Duck, Game, or Chicken Stock (see pages 262 and 149)
Roux (see page 165)

Pluck, singe, and eviscerate (gut) the Mallard. Wash and pat dry.

Peel the artichokes using a swivel-top peeler. Immediately drop each one into a bowl of acidulated water (water with a generous squeeze of lemon juice or a teaspoon of vinegar) to stop them from discoloring as you peel.

Melt the butter in a heavy casserole. Drain the artichokes, cut into ½in slices, toss in the melted butter, and season with salt and freshly ground pepper. Cover with a piece of parchment paper and put the lid on the saucepan. Cook over gentle heat for 10–12 minutes. Turn off the heat and allow the artichokes

to sit in the pan for a few minutes – they cook unevenly.

Preheat the oven to 450°F. Season the cavity of each bird with salt and freshly ground pepper. Divide the artichokes between the two Mallard. Sprinkle a little salt on the breasts, and roast for 20 minutes if you like rare meat, or 30 minutes for more well done.

Allow to rest for 10–15 minutes while you make a little gravy. Deglaze the roasting pan, add the stock, and bring to a boil, whisk in a little roux, just enough to slightly thicken. Taste, season, and taste again. Divide the artichokes between the servings. Garnish with a few sprigs of fresh watercress.

ROAST WILD MALLARD WITH POTATO AND PARSNIP STUFFING

Mix one-third mashed potatoes with two-thirds mashed parsnip, add a little chopped parsley, and lots of pepper. Use to stuff the Mallard as above; the stuffing will be deliciously flavored with the juices from the duck as it roasts.

Rabbit and Hare

Our neighbor Peter Lawton told us how he hunted rabbits as a boy: "Go at night, usually September, October, November – windy nights are better because they don't hear you coming – take a flashlight. Go into a field and shine the light around the field. Immediately, you'll see the eyes shining. The rabbits become dazzled by the light and sometimes they hop toward you. One experienced person keeps dazzling and the partner walks quietly over to pick them up. Hold the rabbit by the back legs – they stay still. Then hit a quick chop with a heavy stick to the back of the neck to kill them. (This breaks the neck.)

Above: *A bunny destined for the pot.*

Hang by the back legs in a cool, airy shed – leave for 3 or 4 days before skinning."

Peter and his friends made pocket money by selling some, or he would bring them home to his mam. If you live in the countryside you may even get them free – squeamish children usually think it's delicious chicken – usually best not to get into too much discussion! Three-quarter grown rabbits are the finest ones for eating and are usually at their best in summer and fall.

I remember Mummy showing me how to judge the age of a rabbit – if the ear tears easily it is young. As a child I took all this for granted: I wasn't the least bit upset, but these days most children would squirm at the thought of tearing the ear of a little bunny. Mummy roasted young rabbits wrapped in bacon and used the older ones for rabbit stew. Wild rabbits have a distinctive gamey flavor that I adore. Until recently, every time I saw rabbit on a restaurant menu I'd want to order it to try and recapture that forgotten flavor. However, I've all but given up, because the modern rabbit is usually farmed and about as interesting as an intensively reared chicken. The flesh of rabbit is pale in color and more delicate in flavor than that of hare, which is rich and dark. Hares are protected in Ireland and can only be shot at specific times of the year – they are best in midwinter. It's not as easy to tell a young hare (leveret) as a rabbit; the best guide is the teeth – white and pointed in a young hare, brown and cracked in an older one. The pelt may also look a bit scruffy. Old

hares are best for pâtés and terrines. Be sure to collect the blood carefully when the hare is paunched – it contains a lot of the flavor.

How to skin a rabbit or hare
Tie a string around one of the hind legs of the rabbit and hang it from a hook or nail or a cupboard handle. Using a small, sharp knife, take one of the hind legs and cut all the way around the "ankle" (below the string) so that the skin can be separated from the flesh.

Now slit the skin down the inside of the leg until you hit the base of the tail. Do the same with the other leg. Pull the skin away from one leg and then the other; if your incisions were precise, the skin should come easily away from the flesh.

When both legs are skinned, slit between them at the base of the tail. Slit down the belly, taking care not to pierce the abdomen. Continue down the length of the chest as far as the neck. Using both hands, continue peeling the skin away from the flesh until you get to the shoulders. The skin is only loosely attached and it should peel off as easily as a glove.

Cut around the forelegs just as you did with the hind legs. Slit the skin along the inside of the forelegs, and then pull it away until it remains attached only at the head. Then chop off the head, and discard the head and skin (or you can use the skinned head in a stock or stew).

Your rabbit should be fully skinned now. With poultry shears or a chopping knife, cut off all four paws and discard (or keep the left hind foot for a lucky charm!)

How to gut a rabbit or hare

Lay the rabbit belly-up on a cutting board. Pinch the belly skin and lift it away from the body so that you don't run the risk of piercing the intestines, and with a sharp, small knife, make a shallow cut down the length of the belly.

Reach inside and draw out the innards, cutting any membranes holding them in place, but leaving the liver and kidneys intact. Discard the innards.

Reach into the animal and feel for the liver, just inside the rib cage close to the neck. Remove it carefully with your fingers. Attached to the liver is the gall bladder. Holding the liver, cut off the gall bladder, making sure not to puncture it. Discard the gall bladder. Leave the kidneys inside the animal.

If you want to save the blood to enrich a sauce (for jugged hare, for instance), put a tablespoon of vinegar into a small bowl (this will prevent the blood, which will have been contained by the diaphragm, from coagulating). Lift up the animal and drain the blood into the bowl; you may need to slit the diaphragm open.

When the chest cavity is clear, pull out the heart and lungs. Cut the esophagus and trachea at the neck end and discard. The heart, liver, and blood can be used in stuffings, pâtés, or sauces.

How to joint a rabbit or hare

FOR 6 OR 7 PIECES:
Detach the legs from the carcass: cut through the muscle on the front of the leg, otherwise the leg will toughen as it cooks. Cut around the forelegs and remove. Chop the saddle into 2 or 3 pieces; there will now be 6 or 7 pieces. Discard the back passage.

FOR 8 OR 9 PIECES:
Prepare as above and then divide the hind legs into 2 pieces.

MUMMY'S RABBIT STEW

We were thrilled when Owen O'Neill, the local hunter, came around with a couple of rabbits slung over his shoulder for Mummy to buy. We all knew how to skin a rabbit and it was a matter-of-fact thing to do; in fact, we'd fight over the opportunity to skin the rabbit and make Davy Crockett hats ·

SERVES 4–6

1 wild rabbit (about 4lb) with liver and kidney
12oz unsmoked bacon, preferably dry-cured (blanch if salty)
a little oil and butter for sautéing
1lb onions (baby ones are nicest)
12oz carrot, peeled and thickly sliced
3 cups Chicken Stock (see page 262)
sprig of thyme
Roux, optional (see page 165)
Wild Mushrooms à la Crème, optional (see page 50)
1 tablespoon chopped parsley

Skin and gut the rabbit. Remove the rind from the bacon and cut into pieces about 1in wide (blanch if salty and pat dry on paper towels). Joint the rabbit into 8 pieces.

Heat a little oil in a sauté pan and sauté the bacon until crisp; remove and put in a casserole.

Add the rabbit pieces to the pan and sauté until golden; add to the bacon in the casserole. Heat control is crucial here: the pan mustn't burn yet it must be hot enough to sauté the rabbit. If it is too cool, rabbit pieces will stew rather than sauté and as a result the meat may be tough.

Next, sauté the onion and carrots, adding a little butter if necessary, then add into the casserole. Degrease the sauté pan and deglaze with stock; bring to a boil and pour over the rabbit pieces. Season well, add a sprig of thyme, and bring to simmering point on top of the stove, then put into the oven for about 30–45 minutes at 350°F. Cooking time depends on how long the rabbit pieces were sautéed.

When the rabbit is just cooked, strain off the cooking liquid, degrease, and pour the degreased liquid into a pan. Bring to a boil and thicken with a little roux, if necessary. Add back to the meat, carrots, and onions and bring to a boil. The casserole is very good served at this point, but it's even more delicious if some Wild Mushrooms à la Crème is stirred in as an enrichment. Serve bubbling hot, sprinkled with chopped parsley.

Variation

RABBIT STEW WITH CHORIZO OR CABANOSSI
4oz chorizo or 6oz cabanossi added instead of the equivalent amount of bacon is a delicious variation.

Left: *Saddle of Rabbit with Cream, Basil, and Caramelized Shallots.*

6 saddle of rabbit (use the legs for
    confit)
4oz pork caul fat
salt and freshly ground pepper
extra virgin olive oil
⅔ cup dry white wine
⅔ cup Chicken Stock (see page
    262)
⅔ cup cream
2oz basil leaves
Caramelized Shallots (see below)

Trim the flap of each saddle, if
necessary (use in stock or pâté).
    Remove the membrane and
sinews from the back of the saddles
with a small knife. Wrap each saddle
loosely in pork caul fat. Season well
with salt and freshly ground pepper.
    Preheat the oven to 400°F. Place
the rabbit pieces in a stainless steel
or heavy roasting pan and roast for
8–12 minutes, depending on size.
Remove from the oven, cover, and
allow to rest. Degrease the pan if
necessary, and put the wine to
reduce in the roasting pan. Reduce
by half over medium heat, add the
chicken stock, and continue to
reduce. Add the cream. Bring to a
boil, season with salt and freshly
ground pepper, and add lots of
snipped basil. Serve the rabbit with
the basil sauce, caramelized shallots,
boiled new potatoes, and a good
green salad.

CARAMELIZED
SHALLOTS

1lb shallots, peeled
4 tablespoons butter

SADDLE OF RABBIT
WITH CREAM, BASIL,
AND CARAMELIZED
SHALLOTS

*The saddle comprises the two loins still
attached to the backbone and is the
choicest part of the rabbit. But it's
really easy to overcook it, in which case
it will be dry and lose its succulence
and appeal. This is a particularly good
way to serve the saddle. I also love to
remove the loins from the bone, season
well, roast for 5–8 minutes in a hot
oven, then coat in well-seasoned flour,
egg, and bread crumbs, deep-fry in hot
oil until crunchy, and serve with a
really good aioli (see page 96) and
a few arugula leaves* · **SERVES 6**

½ cup water
1–2 tablespoons sugar
salt and freshly ground pepper

Put all the ingredients in a small saucepan, and add the peeled shallots. Cover and cook on a gentle heat for about 10–15 minutes or until the shallots are soft and juicy. Remove the lid, increase the heat to medium, and cook, stirring occasionally. Allow the juices to evaporate and caramelize. Be careful not to let them burn.

FILLETS OF HARE WITH MUSHROOMS AND CREAM

Hare fillets are tiny, so be really careful not to overcook them. A little French tarragon is also delicious instead of the thyme leaves, as is fresh marjoram. The sauce can be thickened with a little roux, if necessary. Serve with mashed or boiled potatoes · SERVES 2

1 saddle of hare
salt and freshly ground pepper
8 juniper berries, pounded
1 tablespoon butter
4oz mushrooms, quartered
1 teaspoon of thyme leaves
4 or 5 shallots, finely chopped
glass of dry white wine
1 cup Game Stock
   (see page 149)
¼ cup heavy cream

Remove the eye of the loin from the saddle, giving you two fillets. Cut each fillet into 4 pieces. Season with salt and pepper and the juniper berries.

Put half the butter in a hot sauté pan and add the mushrooms. Season with salt and pepper, add the thyme leaves, and sauté for a few minutes. Remove to a plate.

Melt the remaining butter in the sauté pan, add the hare, and color for a minute or two on each side. Transfer the hare to the plate with the mushrooms. Add the shallots to the pan and cook for a couple of minutes over medium heat, until soft and pale golden. Increase the heat, pour in the wine, and cook for 3–4 minutes to cook off the alcohol. Add the stock and cream, bring back to a boil, add the mushrooms and hare, and allow to bubble gently for 5–6 minutes, until the hare is just cooked. Check the seasoning and serve immediately.

TUSCAN PASTA WITH HARE SAUCE

This is based on the classic pappardelle con la leper *recipe: rich, intense, and delicious. You're unlikely to have a hare very often, but when you do, save some to make this memorable pasta ·* SERVES 6–8

2 tablespoons lard or extra virgin
   olive oil
4oz fat rindless bacon or pancetta,
   cut into ¼in pieces
5oz onions, sliced
1 celery rib, cut into strips
1 garlic clove
2 front and hind legs of hare
5 or 6 dried porcini, soaked in
   ⅔ cup warm water
2–3 sprigs of thyme or marjoram
salt and freshly ground black
   pepper
1 tablespoon all-purpose flour

⅓ cup red wine
1½ cups Game or Chicken Stock
   (see pages 149 and 262)
1 lemon
freshly chopped flat-leaf parsley
1lb pappardelle or noodles
1 heaping cup grated Parmesan

Heat the lard or olive oil in a casserole dish or a deep sauté pan. Add the bacon or pancetta, cook and stir over medium heat for a couple of minutes, until the fat begins to run.

Add the sliced onions, celery strips, and the garlic clove and continue to cook until they begin to color. Then add the joints of hare, the dried porcini and their soaking liquid, and the herb sprigs. Season with salt and pepper.

When the hare colors slightly, sprinkle in the flour. Stir and cook for 2–3 minutes, add the red wine, bring to a boil, and allow to reduce for 3–4 minutes. Add the stock (or use water), and bring back to a boil. Cover the casserole dish and cook for 1¼ hours, or until the hare is almost falling off the bones.

Remove the bones. Add the grated zest of the lemon and a few drops of the juice. Taste, and add lots of chopped parsley.

Meanwhile, bring a large pan of water to a boil and add 2 tablespoons salt for every 6 quarts of water. Add the pappardelle and cook until al dente, 1–1½ minutes for fresh, 10–15 minutes for dried.

Drain well. Place on a hot serving dish. Sprinkle with half the Parmesan and the hare sauce. Toss, scatter with parsley, and serve with the remaining Parmesan.

Venison

There are several varieties of deer available: in Ireland, we can get red deer, fallow deer, Sika deer, and roe deer. The latter is rapidly becoming a pest in parts of Britain. Deer common to the United States include the white-tailed (or Virginia) deer, the black-tailed, and the fallow and red deer. The smaller deer, like the fallow are similar in size to lamb; and it's very easy to work out their anatomy.

Venison is shot with a rifle, shotgun, or bow and arrow depending on season and place.

A hunter who is a good marksman will shoot his animals through the neck, heart, or lungs, leaving the most of the meat intact and ready for use. Unfortunately, a stray shot can hit a bone, and leave portions of the carcass suffused with blood and bone fragments and unsuitable for use.

Deer must be bled immediately after being shot and disemboweled as soon as possible afterward. This means removing the stomach and entrails right up to the diaphragm, but leaving the liver and kidneys in place. This must be done very carefully to avoid penetrating the stomach and flooding the carcass with partly digested food.

The animal is then brought home and hung. At that stage you cut down from the diaphragm as far as the neck, prop open the chest cavity with a special piece of metal (or a short piece of wood) and allow it to drain out completely before putting it in the cold-room to hang.

Special treat – venison liver

At this point, you can remove the liver and kidneys. For a big treat that evening, have the venison liver for supper (see page 148). Really fresh, just fried simply in a little butter and seasoned with salt and pepper, it's one of the best things you can eat.

Skinning and butchering

Deer are hung in the skin, which is only removed when you are about to butcher. Run the blade of a knife down the hind leg (haunch), taking care not to puncture the flesh, and work off the skin by a combination of pulling gently and making small cuts to separate it from the flesh.

Butchering is relatively easy and largely a matter of common sense, but a special one-day course on venison butchery (or even a video or DVD) is never wasted. Deer are not the same as cattle or sheep – the cuts are very different.

Examining the carcass

If you haven't shot the deer yourself, it's important that you buy from a reliable source. You need to know that it has been legally killed, properly bled and disemboweled, and then correctly treated. It must also have been examined by a trained person to ensure that it is safe for human consumption.

It is essential that hunters know how to examine a carcass or have access to a processing facility that can do it. Deer, like cattle and sheep, are prone to diseases such as liver fluke and tuberculosis, and it is essential to ensure that any animal destined for the table is healthy.

If the journey home is a long one, it may be necessary to carry out these steps in the field, with the deer perhaps hanging from a tree, so as to allow the animal to cool down properly before beginning your journey. This can take several hours. An animal shot on a warm day and put immediately into a car for transporting can actually "heat" and go bad very quickly.

Cooking with venison

Venison meat is very lean. The back leg, which is cut off in one piece, is called the haunch. It's a fantastic joint for a dinner party and a haunch from a large fallow or red deer will feed about 20 people. You'll need to be very fussy about not overcooking it or it'll be dry and tough and completely uninteresting.

For the loin, I've come to the conclusion that it's best to take out the "eye," the whole length of the loin, and that can be either sliced and cut into medallions and fried off on a pan quickly, or the whole eye of the loin can be pan-grilled in a piece and then cut into slices while it's still juicy and pink – that's absolutely wonderful.

There's very little meat on the rib cage or belly, but what you can recover can be ground for venison burgers, venison sausages, or venison chile con carne. The best stewing meat comes from the shoulder.

ROAST HAUNCH OF VENISON WITH QUINCE AND ROSEMARY GRAVY

A haunch of venison makes an excellent, easy, delicious, and impressive dish. Venison tends to be very lean – an advantage for those who fear fat. However, some fat is needed to baste the joint while roasting to ensure succulence. The sweet pork caul fat will melt over the joint, basting as it roasts. It virtually disappears · **SERVES ABOUT 20 PEOPLE**

1 haunch of venison, about 6–7lb

TO LARD VENISON
8oz back fat or fatty pork; alternatively, bard the whole joint in caul fat

FOR THE MARINADE
2 tablespoons fresh herbs; I use a mix of thyme and marjoram
4 tablespoons olive oil
½ cup dry white wine

FOR THE GRAVY
3 cups Game or Beef Stock (see pages 149 and 159)
2 tablespoons chopped rosemary

Roux, optional (see page 165)
Quince Compote (see next recipe)

First, lard the venison. Cut the pork back fat into ¼in wide strips. Insert a strip into a larding needle, draw a piece through the meat to make a stitch; trim the end. Repeat the stitches at 1in intervals to make horizontal rows, positioning each row about ½in away from the previous row. Continue with the remainder of the fat.

Put the haunch into a shallow dish, stainless steel or cast iron, but not tin or aluminum. Sprinkle it with the freshly chopped herbs. Pour the olive oil and wine over the meat. Cover the dish or tray and marinate the meat for about 4 hours at room temperature or in the refrigerator overnight, turning the meat occasionally. I also use the marinade to baste the meat during cooking to ensure it doesn't dry out.

Preheat the oven to 350°F. Weigh the venison and calculate 10 minutes to every 1lb. We like our venison slightly pink and still very juicy, so I usually turn off the oven then and allow the meat to relax for 20–30 minutes. Baste every 10 minutes during the cooking time with the oil and wine marinade and turn the joint over halfway through. When the venison is cooked, remove to a serving dish while you prepare the gravy.

Degrease the roasting pan, and add the stock and the rosemary. Bring to a boil, scraping and dissolving the sediment and crusty pieces from the roasting pan. Thicken very slightly with a little roux, taste, and correct the seasoning. Pour into a warm gravy boat. Serve the haunch of venison on a large serving dish surrounded by roast potatoes with the quince compote. Alternatively, a creamy Gratin of Wild Mushrooms and Potatoes (see page 50), or Mashed Celeriac and Parsnip (see page 134) would be very good accompaniments.

Note: it is very easy to overcook venison, mainly because it continues to cook after the oven has been turned off, and the need to prevent this from happening cannot be overemphasized. It is better to allow the meat to cool considerably than to risk overcooking, and for this reason venison is served in thin slices on very, very hot plates, which has the effect of reheating it right at the last moment.

QUINCE COMPOTE

5–6 quinces
1 cup sugar
⅓ cup water
1–2 teaspoons chopped rosemary leaves

Peel, core, and chop the quince into ¾in cubes. Immediately put in the saucepan with sugar and water, cover, and cook over medium heat until soft – this takes about 20 minutes. Add the chopped rosemary, taste, and add a little more sugar and rosemary, as needed.

VENISON SHEPHERD'S PIE

Use every scrap of the leftover cooked meat from the haunch to make this dish. Serve with a dab of herb butter melting into the top · **SERVES 6–8**

1 tablespoon extra virgin olive oil
¾ cup finely chopped onion
4oz mushrooms, finely chopped
1lb ripe tomatoes, peeled and chopped, or 1 x 14oz canned tomatoes

salt and freshly ground pepper
and sugar
2 tablespoons chopped parsley
2 teaspoons chopped thyme
2 teaspoons chopped marjoram
2lb ground cooked haunch of
venison (see page 145)
1 tablespoon all-purpose flour
venison gravy or a rich game stock

2lb mashed potatoes or a mixture
of mashed potatoes, parsnip,
and/or celeriac

Heat the oil in a casserole dish over medium heat. Add the onion, cover, and sweat until soft and pale gold. Increase the heat, add the mushrooms, and cook for 3–4 minutes. Add the tomatoes, season with salt, pepper, and sugar. Add the chopped herbs and allow to bubble and cook uncovered for 8–10 minutes. Add the ground venison. Stir, sprinkle in the flour, and cook for 2–3 minutes. Add the gravy and let bubble. Taste and correct the seasoning.

Spoon into one large or several small pie dishes, cover the top with a layer of mashed potatoes or a mixture of potatoes and parsnip or potato and celeriac purée. Reheat in the oven at 350°F for about 20–30 minutes, or until hot and bubbling. Serve with some broccoli or kale and a green salad.

VENISON STEW WITH CHESTNUTS

When you buy venison, allow time for marinating, and remember that unsmoked bacon or fatty salt pork is essential either for cooking in with the meat (stew) or for larding (roasting or braising), unless the meat has been well hung · SERVES 8

3lb shoulder of venison, trimmed
and cubed into (1½in) pieces

MARINADE
¾ cup red wine
8oz onion, sliced
3 tablespoons brandy
3 tablespoons olive oil
salt and lightly crushed black
peppercorns
bouquet garni made with parsley
stems, 1 bay leaf, and a fine
sprig of thyme

seasoned flour

SAUCE
8oz fat streaky bacon, diced
2 tablespoons olive oil
2 large onions, chopped
1 large carrot, diced
1 large garlic clove, crushed
2 cups Beef or Game Stock (see
pages 159 and 149)
bouquet garni
24 small mushrooms, preferably
wild ones
9oz cooked and halved chestnuts
2 tablespoons extra virgin olive oil
lemon juice or red currant jelly, as
required
salt, freshly ground pepper,
and sugar

3lb mashed potatoes

Season the venison well and soak in the marinade overnight. Drain the meat well, pat it dry on paper towels and toss in seasoned flour.

Meanwhile, brown the bacon in the olive oil in a frying pan, cooking it slowly at first to persuade the fat to run, then raising the heat until crisp on the outside. Transfer to a casserole dish.

Brown first the venison in the fat, then the onion, carrots, and garlic (do this in batches, transferring each ingredient to the casserole dish). Do not overheat or the fat will burn. Pour off any surplus fat, deglaze the pan with the strained marinade, and pour over the venison. Heat enough stock to cover the venison and vegetables in the casserole dish and pour it over them. Add another bouquet garni, bring to a gentle simmer, either on top of the stove or transfer to a preheated oven at 300°F. Cover tightly and continue to cook gently until the venison is tender.

Test after 1½ hours, but you may need longer – up to 2½ hours cooking time. For best results, it is wise to cook this kind of dish one day and then reheat it the next, which improves the flavor and gives you a chance to make sure that the venison is tender.

Sauté the sliced mushrooms in the extra virgin olive oil. Season with salt and pepper and add to the stew with the cooked and halved chestnuts. Finally, taste the sauce; it may need seasoning or perhaps a little lemon juice. It also sometimes benefits from a pinch of sugar or some red currant jelly (be careful not to use too much.)

Serve with lots of mashed potatoes, Champ, or Colcannon (see pages 383 and 384).

VENISON PIE

The skill of covering a pie is really worth mastering; you can use it to cover any meat or game pie. There are always appreciative gasps when I bring them to the table! · SERVES 8

Venison Stew (use previous recipe, minus the chestnuts)
12oz Puff Pastry or Billy's Cream Pastry (see pages 218 and 209)
egg wash (see page 539)

Fill a large pie dish with the stew and cover with puff pastry (see below).

To cover a pie dish with pastry

Preheat the oven to 450°F. Fill a large pie dish with the stew. Roll the pastry into a sheet ¼in thick, and cut several strips wide enough to fit onto the lip of the pie dish. Brush the lip with cold water and press the strips of pastry firmly onto the dish. Brush the pastry strips with cold water and then press the lid of pastry firmly down onto the edges. Trim off the excess pastry. Flute the edges and scallop with the back of a knife, then cut some pastry leaves from the trimmings. Egg wash the pie and decorate with the pastry leaves. Make a hole in the center and egg wash again. Bake in the oven for 10–15 minutes, reduce the heat to 400°F, and continue to bake until the pastry is cooked and the filling bubbling.

Above: *Venison Stew with Chestnuts.*

VENISON AND POTATO PIE

Put the the Venison Stew (see page 146) with or without the chestnuts, in a pie dish and cover with mashed potatoes. Reheat in a preheated oven at 350°F for 20–30 minutes, or until the stew is bubbling and the potato is brown and crusty.

POTTED VENISON WITH JUNIPER BERRIES

Another way to use up cooked morsels of venison in a delectable way. Other leftover game – pigeon, rabbit, hare, wild duck, or pheasant – can also be used up in this way. I sometimes add a few fat raisins or golden raisins soaked in Pedro Ximenez sherry to the potted meat · SERVES 6–8

8oz cooked venison
6 tablespoons butter
1 large shallot
1 small garlic clove
1 tablespoon brandy or gin
5 plump juniper berries
salt and freshly ground pepper
½ cup cream, whipped

Clarified Butter (see page 216)

Cut the meat into small pieces, and process for a few seconds in a food processor; the texture should be rough. Melt the butter in a saucepan, gently cook the shallot and garlic until soft, but not colored. Add the brandy or gin and allow to flame, then add the juniper berries and squash with a wooden spoon in the hot pan. Allow to cool, then scoop the contents of the saucepan

into the food processor with the venison. Season with salt and pepper. Process until smooth, fold the stiffly whipped cream into the venison, taste, and correct the seasoning. Fill into a terrine, cover with a thin layer of clarified butter, and leave for 24 hours. Serve with hot thin toast or crusty white rolls.

VENISON LIVER WITH BUBBLE AND SQUEAK

If ever you have the chance to taste fresh venison liver, do so. It's a revelation, but it must be super fresh. It is best eaten on the same day, but would still be worth trying the following day · SERVES 4–6

fresh venison liver (about 1lb) cut into ½in slices
flour seasoned with sea salt and freshly ground black pepper
4 tablespoons Clarified Butter (see page 216), more if you need it
extra virgin olive oil
Bubble and Squeak (see page 384)
watercress or flat parsley, to serve

Dip the slices of liver in the seasoned flour. Heat some clarified butter or extra virgin olive oil in the pan over high heat. Cook the liver for 30 seconds on each side. Serve immediately on hot plates with freshly cooked Bubble and Squeak and some watercress or sprigs of flat parsley – divine.

Venison liver is also delicious with Champ or Colcannon (see page 383 and 384).

VENISON BURGERS

Another good way to use the stewing meat. Venison is so lean that it benefits from the addition of the fatty pork · MAKES 6

3 tablespoons finely chopped shallot or onion
extra virgin olive oil
1lb venison shoulder or flap, trimmed
6oz fatty pork, rind removed
1 teaspoon or more thyme leaves
1 teaspoon or more marjoram
1 tablespoon sweet chile sauce
salt and freshly ground pepper
caul fat, if available (see page 325)

burger buns

Cook the shallot or onion gently in the olive oil until soft. Allow to get cold. Meanwhile, cube the venison and pork. Chop or grind in batches in a food processor. Mix the meat, cold shallots, fresh herbs, and chile sauce together in a bowl. Season with salt and pepper.

Heat a frying pan. Fry a spoonful of meat to check the seasoning. Adjust, if necessary. Divide the mixture into burgers. Wrap in pork caul, cover, and chill until needed.

Heat a little extra virgin olive oil in a frying pan. Cook burgers for about 5 minutes on each side.

Serve each on a toasted bun with the usual accompaniments. Wild Mushrooms à la Crème (see page 50) and a watercress salad are delicious on the side.

GAME STOCK

This stock will keep for 2–3 days in the refrigerator. It can also be frozen · MAKES ABOUT 2 QUARTS

2–4 game carcasses (pheasant, duck, hare, snipe, venison, etc.)
3–4 onions
3–4 carrots, one stuck with 2 cloves
leek trimmings
1–2 celery ribs
bouquet garni
a few peppercorns
water or Chicken Stock (see page 262) to cover

Preheat the oven to 450°F.

First, chop the carcasses with a meat chopper to release more flavor. Put the carcasses into a roasting pan and roast for 30 minutes, or until the bones are well browned. Add the onions, carrots, leek trimmings, and celery and return to the oven until the vegetables are also browned. Transfer the bones and vegetables to a stock pot with a metal spoon. Add the bouquet garni and a few peppercorns. Degrease the roasting pan and deglaze with some water or chicken stock; bring to a boil and pour over the bones and vegetables. Add the rest of the water and bring slowly to a boil. Skim the stock and simmer gently for 3–4 hours. Strain the stock, allow it to get cold, and skim off all the fat, and chill again before use.

GAME TERRINE

Making a coarse terrine like this is pleasurable and worthwhile, but it does take time and care. It's a good way of using up less desirable bits of scrappy game from a bird that has been peppered with shot. It has a layer of fat over the delicious jellied juices and terrine, which helps to preserve it. Provided it's well covered, it will keep for 7–10 days in the fridge and can be successfully frozen for a couple of months. On the day it is to be eaten, present the terrine, uncut, to your guests and slice it at the table. Serve with Onion Jam and Beet and Ginger Relish (see pages 450 and 439), a watercress salad, lots of sourdough toast, and good a red wine · SERVES 6–8

1lb game livers
9oz fat pork belly
10oz ground rabbit or pheasant, or a mixture of game
7oz bacon, cut in thin slices, or pork back fat or caul fat

FOR THE MARINADE
7 tablespoons Armagnac or brandy
3 tablespoons port
3 tablespoons sherry
4 garlic cloves, chopped
2 tablespoons chopped parsley
1 teaspoon thyme leaves
1 teaspoon marjoram leaves
freshly grated nutmeg
½ teaspoon superfine sugar
2 teaspoons salt
freshly ground pepper
4 sprigs thyme
4 bay leaves

oven-proof porcelain terrine with a lid, 6½ x 4 x 3in

Day 1: preparing and marinating the meat

Trim away all greenish patches from the game livers. Cut the livers in half. Divide the pork belly in two. Cut one half into scant ½in cubes and grind the rest. Put the livers, the pork cubes, and ground meat in a large bowl, and add the ingredients for the marinade – Armagnac, port, sherry, garlic, parsley, thyme, marjoram, nutmeg, sugar, salt, and pepper. Mix all the ingredients together thoroughly, then cover and leave to marinate overnight in the refrigerator. Fry off a little bit on a pan to test the seasoning.

Day 2: filling and cooking the terrine

Preheat the oven to 425°F and prepare a bain-marie.

Line the terrine with some of the bacon, then fill it to the brim with the meat and the marinade. Cover the pâté with the remaining strips of bacon or back fat and lay the sprigs of thyme and the bay leaves on top. Put the terrine in the double boiler and cook uncovered in the oven for 1¾ hours. The top will brown nicely, but cover with a piece of parchment paper if it is getting too dark.

Remove from the oven, and use the upturned lid with a weight on top to compress the terrine. Allow to cool completely and then refrigerate for a day or two to allow the flavor to mature.

Beef

A big roast of beef gets everybody (except for vegetarians) excited and conjures up happy childhood memories of Sunday roast with lots of gravy and crusty roast potatoes. Then there were the pink paper-thin slices of cold roast beef for Monday lunch with horseradish sauce and potato salad, cottage pie on Wednesday and maybe a little potted beef for Thursday's supper, depending on how long it lasted. The skill of thrifty housekeeping was second nature to many of our our mothers and grandmothers and they were masters at making a little meat go a long way. I even remember with great fondness the flavor of dripping on toast.

Farmers and traditional butchers agree with my opinion that there is a considerable and distinct difference in the feel and smell of well-reared meat, whether it be beef, chicken, lamb, or pork. Organic meat is firmer in texture and smells quite different when cooked. In our experience, it's a more stable product and keeps for longer.

One thing to be aware of when buying beef is the breed. The flavor of meat is determined by breed and feed. I personally favor the traditional Irish breeds, which have adapted to the Irish climate and still are finished mostly on grass, at a younger age. I love the flavor of that beef: Hereford, Aberdeen Angus, or Strawberry Roan (as Shorthorn used to be called in Ireland) was my absolute favorite, but nowadays rare indeed. A Poll Angus, which is a cross between Aberdeen Angus and Shorthorn, is today's best option. Some of the Continental breeds are wonderful, too – I particularly love the Chianina, a breed native to Tuscany, and practically make a pilgrimage to Florence once a year to have a *bistecca alla fiorentina* at the Osteria di Benci.

The quality of the grass really matters, but nowadays, most pastures are just made up of a few rye grasses. It stands to reason that animals fed on a diet of just three different things rather than on a mixed pasture of 20 or 30 grasses, herbs, and wildflowers are unlikely to be as flavorsome or as nutritionally complex. Also, electric fences and barbed wire have closed off the hedgerows and riverbanks to animals that used to self-medicate by foraging for plants like cocksfoot and brambles.

Many farmers now use artificial fertilizers, rather than clover, to fix nitrogen. Our former butcher, Michael Cuddigan, a third-generation butcher from Cloyne, now retired, from whom I learned so much about meat and animal husbandry, finished his animals on his own farm, and had a mixture of pastures, new and old – but he always finished them off on old pastures. (Finishing is the term used to refer to fattening an animal before slaughter.) Both he and I are convinced that that was one of the reasons that his meat was so extraordinarily good.

Nowadays, the majority of the feed, when it's grain, is genetically modified, and there is a growing number of people who have a concern about that. We certainly need clarity in this, as well as a choice. People are asking why farmers and butchers don't have to identify that the animals have been fed on genetically modified feed. If there's no problem with it, why can't they be transparent? Research shows that E. coli can be significantly less prevalent in grass-fed or hay-fed animals. Ruminants may get fat quickly on grain-based diets, but such diets produce an acid environment in the animal stomach, encouraging the growth of acid-resistant E. coli (particularly E. coli 0157).

Most people today buy meat from their supermarket. But there are a number of compelling reasons to buy from a local butcher instead. The service they provide, the education they offer and the fact that they're buying locally, are all crucial to sustaining local economies both from the perspective of the producer and the consumer.

Cuts of Beef

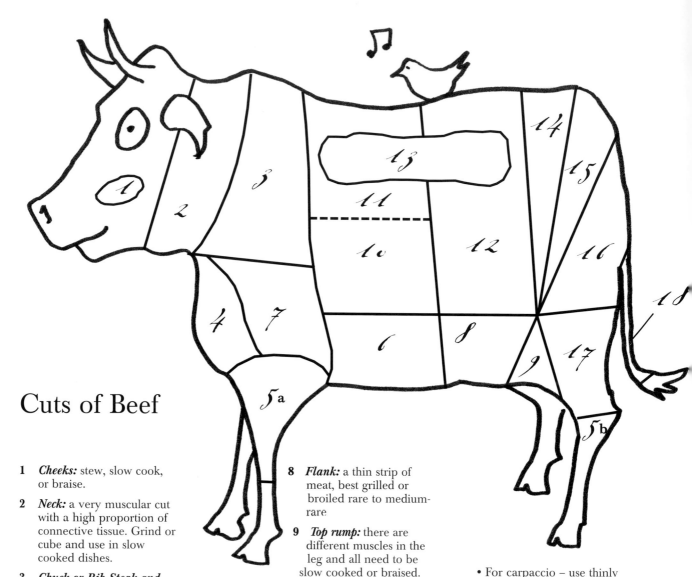

1 ***Cheeks:*** stew, slow cook, or braise.

2 ***Neck:*** a very muscular cut with a high proportion of connective tissue. Grind or cube and use in slow cooked dishes.

3 ***Chuck or Rib Steak and Blade:*** grind or use for stewing. Braise and slow cook the blade.

4 ***Clod:*** grind or cube for slow cooking. Texture is similar to neck.

5 **(a)** ***Foreshin:*** long slow cooking breaks down the collagen. Great for stews and for consommé. **(b)** ***Hindshin:*** tougher than the foreshin and not as meaty but can be cooked in the same way.

6 ***Brisket:*** use for corned beef or grind.

7 ***Toprib or chuck:*** braise or slow roast.

8 ***Flank:*** a thin strip of meat, best grilled or broiled rare to medium-rare.

9 ***Top rump:*** there are different muscles in the leg and all need to be slow cooked or braised.

10 ***Rib roast:*** great roasted or grilled.

11 ***Prime rib or fore rib:*** roast on bone or off bone or cut into rib steaks.

12 ***Sirloin – strip loin:*** roast whole in a piece or cut into sirloin or minute steaks, fry or grill.

13 ***Fillet:*** roast whole or cut into fillet steaks, tournados ½in thick, or medallions ¼in thick.
• Chateaubriand steak is cut from the thicker part of the fillet at the leg end.
• For beef stroganoff – use the chain cut off the fillet.
• For carpaccio – use thinly sliced fillet.
• For steak tartare – use minced fillet.

14 ***Rump:*** grill or slow roast rump steak; carve across the grain.

15 ***Top round:*** very lean cut. Use for corning and spiced beef.

16 ***Eye of round:*** roast to rare and slice thinly.

17 ***Round:*** braise or slow cook.

18 ***Oxtail:*** stew or slow cook.

Note: the highest percentage of "best" cuts come from the hind quarter.

Beef terms

CALF: the young offspring of a cow and a bull.
VEAL: the meat from a calf. More often, these are the male animals of dairy breeds, because they don't fatten as effectively as beef breeds and will never give milk.
HEIFER: female animal who hasn't had a calf yet
COW: mature female animal of the family Bovidae. Raised for dairy, beef, or both.
BULL CALF: young male animal.
BULLOCK OR STEER: a castrated bull.
BULL: mature male adult of the family Bovidae. Raised for beef or dairy breeding.
OX: a bovine animal used as a draught animal, often an adult, castrated male.

Aged meat

When buying meat I always look for dry-aged meat. Aging meat is becoming a forgotten skill. The animal is slaughtered, and nowadays, within a very short time it is butchered, put into Cryovac and "aged" there, so it retains its moisture and thus its weight. Whereas in dry-aging, the prime cuts of meat (those with adequate marbling, or in other words evenly distributed fat) are allowed to begin to deteriorate slowly at cold temperatures, and the enzyme action in the meat breaks down the connective tissue in the muscles, thus tenderizing the meat. Plus, as moisture evaporates, the flavor is concentrated. The fungal genus *Thamnidia* apparently makes for particularly tender and flavorful meat.

Traditional butchers still know about aging, but they're in a dilemma because hanging the meat as long as they'd like to is a costly process, since it causes meat to lose as much as a third of its weight. Plus, the fungal crust that develops on the outside of the meat must be trimmed off. Dry-aging takes much longer (15–28 days) than wet-aging, which only takes a few days. Most customers are not aware of this issue and don't understand why they should have to pay more. If, however, we want well-aged meat, we need to be prepared to pay for it. I personally would be happy to have a choice, and this is exactly what Tim Wilson of the Ginger Pig, an innovative farmer/butcher from the UK, who sells a lot of rare-breed meat, does. He identifies the breed and also hangs the meat for different periods of

time. You can go into his butcher shop and buy something that's hung for two weeks or four weeks and pay accordingly. Meat is expensive, and as far as I'm concerned, we might as well get something delicious.

Well-aged meat will be a crusty dark brown or even almost black rather than rosy pink, particularly on the outside, which puts people off, but it's actually a sign of quality. It could even grow a little mold and still be okay, you can just trim that off. We have our own meat on the farm and have aged it for seven or eight weeks on occasion and it's been wonderful, but no butcher would do this, for economic reasons.

Why buy meat from a local butcher?

Meat sourced locally is a win-win scenario for the consumer, the producer, and the animal, in that the animals are born and reared in the locality, their meat is directly traceable to a particular farm or region, and the animals are less stressed before slaughter, unlike those that have to travel long distances in less than ideal conditions. All of these factors impact on the quality of the meat sold to the consumer. There are still many good, craft-style butchers left and these are people who know their meat. Some even have their own farms and can offer total traceability. These butchers are treasures and should be supported. Many will be happy to enter into discussion with you about the meat and its good qualities. Give them feedback next time you visit. Some butchers buy from local farmers but have their own abattoir and this, again, can be very reassuring. They too identify with their product and are not going to sell anything that reflects badly on them. Wherever you buy you should ask questions: the breed, feed, and hanging time are essential issues which you should investigate.

But not all is well in the craft butcher's world. I'm concerned about the number of butchers, even craft butchers, who are going down what I call the "sweet 'n' sour" route, where so much of their food is tossed in a standard spice mix or gloopy sauce that comes from a supply store. I feel then that there's no point of difference between them and the supermarket anymore. I wish that butchers would have the courage of their convictions, to focus on what they're better at than the supermarkets: buying well, slaughtering appropriately, aging adequately, and selling local meat with pride.

Roasting

Roasting is a very traditional way to cook meat, but today's ovens vary enormously in efficiency. In addition, thermostats are not always accurate and some joints of meat are much thicker than others, so the figures for roasting times below must be treated as guidelines rather than rules. The times below include a 15-minute searing time at 450°F.

For beef on the bone:

Rare: 10 minutes per 1lb
Medium: 12 minutes per 1lb
Well-done: 18 minutes per 1lb

For beef off the bone:
Rare: 8 minutes per 1lb
Medium: 10 minutes per 1lb
Well-done: 15 minutes per 1lb

Is it cooked?

When roasting meat, there are various ways of checking how well the roast is cooked. I insert a metal skewer into the thickest part of the roast, leave it there for about 30–45 seconds, and then put it against the back of my hand. If it still feels cool, the meat is rare, if it is warm it is medium rare, if it is hotter it is medium and if you can't keep the skewer against your hand for more than a second then you can bet it's well-done. Also check the color of the juices: the meat is well done if they are clear as opposed to red or pink for rare or medium.

If you own a meat thermometer, it will eliminate guesswork altogether, but ensure the thermometer is not touching a bone when you are testing the internal temperature.

Rare: 140°F
Medium: 155°F
Well-done: 165°F

TRADITIONAL ROAST RIB OF BEEF WITH HORSERADISH SAUCE, GRAVY AND YORKSHIRE PUDDING

Few can resist a roast rib of beef with horseradish sauce, Yorkshire pudding, lots of gravy and crusty roast potatoes. Always buy beef on the bone for roasting; it will have much more flavor and is not difficult to carve (ask your butcher to saw through the upper chine bone so that the "feather bones" will be easy to remove before carving). Remember to leave at least 15 minutes of resting time so that the juices can redistribute themselves evenly through the meat before being carved ·
SERVES 8–10

1 beef rib roast, preferably dry-aged, about 9lb
salt and freshly ground pepper

FOR THE GRAVY
2¾ cups Beef Stock (see page 159)
2 tablespoons Roux (see page 165), optional
salt and freshly ground pepper

ACCOMPANIMENTS
Horseradish Sauce (see page 24)
Yorkshire Pudding (see opposite)

Preheat the oven to 475°F.

Weigh the roast and calculate the cooking time (see above). Score the fat and season well with salt and freshly ground pepper. Place the meat in a roasting pan with the fat side facing up. As the fat renders in the heat of the oven, it will baste the meat. The bones provide a natural rack to hold the meat above the fat in the roasting pan. Put the meat into a 450°F oven, and after 15 minutes, turn down the heat to 350°F, until the meat is cooked to your taste (see above).

When the meat is cooked, it should be allowed to rest in the pan in the turned-off oven for 15–30 minutes before carving, depending on the size of the roast. The internal temperature will continue to rise by as much as 5°F, so remove the roast from the oven while it is still slightly underdone.

While the meat is resting, make the gravy. Spoon the fat off the roasting tin. Pour the stock into the cooking juices remaining in the tin. Boil for a few minutes, stirring and scraping the pan to dissolve the caramelized meat juices (I find a small whisk ideal for this). Whisk in the roux to thicken if you like. Taste and add salt and freshly ground pepper if necessary. Strain and serve in a warmed gravy boat.

Carve the beef at the table and serve with a fiery horseradish sauce, Yorkshire pudding, the gravy and lots of crusty roast potatoes.

Variation

ROAST ROUND OF BEEF WITH HORSERADISH SAUCE, GRAVY AND YORKSHIRE PUDDING
Prime cuts of beef are now extremely expensive so why not try roasting a well-aged round roast instead? It's a much tougher piece of meat and it needs to age for at least a week longer than rib roast. As in the

previous recipe, score and season the fat well with sea salt and freshly cracked pepper. You'll be surprised by how delicious it is. It has an even beefier flavor than rib roast, but is about one-third of the cost.

YORKSHIRE PUDDING

Simply irresistible with lots of gravy, I cook individual ones which I'm sure would be very much frowned upon in Yorkshire. Heat the muffin pan in the oven before adding the batter. If you want to be more traditional cook it in a roasting pan and cut into squares
• SERVES 8–10

Scant cup all-purpose flour
2 organic eggs
1 cup whole milk
1 tablespoon butter, melted
beef dripping (see page 177) or
**   oil, for greasing pans**

Sift the flour into a bowl, make a well in the center and drop in the eggs. Using a small whisk or wooden spoon, stir continuously, gradually drawing in flour from the sides, adding half the milk in a steady stream at the same time. When all the flour has been mixed in, whisk in the remainder of the milk and the cooled melted butter. Allow to stand for 1 hour.

Preheat the oven to 450°F. Grease hot muffin pans with beef dripping or oil and fill halfway with the batter. Bake in a 450°F oven for about 20 minutes until crisp and golden.

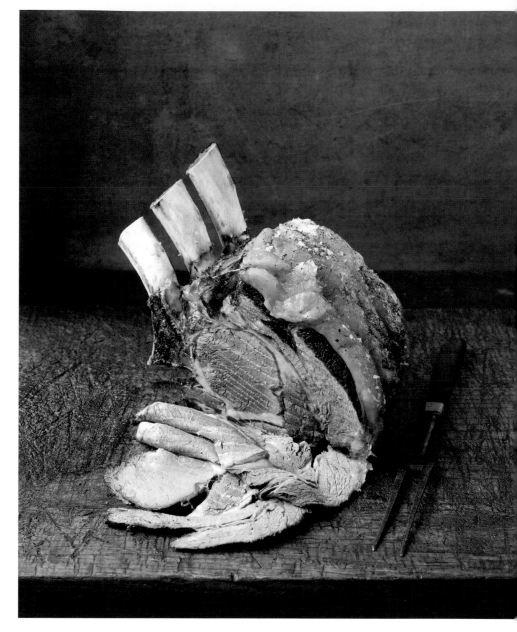

Above: *Traditional Roast Rib of Beef.*

ROAST FILLET OF BEEF

A whole fillet of beef is definitely a special treat, so it's really good to know how to cook it perfectly. If you're serving it hot, the classic combination for roast fillet of beef is a good Béarnaise sauce (see page 173). Or you could try Aioli (see page 96), Horseradish Sauce (see page 24), or I also love a combination of roast peppers and Anchoïade (see page 180). Finally, if you like something rich and creamy, it would be hard to beat Wild Mushrooms à la Crème (see page 50).

Remember to let rest for at least 15 minutes so that the juices can redistribute themselves evenly ·
SERVES 8-10

1 beef fillet (tenderloin) roast, preferably dry-aged, about 6lb
1 garlic clove
sea salt and freshly cracked pepper
pork caul fat (if available – see page 325)
extra virgin olive oil
sprigs of thyme

Preheat the oven to 450°F.

Trim away the chain if it is still attached. You can use the meat for Beef Stroganoff (see page 174). Double over the meat at the tapered end and tie the fillet securely with kitchen string. Alternatively, ask your butcher to do the "butchering" for you.

Rub the fillet all over with a cut clove of garlic and season it well with lots of freshly ground pepper. Wrap the fillet loosely in caul fat, if available, and season well with sea salt.

Alternatively, rub the fillet all over with the cut clove of garlic as before, season well on all sides with salt and freshly cracked pepper and drizzle with extra virgin olive oil. Heat a cast-iron ridged skillet to very hot. Sear the beef until it is nicely browned on all sides. Transfer it to a roasting pan and tuck a couple of sprigs of thyme underneath.

Roast for 25–30 minutes. If you have a meat thermometer, the internal temperature should read 140°F for rare. Alternatively, the meat should feel springy to the touch and the juice should turn to a pale pink when the meat is pierced with a skewer. Remove from the oven to a carving dish. Cover and let rest for 15–20 minutes by which time the juices will have redistributed themselves and the beef will be uniformly medium-rare.

Serve cut in ¼in slices and serve with one of the accompaniments suggested above.

STUFFED BEEF HEART

Many children nowadays can happily watch bloodcurdling scenes on TV, yet would scream with horror if one of my favorite childhood dishes, roast stuffed heart, was put on the table for dinner! This makes a substantial and delicious supper · **SERVES 6**

1 beef heart
salt and freshly ground pepper

FOR THE STUFFING
6 tablespoons butter
1 onion, finely chopped
1 tablespoon chopped chives
1 tablespoon chopped thyme leaves
1 tablespoon chopped marjoram
1 tablespoon chopped parsley
3 cups fresh bread crumbs
salt and freshly ground pepper
chopped parsley, for garnish

FOR THE GRAVY
2 cups Beef Stock (see page 159)
1 tablespoon Mushroom Ketchup (see page 56), optional
2 tablespoons Roux (see page 165)

Trim the heart, cutting away any sinews to make a nice pocket. Then wash the heart thoroughly in cold, salted water. Remove some of the inner tubes to make more room for stuffing and dry well.

Next make the stuffing by following the method in the Roast Chicken recipe on page 260. Let cool.

Preheat the oven to 350°F.

Season the inside of the heart with salt and pepper. Fill with the fresh herb stuffing, piling the extra on the top. Cover with buttered parchment paper and tie with kitchen string if necessary. Put into a deep roasting pan and add the beef stock. Season with salt and freshly ground pepper. Cover and cook for about 3–3½ hours, or until tender.

When the beef heart is fully cooked, transfer it carefully to a serving dish. Bring the cooking liquid to a boil, add a little mushroom ketchup, if available. Thicken with the roux and correct the seasoning. Strain into a sauceboat and serve with the sliced stuffed heart. Sprinkle with chopped parsley and serve.

Stock

Brown beef stock is used for beef and game stews, gravies, and sauces. The browning of the bones and vegetables enhances the flavor and color of the stock. You can use the recipe below to make a more concentrated stock by following the instructions for demi-glace or glace de viande.

BEEF STOCK

This stock will keep for two to three days in the refrigerator. If you want to keep it for longer, boil it for 10 minutes, and then chill it again. It can also be frozen · MAKES ABOUT 3 QUARTS

6lb beef bones or more if you have them, preferably with some scraps of meat on them, cut into small pieces
2 large onions, quartered
2 large carrots, quartered
2 celery ribs, cut into chunks
10 peppercorns
2 cloves
4 unpeeled garlic cloves
1 teaspoon tomato paste
large bouquet garni, including parsley stalks, bay leaf, sprigs of thyme, and a sprig of tarragon

Preheat the oven to 450°F.

Put the bones into a roasting pan and roast for 30 minutes, until nicely browned. Add the onions, carrots, and celery and return to the oven until the vegetables are colored at the edges. Transfer the bones and vegetables to a stockpot. Add the peppercorns, cloves, garlic, tomato paste, and bouquet garni.

Degrease the roasting pan and deglaze with about 1 cup of water. Bring to a boil and then pour over the bones and vegetables in the stockpot. Add enough additional water to cover the bones, about 4 quarts. Bring slowly to a boil. Skim the stock and simmer gently for 5–6 hours, adding more water if necessary. Strain the stock, let cool and skim off all the fat before use.

Variations

DEMI-GLACE
For a more concentrated stock, return the skimmed stock to a saucepan and boil, uncovered, until reduced by half. It will keep for 3–4 days in a fridge or freeze until needed.

GLACE DE VIANDE
Reduce the demi-glace in an uncovered saucepan until it becomes almost syrupy. Pour into a heatproof container and let cool. It will set to a firm jelly with a rich, concentrated flavor. Cover and chill. Cut into cubes as needed and use to enrich sauces, stews, casseroles, and gravy. It will keep for several weeks months in an airtight container in the fridge.

Caramel for gravy
This is how to make your own caramel coloring, which some people like to add to gravy to give it a darker color and a little extra sweetness. Add by the teaspoon to taste. Put ¾ cup of sugar into a heavy saucepan over medium heat. Stir until it begins to melt; continue to stir with a wooden spoon until it caramelizes to a dark chestnut color. When it begins to smoke, add 1 cup of water and let the sugar dissolve. Pour into a bottle and use to color gravy.

How to tell when stock is safe
It's easy to tell when stock has really gone bad, but if you are wary, smell it. You might get a slightly suspect odor. If you're still in doubt, have a taste. Most people's palate will detect a sour taste. If you're still suspicious, put it on to heat. Very often, the smell becomes much more pronounced. But it also becomes slightly foamy on top, and that's a sure sign it's bad. In the summer, we reckon stock will keep 2–3 days in the fridge; in the winter, 4–5 days. So if you don't intend to use stock quite soon, just freeze it. If you think you're going to use it and decide against it, but the stock has been in the fridge for a couple of days, boil it for a few minutes, let it cool again and then refrigerate or freeze it –that should kill off any bacteria.

Taste, taste, taste. It hones your palate and develops your taste memory and gives you a better base for comparison.

BEEF CONSOMMÉ

Consommé is a clear, well-flavored broth that can be made from meat, poultry, game, or vegetables. Even for many trained chefs, it's often a forgotten skill and a real accomplishment when successful. It needs to be made with care and attention. It is the pure essence of beef – simple, elegant, and nourishing. In Ballymaloe we buy an aged beef shin from our butcher. We use the bones to make a rich beef stock and then use the meat to flavor the consommé. For strength of flavor in this, the meat really needs to be aged. Fresh meat will not give you the depth of flavor you need for a good consommé.

The garnish that's served with consommé gives it its specific name. For consommé julienne we serve it with a julienne of vegetables, carrot, leek, and celery, cooked for a few minutes in boiling, salted water, then refreshed · SERVES 4

12oz boneless beef shin, finely chopped and surface fat trimmed
1 small carrot, very finely chopped
green tops of 2 leeks, finely chopped
2 celery ribs, very finely chopped
2 ripe tomatoes, quartered and seeded
3 organic egg whites
1½ quarts well-flavored Beef Stock (see page 159), chilled
salt and freshly ground pepper
1 or more tablespoons medium or dry sherry (optional)

FOR THE JULIENNE GARNISH
small carrot, stalk celery, small white turnip, white part of 1 small leek
½ cup boiling, salted water

Mix the chopped beef, carrots, leeks, celery, tomatoes, and egg whites in a bowl. Pour on the cold stock, whisk well and season. Pour into a deep, stainless-steel saucepan. Bring slowly to a boil on low heat, whisking constantly. This should take about 10 minutes.

As soon as the mixture looks cloudy and slightly milky, stop whisking. Allow the filter of egg whites to rise slowly to the top of the saucepan. DO NOT STIR the consommé; just leave it to simmer gently for 45 minutes–1 hour to extract all the flavor from the beef and vegetables.

Line a wire sieve with rinsed cheesecloth and gently ladle the consommé into it. Do not press the sediment in the sieve or the consommé will not be sparkling clear. Strain it through the cloth a second time if necessary. Add sherry if desired.

To make the garnish, cut the vegetables into very thin julienne strips. Simmer in boiling salted water for about 6 minutes or until tender. Drain and rinse under cold water.

Put the vegetables into a warmed soup tureen or individual soup bowls and pour in the consommé. Do not cook the garnish in the consommé or allow it to boil, as it will become cloudy.

Variation

CONSOMMÉ EN GELÉE
This cool, refreshing starter is perfect for a summer meal. When the consommé is served cold it should be lightly jellied. So chill the consommé well and just before serving, spoon into chilled bowls. Garnish with a chervil sprig and serve with freshly made Melba toast.

BEEF TEA

Beef tea is full of goodness and was often made to help restore people to full strength after a bout of illness.

1lb beef shin, preferably organic
sea salt

Remove every scrap of fat from the meat and cut it into tiny cubes so as much flavor can be released as possible. Put into a deep, earthenware pot and cover with 2 cups of water; then set the pot in a water bath. Put on the lowest heat possible and let to cook gently for 5–6 hours. Add a little salt halfway through. Strain through a wire sieve lined with rinsed cheesecloth and let cool. Skim off any fat before serving. Serve as a hot drink.

Right: *Beef Tea – the ultimate tonic.*

Stewing and Braising

Anybody can slap a steak on a pan, but at times when money is scarce, the forgotten skill is taking a piece of beef shin or short ribs and making something completely delicious from it. Cuts of meat that have the most exercise (chuck, shins, rump) are the toughest and need slow, gentle cooking, whereas the cuts that get less exercise (sirloin and fillet) are more tender and can be roasted, grilled, or fried.

The toughest parts of beef are actually the most flavorful – you just have to coax that flavor out with time over a low heat, while stewing, braising, or otherwise slow cooking.

Long, gentle simmering tenderizes the muscular and gelatinous cuts which have had most exercise in the animal. Stewing gives you the opportunity to add other vegetables to "spin it out"; stewing and braising are low-maintenance ways of cooking that allow you to do other things. They also involve fewer pots. Stewing is a similar cooking method to braising, but for stews the meat is cut into smaller pieces.

BEEF SHIN AND OXTAIL STEW

Another humble dish, which has recently been resurrected by trendy chefs capitalizing on their customers' nostalgic craving for Granny's cooking. Oxtail, or the tail of a beef animal, makes an extraordinarily rich and flavorsome winter soup or stew. If you prefer, you can cover and cook this very gently on top of the stove rather than in an oven · SERVES 8

6oz slab bacon, rindless
1lb boneless beef chuck
2½lb oxtails, cut into 1½–2in pieces
2 tablespoons beef dripping or olive oil
1 onion, finely chopped
4 carrots, cut into ¾in cubes
½ celery rib, chopped
½ cup red wine and 1½ cups Beef Stock (see page 159) OR 2 cups all Beef Stock
1 bay leaf, 1 sprig of thyme, and parsley stalks
1 tablespoon tomato paste
salt and freshly ground pepper
6oz mushrooms, sliced
2 tablespoons butter
1 tablespoon Roux (see page 165)
2 tablespoons chopped parsley

Preheat the oven to 325°F.

Cut the bacon into 1in cubes and cut the beef into 1⅓in cubes. Heat the drippings or olive oil in a frying pan, add the bacon and sauté for 1–2 minutes, then add the onions, carrots, and celery and cook for 2–3 minutes, stirring occasionally. Transfer the bacon and vegetables into a flameproof casserole. Now add the beef and oxtail pieces to the frying pan, a few at a time and continue to cook. When the meat begins to brown, add it to the casserole. Then add the wine and ½ cup of the beef stock to the frying pan. Bring to the boil and use a whisk to dissolve the caramelized meat juices from the pan. Add to the casserole with the herbs, the rest of the stock, and the tomato paste. Season with salt and freshly ground pepper. Cover and transfer to the oven. Cook very gently for 3–4 hours, or until the oxtail is falling off the bones and the vegetables are very tender.

Meanwhile, cook the sliced mushrooms in a hot frying pan in the butter for 2–3 minutes and season with salt and freshly ground pepper. Stir into the oxtail stew and cook for about 5 minutes. Strain the liquid from the meat and vegetables, and keep them warm in a hot serving dish while you thicken the broth. Remove and discard the bay leaves, thyme, and parsley stalks. Bring the cooking liquid back to a boil, whisk in the roux and cook until slightly thickened. Add back in the meat and vegetables. Add the chopped parsley and bring to a boil. Taste and correct the seasoning. Serve in the hot serving dish with lots of Champ (see page 383) or Colcannon (see page 384).

LEFTOVER OXTAIL STEW
The end of leftover oxtail stew, shortribs and other gutsy beef, pork, and lamb stews where the meat has disintegrated into small pieces or shreds is still full of flavor. Don't waste it! It makes a delicious sauce for pasta – particularly with fettucine. I once enjoyed the cold remains of an oxtail stew on hot buttered toast for breakfast – it was memorably delicious.

OXTAIL WITH GRAINY MUSTARD SAUCE

Another great recipe for oxtail; a wonderful, inexpensive forgotten cut that's really worth experimenting with. Serve with lots of fluffy mashed potatoes · **SERVES 4–6**

1¼lb oxtail

about 4 tablespoons extra virgin olive oil

6 onions, peeled and quartered

3 bay leaves

½ **cup Beef Stock (see page 159)**

1 cup heavy cream

1 tablespoon Roux (see page 165)

1 tablespoon Dijon mustard

1 tablespoon grainy mustard

flat parsley sprigs, for garnish

Divide the oxtail into sections, following its natural divisions and season it with salt and freshly ground pepper.

Heat the olive oil in a frying pan. Brown the oxtail on all sides, turning with tongs until it's evenly colored, then transfer to a flameproof casserole. Add the quartered onions to the frying pan and toss in the fat until they begin to color. Add to the oxtail with the bay leaves.

Degrease the frying pan by adding the beef stock and whisking to dissolve the meat juices. Add to the casserole, cover and simmer gently for 2–2½ hours. When the meat is meltingly tender and almost falling off the bones, remove it to a warm serving dish.

Degrease the liquid from the casserole and add the cream. Bring back to a boil, whisk in a little roux to thicken slightly, then add the oxtail and the mustards. Bubble for 1–2 minutes, taste and correct the seasoning. Transfer to an earthenware dish and scatter with lots of flat parsley sprigs and serve with fluffy mashed potatoes.

WINTER BEEF STEW

We make many beef stews, but this is by far the bestseller at the Midleton Farmers' Market, where we have a stall every Saturday morning. We use our own aged organic beef from the farm, but this is an ideal recipe for using the cheaper, forgotten cuts of meat, anything from shin of beef to flank. The red wine helps to tenderize the meat and add extra flavor. The end of a bottle of wine is fine to add, but it does have to be drinkable stuff, not vinegar. Like many other stews, this is even better on the following day, and freezes perfectly · **SERVES 8–10**

4lb boneless beef chuck, round or shin

3 tablespoons extra virgin olive oil

1lb onions, sliced

4 medium carrots, cut into ½**in slices**

2 tablespoons all-purpose flour

¾ **cup gutsy, full-bodied red wine**

¾ **cup Beef Stock (see page 159)**

1 cup Tomato Paste (see page 376), or best-quality canned tomatoes, puréed and sieved

salt and freshly ground pepper

8oz shiitake mushroom caps, sliced

2 tablespoons butter

3 tablespoons coarsely chopped parsley

Preheat the oven to 325°F.

Trim the beef of any excess fat and discard. Cut the meat into 1½in cubes. Heat half the olive oil in a flameproof casserole and sweat the sliced onions and carrots on low heat covered for 10 minutes. Heat the rest of the olive oil in a frying pan until it is almost smoking. Sear the pieces of meat on all sides. Reduce the heat, stir in the flour and cook for 1 minute.

Mix the red wine, beef stock, and tomato paste together and add the mixture gradually to the casserole, stirring all the time. Season with salt and freshly ground pepper. Cover and cook gently in the oven for 2½–3 hours.

Meanwhile, sauté the mushrooms in the butter in a hot frying pan, season each batch with salt and freshly ground pepper and add them to the casserole about 30 minutes before the end of cooking. Just before removing the casserole from the oven, add the chopped parsley and let it bubble for a minute or two. Taste and correct the seasoning if necessary. Serve with mashed potatoes and a green salad.

MARROW BONES WITH FRESH HERB SALAD

The raw marrow can be scooped out and added to stews, hamburgers, and risottos for flavor and embellishment. You'll need one or two marrow bones per person, depending on size.

Ask your butcher to saw the marrow bones (leg bones) into manageable size pieces, about 4in long. Poach the marrow: simply put the bones in a saucepan and cover with cold water, add a little salt, bring to a boil and then simmer for 8–10 minutes until the marrow slips out easily.

Serve the marrow bones with a little fresh herb salad of flat parsley, chervil, and tiny sprigs of tarragon, watercress, arugula, chives, and wild garlic flowers if in season.

AMERICAN BRAISED SHORT RIBS

Beef short ribs are about 3–4in strips of a cross section of rib bones and the meat that links them together. Originally an American cut, they are gaining favor all over the world. This cut cooks out to melting tenderness when slow-cooked, which is why we've chosen braising as the method of cooking and the high percentage of bone adds lots of extra flavor. If at all possible, make this the day before serving – the flavor will be even better and it'll be much easier to remove every scrap of fat when it has solidified on top · **SERVES 6**

Opposite: *Marrow Bones with Fresh Herb Salad.*

6 beef short ribs, trimmed
salt
8oz slab bacon, rind removed
1 tablespoon olive oil
2 carrots, diced
2 celery ribs, diced
8 garlic cloves, cut in half
1 red hot chile, sliced
1 red bell pepper, diced
1 yellow bell pepper, diced
3 large onions, 1 sliced – the other
**   2 chopped**
1 tablespoon tomato paste
¾ cup red wine
1 sprig of rosemary
2 bay leaves
small fistful thyme sprigs
1 cinnamon stick
3 long strips of orange zest
Beef Stock (see page 159) or
**   Chicken Stock (see page 262) to**
**   come halfway up the pot**
Roux (see below), optional

If possible, trim and sprinkle the beef with salt the night before cooking.

Preheat the oven to 300°F. Remove the rind and dice the bacon. Save the rind to cook with the beef as it adds gelatin which gives the sauce extra body. Heat a little oil in a wide frying pan and brown the diced bacon. Transfer to a plate.

Brown the beef in batches (do not overcrowd the pan). Leave 2 tablespoons of fat in pan and use it to sweat the onions, carrots, and celery, stirring to dissolve all the browned bits in the sauté pan. Add the garlic, chile, and peppers, and sweat for 5–6 minutes or until limp.

Place the beef, bacon, and vegetables in a casserole or heavy

braising pot, preferably enamelled cast iron.

Add the tomato paste to the hot frying pan and cook briefly. Add the wine and bring to boil. Pour the over the beef and add the herbs, cinnamon stick, and orange zest. Add enough stock to come halfway up the pot. Cover with buttered parchment paper and a tight-fitting lid and transfer to the oven. Braise until tender, about 3 hours – the meat should be tender and almost falling off the bones.

Remove bay leaves, stalks and stems of the other herbs, and the orange peel and cinnamon stick. Refrigerate overnight. The next day, skim off the solidified fat and discard. Bring back to a boil, add more stock if needed and thicken with the roux if desired. Taste and correct the seasoning.

ROUX

Roux can be stored in a cool place and used as required or it can be made up on the spot if preferred to thicken up a sauce.

8 tablespoons butter
scant cup all-purpose flour

Melt the butter in a pan and cook the flour in it for 2 minutes on low heat, stirring occasionally. It will keep for two weeks in the refrigerator.

BEEF CHEEKS WITH MUSTARD FRUITS

Beef cheeks are a super cut to know about – you'll need to order them ahead from your butcher. They are absolutely packed with meaty flavor, and the mustard fruits perk up the whole thing · SERVES 4 –6

3 tablespoons extra virgin olive oil
2¼lb beef cheeks
4oz rindless slab bacon, cut into lardons
8 onions, chopped
2 carrots, chopped
2 celery ribs, chopped
8 garlic cloves, peeled
6 very ripe tomatoes, peeled and chopped
salt, freshly ground black pepper, and a sprinkle of sugar
1¼ quarts Beef Stock (see page 159)
2 cups full-bodied red wine
¾ cup balsamic vinegar
2 sprigs of rosemary
4 sprigs of thyme
2 bay leaves
4 tablespoons chopped parsley

TO SERVE
mashed potatoes
Mustard Fruits (see page 429)

Preheat the oven to 325°F.

Heat the olive oil in a heavy frying pan. Add the beef cheeks and brown on all sides, then transfer to a heavy casserole. Add the bacon, cook until the fat runs, add to the beef. Toss the onions, carrots, celery, and garlic in the fats left in the frying pan. Cook until they just start to brown. Transfer to the casserole.

Add the tomatoes. Season well with salt, freshly ground pepper, and sugar.

Deglaze the pan with the stock and a bit of the wine, bring to a boil and add to the casserole with the remainder of the wine and the vinegar. Add the herbs and stir well. Bring to a boil, cover and cook in the oven for about 3 hours or until the beef cheeks are falling apart. Strain off the liquid and transfer into a saucepan. Boil over high heat and reduce by about half. Taste and correct the seasoning. Pour the reduced cooking liquid over the beef cheeks and add the parsley. Serve with mashed potatoes and mustard fruits.

BEEF CHEEKS WITH PARSNIP CHAMP

Here is another good recipe for this forgotten cut. It makes a wonderful, gutsy winter stew and is particularly delicious with the parsnip champ · SERVES 8

4 tablespoons olive oil
4oz slab bacon, rind removed, cut into lardons
4lb 8oz beef cheeks, well trimmed
½ cup all-purpose flour, well seasoned with salt, freshly ground pepper, and ½ teaspoon or more smoked paprika
2 onions, sliced
8 large carrots, cut into large chunks
2 cups gutsy red wine
1½ cups Beef Stock (see page 159)
4 large garlic cloves
1 bay leaf
couple of thyme sprigs
lots of flat parsley

ACCOMPANIMENT
Parsnip Champ (follow the recipe for Champ on page 383 but replace half the quantity of potatoes with parsnips)

Preheat the oven to 300°F.

Heat the olive oil in a frying pan and cook the bacon until the fat runs. Transfer the lardons to a casserole. Dip the beef cheeks in well-seasoned flour. Sear the beef cheeks in the oil and bacon fat until they are nicely browned on both sides. Add them to the bacon in the casserole. Then add the onions to the frying pan. Cook and stir until they begin to brown. Add them and the carrot chunks to the casserole.

Deglaze the frying pan with the red wine, bring to a boil and stir to dislodge the caramelized meat and vegetable juices. Pour over the other ingredients in the casserole, add the stock, garlic cloves, a bay leaf, and the thyme sprigs. Bring the casserole to a boil, cover and transfer to the oven. Cook for 2½–3 hours, until the meat is meltingly tender.

Taste and correct the seasoning and scatter with flat parsley. Serve with parsnip champ and a freshly cooked green vegetable.

SCALLOPED POTATO WITH STEAK AND KIDNEY

This is an economical and enormously comforting dish. We used to ask my mother to make it when we came home from college on winter weekends. You can do lots of variations on the theme; bacon is particularly good and shoulder of lamb would also be delicious ·
SERVES 4-6

1 beef kidney, about 1lb
salt and freshly ground pepper
1lb boneless beef chuck or round
3lb baking potatoes – Russets
    or Burbanks, peeled
    and thickly sliced
1 large onion, chopped
4 tablespoons butter, or more
1⅓ cups Beef Stock (see page 159)
    or hot water

GARNISH
freshly chopped parsley

large, oval casserole, 10-cup
    capacity

Preheat the oven to 300°F.

    Remove the skin and white core from the kidney and discard. Cut the flesh of the kidneys into ½in cubes, put them into a bowl, cover with cold water, and sprinkle with a good pinch of salt. Cut the beef into ¼in cubes. Put a layer of potato slices at the base of the casserole. Drain the kidney cubes and mix them with the beef cubes, then scatter some of the meat and chopped onions over the layer of potato.

    Season well with salt and freshly

Above: *Scalloped Potato with Steak and Kidney.*

ground pepper, dot with butter, add another layer of potato, more meat, onions, and seasoning, and continue right up to the top of the casserole. Finish with an overlapping layer of potato. Pour in the hot stock or water. Bring to a boil, cover and transfer to the oven, and cook for 2–2½ hours or until the meat and potatoes are cooked. Remove the lid

of the saucepan about 15 minutes from end of the cooking time to brown the top slightly.

    Sprinkle with chopped parsley and serve in deep plates with lots of butter.

JULIJA'S LITHUANIAN BEEF GOULASH

One day when I was madly busy at the Cookery School, I asked Julija Makejeva, who'd recently arrived from Lithuania with little English, if she could cook. She looked at me as though she hadn't understood the question. So I asked her again and she said, "Of course I cook. Everyone cook."

Afterwards I realized it seemed to her to be the most ridiculous question. She learned how to cook this goulash from her mother, and now I pass it on to you · **SERVES 8**

2½lb boneless beef chuck or round, cut into 1in cubes
3 garlic cloves, crushed
1 tablespoon paprika
¼–½ teaspoon cayenne pepper (depending on how hot you like it)
salt and freshly ground pepper
4 tablespoons sunflower oil
1 onion, sliced
1lb carrots, cut into ½in cubes
⅓ cup all-purpose flour
3 cups Beef Stock (see page 159)

Preheat the oven to 325°F.

Put the cubes of beef in a bowl and add the garlic, paprika, cayenne, and salt and pepper. Mix well and let stand while you prepare the other ingredients.

Heat 1 tablespoon of sunflower oil in a frying pan over medium heat and add the onions and carrots. Fry for a few minutes until slightly soft and beginning to color. Remove from the pan and transfer to a casserole.

Increase the heat under the pan, add more oil and brown the beef in batches. When brown on all sides, transfer the meat to the casserole.

Put the casserole on medium heat, add the flour and cook for 1 minute. Deglaze the frying pan with the stock. Gradually add it to the casserole and bring to a simmer. Transfer to the oven and bake for 2–2½ hours or until the meat is tender. Serve with boiled potatoes or plain, boiled rice.

STEAK AND OYSTER PIE

It may sound new and adventurous, but this is an old recipe dating back to the time when oysters were so cheap they were added to beef stew to spin out the beef. The combination is really delicious. The filling for this pie is perfectly delicious eaten as a stew; just omit the pastry · **SERVES 8**

2lb boneless beef chuck or round
salt and freshly ground pepper
4 tablespoons butter
1 tablespoon olive oil
2 onions, coarsely chopped
2 tablespoons all-purpose flour
2⅓ cups Beef Stock (see page 159)
10oz mushrooms, sliced
16 large oysters
Roux (see page 165), if necessary
12oz Puff Pastry or Billy's Cream Pastry (see pages 218 and 209)
egg wash (see page 539)

Preheat the oven to 325°F.

Cut the beef into 1½in cubes and season. Heat half the butter with the oil in a frying pan and sear the meat over high heat. (When you add a little oil to butter, it raises the smoke point so you can fry things at higher temperatures.) Do this in batches, because if the pan is overcrowded, the meat will stew rather than sear. Transfer the meat to a plate, add the onions to the pan and cook for 5–6 minutes, stirring occasionally. Add the flour, stir and cook for 1 minute. Blend in the stock, add the meat and bring to a boil. Transfer to a casserole, cover and bake for 1½–2 hours.

Meanwhile, sauté the mushrooms over high heat in the rest of the butter, season, and keep aside. Open the oysters (see page 118) and put in a bowl with their juices.

When the beef is tender, thicken the meat juices in the casserole slightly with roux (if necessary). Add the mushrooms, oysters, and the oyster juice to the casserole. Bring back to a boil for 2–3 minutes and taste for seasoning. Let cool.

Increase the oven temperature to 475°F. Put the entire mixture into a deep pie dish and cover the top with pastry (see next page). Then brush with egg wash and cook in the oven for 10 minutes (this quick burst of heat rises the pastry). Then reduce the oven to 350°F and cook for another 15–20 minutes, or until the pastry is puffed and golden.

Opposite: *Steak and Oyster Pie.*

HOW TO COVER A POT PIE WITH PASTRY

Put the filling into a dish. Roll out the pastry into a sheet just less than ¼in thick, cut several strips to fit onto the rim of the pie dish. Brush the rim with cold water and press the strips of pastry firmly onto the dish. Brush the pastry strips with cold water and then press the lid of pastry firmly down around the edges. Trim off the excess pastry. Flute the edges and scallop with the back of a knife. Cut some pastry leaves from the excess pastry, egg wash the pie and decorate it with the pastry leaves. Make a little air hole in the center, egg wash again and bake.

STEAK AND KIDNEY PIE

Like oxtail, beef kidney is brilliant value for money and you get so much flavor in comparison to some other, much more expensive cuts. Growing up, a favorite winter food for me was this pie. As children, we literally fought over the bits of kidney and would count the bits of kidney on our plate. I feel so sorry that so many people's minds are closed to even tasting beef kidney – it's their loss. For this recipe, the stewing beef needs to be aged while the kidneys must be fresh. This filling may be kept overnight before being used (in fact, the flavor improves)

· SERVES 6–8

1 beef kidney, about 1lb
pinch of salt
2lb boneless beef chuck or round
1 large onion
1 large carrot
2 tablespoons butter
2 tablespoons all-purpose flour, seasoned
2 cups Beef Stock (see page 159)
bouquet garni
8oz mushrooms
2 tablespoons Roux (see page 165), optional
8oz Puff Pastry or Billy's Cream Pastry (see pages 218 and 209)

Preheat oven to 300°F.

Peel the kidney, cut out the core and cut the kidney into about ¾in chunks. Cover with cold water and a pinch of salt while you prepare the other ingredients. Cut the beef into 1in pieces. Slice the onion and carrot into ½in slices. Melt half the butter in a frying pan and lightly brown the onions, add in the carrots and transfer to a casserole.

Drain the water off the kidney. Rinse again and dry well. Increase the heat under the frying pan. Toss the meat and dried kidney pieces in seasoned flour and cook in batches in the pan until lightly brown on all sides. Add to the casserole. Next, pour the stock into the frying pan, bring it to a boil and scrape the pan to dissolve the bits of sediment and caramelized juices. Pour this over the meat and add the bouquet garni.

Cover with the lid, bring to a boil and simmer in the oven for 1¼–1½ hours.

Slice the mushrooms thinly and sauté them in the remainder of the butter in a hot frying pan. Add them to the casserole about 20 minutes before the end of cooking. When the meat is cooked, taste the cooking liquid. If it is a little weak, strain it off into another saucepan and reduce it to concentrate the flavor, or if it is too thin whisk in enough roux to thicken to a light coating consistency (remember, the liquid must be boiling when the roux is added otherwise it won't thicken). Taste and correct the seasoning. Pour back over the meat.

To make the pie
Preheat the oven to 450°F.

Cover the pie, following the instructions on the left. Bake for 10–15 minutes. Then reduce the heat to 400°F and continue to bake until the pastry is cooked through and the filling is bubbling. Garnish with a sprig of parsley and serve.

Variation
Colcannon, champ (see pages 383 and 384) or parsnip purée also make a complementary topping for this pie. Or if you prefer, leave the topping out of the equation altogether for a delicious stew.

Ground Beef

Like shepherd's pie, cottage pie was traditionally made from leftover scraps of meat from the Sunday roast – definitely a forgotten and longed-for flavor. In addition, every thrifty cook should have a couple of recipes for freshly ground meat in their repertoire – homemade burgers and meatballs are always family favorites.

COTTAGE PIE WITH GARLIC BUTTER

The cheese in this crust and the lump of garlic butter that melts into the center makes this into something very special. The Worcestershire sauce is also a great help. I have no shares in the company, but ensure you always have a bottle in your cupboard as it gives a welcome lift to many otherwise pedestrian dishes · **SERVES 6**

3 tablespoons olive oil
2 garlic cloves, mashed
1 small onion, chopped
1lb beef, freshly ground
1 teaspoon fresh thyme leaves
½ cup dry white or red wine
1 cup Beef Stock (see page 150)
1 teaspoon Worcestershire sauce
1 tablespoon tomato paste
Roux (see page 165)
salt and freshly ground pepper

FOR THE TOPPING
3lb baking potatoes, unpeeled
1 cup whole milk, boiling
salt and freshly ground pepper
2 tablespoons butter
1 tablespoon chopped chives
 (optional)

¼ cup grated Parmigiano Reggiano cheese
¼ cup grated Cheddar cheese

TO SERVE
Garlic Butter (see page 217)
green salad

Heat the oil in a saucepan. Add the garlic and onion and fry until soft and slightly brown. Increase the heat, add the ground beef and thyme and fry until the beef changes color. Add the wine, half the stock, the Worcestershire sauce, and the tomato paste. Simmer for 10 minutes.

Meanwhile, boil the unpeeled potatoes, then peel them. Add boiling milk and mash the potatoes while they are still hot. Season with salt and freshly ground pepper and add the butter and the chives, if using.

Preheat the oven to 350°F.

Bring the rest of the stock to a boil and thicken it well with roux. Stir it into the beef – it should be thick but still juicy. Taste and correct the seasoning.

Put the meat mixture into one large or six individual pie dishes. Pipe or spread the mashed potato mixture over the top. Sprinkle with the grated cheeses. Bake for 30 minutes, until the top is golden and slightly crispy. Serve with garlic butter and a green salad.

BASIC BEEF BURGERS

The secret of really good hamburgers is the quality of the beef. It does not need to be an expensive cut of meat, but it is essential to use the beef on the day it is ground. A small percentage of fat in the beef will make the hamburgers sweet and juicy. Here we add some more flavors to the burgers for extra deliciousness · **SERVES 4–6**

1 tablespoon butter
½ onion, chopped
1lb freshly ground beef – round or chuck would be perfect
½ teaspoon fresh thyme leaves
½ teaspoon finely chopped parsley
1 small organic egg, beaten
salt and freshly ground pepper
pork caul fat, optional
olive oil

hamburger buns

Melt the butter in a saucepan. Toss in the chopped onions and sweat them until soft but not colored. Let the onions cool. Meanwhile, mix the ground beef with the herbs and beaten egg, season with salt and freshly ground pepper, add the onions and mix well. Fry a tiny bit on the pan to check the seasoning, and correct it if necessary. Then shape the mixture into hamburgers, 4–6 depending on the size you require. Wrap each one loosely in caul fat, if using, which will baste the meat and melt away in the cooking. Cook to your taste on a medium-hot pan or grill pan in a little oil, turning once.

MEATBALLS WITH FRESH TOMATO SAUCE

Meatballs are a favorite family meal loved by everyone from tiny tots to greedy grandmas. Besides serving with spaghetti, you could just serve this with crusty bread or a green salad

· **SERVES 6**

FOR THE MEATBALLS

2 tablespoons extra virgin olive oil
1 onion, finely chopped
1 garlic clove, crushed
2lb freshly ground round beef
2 tablespoons or more of chopped
    fresh herbs, such as marjoram,
    or a mixture of parsley, chives,
    and thyme leaves
1 organic egg, beaten
salt and freshly ground black
    pepper

FOR THE TOMATO SAUCE

3 tablespoons extra virgin olive oil
1 onion, sliced
1 garlic clove, crushed
2lb ripe, peeled and chopped
    tomatoes, or 1 x 28oz can
    chopped tomatoes
salt, freshly ground black pepper,
    and sugar
basil leaves

TO SERVE

3 tablespoons extra virgin olive oil
1lb spaghetti
1 cup (4oz) each grated Cheddar
    and Parmesan cheese
flat parsley sprigs, for garnish

First make the meatballs. Heat the olive oil in a heavy, stainless-steel saucepan over a gentle heat and add the chopped onions and garlic.

Cover and cook for 8–10 minutes until soft and slightly golden. Let cool.

Put the ground beef into a bowl. Add the cooled onion and garlic, the herbs, and the beaten egg. Season the mixture to taste by frying a tiny bit to check the seasoning and adjusting if necessary. Divide the mixture into about 24 round meatballs. Cover and refrigerate.

Meanwhile, make the tomato sauce. Heat the oil in a casserole or a stainless-steel saucepan. Add the sliced onions and crushed garlic and toss until coated. Cover and cook over low heat until soft. Add the tomatoes, mix and season with salt, freshly ground pepper, and a pinch of sugar (canned tomatoes take more sweetening). Cover and simmer for 15 minutes, uncover, add the basil and continue to cook for 15–20 minutes or until thick and unctuous.

Preheat the oven to 350°F.

Heat a frying pan over medium heat and add 3 tablespoons of extra virgin olive oil. Cook the meatballs for 8–10 minutes, turning from time to time. When they are cooked, transfer them to an ovenproof serving dish. Add the hot tomato sauce and turn the meatballs gently to cover. Pop into the oven and bake for 15 minutes.

Meanwhile, cook the spaghetti in a large pot of boiling salted water. Drain and transfer to a hot serving dish. Spoon the meatballs and tomato sauce over the top, sprinkle with grated Cheddar and Parmesan cheese and lots of flat parsley sprigs.

How to Cut Your Own Steaks

It is very easy and relatively cheap to cut your own steaks provided you know what to do with all the parts. A 7lb whole loin with a good amount of fillet should yield you about four strip steaks weighing about 6oz each and three fillet steaks of the same weight or four or five tournedos steaks weighing about 4oz each. In addition to these, there will be over 1lb of bones for the stockpot, 1¾lb of trimmings, and over 1lb of beef suet for suet crust pastry, suet pudding, or dripping. A 7lb piece further down the loin with less tenderloin will give you more strip steaks and the fillets will be much smaller.

Chain
Start by cutting off the chain, which is the thin piece of boneless meat below the "eye" of the tenderloin. This cut should be hung for 7–10 days and then roasted, stewed, corned, spiced, or ground for hamburgers.

Strip loin steaks
With the fat side uppermost, insert the knife in between the top of the meat and the bone. Cut downward, pressing the knife against the bone. You will be able to feel your way between flesh and bone and gradually you will be able to turn the knife sideways and cut the piece off the bone horizontally. It is like cutting the meat off an enormous chop. Divide the top piece into four or more steaks according to the size of your piece.

Right: *From left to right: T-bone, sirloin, minute fillet, and medallions.*

This entire piece is called top loin and may be roasted whole or cut into strip (or shell) steaks. This tender cut is rectangular in shape and about 6in long, with a strip of fat alongside. We cut strip steaks about 1¼in thick.

Thinner slices cut from the strip loin are called minute steaks. They are about ⅓in thick and are so called because they only take a minute to cook on each side on a very hot grill pan.

Fillet and tournedos

Now turn the meat the other way up and cut off the fillet in exactly the same way. There is a good deal of suet around the fillet that will peel off easily. Trim the fillet of all fat and membrane. It may be roasted whole (see Roast Fillet recipe, page 158) or cut into fillet steaks to the thickness of your choice or into ¼in thick slices called medallions.

Fillet steak is roughly round in shape and absolutely lean, except for a little marbling in the tender but less flavorsome flesh.

Beef ribs

You are now left with three or four T-shaped bones. Take the piece of bone and then cut between the ribs, at the natural divisions – they will just pull apart; use for Beef Stock (see page 159) or give to your dogs.

How to know when your steak is cooked

Press with tongs while cooking. Raw or rare meat feels very springy to the touch – it gets gradually firmer as it cooks and is very firm when well done. The juices of rare meats are blood red and get gradually paler as the meat cooks more. The juice of well-done meat will be clear.

PAN-GRILLED STEAK WITH BÉARNAISE SAUCE AND FRITES

Strip loin is more textural than fillet, with lots of flavor, but you can use either here.

Of all the sauces to serve with steak, Béarnaise sauce is the classic combination and my absolute favorite. We find a heavy-ridged cast-iron grill pan best for cooking steaks when you don't need to make a sauce in the pan. If the weight of these steaks sounds small by your standards, the portion size can be increased and the cooking times adjusted accordingly ·

SERVES 6

6 x 6oz strip or fillet steaks
1 garlic clove
salt and freshly ground pepper
a little olive oil

To Serve
Béarnaise Sauce (see page 173)
Hand-cut Potato Fries (see page 386)
fresh watercress (optional)

To prepare the steaks, about 1 hour before cooking cut a clove of garlic in half and rub it on both sides of each steak. This simple step intensifies the beefy flavor. Then grind some black pepper over the steaks and sprinkle on a few drops of olive oil. Turn the steaks in the oil and set aside. If using strip steaks, score the fat at 1in intervals.

Make the Béarnaise sauce and keep it warm. Heat the grill pan, season the steaks with a little salt and put them down onto the hot pan.

The cooking times for each side of the steaks are roughly as follows:

	Sirloin	**Fillet**
RARE	2 mins	5 mins
MEDIUM-RARE	3 mins	6 mins
MEDIUM	4 mins	7 mins
WELL-DONE	5 mins	8–9 mins

When cooking a sirloin steak, be sure to cook the fatty edge too so it can crisp up nicely. Put the steaks onto an upturned plate resting on another plate and leave them for a few minutes in a warm place while you make the frites.

Transfer the steaks onto hot plates. Serve with Béarnaise sauce and a pile of crispy frites.

BÉARNAISE SAUCE

The consistency of Béarnaise sauce should be considerably thicker than that of Hollandaise or beurre blanc, both of which ought to be a light coating consistency. If you do not have tarragon vinegar to hand, use a wine vinegar and add some extra chopped fresh French tarragon · SERVES 8–10

4 tablespoons tarragon vinegar
4 tablespoons dry white wine
2 teaspoons finely chopped shallots
pinch of freshly ground pepper
2 organic egg yolks
8 tablespoons butter
1 tablespoon freshly chopped French tarragon leaves

Boil the first 4 ingredients together in a low, heavy-bottomed, stainless-steel saucepan until completely reduced and the pan is almost dry but not browned. Add 1 tablespoon of cold water immediately. Pull the pan off the heat and let cool for 1 or 2 minutes.

Using a coil whisk, whisk in the egg yolks and add the butter bit by bit over very low heat, whisking all the time. As soon as one piece melts, add the next piece; it will gradually thicken. If it shows signs of becoming too thick or slightly scrambling, remove from the heat immediately and add a little cold water. Do not leave the pan or stop whisking until the sauce is made. Finally, add 1 tablespoon of freshly chopped French tarragon and taste for seasoning.

If the sauce is slow to thicken, it may be because you are excessively cautious and the heat is too low. Increase the heat slightly and continue to whisk until all the butter is added and the sauce is a thick coating consistency. It is important to remember, however, that if you are making Béarnaise sauce in a saucepan directly over the heat, it should be possible to put your hand on the side of the saucepan at any stage. If the saucepan feels too hot for your hand it is also too hot for the sauce!

Another good tip if you are making Béarnaise sauce for the first time is to keep a bowl of cold water close by so that you can plunge the bottom of the saucepan into it if it becomes too hot.

Keep the sauce warm in a heatproof bowl over hot but not simmering water or in a Thermos flask until you want to serve it.

RED WINE SAUCE FOR BEEF AND STEAKS

This is the basic red wine sauce and it should yield enough sauce for 10–12 portions to serve with roast beef or steak. We store it in the fridge for up to a week · SERVES 10–12

⅓ cup finely chopped shallots
3 tablespoons butter
2⅔ cups full-bodied red wine
2 tablespoons port
2 tablespoons Grand Marnier
3 cups Beef Stock (see page 159)
butter, for finishing the sauce

Sweat the chopped shallots in the butter until they begin to soften. Increase the heat, add the wine, and reduce, uncovered, until it is almost completely evaporated. Add the port and Grand Marnier and reduce by half. Add the beef stock and reduce to about one-third of the original amount. Strain through a sieve and discard the shallots.

To finish, reheat when needed, taste for seasoning and whisk in a little butter to enrich it and give it a glossy shine and smooth texture (about 1 tablespoon butter per portion). Serve immediately. This sauce cannot be reheated after the butter has been added.

BEEF STROGANOFF

This is one way to use the chain – the long, narrow piece of meat attached to the side of the fillet. When trimmed, it's a lovely tender piece of meat that may be cut into small chunks, so this dish can be prepared in a matter of minutes in a sauté pan · SERVES 6–8

2 tablespoons butter
salt and freshly ground pepper
1 large onion, chopped finely
4 tablespoons extra virgin olive oil
8oz cremini mushrooms, sliced
freshly grated nutmeg
1lb 10oz beef fillet or the trimmed
    chain, cut into very thin
    strips or little chunks
1 cup sour cream
1 teaspoon Dijon mustard
1 teaspoon grainy mustard
a dash of smoked paprika

Melt the butter in a sauté pan and add the chopped onions. Season well with salt and freshly ground pepper. Cook over low heat for about 10 minutes, stirring regularly, until the onions are soft and slightly colored. Transfer to a plate.

Heat 2 tablespoons of the olive oil in a frying pan over a high heat. Add the mushrooms and season them with salt, freshly ground pepper, and a little grated nutmeg. When well-cooked (I like them to be a little brown at the edges) add to the onions. Add another 2 tablespoons of olive oil to the frying pan. While the oil heats, sprinkle salt and freshly ground pepper over the raw meat. Add the beef in a single layer and stir-fry over a high heat for a minute or two until it is just cooked. Cook the beef in batches, because if you try to fit more than a single layer in the pan, the meat will stew and lose its tenderness. When all the beef is cooked, add the other beef, onions, and mushrooms back into the pan. Stir in the sour cream, both mustards, and the smoked paprika.

Continue to reheat until the stroganoff is just bubbling. Taste, correct the seasoning and serve right away.

CARPACCIO WITH ARUGULA AND PARMESAN

If you have some really good fillet of beef try serving it raw and cut into paper-thin slices. It is the ultimate recipe to make a little beef go a long way. This sophisticated dish was invented in Harry's in Venice and named for Carpaccio, the great 15th-century Venetian painter. There are many good ways to serve it and this one is inspired by a version served at the Cipriani Hotel in Venice, one of the most romantic hotels in the world · SERVES 12

1lb beef fillet, preferably
    Aberdeen Angus (fresh,
    not frozen)
a few arugula leaves per person

FOR THE MUSTARD AND
HORSERADISH MAYONNAISE
2 organic egg yolks
2 tablespoons Dijon mustard
1 tablespoon sugar
2 tablespoons wine vinegar
½ cup olive oil or sunflower oil
1 tablespoon grated fresh
    horseradish
1 generous teaspoon chopped
    parsley
1 generous teaspoon chopped
    tarragon

Make the mustard and horseradish mayo first. Put the egg yolks into a

bowl, add the mustard, sugar, and vinegar and mix well. Whisk in the oil gradually as though you were making mayonnaise. Finally, add the grated horseradish, chopped parsley, and tarragon. Taste and season if necessary.

Cover the meat and place in the freezer for 15 minutes to firm up. It will be much easier to slice.

Slice the beef fillet ⅓in thick with a very sharp knife. Place each slice on a piece of oiled plastic wrap or parchment paper, cover with another piece of oiled plastic wrap or parchment paper. Roll each slice gently with a rolling pin until almost transparent and double in size. Peel the plastic wrap or parchment paper off the top, invert the meat on to a plate, and gently peel away the other layer of plastic wrap or parchment paper.

Arrange the arugula on top of the beef and scatter some very thin slivers of Parmesan over the top. Sprinkle with sea salt and freshly ground pepper. Drizzle with the mustard and horseradish mayo and serve immediately.

Good things to go with carpaccio:
Serve with extra virgin olive oil instead of the mustard and horseradish mayonnnaise, or with the following:
• arugula leaves, slivers of Parmesan, and tapenade
• arugula leaves, slivers of Parmesan, and truffle oil
• arugula leaves with a drizzle of Anchoïde (see page 180)

Suet

Suet comes from the fat that protects the beef kidney. Suet and tallow (the rendered suet) had fallen out of favor, but chips fried in suet and potatoes roasted in it are lovely. The flavor is much better and, incidentally, beef tallow has more vitamin B and despite its reputation is considerably better for you than cheap, trans-fat ridden cooking oils. People now make plum puddings with butter because they're so paranoid of eating the wrong kinds of fat, but I'm still a great fan of the traditional plum puddings made in the classic way with suet, as they have a better flavor and texture. Serve these on hot plates, though, because if suet congeals it's distinctly unappetizing. Many sweet puddings can be made with suet, such as Plum Pudding (page 514), or Marmalade Pudding (see page 512).

You can buy suet ready-prepared in packets but it's very easy to do it yourself at home. Your butcher will probably give you the suet for free because there is so little demand. Celiacs need to be aware that ready-prepared suet usually contains white flour.

Strictly speaking, beef dripping is the fat and the meat juices that render out of a joint of roast beef while it's cooking, whereas suet or tallow is fat just rendered from fat surrounding the beef kidney. However, nowadays the term "dripping" is colloquially used to refer to all of these.

Suet – how to prepare

To prepare suet, start by asking your butcher for the fat that surrounds beef kidneys.

Remove and discard the papery membrane and any red veins or fragments of meat. If you're not meticulous about this, these bits will deteriorate and the suet won't keep properly. The fat will separate into natural divisions. Chop it coarsely and either grind or process it in a food processor for a minute or two until it's evenly grainy (years ago, people used to grate suet on a simple box grater). Refrigerate and use within a couple of days, but if it has been properly trimmed it will keep for weeks in a fridge.

SUET PASTRY

2 cups self-rising flour
¼ teaspoon salt
4oz shredded suet

Put the flour into a bowl and add the suet, salt, and enough water (about 7 tablespoons) to make a soft but not sticky dough. Very little liquid will be required.

HERB DUMPLINGS

Dumplings were originally a way to spin out the meat and add bulk to a stew. They soak up the sauce as well as the flavor, so make sure you allow for that when you're seasoning and adding liquid. Add to any gutsy stew or casserole – they're rib-stickingly good · MAKES ABOUT 48, DEPENDING ON SIZE

2 cups all-purpose flour
1 tablespoon baking powder
2oz shredded suet
2 tablespoons chopped parsley
1 teaspoon chopped thyme leaves
½ teaspoon salt
½–¾ cup whole milk

Put the flour and baking powder into a bowl, and crumble in the suet with your fingers. Add the herbs, salt, and enough milk to bind. Roll into small balls (they will swell during cooking). Poach in stock, stew, or casserole liquid for 6–8 minutes after they float to the top.

STEAK AND KIDNEY PUDDING

When we serve steak and kidney pudding, the most comforting of all the winter dishes we make, everybody goes into a swoon of nostalgia because it's often years since they've tasted it. You can just as well fill the pastry with the mixture for steak and oyster pie or other meat stews. When the juices of the pie soak into it, the steamed suet pastry turns soft and spongy. It's just a wonderful eating experience · SERVES 4–6

4oz beef kidney
2 tablespoons beef dripping
1 small chopped onion
1lb boneless beef chuck, cut into cubes
1 tablespoon seasoned flour
1½ cups Beef Stock (see page 159)
4oz cremini mushrooms, sliced
Suet Pastry (see above)

5-cup capacity heatproof casserole

Prepare the beef kidney: peel the membrane from the outside of the kidney, split in half lengthwise. Using scissors, remove all the tough white bits in the middle. Cut into ½in cubes. Melt the dripping in a saucepan, add the onions, and cook for 1 minute. Transfer the onions to a plate. Toss the cubed beef and kidney in seasoned flour, toss in the pan to seal juices and brown well. Add the beef stock and simmer for 1½ hours. Pour off the cooking liquid except for 5 tablespoons, and save it to serve later. Add the mushrooms to the meat and onion.

Line the heatproof casserole. Sprinkle a little flour on the counter and roll the pastry into a round large enough to line the bowl. Cut out one-fourth of the round, as if it was a clock and you were getting rid of 12 to 3 o'clock. Butter the interior of the pudding bowl. Lift up the pastry, drop it into the bowl and press gently to seal the overlap (connecting, as it were, 12 and 3 o'clock). The pastry should overhang the rim of the bowl by about an inch.

Put the filling into the bowl. It can come to within an inch of the top. Roll out the remaining quarter of pastry into a round. Fold the overhanging pastry in over the filling, brush it with water, lay the lid gently on top, and press the edges to seal. Cover the top with a pleated, double layer of parchment paper. Tie the paper securely underneath the rim with kitchen string and make a string handle on it so it can be lifted easily from the steamer.

Choose a deep pot that will take the bowl neatly. Half fill the pot with water, bring to a boil and put in the pudding. The water should come halfway up the sides of the pudding bowl. Cover and continue to simmer steadily for 1½–2 hours. Keep an eye on the water level and top it up if necessary. When the pudding is cooked, remove the paper lid, wrap the bowl in a white linen napkin in the traditional way, bring to the table, and serve on very hot plates with a little cabbage or Brussels sprouts and serve with gravy.

Beef Dripping

The best beef dripping is made from the fat that encases the beef kidney. Try to buy organic if available. Remove any traces of blood or plumbing. Chop the fat into small pieces. Put into a roasting pan and cook in a very low oven at 300°F for about an hour or until the fat has rendered out of the suet. Pour off the liquid fat into a stainless-steel or enamel bowl at regular intervals. Beef dripping solidifies and will keep for months in a fridge. It can be diced and used to make a delicious old-fashioned cake – see recipe on page 539.

To melt beef fat, simply warm it gently. The fat will liquefy and can be used for roast potatoes or for deep-frying. Myrtle Allen always believed that the best chips were those cooked in beef dripping and I agree – see page 386 for the recipe. It is rich in Vitamin D and, in my opinion, is far preferable both in flavor and health terms to the cheap and low-grade oil that is frequently used to deep-fry.

It's important to strain the beef fat through a fine tin sieve after each use, otherwise the little particles of food will burn when the oil is reheated. Beef dripping can be heated to 450°F provided the oil is strained and does not burn. You can use it up to five times.

DRIPPING ON TOAST

For many young people, the idea of eating dripping is simply gross. Well, don't knock it until you try it. Bread and dripping has nourished many a hungry lad. It's really good and, I suspect, much more nourishing than those bizarre dairy spreads
· SERVES 6

6 thick slices of bread
**dripping with lots of meaty juices
    underneath**
**rosemary or thyme leaves, finely
    chopped**
sea salt

Toast or grill the bread. While it is still hot, spread generously with dripping and meat juices. Sprinkle each slice with a few thyme leaves or a little freshly chopped rosemary and a few flakes of sea salt. Divine.

Veal

When a calf is going to be born on a farm, there's always great anticipation as to whether it's going to be a female or a male. But here on our small organic farm, we welcome them both equally, because the female calf will grow up to be either a dairy cow or a heifer killed for meat. The bull calf will suckle and range freely with its mother, until it's about five and a half months old, when it will be killed for rosé veal or alternatively it will be reared to 30 months and then will be classified as beef.

Rosé veal, also called baby beef, is not as pale and tender as veal intensively reared in small pens in the dark. The public now knows enough about how that kind of veal is produced to reject it. Rosé veal, on the other hand, comes from animals that have been humanely reared, and it has a delicate and sweet-tasting flavor.

ROSÉ VEAL CHOP WITH SAGE LEAVES

I just love a veal chop on the bone, simply served with some pan-fried potatoes or oven-roasted diced potatoes and a little wedge of lemon and arugula leaves. Chopped rosemary is also delicious with veal instead of sage · SERVES 6

6 rosé veal loin chops, 1in thick
extra virgin olive oil

Opposite: *Rosé Veal Chop with Sage Leaves.*

salt and freshly ground pepper
4 tablespoons butter
24–30 fresh sage leaves
6 lemon slices, to serve

Heat a stovetop grill pan. Drizzle the chops with olive oil. Season with sea salt and freshly ground pepper. Cook the chops for 5–8 minutes on the hot grill pan.

Meanwhile, heat the butter in a frying pan over medium heat. Dry the sage leaves if necessary and add to the pan. Cook for 30 seconds to 1 minute, until they frizzle up.

Put the chops onto a hot serving plate, spooning sage leaves over the top. Serve with lemon slices.

ROAST ROSÉ VEAL CHOP WITH MORELS

If you manage to find a few precious morels in the woods in early spring, there could be no more delicious pairing than with these rosé veal chops ·
SERVES 4

1 tablespoon extra virgin olive oil
4 x 1½in thick rosé veal loin chops
salt and freshly ground pepper
1 tablespoon butter
2 sprigs of thyme
2 garlic cloves
1–2 slivers of fresh ginger

FOR THE SAUCE
4oz morels or 1 cup (2oz) dried
    morels (see page 54)
2 cups hot water or Veal Stock
    (see page 182) or Chicken Stock
    (see page 262)
2 tablespoons finely chopped
    shallots
3 tablespoons brandy

1 cup sour cream
2 teaspoons chopped tarragon
2 teaspoons chopped parsley
salt and freshly ground pepper

If the morels are dried, put in a deep saucepan. Cover with hot water or stock and leave to sit for 20–30 minutes or until the morels soften. Strain the liquid through a sieve into a bowl and save for stock or to thin out the sauce if necessary. Press gently on the morels to extract the maximum amount of flavor. Rinse under cold water if still gritty and set aside.

Preheat the oven to 450°F.

Heat a frying pan over high heat. Add the olive oil. Season the rosé veal chops generously on each side with salt and pepper. When the pan is smoking, add the chops and sear well for a couple of minutes on both sides. Remove from the heat.

Add a couple of sprigs of thyme to the pan, 2 garlic cloves, and a sliver or two of ginger. Transfer to the oven and cook for 10–15 minutes until the chops are medium rare and still slightly pink in the center. Put on warm plates and transfer to a warm oven to rest.

Meanwhile, make the sauce. Add the shallots to the used pan, toss quickly and then add the morels and cook for 8–10 minutes. Add the brandy and sour cream. Bring to a boil and add the tarragon and parsley. Bubble for a minute or two. Taste and correct the seasoning. Serve the veal chops on warm plates, surrounded by morels.

CLASSIC BLANQUETTE OF VEAL

Blanquette is another word for a delicate, white stew; the finished stew doesn't have carrots or other vegetables in it. It is enriched with a liaison of cream and egg yolk. The stew is subtle, so serve it with a mild-flavored accompaniment like rice or pasta · **SERVES 6**

3lb boneless veal shoulder
1 large onion stuck with a clove
1 large carrot, peeled and
    quartered
bouquet garni of 1 sprig of thyme,
    2 stalks celery, and 8 parsley
    stalks
pinch of salt
1 quart light Veal Stock (see page
    182) or Chicken Stock (see page
    262) – whichever you have

FOR THE SAUCE
24 baby onions
½ cup Veal or Chicken stock
    (see pages 182 and 262) plus
    an extra ¼ cup
2 tablespoons butter
24 button mushrooms, stemmed
lemon juice
1 tablespoon Roux (see page 165)
salt and freshly ground pepper

FOR THE CROUTONS
½ cup Clarified Butter (see
    page 216)
heart-shaped slices of bread
finely chopped fresh parsley

FOR THE LIAISON
2 organic egg yolks
⅔ cup heavy cream

ACCOMPANIMENT
Rice Pilaf (see page 131)

Trim the veal of all fat and gristle. Cut into 1½in cubes.

Start by blanching the veal. To do this, put the veal in a saucepan, cover with cold water, bring to a boil and simmer gently for 2 minutes. Drain off the water and rinse away the scum that will have risen to the top from the veal. Wash the saucepan.

Put the veal back into a casserole with the onion, carrot, bouquet garni, celery, parsley stalks, salt, and stock. Bring to a boil and simmer gently for about 1–1¼ hours, or until tender.

Meanwhile, to prepare the sauce, peel the onions. Simmer them in a covered casserole for about 40 minutes in ¾ cup stock and 1 tablespoon butter. Toss the mushrooms in the rest of the butter, add a good squeeze of lemon juice and the ¼ cup stock. Simmer in a covered casserole until cooked through, about 10 minutes.

Heat the clarified butter in a frying pan, then sauté the croutons on both sides until golden brown. When the veal is tender, strain off the cooking liquid. Bring the cooking liquid back to a boil and thicken to a light coating consistency with roux. Remove the carrot, onion, celery, and bouquet garni from the veal pieces and discard. Add the veal to the sauce. Taste and correct seasoning.

Simmer for a few minutes, then add the mushrooms and onions, and simmer gently until heated through. Season with salt and pepper and add lemon juice to taste. If preparing ahead, cool quickly, cover and refrigerate.

Just before serving, slowly reheat the veal, onion, and mushroom mixture (if necessary) in a casserole. Make the liaison by whisking the eggs and cream together in a bowl. Whisk in a ladle full of a boiling liquid from the casserole. Stir the egg and cream mixture into the casserole. Be careful not to allow the blanquette to boil once the liaison has been added, otherwise it will curdle.

Serve in a warm dish surrounded by rice pilaf. Dip the ends of the croutons into the blanquette sauce and then into the chopped parsley. Use them to garnish the dish.

What is a liaison?
Liaison is the culinary term used for an enrichment of egg yolk and cream. This is added to the sauce just before serving. Care must be taken to add some of the hot liquid to the cold liaison to warm it gently before adding it to a boiling sauce. Otherwise it will curdle.

ROAST LOIN OF ROSÉ VEAL WITH ANCHOÏDE

The veal is quite delicate in flavor, and the anchoïde really wakes it up. I particularly like this with some Swiss chard · **SERVES 8**

5lb bone-in veal loin
extra virgin olive oil
salt and freshly ground pepper

FOR THE ANCHOÏDE
2 garlic cloves, crushed
2oz can filleted anchovies
1 organic egg yolk
juice of ½ lemon
¾ cup or more extra virgin
   olive oil
1–2 tablespoons hot water

ACCOMPANIMENT
flat parsley salad

Preheat the oven to 425°F.

   Drizzle the veal with extra virgin olive oil and season with salt and freshly ground pepper. Pop the meat into the oven on a roasting pan and cook for 5 minutes. Then reduce the temperature to 350°F and cook for another 45 minutes. Remove from the oven and let rest for 15 minutes.

   Meanwhile, make the anchoïde. Put the garlic, anchovies, egg yolk, and lemon juice into a food processor, turn on and add the oil gradually as if making a mayonnaise. Thin to the required consistency (similar to mayonnaise) with hot water. Cut the veal into chunky slices and serve with anchoïde and a flat parsley salad.

ROSÉ VEAL SAUSAGES

One can use stewing meat from the shoulder or flank for these delicious sausages. They are best eaten within the day because ground veal goes sour quite quickly · MAKES 8

olive oil and butter

FOR THE SAUSAGES
9oz lean rosé veal
3oz slab bacon, rind removed

5oz boneless pork butt
3 anchovy fillets, mashed with
   a fork
1 teaspoon chopped sage
1 teaspoon chopped thyme leaves
1 tablespoon chopped flat parsley
salt and freshly ground pepper

ACCOMPANIMENTS
fresh herb salad
Tomato and Chile Fondue (see
   page 378)

Cut all the meats into 1in cubes. Season with salt and freshly ground pepper. Add the mashed anchovy and then mince all the meats together.

   Put into a wide, chilled bowl. Add the chopped herbs, mix well. Heat a frying pan and fry off a little morsel. Taste and correct the seasoning if necessary.

   Shape into skinless sausages or patties or fill into sausage casings. Cook in a little sizzling olive oil and butter until brown on all sides. Alternatively, chill until later but use within the day. Serve with a herb salad and tomato and chile fondue.

WIENER SCHNITZEL

This just sounds like bits of breaded meat, but the whole is much greater than the sum of its parts. It is a terrific way to make a little veal go a long way. The lemon really adds zing. Serve with skinny French fries. In Switzerland, a butterhead lettuce salad and salad cream are the traditional accompaniment. Every time we killed a bull calf in Ballymaloe we put this on the menu – the sweet rosé veal was a favorite with guests · SERVES 6

1½lb lean veal from the top round
well-seasoned all-purpose flour
salt and freshly ground pepper
1 or more organic beaten eggs
about 2 cups or more fresh white
   bread crumbs (see page 577)
Clarified Butter (see page 216)

TO SERVE
6 lemon wedges

With a very sharp knife, cut the veal into ¼in slices across the grain. Trim any fat or sinews. Put between 2 sheets of plastic wrap and flatten a little more with a meat pounder or rolling pin. The schnitzels are also called scallopini.

   Dip each piece of meat in well-seasoned flour, then beaten egg and then the bread crumbs. Pat off the excess.

   Melt 3 or 4 tablespoons of clarified butter in a wide frying pan. Fry the scallopini a few at a time until crisp and golden on one side, then flip over onto the other side. Drain briefly on paper towels. Serve immediately with lemon wedges.

OSSO BUCCO ALLA MILANESE

There are several good things you can do with veal shank, an inexpensive cut. We have the Italians to thank for this one. Cut the shanks good and thick for Osso Bucco · SERVES 6

16 pieces osso buco (veal shanks),
   about 2in thick and securely
   tied around the middle
4 tablespoons butter
1 finely chopped onion
1 carrot, finely chopped

Beef · 181

1 celery rib, finely chopped
2 garlic cloves, finely chopped
2 strips lemon peel
½ cup vegetable oil
⅔ cup all-purpose flour
1 cup dry white wine
1¼ cups Veal Stock (see page 182),
    Chicken Stock (see page 262),
    or Beef Stock (see page 159)
14oz can plum tomatoes, coarsely
    chopped with their juice
¼ teaspoon fresh thyme leaves
4 leaves fresh basil, chopped
    (optional)
2 bay leaves
2 or 3 sprigs of parsley
salt and freshly ground black
    pepper

FOR THE GREMOLATA
1 garlic clove, very finely chopped
1 teaspoon grated lemon zest
2 tablespoon finely chopped
    parsley

In a heavy casserole just large enough to hold the veal, melt the butter and add the chopped onion, carrot, and celery. Cook over medium heat for 8–10 minutes, until the vegetables are soft. Add the garlic and lemon peel. Remove from the heat.

Heat the vegetable oil in a sauté pan over medium heat. Dust the veal shanks with flour and brown in the sauté pan. When brown on all sides, place the shanks in the casserole on the bed of vegetables.

Pour off almost all the fat in the sauté pan and add the wine. Boil briskly for about 3 minutes, scraping up the residue in the pan. Pour over the veal. In the same sauté pan, add the stock and bring to a boil. Pour it into the casserole. Next, add to the casserole the chopped tomatoes, thyme, basil (if using), bay leaves, parsley, salt, and freshly ground pepper. The liquid should come up to the top of the pieces of veal, so add more stock if necessary.

Preheat the oven to 350°F.

Bring the casserole to a simmer on top of the stove and cover tightly. Place in the lower part of the preheated oven and cook for about 2 hours, turning and basting the veal every 20 minutes. The veal is cooked when it is very tender and the sauce is rich and caramelized. Make some gremolata by mixing together the garlic, lemon zest, and parsley. Sprinkle it over the veal as it finishes cooking. Serve in a hot serving dish over fettucine or mashed potatoes.

VEAL STOCK

Veal stock is a wonderful resource, it can be used in soups, stews, sauces, and of course Blanquette of Veal (see page 180) · MAKES ABOUT 3½ QUARTS

6lb rosé veal bones, cut into
    small pieces
2 large onions, peeled and
    quartered
2 large carrots, peeled and
    quartered
4 celery ribs, cut in 2in pieces
1 head of garlic, cut in half
    crosswise
bouquet garni, made up of
    8 parsley stalks, 2 sprigs of
    thyme, and 1 small bay leaf
10 peppercorns

Put the bones in a deep saucepan, cover with 6 quarts of cold water. Bring slowly to a boil, simmer for 4 or 5 minutes, discard the scummy water, and wash the bones in cold water. Put the bones back into the clean saucepan, add the vegetables, bouquet garni, and peppercorns (no salt). Add enough water to cover the bones generously. Bring to a boil. Skim regularly and simmer uncovered for 4–5 hours. Strain, cool and keep chilled in a refrigerator. It will keep for 2–3 days and can be frozen for 2–3 months.

BROWN VEAL STOCK
Instead of blanching, roast the bones in a hot oven at 450°F for 20–30 minutes until browned, and continue as above.

CALVES' FOOT
Calves' feet are a very rich source of gelatin for the stock pot. If you can get one from your butcher, ask for it to be split it in two (so it will yield its gelatin more readily) and then add it to the stockpot. One calves' foot is the equivalent of two pig's feet, which you can use instead.

Above: *Calves' Livers with Caramelized Onion.*

CALVES' LIVERS WITH CARAMELIZED ONION

Young lamb's liver is also delicious if calves' livers are unavailable. Calves' liver is mild and delicate; as ever, the fresher it is the better. Don't cook until the guests are sitting at the table, it only takes a few minutes to cook ·
SERVES 4

2 tablespoons butter
2 tablespoons olive oil
4 onions, sliced
4 slices veal liver not more than ½in thick, allow 5oz per person
salt and freshly ground black pepper
seasoned all-purpose flour
balsamic vinegar

mashed potatoes or Champ (see page 383)

Melt the butter and olive oil on a hot pan, add the onions and cook until they are soft and slightly golden.

Meanwhile, dip the liver in well-seasoned flour and shake off the excess. Melt the butter in a pan over medium heat. When it foams, add the liver and cook for just a minute or two on each side and then transfer to a hot plate. Add the sautéed onions to the pan used to cook the liver and a dash of balsamic vinegar. Allow to bubble and heat through. Spoon next to the liver on the plate. Serve with fluffy mashed potatoes or scallion champ.

Tripe

Tripe is the lining of beef stomach. The stomach is divided into two parts, and there are three distinct types of tripe: plain tripe, which comes from the first stomach chamber; honeycomb tripe, which comes from the second stomach chamber; and packet tripe, which comes from the far end of the second stomach chamber. Honeycomb tripe is by far the most tender and flavorful, and is my preferred option.

How to prepare tripe for cooking

Wash the tripe very thoroughly in three or four changes of barely warm water. Drain and put it into a bowl. Sprinkle with 1 tablespoon of salt and the juice of a lime. Work the salt and lime well into the tripe, rubbing it between your hands as though you were washing clothes. Leave it to sit for 30 minutes. Wash

Above: *Honeycomb tripe.*

again thoroughly in several changes of warm water.

TRIPE WITH TOMATOES

The traditional way to serve tripe in Cork is with onions in a white sauce, which is definitely an acquired taste. It has its aficionados, but you're more likely to convert the uninitiated with some of the Mediterranean, Indian, or Mexican ways of preparing tripe

· **SERVES 8**

2lb honeycomb tripe
1 tablespoon salt
2 carrots, peeled and coarsely chopped
1 medium onion, quartered
2 bay leaves
2 sprigs of thyme
2 sprigs of parsley
6 black peppercorns
2 tablespoons white wine vinegar

FOR THE SAUCE
2 tablespoons extra virgin olive oil
5 garlic cloves, sliced
1 red chile, deseeded and sliced
2 medium onions, sliced
3 celery ribs, cut into ½in dice
1 red bell pepper, cut into ½in dice
1 green bell pepper, cut into ½in dice
2 teaspoons sweet paprika
1 bay leaf
1 teaspoon thyme leaves
28oz can plum tomatoes, drained and chopped
salt, freshly ground black pepper, and sugar
1 cup Chicken Stock (see page 262)

TO SERVE
flat parsley

First wash the tripe (see above), then drain and put into a bowl. Rub the salt well into the tripe and let stand for 30 minutes. Drain and rinse well.

Put the tripe into a large saucepan with the carrots, onion, bay leaves, thyme, parsley, peppercorns, and white wine vinegar. Cover with cold water. Bring to a boil and leave to simmer for 1½–2 hours or until the tripe is tender. Remove the tripe from the cooking liquid and slice into 2in x ½in slices.

Meanwhile, prepare the sauce. Heat the olive oil in a saucepan, add the garlic, chile, onion, and celery. Cook over low heat for 5 minutes. Then add the red and green bell peppers and cook for another 5 minutes. Next add the paprika, bay leaf, and thyme, stir and cook for 1 minute. Add the canned tomatoes and cook uncovered for 10 minutes. Season with salt, freshly ground pepper, and sugar. Add the tripe and chicken stock and simmer until slightly reduced, about 10–15 minutes. Scatter with flat parsley and serve with plain boiled rice, pasta, or potatoes.

Variation
TRIPE WITH ONIONS
Cook the tripe as above. Meanwhile, cook an onion sauce (see page 389). Add the tripe to the onion sauce, add lots of parsley, and serve.

Dried Meat Jerky and Biltong

Bacteria need moisture to grow, so drying is a time-honored way of preserving food. The two main types of dried meat are jerky, from the tradition of North American Indians, and biltong, a South African speciality. For both cultures, the meat was dried in the sun and provided an invaluable, easily transportable source of protein.

Both jerky and biltong are typically made from thinner strips of meat, but jerky is not cured before drying and originally was made from buffalo meat. Traditionally jerky was not flavored, whereas nowadays many flavors are introduced, such as Worcestershire sauce, Tabasco, soy, or chile.

Biltong is made from several types of venison, ostrich, or beef and is usually flavored with salt, sugar, spices, and vinegar.

For those unaccustomed to it, the chewy texture and strong, spicy flavor, can be an acquired taste but soon become addictive. There are many commercial versions available, but it is still worth making your own.

BILTONG

This is an excellent way to preserve meat. For those who are unfamiliar with biltong, it is an acquired taste that soon becomes addictive. Arrange in a single layer on a wire rack over a baking tray and store in a dry place. If you live in a hot, dry climate, biltong or jerky can be air- and sun-dried in the traditional way – just hang it from a clothes line in a sunny breeze. Alternatively, a convection oven, though less romantic, does a terrific job – just hang each piece with meat hooks or string from a rack close to the top of the oven. Put a sheet of foil on the base of the oven to catch the drips · MAKES ABOUT 40 PIECES

2¼lb beef or venison top round steak
½ cup sea salt or kosher salt
2 tablespoons light brown sugar
1½ tablespoons coriander seeds, toasted and coarsely ground
1 tablespoon black peppercorns, coarsely ground
¼ cup red wine vinegar

First, put the piece of meat in the freezer for 2–3 hours. It will be much easier to slice if it's semi-frozen first. Using a sharp cook's knife, slice the meat into 1in strips along the grain.

Sprinkle the meat on both sides with salt and leave for an hour or so. This will extract some liquid. Shake off the excess salt.

Mix the sugar, coriander, and pepper in a bowl, sprinkle over both sides of the meat. Arrange a layer of meat in a sterilized earthenware dish. Layer up the rest of the meat, sprinkling a little vinegar over each layer. Cover and let marinate in a fridge for 6–8 hours. Turn once or twice to ensure even curing.

Remove the meat from the marinade and place on a wire rack on a baking tray; be sure the pieces are not touching. Alternatively, hang from meat hooks as described in the recipe introduction.

Turn a convection oven to the lowest setting and let the meat dry slowly and evenly, about 15 hours or overnight. When fully dried, the biltong will be dark, dry, and wizened and will have lost 40–50 percent of its weight.

JERKY

Originally this would have been dried in the open air in the sun but I have to say that drying it out in a fan oven works brilliantly and totally takes the guesswork out of it. We find that the grandchildren love to chew it and it's great to have in a backpack when you're hiking · MAKES ABOUT 1LB

2lb beef top round steak
1 onion, finely chopped
2 garlic cloves, crushed
2 tablespoons white wine vinegar
2 tablespoons dark brown sugar
½ teaspoon cayenne pepper, or more if you like it hotter
1 teaspoon freshly ground black pepper
¾ cup soy sauce

Cut the beef into thin ¼in strips along the grain. Mix all the ingredients for the marinade together in a bowl. Add the meat and marinate for 6 hours in the fridge.

Remove the meat from the marinade and place on a wire rack on a baking tray, making sure that the meat pieces are not touching. Place in a convection oven at its lowest setting for 15 hours or overnight until the meat is fully dried.

Brining Beef

Many craft butchers still keep a brine or pickle barrel going where tougher cuts of beef are submerged for several days to absorb flavor and prolong their keeping time. It's not only a method of preservation, it's a really tasty way of using a cheap cut of meat. Corned, or brined, beef falls into this category.

Both corned beef and spiced beef are Cork specialities, as butchers would have prepared them for long sea voyages. Cork has a long tradition of corning beef – in fact, corned beef was a huge Cork export for much of the 17th century, and during the Napoleonic Wars Cork supplied the British army with corned beef.

Our revered family butcher, Michael Cuddigan, showed us how to make his specialities, so now we are passing on this skill to you, so you can just enjoy making your own – it couldn't be simpler.

HOW TO MAKE CORNED BEEF

Order an untrimmed 5lb beef brisket from your butcher. The first cut (deckle) is thin and slices well, but the thicker second cut has interior marbling that provides flavor. A beef round roast, trimmed of surface fat, can also be brined.

In a large, stainless-steel saucepan, prepare a brine with 6 quarts of water and 3½ cups salt. Stir the brine to help the salt to dissolve.

It'll be easier to cut the beef into perfect slices if you tie it into a neat shape with three pieces of kitchen string (this is optional).

Put the chosen cut of beef in the brine and sprinkle the top with another ½ cup salt. Put a cold, sterilized plate on top of the beef and a weight on top of the plate so that none of the meat is exposed to the air (we use a Pyrex measure filled with water). Leave the meat in the brine for five days; after that, cook and serve as desired (see instructions below).

Top Tip: the used brine makes a great weed-killer for gravel paths.

CORNED BEEF AND CABBAGE

The skill of corning beef is still known, but eating corned beef has gone out of favor. Our local butcher Michael Cuddigan showed Myrtle Allen and her chefs how to corn beef before he retired, and they serve it in Ballymaloe for Sunday lunch · SERVES 8

4lb beef brisket, corned
  (**see left**)
4 large carrots, cut into large
  chunks
8 small onions
1 teaspoon dry English mustard
6 whole black peppercorns
bouquet garni of fresh thyme and
  parsley stalks
1 large or 2 small cabbages
no salt

Put the corned beef into a deep saucepan with the carrots, onions, mustard, peppercorns, and the bouquet garni. Cover with cold water. Bring to a boil, cover and simmer gently for 2 hours. Discard the outer leaves of the cabbage, cut into quarters and add to the pot. Cook for another 1–2 hours, or until the meat and vegetables are soft and tender.

Serve the corned beef, cut into slices and surrounded by the vegetables. Serve lots of boiled potatoes and freshly made English mustard as an accompaniment.

PASTRAMI

Pastrami is smoked corned beef. This staple of New York delis like Zabar's, is cured, smoked, and then cooked. It has a long history and has its roots in Romania and Turkey. The saltpeter in this recipe gives the pastrami its characteristic pink color, but if you can't find it then leave it out (though the pastrami will be gray instead of pink). Note that you will need a cold smoker for this (see page 472).

6lb beef brisket
1 cup kosher salt
5 garlic cloves, crushed
1in piece fresh ginger,
  peeled and grated
4 tablespoons black peppercorns,
  coarsely ground
2 tablespoons coriander seeds,
  coarsely ground
1 teaspoon saltpeter (potassium
  nitrate)

First, put the beef into a shallow Pyrex dish. Rub 6 tablespoons of the salt into the entire surface of the meat. Cover and refrigerate for 2 hours.

Rinse the meat and dry it thoroughly, and wash and dry the dish. Mix the rest of the salt and the remaining ingredients together. Rub well into the surface of the meat, and return to the clean dish. Cover and refrigerate for 12–14 days. Turn the joint every couple of days.

Lift out the meat; don't rinse it but just pat it dry. Then insert a sterilized meat hook into the joint and hang it to dry in a cool, airy place at 42–46°F or in a cold-room. When it's fully dry, cold smoke the joint (see page 472) at 85°F for 5–6 hours at a temperature not higher than 95°F.

To cook: put the pastrami into a deep saucepan, cover with cold water, bring to a boil, and cover and simmer for 3–4 hours, or until tender (a skewer will go through easily). Serve warm or cold. If you want to serve the pastrami cold, put it in a dish and cover it with a board to compress – it will be easier to slice. Cover and keep in a fridge.

Serve the pastrami in a Reuben sandwich with sauerkraut, or however else you fancy.

MICHAEL CUDDIGAN'S PICKLED OX TONGUE

Every country-house sideboard would have featured pickled ox tongue occasionally. There's a great saying around Cork, applied to someone who is out of favor – particularly after a night of liquid socializing: "Ah, there'll be nothin' but hot tongue and cold shoulder for you for dinner!" · **SERVES 8–10**

For this recipe, use one or two fresh ox tongues (the amounts below should be sufficient for 2). Alternatively, one can freeze fresh

tongue until later and then pickle it. As with corned beef, start by preparing a brine in a stainless-steel saucepan with 6 quarts of water and 3¼ cups of salt.

Cut any excess fat away from the tongue and discard. If the forked bones that connect the root of the tongue to the rest of the animal are still attached to the tongue, carve them out and discard them too. Turn the tongue so that the underside faces up. Cut a 1in slit the length of the tongue and pack it with salt. Put the tongue or tongues into the brine and let them cure for five days. Remove from the brine. Then follow the instructions below.

1 pickled ox tongue
no salt

Put the tongue into a deep saucepan. Cover it completely with cold water. Bring to a boil, cover the saucepan and simmer for 3–4 hours, or until the skin will easily peel off the tip of the tongue. Remove the tongue from the pot and set aside the liquid. As soon as the tongue is cool enough to handle, peel off the skin and discard. Remove all the little bones at the neck end. Sometimes I use a skewer to prod the meat to ensure no bones are left behind. Curl the tongue and press it into a small, plastic bowl. Pour a little of the cooking liquid over, put a side plate or saucer on top and weigh down the tongue. Tongue will keep for up to a week in the refrigerator.

Traditionally, cold tongue is thinly sliced horizontally into rounds. Use a very sharp knife with a long blade. Thinly slice the tongue

and serve it with red currant jelly.
SPICED OX TONGUE
"Spiced Tongue" was a common 19th century dish on the tables of the middle classes. It was spiced with cloves and flavored with onion, thyme, parsley, pepper, and salt. You can use the spiced beef recipe and apply it to the tongue.

BALLYMALOE SPICED BEEF

There are lots of recipes for spiced beef, traditionally eaten at Christmas, and many of them corn or brine the beef first. This recipe, which has been handed down in Myrtle Allen's family, is for dry-spiced beef. The recipe called for round, but you can also use first or second cut brisket. The recipe also includes saltpeter, which should only be used in moderation. If you can't find it, just leave it out. The meat will be slightly more gray in color rather than the rosy pink that comes from the saltpeter cure. The recipe below makes enough spice to cure five pieces of beef, about 4lb each in size. Spiced beef keeps for immeasurably longer than ordinary cooked or roast beef. Store the spice mix in a screw-top jar. It will keep for months, so make the full quantity even if it is more than you need at a particular time. To serve, cut it into thin slices and serve in sandwiches or with freshly made salads and homemade chutneys · **SERVES 12–16**

4lb lean beef round roast

BALLYMALOE SPICE FOR BEEF
1 cup plus 2 tablespoons
   Demerara sugar
1¼ cups salt

½oz saltpeter (potassium nitrate)
3oz whole black pepper
3oz whole allspice
3oz whole juniper berries

Grind all the spice ingredients (preferably in a food processor) until fairly fine.

Trim away any unnecessary fat from the surface of the beef. Rub a little spice well over the surface of the beef and into every crevice. Put into an earthenware dish and leave in the fridge for 3–7 days, turning occasionally. (This is a dry spice, but after a day or two some liquid will come out of the meat.) The longer the meat is left in the spice, the more spicy the flavor and the longer it will last.

Just before cooking, remove the spiced beef from the earthenware dish. The salt and sugar will have extracted some liquid, which should be discarded. Tie the meat neatly with kitchen string into a compact shape. Put it into a deep saucepan, cover generously with cold water, bring to a boil and simmer for 3–4 hours or until tender and fully cooked. If it is not to be eaten hot, then press the meat by putting it on a flat roasting pan or into an appropriate sized loaf pan and covering with a board and weight. Chill for 12 hours in the fridge. Spiced beef will keep for 3–4 weeks in the fridge.

SPICED BEEF WITH ARUGULA LEAVES AND GUACAMOLE

If you have a tiny bit of spiced beef left over, you can pot it like you would tongue. It's really good spread on a little hot toast, or with guacamole
· SERVES 8

10oz cooked spiced beef
wild arugula leaves
24 crostini, warmed

GUACAMOLE
2 or more ripe avocados
2 tablespoons freshly squeezed lime
2 tablespoons extra virgin olive oil
2 tablespoons freshly chopped cilantro
sea salt and freshly ground pepper

First make the guacamole. Scoop out the flesh from the avocado and mash it with a fork. Add the lime juice, olive oil, cilantro, salt, and pepper to taste. Serve immediately or cover the surface of the guacamole with a sheet of plastic to exclude the air, keeping cool until needed.

To serve, put a blob of guacamole on each warm crostini and top with a little spiced beef and a sprig of arugula. Serve as finger food with drinks.

BRESAOLA

Bresaola – a classic Italian starter made from cured beef – is salted and air-dried beef that is eaten thinly sliced. The original and best examples hail from the Valtellina region on the borders of Italy and Switzerland ·
SERVES ABOUT 20

1 beef rump roast, about 4lb 8oz, tied tightly with string
cheesecloth, as needed
red-wine vinegar, for washing

FOR THE MARINADE
1¾ cups red wine (e.g. Chianti)
2 teaspoons red chili powder
4 garlic cloves, crushed
6 bay leaves, shredded
3 cups coarse salt
1 tablespoon coarsely ground black pepper
10 sprigs of rosemary, roughly bruised
10 sprigs of thyme, roughly bruised
3 tablespoons sugar

Mix all the marinade ingredients together. Put the beef into a large plastic container and cover it with all the marinade. Cover and leave the meat to marinate in the fridge for 1 week, turning it over every day to ensure even curing.

After 1 week, brush the marinade off the beef and wrap it in clean cheesecloth. Hang it in a dry, cool place for 1 month. It will drip for a day or two, so put a plate or bowl underneath.

The bresaola will have matured when it feels firm to the touch. When it is ready, wash it with red-wine vinegar, then dry it with a clean cloth. You can then store it in the fridge, preferably in a covered container, for up to 1 month.

To serve, cut it into thin, succulent, almost translucent ruby-red slices and serve with olive oil, lemon juice, and Parmesan.

Right: *Bresaola marinating.*

Dairy

Milk is a magic ingredient, literally the fat of the land, converted by the mammal into a complete food capable of sustaining life. I have fond memories of a little black Kerry cow my parents kept as a house cow when I was a child. She became progressively wickeder, and eventually terrorized our workman to the point at which he refused to milk her. As children, we loved watching her antics from the safety of the wooden gate and were delighted when she kicked the stool or knocked over the bucket. After the cow was banished, we'd run down the hill to Bill Walsh's farm every morning and evening to collect our milk. At that time, and since the turn of the century, the milk was taken by horse and cart to small local creameries to be pasteurized before being sold in glass bottles, and the cream was churned into butter. Soon tankers started to collect the milk. Many small creameries began to close, and skilled butter makers lost their jobs. Some farms continued to make their homemade butter on a small scale into the mid-1950s, and this had more of a ripened flavor. But the milder-tasting creamery butter, which was available in every village shop, soon outsold homemade butter.

Years later, while looking at a herd of black Kerry cows on a summer's day overlooking Dunmanus Bay in lovely West Cork, I suddenly had a desperate yearning to breed my own cattle. I wanted my children and grandchildren to have the opportunity to drink raw milk. It was suggested that I should consider Kerrys because they were almost an endangered species. The word went out among the Kerry breeders, and within a few weeks I was the proud owner of a Kerry cow.

Recently I've noticed that there's a deep craving among my students to learn dairy skills; not only that, but I've been astounded by the number who get out of bed at 6.30 in the morning so they can learn how to milk a cow, even though they may never need or have the opportunity to do so again. They are intrigued to find out where milk comes from. In fact, they are sometimes disappointed when they discover that we have a little milking machine rather than a three-legged stool and a bucket. They joke that it will look good on their resume – "can milk a cow" is guaranteed to get the conversation going at a job interview!

In his book *The Tailor and Antsy,* Eric Cross describes the importance of cow's milk: "If you had not the cow you would not be able to live at all ... She provides us with milk. Milk to drink and "coloring" for the tea. Then she provides us with the thick milk and with the buttermilk. How could you eat the potatoes without the thick milk; and how could you bake the cake without the buttermilk; and how could you get through the heat of the summer without the buttermilk – the best drink a man ever had – almost … Next comes the butter ... the cow is a miracle entirely, so that a man could scarcely live without her. It would be like trying to hang your hat upon a rainbow, as to be trying to live without a cow."

Of course, you don't have to have your own cow to make your own butter, cheese, and yogurt, but it's not worth the effort unless you have really good milk. The quality of the milk will reflect what the cow's had to eat, but shopping for good milk can be tricky. Remember, "natural" is not a word that means much on food packaging, and "organic" doesn't necessarily mean the cows are eating grass, which they were designed to do.

The breed of cow will also affect the milk composition – for example milk from high-yielding breeds like Friesians has less fat (and less flavor) than milk from low-yielding cows like Ayrshires, Jerseys, and Kerrys.

I hope this chapter will whet your appetite at least to make your own yogurt or cottage cheese, and if perchance you overwhip cream, don't dream of getting rid of it – make it into butter!

Milk Types

There are two types of milk – unpasteurized and pasteurized. Unpasteurized (or raw) milk is milk in its elemental form, right after it comes out of the animal, while pasteurized milk has had heat applied to it.

Unpasteurized Milk

The flavor and mouthfeel of unpasteurized (raw) milk far exceed those of industrially processed milk, and one taste usually forms converts. I was reared on raw milk, and I feel very strongly about the importance of drinking it – or at least having the choice to do so. It goes without saying that the milk must come from healthy animals from a TB-free and Brucellosis-free herd. We keep two organic Jersey cows here on the farm; the milk for the Cookery School is of course pasteurized as required by law, but at home we all enjoy raw milk.

Most people have never tasted raw milk as government regulations have made it increasingly hard to find. The reason for the controversy surrounding raw milk is the potential presence of harmful micro-organisms, which have certainly been problematic in the past and continue to be so in unhealthy animals. But farmers who don't pasteurize their milk must adhere to stricter bacteriological standards than those whose milk will be pasteurized, and are inspected more regularly. Contrary to popular belief, most of the cases of people getting sick from milk involve pasteurized milk rather than raw milk (though of course, there is more of the former). When you think about it, pasteurized milk is a blank slate easily colonized by pathogens (bad bacteria), whereas pathogens in raw milk face far more competition before they claim victory. That said, dairy products are generally quite safe and outbreaks are rare.

In the US, some people belong to "cow shares," where each of them "owns" part of a cow and thus can legally drink the raw milk. In Italy, buying raw milk is legal as long as you buy directly from the dairy farm. An artisan supermarket called Eataly in Turin has circumvented the process by having sealed a big tank with raw milk; after popping in a euro for the farmer, people can fill bottles with raw milk in the store.

Pasteurized milk

Pasteurization, invented by Louis Pasteur in 1862, involves the application of heat to destroy micro-organisms. This is an essential process when you're dealing with a large volume of milk from variable sources liable to be tainted with bad bacteria. However, if a farmer is scrupulous about the health of his or her herd and the cleanliness of the production facility, raw milk production can be perfectly safe as well.

Pasteurization can be applied to many foods, but when milk is involved, it means heating the liquid at 145°F for at least 30 minutes or at 161°F for 15 seconds, at 192°F for 1 second, or, for ultra-pasteurization, 2 seconds at 280°F. Ultra High Temperature (UHT) pasteurization means filling hermetically sealed packaging with heated milk under aseptic conditions, which stabilizes the product to a point where it does not need refrigeration until opened. The UHT process prolongs shelf life for up to 12 months, but it damages the protein structure of the milk and takes away most of the flavor. Unless you were going camping or into space, why would you subject milk to this process?

There's a lot of speculation about whether pasteurization diminishes milk's nutrient content. Even though cow's milk is over 80 percent water, good milk is rich in calcium and vitamins A and B, with significant amounts of vitamins C and D. But heat treatment causes proteins and minerals, including calcium, to interact, which may reduce the bioavailability of minerals in heated milk. When milk is heated to above 176°F, the process undermines the calcium, as well as vitamins A, D, C, E, B1, B6, and B12. This may partly explain why there is a growing osteoporosis problem in younger people despite the fact that they are eating more dairy products. Many of us in older generations have fewer such problems and were reared on raw milk. Recent research suggests that a few glasses of raw milk per week reduce a child's chances of eczema and hay fever. The researchers' hunch is that children who drink raw milk are exposed to bacteria that strengthen their developing immune systems. I expect we'll see a lot more research that arrives at the same conclusion.

Homogenized milk

Homogenization is another process to which commercial milk is usually subjected. In homogenization, the cream is dispersed through the milk by forcing it through small orifices at high pressure. This process reduces the size of the fat globules into uniform particles – about a quarter of their original size. After homogenization, fat globules no longer rise to the top but remain suspended in the milk. Homogenized milk has a longer shelf life than raw or pasteurized milk – about 11 days as opposed to 3–4 or 9 days, but is less good for cheese making than raw or pasteurized milk.

Most milk sold commercially is both pasteurized and homogenized. Milk that's pasteurized but not homogenized is very difficult to find, although there is a growing demand for it, as research has indicated that homogenized milk is digested in a different manner to raw or unpasteurized milk. Beyond the health aspect though, which is still being debated, to me, unhomogenized milk has a completely different mouthfeel: it is both smoother and more unctuous.

Organic milk

A Danish study conducted in 2005 found that organic milk contained 50 percent higher levels of vitamin E, 75 percent more beta-carotene, and two to three times more omega 3 essential fatty acids and antioxidants than conventionally produced milk (levels of calcium or vitamin B12 did not differ). Milk from cows that have fed on grass is usually yellower and tastes more delicate, as it showcases the carotene (not to mention the wildflowers, herbs, and so on) the cows have eaten.

In some countries, organic cows may not necessarily have been on grass, instead being given organic feed. However, milk from cows that have been feeding on rich mixed pasture is much better in terms of both flavor and nutrient content.

Fat content of commercial milk

Whole milk has approximately 4 percent fat, while 2 percent milk has 2 percent fat, and lowfat (skim) milk has hardly any fat at all.

Milk from other animals

Cow's milk is not the only type of milk we drink here in Ballymaloe. Goat's milk comes naturally homogenized (i.e. the fat does not rise to the top) and can be enjoyed by people who have difficulty digesting cow's milk. Goat's milk also makes delicious cheese and yogurt, as does sheep's milk.

A milk cow will give about 15 quarts of milk a day (or twice that, if hormones and other methods of intensive farming are used), whereas a goat will give about 3–4 quarts and sheep give about 2 quarts, but their milk has a much higher fat content.

How to warm or heat milk

Put the milk in a heavy-bottomed saucepan and heat it gently. It's important to be extra conscientious about hygiene when warming milk, especially raw milk, as bacteria thrive in a warm environment. If the heat is too intense or the saucepan is too light, it will damage and scorch the milk, which produces a burnt flavor and also adversely affects the nutritional makeup. Note that milk will curdle as it heats if it is slightly sour. Don't throw it out though – you can use it for soda bread.

How to store milk

Ideally, all milk should be stored in reusable glass bottles in a fridge out of the direct light, because the flavor of the milk is adversely affected by sunlight.

Recent research indicates a concern that bisphenol A, a major ingredient in many plastics, may leach into food, particularly dairy products, and promote breast cancer cell growth or lower sperm count. This is a problem, as most milk comes in plastic containers! If you have a concern in this regard, as I do, simply transfer milk you buy in plastic containers into sterilized glass bottles, which can then be kept refrigerated. Ideally, always keep bottled (and plastic carton) milk in the dark to prevent vitamin D degradation.

Beestings

"Beestings," or colostrum, also known as "cherry curds," is the name given to the very rich milk the cow produces after a calf is born to pass on precious antibodies. In some parts of Ireland it was never used for human consumption, but in others it was highly prized and was shared with the neighbors. It was made into pancakes and beestings curds. For some reason, the third milking was considered to be the best for these recipes, but in fact the five first milkings after a cow has given birth are all considered colostrum.

How to make beestings curd

Strain the beestings into a pie plate. Place on the bottom shelf of a cool oven. It will thicken gradually over several hours.

Cut the curd into cubes with a clean knife. Pour them into clean cheesecloth and allow to drain a little.

Serve the curds with herbs such as parsley or chives, or with softly whipped cream and poached fruit.

BEESTINGS PANCAKES

To my great delight, when my own Kerry cow first produced her heifer calf, much to the amusement of our neighbors and friends, I had the opportunity to try these beestings pancakes. They are fantastically good
· **MAKES 12-14 SMALL PANCAKES**

2 cups all-purpose flour
1 teaspoon baking soda
pinch of salt
1 tablespoon sugar
2–2½ cups beestings, depending on thickness
butter, for frying

Sift the flour, baking soda, and salt into a bowl. Beat in enough beestings to make a thin or slightly thicker batter, depending on whether you want thin or thick pancakes.

Melt a little butter in a heavy pan over medium heat. Spoon on the batter (we use a tablespoon). Cook several at a time until golden on one side, then flip over and continue to cook on the other side. Serve hot with butter and maybe a sprinkling of superfine sugar.

Cooking in Milk

Few people know that soaking chicken breasts or pork cutlets in milk before cooking greatly improves the texture. The lactic acid in milk has a tenderizing and moistening effect on meat while it is cooking.

PORK COOKED IN MILK

Cooking pork in milk produces the most delicious curdy liquid. There is honestly no point in attempting this recipe, however, if you cannot find really good free-range pork · **SERVES 10-12**

4lb loin of pork (free range and organic if possible)
sea salt and freshly ground pepper
dash of extra virgin olive oil
thinly sliced peel from 1 unwaxed lemon
1 teaspoon coriander seeds, slightly crushed
4 garlic cloves, cut in half
about 2½ cups milk
sprig of marjoram

Remove the rind and almost every scrap of fat from the pork. Season generously with sea salt and freshly ground pepper. Heat a few tablespoons of olive oil in a flameproof casserole just large enough to fit the pork. Brown the pork well on all sides. Place the pork on a plate and pour out all the oil and fat from the casserole. Add the lemon peel, coriander seeds, and garlic.

Return the pork to the casserole and add the milk; it should come about halfway up the meat. Add a sprig of marjoram and bring to a boil. Simmer for 1½–2 hours with the pan partially covered – after about an hour the milk will have formed a golden skin. Scrape all this and what has stuck to the sides back into the milk and continue to cook, uncovered.

The liquid should simmer very gently all the time. The whole object of this exercise is to allow the milk to reduce and form delicious pale café-au-lait colored "curds" and a golden crust while the meat cooks. When the pork is cooked, slice the meat and carefully spoon the precious curds over the top.

CHICKEN BREASTS WITH MUSHROOMS AND GINGER

We often serve this recipe with orzo, a pasta that looks like grains of rice. I sometimes replace the ginger with a teaspoon of chopped rosemary or a tablespoon of chopped marjoram – both are also delicious · SERVES 4

4 organic chicken breasts
about 1¼ cups whole milk
salt and freshly ground pepper
1 tablespoon butter
2 tablespoons chopped shallots
    or scallions
extra virgin olive oil
4oz mushrooms, sliced
⅔ cup Chicken Stock (see
    page 262)
⅔ cup heavy cream
1 teaspoon freshly grated ginger
Roux (see page 165)
1 tablespoon chopped parsley
sprigs of parsley, for garnish

Soak the chicken breasts in milk, using just enough milk to cover them, for about 1 hour (save the milk to make a Béchamel Sauce – see page 116). Dry the chicken breasts with paper towels. Season with salt and pepper.

Heat the butter in a wide frying pan until it foams. Put in the chicken breasts and turn in the butter but do not brown them. Cover with a round piece of parchment paper and place the lid on the pan. Cook over low heat for about 5–7 minutes, until they are just barely cooked.

Meanwhile cook the shallots gently in a pan in a little butter, then remove to a plate. Raise the heat, and add a little extra virgin olive oil and the mushrooms. Season with salt and pepper and cook for 3–4 minutes. Remove from the pan and add to the onions.

When the chicken breasts are cooked, remove them to a plate. Add the chicken stock, cream, and ginger to the pan. Bring to a boil and thicken by whisking in a little roux.

When you are happy with the flavor and texture of the sauce, return the chicken breasts and the mushroom mixture to the pan, add chopped parsley, and simmer for 1–2 minutes. Taste and correct the seasoning. The cooked chicken breasts may be cut into strips or chunks if preferred.

Serve immediately garnished with sprigs of fresh parsley and with freshly cooked orzo or rice.

Sour Milk and Buttermilk

When I was little, we always had a sour milk jug into which we'd pour the raw milk we hadn't used at the table. In the heat of the kitchen, it would become more acidic and "sour" quickly; sometimes this would even happen overnight. As a result, we had a constant supply of sour milk for soda bread – one reason why the tradition of making these quick breads developed in Ireland.

Even today, we still have a sour milk crock at home to which we add raw milk continuously. However, it's good to remember that once the milk sours it should be refrigerated because, if left to its own devices, the curds continue to thicken, the whey begins to separate, and it can become too sour. If that happens, we throw it out (the hens love it), sterilize the container, and start over. The texture of freshly soured milk is similar to yogurt.

Can I sour pasteurized milk?
Be aware that pasteurized milk stays fresh for longer than raw milk, but left to its own devices it goes rotten rather than sour and should be thrown out. However, you can follow the steps below to make buttermilk if you need it for any of the following recipes.

Buttermilk vs sour milk
The term *sour milk* is often used interchangeably with *buttermilk*. Originally, however, buttermilk was the liquid remaining in the churn after butter was made. In olden times, this type of buttermilk was considered to be "the cure for all ills," and a visitor to a farmhouse would invariably be offered a mug of buttermilk.

During turf-cutting, haymaking, and harvesting, buttermilk was considered to be the best drink to give energy, slake the thirst, and cure a hangover. Young girls washed their faces in buttermilk to improve their complexion, while their mothers and grandmothers used it to make bread.

Nowadays, buttermilk often refers to a cultured product made from pasteurized milk inoculated with lactic acid bacteria, and is almost always made from low-fat milk. Raw milk can ferment on its own, but pasteurized milk needs the added bacteria to help it to sour. Commercial buttermilk works fine, and you can find it in virtually every village shop in Ireland, which cheers me up because it means the baking tradition is still alive. It's also widely available in the US. However, don't believe that it will have the same microbiological advantages as raw, sour whole milk.

Both sour milk and buttermilk (from the butter churn) are high enough in acidity to use in any of the buttermilk or soda bread recipes mentioned below. If you're buying low-fat buttermilk but want the full flavor of the original, supplement each 2 cups with 2–3 tablespoons of heavy cream.

HOMEMADE BUTTERMILK

If you can't buy commercial buttermilk easily, or want full-fat buttermilk, here is a simple method for producing your own. Commercial buttermilk is usually made with low-fat milk. This version, made with whole milk, will give you rich, thick buttermilk. To make low-fat buttermilk, use low-fat milk and 1 tablespoon of white vinegar ·
MAKES 2 CUPS

2 cups whole milk
1 tablespoon freshly squeezed lemon juice

Combine the milk and lemon juice in a deep bowl and let stand at room temperature for about 15 minutes. The milk will start to curdle. Stir well before using and store in a fridge in a covered container. The buttermilk will keep for a couple of days.

MUMMY'S BROWN SODA BREAD

In our household of nine children, Mummy made this bread virtually every day of her life, well into her 80s. She always had a light hand at baking. Wherever we were, her bread was one of the things that we looked forward to when we came home for a few days. So many happy memories are made at the kitchen table ·
MAKES 1 LOAF

2 cups wholewheat flour
2 cups all-purpose flour
1 teaspoon salt
1 teaspoon baking soda, sifted
1½–2 cups buttermilk (depending on the consistency of buttermilk)

Preheat the oven to 450°F.

Mix the flours in a large, wide bowl, then add the salt and baking soda. Lift the flour up with your fingers to distribute the ingredients evenly.

Make a well in the center and pour in the buttermilk. With your fingers stiff and outstretched like a claw, stir in a circular movement from the center to the outside of the bowl in ever-increasing concentric circles. When you reach the outside of the bowl seconds later, the dough is made.

Sprinkle a little flour on the countertop. Place the dough onto the flour. (Fill the bowl with cold water now so it will be easy to wash later.) Wash and dry your hands to make it easier to handle the dough.

Sprinkle a little flour onto your hands. Gently tidy the ball of dough, tucking the edges underneath with the inner edge of your hands. Pat the dough gently with your fingers to flatten it slightly into a round loaf about 1½in thick. Slide one hand underneath and with your other hand on top transfer the dough to a baking sheet.

Cut a deep cross into the bread (this is called "blessing the bread") and then prick it in the center of each of the four sections to "let the fairies out." There's also a practical reason for doing this – the last part of the loaf to bake fully is the center, so cutting the cross opens out the center during cooking, allowing the heat to penetrate more evenly.

Bake for 15 minutes, then reduce the heat to 400°F and cook for a further 15 minutes. Turn the bread upside down and cook for a further 5–10 minutes, until cooked (the bottom should sound hollow when tapped). Cool on a wire rack.

BUTTERMILK ONION RINGS

A great way to use up some buttermilk · **SERVES 6**

1 large onion, sliced into ¼in rings
¾ cup buttermilk
1 cup all-purpose flour, cornmeal, or polenta, lightly seasoned with salt, pepper, and a pinch of cayenne
good-quality oil or beef fat for deep-frying

Separate the sliced onion rings and cover with buttermilk until needed.

Just before serving, heat the oil or beef fat to 350°F. Toss the rings a few at a time in lightly seasoned flour. Deep-fry until golden, a few rings at a time, in the hot oil. Drain on paper towels and serve hot.

Variation

BUTTERMILK FRIED CHICKEN
My friend Canice Sharkey was given this recipe by a lady in Alabama. Buttermilk tenderizes meat in a similar way to milk. Poach chicken legs (wings are great too) gently in buttermilk for 30–40 minutes, depending on size. Cool, dip in beaten egg thinned with a little water, and then in flour seasoned with pepper, salt, and some paprika and cayenne. Fry until crisp and golden in ¼in sunflower oil. Serve with a tomato salad and homemade Mayonnaise (see page 252).

RUSSIAN FLUFFY PANCAKES

Julija Makejeva, who works with us at the Cookery School, taught me how to make these pancakes, known as oladushki *in Russian* · **SERVES 6**

2 cups buttermilk
1 teaspoon baking soda
2 organic eggs, beaten
scant ½ teaspoon salt
2 teaspoons superfine sugar
2¼ cups all-purpose flour
2 tablespoons vegetable oil

Put the buttermilk into a bowl, sprinkle the baking soda on top, and leave for 3–4 minutes to allow the mixture to bubble.

Beat the egg, salt, and sugar into the buttermilk mixture. Slowly add the flour to the batter, beating all the time, until the mixture has an even consistency. The batter should be very thick and reluctantly fall off the spoon.

Heat a wide frying pan on medium heat. Add the vegetable oil. Pour a tablespoon of batter into the pan and repeat – you should be able to fit about 5 more pancakes in the pan, spaced evenly apart. Cook until golden brown on one side, and flip over once bubbles have appeared on the surface and popped. Repeat the process until all of the batter is used. Serve with sour cream mixed with raspberry jam or sour cream sprinkled with brown sugar.

BUTTERMILK PANNA COTTA

Buttermilk adds real interest to this classic Italian dessert while cutting the richness · **MAKES ABOUT 12**

3 teaspoons powdered gelatin
3 cups heavy cream
1 vanilla pod, split
1 cup superfine sugar
2 cups buttermilk
juice of 1 large lemon

3in molds

Put 3 tablespoons of cold water into a small bowl, sprinkle in the powdered gelatin, and leave to sit for 5–10 minutes, until the gelatin has absorbed the water. (This is called sponging the gelatin, and helps it dissolve more easily.)

Combine the cream and split vanilla pod in a saucepan. Warm gently, then add the sugar and stir to dissolve. Remove the vanilla pod, and scrape the seeds into the cream. Save the pod to make Vanilla Sugar (see page 527). Add the gelatin and stir to dissolve. Remove from the heat and allow to cool. Stir in the buttermilk and lemon juice. Pour into the molds, cover, and chill for several hours or overnight to set completely. Dip the molds in hot water, then turn onto a wide soup bowl or a flat plate and serve with fruit compote.

BUTTERMILK CHOCOLATE CAKE

At Ballymaloe we used to call this Cynthia's chocolate cake, after a young American woman who came on an international youth farming exchange program in 1955. They would have competed to come, so the ones who came were very skilled in farm and home crafts. One day she offered to cook lunch and made this chocolate cake. I wonder if Cynthia could ever imagine how many people we've passed this recipe on to since. This is one of those cakes made by the all-in-one method in which ingredients are progressively added to the same bowl

· **SERVES 10**

2 cups flour
1 teaspoon baking powder
pinch of salt
¼ teaspoon baking soda
½ cup cocoa
1½ cups superfine sugar
8 tablespoons softened butter
1 cup buttermilk
1 teaspoon vanilla extract
2 organic eggs

FOR THE FROSTING
2 cups heavy cream
8oz semisweet chocolate,
   chopped

3 x 7in cake pans, lined (see
   page 524)

Preheat the oven to 350°F.

Sift the dry ingredients into the bowl of an electric mixer. Add the butter, buttermilk, and vanilla extract. Beat for 2 minutes. Add the eggs and beat for another 2 minutes.

Divide the mixture between the three pans, making the sides higher than the center because it will rise more. Bake for 20–25 minutes. When the cakes have begun to shrink in slightly from the sides of the pan, remove from the oven, cool in the pan for a couple of minutes, then turn onto a wire rack. Remove the paper and let cool.

While the cakes are cooking or cooling, make the chocolate frosting. Combine the cream and chocolate in a saucepan. Stir over a low heat. The mixture will look curdled at first but fear not; if you continue to stir, it will become smooth and shiny. Let cool.

Sandwich the three layers together with some of the frosting and place the cake on an upturned plate sitting on a wire rack over a baking sheet.

Beat the remaining frosting for a minute or two, until it thickens slightly. Pour the frosting onto the center of the cake and allow it to flow down the sides. Use an offset spatula to touch up any uneven areas.

Collect the frosting that has dripped into the baking sheet and put it back into a bowl. Whip it to piping consistency with a wire whisk and spoon it into a piping bag. Decorate the top of the cake with rosettes and swirls.

SLEEPY MILK

One of my happiest childhood memories is of having a glass of milk and eating a cookie in my pajamas beside the fire before I went to bed – then off to brush my teeth before I curled up under my flowery quilt. I understood this drink would help me to sleep well. The milk came from cows milked right before dawn.

Recently, I discovered that this milk is, indeed, considerably higher in melatonin, the natural hormone that helps baby calves develop a daily rhythm, and one that in humans allows us to relax and sleep – so there was definitely something in the old wives' tale, after all.

Several dairy farms now sell morning milk under various brand names. Many people find this natural remedy more effective than sleeping pills as it helps to establish a good sleeping pattern.

Cream

The breed of the animal, the feed, and the stage of lactation all determine the fat content of milk. The higher the milk is in fat, the more cream and butter it can produce.

Separating cream from milk

At the Cookery School, we separate milk from cream in an old Alfa Laval mechanical separator. This is strenuous work and it's important to turn the handle fast; otherwise the milk and cream don't separate properly.

Years ago, aluminum skimming bowls were sold in dairy supply stores. When the cream would rise, the milk would pour out through a spout below the cream, like in a gravy strainer. This was an invaluable utensil, not only for skimming milk, but also for degreasing stock. If you ever come across one, snap it up.

How to skim cream from milk

If you are lucky enough to get your hands on fresh raw or pasteurized (and unhomogenized) milk, simply pour it into a wide, shallow bowl or basin, preferably with sloping sides (you can sometimes find beautiful old Delft milk bowls in antique shops). Leave in a cold place overnight. The cream or "butter fat" is lighter than milk and as a consequence will rise to the surface.

The next day, skim the layer of cream off the top of the milk with a large, shallow spoon. The amount of cream will depend on the fat content of the milk. Using 4 quarts of milk will usually yield about 1 cup of cream.

Store both milk and cream in sterilized glass bottles in the fridge and use as required. It's very important that milk, cream, and butter are covered in the fridge, otherwise they will absorb flavors from other foods. The flavor of milk is also tainted by sunlight.

Different creams

Sometimes people are confused about the different types of cream – which ones whip and which don't – so here is a little guide.

Remember, the more air that is incorporated into the cream, the more diluted the flavor becomes, so bear this in mind when deciding what kind of cream to serve with desserts. I prefer softly whipped cream because it retains the flavor of cream but has the light texture of whipped cream.

Light cream: is around 20 percent fat and doesn't whip.
Heavy cream: is around 36–40 percent fat and very thick and can be whipped. This is the cream I normally use.
Whipping cream: cream that has enough butterfat (30–36 percent) to be whipped.

Top: *Our ancient Alfa Laval separator, which I bought secondhand from Nancy Roberts in the village where I grew up, continues to separate the milk from the cream in the time-honored way. Today one can buy electric separators on the Internet.*
Above: *Hand-skimming rich Jersey cream from the top of milk from our two cows.*

How to whip cream

Before you start, be aware of the importance of keeping cream refrigerated. If it is left at room temperature for even a short period of time, particularly in the summer, it will not whip properly.

Pour chilled heavy cream or whipping cream into a large bowl – it needs to be large enough to allow for whisking in lots of air to lighten the cream. If you tilt the bowl sideways, it's easier to incorporate air into the cream. Use a metal balloon whisk, and beat with a flicking, circular movement until the cream thickens to the required consistency. For softly whipped cream, stop whisking when it just holds a peak (as in the picture). For stiffly whipped cream, continue to whisk until it is so stiff that it will hold its shape when piped. An electric whisk may also be used, but be careful not to overwhip or you will soon have butter! Cover and keep chilled until needed. Whipped cream will become granular and may separate if left in a warm kitchen.

Cooking with cream

Heavy cream can be added directly into boiling stocks or sauces to make them smoother and richer. If, however, the base contains wine, the sauce should be reduced well before any cream is added, or the acid may cause the cream to curdle. If you're not sure how rich the cream is or if it's light cream, it is best heated before being added to a hot liquid.

NOTE: our Jersey cream is very rich (about 55 percent fat), so we sometimes add ⅔ cup of whole milk to whipped cream to lighten the texture and make it a little less rich.

Above: *Softly whipped cream is perfect to serve with desserts.*

CRÈME ANGLAISE

This, the classic French version of custard sauce, is usually flavored with pure vanilla, but can also be flavored with lemon, orange rind, mint, coffee, chocolate, or pistachio nuts. Apart from being used as a sauce, it can also be the base of ice cream, though in that case the proportion of sugar is much higher · **SERVES 10–12**

2½ **cups whole milk**
vanilla pod (or other flavoring)
6 **organic egg yolks**
¼ **cup sugar**

Bring the cold milk almost to a boil with the vanilla pod. Then beat the egg yolks with the sugar until thick and light. Pour in half the hot milk and then beat the mixture back into the remaining milk. Cook over very low heat, stirring constantly with a wooden spoon, until the custard thickens slightly. When the custard is at the perfect stage, your finger should leave a clear trail when drawn across the back of the spoon.

Remove from the heat at once and strain. Remove the pod. Cool, then cover tightly and chill. The custard can be kept for up to 2 days in the refrigerator.

Variations
CHOCOLATE CRÈME ANGLAISE
Melt 8oz of dark chocolate in a Pyrex bowl over hot but not simmering water. Stir the melted chocolate into the crème anglaise while still warm.

COFFEE CRÈME ANGLAISE
Add 2 tablespoons of instant coffee dissolved in 1 tablespoon of hot water to the crème anglaise.

CLASSIC CRÈME BRÛLÉE

Some recipes tell you to cook crème brûlée in the oven, but this old-fashioned method was taught to me by my mother-in-law, Myrtle Allen. You have to really pay attention while you're making this, because if you let it get too hot, you'll have very expensive, sweet scrambled eggs. You'll need to make the custard the day before the crème brûlée is needed, and use the very best eggs and cream. I like to serve this with fruit compote.

The alternative way to make the topping is to sprinkle the top with a layer of white superfine sugar or light brown sugar, spray with a film of cold water, and then caramelize with a blowtorch. "Crème brûlée," after all, means "burnt cream" · **SERVES 4**

FOR THE CUSTARD (DAY 1)
2 **large organic egg yolks**
½ **tablespoon sugar**
1¼ **cups heavy cream**
half a vanilla pod (optional)

FOR THE CARAMEL TOPPING (DAY 2)
½ **cup sugar**
½ **cup whipped cream (optional)**

4 **shallow ramekins**

Mix the egg yolks with the sugar. Heat the heavy cream in a saucepan with the vanilla pod until it just about starts to get a skin on it and gets "shivery" on top, but do not allow it to boil. Pour it slowly onto the egg yolks, beating all the time.

Return the mixture to the saucepan and cook over medium heat, stirring until it is thick enough to coat the back of a spoon. Again, it must not boil. Remove the vanilla pod, pour the custard into a serving dish or ramekins, and chill overnight. Be careful not to break the skin that will form on top of the cream as it sets, or when you add the caramel later it may sink.

Next day, make the caramel. Heat the sugar with ⅓ cup of water until dissolved. Then bring to a boil and cook until it caramelizes to a chestnut-brown color. Remove from the heat and immediately spoon a thin layer of caramel over the custard.

Leave the crème brûlée to get cold. If desired, pipe a line of whipped cream around the edge to cover the joint where the caramel meets the side of the dish. Serve within 12 hours, or the caramel will melt.

To eat, crack the top by knocking it sharply with the back of the serving spoon.

NOTE: two yolks only just set the heavy cream so try to use large eggs and measure your cream slightly short of 1¼ cups.

The heavy cream takes some time to thicken and usually does so just under boiling point.

If the custard is not properly set, or if the skin that forms on top while cooling breaks, the caramel will sink to the bottom of the dish. If this happens, freeze the pudding for 1–2 hours before spooning on the hot caramel.

Variations

CRÈME BRÛLÉE WITH PRALINE TOPPING

Follow the instructions for making praline as in Ballymaloe Praline Ice Cream (see page 208). Then, instead of using the caramel topping as in the recipe, sprinkle the finely crushed praline over the top of the chilled crème brûlée not more than 30 minutes before serving.

LAVENDER CRÈME BRÛLÉE

Add 1 teaspoon of dried lavender, tied in cheesecloth, to the heavy cream instead of the vanilla pod. Infuse for 15 minutes. Strain and proceed as above.

PEACH LEAF CRÈME BRÛLÉE

I was enchanted to discover that I could cook with peach leaves, which have a delicate, almondy flavor. Put ½oz of peach leaves into the cold heavy cream instead of the vanilla pod. Heat to the shivery stage, then leave to infuse off the heat for 30 minutes. Strain, discard the leaves, and continue as above.

CRÈME BRÛLÉE ICE CREAM

If you have leftover crème brûlée, don't let it go to waste. Mix it up so that the caramel top cracks into pieces and freeze for a delicious ice cream. There is no need for an ice cream maker for this, you will just need patience waiting for it to freeze!

Above: *Ingredients for Peach Leaf Crème Brûlée.*

BAKED BAY LEAF CUSTARD

In this old-fashioned dessert, custard is flavored and then baked. We use bay leaves to flavor it, as my grandmother did, but you can use peach leaves, verbena, rosemary, ginger, or spices like cardamom or cinnamon. For peach leaf custard, I use half milk, half heavy cream to make it a little richer and round off the slightly bitter flavor of the peach leaves · SERVES 6

2½ **cups whole milk**
3 **bay leaves**
2 **organic eggs plus 2 organic egg yolks**
2 **tablespoons superfine sugar**

6 x 3in **ramekins OR 5 cup pie plate**

Combine the milk and bay leaves in a saucepan and bring slowly to the shivery stage over medium heat. Remove from the heat and leave to infuse for 15–20 minutes.

Preheat the oven to 350°F. Beat the eggs with the egg yolks and add the sugar. Add the milk, whisking gently. Strain the mixture into the ramekins or large pie plate. Bake in a bain-marie in the oven for 35–40 minutes for the ramekins or about 1 hour for the pie plate.

Serve the custards chilled, alone or with a fruit compote. Sugared peaches or apricots poached in a lemon verbena-flavored syrup are a delicious accompaniment.

Left: *Ballymaloe Vanilla Ice Cream.*

BALLYMALOE VANILLA ICE CREAM

Really good cream makes really good ice cream. This recipe is made on an egg-mousse base with softly whipped cream. It produces a deliciously rich ice cream with a smooth texture that does not need further whisking during the freezing period. This ice cream should not be served frozen hard; remove it from the freezer at least 10 minutes before serving. You can add other flavorings to the basic recipe: liquid ingredients such as melted chocolate or coffee should be folded into the mousse before adding the cream. For chunkier ingredients such as chocolate chips or muscatel raisins soaked in rum, finish the ice cream, semifreeze it, and then stir them through, otherwise they will sink to the bottom · SERVES 12–16

4 **organic egg yolks**
½ **cup sugar**
1 **teaspoon pure vanilla extract OR seeds from 1 vanilla pod**
5 **cups softly whipped cream (measured after it is whipped, for accuracy)**

Beat the egg yolks until light and fluffy (keep the whites for meringues).

Combine the sugar with 1 cup of water in a small heavy-bottomed saucepan. Stir over heat until the sugar is completely dissolved, then remove the spoon and boil the syrup until it reaches the "thread" stage, about 223–235°F: it will look thick and syrupy, and when a metal spoon is dipped in, the last drops of syrup will form thin threads. Pour this boiling syrup in a steady stream onto the egg yolks, beating all the time by hand. (If you are beating the mousse in an electric mixer, remove the bowl and beat the boiling syrup in by hand; otherwise it will solidify on the sides of the bowl.)

Add the vanilla extract or vanilla seeds and continue to beat the mixture until it becomes a thick, creamy white mousse.

This is the stage at which, if you're deviating from this recipe, you can add liquid flavorings such as coffee. Fold the softly whipped cream into the mousse, pour into a bowl, cover, and freeze.

BLACK CURRANT SWIRL ICE CREAM

The strong, tart taste of black currants marries perfectly with the velvety texture of vanilla ice cream · SERVES 12–16

Ballymaloe Vanilla Ice Cream (see above)
12oz **fresh black currants (frozen black currants may be used instead)**
⅔ **cup Stock Syrup (see page 468)**

Make the Ballymaloe vanilla ice cream as above and freeze.

Meanwhile, make a black currant coulis. Combine the black currants in a small saucepan with the stock syrup. Bring to a boil, cover, and simmer until the black currants have completely burst. Purée in a blender and pass through a nylon sieve. Let cool and then refrigerate.

When the ice cream is semifrozen, pour ⅔ cup of the chilled coulis over the top and swirl through the ice cream with a tablespoon. Return the ice cream to the freezer and freeze it until set. Scoop out and serve alone or with the remaining coulis.

SEVILLE ORANGE MARMALADE ICE CREAM

Here is a great way to show off your homemade marmalade. Remove this ice cream from the freezer at least 10 minutes before serving · **SERVES 12–16**

Ballymaloe Vanilla Ice Cream (see previous page)
zest of 2 organic oranges
4 tablespoons Seville Whole Orange Marmalade (see page 454)

FOR THE SAUCE
½ cup Seville Whole Orange Marmalade (see page 454)
juice of 1 orange

Make the Ballymaloe vanilla ice cream, adding the orange zest to the mousse before folding in the softly whipped cream. Pour into a bowl, cover, and freeze.

When the ice cream is semifrozen, remove it from the freezer. Chop the marmalade peel into ¼in pieces and fold with the rest of the marmalade into the ice cream. Cover and freeze.

Serve with a little sauce made by thinning the marmalade with orange juice.

BALLYMALOE PRALINE ICE CREAM

The praline can be made from hazelnuts, pecans, or even salted peanuts as well as almonds · **SERVES 12–16**

Ballymaloe Vanilla Ice Cream (see previous page)
1 cup unskinned almonds
½ cup sugar

Make the Ballymaloe vanilla ice cream and freeze.

Meanwhile, make the praline. Heat the almonds and the sugar in a heavy saucepan over low heat until the sugar gradually melts and turns a caramel color – DO NOT STIR. When this stage is reached and not before, carefully rotate the pan until the nuts are all covered with caramel. When the nuts go "pop," pour this mixture onto a lightly oiled baking sheet or marble slab. Leave until cold. When the praline is hard, crush in a food processor or with a rolling pin. The texture should be coarse and gritty.

After about 1½ hours, when the ice cream is just beginning to set, fold in 8 tablespoons of the praline mixture and freeze again. If you fold in the praline too early, it will sink to the bottom of the ice cream.

To serve, scoop into balls and sprinkle with the remainder of the praline mixture.

BROWN BREAD ICE CREAM

This is also known as "poor man's praline ice cream" because it gives a similar texture but uses cheaper

ingredients. This is a great way to use up brown soda or wholewheat bread crumbs that would otherwise be wasted · **SERVES 12–16**

Ballymaloe Vanilla Ice Cream (see previous page)
2 cups brown soda or wholewheat bread crumbs
½ cup vanilla sugar (see page 527)
½ cup soft dark-brown sugar

Make the Ballymaloe vanilla ice cream and freeze.

Preheat the oven to 450°F.

Spread the chunky bread crumbs on a baking sheet. Sprinkle with sugar and toast in the oven for 10–15 minutes. Stir every 4 or 5 minutes until the sugar caramelizes and coats the bread crumbs. Spread onto a Silpat mat and let cool. Then pulse the caramelized bread crumbs into small, chunky bits in a food processor.

When the ice cream is semifrozen, fold in the bread crumbs and freeze until fully frozen.

RUM AND RAISIN ICE CREAM

Very retro – an all-time favorite · **SERVES 12–14**

Ballymaloe Vanilla Ice Cream (see previous page)
2 cups plump raisins
Jamaica Rum, enough to cover the raisins

Make the Ballymaloe vanilla ice cream and freeze.

Put the raisins into a small stainless-steel saucepan and cover with rum. Warm gently. When almost boiling, turn off the heat and allow the raisins to macerate for several hours.

When the ice cream is semifrozen, fold in the rum and raisins and freeze until fully frozen.

GLENNY'S ELDERFLOWER AND LEMON ICE CREAM

This recipe is a variation on a custard-based ice cream. Unlike the Ballymaloe Vanilla Ice Cream, this method uses an ice-cream machine. Glenny Cameron, one of our students, made this version for her final exam at the Cookery School. When I tasted it I thought it was so delicious that I asked for the recipe immediately – and Glenny was delighted to share it with me. For information on foraging for elderflowers, see page 34 ·
MAKES 2½ CUPS

¾ cup whole milk
¾ cup heavy cream
8 large elderflower heads
4 organic egg yolks
6 tablespoons sugar
2 tablespoons freshly squeezed
   lemon juice, or more to taste

Combine the milk, cream, and elderflower heads in a heavy saucepan. Warm gently to just below boiling point and remove from the heat. Cover and leave to steep for 15–20 minutes. Strain.

Beat the egg yolks and sugar together. Add the warm, infused milk mixture gradually, stirring continuously until it is all added. Return to the saucepan and cook over low heat, stirring continuously, until the custard coats the back of a spoon. Mix in the lemon juice to taste.

Pour the cream into a large bowl, then chill thoroughly. Freeze according to the directions of your ice-cream machine.

Variation

VANILLA BEAN ICE CREAM
Follow the previous recipe, but substitute a vanilla pod for the elderflowers. Split the pod, scrape out the seeds, and infuse in the milk and cream. Continue as above but omit the lemon juice.

BILLY'S CREAM PASTRY

Billy Motherway has been a chef in Ballymaloe for more than 30 years. I don't know whether he's the one who dreamed this pastry up, but it's definitely one to add to your repertoire. It uses butter and cream, sounds horrifyingly rich, but in fact it is terrifically delicious and cooks to a light, flaky texture. So actually it's a more economical way to get the results you might get from puff pastry. Use it in savory or sweet tarts or in pies, such as Ballymaloe Gooseberry and Elderflower Tart (see page 501) ·
MAKES ABOUT 3LB PASTRY

1lb butter, chilled
4 cups all-purpose flour
2½ cups heavy cream

Cut the butter into cubes, then rub it into the flour until the texture resembles coarse bread crumbs. Add just enough cream to combine. Turn onto a floured sheet of silicone paper. Pat into a round and wrap like a parcel. Chill in the fridge and use as required.

TRADITIONAL CREAM DRESSING

This dressing was used in the days before mayonnaise was commercially available, which wasn't as long ago as you might think. Cream dressing was traditionally served for high tea or supper with a couple of slices of cold leftover roast beef · **SERVES ABOUT 4**

2 hard-boiled organic eggs
1 tablespoon soft dark-brown sugar
pinch of salt
1 teaspoon dry English mustard
1 tablespoon brown malt vinegar
   or cider vinegar
½ cup heavy cream, or more

Cut the eggs in half, put the yolks in a bowl, and combine with the sugar, salt, and mustard. Blend in the vinegar and cream to a pouring consistency. Chop the egg whites and add to the sauce. Cover until needed.

OLD-FASHIONED SALAD WITH TRADITIONAL CREAM DRESSING
Assemble individual salads from butter lettuce leaves, quartered ripe tomatoes, hard-boiled egg quarters, and slices of cucumber, radish, and home-pickled beets. Garnish with scallions and watercress and place a tiny bowl of dressing in the center of each plate.

Sour Cream

As with sour milk, the best sour cream is made by leaving unpasteurized cream to sour naturally at room temperature for two or three days. I use Jersey cream from our two house cows.

If I want to slightly speed up the process, I add a tablespoon of natural yogurt to every 2½ cups of heavy cream, and leave it in a warm place overnight.

Store sour cream in covered, sterilized glass jars in a refrigerator. Sour cream makes delicious dips, salads, and spreads.

How can I sour cream even faster?

This is a bit more drastic, but if you add a teaspoon of freshly squeezed lemon juice or white wine vinegar to every 2½ cups of heavy cream and leave it in a warm kitchen for an hour or two, it will thicken and become more acidic. Use it immediately or cover and store in a fridge.

Should I use cream that has soured on its own?

As with milk, this depends whether it's pasteurized or raw. If it's raw, it's probably soured nicely – just taste it and see. If it's pasteurized, however, it's probably spoiled rather than gone sour and can contain undesirable bacteria, so get rid of it.

Get in the habit of smelling and tasting and soon you'll be able to trust your own judgement rather than relying on sell-by dates.

SOUR CREAM SHORTCRUST PASTRY

Sour cream makes a truly delicious crumbly pastry. I particularly love it in Tarte Tatin (see recipe below) · **MAKES ABOUT 2¼LB**

4½ cups all-purpose flour
½ cup confectioners' sugar
1½ cups butter
1 cup sour cream

Put the flour and sugar into a large bowl. Dice the butter and rub into the flour until it resembles coarse bread crumbs. Add enough sour cream just to bring it together.

Divide the pastry into two pieces, wrap, and put in the fridge. Chill for at least 30 minutes before rolling out. Use for tarts, pies, or tarte Tatin.

TARTE TATIN WITH SOUR CREAM SHORTCRUST PASTRY

This is a recipe for classic tarte Tatin, but it is made with a pastry that uses sour cream. The Tatin sisters, Stephanie and Caroline, ran a restaurant at Lamotte-Beuvron in the Sologne at the beginning of the 20th century. They're credited with this tart, and there are many apocryphal stories about its creation. However, it came about, it is a triumph – soft, buttery caramelized apples (or indeed you can also use pears) with crusty golden pastry underneath. It is unquestionably my favorite French tart!

One can buy a copper Tatin tin made especially for this tart, but a heavy, stainless-steel pan is a perfectly good substitute · **SERVES 6-8**

6oz Sour Cream Shortcrust Pastry (see previous recipe)
8–9 Golden Delicious or Macintosh apples, depending on size
8 tablespoons unsalted butter
1 cup superfine sugar

heavy 8in Tatin mold or copper or stainless-steel sauté pan with low sides

First make the pastry and chill it for at least 30 minutes in a fridge. Roll 6oz of pastry into a circle slightly larger than the sauté pan or Tatin mold. Prick it all over with a fork and chill until needed.

Peel, core, and halve the apples. Melt the butter in the sauté pan or Tatin mold, add the sugar, and cook over medium heat until it turns a rich golden-fudge color. Remove from the heat. Place the apple halves upright on top of the caramel, packing them in very tightly around the edge and in the center so that they are nested around each other securely.

Replace the pan on low heat and cook until the sugar and juice are a dark-caramel color. This process can take 15–30 minutes, depending on how juicy the apples are. Hold your nerve; otherwise the tarte Tatin will be too pale.

Preheat the oven to 350°F.

When the juices in the sauté pan or Tatin mold have caramelized to a dark-chestnut color, bake for about 15 minutes.

Remove from the oven, cover the apples with the pastry, tucking it into the edges. Return the sauté pan or Tatin mold to the oven and bake until the pastry is cooked, about 25–30 minutes, until the apples are soft.

Remove from the oven and let rest for 5–10 minutes or longer if you like. Put a plate over the top of the sauté pan or Tatin mold and flip the tart onto the plate. (Be careful–this is a rather tricky operation because the hot caramel and juice can ooze out).

Reshape the tart if necessary and serve warm, with softly whipped cream – divine.

Clotted Cream

Clotted cream is not a part of my own traditional food culture but it is a forgotten skill in everyday cooking and is so gorgeous and so easy to make that it is really worth doing every now and then.

You can make clotted cream on any stove or in a cool oven, just make sure the heat is low. Even a temperature as low as 110°F will do!

It's best to use unpasteurized cream like they do in Devon and Cornwall, where clotted cream has its own appellation.

CLOTTED CREAM

You can use gently pasteurized cream, but homogenized cream or cream that has been ultra-pasteurized will not work for this recipe · **MAKES ABOUT** 1¼ **CUPS**

5 cups heavy cream

Heat the cream in a heavy sauté pan and gently on the lowest heat for 5–6 hours, by which time it will have a rich, deep-yellow, wrinkled crust (use a diffuser mat if necessary). The cream must not boil or simmer.

Let the cream cool overnight, but preferably not in a fridge (I leave it in a cold pantry).

Next day, lift off the crust, or "clout" as my Cornish son-in-law calls it. Spoon the cream into sterilized glass jars, cover, and store in the fridge. The clotted cream is on top; thick cream left over when the clotted cream is removed can be used as heavy cream and it keeps for ages – several weeks at least.

If your stove doesn't go low enough, then put the cream into an earthenware bowl, set it in a bain-marie, and proceed as above.

CHEAT'S METHOD – CLOTTED CREAM

If you own a thermometer, you can take the guesswork out of the whole process of making clotted cream · **MAKES ABOUT** 1¼ **CUPS**

5 cups heavy cream

Put the cream into a double boiler, or put a heavy bowl (with the cream in it) into a saucepan of hot water. Heat until the temperature of the cream reaches 170–180°F. It mustn't go above 190°F or boil.

Keep the cream at this same temperature for 45 minutes to an hour. After an hour, transfer the saucepan into a bowl of iced water to cool quickly.

Leave overnight, decant into jars, cover, and refrigerate as above.

Variations
SCONES WITH CLOTTED CREAM AND JAM
Make a batch of Mummy's Sweet White Scones (see page 538) and, in the Cornish tradition, serve with homemade jam and a blob of clotted cream.

TOAST WITH CLOTTED CREAM AND MARMALADE
Slather clotted cream over hot toast and top with marmalade for a particularly luxurious breakfast. My Cornish son-in-law, who told me about this delicious combination, would live on it if he got half a chance, but my daughter Lydia is watching his waistline!

CLOTTED CREAM ACCOMPANIMENTS
· Chocolate tart
· Poached plums
· Any fruit compote

Butter

One morning at the Cookery School, one of the students was whipping cream for dessert. She left it to whip merrily in the food mixer while she went off to put the finishing touches to the rest of her meal. Suddenly there was a sloshing sound. The cream had over-whipped and she was astonished to see what was essentially butter and whey in the bowl. She was just about to dump it when I came around the corner and managed to save it before it went into the hens' bucket. I gathered the other students around and showed them the miracle of how cream turns into butter. Their amazement and delight made me realize that over half the group didn't know that butter comes from cream, or how easy it is to make butter at home without any special equipment. This is definitely a forgotten skill.

When I was a child, butter was part of everyday life on dairy farms, and I learned the simple art of making it from my Great-Aunt Lil, who lived in County Tipperary. Every farm had a churn, but you don't need a churn or any specific equipment to make butter; in fact, if you over-whip cream, like my student did, you can quite easily make butter by accident. (I've done it on many occasions!) Then all you have to do is drain and wash it several times, knead it until the water runs clear, and then add some salt to preserve it. A food mixer is an advantage, though not essential. You can also turn cream to butter by shaking the cream in a jar, though it begins to be hard work.

I'm very fortunate to live in a country renowned for its wonderful butter. In Ireland we grow grass like nowhere else in the world, because our climate is ideal for it – all that lovely soft rain. The Cork Butter Market, which opened in the 1770s and continued to trade for 150 years, was the biggest in the world and exported Irish butter as far as the Caribbean. The butter was packed in hardwood casks called firkins and brought by horsedrawn cart from Kerry and West Cork along roads still known today as butter roads.

Originally home butter makers didn't understand the science of butter making, but were well aware that it sometimes inexplicably could go wrong, so many *piseogs* (superstitions) prevailed. Butter luck required following all sorts of rituals, like placing a horseshoe below the churn or sprinkling primroses on the threshold of the churning room, though only if they'd been picked before sunrise. In County Mayo, using a dead man's hand to stir the churn was highly recommended!

Nowadays, butter has to compete with a bewildering variety of spreads. I prefer good, honest butter. We know where it comes from and it has no additives, nor does it require any complicated processing.

Butter stamps

Butter stamps (below) were a traditional way of marking butter. People often used a flower or plant motif etched into a wooden stamp. They would dip the stamp in cold water then press it onto little butter pats to make their butter completely unique.

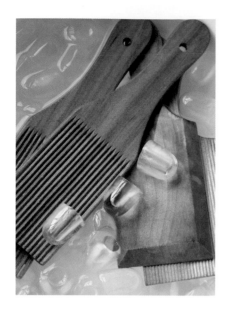

Left: *Butter bats, or hands, soaking in iced water.*

UNSALTED BUTTER

You don't absolutely need butter bats (pictured above) to make butter, but they do make it much easier to shape the butter into blocks. They're more widely available than you might think, considering butter making is certainly an alternative enterprise, but keep an eye out in antique shops and if you find some, snap them up. A good pair will bring you butter luck.

Unsalted butter should be eaten within a few days, but the addition of salt will preserve it for two to three weeks. Also, you can make butter with any quantity of cream but the amount used in the recipe below will keep you going for a week or so and give you enough to share with friends (though not in my house!).

Remember, sunlight taints butter (and milk) in a short time, so if you are serving butter outdoors, keep it covered · **MAKES ABOUT 2¼LB BUTTER AND 1 QUART BUTTERMILK**

2½ **quarts unpasteurized or pasteurized heavy cream at room temperature**
2 **teaspoons pickling salt** (**optional**)

pair of butter bats or hands

Soak the wooden butter bats or hands in iced water for about 30 minutes so they do not stick to the butter.

Pour the heavy cream into a cold, sterilized mixing bowl. If it's homogenized, it will still whip, but not as well. If you're using raw cream and want a more traditional taste, leave it to ripen in a cool place, where the temperature is about 46°F, for up to 48 hours.

Beat the cream at medium speed in a food mixer until it is thick. First it will be softly whipped, then stiffly whipped. Continue until the whipped cream collapses and separates into butterfat globules. The buttermilk will separate from the butter and slosh around the bowl.

Tip the mixture into a cold, spotlessly clean sieve and drain well. The butter remains in the sieve while the buttermilk drains into a bowl. The buttermilk can be used to make soda bread or as a thirst-quenching drink (it will not taste sour). Put the butter back into a clean bowl and beat for a further 30 seconds to 1 minute to expel more buttermilk. Remove and drain as before.

Fill the bowl containing the butter with very cold water. Use the butter bats or your clean hands to knead the butter to force out as much buttermilk as possible. This is important, as any buttermilk left in the butter will sour and the butter will spoil quickly. If you handle the butter too much with warm hands, it will liquefy.

Drain the water, and wash twice more, until the water is completely clear.

Weigh the butter into 4oz, 8oz, or 1lb slabs. Pat into shape with the wet butter hands or bats. Make sure the butter hands or bats have been soaked in ice-cold water for at least 30 minutes before using to stop the butter sticking to the ridges. Wrap in parchment or waxed paper and keep chilled in a fridge. The butter also freezes well.

Variations

SALTED BUTTER
If you wish to add salt, you will need ¼ teaspoon of pickling salt for every 4oz of butter. Before shaping the butter, spread it out in a thin layer and sprinkle evenly with dairy salt. Mix thoroughly using the butter pats, then weigh into slabs as before.

SPREADABLE BUTTER
I much prefer unadulterated butter, rather than butters with additives that change the texture. So if you want to be able to spread butter easily, simply leave it out of the fridge for a few hours in a covered container.

Above: *Stop beating as soon as the butter starts to look like scrambled eggs. To drain the butter, use a fine sieve or piece of cheesecloth. Knead the butter to force out all the buttermilk – this can be done with butter bats if you prefer.* **Below:** *Wash the butter twice more, until the water runs clear. When patting the butter into blocks, keep the quantities small to make it easier to work with.*

and residual milk are removed. Butter starts to burn at 350°F, whereas clarified butter can withstand temperatures of up to 485°F. Use clarified butter for recipes when you want the flavor of butter without the risk of burning, like in a French omelette, when cooking fish à la meunière, frying eggs, and so on.

To make clarified butter, melt butter gently in a saucepan or in a Pyrex cup in a very low oven, at 300°F. Let stand for a few minutes, then spoon the crusty white layer of salt particles off the top. Underneath this crust there will be a clear liquid butter – the clarified butter. The milky liquid at the bottom can be used in a white or parsley sauce.

BUTTER BALLS OR "PATS"

This is a traditional way of serving butter for the table and at Ballymaloe House, staff members make butter balls every day and butter is still served in this way. Put the butter bats or hands into a deep container of iced water for about 30 minutes. Dice the cold butter. Pick up a piece with the butter bats. Hold one bat flat with the ridged side upward and the knob of butter on top, then roll the other bat around over the butter to form a ball. Drop each into a bowl of iced water.

CLARIFIED BUTTER

Clarified butter is excellent for cooking because it can withstand a higher temperature when the salt particles

GHEE

Ghee is clarified butter from India, usually slightly soured and made from either cow's or water buffalo's milk. It cooks longer, hence it keeps longer, and has a lovely nutty flavor.

To make ghee, melt butter in a heavy-bottomed saucepan over gentle heat for about 45–60 minutes, by which time the sediment will have settled on the bottom of the pan. Strain through cheesecloth into a sterilized jar, cover, and store in a fridge.

MAÎTRE D'HÔTEL BUTTER

This is one of the oldest classic flavored butters, I remember it as a child at the Clarence Hotel in Dublin. People add

all kinds of ingredients to butter today, but originally it was served this way. It is good served with a piece of grilled fish or steak.

8 tablespoons butter
2 tablespoons finely chopped parsley
a few drops of freshly squeezed lemon juice

Whip the butter, then add in the parsley and a few drops of lemon juice at a time.

Roll into butter pats or form into a roll and wrap in parchment paper or tin foil, twisting each end. Refrigerate to harden.

Variations

WATERCRESS BUTTER
Substitute watercress for parsley in the above recipe. Serve with Pan-Grilled Fish (see page 82), using 8 x 6oz fresh John Dory filets.

WILD GARLIC BUTTER
Substitute wild garlic for the parsley in the recipe above. Serve with grilled fish or meat.

FRESH HERB BUTTER
Substitute a mixture of chopped fresh herbs, e.g. parsley, chives, thyme, fennel, or another herb for the parsley. Serve with grilled fish.

MINT OR ROSEMARY BUTTER
Substitute 2 tablespoons of finely chopped mint or 1–2 tablespoons of rosemary for the parsley, and serve with grilled lamb chops.

DILL OR FENNEL BUTTER

Substitute dill or fennel for the parsley. Serve with fish.

MUSTARD AND PARSLEY BUTTER

Add 1 tablespoon of course-grained Dijon mustard to the basic recipe. Serve with herring.

NASTURTIUM BUTTER

Substitute 3 tablespoons of chopped nasturtium flowers (red, yellow, and orange) for the parsley. Serve with grilled fish.

GARLIC BUTTER

Add 3–5 cloves of crushed garlic. Slather over bruschetta or toast. Also great with grilled fish, meat, or vegetables.

ANCHOVY BUTTER

Add six anchovy filets and mash them in. Serve with grilled fish or fresh radishes.

BRANDY OR RUM BUTTER

If you have a food processor, use it for this recipe and you will get a wonderfully light and fluffy butter.

6 tablespoons unsalted butter
¾ cup confectioners' sugar
2 tablespoons brandy or Jamaica rum, or more to taste

Beat the butter until it is very light. Add the sugar and beat again. Then beat in the brandy or rum, drop by drop. Serve with plum pudding or mince pies.

Above: *Maître D'Hôtel Butter.*
Opposite: *Butter balls or "pats."*

TRADITIONAL COUNTRY BUTTER

As farmers rarely had enough cows to yield sufficient cream for one batch of butter in a single milking, traditional country butter was usually made from cream derived from several milkings. As the cream accumulated over a couple of days, it would ripen in the cool dairy, where temperatures were about 46°F. This ripening process enriched the flavor of the butter. This kind of butter can be an acquired taste for those who are familiar only with creamery butter, but for those of us who remember it from childhood, it's a longed-for, almost forgotten flavor.

BUTTER COOKIES

These butter cookies melt in the mouth and keep very well in a tin for several days to nibble when you feel peckish! Use your own butter or buy good butter because the flavor of the butter really shines through · **MAKES ABOUT 40**

1½ **cups unsalted butter, softened**
1 **cup superfine sugar**
4½ **cups all-purpose flour**
confectioners' sugar

Preheat the oven to 325°F.

Process the butter with the superfine sugar and flour in a food processor for a few seconds to make a soft dough. Roll into walnut-sized balls and flatten slightly. Arrange on a baking sheet about 1in apart (they will spread out).

Bake for about 25 minutes. They should still be pale – not at all colored. They will seem very soft and uncooked, but they will firm up when they cool. Remove from the baking sheet only when they have firmed up. Dredge in confectioners' sugar.

Variations

SPICED BUTTER COOKIES
Add 1 teaspoon of cinnamon or freshly ground cardamom to the dough.

NUT AND BUTTER COOKIES
Press a pecan, hazelnut, or blanched almond on top of each ball before baking.

ORANGE BUTTER COOKIES
Add 2 teaspoons of orange zest to the dough.

PUFF PASTRY

Homemade puff pastry takes some time to make, but it is more than worth the effort. Butter is the secret to this beautifully flaky puff pastry. Sometimes people are shocked that it uses equal quantities of butter and flour, but the delicious, light pastry that results tastes wonderful. The commercial equivalent may look spectacular, but because it is made with inferior pastry margarine, it tends to leave you with a greasy feeling in the mouth.

A slab of chilled marble is a real advantage for pastry making, particularly for puff pastry because of its high butter content. It can even be kept as a shelf in your fridge. If you don't have a marble slab, just use your kitchen countertop. In summer a roasting tray filled with ice can be used to chill the surface · **MAKES ABOUT 2½LB**

4 **cups chilled bread flour**
pinch of salt
squeeze of lemon juice (optional)
1lb **butter, firm but pliable**

Sift the flour and salt into a bowl and mix to a firm dough with 1–1¼ cups of cold water (depending on the flour) and the lemon juice, if using. This dough is called *détrempe*. Cover with parchment paper or plastic wrap and let rest for 30 minutes in the fridge. Then roll the *détrempe* into a square about ½in thick.

If the butter is very hard, then hit it (still in the wrapper) with a rolling pin until pliable but not sticky. Unwrap the butter and shape into a slab roughly ¾in thick. Place in the center of the dough and fold over the edges of the butter to make a neat parcel.

Make sure your marble slab or countertop is well-floured, then flatten the dough with a rolling pin, and continue to roll out into a rectangle about 18in long and 6½in wide (this is approximate so don't worry if it's not exact). Fold neatly into three with the sides as accurately aligned as possible.

Seal the edges with a rolling pin.

Give the dough a one-quarter turn (90°), it should now be on your countertop as though it was a book with the open ends facing north/south. Roll out again, fold in three and seal the edges with the rolling pin. Cover with plastic wrap or parchment paper and let rest in the fridge for 30 minutes.

The pastry has now had two rolls or "turns." Repeat the rolling process another 2 times to give the dough 6 rolls altogether with a 30-minute rest in the fridge between every two turns. (In hot weather it may be necessary to chill the pastry slightly longer between rollings.) Each time you start to roll the pastry, place it on the countertop with the open ends north/south as if it were a book. Chill for at least 30 minutes before using.

FRENCH WAFERS

Here is a delicious way to use up scraps of puff pastry. Nibble with coffee or sandwich together with jam and whipped cream · MAKES ABOUT 30

scraps of left-over puff pastry
1 organic egg white, lightly beaten
granulated sugar

Preheat the oven to 450°F.

Roll the pastry thinly. Cut into rectangles. Brush the pastry with the egg white, and sprinkle with sugar. Bake in the oven for 10–12 minutes or until crisp and golden. Cool on a wire rack.

ELEPHANTS' EARS

Also called palmiers, these are another great way to use up puff pastry.

puff pastry scraps
confectioners' sugar

Preheat the oven to 400°F.

Sift some confectioners' sugar over the countertop. Roll the puff pastry scraps out into a rectangle about 1/8in thick. Dredge heavily in confectioners' sugar.

Lightly fold the pastry in half lengthwise, then open it out again to show the center fold.

Take one of the long edges of the rectangle and fold it once, then twice toward the center fold. Do the same with the other long edge, so both long edges are folded into the center. Then fold the entire thing in half lengthwise to make a long roll.

Cut the roll of pastry into 1/2in slices (these are your elephants' ears) and space them out well on a baking sheet. Pinch the ends out slightly so they will spread a little in the oven.

Bake for 8–10 minutes and when golden on one side, flip them over and continue to cook for a few minutes longer until caramelized on both sides.

CHEESE STRAWS

My friend Alicia Wilkinson from Silwood Kitchens Cooking School in Capetown, South Africa, gave me this fantastic recipe for cheese straws. It's the best I know and is a delicious way to use up both puff pastry scraps and leftover grated cheese · MAKES ABOUT 12

9oz chilled puff pastry – scraps
are fine
1 organic egg white, lightly
beaten
1 cup grated Parmesan cheese
1 cup grated Cheddar cheese
pinch of cayenne pepper

Preheat the oven to 375°F.

Roll the puff pastry into a large rectangle on a floured surface. Brush the lower half with egg white.

Mix the finely grated cheeses with the cayenne pepper. Sprinkle half of this mixture over the egg white and press down gently.

Fold the upper half of the pastry down over the lower half and press with a rolling pin to seal. Then roll out the pastry to the original size. Paint the entire sheet with egg white and cover with the remaining cheese and spice mixture.

Chill for about 10 minutes. Cut into thin strips of 1/2in and twist into straws. Bake for 10–15 minutes or until golden brown and cooked through. Leave to cool on a wire rack.

Yogurt

For many of us, yogurt is a relatively new thing. But of course in the Middle East, Mediterranean, and Asia, yogurt has been part of the food culture for centuries and is made from cow's, goat's, sheep's, and even water buffalo's milk.

I first came across yogurt when I was working as an au pair in France in the late 1960s, and I must admit I wasn't very keen on it then. Now, of course, I couldn't live without it.

Yogurt has better keeping qualities than milk, due to its acidity, a most useful attribute in the days before refrigeration. The health benefits of yogurt have been known for centuries. It keeps the gut healthy and is especially good after a course of antibiotics because it helps to rebuild good intestinal flora. In fact, when I travel in India, I make sure I eat natural yogurt, which they call "curd," every day to help keep stomach troubles at bay. Probiotics such as *Streptococcus thermophilus* and *Lactobacillus bulgaricus* – good bacteria found in yogurt and other cultured products – can help prevent lactose intolerance and other allergies, and stimulate disease-fighting cells. People in yogurt-eating regions such as Bulgaria, Turkey, India, Georgia, and Armenia are renowned for their longevity.

So why make yogurt at home? Homemade yogurt is infinitely more delicious and more valuable nutritionally than virtually anything you can buy in a store – the commercial version tends to be thinner and usually has added sugar. Then, of course, there's the buzz and satisfaction you get from making your own yogurt – and yet it's so easy to do.

If you want to make yogurt on a slightly larger scale, you might want to consider purchasing customized starter bacteria direct from cheese-making suppliers (see Resources, page 584).

YOGURT

As with any dairy product, your raw materials must be of the finest quality. The yogurt you start with needs to be very fresh; otherwise the finished product will have a slimy, ropey consistency. As ever, one must be meticulously careful about hygiene. All your equipment must be sterilized, or you run the risk of unwanted bacteria getting in. I use our own rich, full-cream Jersey milk, but if you're starting with low fat milk, you will need to add some cream to enhance the flavor (use at least ⅔ cup for every 2½ quarts of milk; for really unctuous yogurt 1¼ cups is better). You also need a heavy, stainless-steel saucepan; otherwise the milk will scorch when you are reducing it · MAKES ABOUT 6 CUPS OF YOGURT

2½ **quarts whole milk**
1¼ **cups heavy cream**
1 **cup live, very fresh, natural yogurt**

Put the milk into a large, stainless-steel saucepan and bring to a boil. Turn the heat down to a simmer and stir gently and regularly until the milk reduces by one third. Remove from the heat and pour into a bowl – I use a ceramic bowl to retain the heat. Stir in the cream and let cool.

When the mixture has cooled to the point where you are able to hold your finger in it for a count of 10, add the yogurt and stir well. It is important that the milk is not too hot when the yogurt is added; heat over 145°F will kill the bacteria. On a dairy thermometer, the optimum temperature is 104–108°F.

Cover with plastic wrap, then wrap the whole thing in a towel and keep it in a warm place until the milk coagulates – a minimum of 5 hours, or better still, overnight. The optimum temperature is 104°F, but if it's a bit cooler than that it doesn't matter; it will just take longer to coagulate. When the yogurt is set, transfer it to the fridge. It will keep for 7 to 10 days.

Above, left: *First bring the milk to a boil and reduce by one third.* **Above, right:** *Pour into a good thick bowl – preferably ceramic but Pyrex will be fine.* **Below, left:** *Stir the cream and yogurt into the barely warm milk.* **Below, right:** *The net result will be gorgeous, thick, unctuous natural yogurt with a layer of cream on top.*

EASY HOMEMADE YOGURT

Eddie O'Neill, artisan food specialist for the Dairy Research Station in County Cork, is a mine of information. He taught us this easy and, dare I say, foolproof method for making gorgeous yogurt. Adding a little powdered milk helps to enrich the yogurt and adds extra protein.

We have a few favorite spots where we keep the yogurt warm – on the countertop close to the oven, on a shelf over the radiator in the office – but I'm sure you'll find your own!

2 quarts whole milk
2 tablespoons powdered skim milk
2 teaspoons very fresh, live natural yogurt

Heat the milk in a heavy, stainless-steel saucepan. When it is lukewarm, stir in the powdered milk. Continue to heat until the milk begins to froth, at about 195°F.

Turn off the heat and let stand for 15 minutes, by which time the mixture should have cooled to about 104–108°F. Having a dairy thermometer takes the guesswork out of this, but alternatively you can test it in the time-honored way, by inserting a clean finger into the milk. You should be able to leave your finger for a count of 10 without it getting too hot. At this point, stir in the live yogurt and then transfer the mixture into a heavy ceramic bowl.

Wrap the entire bowl in a towel and keep it in a warm place until the milk coagulates, a minimum of 5 hours or, better still, overnight.

One way or another, you need to keep the bowl warm. The optimum temperature should be around 104°F, but if it's a bit cooler than that it doesn't matter; it will just take longer to coagulate. The longer the mixture is kept warm, the better the flavor.

When the yogurt is set, transfer to the fridge and use as required.

Variation

FLAVORED YOGURTS
Put ¼ cup of Apple and Rose Geranium Sauce (see below), stewed rhubarb, or other fruit purée into 6fl oz sterilized jars. Top with semiset yogurt, cover, and chill.

Above: *Flavored Yogurts with Apple and Rose Geranium Sauce.*

APPLE AND ROSE GERANIUM SAUCE

Rose geranium leaves infuse this apple sauce with a delicious haunting flavor
· **SERVES 6**

1lb cooking apples
¼ cup sugar, or more
2–4 rose geranium leaves (Pelargonium graveolens)

Peel, quarter, and core the apples, then cut the pieces in two. Put into a small stainless-steel or cast-iron saucepan with the sugar, about 1–2 tablespoons of water, and the rose geranium. Cover and put over low heat. As soon as the apple has broken down, stir and taste for sweetness. Serve warm.

BEET TZATZIKI

A good way to showcase the yogurt you've made. Serve with lamb or chicken, or as a dip · MAKES 1LB

⅔ **cup cooked and grated beets**
8 **tablespoons natural yogurt**
2 **tablespoons freshly chopped mint**
sea salt and freshly ground pepper
pinch of superfine sugar

Mix everything gently in a bowl. Season with salt, pepper and sugar and taste – tweak if necessary.

POMEGRANATE AND CUCUMBER RAITA

This raita makes a addictive dip with poppadums or naan bread. It will taste especially good if you use your own yogurt · MAKES 1 CUP

1 **pomegranate**
¼ **cucumber, peeled, seeded, and**
  finely diced
1 **tablespoon coarsely chopped**
  fresh cilantro
1 **tablespoon coarsely**
  chopped mint leaves
1 **cup natural yogurt**
salt

Split the pomegranate in half around the equator. Place the cut side down on the palm of your hand. Hold over a container and tap vigorously with the bowl of a wooden spoon; the

seeds will dislodge and fall into the bowl. Add the cucumber, cilantro, and mint to the bowl. Stir in the yogurt, season with salt, and serve.

SRIKHAND

Everyone should know about this exceptionally delicious Indian pudding as it's a great way to embellish yogurt · SERVES 8–10

4 **cups thick homemade or Greek**
  yogurt
generous pinch of saffron strands
4 **whole cardamom pods**
2 **tablespoons coarsely chopped**
  pistachio nuts
1½ **cups superfine sugar**

piece of cheesecloth

If using homemade yogurt, put the square of cheesecloth into a bowl and pour in the yogurt. Tie the ends and allow to drip overnight in a cool place. Next day, transfer the dripped yogurt into a clean bowl. (Save the whey to make soda bread.)

Put the saffron in a small bowl with 1 tablespoon warm water and allow to infuse for a few minutes. Then stir every last drop into the dripped or Greek yogurt. Remove the seeds from the cardamom pods, and crush lightly. Add ¼ teaspoon of the crushed seeds to the yogurt along with the sugar. Mix well.

Pour into a serving bowl, cover, and chill in the fridge for at least 15 minutes. Sprinkle the top with pistachio nuts and serve on its own, or with summer or autumn berries.

USES FOR YOGURT

Yogurt is incredibly versatile. Here are a few ideas to show it off.

• In many countries, notably in the Middle East and India, yogurt is used as a marinade. The lactic acid has the effect of tenderizing tough meat. In India, fish is sometimes cooked as well as marinated in yogurt.

• In India, yogurt-based raitas are served with many spicy dishes. A bowl of curd, as yogurt is called in India, is part of virtually every meal, as it is in Bulgaria, too.

• In the Middle East, yogurt is added to soups, braises, and stews to give a silky richness.

• Yogurt can be served as an alternative to cream with soups and desserts.

• Yogurt, particularly flavored yogurt, makes a delicious, light ice cream.

• Make yogurt into a drink similar to Danish ymer and Indian lassis. Yogurt drinks can be natural or flavored with fresh or dried fruit purées and sweetened with sugar syrup or, preferably, honey. The texture is similar to a light custard and one can drink them through a straw.

• Yogurt can be cooked as in the Bhapa Doi recipe on the next page.

BHAPA DOI (STEAMED SWEETENED YOGURT)

This isn't exactly a traditional recipe, but steamed puddings are certainly a forgotten skill. I ate the most sublime steamed yogurt in terra-cotta bowls at Kewpie's restaurant in Calcutta. This isn't exactly the same, but it is as delicious. This recipe comes from The Calcutta Kitchen, *with kind permission from Simon Parkes.*

The sweetness of the condensed milk works wonderfully with the acidity of the plain yogurt. In fact, it's the sucrose in condensed milk that gives it its long shelf life. This creamy pudding is similar to a crème caramel – one of my favorites · SERVES 8

3 cups natural yogurt
1¼ cups sweetened condensed milk
seeds of 6 green cardamom pods, powdered in a mortar and pestle
10 saffron strands

GARNISH
sliced pistachio nuts
rose petals

Heat some water in a steamer, such as a bamboo steamer over a wok, but any multitiered steamer will work. If you do not have a steamer, invert a small, metal, flat-bottomed bowl inside a larger pot with a close-fitting lid. Pour water into this and bring to a simmer.

Mix the natural yogurt and other ingredients in a bowl and whisk to incorporate some air, but don't overdo it or the whey will separate. Pour into 8 small serving bowls. Cover with plastic wrap and put in the steamer or, if not using a steamer, on top of the inverted bowl in the pot. Cover with the lid and steam on a steady simmer for 35–40 minutes.

Carefully remove the bowls and let cool. Remove the plastic wrap and chill.

Serve chilled, sprinkled with the sliced pistachio nuts and rose petals.

YOGURT CAKE WITH LEMON CURD AND SOUR CREAM

Yogurt isn't necessarily something you put into cakes (or much less pair with lemon), but this recipe is a real find. It's easy to make and you can serve it as a pudding or cake · SERVES 10–12

1½ cups all-purpose flour
1 teaspoon baking powder
½ teaspoon salt
4 small organic eggs, beaten
1 cup natural yogurt
1 cup superfine sugar
zest of 2 organic lemons, about 2 teaspoons
½ teaspoon pure vanilla extract
½ cup sunflower oil

FOR THE GLAZE
½ cup superfine sugar
⅓ cup freshly squeezed lemon juice

ACCOMPANIMENT
homemade Lemon Curd (see next recipe) OR summer berries OR Green Gooseberry and Elderflower Compote (see page 35)
sour cream or softly whipped cream

8in springform pan, lined with baking parchment (see page 524)

Preheat the oven to 350°F.

Sift the flour into a bowl and add the baking powder and salt. Beat the eggs in a separate bowl, adding yogurt, sugar, lemon zest, and vanilla extract. Beat well and then add the dry ingredients. Mix thoroughly, and finally beat in the oil in a steady stream.

Pour the cake mixture into the pan and bake for 1–1¼ hours. Test by putting a skewer into the center, which should come out clean rather than moist and sticky.

Meanwhile, mix ½ cup of sugar and the freshly squeezed lemon juice together to make a glaze.

When the cake is cooked, spoon the glaze over the top of the cake. Leave to cool in the pan.

Serve with homemade lemon curd, fresh berries, or a compote of your choice, and sour cream or softly whipped cream.

LEMON CURD

Tangy, delicious lemon curd can be made in a twinkling and smeared over a sponge cake or onto fresh bread, buttery scones, or meringues. It is best eaten within two weeks · MAKES 2 X 7FL OZ JARS

4 tablespoons butter
½ cup superfine sugar
grated zest and juice of 2 lemons
2 organic eggs and 1 organic egg yolk, beaten

Melt the butter on very low heat. Add the sugar, lemon zest and juice, then add the eggs. Stir carefully over low heat with a wooden spoon until the mixture coats the back of it.

Remove from the heat and pour into a bowl or sterilized jar (it will thicken further as it cools). Cover when cool and refrigerate.

YOGURT ICE CREAM

This is another recipe where really good yogurt (your own perhaps?) makes a great difference. This is more of a new skill rather than a forgotten skill, but it's well worth trying and experimenting with flavorings ·
SERVES 6–8

1¾ **cups whole, unsweetened natural yogurt**
½ **cup heavy cream**
¾ **cup superfine sugar**
1 **teaspoon pure vanilla extract**

Mix the yogurt with the cream, then add the sugar and the vanilla extract. Pour the mixture into an ice-cream machine or *sorbetière* and freeze according to manufacturer's instructions – about 30–35 minutes. Eat immediately or store in a covered container in the freezer.

Variations
FLAVORED YOGURT
ICE CREAM
Sweetened fruit purées, like strawberry, raspberry, blackberry, and mango, may be added to the base mixture before churning.

SOFT YOGURT CHEESE – LABNE

This thick, creamy, soft cheese from the Middle East is so easy to make and so wonderfully smooth that your friends will be mightily impressed if you produce it for a dinner party. This is an old recipe. I believe that dairy items like these were once made everywhere in Europe and elsewhere over many centuries and then forgotten at some stage, probably during industrialization, so I have borrowed from those places where the traditions survived. Labne is a real treat and an easy way to dabble in cheese making. It is also much-loved by children and is a good way for you to pass on your knowledge of old skills to them. It can be used for sweet or savory dishes.

Use whole-milk yogurt for a creamier cheese – this can be made from cow's, sheep's, or goat's milk. You can also use commercial yogurt
· **MAKES 18OZ LABNE**

4 **cups natural yogurt**

Line a strainer with a double thickness of sterilized cheesecloth. Place it over a bowl. Pour in the yogurt. Tie the four corners of the cheesecloth to make a loose bundle and suspend this bag of yogurt over a bowl. Leave it in a cool place to drip into the bowl for 8 hours. Then remove the cheesecloth and put the labne in a bowl. Refrigerate overnight, and store until needed in a covered glass or plastic container. The liquid whey that has drained off can be fed to pigs or hens.

LABNE BIL ZEYT (MARINATED LABNE)

Make the labne in the usual way, then marinate it. You don't have to dry the labne – you could just pop them into the jar immediately if you prefer
· **MAKES ENOUGH TO FILL A 1 QUART JAR**

18oz **cows', sheep's, or goats' milk Labne (see previous recipe)**
1 **teaspoon salt**
1 **red chile**
3 **sprigs of thyme or 1 sprig of rosemary**
extra virgin olive oil

Next day, unwrap the labne, put it into a bowl, sprinkle with salt, and mix well so it is evenly distributed. Shape the labne into small, walnut-sized pieces. If you like, put them out on a clean kitchen towel and leave to dry for a day or two in a cool place. Then fill into a sterilized jar, tucking the herb sprigs and chile in between the cheeses. Cover with olive oil and put on the lid.

Store in a cool, dark place, and the labne will keep for one to two months. Eat with crusty bread.

Variation
LABNE WITH FRESH HERBS
Add 4 tablespoons freshly chopped mint, parsley, and chives to the labne and serve with homemade crackers (see page 231).

Cheese

Cheese, like butter, was traditionally made on small farms in many parts of the world. Those who had surplus milk would have made not only butter, but one or maybe several cheeses for home use and local markets. Sadly, the Industrial Revolution virtually put an end to farmhouse cheese making. Economies of scale, price supports, and changing tastes led to the migration of cheese making and butter making from farms to creameries. Pasteurization soon followed.

The back-to-the-land movement of the 1960s and 1970s revived interest in traditional cheese making. A new generation of farmhouse cheese makers emerged, many of whom used raw milk from their own animals. Over the years, some cheese makers either decided or were forced to pasteurize under pressure from stringent national and EU hygiene regulations. Some cheese makers persisted, though, and the international Slow Food movement, recognizing their importance, created a raw-milk cheese presidia to protect them. The emergence of this farmhouse cheese movement is one of the most exciting developments on the food scene in recent times.

Even though some truly beautiful cheeses are available these days, it's still worth experimenting at home. There are many simple ones that are easy – and lots of fun – to make. There's also the satisfaction of being in control of the process and ingredients. In fact, it can become an enduring obsession.

Dairy hygiene

A dairy would always have been sited in a cool place, usually on the north side of a building. Marble or slate work surfaces kept temperatures low. Hygiene is crucial to successful cheese making, whether you're using raw or pasteurized milk. Utensils must be kept meticulously clean. You don't need to use chemicals to sterilize your equipment; simple boiling water will do as long as you are thorough.

What do I need to make cheese?

You don't need any special equipment to make a simple cheese at home, although if you're going to experiment with a variety of cheeses, you'll need rennet, starter cultures, and a few molds.

You will, of course, also need milk. Cheese connoisseurs believe that truly great cheese can only be made from unpasteurized milk, since it contains the natural bacteria that contributes to the unique character and flavor of the finished cheese. The debate rages on but the recipes that follow can be made with either raw or pasteurized (but not homogenized) milk.

Cheese-making equipment

To get started making cheese at home, you'll need the following:

- Large stainless-steel saucepan with a heavy bottom
- A thermometer, while not essential, can be very useful. Dairy thermometers have a range from 32–212°F and can be clamped to the side of a saucepan for ease of reading.
- Piece of cheesecloth for draining the curds (this can be reused). A linen napkin may also be used. You'll also need string to tie your cheesecloth bag and a hook to hang it from.
- Strainer
- Ladle
- Long-bladed knife to cut the curd. The blade should be 10–11in long and preferably have a rounded rather than pointed end; a stainless-steel spatula will suffice to begin with.
- A few simple cheese molds are useful, or even baskets or little bowls in stainless steel or plastic.

What are curds and whey?

Milk coagulates in the process of making cheese, and separates into solids (curds) and liquid (whey) during the cutting process. Whey can be used to make other cheese (e.g. Italian ricotta or Norwegian *gjetost*), used as food for calves or pigs, or as fertilizer for fields. At the Cookery School we boil the whey and then collect the milk solids to make ricotta. Many food manufacturers use whey powder, a product of industrial cheese making, in processed foods and supplements.

HOMEMADE COTTAGE CHEESE

Cottage cheese, formerly known as "curds and whey," is curd cheese drained of most but not all of its whey. It's not pressed, either, so the consistency remains loose and crumbly. The homemade version is so worth making yourself – it is smoother and tastes so much better than the slightly granular kind you buy in the store. But you must use good milk.

Cottage cheese is very versatile and is great to have in the kitchen to use in sweet and savory dishes. You will need to start one day ahead ·

MAKES ABOUT 1½ CUPS

2½ **quarts whole milk**
½ **teaspoon GM-free liquid rennet, mixed with 2 tablespoons water**

good-quality cheesecloth, sterilized in boiling water

Heat the milk in a spotlessly clean, stainless-steel saucepan very gently, until it is barely tepid. Sprinkle the rennet over the milk and stir in well. Don't be tempted to add more rennet to coagulate the milk more quickly as too much will result in a tough, acidic curd.

Cover the saucepan with a clean kitchen towel and the lid (the towel prevents the steam from condensing on the lid of the pan and falling back onto the curd). Leave undisturbed somewhere in your kitchen for 2–4 hours, by which time the milk should have coagulated and will have formed a solid curd, or "junket."

Dice the curd with a spotlessly clean, long-bladed knife, and you'll see the whey starting to exude. Put the curd back into the saucepan on a very low heat, and warm gently for a couple of minutes until the whey starts to run out of the curds. It must not get hot or the curds will tighten and toughen.

Ladle the curds and whey into a cheesecloth-lined colander placed over a bowl. Tie the corners of the cloth and leave it to drip overnight.

Next day, the curds can be used in all manner of ways, for example in *Coeur à la Crème* (see page 228) or Baked Cheesecake (see page 229). The whey can also be used – in soups, added to buttermilk for soda bread, to make ricotta cheese, or added to animal feed.

Variations

HOMEMADE COTTAGE CHEESE WITH FRESH HERBS AND OATCAKES

Strain the cottage cheese into a bowl. Then add 2–4 tablespoons of freshly chopped herbs – e.g. parsley, chives, chervil, lemon balm, and perhaps a little tarragon and thyme. Also add 1–2 crushed garlic cloves, if you like. Mix well and season to taste. It may even need a pinch of sugar if it tastes a little acidic. Spoon the cottage cheese into a pretty bowl and serve with homemade Oatcakes or Crackers (see pages 549 and 231). Sometimes a few tablespoons of heavy cream help to enhance the flavor and texture.

WHAT IS RENNET?

Rennet is a cluster of enzymes that is produced in the lining of a calf's stomach. It causes its mother's milk to coagulate and separate into curds (solids) and whey (liquid), thereby making it easier for the calf to break down. Rennet is traditionally used in cheese making to speed up the process of separating curds and whey.

In the olden days, a dried strip of calf's stomach would have been dipped in the vat of milk, but today rennet is extracted in laboratories and is more likely to come in bottles with an eyedropper. Rennet was one of the first products to be genetically modified, and I always specify non-GM rennet in my recipes.

Rennet is unsuitable for vegetarians, but rennet from non-animal sources, like lady's bedstraw, thistles, or cardoons, is widely available. All types of rennet are available in liquid, tablet, or powdered form from cheese-making suppliers (see Resources, page 584).

COTTAGE CHEESE WITH NASTURTIUM FLOWERS

Nasturtium flowers add a wonderful peppery flavor to cottage cheese. Gently stir in 1–2 tablespoons of shredded red, yellow, and orange flowers. Then garnish with whole nasturtium leaves and flowers.

HOMEMADE CREAM CHEESE

You know that slightly boiled flavor you get from commercial cream cheese? Homemade cream cheese doesn't have that, which is reason alone to make it · SERVES 4: MAKES ABOUT 1½ CUPS

1 quart whole milk
¾ cup heavy cream
lemon zest
1 teaspoon non-GM rennet, mixed with 2 tablespoons water

Heat the milk, cream, and fine lemon zest to blood temperature, then remove from the heat and stir in the rennet. Cover and leave in a warm place for 3 hours, until set.

Cut the curd into squares with a clean knife. Line a colander with a double layer of cheesecloth. Gently scoop the curds with a large spoon into the cloth, taking care to break them as little as possible. Leave it to drain for at least 12 hours.

COEUR À LA CRÈME WITH SUMMER BERRIES

I had to battle my editor to keep this in the book because I've published this recipe before. But if you go to the trouble of making your own cottage or cream cheese, this is one of the nicest ways to use it. Use individual or one large mold (in France they are traditionally heart-shaped). The molds must be well perforated to allow the cheese to drain · SERVES 4

1 cup homemade Cottage Cheese (see page 227) OR unsalted homemade Cream Cheese (see previous recipe)
1¼ cups heavy cream, softly whipped
2 tablespoons superfine sugar
2 organic egg whites, stiffly beaten

ACCOMPANIMENT
summer berries, *fraises du bois*, strawberries, raspberries, loganberries, blackberries, red currants, blueberries...
Strawberry, Raspberry, or Black Currant Coulis (see next recipes)
1¼ cups heavy cream, softly whipped
superfine sugar
fresh mint leaves, for garnish

Press the cheese through a fine-mesh nylon sieve and blend it gently with the heavy cream. Stir in the sugar and lightly but thoroughly fold in the stiffly beaten egg whites. Spoon the mixture into cheesecloth-lined, heart-shaped molds. Stand them on a wide plate, cover with a large plastic bag, and leave in the refrigerator overnight to drain.

Just before serving, turn the molded *coeurs à la crème* out onto white plates. Then scatter a selection of summer fruits around them.

Serve with a strawberry, raspberry, or black currant coulis, softly whipped cream, and superfine sugar. Decorate with sprigs of mint. It is also delicious with any fruit compote.

FRESH STRAWBERRY COULIS

SERVES 8

14oz fresh strawberries
½ cup confectioners' sugar
lemon juice

Clean and hull the strawberries, then place in a blender with sugar and blend. Strain, taste, and add lemon juice if necessary. Use as soon as possible or store in a fridge for no more than 2 days.

RASPBERRY COULIS

8oz raspberries
3–6 tablespoons sugar
lemon juice (optional)

Make a syrup of the sugar and 8 tablespoons water. Cool and add to the raspberries. Purée and sieve. Taste and sharpen with lemon juice if necessary. Use as soon as possible or store in a fridge for up to 2 days.

BLACK CURRANT COULIS

8oz black currants
1 cup Stock Syrup (see page 468)

Pour the stock syrup over the black currants and bring to a boil. Cook for 3–5 minutes until the blackcurrants burst. Purée and put through a nylon sieve. Leave to cool. Add ½–⅔ cup of water. Store in a fridge. Black currant coulis keeps for weeks and freezes very well.

ALISON HENDERSON'S BAKED CHEESECAKE

I hate cheesecake with a passion, and this is the only one that has ever made me understand why people bother to make it. Thank you, Alison. The top usually cracks as it cools but don't worry – this doesn't affect the flavor ·
SERVES 8

6oz (about 25) **Gingersnap Cookies (see page 548), reduced to a powder in a food processor**
4 tablespoons **butter, melted**
1 cup **homemade Cream Cheese (see previous page) OR well-drained Cottage Cheese (see page 227)**
3 large **organic eggs, separated**
½ cup **superfine sugar**
¾ cup **natural full-fat yogurt**
⅓ cup **raisins**
¼ cup **whole peeled almonds to decorate**

FOR THE APRICOT GLAZE
1 cup **Apricot Jam (see page 448)**
juice of a quarter lemon

8 x 3in cake pan with a removable base

Mix the powdered cookies with the melted butter and press into the base of the cake pan. Chill for 30 minutes.

Preheat the oven to 325°F.

Combine the cream cheese or cottage cheese, egg yolks and ¼ cup of the sugar into a bowl. Add the yogurt and beat until smooth. Add the raisins. Next beat the egg whites in a large, clean, dry bowl until they reach stiff peaks. Gradually add the

remaining sugar, and beat until stiff and glossy. Carefully fold the egg white and sugar mixture into the cheese mixture.

Pour into the cookie base and decorate with the almonds. Bake for 45 minutes until golden, risen, and set. Remove from the oven.

Meanwhile, make the apricot glaze. In a small, stainless-steel saucepan, melt the apricot jam with 1–2 tablespoons of lemon juice or water. Push the hot jam through a fine sieve.

Once the cake has cooled 5 minutes, run a sharp knife around

Above: *Alison Henderson's Baked Cheesecake.*

the edge of the cheesecake to loosen it and minimize surface cracking. When cool, top with the apricot glaze (melt and stir it before use if necessary). Store any leftover glaze in a sterilized airtight jar.

STARTERS

All cheeses rely on some kind of bacteria, or "starter," to ferment the milk and turn it into cheese. Some recipes rely on bacteria from the air but commercial cheese makers don't leave things to chance and use custom-made starters. These introduce specific bacteria that give the cheese its unique character.

They are divided into two basic groups: thermophilic and mesophilic. Thermophilic cultures are heat-loving and are used to make Swiss cheese and Italian cheeses such as Parmesan and mozzarella. Yogurt is also made with thermophilic culture.

Mesophilic cultures thrive at cooler temperatures and are used in about 90 percent of cheese making.

MASCARPONE

Mascarpone, originally from the area southwest of Milan, isn't really a cheese – it's a result of a curdling agent being added to cream. Some store-bought Mascarpone can have a synthetic taste, but it's lovely when you make it at home – creamy, and just slightly sour. We've found that the secret is to leave it to rest overnight in the first stage, rather than just an hour, which is what most recipes call for.

Mascarpone will keep for a week to 10 days in the fridge · **MAKES 8½ CUPS**

2½ **quarts heavy cream**
1oz **citric acid OR 4 tablespoons lemon juice**

Heat the cream in a spotlessly clean stainless-steel saucepan, stirring constantly. As soon as the temperature reaches 185°F, turn off the heat.

Add the citric acid or lemon juice, stir for a minute, then let cool to room temperature. Cover and leave in the fridge overnight. It will set to the consistency of a thick yogurt.

Next day, put a sieve or colander over a bowl, line it with a square of cheesecloth and ladle the curds in carefully. Tie the ends of the cheesecloth, put in the fridge, and leave to drip overnight. It picks up flavors very easily so make sure there are no other strong smells in the fridge.

Next day, transfer the fresh Mascarpone to a sterilized container. Cover tightly, refrigerate, and use as required. We give the leftover whey to the hens or pigs, or you can use it for Soda Bread (see page 561).

TIRAMISU

The name means "pick-me-up" – not surprising, considering the amount of booze in it! This is a fairly recent Italian dessert that seems to have originated in Venice but is now served in restaurants all over Italy, and it always tastes different. We've had rave reviews for this version, which is very easily put together · **SERVES 8**

1 **cup strong coffee – espresso is best**
2 **tablespoons brandy**
2 **tablespoons Jamaica rum**
3oz **dark chocolate**
3 **organic eggs, separated**
4 **tablespoons superfine sugar**
1 **heaping cup Mascarpone cheese**
38–40 **ladyfingers**
unsweetened cocoa

8 x 10in **dish with low sides OR a 1lb loaf pan 4 x 8in, lined with plastic wrap**

Mix the coffee with the brandy and rum. Roughly grate the chocolate (we do it in the food processor with the pulse button).

Beat the egg yolks with the sugar until the mixture falls off the whisk as "ribbons" and is light and fluffy, then fold in the Mascarpone one tablespoon at a time. Beat the egg whites to stiff peaks and fold gently into the cheese mixture. Now you are ready to assemble the tiramisu.

Dip each side of the ladyfingers one at a time into the coffee mixture and arrange side by side in the dish or pan. Spread half the Mascarpone mixture gently over the ladyfingers, sprinkle half the grated chocolate over the top, then add another layer of soaked ladyfingers, and finally the rest of the Mascarpone. Cover the whole dish or loaf pan carefully with plastic wrap, or, better still, slide it into a plastic bag and twist the end. Refrigerate for at least 6 hours (I usually make it the day before I serve it).

Just before serving, scatter the remainder of the chocolate over the top and sprinkle with cocoa.

Tiramisu will keep for several days in a fridge, but make sure it is covered so that it doesn't pick up "fridgy" tastes.

JUNKET

Junket is nearly cheese – it involves rennet, but is still really easy and requires no special equipment to make. A delicate and delicious pudding, it has a gorgeous, tender texture that further enhances the enjoyment of eating it. Junket is a very old recipe, mentioned in The Boke of Nurture, Folowyng Englodis Gise, *by John Russell, circa 1460. In the more recent book* English Food, *by Jane Grigson, Devonshire "junket" includes two tablespoons of brandy* · SERVES 6

3 cups whole milk
1 tablespoon superfine sugar
1 teaspoon non-GM rennet
softly whipped cream
freshly grated nutmeg or soft
    brown sugar (optional)

Warm the milk gently for a couple of minutes until it is neither hot nor cold to the touch. Add the sugar and stir until dissolved. Remove from the heat.

Sprinkle the rennet over the surface and stir. Pour into a shallow pie dish and leave at room temperature until set.

Spoon a thin layer of very softly whipped cream over the top just before serving. Some people like to dust the surface with a little freshly grated nutmeg or soft brown sugar.

Serve the junket on its own or with a fruit compote.

SOFT GOAT CHEESE

This recipe came to me from former student Mike Hanrahan. He got it from local cheese maker Jane Murphy of Ardsallagh farm who says that, though she prefers raw milk, pasteurized goat's milk is fine and needs less setting time. The raw goat's milk, which can prove very hard to come by, makes a much creamier, tastier cheese, which will be ready to eat in four days · MAKES ABOUT 6OZ

2 quarts raw goat's milk
1 heaped teaspoon goat cheese
    starter
a drop of non-GM rennet
perforated cheese molds 3in wide
    x 2¼in deep

Day *1*
Warm the goat's milk in a heavy, stainless-steel saucepan over low heat. When the temperature reaches 160°F, turn off the heat (do not boil) and let cool to 80°F.

Scatter the starter over the surface of the milk. Stir gently and leave for 1 hour at room temperature.

Then add the rennet and stir slowly for 2 minutes. Cover and

leave at room temperature for about 24 hours.

Day *2*
Ladle the goat's milk mixture carefully into 2 molds. Let drain (a wire rack over a basin is ideal for this).

Day *3*
Gently turn the cheeses over in their molds and let drain for another 24 hours.

Day *4*
The goat cheese is now ready to eat. Serve and enjoy with homemade crackers (see below).

HOMEMADE CRACKERS

These light crackers taste delicious with butter alone, or with butter and a soft cheese. The thinner you can roll them the better · MAKES 45–50 CRACKERS

2 cups all-purpose flour
2 tablespoons butter
pinch of salt
around ¾ cup hot milk

Preheat the oven to 425°F.

Rub the first three ingredients together. Mix to a dough with the hot milk, it should be firm but soft. Knead well. Roll out small bits of the dough to paper thinness – it will look and feel like a piece of cloth. Cut into 3in rounds with a plain or fluted scone cutter and bake for about 5 minutes, until slightly browned and puffed up. Cool and store in an airtight box.

Left: *Paneer.*

the ends of the cheesecloth and let drain. Then put the cheese into a round or rectangular mold with holes, cover with a plate, and press down gently. The paneer can be used soon after.

Good things to serve with paneer:
• Tomato salsa
• Tomato and Chile Fondue (see page 378) and peas
• Spinach and olive oil

SEMIHARD CHEESE

If you'd like to try your hand at a simple semihard cheese, have a go at this recipe that Philip Dennhardt showed us how to make at the Cookery School. Students occasionally ring the changes by adding cumin seeds, black peppercorns, or fenugreek seeds. It always fascinates me that each student sees exactly the same demonstration and follows the same recipe using the same batch of milk – yet every cheese turns out slightly differently, reflecting the student's interpretation.

Remember, cheese making can't be hurried, so slow down and enjoy the process. You are working with live bacteria, which are sensitive to heat: if the milk gets too hot they'll die; if it's too cold they won't multiply
· **MAKES ABOUT 12OZ**

3½ **quarts whole milk, preferably unpasteurized**
2 **teaspoons live natural yogurt**
1 **teaspoon liquid rennet OR**
  ½ **teaspoon powdered non-GM rennet**

PANEER

Here is another very simple cheese that I'm borrowing from India. Paneer is a fresh curd cheese made extensively in north India and less so in the south, where there are fewer cows. It is used in a myriad of Indian vegetable dishes. If you're slightly intimidated by the prospect of cheese making, paneer is a good place to start. It requires no special ingredients or equipment and, most importantly, is easy to make. All you need is a saucepan! Paneer can be kept refrigerated for two to three days
· **SERVES 4–6**

7⅔ **cups whole milk**
3–4 **tablespoons lemon juice or white wine vinegar**

Bring the milk to a boil in a large deep-sided, stainless-steel saucepan. When it looks as though it might boil over, add 3 tablespoons of lemon juice or vinegar. Stir and turn off the heat; the milk should start to curdle immediately. Stir the curds until they separate from the whey. Put a large sieve, strainer, or colander over a deep bowl lined with a double layer of cheesecloth. Pour the curds and whey into the cheesecloth, leaving the whey to drain away. Alternatively, gather up

1 teaspoon sea salt or
   pickling salt

2 x molds 6in deep x 12in wide

Slowly heat the milk in a deep, heavy-bottomed, stainless-steel saucepan to 72°F, then remove from the heat and stir in the yogurt. Leave for 15 minutes. The yogurt cultures will help to create acidity, which the rennet needs to work.

Mix the rennet with 4 tablespoons of cold water. If using powdered rennet, dissolve it in the water.

Return the saucepan to the heat and when the milk reaches 86°F, turn off the heat. Add the rennet, stir gently, cover, and leave at room temperature for up to 45 minutes, until the curd is set.

Take a knife with a long, sterilized blade and cut lengthwise and then crosswise, over and over again until the curd is cut first into small cubes and eventually is about the size of peppercorns. The cutting should be done slowly and gently and takes about 15 minutes. The curds (the thick part) and the whey (the liquid) will separate.

Put the saucepan over a gentle heat and stir the curds and whey slowly with your clean hand until they start to become too hot to bear (about 105–115°F). Remove from the heat, then stir for another 10–15 minutes, until the curd becomes slightly rubbery in texture. Using a perforated spoon, gently ladle the curds into a mold. Then, using your hands or a spoon, press the curd down so that more whey drains out. An unpressed cheese will be much

softer and won't keep as long.

Turn the cheese onto a cold, upturned, sterilized dinner plate, so the whey can drain away easily. Lightly sprinkle salt or over the top and around the sides. This draws out moisture and inhibits the growth of bacteria. Leave in a cold, dry place overnight.

Next day, turn the cheese over on the plate. Sprinkle salt on the top (formerly the bottom), so that all sides of the cheese have been salted. Turn the cheese over every day, making sure that it doesn't sit in its own juice (dry the plate with paper towels if necessary). Better still, transfer the cheese to a sterilized cutting board or shelf.

After about 10 days a rind will have formed and in 4–5 weeks the cheese should be ready to cut. If a mold grows on the outside, don't panic. Just wash it in brine (1 tablespoon of salt to 2½ cups of water) and put it back on the plate or cutting board. Let it dry out for a couple of days and enjoy the fruits of your labor with some crusty white bread or crackers.

NOTE: if the milk does not coagulate, something may have gone wrong:
• Too little rennet may have been used. Increase the amount in the next batch but don't overdo it, too much rennet produces a tough, acidic curd.
• The rennet may have been stale. Buy rennet in small quantities because it gradually loses potency.
• If the water used to dilute the rennet was too hot, it may have killed the rennet. A temperature of about 50–59.9°F is the maximum.

DOUNE MCKENZIE'S CHEESE CRISPS

This is a brilliant recipe for using up leftover cheese. A little soft cheese may also be added, but you will need to balance the flavor with hard cheese. Delicious to nibble with a glass of wine or to tuck into a lunch box.

**Cheddar, Parmesan, Gruyère, or
   other cheese of your choice**
butter
all-purpose flour

Weigh the cheese, then use the same weight of butter and flour.

Preheat the oven to 475°F.

Grate the cheese – rinds and all. Dice, then whip the butter. Stir in the flour and grated cheese and form into a roll like a long sausage, about 1½in thick. Alternatively process in a food processor until it forms a dough – shape using a little flour if necessary. Chill in the refrigerator for 1–2 hours, until solid.

Slice into rounds about ⅓ in thick. Arrange on a baking sheet and bake for about 5 minutes or until golden. Cool for a couple of seconds, then transfer to a wire rack. These crisps are best eaten on the day they are made as they soften quite quickly.

Eggs and Poultry

Of all the Forgotten Skills courses that we've been running since 1990, "How to keep a few chickens in your garden" has always generated the greatest excitement, but in recent times the interest has totally skyrocketed. Every course seems to be oversubscribed and the participants come fired up with enthusiasm and ready to go with chickens, coop, and feeder.

Years ago, it was very common for people to keep hens – nearly every farm or cottage would have had a few scratching around the yard. There used to be a poultry instructor in every county, but by the early 21st century there was not a single one left. We were in a catch-22 where anyone who actually wanted to keep poultry had nobody to advise and support them. Now, I am happy to say this valuable service is becoming available again.

My family has kept hens for as long as I can remember. In one of my earliest memories, I am taking my little bucket full of scraps down to the hen run at the end of the garden, clutching Mummy's hand tightly. I remember the feeling of apprehension as the hens ran toward me. I must have been very tiny because they came up to my waist. It was a really holistic system: hen manure went onto the compost heap, and the aged compost went into the vegetable garden to make the soil more fertile to grow nutritious vegetables. Food scraps from the house were fed to the hens and came back as eggs a few days later. It was win-win all the way.

So why should you bother keeping hens? Despite the availability of eggs claiming to be free-range and organic, it is really difficult to find eggs laid by hens that are actually ranging freely on fresh green grass. Keeping your own hens is something you can do even in an urban setting – maybe not on your balcony, but people in London, Dublin, and San Francisco are all doing it, and you can, too.

Provided you're not doing it on a big scale, it's not complicated to rear a few chickens for the table either. You'll need more land, but anyone who, like me, remembers what chickens used to taste like will tell you that it's certainly worth the effort. Keeping ducks and geese has lots of extra bonuses for the gardener, too. Ducks gobble up slugs and worms, and geese make wonderful country watchdogs.

When I was a child, our family operated the post office in our little village. At Christmas, I remember people bringing in ducks and geese plucked and neatly sewn in calico flour bags, with the head and feet sticking out and the label tied around the neck, and sending these packages off to relatives in Dublin. If you did that today it would probably make the news. I actually called the post office to see if this was still allowed; the man I spoke with said that they never officially discontinued the practice, but it was unlikely that the package would make it through if you tried that sort of thing today!

At the Cookery School, we keep three flocks of hens, and the students feed them daily with the scraps from the morning's cooking. Initially, some are terrified of the hens, never having never been up close and personal with a hen in their entire lives. On one course, I discovered that several of the girls were paying an American student to feed the hens when their turn came up. Apparently they were traumatized by the hens running toward them when they arrived with the buckets full of scraps. They didn't seem to realize that the hens were not in the least interested in them, it was the food they were after. When I asked Steve, the American, why he enjoyed feeding the hens so much, he quipped, "I love it when all the hens run toward me when I appear around the corner – to tell you the truth, they are the only appreciative females I've ever encountered in all my life." Therein must lie a tale!

Keeping Hens

Why bother keeping hens?

1 To have a supply of fresh, free-range, and possibly organic, eggs. Research has shown that organic, free-range eggs are considerably lower in cholesterol than eggs from intensive production systems.

2 To generate a supply of nitrogen and phosphate-rich manure that will turn into a rich compost for your garden.

3 For pest and weed control. I open the garden gate to allow our hens into the vegetable gardens in the winter to gobble up slugs and insects.

4 Because children love to collect eggs and it helps to connect them with the reality of how food is produced.

5 Because from a cook's point of view, the quality of an egg hugely affects the flavor and texture of food. There is no comparison between the taste of free-range, organic eggs and intensively produced eggs from a battery system.

6 For divine Mayonnaise (see page 252), Hollandaise (see page 248), Béarnaise (see page 173)… nowadays a really good soft-boiled egg with toast is a forgotten flavor for many people.

7 For the sheer joy of keeping a few hens. They are intriguing creatures and many breeds are truly beautiful – decorative as well as functional, although it must be said that the fancier they are, the fewer eggs they lay, in most cases.

How many hens do I need?

Five or six hens will provide plenty of eggs for an average household. Depending on the breed, a hen will lay up to 300 eggs a year.

Where do I start?

If you live in a city or town, you may first want to check planning regulations in your area. Usually regulations do not expressly forbid the keeping of livestock in your garden. Most authorities accept that if they are for family use and not for business purposes they fall into a category referred to in the planning phrase: "part of the enjoyment of the dwelling."

Where can I buy chickens?

Chicken are sometimes sold at livestock markets, farmers' markets, or after summer agricultural shows. Buy from a reputable supplier and ask for a certificate to prove they are disease-free. Transport birds in large cardboard boxes with lots of ventilation.

If you buy day-old chickens, you will need an infrared lamp. Point of Laying (POL) pullets, or young hens, will arrive in large, plastic crates, four to six birds to a crate. These birds are 16–18 weeks old, but they probably won't start to lay eggs for another two to three weeks.

Pets will get accustomed to your hens, but let them do so gradually. Keep the chickens confined to the coop and run them for four or five days until they get acclimatized.

How long do hens live?

Hens in intensive systems are killed after a year, but happy, lazy free-range hens can live from five (Bantams) to 10 years (full-size birds).

What do hens eat?

Hens are not vegetarian. Chickens love food scraps from the house, particularly if they are mixed with mash, but it is both unwise and unethical to feed them chicken products. Scraps greatly enhance the flavor of eggs. In our experience, hens have a preference for cooked scraps – cooked cauliflower stems will be gobbled up while raw ones will remain on the ground to rot. Giving them raw produce only attracts vermin and looks unsightly. Also, observe your hen's appetite. Feeding it more than is necessary will simply result in waste and attract vermin.

Hens are pretty fussy, so keep an eye on what they discard and that will give you an indication of their likes and dislikes. They don't eat citrus peel, so these are best composted, dried, or made into Candied Peel (see page 458). There really is no point in feeding them foods they dislike, as it'll just make a mess and encourage rodents.

Laying an egg requires a lot of energy, so you may want to supplement your hen's diet with a specially formulated layers' mash, a mixture of wheat, barley, oats, maize, and soy with added vitamins and minerals. Each hen needs 3½–5½oz of feed every day. Ensure that

Above: *Ladies with attitude – traditional breeds such as Marran, Light Sussex, and Rhode Island Red are suited to free-range production.*

it is GM-free. There are also different feed formulations for chicks, pullets, and hens. Buy food in small quantities to ensure a quick turnover and freshness.

Grass is essential for healthy birds and good-quality eggs. If they have access to grass and can range freely, they are very effective at balancing their own nutritional requirements and are capable of finding a good proportion of their daily food needs. They will eat grass and other greenery, worms, and insects. Provide some grit, too, like crushed oyster shells, to strengthen their shells.

Hens have no teeth, hence the expression "as rare as hens' teeth." They swallow small stones and grit to help them to grind up the food in their gizzards. Foraging,

then, is good for them because ingesting pebbles is good for their digestion.

On a hot day, a chicken can drink more than 2 cups of water, so be sure to provide enough. Special food and drinking containers can be bought from specialist suppliers and should be washed regularly.

Food storage

Store your poultry feed and grain in galvanized pails to protect it from vermin. If possible, cover the feeding area to exclude birds, pigeons, and crows. We cover our feeding area with netting to exclude other birds. They can eat incredible amounts of feed, which you'll soon see proves to be expensive!

What about housing?

Provide as much space as is feasible. A mobile coop is a good idea, and there is a variety of houses available, from the tiny eglu and movable coops to larger portable henhouses (see Resources, page 584).

Chickens need to perch. The bar should be 1–1¾in wide and positioned toward the back of the house. Chickens excrete half their droppings at night, so you may want to position a removable tray underneath for ease of cleaning.

Henhouses can be decorative as well as functional: covered with trellis, for example. Our own *Palais des Poulets* has roses and honeysuckle tumbling all over it.

How often should I clean the henhouse?

Clean out a small coop weekly. Occasionally, a large henhouse can be whitewashed, preferably with hydrated lime. We also scatter dry barn lime on the floor and top with fresh straw. Most problems are caused by the trauma of overcrowding. If your birds have a happy, lazy life and adequate food and water, you should have few problems.

What should I use as bedding?

Use straw, shredded paper from the office, dry leaves, or a mixture. Clean out the henhouse regularly and add the straw and hen manure to the compost heap. Put in fresh straw every one or two weeks, depending on the size of your henhouse.

How many nesting boxes do I need?

Provide at least one nesting box for every four chickens. Use straw or shredded paper to line the nesting boxes. Put them in the darkest part of the henhouse, as a hen's aim is to hide the eggs from you!

Do I need to have a rooster with my hens?

It is not essential to keep a rooster; hens like to have a cockerel around but it doesn't affect how they lay. It might be best not to have a rooster in a built-up area; otherwise neighbors may complain! A regular gift of a few eggs can work wonders, though.

What about chicks?

If you want to have chicks, you must have a cock so the eggs will be fertilized – and you also need a broody hen to hatch them out. Alternatively, you can hatch the eggs in an electric incubator, but then they must be kept under an infrared heat lamp and fed daily (see below). Slipping a few fertilized eggs under the hen doesn't mean she'll sit and hatch them; rather, she must be in the humor.

How long is the incubation period?

For hen's eggs, the incubation period is 21 days; for ducks and geese, it's about 28–30 days. When the chicks hatch, they will probably stay tucked in under the mother hen for a couple of days. They can survive for 24 hours without food.

When they venture out, give them some water in a shallow dish that cannot be tipped over, as chicks can drown easily (we always put a large stone in the center). Feed them with some chick meal or oatmeal. The hen will show the chicks how to scratch and forage – mother hens are very protective of their brood and will defend them gallantly from any predator: human or animal.

Will I have male and female chicks?

A clutch of chickens will be a mixture of male and female. After five or six weeks feathers will start to replace the downy fluff. Cocks grow little tails, which makes them easy to identify. The cocks can be reared for the table and killed after about 14 weeks – one cock is enough for a small flock; otherwise they fight and the hen gets exhausted from all the attention.

What is a broody hen?

In spring or early summer, some hens become "broody" and lay a clutch of eggs, usually between 9 and 15. A broody hen sits and sits on the nesting box and will usually react angrily if you disturb or try to remove her. She may even peck you and will want to hop straight back into the nest. If you don't want chicks, take the eggs away and prevent her from nesting, and eventually she will give up.

You can stop a hen from being broody by putting a light wooden box over her for a week or so until the humor goes off her, but it's really much better just to let nature take its course. Move the hen plus the eggs into a strong, straw-lined box. She will come out once a day for about 15 minutes to eat and drink and perform her ablutions. A lot of the hybrid varieties have actually had the broodiness bred out of them. That's one of the lovely things about the old breeds and bantams; they still have that instinct.

What if I don't have a broody hen?

Eggs can, of course, be hatched without a hen. An incubator will maintain a constant temperature and turn the eggs automatically every couple of hours, although it may take them a day or two longer than the usual incubation period to hatch. If you do not have a broody hen, you will then need to move the newly hatched chicks to a brooder (a small enclosed area) with an infrared heat lamp for warmth. You will also need food and water containers. This is much more work than simply allowing nature to take its course, but beware, hatching chicks can become addictive. It can also become a lucrative hobby as more and more people want to keep a few hens in their garden.

You don't necessarily have to hatch out the chicks yourself. You can also buy day-old chicks from specialist hatcheries or the growing number of enthusiast breeders. Choose the breed carefully – avoid hybrids that are bred for intensive production and choose traditional breeds instead that are suited to free-range organic production systems. Mummy always reared Rhode Island Red cockerels for the table, and they made fantastic eating. You will need to put day-olds under an infrared heat lamp, which you can buy especially for this purpose in a local farm-supply store or poultry suppliers. Gradually increase the space as they grow. Feed them organic chick mash for the first few days, then wheat or oatmeal mixed with milk and a hard-boiled egg mashed with a little milk can be added to their ration.

After five to seven weeks they can roam out onto grass for a few hours a day, for access to grit. By eight and a half weeks, they will weigh about 2½–3½lb and are called broilers. Their flavor will be even better if you fatten them up for 14–15 weeks.

Top right: *The eglu, light and easy to move around a suburban backyard.* **Bottom right:** *Another, more traditional, moveable coop.*

How can I protect my flock from predators?

A fox is not the only enemy; dogs, hawks, raccoons, and coyotes are also a menace in some areas. A low electric fence is the best deterrent.

For total protection from predators, a 6.5ft wire netting fence is advisable. Dig the bottom 6in into the ground for fox and dog protection. Our busy little Jack Russell and Border terriers also help to keep the foxes at bay.

If you need to confine your hens, or if they are flighty and try to escape, their wings can be clipped. It may sound a bit drastic, but you only need to trim the first three or four feathers on one wing. This can be done with strong scissors.

Should I let them dust bathe?

Hens need to have a dust bath regularly to keep away mites. When they range freely they will scratch in the dry earth.

Why are their feathers falling out?

All hens molt automatically in late summer, when they stop laying. Hens lose their feathers, but fear not, they will grow another layer of feathers. Molting lasts about four weeks. Outside this period, if a chicken is molting give it a once over to make sure it's not unwell.

How do I know if I have a sick chicken?

Sick chickens hunch up and stand in one place for a long time, looking into space. They go off their food and sometimes have runny noses. Combs on a sick chicken might look pale pink rather than red (a red comb usually indicates a chicken is in prime condition and laying well) and their droppings may be runny rather than solid.

What do I do if I have a sick chicken?

If a bird becomes ill, call your vet (check that the bird has a clean beak and that its nostrils are clear, etc). Free-range hens are healthier and have fewer problems with disease and mites.

If they seem off-color, try a crushed garlic clove or a half-teaspoon of Epsom salts in the drinking water. A couple of spoonfuls of cod liver oil mixed with food is also a tried-and-tested tonic, especially during the molting season.

Like many animals, chickens can pick up worm eggs while they are feeding. These hatch out and live in the intestines of the bird. Hens will increase their food intake, lay fewer eggs, or may stop laying altogether. If you suspect that your chickens have worms, buy a worming treatment from your vet and mix it with the feed. It's probably a good idea to worm your flock twice a year as a precaution.

How do I keep my hens healthy?

It is not advisable to put a batch of hens on the same ground as the previous flock. It is prudent to allow a hen run to recover for six months to eliminate any disease or parasites that may have built up, particularly if the flock was confined to a small area.

Salmonella

Even free-range organic chickens can pick up salmonella occasionally, particularly if wild birds share their food. It is prudent to send a small sample of feces to a laboratory to be tested once or twice a year. It may cost a small fee, but it's worth it for peace of mind.

A day in the life of a chicken

Hens usually lay their eggs in the morning. They are sensitive to light, so they lay more in warmer weather than in winter. Hens also eat most of their food in the morning and drink lots of water, up to 2½ cups of fresh clean water per day. Remember, chickens are naturally forest-dwellers, so if possible, provide some trees or shrubs to shelter them from the rain and direct sun.

Hens usually peck grass before they go in to roost at sundown and will go indoors themselves at night. The door must be shut though; otherwise the foxes will gobble them all up! Foxes are most active early in the morning and are most daring when they have hungry young.

Good breeds for free-range production

Seek out poultry that are bred for free-range production. As a general rule, the fancier and more ornamental breeds are more decorative than functional. They lay fewer eggs but they also look gorgeous in your garden!

As a rough guide, hens lay between three and six eggs each week, depending on the breed. Also depending on breed, eggs can be brown, white, speckled, or even turquoise, as with the Araucanas. The main laying season is from Valentine's Day to Halloween. Main breeds include:
• Rhode Island Reds (lay about 260 eggs per year)
• Light Sussex (lay about 260 eggs per year)
• Marans (a French breed of several varieties – lay about 200 eggs per year)
• Welsummers (a crossbreed – lay about 200 eggs per year)
• Orpington (Buff or Black – they have cute fluffy legs but are not great layers. Their eggs are terra-cotta colored.)

HYBRIDS

Hybrids are less expensive than pure breeds. There are many to choose from, and they generally lay more than 300 eggs each year:
• Rhode Island Red hybrids (lay 300 eggs per year)
• White Stars (lay about 300 eggs per year)
• Black Rocks (lay about 320 eggs per year)
• Speckledys, a mixture of Rhode Island Reds and Marans (lay about 250 eggs a year)
• Hepden Blacks (lay about 250 eggs per year)

BANTAMS

The name *bantam* comes from the village of Bantam in Java. After a trading boat from the East Indies arrived in Great Britain carrying lots of miniature chickens, the Victorians used the name bantam to denote any small chicken. Bantams are a brilliant choice for keeping, particularly if space is restricted.

There are lots of bantam breeds to choose from. They make great mothers and will hatch out clutch after clutch of chickens that will enchant your family and friends. They make great layers, too. Of course they lay smaller eggs, which children particularly adore. I love to serve them for children's breakfast: a fried bantam egg with a small piece of bacon, some cherry tomatoes, and little sausages.

Bantams can live for up to five years. Types of bantam include:
• Pekin Bantams
• Japanese Bantams
• Polish Bantams; these have a head of bushy feathers and we call them "Tiny Turners"
• Maran Bantams; these lay better than standard-sized Marans
• Plymouth Rock Bantams
• Lace Wing Bantams
• Silkies

Poultry terms

Chicken: a chicken at any age may be referred to as a chicken.
Pullet: before she lays her first egg at 20–24 weeks, a female chicken is called a pullet, so a pullet is a young female.
Hen: after the momentous event of laying her first egg, a pullet officially becomes a hen. A hen is a female who lays eggs.
Cockerel: a young male is called a cockerel. They are usually fattened up for the table in 39 to 100 days, depending on the intensity of production system.
Cock: a cock is a fully grown male. Cocks fertilize hens' eggs.
Poussin: a poussin is a young chicken killed between two and four weeks, long before they have time to develop any flavor. They look sweet but are usually a waste of time as far as eating is concerned. Having said that, they are very appealing as a main course for one person if you add lots of spices or Moroccan flavors – you can have a tasty meal.
Capon: a capon is a castrated male reared for the table. They grow slowly and accumulate more body fat. They are marketed around 15 to 18 weeks of age, when they have reached a weight of 6–8lb.
Broiler: commercial broiler chickens are sent to market when they are as little as six weeks old.

Eggs

If keeping hens is not an option, here are some guidelines on buying eggs.

Free-range vs organic
People are often confused about the terms free-range and organic when it comes to eggs, and understandably so. Organic eggs must come from chickens that are allowed to range freely on grass, but the term "free-range" alone on a label is quite elastic. For example, the regulations allow producers to label their eggs free-range provided there are no more than a certain number of chickens in a house.

In addition, organic eggs come from hens fed on a special feed that does not contain any animal materials, any products derived from genetically modified organisms, or any raw materials produced by chemical processes. This diet costs about 60 percent more than conventional feed. Organic eggs are expensive to produce but to my mind are worth every penny. This is why I always specify organic eggs in my recipes.

How can I tell whether eggs are fresh?
Fresh eggs sink in water, while staler eggs (over a week old) will float. If you crack an egg onto a plate, a fresh egg will have three distinct layers: a little runny albumen around the edge; the rest of the

Above: *A bowl of freshly laid hens' eggs.*

albumen, which is firm and jelly-like; and the yolk firmly in the center on top. The staler the egg, the more liquid the albumen will become.

Only really fresh eggs should be used for boiling or poaching. Staler eggs may be used for cooking, but the difference in quality of the finished article is easily discernible, so the fresher the better. It is anathema to me to read that you can eat eggs that are three or four weeks old.

You can tell if an egg is boiled or raw by spinning it on a countertop! Cooked eggs spin much faster than raw ones.

How should I store eggs?

Eggs should be stored in a cool place; we store them in the egg cupboard in a cool larder. For most households, the fridge is the most practical place for eggs. Store them pointy end down in their cartons. This stops the yolks from rising to the air pocket in the egg.

The shells are porous, which means that the eggs will absorb tastes and smells of strong foods, like onions, garlic, smoked fish, or strawberries. If, however, you are fortunate enough to get your hands on a fresh truffle, take advantage of the porous shell. Store the eggs with the truffle in a sealed container for 24 hours, and then you can feast on truffled scrambled eggs.

Remove eggs from the fridge 30 minutes before cooking; otherwise, they may crack on contact with boiling water. If you are in a rush, put the eggs into warm water for a few minutes before cooking.

APPROXIMATE WEIGHT OF EGGS
Quail eggs: ½ oz
Hen's eggs: 2oz for small and 3oz for extra large
Duck eggs: 3oz
Turkey eggs: 3oz
Goose eggs: 7oz

SOFT-BOILED EGGS WITH SODA BREAD "SOLDIERS"

Most people have given up on soft-boiled eggs because eggs from battery chickens, kept in a holding pattern for a couple of weeks, aren't worth serving as the centerpiece of a breakfast or dinner. But those of us who are fortunate enough to have some space to keep a few free-range hens are blessed indeed. The eggs laid by my happy, lazy hens are quite a different thing from those you will find in an average supermarket.

When you have access to eggs of this quality, treat yourself to a soft-boiled egg – absolute perfection but sadly a forgotten flavor for so many people. Little fingers of toast called dippies or soldiers are the traditional accompaniment, but I love brown soda bread with my boiled eggs.

When people drop in, even if we don't have anything much in the house, there's always the option of freshly laid eggs. So I might just pop a loaf of soda bread into the oven and boil a couple of eggs. It doesn't sound like much, but people are totally amazed by how good it is. One friend says that one of the best meals she ever had in our house was three boiled eggs and a big glass of whisky!

It may sound like a really simple thing, but few people can cook a really good boiled egg. It is imperative that the egg is at room temperature, because if you take the eggs out of the fridge and drop them in boiling water, they're likely to crack from the temperature shock. If you're worried about them cracking, another option is to use a darning needle to poke a hole in the eggshell before boiling it · SERVES 2

2 fresh organic eggs
sea salt and freshly ground pepper
butter
brown soda bread

Bring a small saucepan of water to a boil, add a little salt, and gently slide in the eggs.

Bring the water back to a boil and simmer for 4–6 minutes, according to your taste. A 4-minute egg will be still quite soft, 5 minutes will almost set the white while the yolk will still be runny, and 6 minutes will produce a boiled egg with a soft yolk and solid white.

Meanwhile, slice the soda bread and spread with butter. Then cut into strips.

As soon as the eggs are cooked, pop them into egg cups on plates and cut the top open or they will continue to cook.

Put the bread on the side and serve with a pepper mill, sea salt, and a few pats of butter. Eat boiled eggs with a stainless-steel teaspoon – as silver or silverplate cutlery will react with the egg and give it a nasty taste.

HARD-BOILED EGGS

Many people hard-boil eggs in a somewhat haphazard way. To avoid that black ring around the yolk (a sign of overcooking) you need to time them. Really fresh eggs are not ideal for hard-boiling because peeling their shells is a nightmare; the best eggs to use are a few days old. As with soft-boiled eggs, it's important to use room-temperature eggs, and they should be cooked in salted water; their shells are porous, so the flavor will benefit.

organic hen or duck eggs

Bring a small saucepan of water to a boil, gently slide in the eggs, bring the water back to a boil and simmer for 8–10 minutes (12 minutes for duck eggs), according to your taste. Drain and then cover with cold water to stop the cooking.

CRISPY EGGS WITH BACON AND TOMATO FONDUE

Duck eggs are delicious cooked in this way. Chorizo is also really good with this, instead of the bacon · **SERVES 4**

cooking oil
4 semi hard-boiled eggs
   (8 minutes)
flour, well seasoned with salt,
   freshly ground pepper, and a
   pinch of cayenne
1 organic egg, beaten
bread crumbs
4 tablespoons Tomato Fondue with
   Chile (see page 378)

6oz (about 4) thick slices
   home-cured bacon, cut into
   ¼in pieces
watercress sprigs

Heat the oil to 350°F in a deep fryer.

Peel the eggs and roll in the seasoned flour, followed by the egg and bread crumbs.

Meanwhile, heat the tomato and chile fondue and cook the bacon in a frying pan until crisp. Cook the eggs in the deep fryer for 2–3 minutes or until crisp and golden.

Put a little tomato and chile fondue on the plate and top with the watercress. Place a crispy egg on top and sprinkle with the bacon. Eat immediately.

SCRAMBLED EGGS

Perfectly scrambled eggs are rare indeed, though people's perception of "perfect" varies wildly. However, for ideal scrambled eggs (in my case, soft and creamy), really fresh organic eggs are essential.

Nowadays, it's become common practice to put the eggs into a hot pan, which gives a tough curd if you're not careful. I prefer the old-fashioned way that my mother taught me: putting the eggs into a cold saucepan, whereby they scramble gently and slowly on a low heat, and yield a softer, creamier curd. Scrambled eggs should always be served on warm plates but beware – if the plates are too hot, the scrambled egg can overcook between the stove and the table · **SERVES 2**

4 organic eggs
2 tablespoons whole milk
a knob of butter
salt and freshly ground pepper

Break the eggs into a bowl, add the milk, and season with salt and pepper. Mix until the whites and yolks are mixed well. Put a blob of butter into a cold saucepan over a low heat, pour in the egg mixture, and stir continuously, preferably with a flat-bottomed wooden spoon, until the eggs have scrambled into soft creamy curds. Serve immediately on warm plates with lots of hot buttered toast or fresh soda bread.

Really great scrambled eggs need no further embellishment, except perhaps a slice of hot, thin toast. Having said that, here are some great additions and accompaniments:

Variations
Good things to serve with scrambled eggs:
· Chopped watercress or arugula leaves with a little grated cheese
· Diced, cooked chorizo – add just at the end with some flat-leaf parsley
· Crispy smoked bacon or a little cooked ham
· For a Mexican flavor, add a little diced onion and chile; then add diced tomato and lots of cilantro at the end of cooking
· A few cooked wild mushrooms, perfumed with a little tarragon or thyme leaves
· Smoked fish such as smoked salmon, mackerel, or eel
· Cooked shrimp

PERFECT POACHED EGGS ON TOAST

No fancy egg poachers or molds are needed to produce a perfect result – simply use a really fresh egg laid by a happy, lazy duck or hen. The tips you hear about putting the vinegar in the water are really only valid for eggs that aren't so fresh – if you have a fresh, organic egg, the albumen is strong enough to hold together. And in my book, what could possibly be the point of poaching an egg that wasn't any good to start with? · SERVES 1

2 organic eggs
toast, freshly made

Bring a small saucepan of water to a boil. Reduce the heat, swirl the water, crack the egg into a tiny bowl, and slip the egg gently into the whirlpool in the center. This avoids burning the tips of your fingers as you drop the egg into the water. The water should not boil again but bubble very gently just below boiling point. Cook for about 3–4 minutes, until the white is set and the yolk is still soft and runny.

Meanwhile, make a slice of toast. Cut off the crusts, butter the toast, and pop it onto a hot plate. Lift out the poached egg with a slotted spoon; drain and place on top of the toast. Serve immediately. Or you can poach the eggs ahead of time and then reheat them briefly in boiling water. Just cook them for a minute less than usual, and slip them into a bowl of cold water to stop them from cooking further.

To reheat the poached eggs, bring a saucepan of water to a boil, take off the heat, and slip the egg back into the water for a minute or two until hot through.

CRISPY DEEP-FRIED EGGS

Some people love eggs cooked over low heat with a tender white, but this method is for those who adore their eggs crispy. This technique takes a bit of practice but the crispy edges are simply irresistible.

generous amount of extra virgin olive oil or sunflower oil
really fresh organic eggs
salt and freshly ground pepper
Croutons (see page 579)
Tomato and Chile Jam (see page 450)
arugula leaves

Heat 1in of oil in a deep-sided frying pan. It should be really hot; test by dropping in a tiny bread cube – it should brown in seconds.

Break an egg into the hot oil. Tilt the pan immediately so the egg slides down into a pool of oil. Use a tablespoon to lift the white over the yolk so the yolk is completely enclosed between two layers of white. This will prevent the yolk from overcooking and allows the white to get deliciously crisp and slightly golden. Cook for a minute or two more.

Lift the egg out of the oil with a slotted spoon and drain well on paper towels. Season with a few flakes of sea salt and freshly ground pepper. Serve on warm, crisp croutons with tomato and chile jam and some arugula leaves.

Above: *Crispy Deep-fried Eggs.*

EGGS BENEDICT

This recipe is a combination of two forgotten skills: poaching eggs and making Hollandaise sauce (which also involves eggs). It is the perfect breakfast for a lazy weekend · SERVES 4 (OR 2 IF VERY HUNGRY)

Hollandaise Sauce (see below)
4 organic eggs
4 slices good sourdough bread
  or 2 English muffins or 2 bagels
butter
4 slices home-cooked ham or
  8 slices good bacon, cooked

First, make the Hollandaise sauce and keep it warm. Poach the eggs (see page 247). Meanwhile, toast the bread, muffins, or bagels. Slather a little butter on the hot bread and lay a slice of ham or freshly cooked bacon on the base. Prop a beautifully poached egg on top, and coat generously with the Hollandaise sauce.

HOLLANDAISE SAUCE

A classic Hollandaise is based on a reduction of dry white wine, vinegar, and finely chopped shallots. In the version we make at the Cookery School we simply emulsify rich butter with egg yolks by whisking and then sharpen with a little lemon juice. Unless you have a heavy-bottomed saucepan, don't attempt this recipe without a double-boiler. Even on the lowest heat, cooking a Hollandaise sauce in a pot that isn't heavy-bottomed may scramble the eggs.

Once the sauce is made, it must be kept warm, though the temperature should not go above 180°F, or the sauce will curdle. A thermos can provide a simple solution on a small scale; otherwise put the sauce into a bowl in a saucepan of hot, but not simmering, water. Hollandaise sauce cannot be reheated very successfully so it's best to make just the quantity you need. If, however, you have a little left over, use it to enrich other sauces or mashed potatoes. When it solidifies, it makes a delicious Hollandaise butter to melt over fish · SERVES 4–6

2 organic egg yolks
10 tablespoons butter, cut into dice
1 teaspoon freshly squeezed lemon
  juice

Put the egg yolks in a heavy-bottomed, stainless-steel saucepan over low heat or in a bowl over hot water. Add 2 teaspoons water and whisk thoroughly. Add the butter bit by bit, whisking all the time. As soon as one piece melts, add the next piece. The mixture will gradually thicken, but if it shows signs of becoming too thick or slightly scrambling, remove from the heat immediately and add a little cold water to cool it quickly. Do not leave the pan or stop whisking until the sauce is made. Finally add the lemon juice to taste.

If the sauce is slow to thicken, it may be because you are excessively cautious and the heat is too low. Increase the heat slightly and continue to whisk until the sauce thickens to coating consistency.

It is important to remember that if you are making Hollandaise sauce in a saucepan directly over the heat, it should be possible to put your hand on the side of the saucepan at any stage. If the saucepan feels too hot for your hand, then it is also too hot for the sauce.

Another good tip if you are making Hollandaise sauce for the first time is to keep a bowl of cold water close by so you can plunge the base of the saucepan into it if becomes too hot.

CLASSIC FRENCH OMELETTE

An omelette is the ultimate fast food but many bizarre creations are served in its name. In reality a simple French omelette takes 30 seconds to make or 45 seconds if you're adding a filling. At the Cookery School, students never believe me when I tell them this, and when I demonstrate they are there with their watches ready to catch me out! In no time they are turning out tender golden 30-second omelettes themselves. The whole secret is to have the pan hot enough and to use clarified butter if at all possible. Ordinary butter will burn if your pan is as hot as it ought to be. It's also important to use the right size pan, otherwise the omelette will be too thick or thin and consequently overcooked or undercooked, so use the pan size specified below for a two-egg omelette. Your first omelette may not be a joy to behold but persevere – practice makes perfect! · SERVES 1

filling of your choice (optional)
2 organic eggs
2 teaspoons milk or water
salt and freshly ground pepper
2 teaspoons Clarified Butter (see
  page 216) or olive oil

omelette pan, preferably nonstick,
  9in diameter

Warm a plate in the oven.

Meanwhile, heat the omelette pan over a high heat. If using, have your chosen filling ready beside you, along with a spoon.

Beat the eggs with the milk or water in a bowl, until thoroughly mixed but not too fluffy. Season with salt and freshly ground pepper. Put the warm plate beside the stove because you won't have time to go looking for it.

Add the clarified butter or oil to the pan. As soon as it sizzles, pour in the egg mixture. It will start to cook immediately so quickly pull the edges of the omelette toward the center with a metal or plastic spatula, tilting the pan backward and forward then up and down for another few seconds so that the uncooked egg runs to the sides. Continue right around until most of the egg is set and will not run any more. The center should still be soft and moist – don't worry, it will be perfectly set by the time it gets to the table. If you are using a filling, spoon the hot mixture in a line across the center of the omelette, perpendicular to the pan handle.

To fold the omelette: flip the omelette edge nearest the handle of the pan over the filling, toward the center. Then change your grip of the handle so you are holding it from underneath, this will make it more comfortable for you to hold the pan almost upright so the omelette can roll toward the bottom of the pan. Half-roll and half-slide the omelette onto the plate so that it lands folded into three. Serve immediately.

Variation

OMELETTE FINES HERBES
Add 1 teaspoon each of freshly chopped parsley, chives, chervil, and tarragon to the eggs just before cooking – divine!

Good things to serve with an omelette:
· Wild Mushrooms à la Creme (see page 50)
· Cooked lamb's kidneys and chopped parsley
· Smoked mackerel or smoked salmon and chives
· Peperonata or Tomato Fondue (see pages 87 and 378)
· A little crispy chorizo and flat-leaf parsley

CHEESE SOUFFLÉ OMELETTE

After a funeral many years ago, we stopped in a little country guesthouse in Borris in Ossory and ordered what was listed on the menu as a cheese omelette. It took ages to arrive and I wondered what on earth they were up to in the kitchen. When it finally came, I was surprised to be served a puffed-up, fluffy omelette. I still remember the taste and the fluffy texture of it, clear as day. I often wondered where this country cook had learned how to make a soufflé omelette and I wish I'd asked at the time.

A perfect soufflé omelette is a special treat and takes only a few minutes longer to make than a French omelette, but it is well worth the effort. This is definitely a forgotten skill, and Irish farmhouse cheeses in particular are utterly delicious in this recipe · SERVES 1-2

3 organic eggs, separated
salt and freshly ground pepper
2 tablespoons finely grated cheese
  – Gruyère, Parmesan, Irish farmhouse cheese, or a mixture
1 teaspoon finely chopped chives or scallion tops (optional)
2 tablespoons butter

omelette pan, preferably nonstick,
  9in diameter

Whisk the egg yolks until light. Season well with salt and pepper, and add the cheese and chives, if using.

Whisk the egg whites until they hold a stiff peak, stir a little of the whites into the yolks, then very lightly, very carefully, fold in the rest with a metal spoon.

Melt the butter in the omelette pan, shaking it gently so that the sides are covered with butter, too, and as it foams add the egg mixture and level it off with an offset spatula.

Cook the omelette very gently for about 3–4 minutes. The bottom should be golden when you lift the omelette with the offset spatula to have a peek, and it should have started to fluff up. Then put the pan under a broiler about 4in from the heat. Cook very gently for 3–4 minutes longer, until the omelette is well risen and just set. Remove at once, loosen the edges with the offset spatula, and if you want to fold it over, first score it lightly across the center. Then slide it out gently onto a hot plate and serve with a green salad.

BUTTERED EGGS

This ancient Irish way of preserving eggs in times of glut deserves to be more widely practiced, not just for preservation, but actually for the gorgeous flavor and texture the cooked eggs produce. If you've got access to really fresh, still-warm eggs, you can try it yourself.

Gerry Moynihan, who still sells buttered eggs in the English Market in Cork, told me that the whole secret is that the shells must be sealed with butter while the egg is still warm or, as he puts it, "before the hen misses the egg." The warm egg and your warm hands will cause the butter to form a coating around the egg. The freshness is sealed in and the albumen stays soft and curdy when boiled or poached.

Buttered eggs can be kept up to two months, but now that we all have constant access to eggs, the reason people continue this tradition is for the flavor and texture it produces. I've also heard of people dipping eggs in lard, melted wax, or flaxseed oil.

QUICHE LORRAINE

Named after the Lorraine region of northeast France, this classic quiche is delicious served with a green salad and tangy relish. It tastes great cold, too. The sweetness of well-sweated onions is a fine addition · **SERVES 6**

1 x quantity Basic Shortcrust Pastry (see next recipe)
1 tablespoon extra virgin olive oil
6oz bacon, cut into ½in slices
¾ cup chopped onion
3 organic eggs and 2 egg yolks
1¼ cups heavy cream
1 tablespoon chopped parsley
1 tablespoon chopped chives
½ cup grated Cheddar cheese
½ cup grated Gruyère cheese
salt and freshly ground black pepper

tart pan 9in in diameter

Preheat the oven to 350°F.

Roll the pastry out on a lightly floured board until quite thin, then fit into the pan, bringing the pastry just a little above the rim. Line the tart shell with parchment paper and fill it to the top with dried beans to hold the paper in place. Bake for 20 minutes. Remove the paper and beans and save to use another time.

Heat the olive oil in a frying pan and cook the bacon until crisp and golden. Remove and dry on paper towels. Then sweat the onions gently in the oil for 10 minutes.

Meanwhile, beat the eggs and egg yolks in a medium bowl. Add the cream, herbs, cheeses, and bacon and onions. Mix and season.

Pour the filling into the pastry base and return it to the oven. Cook for 30–40 minutes or until the center has just set. Serve warm with a green salad.

BASIC SHORTCRUST PASTRY (SAVORY)

The aim is to make a crisp, crumbly, but not brittle pastry · **MAKES ENOUGH PASTRY TO LINE A 9IN TART PAN**

1½ cups all-purpose flour, spelt, or wholewheat flour, sifted
6 tablespoons butter
pinch of salt
beaten egg or water (to bind)

Sift the flour and salt into a large bowl. Cut the butter into cubes, toss into the flour, and then rub in with your fingertips. Keep everything as cool as possible; if the fat is allowed to melt, the finished pastry may be tough. When the mixture looks like coarse bread crumbs, stop.

Beat the egg or egg yolk and add some water. Using a fork to stir, add just enough liquid to bring the pastry together, then discard the fork and collect it into a ball with your hands, this way you can judge more accurately if you need a few more drops of liquid. Although rather damp pastry is easier to handle and roll out, the resulting crust can be tough and may well shrink out of shape as the water evaporates in the oven. The drier and more difficult-to-handle pastry will give a crisper, shorter crust.

Flatten into a round, cover the pastry with plastic wrap and leave to rest in the fridge for at least 15 minutes. This will make the pastry much less elastic and easier to roll.

Right: *Quiche Lorraine.*

HOW TO WHISK
EGG WHITES

Use a stainless-steel, glass, ceramic or unlined copper bowl. Make sure that the bowl is spotlessly clean and dry (to clean unlined copper, see page 583). Put the egg whites into the bowl; they must be free of any egg yolk, oil, grease, or water. Turn the bowl onto its side and start to whisk, using a light balloon whisk or a coil whisk, slowly at first and then faster until the egg whites are stiffly beaten. They will form a stiff peak on the end of the whisk when lifted out of the bowl. At this point change the angle of the whisk and stir in a full circular movement to tighten the egg white and make it more stable. It should be possible to turn the bowl upside down at this stage without the egg whites falling out. Overwhisked egg white will become granular. If egg whites separate and become grainy, add 1 unbeaten egg white for every 4 in the bowl and continue to whisk for 30 seconds. This should re-emulsify the problem egg whites.

CHEDDAR CHEESE
SOUFFLÉ WITH CHIVES

A soufflé sounds very grand, like the sort of thing a fancy chef would make, but you mustn't be put off. A soufflé is just a combination of three basic techniques: making a white sauce, whipping egg whites, and folding in the egg whites. These little Cheddar cheese soufflés are the most delicious thing for supper. Children absolutely love them, but they're also elegant enough for entertaining.

When I was doing the research for my Irish Traditional Cooking *book, I noticed that nearly every country-house cookbook that I went through had a soufflé recipe in it – this would've been the pride of country-house cooks. Then, with uncalibrated, drafty ovens, soufflés would have been much more of a hit-and-miss affair, and that's probably where they get their difficult reputation.*

With today's ovens, though, soufflés are a walk in the park. Just remember that the egg whites must not be whisked until you are about to cook the soufflé, otherwise they will lose volume. And if, after eating, you have some of the soufflé left over, you can spoon it into a little gratin dish, add a couple of tablespoons of cream and some cheese over the top, and put the dish back into the oven for a delicious, if rather inelegantly named, twice-baked soufflé · **SERVES 6–8**

2 tablespoons butter
2 tablespoons all-purpose flour
1¼ cups milk
3 organic egg yolks
1 level teaspoon salt
½ teaspoon Dijon mustard
1 teaspoon finely chopped chives
   (**optional**)
1½ cups grated Cheddar cheese
4 organic egg whites

**7-cup soufflé dish or 6–8 individual
   soufflé dishes**

Melt the butter in a heavy-bottomed saucepan. When it has stopped foaming, add the flour and stir well. Cook gently for 2 minutes. Remove the saucepan from the heat, whisk in the milk slowly, return to the heat, and cook until the sauce boils and thickens. Remove from the heat once more and beat in the egg yolks, one by one. Then add the salt, mustard, chives, and all but 2 tablespoons of the cheese (set aside to sprinkle over the top). The recipe can be prepared ahead to this stage but must be warmed gently before the egg whites are folded in.

Preheat the oven to 400°F.

Grease the soufflé dish or dishes with melted butter and sprinkly with fine, dried bread crumbs. Whisk the egg whites until they reach a stiff peak. Stir about one third of the whites into the cheese mixture, then fold in the remainder carefully. Spoon into the soufflé dish or dishes

Sprinkle grated cheese on top and bake for 30–35 minutes for a large soufflé, or 9–10 minutes for individual soufflés. They should be well-risen and golden on top yet slightly soft in the center. Serve immediately on hot plates.

MAYONNAISE

Most people don't seem to be aware that mayonnaise can be made even with a hand whisk in less than five minutes, and if you use a food processor the technique is still the same but it is even faster. The great secret is to have all your ingredients at room temperature and to drip the oil very slowly into the egg yolks at the beginning. The quality of your mayonnaise will depend totally on the quality of the egg yolks, oil, and vinegar, and it's perfectly possible to make a bland mayonnaise if you use poor-quality ingredients.

Mayonnaise is the "mother" of all the cold emulsion sauces, so once you can make a mayonnaise you can make any of the "daughter" sauces such as tartare, aioli, garlic mayo, dill mayo, wholegrain mustard mayo... Just add extra ingredients as required ·
MAKES 1½ CUPS

2 organic egg yolks
pinch of English dry mustard or
    ¼ teaspoon French mustard
¼ teaspoon salt
2 teaspoons white wine vinegar
1 cup oil (sunflower or olive
    oil or a mixture) – we use
    ¾ cup sunflower oil and
    ¼ cup olive oil

Put the egg yolks into a bowl with the mustard, salt, and white wine vinegar. Measure out the oil into a jug. Take a whisk in one hand and the oil in the other and drip the oil onto the egg yolks, drop by drop, whisking at the same time. Within a minute you will notice that the mixture is beginning to thicken. When this happens you can add the oil a little faster, but don't get too cheeky or it will suddenly curdle because the egg yolks can only absorb the oil at a certain rate. Taste and add a little more seasoning and vinegar if necessary.

If the mayonnaise curdles, it will suddenly become quite thin, and if left sitting the oil will start to float to the top of the sauce. If this happens you can quite easily rectify the

situation by putting another egg yolk or 1–2 tablespoons of boiling water into a clean bowl and whisking in the curdled mayonnaise, a half-teaspoon at a time until it emulsifies again.

PICKLED EGGS

Pickled eggs are a living tradition still served in many country pubs. Originally, pickling would've been yet another way of preserving the eggs in times of glut, but the pickle added interest and flavor, so just because we have fridges now doesn't mean we shouldn't pickle eggs any more.

3½ cups white wine vinegar
1in piece fresh ginger
1½ tablespoons white peppercorns
1½ tablespoons black peppercorns
1 chile
12 organic eggs, hard-boiled

Put the vinegar, ginger, peppercorns, and chile into a stainless-steel saucepan and bring to a boil. Simmer for 5 minutes, strain, and let cool.

Peel the eggs, run under cold water to remove any traces of shell, and put into a sterilized jar. Pour in the spiced vinegar. The eggs must be completely covered; otherwise they won't keep. Seal the jar and keep for 3–4 weeks before using. These are great eaten in the traditional way with a beer, but I like them on a salad of organic leaves or watercress, mint, cherry tomatoes, and cucumber sticks.

USES FOR LEFTOVER EGG WHITES

- Egg-white omelette
- Meringues, pavlova, meringue roulade
- *Oeufs à la neige*
- Angel food cake
- To lighten mashed potato, which then becomes *pommes mousseline*
- Added to the milk in onion rings to make the batter crispier
- Macaroons
- Marshmallows
- Seven-minute frosting
- Baked Alaska

USES FOR LEFTOVER EGG YOLKS

- Mayonnaise
- Caesar dressing
- Hollandaise sauce
- Béarnaise sauce
- *Sauce de Quimper*
- Lemon or passion fruit curd
- Ice cream
- Shortcrust pastry
- Liaison to enrich sauces
- To enrich mashed potatoes
- As an egg wash

basil or marjoram leaves, chopped
12 spears of asparagus
4 organic duck eggs
4 small handfuls of frisée or mixed
  leaves
2 tablespoons grated Parmesan
  cheese
chopped chives

For the Dressing
1oz anchovies from a can
1 organic egg yolk (duck or hen)
½ tablespoon lemon juice
½ garlic clove, crushed
tiny pinch of English dry mustard
½ tablespoon Worcestershire sauce
½ tablespoon Tabasco
⅓ cup sunflower oil
2 tablespoons extra virgin olive oil
2 tablespoons cream or cold water
salt to taste

Duck Eggs

Duck eggs deserve to be more
widely known and used. They're
about twice the size of hen's eggs,
and the two can be used
interchangeably. Because of the
structure of the albumen, the whites
take slightly longer to whip up and
they make wonderfully light sponge
cakes and meringues, while the
yolks make delicious ice cream and
lemon curd. The texture makes
gorgeous creamy hard-boiled eggs.
Some people who have allergies to
hen's eggs find that they can tolerate
duck eggs. Many chefs have
rediscovered them and are finding
creative ways to serve duck eggs.

SALAD WITH DUCK EGG, PARMESAN, ROASTED RED PEPPER, AND ASPARAGUS

*Follow the method for poaching eggs on
page 247 but allow 5–6 minutes for
duck eggs. The dressing here is
essentially a Caesar dressing, and we
use it over lots of little winter salads.
It keeps for 10 days or longer in the
fridge. I use the first few spears of
asparagus as a treat when in season,
but broccoli florets are a good
alternative in autumn or winter ·*
SERVES 4

1 red or yellow bell pepper
salt and pepper
olive oil

Preheat the oven to 350°F.

Season the red or yellow bell
pepper with salt and pepper, add a
little olive oil, and roast on a baking
sheet until tender. This can take up
to 45 minutes. Turn occasionally
during cooking and don't allow the
peppers to get charred.

When tender, place in a bowl.
Cover with plastic wrap and let cool.
When cool, peel, seed, and season.
Add a little chopped basil or
marjoram and olive oil if you have it
to hand.

Cook the asparagus spears in a
little boiling salted water, until just
tender. Dress with a little olive oil –
use just enough to coat – and let
cool.

To prepare the dressing, drain the anchovies and wash under cold water. Dry and mash with a fork. Combine in a bowl with the egg yolks, lemon juice, garlic, mustard, Worcestershire sauce, and Tabasco. Whisk together. As you whisk, add the oils to form an emulsion. Finally, add the water or cream and salt to taste.

To assemble the salad, poach the duck eggs in gently simmering, salted water. Dress the leaves, peppers, and asparagus and place onto four warmed plates. Place a softly poached egg on each salad. Drizzle with a little of the dressing, sprinkle the chives and Parmesan on top, and serve immediately. Save the remainder of the dressing for another time.

DUCK-EGG SPONGE CAKE

Duck eggs are renowned for making a lighter, more yellow sponge cake than hen's eggs, and are, as such, much sought after. This sponge cake is interesting because the whites, rather than the yolks, are beaten with the sugar, which is opposite to the way most sponge cakes are made. This recipe was given to me by a neighbor named Winnie Cowhig · SERVES 8

¾ **cup all-purpose flour, sifted, plus**
    2 teaspoons for dusting
3 **organic duck eggs**
6 **tablespoons superfine sugar**

2 x 7in **round cake pans, lined**
    (see page 524)

Preheat the oven to 350°F.

Brush the base and sides of the pan with melted butter and dust with the 2 teaspoons flour.

Separate the egg whites from the yolks. Put the whites and sugar into a bowl and whisk until stiff, preferably in an electric mixer. Whisk in the yolks one by one and then fold in the sifted flour, making sure not to deflate the mixture. Divide the mixture between the prepared pans.

Bake for 20–25 minutes. Turn out carefully and let cool on a wire rack. Sandwich together with cream and homemade jam or fresh berries. Sprinkle a little superfine sugar or confectioners' sugar over the top and enjoy with a cup of tea.

Quail Eggs

Quail eggs are available all year round, and keep for an incredibly long time, up to six weeks. I've always thought the reason they kept for so long was because their shell was tough, but in fact it's the film inside the shell that's very strong, so you can boil a quail egg even if it's cracked.

To hard-boil quail eggs, put them into a saucepan of cold water and bring to a boil. Once the water is boiling, the eggs need about 2 minutes until they're hard-boiled. The speckled shells are so beautiful I can hardly bear to peel them. Because of their small size they make an adorable snack for children. They're also irresistible atop crostini with a piece of crispy chorizo as a nibble for drinks.

A SALAD OF QUAIL EGGS WITH SMOKED VENISON AND AVOCADO

Quail eggs are wonderful in this bitter leaf salad · SERVES 6

18 **quail eggs**
1 **slice white bread cut into**
    ¼in **cubes for croutons**
3 **tablespoons walnut oil**
4oz **curly endive**
2oz **mache lettuce or purslane**
1 **head of chicory**
2oz **red-leaf lettuce**
12 **sprigs of watercress**
French Dressing (see page 374)
1 **avocado, diced or sliced**
4oz **smoked venison, cut into**
    strips, or use smoked salmon
tiny scallions or chives
a few chive, nasturtium, or wild
    garlic flowers

Hard-boil the quail eggs in boiling salted water for about 3–4 minutes. Put them in cold water and shell when required, keeping six still in their shells so guests can peel them. Cook the bread cubes in the oil over medium heat until crisp and golden. Keep warm.

Toss the salad leaves in a little dressing, the leaves should just glisten. Divide among 6 plates. Brush the avocado with a little dressing and add a few slices to each plate. Put 3 eggs on each plate, perhaps 2 peeled and 1 unpeeled. Sprinkle with warm croutons and the strips of smoked venison or salmon. Garnish with the herbs and flowers and serve.

Poultry

One of the most satisfying things is to rear a few chickens for the table, certainly not something you can do in downtown New York or Dublin, but for those who have some space, the rewards in terms of flavor and tasty chicken broth are immense.

It's still quite a challenge to find breed stock that are bred for free-range production. Even the best chickens available commercially are so closely related to breeds reared to fatten fast that, by the time they get to the end of lives, they are almost too fat to walk, which is very disturbing. So there is a business opportunity there if someone wants to bring the classic breeds back. Many people would be eternally grateful to a chicken breeder who would supply chickens to rear for the table in small lots.

There's a discernible difference between intensively reared birds and organic, free-range ones. They have different textures, different water content, different smells, and of course different flavors.

Many people these days don't realize that age means flavor. In France, chickens are often sold with information about their age at slaughter. People there expect to pay more for an older chicken – something that isn't at all a part of our buying culture. Our local organic chicken farmer has chosen the Hubbard breed and rears them to 98–100 days. By contrast, intensively reared chickens are killed at 37–45 days old.

How to kill a chicken

Killing a chicken may not be everyone's "cup of tea," but I am always surprised by the number of people who request a demonstration on how to kill a chicken quickly and humanely. This is the sort of skill that many people had when I was a child. Mummy would just ask Joe, one of our workmen, to kill and pluck a chicken, which he would do without batting an eyelid. Mummy would bring a few cockerels indoors to fatten them up for 2–3 weeks beforehand. Joe would catch them one at a time. He'd feel the breast to ascertain which was the plumpest and then simply pull their necks. The bird would flap about for a minute or two and then it was bled and hung up by the legs.

Hold the bird by the legs with your left hand. Grab the neck with your right hand so it protrudes through your middle finger and the head is cupped in the palm of your hand. Quickly push your right hand downwards and twist so the chicken's head is bent backward. Stop as soon as you feel the backbone snap or you may pull the head off. Cut through the skin at the back of the head to allow it to bleed. You can also get a wall-mounted humane dispatcher or a cone tripod poultry dispatcher (see Resources, page 584), which I first saw in France when I went to investigate production of the famous French chickens *poulets de Bresse*. Free-range birds benefit from being hung for two or three days.

Plucking

You might have access to a chicken-plucking machine, but if you're just doing one at a time, it'll take all of 20 minutes. Pluck outdoors or in a garage. It's easiest if you start while the bird is still warm. Pinch a little clump of feathers between your thumb and first two fingers and tug gently. The tail and wing feathers are tougher and will need to be plucked one at a time. When the bird gets cold, it is more difficult to dry-pluck because the feathers are much harder to get out without tearing the skin. Another method is to immerse the bird in a bucket of boiling water for 2 or 3 seconds and then immediately plunge into a bucket of ice-cold water. This loosens the feathers and it becomes easy to pluck. Be careful not to leave the bird in water for more than a few seconds or the skin will start to cook and the bird will deteriorate faster. If you're plucking on any kind of scale, you might want to invest in an electric chicken plucker (see Resources, page 584).

Singeing

Ducks and geese have a double layer of plumage: an outer layer of feathers and an inner layer of down. It is difficult to pluck the last little bits of down, so you'll need to singe it with a gas torch, over a gas jet, or with a rolled-up piece of newspaper set on fire (be careful!).

Chopping off the feet, head, and neck

Put a couple of sheets of newspaper on a chopping board and put the bird on top. With a cleaver or a poultry shears, chop off the feet, either at the knuckle or 1in below.

Chop off the head where it meets the neck. You can use it for stock if you like – it will add lots of flavor and extra gelatin. Otherwise, just discard it.

Flip the bird over. Slit the skin down the length of the underside of the neck. Peel the skin back away

from the neck, toward the carcass. Then chop off the skinned neck as close to the carcass as possible, making sure the skin stays attached. The windpipe is a tube that runs alongside the neck. Remove and discard it.

Find the crop, or craw, tucked inside the neck end of the bird. In table birds, which are fasted before slaughter, this is usually empty of food, but in wild birds that are shot on the wing, the crop will be filled with the contents of their last meal, some of which may be poisonous or at least unpleasant to humans, so remove and discard it.

Flip the bird back over so that it's breast side is upward. Fold the neck flap underneath the bird and secure by twisting the wings and then tucking the pinions under the carcass at either side.

Gutting a chicken, guinea hen, pheasant, turkey…

Cut a slit, 3–4in long, either widthwise or lengthwise, just above the vent of the chicken (the other end from the neck), large enough to fit your hand. Touch your thumb and pinky to each other to make your hand a little narrower and insert your hand, keeping all fingers straight, under the breastbone as far as you can get toward the neck.

Curl your fingertips and scoop out all the intestines. Ideally, they should come out in one clump. They will still be attached to the vent end. Cut around the vent and discard it. Put the intestines on a clean, newspaper-covered part of the cutting board. If the heart hasn't come out with the intestines, insert

your hand again and feel around toward the right, near the neck. Bring that out, too, squeeze it to eliminate any remaining blood, rinse it in cold water, and put it on a clean plate.

Go back to the intestines and, using a small sharp knife, detach the two brown lobes of the liver very carefully, leaving the gall bladder behind. The gall bladder is a little green sac very close to the liver, so be careful not to pierce it, as doing so will discharge a bitter liquid that will ruin the liver and render anything else that it comes into contact with it unusable. Add to the plate with the heart.

The gizzard is a gray-blue sac that's part of the chicken's digestive system. It is larger than the liver, sometimes with a bit of fat attached, Use your knife to detach the gizzard from the intestine, too.

Place the gizzard on the newspaper-covered board. Between the two lobes you'll notice some connective tissue that is paler in color. The trick is to barely cut down this connective tissue without piercing the inner sac. Use your hands to further pry open the gizzard and remove and discard the wrinkly inner sac, which still contains grit and undigested food, still intact, if at all possible. Rinse the gizzard in cold water. Trim off the fat. The gizzard can be added to stock or used for *Salade de Gésiers* (see page 283).

The lungs, which are a pale, pinky-red color, may have come out with the intestines, but if, upon examination, you discover they haven't, you'll find them in the bottom of the carcass, close to the neck end. Insert your hand again and scrape them out with the tips of your fingers.

Rinse the gutted bird in cold water, paying particular attention to the vent end, then put it on a clean chopping board. Wrap the lungs and intestines in the newspaper and discard. Go back to the vent end of the bird and take out the two little chunks of fat you'll find tucked inside at either side. Provided you've got a well-reared bird (free-range, organic) this fat is precious and can be rendered down (see page 276) and added to Chicken Liver Pâté (see page 268) or used for sauté or Roast Potatoes (see page 382).

A free-range organic chicken will keep in a fridge for four or five days; an intensively produced chicken needs to be used earlier.

Gutting a duck or goose

The fat chunks near the vent end are much larger in ducks and geese and are worth rendering for their fat. In game birds, look out for shot and remove it with your fingers.

Giblets

The giblets are the neck, gizzard, heart, and liver. The first three can be added to the stockpot, but the liver adds bitterness, so leave it out. The liver is best saved for pâtés and terrines. In France, one of my favorite bistro appetizers is a *Salade de Gésiers* (see page 283), which includes the gizzards and sometimes the extra bonus of heart and liver.

Trussing a bird

Birds are trussed to give them a neat shape. Generally, I don't truss a bird very tightly, as I find it's more difficult for the heat to penetrate and the bottom of the legs don't cook properly. I tie kitchen string around the little pointy bit at the back end (called the pope's or parson's nose), and then tie the two leg tips loosely together to make a neat shape.

How to cut a chicken into four pieces:

Use a fileting or boning knife, and put your index finger along the back of the blade. Use the thumb of your opposite hand as a guide so you can feel where to cut.
• Put the chicken on a chopping board with its legs away from you.
• Remove the wishbone from the neck end (add to the stockpot).
• Turn the chicken around with the legs and cavity toward you.
• Cut through the loose skin between the left leg and the breast.
• Push the left leg down with your thumb and upwards with your four fingers to break the ball-and-socket joint.
• Turn the bird onto its side and cut around the oyster piece so it remains attached to the leg. Ideally remove the drumstick, thigh, and oyster in one piece, leaving as little meat as possible on the carcass.
•   Cut along the edge of the left side of the breastbone to loosen the white meat. Using long, sweeping movements, remove the breast in one piece with the wing attached. (Alternatively use a poultry shears to cut through the breastbone and ribs.

This adds extra flavor – particularly for a casserole.)
• Chop off the pointed wing tips and discard if the chicken has been intensively reared; otherwise use in the stockpot or use for a chicken wing recipe.
• Cut off the pinion at the first joint and keep for the stockpot.
• Turn the chicken around and repeat on the other side.
• Chop the carcass and put into the stockpot.

How to cut a chicken into eight pieces:

• Joint the chicken as per the above instructions.
• Put one leg skinside down on a chopping board.
• Divide the leg into two by cutting through the line of fat at the knuckle between the thigh and drumstick. Repeat with the other leg.
• Cut the wing from the breast.
• If desired, detach the skin from the breast by pulling it gently away from the flesh.
• Cut the breast into two pieces at an angle.
• Repeat with the second breast.

To prepare a chicken breast

Detach the tender and cook it separately or use it for another recipe, such as a stir-fry or pasta dish. If the chicken breast is to be pan-fried, you may want to remove the skin; however, if the chicken is free-range and organic the skin is delicious when slowly cooked in a low oven for 20 minutes or so, until crisp.

To prepare chicken wings

If still attached to the carcass, cut the entire wing off the chicken. With the blade of the knife at an angle, cut through the cartilage between the third and second joint. Detach the first joint pinion from the middle joint with a quick chop and add it to the stockpot.

To make Chinese drumsticks or buffalo wings, use the wing piece closest to the body. If you have a cleaver, chop the end off the narrow bone. Alternatively, cut through the skin around the narrow end of the bone (closest to the middle joint). Push the flesh back down along the bone with the back of your knife, and turn it inside out so it covers the bone at the other end. Marinate and cook as desired.

How to bone a bird

All birds have a similar anatomy, so they are generally boned in the same way. Sometimes they are partially boned, leaving the leg and wing bones to add shape when stuffing is added – this is more common for small birds. For galantines and ballotines, the bird is boned completely. For boning, choose a bird with the skin intact, so it can be kept whole.

How to bone a bird partially

Use a poultry shears or a Chinese cleaver, cut off the wing tip and middle section, leaving the largest wing bone still attached to the carcass.
• Put the bird breastside down onto a chopping board. Use a small knife with a point to slit the skin in a line along the backbone from neck to tail and expose the backbone.
• Cut the flesh and skin away from the carcass, working with short, sharp, even strokes of the knife. After each stroke, carefully ease the flesh and skin away from the carcass with your left fingers.
• Cut the flesh from the saber-shaped bone near the wing. As you reach the ball-and-socket joints connecting the wing and thigh bones to the carcass, sever them. The wing and thigh are thus separated from the carcass but are still attached to the skin.
• Using longer strokes of the knife, continue cutting the breast meat away from the bone until the ridge of the breastbone, where the skin and bones meet, is reached. (Take great care not to sever the skin here as it is very thin and close to the tip of the breastbone.)
• Turn the bird around and repeat on the other side. When the skin and meat have been freed from the carcass on both sides of the bird, they will remain attached only along the breastbone.
• Lift up the carcass of the bird in one hand so that the skin and meat hang loose from the breastbone.
• Cut against the ridge of the breastbone to free the shin and pull to remove the breastbone and the carcass from the flesh. Be careful – the skin here is easily pierced or torn.
• Spread the chicken skinside down on the chopping board. The bird is partially boned, with the wing and leg bones still in place.

How to bone a bird completely

• For the wing bone, hold the end of the wing bone in one hand, cut through the tendons, and scrape the meat from the bone, drawing the skin away inside out. Pull out the bone, using the knife to free it.
• For the leg bone, hold the inside end of the thigh bone firmly in the left hand and cut through the tendons attaching the flesh to the bone. Use the knife to scrape the meat from the thigh bone, pushing the meat away from the end of the bone. When you reach the joint between the thigh and drumstick, stop; then start from the other end.
• Cut through the skin around the foot end of the drumstick, then push the meat up toward the knuckle loosening inside with your thumb. Be careful of the splinter bone, which runs downward, close to the bone. Then with the tip of a small sharp knife, cut the meat from around the knuckle, using your fingers as a guide to feel whether it is free. The thigh bone and drumstick should come out in one piece, drawing the skin inside out.
• Repeat on the other side.
• Push the skin from the legs and wings rightside out. The completely boned bird will now be flat.

HOW TO CARVE

You will need a carving fork and a really sharp knife. Carve into four or six portions depending on the size of the chicken. Each portion should have some brown and white meat and bone.

First, carve off the leg. Separate the drumstick from the thigh, and if the leg is big, the thigh can be divided into two portions, one piece with a bone and one without. Put on a hot serving dish.

Carve off a generous piece of white meat with the wing attached and serve with the piece of thigh with no bone to make one portion. Then carve the remainder of the white meat into slices; put some with the drumstick and some with the thigh piece with a bone to make two more portions.

Repeat on the other side. Save the cooked carcass for stock (see page 262).

TRADITIONAL ROAST STUFFED CHICKEN

A gorgeous stuffed roast chicken with all the side dishes is the ultimate comfort food. But if you want to recapture forgotten flavors, then source a genuine organic chicken. The stuffing is equally good with roast turkey – just multiply the quantity by three or four. It is also good with guinea hen or a boned loin of lamb · **SERVES 4–6**

4½lb free-range chicken
salt and freshly ground pepper
2 tablespoons butter
sprigs of flat-leaf parsley,
    for garnish

FOR THE GIBLET STOCK
giblets from the chicken (the neck, heart, gizzard, and liver – the latter will make the stock bitter so use for a chicken liver pâté)
1 carrot, sliced
1 onion, sliced
1 celery rib
parsley stems and a sprig of thyme

FOR THE STUFFING
1 small onion, chopped
3 tablespoons butter
1½ cups soft white bread crumbs (see page 577)
2 tablespoons fresh herbs, e.g. parsley, thyme, chives, and annual marjoram, finely chopped
salt and freshly ground pepper
soft butter
Roux (see page 165), optional

Preheat the oven to 350°F.

Weigh the chicken and calculate 20 minutes per pound and 20 minutes over for the cooking time.

Remove the wishbone from the neck end of the chicken (this isn't essential but it does make carving much easier later on). Tuck the wing tips underneath the chicken to make a neat shape.

To make the stock (which you will use for the gravy) put the wishbone, giblets (apart from the liver), carrot, onions, celery, and herbs into a saucepan. Cover with cold water, bring to a boil, skim, and simmer gently while you prepare and roast the chicken.

Next make the stuffing. Sweat the onion gently in the butter until soft – about 10 minutes. Remove from the heat and stir in the bread crumbs, herbs, and a little salt and pepper to taste. Cool completely. If necessary, wash and dry the cavity of the bird; then season and fill it halfway with cold stuffing. Season the breast and legs, smear with a little soft butter, and put in the oven in a roasting pan for about 1½ hours.

Baste the bird a couple of times during the cooking with the buttery juices. To test if it's done, prick the thickest part at the base of the thigh and examine the juices: there should be no trace of pink. Remove the chicken to a carving board and keep it warm.

To make the gravy, spoon off the surplus fat from the roasting pan. Deglaze the pan juices with the giblet stock (you will need about 2 cups, depending on the size of the chicken). Stir and scrape the pan to dissolve the caramelized meat juices. Boil it, season, and, if you like, thicken with a little roux. Taste and correct the seasoning and serve in a warm gravy boat.

Serve the chicken on a nice carving dish surrounded by crispy roast potatoes and some sprigs of flat-leaf parsley; then arm yourself with a sharp knife and bring it to the table. Carve as best you can following the instructions in the box. Serve with gravy and whatever else you fancy.

Opposite: *Traditional Roast Stuffed Chicken.*

Stock

Making stock is really just thrifty housekeeping. Instead of absent-mindedly flinging things into the garbage, keep your carcasses, giblets, and vegetable scraps and use them for your stockpot. Nowadays some supermarkets and butchers are happy to give you chicken carcasses and often giblets as well just for the asking because there is so little demand.

There are some vegetables that should not be put in the stock, such as potatoes, because they soak up flavor and make the stock cloudy. Parsnips and beet are too strong, and the dye from the latter would produce a red stock. Cabbage and other brassicas give an off-taste on long cooking. A little white turnip can be an asset, but it is very easy to overdo it. I also ban bay leaf in my chicken stocks because I find that their flavor can predominate easily and add a sameness to soups made from the stock later on.

Salt is another ingredient that you will find in most stock recipes, but not in mine. That's because if I want to reduce the stock later to make a sauce, it very soon becomes oversalted.

I usually advise people making stock at home to cover the pot, otherwise the whole house will smell of stock, which may put you off making it on a regular basis.

Giblet stock

Any time you buy a fowl, buy it complete with giblets (heart, liver, neck, and gizzards). You can use these to make a little stock while the bird is roasting and use this as a base for your gravy as in Traditional Roast Stuffed Chicken (see page 260). The liver shouldn't go into the stockpot because it will make the stock taste bitter. It can be saved to make a smooth pâté or terrine.

CHICKEN STOCK

This recipe is just a guideline. If you have just one carcass and can't be bothered to make a small quantity of stock, why not freeze the carcass and save it up until you have six or seven carcasses and giblets, then you can make a really good-sized pot of stock and get best value for your fuel.

Stock will keep for several days in the refrigerator. If you want to keep it for longer, boil it up again for 5–6 minutes every couple of days; allow it to get cold and refrigerate again. Stock also freezes perfectly. For cheap containers, use large yogurt cartons or plastic milk bottles, then you can cut them away from the frozen stock without a conscience if you need to defrost it in a hurry! · MAKES ABOUT 15 CUPS

2–3 raw or cooked chicken
    carcasses or a mixture of both
giblets from the chicken (neck,
    heart, gizzard – save the liver
    for a different dish)
1 onion, sliced
1 leek, split in two
2 outside celery ribs or
    2 lovage leaves
1 carrot, cut into chunks
a few parsley stems
sprig of thyme
6 peppercorns

Chop up the carcasses as much as possible. Put all the ingredients into a saucepan and cover with about 3½ quarts cold water. Bring to a boil. Skim the fat off the top with a tablespoon. Simmer for 3–4 hours. Strain and remove any remaining fat. Do not add salt.

Variations

DEMI-GLACE
For a stronger flavor, boil down the liquid in an open pan until it reduces to about half of the original volume. Do not add salt.

TURKEY STOCK
Keep your turkey carcass to make a stock that may be used as the basis of a delicious soup or in turkey pot pie. This is definitely the best-flavored stock of all and it can be made in the same way as the chicken stock. I'm always discouraging my friends from making this so that they give me their turkey carcasses!

PHEASANT OR GUINEA HEN STOCK
Pheasant or guinea hen stock is also made on the same principle as chicken stock. Use appropriately in game dishes.

GOOSE OR DUCK STOCK
Goose or duck stock may be made in the same manner as chicken stock. However, some chefs like to brown the carcasses first for a richer flavor and darker stock. Use for goose and duck recipes such as Duck, Ginger, and Noodle Broth (see page 279).

CHICKEN BROTH FOR THE SOUL

Sometimes, when I'm weary at the end of a busy day, I sneak into the kitchen where the stockpot may still be bubbling and gently concentrating in flavor. I ladle out some broth, wait for a minute or two until the chicken fat rises to the top so I can skim it off, cut one or two thick slices of white bread, slather butter on top, and then tear it into big chunks into the bowl. The bread soaks up the broth and becomes soggy and so delicious. I grab a soup spoon and hide in a corner to enjoy this most comforting of all foods.

Casserole Roasting

This is a brilliant, almost forgotten skill that we use for turkey, guinea hen, chicken, and pheasant. Because they're cooked in a steamy atmosphere that's moist, it's also particularly good for game birds that are a little long in the tooth (or spur!). The bird is cooked inside a covered casserole or, in the case of turkey, a large saucepan with a tight-fitting lid that fits into the oven. We usually slather the breast and legs with some herb butter and pop a couple of herb sprigs into the cavity to perfume the bird.

During cooking the birds exude lots of delicious juice in the steamy atmosphere of the casserole, and this can be the base for a delicious sauce to which we add some stock, fresh herbs, and a little cream.

POULET À L'ESTRAGON

This is the classic French tarragon chicken recipe, using the casserole roasting technique. There are two kinds of tarragon, French and Russian, but I prefer to use French tarragon in this recipe because it has far superior flavor. Unfortunately, French tarragon is more difficult to come by than Russian because it is propagated by root cuttings – you can't just grow it from seed like the Russian variety. French tarragon grows to a height of about 9in and Russian will grow to about 4ft in the summer.

Some chickens yield less juice than others, so if you need more sauce just add a little stock to the cream. If the sauce is thickened with roux, this dish can be reheated. It is also delicious without cream, just made with chicken juices, stock, and fresh herbs ·

SERVES 4–6

4½ lb free-range chicken
salt and freshly ground pepper
2 **tablespoons French tarragon, freshly chopped, plus a few extra sprigs**
2 **tablespoons butter**
⅔ **cup cream**
⅔ **cup Chicken Stock (see previous page), optional**
Roux, optional (see page 165)

oval casserole dish with a capacity of 9 cups

Preheat the oven to 350°F.

Remove the wishbone from the chicken and keep it for the stock. Season the cavity of the chicken with salt and freshly ground pepper and stuff a sprig of tarragon inside.

Mix 1 tablespoon of the remaining tarragon with two thirds of the butter. Smear the remainder of the butter over the breast of the chicken, place breastside down in a casserole, and brown over low heat.

Turn the chicken breastside up and smear the tarragon butter over the breast and legs. Season with salt and pepper.

Cover the casserole and cook for 1¼–1½ hours in the oven.

To test if the chicken is cooked, pierce the flesh between the breast and thigh. This is the last place that cooks – so if there is no trace of pink here and if the juices are clear, then the chicken is certainly cooked. Rest on a carving board for 10–15 minutes before carving.

Spoon the surplus fat from the juices into a saucepan, add the remaining tablespoon of chopped tarragon, the cream, and stock, if using, then boil the sauce until it thickens slightly. Alternatively, bring the liquid to a boil and whisk in just enough roux to thicken the sauce to a light coating consistency. Taste and correct the seasoning.

Carve the chicken into 4 or 6 helpings; each person should have a portion of white and brown meat. Arrange on a serving platter, spoon over the sauce, and serve garnished with sprigs of fresh tarragon.

Variation
Substitute annual marjoram for tarragon in the above recipe.

BASTING

Large birds such as turkey benefit from being covered or partially covered during cooking to protect the breast, which cooks faster than the legs in the intense heat. Cooks have developed a variety of ways of protecting the breast meat. Sometimes slices of bacon cover the breast, which baste and protect the meat as it cooks (and the crispy bacon is delicious to nibble). Another way is to cover the breast with a sheet of parchment paper or aluminum foil to shield the meat from the direct heat.

There is also the cheesecloth method, which works brilliantly, not only for a turkey but also for guinea hen, pheasant, or even chicken. Simply soak a sheet of cheesecloth in melted butter. Then enclose the bird in the butter-soaked cheesecloth. Cook in the oven at 350°F. There is no need to baste and the bird will cook beautifully and be moist and golden when the cheesecloth is removed. The cheesecloth can be washed and reused several times.

ROAST CHICKEN SUPPER IN A DISH

I bring this to the table in a big black roasting pan and it's a whole meal in one dish. It's perfect for nights when you just want something warm and homely that won't create too much mess! · SERVES 8

4½lb organic chicken
1¼lb slab bacon
2 tablespoons sunflower oil
flour, well seasoned with salt and freshly ground black pepper
2½ cups finely sliced or chopped onions
1lb carrots, sliced ¼in thick
5lb large potatoes
salt and freshly ground pepper
5 cups Chicken Stock (see page 262)

TO GARNISH
1 tablespoon freshly chopped parsley,

deep roasting pan about 15in square

Preheat the oven to 450°F.

Cut the chicken into 8 pieces (see page 258), separating the wing joints so they will cook evenly.

Cut the rind around half the bacon into ½in pieces and the remainder into ¼in slices.

Heat the oil in a wide frying pan and cook the lardons until the fat begins to run and they are pale golden; transfer to a plate.

Toss the chicken pieces in the seasoned flour and sauté in the bacon fat and oil until golden on both sides. Remove from the pan

and put on a second plate. Then toss the onions and carrots in the bacon fat for 1–2 minutes and add to the lardons.

Peel the potatoes and slice a little less than half of them into ¼in slices. Arrange a layer of potato slices on the base of a deep roasting pan. Season with salt and freshly ground pepper. Sprinkle the carrots, onions, and bacon pieces over the potatoes and arrange the chicken on top. Season again with salt and freshly ground pepper. Pour over enough hot stock to almost cover.

Cut the remaining potatoes into thick slices lengthwise, about 1½in thick, and arrange them cut-side up on top of the chicken so that the whole top of the dish is covered with thick potato slices. Season with salt and freshly ground pepper.

After 30 minutes of cooking, put the slices of bacon on top of the potatoes so they get deliciously crisp. It should bake for about 1 hour, but check it after that time because it may take a little longer. If it's not done but the top is getting too brown, cover loosely with parchment paper or aluminum foil near the end of the cooking.

Sprinkle with lots of chopped parsley and serve at the table, followed by a good green salad.

PASTA WITH ROAST CHICKEN, RAISINS, PINE NUTS, AND PARSLEY

I love this comforting supper cooked in a roasting pan. It's a filling meal that uses both the drumsticks and thighs. It's inexpensive, really tasty, and will feed eight people generously · **SERVES 8**

8 organic chicken thighs or drumsticks, or a mixture
salt and freshly ground pepper
extra virgin olive oil
2 tablespoons rosemary leaves, chopped
1 tablespoon smoked paprika, or more
½ cup raisins, or more
1lb linguine or spaghetti
¾ cup pine nuts, toasted

To Garnish
4 tablespoons coarsely chopped flat-leaf parsley

Preheat the oven to 400°F. Season the chicken with salt and pepper.

Drizzle a roasting pan with olive oil, then add the chicken thighs in a single layer. Sprinkle with the rosemary, smoked paprika, and a bit more olive oil. Cook for 25–30 minutes, until the meat is cooked through and the skin is crisp.

Cover the raisins with boiling water and leave them to plump up while the chicken is cooking.

Bring a large pan of salted water to a boil – 5 quarts to 2 tablespoons salt. Add the pasta, stir, and cook until al dente. When the chicken is cooked, remove the meat from the bones. Cut the meat and skin into chunks and return to the roasting pan. Drain the pasta, add to the roasting pan with the drained raisins and pine nuts. Toss well in the juices.

Put back on the stove, stir, and toss again. Season with lots of freshly ground pepper. Taste and check the seasoning. Spoon into a hot serving dish and serve, sprinkled with the parsley.

Old Hens

Old hens, or casserole roasters, are almost impossible to buy nowadays, but they make terrific eating. So if you keep your own hens, they are a real bonus. These are hens that have laid for a year or more. They have a rich, gamey flavor and should be poached or casserole roasted (see page 263) rather than roasted in the oven. They are perfect for *Coq au Vin* (see page 267) as the meat is first marinated and then gently simmered to melting tenderness.

OLD HEN WITH PARSLEY SAUCE

Before the days of mass-produced chicken, most farmers' wives kept at least a few hens and sold the eggs for "pin money." Broody hens would hatch out a clutch or two of chicks hidden in the hay rick or the back of the haggard (a field at the back of the house where the threshing took place and the hay ricks were built) in the summer. The females grew into hens, and the cocks were fattened up for the pot and cooked for special occasions. Hens no longer in the first flush of youth were often poached gently and served with a parsley sauce. They are packed with flavor but need to be cooked more slowly. In this recipe you can make a liaison to thicken and enrich the sauce using an egg yolk and cream – another forgotten skill · **SERVES 8**

boiling fowl or good organic chicken, about 4lb
salt and freshly ground pepper
1 large carrot, sliced
3 celery ribs
1 large onion, sliced
a bouquet garni with a sprig of thyme, parsley stems, a tiny bay leaf, and 5 peppercorns
2 cups Chicken Stock (see page 262), hot water or water and white wine
¾ cup cream or whole milk (optional)
1oz Roux (see page 165)
4 tablespoons chopped parsley

For the Liaison **(optional)**
1 organic egg yolk
¼ cup heavy cream

Season the chicken with salt and freshly ground black pepper; then put into a heavy-bottomed casserole with the carrot, celery, onion, and bouquet garni.

Pour in the stock, water, or water and wine. Cover, bring to a boil and simmer on top of the stove or in the oven for 1½–2 hours, depending on the age of the bird. When cooked, remove from the casserole.

Strain and degrease the cooking liquid and return it to the casserole. Discard the vegetables: they have already given their flavor to the

cooking liquid. If it tastes a little weak, reduce the sauce in the uncovered casserole for a few minutes. Add the cream, bring to a boil, and reduce it again. Use roux to thicken it to a light coating consistency. Taste and adjust the seasoning.

Skin the chicken and carve the flesh into 2in pieces, then add the meat and the chopped parsley to the sauce and let it heat through and bubble up.

Finally, if using, prepare the liaison just before serving. Mix the egg yolk with the cream. Add some of the hot sauce to this mixture and then carefully stir it into the chicken. Taste, adjust the seasoning, and stir well but do not allow to boil further or the sauce will curdle. Serve with Rice Pilaf (see page 131).

COQ AU VIN

This delicious version was given to me by Lionel Babin who comes from near Angiers in France and serves this at his restaurant, Nautilus, in Ballycotton, Ireland. Originally, this recipe would have been prepared with a capon or rooster, but if you have an old hen spent after a long life of laying, this is a great way to use her. A "mature" bird tenderizes as it cooks long and slowly in rich red wine. However, one can also get a very good result with a good organic chicken and a bottle of Beaujolais. It tastes even better the next day, once the flavors have had a chance to meld together. Serve with mashed potatoes · **SERVES 6-8**

Opposite: *Coq au Vin.*

1 old hen or large organic
    chicken, about 4½lb – keep
    the liver for the end
salt and freshly ground pepper
1⅔ cups sliced carrots
1⅔ cups sliced onions
5 garlic sliced cloves
1 bouquet garni made up of the
    green of leeks, thyme,
    rosemary, bay leaves, and
    celery
¾ cup cognac
2 cups extra virgin olive oil
4¼ cups red wine (Lionel uses
    Anjou rouge, but Bordeaux
    is good, too)
duck fat (see page 276)
¼ cup all-purpose flour
1 cup Chicken Stock (see page 262)
7oz pearl onions, peeled
1¼lb button mushrooms, cut into
    quarters
10½oz bacon or pancetta, cut into
    ¼in strips

TO GARNISH
flat-leaf parsley leaves

Cut the chicken into 8 large pieces. Season with salt and freshly ground pepper. Put into a big bowl with the sliced carrots, onions, garlic, bouquet garni, cognac, olive oil, and red wine. Mix and leave in the fridge, covered, to marinate for at least 12 hours.

Preheat the oven to 325°F.

Strain and separate the chicken and vegetables. Set aside the marinade. Heat a little of the duck fat in a casserole and brown the chicken. Add the vegetables and cook for a few minutes. Skim off the excess fat. Add the flour, mix, and

put in the oven for 5 minutes (to cook the flour). Add the chicken stock and the marinade. Add more wine to cover the chicken completely. Bring to a boil, then transfer to the oven and cook for 45 minutes to 1½ hours, depending on the age of the bird.

Meanwhile, cook the pearl onions in a little salted water and butter in a covered saucepan until cooked but still firm. Cook the mushrooms in the same way in a separate pan, with a little lemon juice as well. Blanch the bacon pieces (cover in cold water, bring to a boil, and then strain and dry well on paper towels). Melt a little butter and oil and sauté the bacon, onions, and mushrooms together for a few minutes. When the chicken is fully cooked, transfer the pieces to a serving dish. Cover with the onions, mushroom, and bacon and keep warm.

Strain the sauce and bring it back to a boil. Skim any fat that rises to the surface, turn the heat down, and add the finely chopped liver to thicken and enrich the sauce slightly. Taste and correct the seasoning. Spoon the sauce over the chicken, sprinkle with parsley, and serve with lots of fluffy mashed potatoes and a glass of good Burgundy or Bordeaux.

CRISPY CHICKEN LIVERS WITH LIME

This little recipe sounds most unlikely, but you can't imagine how delicious it is. Chicken livers are inexpensive so its good to have lots of different ways to serve them. They're great quickly tossed in a hot pan with freshly grated ginger – or with marjoram, sage, thyme, or rosemary leaves for appetizer salads · **SERVES 4–6 AS AN APPETIZER**

12oz organic chicken livers
whole milk
oil for frying
seasoned all-purpose flour
lime or lemon wedges

Wash and trim the chicken livers. Divide each one into 3 or 4 pieces. Cover with milk and allow to soak for a minimum of 10 minutes.

Just before serving, heat the oil in a deep fryer. Drain the chicken livers, toss each one in seasoned flour, then fry until crisp on the outside. Serve with lime or lemon wedges.

BALLYMALOE CHICKEN LIVER PÂTÉ WITH MELBA TOAST

This recipe has certainly stood the test of time. It has been our house pâté at Ballymaloe since the restaurant opened in 1965. It is served in many different ways – and its success depends on being generous with good butter. It is essential to cover chicken liver pâté with a layer of clarified or even just melted butter; otherwise the pâté will oxidize and become bitter in taste and gray in color · **SERVES 10–12**

8oz fresh organic chicken livers
2 tablespoons brandy
2–2½ tablespoons butter depending on how strong the chicken livers are), cut into cubes
1 tablespoon fresh thyme leaves
1 large garlic clove, crushed
freshly ground pepper
Clarified Butter (see page 216), to seal the top

Wash the livers and remove any membrane or green-tinged bits. Melt a little butter in a frying pan. When it foams, add the livers and cook over low heat. All trace of pink should be gone, but be careful not to overcook them or the outsides will get crusty. Put the livers either through a sieve or into a food processor.

Deglaze the pan with brandy and allow it to flame. Add the crushed garlic and thyme leaves, scraping everything into the bowl with a spatula. Add to the livers. Purée for a few seconds. Let cool.

Add 2 sticks of butter and the fresh thyme leaves. Purée again, until smooth. Season carefully, taste, and add more butter if necessary. This pâté should taste fairly mild and be quite smooth in texture.

Put into ramekins or into one large terrine and knock out any air bubbles. Then pour clarified butter over the top of the pâté to seal.

Serve with melba toast or hot white bread. This pâté will keep for 4 or 5 days in a refrigerator or it can be frozen for a month or so. Eat immediately after it is defrosted.

Variations

CHICKEN LIVER PÂTÉ WITH CARAMELIZED ONIONS
Mix in ¼ cup of caramelized onions before putting it in the terrine.

CHICKEN LIVER PÂTÉ WITH MUSHROOMS
Finely chop 4oz of mushrooms. Heat a little extra virgin olive oil in a heavy frying pan and cook over high heat. Season with salt and pepper. Cool and fold the mushrooms into the pâté before putting it into the terrine.

TERRINE OF CHICKEN

We make several delicious versions of Pâté de Campagne but this is the best of them all. It keeps for up to a week in the fridge but I doubt it'll last that long. Cut into thick slices and serve whole for a main course or half a slice as an appetizer, with a couple of cornichons, dressed salad leaves, and some toast · **SERVES 10–20**

8oz organic chicken livers
½ cup brandy or madeira
2 teaspoons ground white pepper
3½lb organic chicken
½lb bacon
½lb cooked ham
caul fat (or *crépine* in French) or thin slices of bacon (or the intact chicken skin) to line the terrine
salt to taste
1 tablespoon chopped marjoram
1 organic egg, beaten
a sheet of very thin bacon fat or very fatty bacon
sprig of thyme and a bay leaf
luting paste (see below)

1 oval casserole or ceramic terrine, 4in deep x 9½in wide, with a lid

Divide the chicken livers in half and remove any membrane or green-tinged bits. Wash the livers, pat dry with paper towels, and put into a little bowl to marinate in the brandy or madeira. Add the ground white pepper (yes, you need it all). Marinate for 2 hours if possible.

Preheat the oven to 350°F.

Cut up the chicken. Remove the skin from the breasts but keep them intact. Save the wings for another recipe. Remove the skin from the drumsticks and thighs, take all the meat from the bones, and purée in a food processor. Purée the bacon as well.

Cut the ham in long, chunky strips the length of the terrine. You'll need 4–6 strips.

Put the chicken and bacon into a mixing bowl. Mix well using your hands. Add the marjoram, egg, and every drop of the marinade from the livers.

Line the terrine with the caul fat, bacon, or the intact chicken skin. Cut the chicken breast into long strips, too. Spread one third of the farce (the puréed chicken and bacon mixture) on the bottom of the terrine, then arrange half of the well-seasoned breasts interspersed with strips of ham and chicken livers lengthwise in the middle. Repeat by covering with another layer of farce, chicken breasts, ham, and livers as before. Cover with the rest of the farce and then with a sheet of bacon fat. Place a thyme sprig and bay leaf on top.

Cover the terrine and seal with luting paste (see below). Put the terrine in a roasting pan and transfer to the oven. Pour boiling water around the roasting pan until it comes halfway up the terrine. Cook for about 2 hours, ensuring that it does not boil dry. The cooking time varies according to the contents of the terrine. When the terrine is cooked, it will shrink in from the edges and the juices will run clear. If the fat and cooking juice appear cloudy, it is not yet cooked. Remove the terrine from the roasting pan. Press with a board and leave for 3 days.

LUTING PASTE

Sealing terrines or casseroles with luting paste is an inexpensive and time-honored solution to keeping in the flavor and precious juices.

2 cups all-purpose flour

Mix the flour with ⅔–¾ cup water into a dough firm enough to handle. Roll into a rope and use to seal the lid onto the casserole to prevent the steam from escaping during cooking.

CHICKEN WINGS WITH SWEET CHILE SAUCE

An inexpensive and delicious little recipe · **SERVES AS MANY AS YOU LIKE – ALLOW 5 OR 6 WINGS PER PERSON**

chicken wings
Sweet Chile Sauce (see page 433)
soy sauce
toasted sesame seeds
fresh cilantro leaves

Preheat the oven to 350F°.

Put the chicken wings into a bowl. Drizzle with sweet chile sauce. Spread in a single layer on a baking sheet. Cook for 25 minutes. Add more sweet chile sauce and a generous dash of soy sauce, and toss again. Cook for a further 5–10 minutes, depending on size.

Sprinkle with toasted sesame seeds and lots of fresh cilantro and serve.

CRISPY CHICKEN SKIN WITH PLUM OR SWEET CHILE SAUCE

This recipe is only worth doing with an organic chicken. The idea of eating chicken skin may frighten some, but it's soooo yummy. You'll soon become addicted – just don't live on it!

skin from organic chicken breasts
sea salt
plum sauce or Sweet Chile Sauce (see page 433)

Peel the skin off the chicken breasts. Cut the skin into pieces about the size of a business card (if the pieces are reasonably even they will be more manageable to eat later).

Preheat the oven to 350°F. Spread the chicken skin upwards on a wire cooling rack on a baking tray.

Cook for 25–30 minutes, until the skin is irresistibly crisp and the fat has rendered out.

Sprinkle with sea salt and serve with a little bowl of plum or sweet chile sauce for dipping.

Turkey

Unlike geese, turkeys can be reared under intensive conditions, and so they often are. In Ireland in the past there was a great tradition of farmers' wives rearing turkeys for the holiday table. They'd get a couple of dozen poults in early autumn and fatten them up. You could buy them "New York dressed," or plucked but with the insides intact. They'd be sold several weeks before Christmas at cattle markets around the country, and the prices would be announced on the radio. It was a great social occasion – all the neighbors would help pluck the turkeys, and this was an important source of income for Christmas.

Then, along came the Health and Safety people and decided this was no longer acceptable. One can understand why they thought the cattle markets weren't the ideal location to have turkey sales (despite the fact that there was no evidence of anyone suffering ill effects from a turkey purchased there), but they left consumers with no alternative other than an intensively reared bird.

The net result of it all was that a valuable part of a food tradition was lost, the skills were forgotten, and the consumer was left with very little choice. Turkeys used to be something you could only get at Christmas, but now you can buy them all year round and the specialness of turkeys has disappeared. In fact, turkey took on a taste of cotton balls most of the time.

In the past few years, however, some people have started to rear turkeys in the traditional way to satisfy the deep craving and growing demand for flavorsome and humanely reared birds. Ask around at your local farmers' market for these birds.

BRINING A TURKEY

A period of brining greatly enhances the flavor of a turkey. I wouldn't necessarily do this with an organic turkey, but a less noble bird will benefit tremendously from 24 hours in brine.

10oz pickling salt

Dissolve the salt in 3¼ gallons of water. Put the turkey into a clean, stainless-steel saucepan, plastic bucket, or pail. Pour over the brine, cover, and chill for 24 hours. If you want to speed up the process, double the salt and brine the bird for 10 hours. Drain, dry, stuff, and roast as in the recipe below.

OLD-FASHIONED ROAST TURKEY WITH CHESTNUT STUFFING AND BREAD SAUCE

The turkey, being a New World animal, did not make its appearance in Ireland until Elizabethan times. For most of the twentieth century, it was associated almost exclusively with Christmas feasting. Like many other festive foods, however, it has now become commonplace and it is not at all unusual to find turkey on the table for many family meals or celebrations.

To recapture the rich, sweet flavor of the roast turkey of years past, search for a naturally reared, free-range bird, preferably the old Bronze variety. This type of turkey may be expensive, but you economize on other ingredients that help fill up your guests, like the stuffing, that are delicious besides.

One dilemma that confronts most households when cooking a traditional holiday dinner with all the side dishes is the oven space crisis just before the meal is served. You've got plates warming, vegetables warming, and the turkey needs to rest but also be kept warm after cooking while you make the gravy. We transfer the turkey onto a carving board, cover it with aluminum foil, and place a folded bath towel over the foil, tucking it tightly underneath the plate. Years ago, country houses would have used silver cloches for this purpose · SERVES 12

10lb free-range turkey with giblets

FOR THE GIBLET STOCK
neck, gizzard, heart (save the liver for pâté)
2 carrots, sliced
2 onions, sliced
1 celery rib
bouquet garni
4 peppercorns

FOR THE CHESTNUT STUFFING
1lb chestnuts
1½ sticks butter
2 cups onions, chopped
9 cups soft bread crumbs (see page 577)
1½ cups freshly chopped herbs, e.g. parsley, thyme. chives, marjoram, savory, lemon balm
salt and freshly ground pepper

melted butter

**large stems of fresh parsley or
    watercress**

Remove the wishbone from the neck end of the turkey to make carving easier later. Make the giblet stock by covering with cold water the neck, gizzard, heart, wishbone, vegetables, bouquet garni, and black peppercorns. Bring to a boil. Simmer for 3 hours while the turkey is being prepared and cooked.

To make the stuffing, bring about 5 cups of water to a boil in a saucepan. Throw in the chestnuts and boil for 5–10 minutes, until the shell and inside skin peel off easily; the flesh should be soft. Take them out one at a time and chop them finely. Melt the butter, and sweat the onions and chestnuts in it until soft. Add the bread crumbs and herbs, taste and season carefully, mix well.

Preheat the oven to 350°F.

Weigh the turkey and calculate the cooking time, allowing about 15 minutes per 1lb and 15 minutes over. Brush the turkey with melted butter (alternatively, smear well the breast, legs, and crop with soft butter) and season with salt and freshly ground pepper. Cover loosely with parchment paper and roast for about 2½–3 hours.

The turkey is done when the juices run clear. To test, prick the thickest part at the base of the thigh and examine the juices to ensure they are clear. Put the turkey on a carving board, keep it warm, and let it rest while you make the gravy.

To make the gravy, spoon off the surplus fat from the roasting pan. Deglaze the pan juices with the giblet stock. Using a whisk, stir and scrape well to dissolve the caramelized meat juices from the roasting pan. Boil, season, and thicken with a little roux if you like. Taste and correct the seasoning and serve in a warmed gravy boat.

If possible, present the turkey on your largest serving dish, surrounded by golden crispy potatoes and garnished with large stems of parsley or watercress and maybe a sprig of holly (make sure no one eats the berries though).

Serve with Bread Sauce and Cranberry Sauce (see below).

BREAD SAUCE

Bread sauce sounds so dull. If I hadn't been reared on it I might never have tried it. It is another ingenious way of using stale bread, I even love it cold! ·
SERVES 12

2 cups whole milk
**2½ cups bread crumbs
    (see page 577)**
2 onions, each stuck with 6 cloves
2 tablespoons butter
salt and freshly ground pepper
½ cup heavy cream

Bring to a boil in a small, deep saucepan all the ingredients except the cream, and season with salt and freshly ground pepper. Cover and simmer gently over very low heat or cook in the oven at 325°F for 30 minutes. Remove the onion and add the cream just before serving.

Correct the seasoning, and add a little milk if the sauce is too thick. Serve hot.

SPICED CRANBERRY SAUCE

This delicious combination of turkey with cranberry sauce is classically American. I've added spices to the traditional version to give extra bite. If you prefer you can put all the spices in a cheesecloth bag to save fishing out the hard spices at the end of cooking. This sauce is also delicious served with game and some rough pâtés and terrines and will keep in your fridge for several weeks · **SERVES ABOUT 6**

1¼ cups granulated sugar
½ cup white wine vinegar
½ stick cinnamon
1 star anise
6 cloves
2in piece of fresh ginger, peeled
1 chile, split and seeded
1lb cranberries
lemon juice

Put the sugar, vinegar, cinnamon, star anise, cloves, ginger, and chile in a stainless-steel saucepan with 1 cup of water. Bring to a boil. Add the cranberries, bring back to a boil and simmer very gently until the cranberries burst. Lift out the hard spices with a slotted spoon. Add a little lemon juice to taste. Serve warm or cold.

Guinea Hens

Guinea hens are beautiful birds with dark-gray feathers speckled with white. Sadly, not quite as many people keep them as hens, because the high-pitched sound they make can be irritating and, according to my poultry man, disturb the laying capacity of other poultry. I have never quite believed him, though.

I was once given a present of some guinea hens. I was so excited and followed the instructions to keep them in for four days or so until they became acclimatized. As soon as I let them out, they ran off; they were seen a few nights later roosting in the woods outside the village – and thereafter were never seen again. If you want to keep them, you need to hatch them out yourself, which I plan on doing one of these days. In the meantime, we fortunately have a local farmer who rears guinea hens for us. They taste like a cross between a wild pheasant and a chicken – with just a touch of gamey flavor. Try the recipe below or use the legs of the guinea hen in place of the chicken in the Pasta with Roast Chicken recipe on page 265.

PAN-ROASTED GUINEA HENS WITH PARSLEY SAUCE

Many pheasant and chicken recipes work really well for guinea hens, too. But if you want to really enjoy the mild gaminess, don't mask it with an overpowering sauce. Try this delicious recipe, kindly given to me by Skye Gyngell when she came to teach at the cookery school · **SERVES 6**

6 guinea hen supremes (whole breasts with a little bit of wing attached)
sea salt and freshly ground black pepper
a little light olive oil, for cooking

FOR THE PARSLEY SAUCE
2⅓ cups curly parsley, stems removed, plus extra for serving
2 cups heavy cream
freshly grated nutmeg
1½ teaspoons finely grated lemon zest, or to taste
salt and freshly ground pepper

First make the parsley sauce. Put a pan of well-salted water on to boil (it should be as salty as the sea).

Plunge the parsley into a boiling water for 30 seconds. Remove and refresh in iced water (to keep your parsley a beautiful, bright color). Drain and set aside.

Pour the cream into a heavy-bottomed pan and bring almost to a boil. Turn down the heat and leave it to bubble and reduce by about one-third, until it has thickened enough to coat the back of a wooden spoon. Add the blanched parsley and boil for a moment longer. Remove from the heat and purée in a blender until you have a beautiful fine texture.

Add a generous grating of nutmeg and the lemon zest, then season well with salt and a good grinding of pepper. Your sauce is now ready; keep it warm.

Preheat the oven to 425°F.

Season the guinea hens generously with salt and freshly ground pepper all over. Place a heavy-bottomed frying pan over medium-high heat and heat until smoking. Pour in about 1 tablespoon of olive oil. Then brown the guinea hens in batches by laying 2 supremes in the pan, skinside down, and leaving to color for 3 minutes (resist the temptation to play with them). Transfer the supremes to a baking sheet (without turning them) and brown the rest of them in the same way.

Finish cooking the guinea hens in the oven for 8 minutes, until the skin is crisp and crunchy and the breast meat is succulent, moist, and cooked through. Rest in a warm place for 5 minutes.

Arrange the guinea hen supremes on warm plates, on a bed of rutabaga purée if you like, and ladle the warm parsley sauce generously over the top. Scatter chopped parsley on top and serve.

Quail

Quail are cute little birds, and are perfect to serve for an appetizer, but you may need two or three per person for a main course. They still roam freely in many countries but the ones that we now have access to in shops and restaurants are mostly farmed and are consequently fairly mild in flavor. However, this gives you an opportunity to be creative and add lots of exotic flavors. They're also easy to spatchcock and barbecue or pan-grill. Don't be shy to pick them up and eat them with your hands so you can nibble every last morsel – remember, though, that you'll need to offer a finger bowl to your guests.

How to spatchcock a bird

Insert a heavy chopping knife into the cavity of the bird from the back end to the neck. Press down sharply to cut through the backbone. Alternatively place the bird breast- and skin-side down on the chopping board, and using poultry shears, cut along the entire length of the backbone, as close to the center as possible. Open the bird out and flatten as much as possible.

SPATCHCOCKED QUAIL

Spatchcocking is a technique used to open out the carcass of white meat poultry (chicken, pheasant, or guinea hens) so that it cooks faster and more evenly. Anybody can do it at home — you just need a large chopping knife. Cornish hens may also be used in this recipe · **SERVES 6 AS AN APPETIZER**

6 quails
6 tablespoons olive oil
2 teaspoons chile flakes
1 tablespoon rosemary or
 marjoram
salt and freshly ground pepper

Preheat the oven to 350°F.

Put the birds on a chopping board and prepare as instructed above. Push a skewer through both the wings and thighs of each quail. Mix the oil with the chile flakes and herbs. Drizzle over the quail, turning to coat both sides, and marinate for 30 minutes to an hour. Season with salt and pepper.

Cook the quails, cutside down first for 8–10 minutes, depending

Above: *Spatchcocked Quail.*

on size. Then turn over and cook on the other side until crisp and golden. Serve with a good green salad and spicy mayonnaise.

Duck

For those who have some space, ducks are easily reared either for egg production or for the table. I am continually surprised by the demand for duck and even goose eggs at our local farmers' market in Midleton. Of course they're not mainstream like hens' eggs, but duck eggs have their devotees and because they are so rarely found in shops nowadays people will travel to find them.

My favorite breed of duck is the old-fashioned Aylesbury duck, which is what we have here, but now Muscovy ducks are mass-produced for restaurants – chefs love them because the breasts are bigger, but I don't think they hold a candle to well-reared Aylesbury ducks. The giblets (neck, gizzard, and heart) of both ducks and geese make a fine broth and their liver a pâté.

Why should I keep a few ducks?

Duck eggs are great – they are delicious to eat and they really add extra oomph to your cakes. Ducks gobble up snails and help fertilize the ground, and keep down weeds without being destructive. Do keep them out of your vegetable garden during the growing season, though – their big flat feet can crush unprotected seedlings.

How many do I need?

The number you keep depends on whether your ducks are for egg or table production. Stocks as small as five or six birds can be functional as well as decorative. They are creatures of habit and thrive and perform much better when feeding times are regular.

Indian Runners and Khaki Campbell are excellent layers and can be expected to produce 225–300 eggs per year. Aylesbury are poor layers, but can produce 140–150 white and pale-green eggs weighing from 2½–3oz in the first year.

Which breed should I choose to rear for the table?

Aylesbury ducks, the beloved of my Grandpoppy, are still my favorite. This breed, which originated in the south of England, is an outstanding table breed with excellent flavor and texture. They are good food converters, grow fast and can be ready for the table or market in about eight weeks, weighing 5½–7lb in live weight.

Pekin are also excellent and would be my second choice. These smaller, creamy-white birds with deep-yellow breast plumage and bright-orange beaks and feet are of Chinese origin. They take a week or two longer to mature than the Aylesbury. The flesh is yellower in color but again the flavor is excellent. They tend to be slightly better layers than the Aylesbury, laying on average 150–200 eggs per year.

Another sought-after table breed is Muscovy. It is native to Brazil and is characterized by its rich gamey flavor.

Do ducks need water?

Ducks, of course, love water and will be happier if they have access to even a small plastic or artificial concrete pond about 4–6ft in diameter and 12–15in deep.

Ducks can often be kept where other animals cannot. For example, ducks can be kept on wet, marshy land that would be totally unsuitable for other poultry. An old farmer once told me that land infested with liver fluke, a parasite that affects the livers of livestock like cows and sheep, can be cleared of the problem by keeping a flock of ducks.

If you are providing a pond, something like an old bathtub is ideal because you can let the water out through the drain to give it a regular clean.

Do I need a drake?

Ducks are happier with a drake around but as with hens, a drake is not essential, although (needless to say) you won't have fertile eggs. A drake will mate with seven or eight ducks.

How long do duck eggs take to hatch?

Most breeds will hatch in about 28 days. However, Muscovy ducks take 35–36 days. Ducks usually make rotten mothers and sometimes abandon their nest even before the eggs are hatched. Muscovy ducks, however, make excellent "sitters" and mothers.

Right: *A cute Aylesbury duck.*

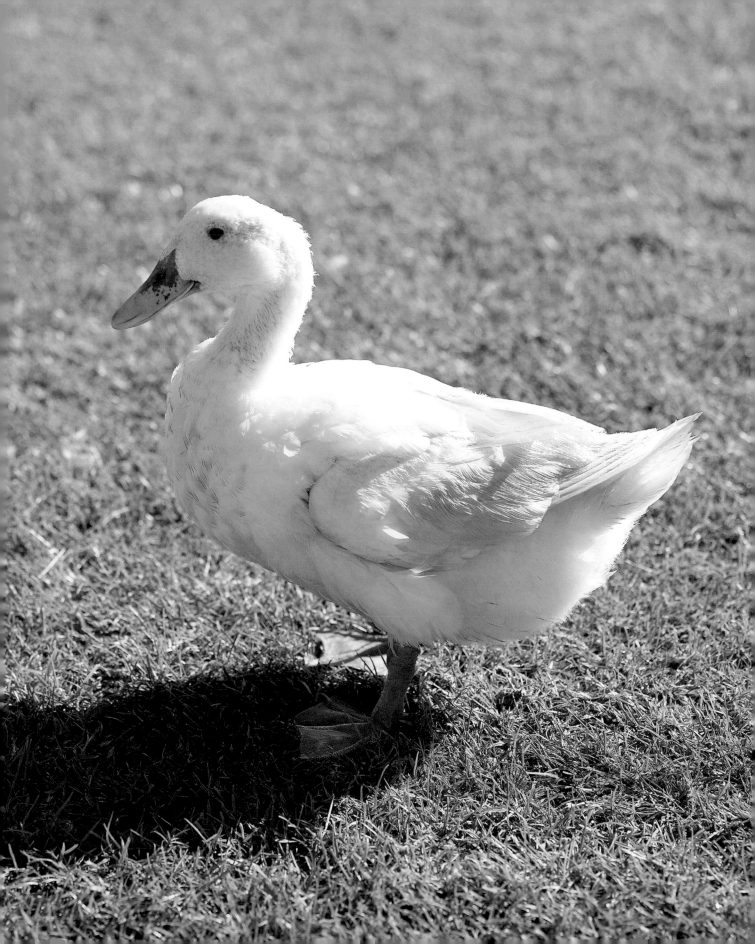

Above: *Goose fat.*

How to cut up a duck to make the most of every morsel

• First remove the wishbone from the neck end.
• Next remove the wings and add them to the stockpot.
• Remove the legs – roast or use for duck confit.
• Remove the duck breasts. Tear off the inside fillet, sauté quickly, and use on a salad.
• Trim any excess fat off the duck breasts, legs, and carcass and save it to render down for duck fat (below).
• You are now left with the duck carcass. Use a cleaver to chop the carcass into smaller pieces for Duck Stock (see page 262), also adding the duck wings and giblets (though save the liver for pâté).
• After the stock is made, scrape every last morsel of meat off the carcass to make Duck Rillettes (see page 278).
• Use the duck liver for pâté or warm salad.
• Use the duck gizzards for *Salade de Gésiers* (see page 283).

How to render duck fat

Remove the remainder of the duck fat from the raw carcass – particularly the pieces near the tail end inside the carcass. Cut it into small pieces and put on a roasting pan in a cool oven at 225°F. The liquid fat will render out slowly over several hours.

Grillons or duck scratchings

The morsels of skin will gradually become crisp and golden as the fat renders. In France these are called *grillons* and are sprinkled over salads. We call them duck scratchings and sprinkle them with sea salt and nibble them with drinks or add them to White Soda Scones (see page 261).

When all the liquid fat has rendered out, pour it into glass jars or ceramic crocks. Cover and store in the fridge. Use in Duck Rillettes (see page 278) or to cook roast potatoes. Duck fat keeps for about six months.

The use of duck (or goose) fat, lard, or dripping has fallen out of favor completely during the last 30 to 40 years as the paranoia around low-fat eating gathered momentum. Now, thanks in great part to some celebrity chefs, people realize that it is in some ways healthier and has markedly better flavor than most of the cooking oils that were lauded as an alternative for many years. Now the demand for duck fat is so enormous that shops regularly sell out and customers at our stall in Midleton Farmers' Market can't get enough of it.

Roasting potatoes in duck or goose fat

Everybody loves roast potatoes, yet people ask over and over again for the secret to making them golden and crispy. The type of fat really matters: duck or goose fat adds delicious flavor. Good-quality pork fat or lard from free-range pigs is also worth saving for roast or sauté potatoes. All will keep for months in a cold larder or fridge.

When making roast potatoes always buy good-quality "old" potatoes. New potatoes are not so good for roasting. The skin gets leathery rather than crisp. See page 382 in the vegetable chapter for the roast potatoes recipe.

How to prepare a duck or goose for the oven

1 Gut the bird if necessary and clean well.

2 Singe carefully over a gas burner.

3 Remove the wishbone from the neck end.

4 For a goose, tuck the wings in close to the body; for a duck, use a sharp cleaver to trim the wings just above the first joint nearest the body. See duck wing recipe, page 278.

5 For a goose, leave the legs intact; for a duck, you may wish to chop off the knuckle just above the "knee."

6 Season the cavity. Stuff with cold stuffing just before the bird goes into the oven.

7 Truss loosely with cotton string. Note: it is not essential that you chop the wings and legs off a duck unless you want a more formal restaurant presentation.

How to pan-grill a duck breast (*magret de canard*)

Score the fat of the duck breasts and put skinside down on a cold grill pan. Cook over low heat for 15–20 minutes. When the fat is thin and crisp, turn over onto the flesh side (the duck breast should be about half-cooked). Sprinkle with a little salt and continue to cook until it reaches the required degree of doneness – medium to well-done is many people's preference. I personally find that rare duck, which was very fashionable when nouvelle cuisine was all the rage, can be unpleasant and tough.

Above: *Potatoes roasted in goose fat.*

Good things to serve with duck breast

• Puy or Castellucio lentils, or haricot beans with rosemary
• Cubed potatoes fried in duck fat
• A salad of organic leaves and green beans
• A compote of green gooseberries or kumquats in season

Good things to serve with duck legs

• Onions with thyme leaves
• Cannellini or borlotti beans with olive oil
• Lentils with chile and parsley

DUCK RILLETTES

I came across this dish in a little restaurant in the French countryside and the thrifty chef shared the secret with me. This recipe uses every last scrap of duck meat from the carcass after yielding its flavor in a stockpot.

duck meat from a cooked carcass
salt and freshly ground pepper
quatre épices (a spice blend of
  ground pepper, cloves,
  nutmeg, and ginger)
duck fat
fresh thyme

Tear the duck meat salvaged from the cooked carcass into shreds and put into a bowl. Season with salt, freshly ground pepper, and a little quatre épices.

Add a few tablespoons of duck fat and a little fresh thyme to the duck meat mixture. Mix it together, then taste and correct the seasoning.

Pack the rillettes into little ramekins, cover, and chill. Serve with hot, thin toast.

TRADITIONAL ROAST DUCK WITH SAGE AND ONION STUFFING AND APPLE SAUCE

Follow the recipe for Traditional Roast Stuffed Chicken (see page 260). Make the stuffing in the same way but substitute 2 teaspoons of freshly chopped sage for the fresh herbs. Sprinkle a little salt over the skin, omit the butter and roast for about 1½ hours. Serve with Apple Sauce (see page 298).

DUCK WITH SEVILLE ORANGE MARMALADE SAUCE

You can make this sauce ahead of time for a dinner party. The orange marmalade cuts the richness of the duck in a very appealing way and it gives you an opportunity to show off your homemade marmalade. Watercress salad is a particularly good accompaniment for this recipe
· SERVES 4

1 free-range duck
2 stems of marjoram
2 tablespoons butter
salt and freshly ground pepper
½ cup Seville Whole Orange
  Marmalade (see page 454)
2 oranges
⅔ cup Duck Stock or Chicken
  Stock (see page 262)
a little sugar (optional), to taste
4 tablespoons chopped parsley

enamel or Pyrex roasting pan

Preheat the oven to 350°F.

First, remove the excess fat from around the vent end of the duck. Render it down (see page 276) and set aside. Tuck the marjoram into the cavity of the duck and season with salt and freshly ground pepper.

Transfer the duck to an enamel or Pyrex roasting pan. Spread the breast and legs of the duck with butter and then cover generously with the marmalade. Juice the oranges and add to the roasting pan with the duck or chicken stock.

Cook for 1¼–1½ hours, depending on the size of the bird.

Transfer to a serving dish and let rest.

Meanwhile, boil up the juices and marmalade. Taste and add a little sugar and a few more tablespoons of marmalade, if necessary. Taste again, correct the seasoning, and add the chopped parsley.

Carve the duck and serve with the marmalade sauce.

RAGOUT OF DUCK WINGS

This recipe was given to me by Carmel Somers, who runs an iconic restaurant called Good Things Café just outside of Durrus in West Cork. I was amused to read her introduction (see below). It's a fantastic recipe for using duck wings, which might otherwise be discarded. They are surprisingly meaty and succulent. Carmel serves them with a big bowl of pasta.

Carmel wrote: "This recipe evolved in the café last summer as a result of the lack of sunny days. I decided we needed a comfort dish to appeal to customers feeling a bit washed out by our unpredictable Irish weather. We had lots of duck wings, nice streaky bacon, and a selection of spices. The wait staff were rather dubious of its popularity – a stew of duck wings! Darina Allen from Ballymaloe Cookery School was in for lunch that day and I knew this was her kind of dish. So the kitchen/front of house bet was laid and we sold six portions that day, with many requests for the recipe. It became our most popular dish after the Durrus cheese pizza."

Always try to have some duck or

chicken stock in the freezer as it is really the ingredient that gives this stew its rich flavor and makes the dish seem uncomplicated · SERVES 6–8

12 whole duck wings (include 2 joints)
salt and freshly ground pepper
extra virgin olive oil
2oz slab bacon, cubed
2 large onions, finely chopped
2 celery ribs, finely chopped
1⅔ cups Duck Stock or Chicken Stock (see page 262)
1 x 14oz can of tomatoes, roughly chopped
4 large garlic cloves
1 red hot chile, dried and finely chopped
¼ teaspoon ground cloves
a good grating of nutmeg
1 cinnamon stick
1 x 14oz can of chickpeas or 1 cup dried chickpeas, soaked and cooked

TO GARNISH
lots of flat-leaf parsley

While you heat a large, heavy-bottomed saucepan, dry the wings with paper towels, put them into a large bowl, and season with salt and pepper.

When the saucepan is warm, add a little extra virgin olive oil and cook the bacon on medium heat until the fat softens. Remove the bacon and set to one side. Add the duck wings and brown on both sides (you might need to do this in two batches). Remove from the saucepan and set aside.

Add the onions and celery and cook on medium heat for 4–5 minutes or until they start to soften. Then return the bacon and wings to the saucepan and add the stock. Bring to a boil and add the chopped tomatoes, garlic, chile, and spices. Reduce the heat to a gentle simmer and cook for 1½ hours, until the meat starts to fall off the bone.

Keep the wings warm in the saucepan while you reduce part of the sauce. Pour about half of the sauce into a shallow saucepan or a deep-sided frying pan. Boil over high heat for at least 10 minutes to reduce and improve the flavor. Pour back into the saucepan over the wings and add the cooked chickpeas.

Serve the wings and sauce directly from the pan with a big bowl of pasta scattered with lots of parsley.

DUCK, GINGER, AND NOODLE BROTH

This recipe uses up any morsels of leftover meat from a roast duck carcass. In addition, it is a good use of duck stock, which is less versatile than chicken stock because of its distinctive "quacky" flavor · SERVES 6–8

7½ cups Duck Stock (see page 262)
2½in piece of fresh ginger, thinly sliced
3 star anise
4–6 scallions, depending on size, roughly chopped
1 teaspoon black peppercorns
2 tablespoons nam pla (fish sauce)
3½oz rice noodles
1½ cups cabbage or Chinese cabbage, thinly sliced
2⅔ cups or more cooked duck meat, shredded
6 tablespoons fresh cilantro leaves OR Thai basil leaves
2 red chiles, thinly sliced
⅔ cup shallots, sautéed to a crisp

Bring the duck stock slowly to a boil with the ginger, star anise, scallions, and peppercorns. Simmer gently for 30 minutes. Strain the broth. Add the fish sauce to the strained broth. Taste and correct the seasoning.

Pour boiling water over the rice noodles. Add the cabbage and simmer for 3–4 minutes. (If you use Chinese cabbage, you don't need to cook it; you can just shred it finely and divide it between the bowls with the noodles.) Strain.

Divide the noodles and cabbage between the six or eight serving bowls and top with the duck pieces. Finally ladle the broth over the noodles and duck and top with the cilantro or Thai basil leaves. Scatter with thinly sliced chile and crispy shallots. Serve as soon as possible.

Confiting

Confit is an almost exclusively French way of preserving. First the meat is salted and then it is cooked, long and slowly, in fat. Originally, confit was made to preserve meat, particularly goose and duck for the winter, but nowadays this essentially peasant dish has become very fashionable.

Confit is stored in sterilized jars that are completely covered with fat to seal them from the air. The meat takes several weeks to mellow and needs to be stored in a cool, dry place.

To extract the pieces of meat from the fat, put the jar in a saucepan of hot water. The fat will melt and the meat can then be extracted easily. After taking what you need, leave the fat to solidify over the remaining pieces and continue to refrigerate. Confit keeps for three to four months. One can, of course, also confit goose, which is an important part of the French culinary heritage.

CONFIT DE CANARD

Serve duck confit hot and crisp on a green salad, add to a cassoulet, or serve it simply with a generous helping of Puy lentils and some thickly sliced potatoes sautéed in duck fat · MAKES 4

4 duck (or goose) legs, preferably free-range
a cut garlic clove, for rubbing
1 tablespoon sea salt
1 teaspoon freshly cracked black peppercorns
a few gratings of fresh nutmeg

1 teaspoon thyme leaves
1 crumbled bay leaf
2lb duck fat (see page 276) or goose fat
1 bay leaf
2 sprigs of thyme
sprigs of parsley
6 garlic cloves, unpeeled

Cut the legs off the duck carcass (use it to make stock, see page 262). The breasts can also be used for confit but you may prefer to use them for another recipe.

Rub the duck legs all over with the cut clove of garlic. Mix together the salt, pepper, nutmeg, thyme, and bay leaf, sprinkle the duck legs sparingly with the mixture, and put into a ceramic dish. Cover and leave overnight in a cold pantry or fridge.

Meanwhile, cut every scrap of fat from the duck carcasses (you will need about 2lb). Render the fat in a low oven, strain, and set to aside.

Next day, melt the fat on low heat in a wide saucepan. Wash the cure off the duck legs, dry them, and put them into the fat (there should be enough to cover the pieces). Bring to a boil, add the fresh herbs and garlic and simmer on low heat until the meat is very tender, about 1–1¼ hours (it is ready when a bamboo skewer can go through the thickest part of the leg with no resistance).

Remove the legs from the fat. Strain the fat, and let rest for a few minutes. Pour the fat off the meat juices. When the meat is cold, pack it into a sterilized earthenware jar, and pour the cooled fat over it so that the pieces are completely submerged. Store in the fridge until

needed, leaving for at least a week at first to mature. When needed, melt the fat to remove the confit.

Variations

CONFIT OF CHICKEN LEGS
Sprinkle the chicken legs with salt and a few thyme leaves and leave for 4–5 hours or even overnight. Next day, wash and dry the chicken legs. Put into a stainless-steel saucepan or casserole and cover completely with melted duck fat. Heat slowly and cook very gently until a skewer will penetrate the flesh easily.

To serve, pop the chicken back into a very hot oven to crisp on the outside and barely heat through. Shred and serve on a salad of seasonal leaves with a few caramelized shallots and Yukon Gold potatoes, or whatever you have to hand. Or try a little diced pickled lemon or Mustard Fruits (see page 429).

CONFIT OF DUCK LEGS WITH PUY LENTILS, ROAST PARSNIPS, AND ROAST POTATOES

This recipe is an earthy, winter combination of classic flavors · SERVES 6 AS A MAIN COURSE

2⅓ cups (1lb) Puy lentils
1 carrot
1 onion, stuck with 2 cloves
bouquet garni
butter or extra virgin olive oil
freshly squeezed lemon juice
3 tablespoons or more freshly chopped herbs e.g. marjoram or parsley

sea salt and freshly ground pepper
6 large confit duck legs (see above)

TO GARNISH
Rustic Roast Potatoes (see page
    383), sprinkled with rosemary
    and cut into large dice
roast parsnips
whole roasted garlic cloves (see
    page 426), optional
fresh rosemary

Follow the recipes to roast the
potatoes, parsnips, and garlic.

Meanwhile prepare the lentils.
Put them into a saucepan and cover
with cold water. Add the carrot,
onion, and bouquet garni, bring
them slowly to a boil, reduce the
heat, and simmer very gently for
10 minutes, testing regularly. The
lentils should be al dente but not
hard. Drain, remove and discard
the carrot, onion, and bouquet garni.
Add a good dab of butter or some
extra virgin olive oil to the lentils,
then add lots of lemon juice and
some chopped herbs. Season with
sea salt and freshly ground pepper.

Preheat the oven to 450°F.

Melt the duck fat in the confit
and remove the duck meat. Roast
the meat in the oven until hot and
crisp (about 15 minutes).

To serve, put a portion of lentils
on each hot plate and top with a
piece of duck confit. Serve with
crispy roast parsnips and rustic roast
potatoes. Garnish with roasted
whole garlic cloves, if you like, and
fresh rosemary.

DUCK CONFIT QUICHE

*When Nathalie Jordi, my research
assistant, told me about this
combination, I thought it sounded a
bit unlikely, but we reconstructed it
based on her taste memory and it
was delicious. We use dried beans to
weigh down the pastry base and keep
up the sides when baking blind. They
can be used over and over again ·*
SERVES 4–6

1 quantity Shortcrust Pastry (see
    page 250)
2 organic eggs plus 1 organic egg
    yolk
1 cup heavy cream
1½ cups duck confit in chunks,
    pulled apart
3 tablespoons freshly grated
    Parmesan cheese
1 teaspoon chopped thyme
1 teaspoon chopped parsley
1 teaspoon chopped chives
salt and freshly ground pepper

1 x 8in tart pan

Preheat the oven to 350°F.

Line the tart pan with the pastry.
Line with parchment paper and
baking beans and bake blind for
15–20 minutes, until the pastry is
half-cooked. Remove the beans from
the pastry.

Beat the eggs with the cream and
add the chunks of duck confit. Add
the cheese and chopped herbs and
season well. Pour into the pastry
case and bake for about 30 minutes
until puffed up and golden. Serve
with an heirloom tomato salad and a
green salad.

CURED DUCK HAMS

*This is yet another interesting way of
using the duck legs – by curing them.
It adds extra interest and helps
preserve them for longer. They can be
served in a variety of ways – with
beans, lentils, or sliced over a salad ·*
MAKES 6 DUCK HAMS

6 free-range duck legs

FOR THE BRINE
2 heaping tablespoons pickling salt
½ teaspoon black and white
    peppercorns, mixed
3 juniper berries
1 bay leaf
a sprig of thyme
2–3 cloves
pinch of saltpeter (potassium
    nitrate), if available

Dissolve the salt in 4 cups of hot
water and let cool. Then transfer the
brine to a nonreactive bowl. Once it
is completely cold, add all the other
brine ingredients.

Meanwhile, trim the duck legs
of excess fat. Duck fat is a really
valuable asset, so chop it up, render
it (see page 276), and save it for
later. Add the duck legs to the
brine. They must be completely
submerged in the liquid. Cover
and refrigerate for 2–6 days. Use
as required.

DUCK HAMS WITH WHITE BEANS

The cannellini beans are a delicious foil to the salty duck hams · SERVES 6

6 Duck Hams (see previous page)
1 medium onion, cut in quarters
1 large carrot, cut in half
2 celery ribs, cut in half
a sprig of thyme
4 parsley stems
3 peppercorns
bay leaf
4 tablespoons extra virgin olive oil
3 garlic cloves, finely chopped
1 medium onion, sliced
1 teaspoon roughly chopped
    thyme leaves
1 teaspoon roughly chopped
    rosemary
14oz can of cannellini beans,
    drained and rinsed
salt and freshly ground black
    pepper
2 tablespoons roughly chopped
    flat-leaf parsley

Lift the duck legs out of the brine. Discard the brine (use it to kill weeds on a path or drive). Put the duck hams into a deep saucepan and cover with cold water. Add the quartered onion, carrot, celery, sprig of thyme, parsley stems, peppercorns, and bay leaf.

Bring to a boil, skim off the foamy scum, and then simmer for 30–40 minutes, until the duck legs are tender and the meat lifts easily from the bone. Remove and put on a baking sheet. Strain the broth and save to cook beans or lentils.

Left: *Cured Duck Hams.*

Heat 2 tablespoons of the oil in a saucepan, add the garlic and onion, and cook for 5–6 minutes until soft. Then add the thyme leaves and rosemary and continue to cook. Add the cannellini beans and heat through for 2–3 minutes. Transfer to a food processor and pulse a few times. Add 2 tablespoons of olive oil and enough cooking water to achieve the consistency of whipped cream. Season with salt and pepper. Add the parsley and serve immediately with the warm duck hams (The beans will keep for 2–3 days in the fridge).

DUCK GIZZARDS COOKED IN DUCK FAT

I so love gizzards and hearts, too – either duck, goose, turkey, or chicken. Cooking gizzards in duck fat gives them an extra succulence.

duck gizzards
duck fat

Cut the lobes off the gizzards and wash and dry. Put into a casserole and cover with duck fat. Cook on the lowest possible heat (use a heat diffuser mat on a gas burner) for about 2 hours, until a knife goes through the meat easily. Store in a sterilized Mason jar or bowl covered with duck fat for several weeks in a cold place.

SALADE DE GÉSIERS

When I go to Paris, one of the first things I do is to seek out a little bistro or brasserie that serves salade de gésiers. *The French could teach us a thing or two about using every scrap* · SERVES 4

8 duck gizzards cooked in duck fat
    (see left)
4oz green beans
duck fat for frying
4 duck hearts (optional)
salt and freshly ground pepper
a selection of salad leaves

FOR THE DRESSING
3 tablespoons extra virgin olive oil
1 tablespoon red wine vinegar
1 small garlic clove, crushed
salt and freshly ground pepper
¼ teaspoon Dijon mustard

TO GARNISH
sprigs of chervil and wild garlic or
    chive flowers (if in season)

Remove 8 pieces of duck gizzard from the duck fat.

Whisk together the ingredients for the dressing. Blanch the green beans in boiling salted water for 2–3 minutes; drain, refresh in cold water, and drain again well.

Heat a little duck fat in a frying pan over medium heat. Remove the gizzards from the fat. Slice each one into 2–3 pieces and toss in the hot fat until hot through and slightly brown at the edges. Slice the duck hearts, if using. Season with salt and pepper and cook quickly in the duck fat. To serve, add the green beans to the salad leaves. Toss in some dressing to coat the leaves. Divide between four plates and scatter the hot duck gizzards and hearts (if using) on top with the garnish.

Goose

Geese are wonderfully inquisitive birds. They will not thrive in confinement, so they are always free-range. This is a great advantage over turkey, because most turkey is now mass-produced and as a result is depressingly boring. If I have to choose between turkey and goose for Christmas, I choose goose, because I so love dark meat.

A neighbor who keeps geese sometimes has a surplus of goose eggs so we sell them for her at the Midleton Farmers' Market – they sell like hotcakes. Children are intrigued by them because we call them dinosaur eggs – they are about four times the size of hens' eggs and would make a fine omelette for a hungry chap, or a good-sized frittata for two.

Uses for Goose Fat
• Rub goose grease on your hands, it's very good for the skin.
• Use goose fat to keep leather soft on the mainsail of a boat.
• Of course, it's always great for roasting potatoes.

TRADITIONAL ROAST GOOSE WITH POTATO STUFFING AND APPLE AND ROSE GERANIUM SAUCE

After the harvest, geese were traditionally ushered into the stubble and would gorge themselves on the loose grain that remained on the ground. They love to graze, and their droppings would enrich the soil. By the end of September, they'd be fat, juicy, and tender: perfect for the table. Roast Goose with Potato Stuffing is almost my favorite winter meal. However, just a word of warning: a goose looks enormous because it has a large carcass. Many people have been caught out by imagining that it will serve more people than it does. Ensure that you allow 1lb in cooked weight per person · **SERVES 8-10**

goose, about 10lb
salt and freshly ground pepper
Roux (see page 165) for the gravy
(optional)

FOR THE GIBLET STOCK
goose giblets
1 onion, sliced
1 carrot, chopped
bouquet garni
a sprig of thyme
4 parsley stems
3 celery ribs, sliced
6 black peppercorns

FOR THE POTATO STUFFING
2 tablespoons butter
4 medium onions, chopped
2–3 cooking apples, peeled and chopped
1 teaspoon thyme
1 teaspoon lemon balm
2 tablespoons fresh orange juice
4 medium potatoes, unpeeled
¼ teaspoon orange rind, finely grated
salt and freshly ground pepper

TO SERVE
Apple and Rose Geranium Sauce (see page 222)

To prepare the goose, gut the bird and singe off the pin feathers and down if necessary. Remove the wishbone from the neck end. Combine the wishbone with the other stock ingredients in a saucepan, cover with cold water, cover the pan, and simmer for 1½–2 hours. Season the cavity of the goose with salt and freshly ground pepper; also rub a little salt into the skin.

To make the potato stuffing, melt the butter in a heavy-bottomed saucepan. Add the onions, cover, and sweat on low heat for about 5 minutes. Then add the chopped apples, herbs, and orange juice. Cook, covered, until the apples are soft and fluffy. Meanwhile, boil the potatoes in their skins until cooked, peel, mash, and add to the fruit and onion mixture. Add the orange rind and seasoning. Let cool completely.

Preheat the oven to 350°F.

Stuff the goose loosely, then roast it for about 2 hours or until the juices run clear. Prick the thigh at the thickest part to check the juices. If they are still pink, the goose needs to cook a little bit longer. When cooked, remove the bird to a serving dish and put it in a very low oven while you make the gravy.

To make the gravy, spoon off the surplus fat from the roasting pan (save it for sautéing or roasting potatoes – it keeps for months in a fridge). Add about 2¼ cups of the strained giblet stock to the roasting pan and bring to a boil. Scrape the roasting pan well to dissolve the meaty deposits, which are full of flavor. Taste for seasoning and thicken with a little roux if you like a thickened gravy. If the gravy is weak, boil it for a few minutes to concentrate the flavor; if it's too strong, add a little water or stock. Strain and serve in a hot gravy boat.

Carve the goose. Serve it alongside the apple and rose geranium sauce and gravy.

Variations

ROAST GOOSE WITH QUINCE
I sometimes serve a warm compote of cooked quince with a simple roast stuffed goose instead of apple sauce, and I find it to be a surprisingly good combination for a change.

ROAST DUCK WITH POTATO STUFFING
Substitute a duck for a goose in the above recipe and use a quarter or one-third of the potato stuffing recipe instead, depending on the size of the duck. Serve with plain apple sauce.

GOOSE, POMEGRANATE, AND PECAN SALAD

You can also use up your leftover morsels of turkey, duck, or goose in this delicious way · SERVES 8

1½lb (5 cups) freshly cooked goose (or duck or turkey)
1 pomegranate
½ cup fresh pecans or walnuts, or more
a selection of salad leaves including watercress, frisée, and arugula leaves

FOR THE DRESSING
6 tablespoons extra virgin olive oil or walnut oil
2 tablespoons best-quality wine vinegar
1 teaspoon honey

½ teaspoon coarse mustard
salt and freshly ground pepper

If the goose has been refrigerated, bring it back to room temperature. Whisk all the ingredients for the dressing together. Cut the pomegranate in half and flick the seeds into a bowl – be careful not to include any astringent pith.

Roast or toast the walnuts or pecans briefly and chop coarsely. Just before serving, sprinkle a little of the dressing over the salad leaves in a deep bowl. Toss gently. There should be just enough dressing to make the leaves glisten (save the rest for later). Then add some dressing to the pomegranate seeds and toss. Taste and correct the seasoning if necessary.

Slice the goose into chunky pieces. Sprinkle a little dressing over the pieces and toss gently. Combine the goose, pomegranate seeds, and salad leaves. Divide pleasingly between 8 large white plates. Sprinkle with the chopped pecans or walnuts and serve immediately with crusty bread.

CASSOULET

This whole comforting meal in one pot has to be one of my favorite winter recipes for entertaining family and friends. To make the goose confit that appears below, simply follow the recipe for Confit de Canard *(duck confit) on page 280 – or just substitute duck confit* · SERVES 8

3½ cups dried navy beans
1 carrot
4 onions, sliced

2 x bouquet garni
8oz slab bacon
3 tablespoons extra virgin olive oil
5 garlic cloves, crushed
1 x 14oz can of tomatoes in their juice or 6–8 very ripe tomatoes, peeled and chopped
salt and freshly ground pepper
5 cups Chicken Stock (see page 262)
2 pieces *confit d'oie* (goose confit)
1lb shoulder of lamb in 4 thick chops cut into 8 pieces
1lb pork sausages (such as Italian or Toulouse), I sometimes use 1 chorizo as well
fresh bread crumbs (see page 577)
flat-leaf parsley

Soak the navy beans overnight in plenty of cold water. Next day, cover with fresh water and add the carrot, one of the onions, and one bouquet garni. Cover and cook for half an hour or 45 minutes, until the beans are almost cooked. Drain and remove the vegetables and bouquet garni.

Meanwhile, cut the bacon into 1in cubes. Heat the olive oil in a casserole, add the bacon, and cook until beginning to turn golden. Add the rest of the onions, garlic, tomatoes and their juice, salt, pepper, and the other bouquet garni. Cook for a minute or two, add the stock, bring to a boil and simmer for 15 minutes.

Preheat the oven to 300°F.

Remove the bouquet garni from the casserole, then add the goose confit, the shoulder of lamb, the sausage, and finally put the beans on top. Bring the cassoulet to a boil, then spread a layer of bread crumbs over the top. Put the pot into a low oven, uncovered, and continue to cook for 1 hour or so until the beans and meat are fully cooked. By this time a crust will form and the beans will have absorbed most of the stock.

Sprinkle with chopped parsley and serve from the casserole with a good green salad.

STUFFED GOOSE NECK

I came across variations of this in France and Italy, where crafty cooks know how to use every last bit of the bird. This may not be everyone's idea of fun, but I love making any kind of charcuterie. The flavor is delicious and a skill that was developed to use every scrap results in a delicious dish ·

SERVES 4–6 AS AN APPETIZER

giblets from 1 goose (neck, gizzard, and heart)
1 onion, quartered
1 carrot, cut into chunks
1 celery rib, cut into chunks
a sprig of thyme
4 parsley stems
4 black peppercorns
1 goose neck skin
1 goose liver
¼lb belly of pork, ground
¼ cup white bread crumbs (see page 577)
1 teaspoon thyme leaves
1 tablespoon parsley leaves, chopped
2 sage leaves, finely chopped
1 tablespoon brandy or port
2 cups goose fat (supplement with duck fat or lard if you don't have enough)
salt and freshly ground pepper

Chop the neck off the goose as close to the body as possible, including as much of the neck skin close to the wishbone as you can. Then chop off the head and discard or add to the stockpot. Peel the skin off the neck in one piece. Be careful not to tear it because this is the "sausage" casing. Remove the windpipe and discard. If there is excess fat inside, remove and render it down to add to your store of goose fat.

Put the heart, neck, and gizzard into a small, deep saucepan. Add the onion, carrot, celery, sprig of thyme, parsley, and peppercorns.

Cover the contents of the saucepan with cold water and bring to a boil. Skim and continue to simmer for 1½ hours, until the giblets are soft. Strain and save the liquid for goose gravy.

When the giblets are cool enough to handle, pick every scrap of meat from the neck, then chop the gizzard and heart into small pieces and put into a bowl. Chop the goose liver finely and add to the bowl with the ground belly of pork, bread crumbs, thyme, parsley, and sage. Add the brandy or port. Season and mix well.

Cook a little morsel of the stuffing in a frying pan over medium heat. Taste and correct the seasoning if necessary. Tie, or better still, sew the narrow end of the neck securely with strong cotton thread. Fill the neck with the stuffing. Don't overfill, or it may burst while cooking. Sew the wide end to enclose the stuffing. Prick the neck in several places with a big needle.

Preheat the oven to 250°F.

Melt the goose fat in an ovenproof dish and carefully lower in the goose neck. It should be submerged in the fat. Cover and cook for about 1–1¼ hours, then remove the goose neck from the fat. It can be eaten warm or cold. For the latter, leave it to cool completely. Then wrap the neck in wax paper and refrigerate for a day or two. Serve in thick slices with some salad leaves, a few cornichons, and crusty bread.

GOOSE LIVER PÂTÉ

Follow the recipe for Ballymaloe Chicken Liver Pâté with Melba Toast on page 268 and adjust the proportions accordingly. Use a little Madeira as well as the brandy if available.

USING THE WHOLE GOOSE

Geese have a layer of feathers and an inner layer of down. When my husband and I were newly married, and duvets were both exotic and expensive, we saved the down from the geese destined for dinner in Ballymaloe House and made a delicious light "feather bed." The fine feathers can be used for pillows but make sure to get the feathers purified first, something we learned the hard way.

MAKING "A WING"

Goose wings were always saved for cleaning awkward corners. The pointed feathery end reached into places no mop or brush could reach. They were simply referred to as "a wing."

To make a wing, you'll need the pinion from a goose wing (the last joint), complete with feathers. Break off the wing at the joint and trim off any fragments of meat. Leave to dry in a warm place, for example on top of a radiator.

We leave it at the back of the Aga for several weeks until the bone is completely dry. Store in a dry place. A wing will last for years and will become an invaluable part of your cleaning kit.

Pig

The last time I actually bought pork was in the mid-80s. I was particularly partial to those center loin chops that had a little piece of kidney attached, so I asked the butcher to cut them nice and thick and looked forward to frying them quickly in a hot pan and eating them with apple sauce. Despite my best efforts, though, the meat was dry and dull – nothing like the sweet, juicy succulent pork of my childhood. I made a decision there and then to rear a couple of pigs myself in an effort to recapture the flavors of my childhood.

My first pig was a boar that I bought during a hill-walking expedition on the Knockmealdown Mountains in Ireland. Next we received a companion gilt from an organic farmer in West Cork. My family threw up their hands in horror, but about six months later, when they tasted the pork, there was no going back. Friends, too, were gobsmacked by the flavor, and we sold the surplus at the local farmers' market.

One customer who was appalled by the price in comparison to the supermarket agreed rather grudgingly to try a piece. He came bouncing back the following week wanting to buy half a pig. "Have you any idea what that will cost?" I asked in astonishment. "I don't care – I haven't tasted pork like that for 20 years," he said. It smelled different, looked different, felt different and, of course, tasted different.

Because there is such a paranoia about fat these days, pigs are bred to be lean. Supermarkets stock only lean pork because they claim that's what consumers want. But fat adds flavor, juiciness, and succulence, and is an integral part of the meat. You don't need to eat the fat, but it has to be there while the meat is cooking, otherwise the end result will be disappointing. It's not surprising that people are joining "meat clubs" to get traditional breeds of pork at a better price. Or they go in and buy a whole pig together, then use or split up the parts. Although buying a whole pig may seem expensive, it can be used to make so many different things that it ends up being quite economical.

The domesticated pig truly is an amazing animal: it eats a varied diet, grows reasonably fast, can be bred in captivity, has a pliant disposition, and doesn't act territorial. In fact, pigs were domesticated much earlier than cattle, and can be kept in much smaller areas. In the days before intensive farming, pigs would've been left outside for seven to nine months, then selected and brought into a shed to fatten for five or six weeks.

Our own happy, lazy pigs are born in the fields and live freely all their lives – rooting in the ground and eating organic meal and surplus greens from the gardens and greenhouse. When they are five or six months old, depending on breed and feed, we take them two at a time into our butcher, who slaughters them. They are inspected by the vet, we bring them home a few days later, hang them in a cold-room, and work our way from the nose to the tail, using every scrap.

A new generation of passionate farmers are beginning to rear a few animals. In the area around the Ballymaloe Cookery School, five young couples (only one is actually a farmer) are fattening a couple of weanlings. They've chosen old breeds like Saddleback, Red Duroc, Black Berkshire, and Gloucester Old Spot. They rear the pigs outdoors, feeding them on organic grain and surplus from their vegetable garden.

Eventually, the pigs are slaughtered and hung by a local butcher. When they get the pig back, my friends invite their pals over, and gather round the kitchen table to make sausages, salami, terrines, and a variety of cured meats and pickles. They experiment, taste, and learn as they go. A pig or hog roast is a must-have part of this ritual, which has even become a popular attraction for some society weddings.

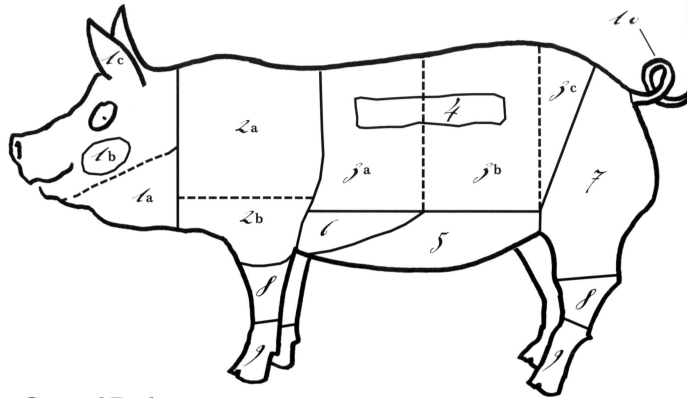

Cuts of Pork

1 **Head:** brine then boil. Serve with parsley sauce or make headcheese.
(**a**) *Jowl:* use for Guanciale.
(**b**) *Cheeks:* use lean pig's cheeks for slow-cooked stews
(**c**) *Ear:* use for headcheese, or boil, then flour, egg, crumb, and deep-fry until crispy.

2 **Shoulder:** made up of 2a and 2b. Eat fresh – slow roast shoulder or alternatively cure for bacon. Grind fresh for sausages or cube for stews.
(**a**) *Neck and collar:* a choice, well-marbled cut, slow roast pork or cut into chops, marinate, and cook on the grill. Alternatively, the cut may be cured for bacon.
(**b**) *Hand and spring:* grind or roast slowly.

3 **Loin:** roast fresh, cure and boil, or slice thinly for breakfast bacon. Loin made up of:
(**a**) *Side loin with ribs:* roast whole on or off the bone or cut into chops and fry or grill.
(**b**) *Center loin with T bones:* roast whole on or off the bone or cut into chops and fry or grill.
(**c**) *Chump or oyster cut:* a V-shaped meaty cut between the center loin and leg, roast whole on or off the bone or cut into chops and fry or grill.

4 **Fillet or pork steak:** this tender cut is tucked inside the center loin. Sauté or roast.

5 **Belly of pork:** slow roast or stuff and roll or cut into slices and fry or pan-grill. Bacon: cure the belly for bacon and pancetta. Cook whole or cut thinly for sliced bacon.

6 **Fresh spare ribs:** roast or BBQ. Cured spare ribs are called "bodice" in Ireland because they resemble an old-fashioned woman's bodice.

7 **Leg:** fresh – slow roast, casserole roast, or braise. Butterfly, roast, or BBQ. Cure for ham and boil or smoke first then boil. Cure and air dry for prosciutto-type hams.

8 **Hocks:** fresh – roast slowly or boil. Brine and boil slowly or smoke first then boil.

9 **Trotters:** cook slowly until the meat is falling off the bones.

10 **Tail:** fresh or cured – boil and eat; or flour, egg, crumb, and deep-fry until crispy.

Left: *Philip Dennhardt with one of our free-range pigs.*

The tradition of a pig slaughter

When I was a child, a few people skilled in pig-killing could be found in every parish and they would have gone from farm to farm to slaughter pigs. When the pig had its nose in the trough, they would stun the pig by hitting it with a sledgehammer on the forehead, then put a rope over the back legs and hoist the animal up. They'd cut the pig's throat, at which point it died, and put a clean bucket underneath to catch the blood. The blood was stirred, covered, and salted so it didn't coagulate, and was used to make bloody sausages.

While the pig was still twitching, two or three others would shave the hair off while the pig was still warm. Sometimes they would pour boiling water over it and then shave it. Occasionally at the farmers' market, I get asked by old timers for hairy bacon, by which they mean old-fashioned, home-cured bacon with a bit of hair on it, but most people today prefer their bacon bald, so ours are clean-shaven.

The head would be cut off first and salted or brined. Half of it would be cooked with turnips or cabbage and the other would be used to make headcheese. Then the animal was slit down the stomach and its contents fell into a clean tub. The liver and heart were removed and the intestines were washed, over and over, in spring water, turned inside out, scraped of excess fat and then used as casings for sausages. The bladder was given to the children as a football. The liver was eaten for lunch, fried with onions.

In the days before refrigeration, fresh meat couldn't be kept for more than a couple of days, so some of the pork was shared with neighbors and friends who helped with the killing and curing, and the rest was enjoyed by the family. The remainder of the animal was salted down to provide meat for the months to come.

The pig was left hanging outside in the shade, and two or three strong sticks were used to keep the stomach open to allow the air to dry the inside. Then the pig was taken indoors and hung from the rafters, covered with a white sheet in a cool and airy shed, and left hanging for three or four days.

Someone would saw the pig in half down the middle. It would then be butchered and the hams, shoulder, trotters, and some of the other joints would be salted in a timber barrel. *Crubeens*, the Irish word for brined pigs' trotters, were eaten cooked fresh or salted and then boiled until the meat was almost falling off the bones.

Pig meat definitions

Pork is the fresh meat from the pig. Bacon is cured (either dry-cured or wet-cured) and sometimes smoked, and comes from any part of the pig that isn't the ham or gammon. Gammon is the back leg of the pig when it is cured (usually brined, sometimes dry-salted) on the bone (in earlier times, it would have been cured still attached to the carcass). A raw ham is the detached, cured back leg of a pig, either bone-out or bone-in, whereas gammon is always cured on the bone. Dry-cured hams like Prosciutto di Parma or the famous Spanish serrano ham are also made from the back leg, but the curing process is different. When uncured, the back leg of the pig is just leg of pork. Green bacon or ham is a slightly old-fashioned term for a piece of bacon or a ham that has been cured but not smoked.

HOW TO MAKE CRACKLING

If you want crackling, you must buy pork with the rind still attached. You may have to order it ahead of time, as nowadays much of the pork comes to the store already rindless.

When you roast pork skin it becomes crisp and crunchy, but it's difficult to cut, so you need to score it beforehand for ease of carving. Use a small knife with a sharp blade (a sanitized box cutter is perfect for this). Lay the piece of meat on the cutting board. Hold the knife like a dagger and cut through the rind at ¼in intervals in the direction you plan to carve it. Exert enough pressure to cut through the rind but not too deeply into the fat. Some chefs like to score the rind in a fancy diamond pattern which looks good, but causes problems when it comes to carving.

ROAST PORK WITH CRACKLING AND RHUBARB SAUCE

Ask your butcher to cut the loin as long as possible so that you have enough of a surface to spread the herbs over the top. Your butcher should also be able to advise you on tying · SERVES 6–8

5lb loin of organic free-range pork with rind intact

salt and freshly ground black pepper
2 tablespoons chopped herbs (parsley, thyme, chives, marjoram, savory, perhaps very little sage or rosemary)
arugula, for garnish

FOR THE RHUBARB SAUCE
1lb red rhubarb, cut into 1in pieces
½ cup sugar

Preheat the oven to 375°F.

First, score the skin at ¼in intervals running with the grain – ask your butcher to do this because the skin, particularly of free-range pork, can be quite tough. This will give you really good crackling and make it easier to carve later.

Next, prepare the joint. Put the pork skin-side down on a cutting board, season with salt and pepper, and sprinkle with freshly chopped herbs. Roll the joint tightly and secure with a slipknot, then repeat at the other end of the loin. Work your way toward the center, tying the joint at about 1½in intervals.

Sprinkle some salt over the rind and roast the joint on a wire rack in a roasting pan. Allow 25–28 minutes per 1lb. Baste now and then with the rendered pork fat.

Meanwhile, make the rhubarb sauce. Place the rhubarb in a stainless-steel saucepan, add the sugar, and cook over low heat until soft. Taste and add more sugar if necessary.

Just before the end of the meat's cooking time, transfer the pork to another roasting pan. Increase the oven temperature to 450°F and

return the joint to the oven to further crisp the crackling. The joint is cooked when the juices run clear.

Place the pork onto a hot carving dish and let it rest for 10–15 minutes in a low oven before carving. Serve two slices of pork per person with some warm rhubarb sauce and garnish with arugula. Rustic roast potatoes and a good green salad would also be great.

POT-ROASTED PORK STEAK (FILLET)

Mummy used to make this a lot when I was a child, and for some extraordinary reason it was called "Mock Duck." The traditional stuffing was potato, but here I've combined that with a duxelle stuffing · SERVES 4–6

2 fresh organic pork fillets
salt and freshly ground black pepper
2 tablespoons good-quality lard (see page 316) or soft butter
1 tablespoon all-purpose flour
2 tablespoons Roux (see page 165)
1 cup Chicken Stock (see page 262)

FOR THE DUXELLE STUFFING
⅓ cup chopped onion
1 tablespoon butter
4oz mushrooms, finely chopped
salt and freshly ground black pepper
4oz cooked ham or bacon, chopped
12oz potatoes, mashed
2 teaspoons in total of freshly chopped parsley, chives, and thyme

Opposite: *Roast Pork with Crackling.*

Apple Sauce (see page 298)
sprigs of parsley, for garnish

Preheat the oven to 350°F.

First make the stuffing. Cook the onion in butter in a saucepan until soft but not colored, then increase the heat and add the mushrooms. Season with salt and freshly ground pepper. Toss until cooked, add the chopped ham or bacon and the mashed potatoes and freshly chopped herbs. Mix well, taste, and correct the seasoning.

Trim the fillets of gristle only, unless they are very fatty which is most unlikely nowadays. Leave what little fat there is on the fillets. Split each fillet down one side and open it out flat. Season with salt and freshly ground pepper. Spread the stuffing over one fillet. Lay the other fillet on top and tie it at the edges with kitchen string. Smear with good lard or soft butter.

Heat a heavy, preferably oval-shaped casserole over low heat, and brown the fillets on each side. Cover with a buttered parchment paper and the lid of the casserole.

Bake for 45 minutes to 1 hour, basting every now and then. To serve, transfer the stuffed fillets to a serving dish. Degrease the cooking juices and return the liquid to the casserole. Add the flour and stir well. Return to the heat and cook for a minute or two, then add the chicken stock. Bring to a boil, stirring all the time with a little whisk to dissolve any caramelized sediment (add some roux if you want it thicker). Taste and correct the seasoning, strain through a sieve into a gravy boat, and serve with the pork fillets and apple sauce, garnished with sprigs of parsley.

SLOW-ROASTED PORK CHUMP WITH BRAISED FENNEL

The chump is the V-shaped piece between the loin and the leg. It is meatier in the pig than in the lamb and is a lean and succulent joint of meat · **SERVES 8**

5lb 8oz pork chump, including
  rind and bone
2 teaspoons sea salt
1 teaspoon freshly ground black
  pepper
2 teaspoons fennel seeds
good pinch of red hot chile flakes
½ cup Chicken Stock (see page 262)
½ cup dry cider
4 large or 6 small fennel bulbs
2 tablespoons extra virgin olive oil
zest of 1 organic lemon

Preheat the oven to 300°F.

Score the rind of the pork chump with a small, sharp knife or sanitized box cutter. Mix the sea salt, freshly ground pepper, fennel seeds, and chile flakes together in a bowl. Then rub the mixture well into the scored rind.

Transfer to a deep roasting pan. Pour the stock and cider around the joint and cover with aluminum foil, tucking it well under the lip of the roasting pan. Cook for 3 hours. Then take the pork out and transfer it to a plate while you prepare the fennel.

Increase the heat to 400°F.

Quarter the fennel bulbs and add them to the roasting pan. Drizzle with extra virgin olive oil. Scatter with the zest of a lemon, season with salt and freshly ground pepper, and toss. Put the roasting pan, now with just fennel in it, back into the oven and place the pork on a wire rack on a rack above the roasting pan so that the juices drop into the fennel as the meat crisps. Continue to cook, uncovered, for 30–45 minutes, until the pork is crisp and crackly on top.

Serve the pork cut into slices, with the braised fennel.

PORK AND APPLE BURGERS

Allow at least 10 percent of your burger to be fat, as homemade sausages or burgers need some fat to keep them juicy and succulent · **MAKES 10-12**

1lb ground pork (shoulder or
  shoulder and belly mixed)
8oz grated apple
2 tablespoons chopped parsley
1 teaspoon finely chopped
  rosemary
salt and freshly ground black
  pepper

Mix the ground pork with the grated apples and chopped herbs. Season well and cook a morsel to taste and correct the seasoning. Shape into 2oz patties and dry-fry for 3–4 minutes on each side.

Serve on warmed plates with Colcannon (see page 384) or Champ (see page 383).

Sausages

If you want to revive the forgotten skills of a pig slaughter, but don't want to go "the whole hog," as it were, then you can start by making sausages. This is something that can be attempted in virtually any kitchen. Making your own sausages is a lot of fun; moreover, you'll know exactly what's in them!

To make your own sausages, you'll need a grinder or freshly ground meat, and a sausage attachment to stuff them. These are available in many shops or online; alternatively you can make them into skinless sausages.

There is nothing more logical – faced with a recently slaughtered animal that will quickly deteriorate the longer you leave it – than making sausages. You can use the shoulder, belly, all the scraps of lean and fat – and the intestine makes a perfect casing. So it's not surprising that the sausage was one of the earliest prepared foods, made thousands of years ago by the Sumerians, the Romans, and the Chinese.

Of course, you don't need to have your own pig to make sausages and salami, but it is important to ensure that you use really good-quality meat; otherwise it won't be worth the effort (I favor free-range, traditional breeds). Sausage can be eaten fresh or, in the case of charcuterie, preserved so it can be kept longer.

Homemade sausages are best hung in a cool place for a few hours or overnight to dry before being packed. Otherwise they tend to be quite wet. Wrap in parchment paper, chill, and use within a couple of days or freeze.

Casings for sausages

Natural casings are made from the intestines of beef, lamb, or pork. They normally come in 7oz packages, preserved in salt. Natural casings must be washed thoroughly before using, and they keep for years in a fridge. Choose the appropriate size for the sausage or salami you plan to make. Use larger casings for plump sausages and smaller ones for salami.

How to wash casings

To wash natural casings, place them into a large bowl of fresh, cold water in the sink. Slosh them around with your clean hands to rinse off the salt. Drain them, then run the cold tap through each one to flush out any salt. When they feel soft and slippery, they are ready for use. Keep them in a bowl of cold water in the fridge until needed.

How to fill sausages

Sausage-making attachments can be bought for many electric stand-alone food mixers. Alternatively, you can buy a hand-operated or electric sausage machine from specialty stores or online. While it is not essential to have an electric or manual sausage filler, it certainly makes the whole operation much easier and faster.

Start by taking a length of well-washed casing. Open one end and slide it onto the opening of the nozzle. Continue until almost all the casing is gathered onto the nozzle.

You'll need to tie the end for blood sausages and salami, but there is no need to tie the end for normal sausages.

Fill the container with the mixture. Then turn on the machine or turn the handle so the sausage meat starts to exude from the funnel into the casing. Even with an electric machine it's good to have some help, but with a hand operated sausage filler, one person can turn the handle while the other regulates the flow. It definitely takes practice to fill the casings evenly and to avoid air pockets. If the casings are too full, they will burst while cooking.

How do I make skinless sausages?

If you don't have a sausage-filling device, you can roll sausages yourself. Simply make the mixture, taste, and adjust the seasoning. Dip your hands in cold water. Take 1–2oz of sausage meat in your hands. Shape, arrange on parchment paper, and chill.

How long will homemade sausages keep?

Homemade sausages do not contain any preservatives apart from salt, so they need to be refrigerated and eaten as soon as possible, certainly within a couple of days. Alternatively they will keep in the freezer for several months.

Suppliers of sausage casings

See the Resources page in the back of the book for places to buy sausage casings.

BALLYMALOE HOMEMADE SAUSAGES

Sausages made from 100 percent lean meat may sound good, but for sweetness and succulence they need some fat. The addition of bread crumbs is not just to add bulk, it greatly improves the texture, too · SERVES 8 (MAKES 16 SMALL OR 8 LARGE SAUSAGES)

1lb good, fat pork (rindless)
2 tablespoons mixed fresh herbs
    (e.g. parsley, thyme, chives,
    marjoram, rosemary, and sage)
¼ cup plus 1 tablespoon soft white
    bread crumbs (see page 577)
1 large garlic clove
1 teaspoon salt and freshly ground
    black pepper
1 organic egg (optional – helps
    to bind; reduce bread crumbs
    to ¼ cup if omitting egg)
oil, for cooking

2oz natural sheep or hog casings
    (optional)

Grind the pork on the first or second setting, depending on the texture you like. Chop the herbs finely and mix with the bread crumbs. Crush the garlic to a paste with a little salt and add to the mixture. Whisk the egg, and then mix into the other ingredients thoroughly. Season with salt and freshly ground pepper. Cook a spoonful of the mixture to check the seasoning. Adjust if necessary.

Fill the mixture into natural sausage casings and tie. Twist into sausages at regular intervals. Alternatively, divide into 16 pieces and roll into lengths to make skinless sausages. Cover and chill. Homemade sausages are best eaten fresh but will keep refrigerated for a couple of days.

When ready to eat, cook gently on a barely oiled pan over medium heat until golden on all sides. These sausages are particularly delicious served with Apple Sauce (see below) and Potato Cakes (see page 384).

NOTE: for breakfast sausages, omit the herbs and garlic.

Variations

· Replace the fresh herbs with 1 tablespoon of freshly grated ginger and 4 tablespoons of chopped scallions
· Add 1 tablespoon of nam pla (fish sauce) to the recipe above
· Add 1 tablespoon of Harissa (see page 342) and 2 tablespoons of chopped cilantro
· Add 1 tablespoon of freshly ground cumin seeds and 1 tablespoon of freshly ground coriander seeds

APPLE SAUCE

The secret of really good apple sauce is to use a heavy-bottomed saucepan and very little water. The apples should break down into a fluff during the cooking · SERVES 6

1lb cooking apples
2 teaspoons water
¼ cup sugar, or more depending
    on tartness of the apples

Peel, quarter, and core the apples, then cut the quarters in two and place in a small stainless-steel or cast-iron saucepan. Add the sugar and water, cover, and cook over low heat. As soon as the apple has broken down, stir so it's a uniform texture and taste for sweetness. Serve warm.

CUMBERLAND SAUSAGES

Normally you make Cumberland sausages into a long continuous coil, but you can, of course, make the mixture into individual sausages if you prefer · SERVES 8-10

2lb pork belly (boneless)
3 teaspoons salt
2 teaspoons freshly ground black
    pepper
¼ cup white bread crumbs
1 teaspoon finely chopped
    rosemary or sage, or
    1 teaspoon chile flakes, or
    1 tablespoon English mustard
    powder

6ft natural sausage casings

Remove the rind from the pork belly and use the rind for stock. Cut the pork belly into cubes, grind, or pulse in a food processor. Season with the salt and ground pepper and add the dried bread crumbs and flavorings of your choice: fresh herbs, chile, or mustard. Mix well, then cook a spoonful to check and adjust the seasoning.

Rinse the casings several times in cold water. I often run the cold water from the tap through the casings.

Tie one end of the casing with kitchen string. Fill the mixture into

Above, left: *To make Ballymaloe Homemade Sausages, first grind the pork.* **Above, middle:** *Add the other ingredients and mix well.*
Above, right: *Rinse the sausage casings.* **Below, left:** *Fill the well-seasoned sausage meat into the casings.* **Below, middle:** *Twist into sausages.* **Below, right:** *Sausages sizzling in the frying pan.*

the casing with a sausage-filling machine, a piping bag, or a nozzle and the handle of a wooden spoon. Prick here and there with a sterilized needle so that it doesn't burst during cooking and roll into a loose coil.

To cook, transfer the coiled sausage onto a hinged grill rack or use two wire racks. I usually crisscross two kebab skewers through the sausage to keep it flat during cooking. Grill for 8–10 minutes on each side, or cook the whole thing in a frying pan. Serve with crusty bread and relishes.

NOREEN CONROY'S HOMEMADE SAUSAGES

Noreen Conroy is a local pig farmer who, along with her husband, Martin, rears rare-breed pigs. They grow their own grain, turnips, and kale to feed the pigs, and the meat is wonderful. Noreen and Martin often provide demonstrations on how to make sausage. Noreen loves to experiment, and these are just a few of the different sausages she makes · **MAKES ABOUT 32 SAUSAGES**

4lb 8oz freshly ground pork from the belly and shoulder, preferably organic
¾ cup dry bread crumbs
4 teaspoons salt
2 teaspoons freshly ground black pepper
2 teaspoons Dijon mustard
½ teaspoon freshly grated nutmeg
good pinch of cayenne
oil, for frying

7oz natural sheep casings (see Resources, page 584)

Place the meat into a large bowl, sprinkle the other ingredients evenly on top, and mix very thoroughly with clean hands. Cook a spoonful morsel in a frying pan, taste, and adjust the seasoning if necessary.

Load the casing onto the nozzle of a sausage filler and fill the length of the casing, twisting it every 3–4in, depending on the size you want. Store in the fridge and eat within two days.

If you don't have a filler, roll into skinless sausages using about 1oz of the mixture per sausage. Store in a fridge and use within a day or two.

Heat the oil in a heavy frying pan over moderate heat and cook the sausages until golden on all sides and cooked through to the center.

Variations

SAGE SAUSAGES
Add 10–12 freshly chopped sage leaves to the above recipe for every 18oz of minced pork.

GARLIC AND PARSLEY
Add 2 crushed garlic cloves and 4 tablespoons of chopped flat-leaf parsley to every 18oz of meat. Season well.

SAUCISSONS DE TOULOUSE

As with all sausage making, it is important to keep the meat well-chilled. This is a simple sausage that can be poached in a cassoulet or bean stew but also cooked in the usual way · **MAKES 6**

1lb 12oz pork shoulder
8oz pork fat
2 teaspoons salt
½ teaspoon freshly ground black pepper
generous grating of fresh nutmeg
1 garlic clove, freshly chopped

3½oz of hog casings, about 1½in in diameter

Cut the very well-chilled meat and fat into 1in cubes. Mix the salt, freshly ground pepper, and nutmeg together, and sprinkle over the meat with the chopped garlic. Mix well. Cover and chill in a fridge overnight (not essential but, if you have time, this gives a good result). The next day, grind the meat and fat coarsely just once. Knead the mixture until it begins to stick together. Cook a spoonful to check the seasoning and adjust if necessary. Keep the meat chilled while you prepare the casings.

Wash the hog casings in iced water. Tie one end, then fill the chilled mixture into the casings (see page 297), twist or tie the other end at about 5in lengths, or link them into smaller sausages. Leave them to dry in a fridge overnight and use within 3 days.

SALSICCIA E FINOCCHIO

In Tuscany, fennel is added to the sausage mixture, which is wonderful. This sausage is also irresistible when fried in lard until it begins to brown and then tossed into pasta · **MAKES ABOUT 20 X 2OZ SAUSAGES**

2lb pork
1 teaspoon pickling salt
½ teaspoon freshly ground black
    pepper
1½–2 teaspoons crushed fennel
    seeds
1 teaspoon hot red pepper flakes
2 large garlic cloves, crushed
2 tablespoons finely chopped
    parsley

3½oz natural sheep casings

Place all the ingredients in a bowl
and mix well. Heat a frying pan.
Cook a spoonful of sausage meat.
Taste and adjust the seasoning.

Fill the mixture into sausage
casings (see page 297) or hand-roll
them into skinless sausages. Cover,
chill, and use within 2 days. The
sooner you eat them, the better they
will taste.

PHILIP DENNHARDT'S HOMEMADE FRANKFURTERS

*Philip Dennhardt is a young German
butcher who teaches a course called
Forgotten Skills to young chefs. This is
his recipe for homemade frankfurters.
These are much paler in color than the
commercial frankfurters, but the flavor
is fantastic. The recipe involves cold-
smoking homemade sausages for an
hour or more* · MAKES 20-25

18oz lean pork (shoulder or leg)
18oz pork fat (neck or back fat)
2 tablespoons salt
a pinch of white pepper
1 teaspoon ground coriander
1 teaspoon ground nutmeg

1 garlic clove, finely crushed
about 3½oz natural sheep casings,
    ½in in diameter

Cut the meat and fat into ¾in chunks.
Mix all the ingredients together
quickly in a chilled, wide bowl. It is
important to keep the mixture cold
in the beginning, otherwise the
emulsion of meat, fat, and water will
not work.

Put everything through the grinder
twice, using a small disc. Then put the
meat mixture in a food processor
with sharp blades and process for
about 4–6 minutes, until it has a very
smooth texture. The consistency
should be smooth and sloppy.

Fill into thin casings and twist
the sausages to a length of about 7in
each (see page 297). Dry in a
convection oven (we hang them
from a rack over a baking sheet).
They must not touch each other.
Turn the convection oven to 122°F
and allow to dry for 20 minutes. If
you don't have a convection oven,
use a hairdryer to dry the sausages.

The outside of the casings must
be dry; otherwise the smoke won't
stick to them. When they are dry
to the touch, transfer them into
a smoker. Cold-smoke at a
temperature not higher than 140°F
for an hour.

After smoking, transfer the
frankfurters into a saucepan of hot
water. Cook at the gentlest simmer
for 20 minutes at 80°C (180°F). On
no account must the water boil, or
the frankfurters will burst. Eat the
frankfurters immediately with
medium spicy mustard and crusty
sourdough bread. Otherwise put
into an ice-water bath for quick

cooling and refrigerate until needed.

To reheat, just put into hot water
at 180°F for 6 minutes. The
frankfurters will keep for 5 days in
the fridge or 6 months in a freezer.

They are best served with
Colman's mustard and Sourdough
Bread (see page 574).

PAPRIKA SAUSAGES

*The paprika really perks up the flavor
and has anti-bacterial properties as
well* · MAKES 1 COIL; SERVES 4-6

1lb pork, rind removed
2 teaspoons salt
1 teaspoon freshly ground black
    pepper
2 teaspoons paprika
1 red chile pepper, seeded and
    chopped
½ cup water
4 garlic cloves, crushed
oil, for frying

3ft sausage casings
bamboo skewers, soaked in cold
    water for 30 minutes

Wash and prepare the sausage
casings (see page 297).

Cut the pork into cubes, sprinkle
with the salt, freshly ground pepper,
paprika, chile, garlic, and water.
Transfer to the bowl of a food
processor and pulse until the meat
is ground and the mixture melds
together.

Fill the sausage casings until the
meat is used up. Shape into a large
coil. Push 2 skewers through each
sausage to keep it flat. Prick the
sausages and cook on a stovetop or
grill. Serve with relish.

BRATWURST

This is a great all-purpose sausage that can be eaten fresh or smoked, and is delicious with lots of German mustard, in a bun like a hot dog · MAKES ABOUT 3LB, OR 12 SAUSAGES

2¼lb pork shoulder
8oz fat pork belly
4oz pork fat
1 tablespoon salt
1½ teaspoons freshly ground black pepper
1 teaspoon sugar
1 teaspoon Colman's mustard powder
½ teaspoon freshly grated nutmeg
1 teaspoon finely chopped sage
3 tablespoons whole milk

about 3½oz natural casings

Remove the rind (use for stock) and cut the pork and fat into cubes; refrigerate. When well chilled, grind the meat and fat. Spread out on a baking sheet. Sprinkle the rest of the ingredients, including the milk, evenly over the top. Mix well and thoroughly. Cover and chill immediately for 30 minutes.

Heat a pan and cook a spoonful to test the seasoning. Adjust if necessary. Fill into the sausage casings and then chill. Cook or poach as needed. Eat fresh or cold-smoked.

Opposite: *Hanging homemade salami.*

Salami

For years, I used to say with the arrogance of the ignorant that you couldn't make salami in Ireland, as I was convinced the Irish climate was too damp. But I now know that's not true at all. I was always longing to give it a try, and an Italian student convinced me to do it. I said, "But where can I maturate it?"

"All you need is a dry, airy place," he said. He walked around my cookery school with me and pointed out a well-ventilated place in the pantry, between a door and a window, where we could hang them up. You don't need to put them in the fridge, and flies don't land on them because they have such a high salt content. Now we cure salamis in the time-honored way.

If you live in a temperate climate, you can make salami any time. If the summer is very hot, put the salamis in the fridge until they cool again. Once you've made salami once or twice, the mystery is taken out of it and you can play with the spices and marinades and other options. Just ensure you have the right proportion of salt, and be very picky about the quality of the meat you use.

There are several different types and sizes of casing, both natural and synthetic – personally I prefer to use natural casings, which are made from animal intestines. Your salamis will be differently sized depending on the casing you use. The smaller the casing, the quicker the salami will be ready, but it'll also dry out quicker. So think about what size you want your salami to be before you stuff it.

Salami can be an extraordinarily scientific process, and if you want to make one of the huge salamis like *soppressata,* it's best to use cultures so that the meat cures all the way through rather than curing on the outside and remaining raw and, later, rotting. If you really get into salami-making seriously, it's best to buy cultures, but you won't need them for the elementary charcuterie. Salami and chorizo take less time to cure than air-dried hams – eight to 10 weeks rather than months.

Here again, salt is the preservative. The correct percentage of salt to meat is vitally important. Use 2–2.5 percent salt by weight – in other words, ¾–1oz of salt is used for every 2lb of meat. We use 10 percent of finely diced back fat to 90 percent coarsely ground lean meat. A variety of other flavorings can be added – for example, garlic, wine, black peppercorns, fennel seeds, mustard seeds, and pistachio nuts. Chorizo include lots of one or more types of paprika.

Drying in the air

Air-drying is a way of maturing meat that has already been cured, either by dry-salting or in a brine solution. As the meat hangs in the air, it continues to dry and its natural flavors, along with any aromatics introduced into the cure, intensify over time. Most air-dried meats are intended to be eaten raw and are very thinly sliced. But in some instances – particularly if they end up being unpalatably salty – they can be used for cooking.

Tips for Making Salami

Choosing casings

Extra large natural casings made from salted cow intestines are the perfect size and strength for making small salami. They will end up 1¼–1½in in diameter. For larger salami, beef middles taken from further down the intestine will result in salami of about 3in. Smaller salami mature faster. For cabanossi or chistorra one can use larger-sized pork sausage casings. Salami made with them matures very quickly and should be eaten soon because it will harden and not keep very well. The size of your casing will determine the end result of your salami, so be sure to choose judiciously.

Filling casings

When all your ingredients are thoroughly mixed, fill a sausage-making machine with the mixture. Take a length of well-washed casing in your hand, and slide it onto the nozzle of the sausage filler. Double tie the end of the casing. To do this, tie a knot around the casing using butcher's twine (white cotton string), then fold the short end over the knot and tie again. Finish by tying the twine into a loop for hanging. Fill the casing with the mixture until you have a length about 16–20in. Then cut the casing, leaving enough unfilled casing to tie another double knot. Again, use enough string to make a loop. Hang to dry and mature.

Hanging

Hang the salami individually in a cool, well-ventilated place where the temperature is no higher than 54°F.

The salami must not touch one another. They will take anything from three to 10 weeks to mature, depending on size, weather conditions, and your preference. They can be eaten once they are fairly firm to the touch, and they will continue to dry out and harden.

Using cultures

Acidophilus is a natural enzyme that speeds up the development of the correct mold on the skin of the salami. It is meant to encourage the salami to develop particular flavors (the same is done with cheese).

Cultures are available in a powder form from butcher suppliers or online. It is not essential to use cultures, but you will get a more consistent result. Another way to encourage the benign mold growth is to hang new salami close to maturing salami that already have a bloom of mold on the natural casing.

Salami can have a variety of molds, or none, as they mature. They may turn white, gray, green, or even orange, so be patient and observe as they change. The molds exist naturally. Provided that you are using good-quality pork and the correct proportion of salt, nature will take its course.

HOMEMADE SALAMI

Our German butcher, Philip Dennhardt, who gave me this recipe, explains the important difference between sausage and salami: salami has a higher salt content, which means that it can be hung and dried, as the salt helps leach moisture out and prevents the meat from spoiling. Salami must have 2.5 percent salt by weight. This makes a fairly smooth textured salami. You can make all kinds of additions to the basic mix here, including pistachios, herbs, and spices (e.g. fennel seeds and mustard seeds, caraway, etc). Observe and record, and once you have mastered the basic technique, you can experiment · **MAKES 2-3 SALAMI, DEPENDING ON SIZE**

about 3½ oz natural hog casings

FOR THE SALAMI
- **2¼lb organic free-range pork (65–70 percent lean, 30–35 percent fat)**
- **2 tablespoons sea salt (sea salt is the best salt to use because of its natural nitrite content)**
- **½ teaspoon crushed black pepper**
- **1 garlic clove, crushed**
- **¾ cup red wine, whiskey, or sherry (optional – the alcohol kills off some bacteria and adds flavor)**

butcher's twine

First, clean and prepare the casings and keep them cold (see page 297). Cut all the meat and fat into 1in cubes and chill well. The temperature of the meat should be below 40°F. Mix all the salami ingredients together thoroughly in a large bowl (using clean hands is most effective for this).

Put the mixture through a grinder. Fill into the casings. Let the salami hang in a dry and cool place for 4–6 weeks. Water will drip out of the salami as they harden. Serve sliced in their skins.

PORK AND BEEF SALAMI

Use these salami as you need them. They will gradually become drier and harder. The outside slices can be trimmed off – simply slice off what you need and hang again. Note that large salami will benefit from being trussed or netted so they keep an even shape ·
MAKES 1-3 SALAMI

8oz pork, rindless
1½lb pork shoulder
1lb lean beef (chuck)
8oz hard pork fat
¼ cup sea salt
½ teaspoon saltpeter (potassium nitrate)
1 teaspoon sugar
freshly ground black pepper
1 teaspoon roasted and ground cumin seeds
1 teaspoon roasted and ground coriander seeds
½ teaspoon coarsely cracked black peppercorns
¼ teaspoon freshly grated nutmeg
1 teaspoon thyme leaves
1 tablespoon brandy

6ft natural casings
cotton butcher's twine

Cut the pork and beef into 2in cubes. Place on separate trays. Slice the pork fat thinly and put on a third tray. Mix the salt and saltpeter with the sugar. Sprinkle a little over the pork fat, then divide the remainder between the pork and beef. Toss, cover, and refrigerate for 24 hours.

Dice the chilled back fat into ⅛in cubes. Mix the chilled pork and beef together in a wide mixing bowl or rectangular pan. Season with freshly ground pepper, cumin seeds, coriander seeds, cracked peppercorns, nutmeg, thyme, and brandy. Sprinkle the chilled, diced pork fat over the top. Mix well with your fingers. Chill the mixture while you prepare the sausage casings.

Soak the sausage casings in a bowl of cold water with a dash of vinegar for about half an hour. Then attach one end of each sausage casing to a cold water tap and run water through it, watching out for holes (cut out any punctured sections and discard).

Cut the twine into 12in lengths. Tie a knot about 3in from one end of each casing. Fold the short end of the sausage casing over the knot and tie again, then tie the string into a loop for hanging.

Remove the chilled mixture from the refrigerator. Fill it into the casings – you can make them any size you like, but ensure they're well packed and allow an extra 3in at the end of each casing to double-tie and make a loop.

Suspend each salami from a meat hook and hang in a cool airy place. We hang them in our pantry. Leave to cure for 5–7 weeks, depending on size. They will gradually firm up and shrink. It's a good idea to turn them upside-down every 2 or 3 weeks.

Variation

 A VARIED TEXTURE
When you remove the meat after chilling for 24 hours, you can create a more interesting texture by grinding the beef and two thirds of the pork shoulder, and cutting the remainder of the pork fat into scant ¼in cubes.

To cut the fat, put it into the freezer first until it is quite firm, then use a warm knife to cut small cubes.

CHORIZO

This spicy, Spanish-style sausage is flavored with paprika – and the best version is made with smoked paprika. This makes it taste as if the whole sausage has been smoked and you should be able to find it in well-stocked, Spanish delis. When it is young and still soft, chorizo should be cooked, but mature chorizo can be eaten raw · **MAKES 3 LARGE CHORIZO**

1lb 12oz ground pork
7oz pork fat – cut into ½in cubes
½ teaspoon freshly ground black pepper
1½ teaspoons cayenne pepper
1 teaspoon ground fennel
2 teaspoons sweet or smoked paprika
1 clove garlic, crushed
2 tablespoons sea salt

7oz natural casings
butchers' twine

Prepare the casings (see page 297).
Mix all the thoroughly chilled ingredients in a large bowl. Cook a spoonful to taste the seasoning (it should taste spicy), adjust as necessary. Fill into the prepared casings and tie the ends with a double loop like salami with the twine. Hang in a cool, airy place for 4–6 weeks to cure.

Curing

Before refrigeration, curing was the only guaranteed method of preserving perishable food. Around the world, people quickly realized that salt not only draws out moisture but also preserves meat and makes it resistant to flies – plus, it adds flavor. Consequently, every culture with access to salt has used it to preserve food.

Home curing techniques are neither difficult nor time-consuming, and the ingredients – fresh air and salt – are readily available. There are two methods: dry-curing, also known as dry-salting, and wet-curing, which includes brining and pickling. Sometimes a combination of both techniques is used on the same piece of meat.

The curing process is a learning curve – every time you experiment you will become more confident. Be observant and make notes so you can gradually add to your store of knowledge and expertise. People have been curing meat and fish for thousands of years, often in primitive conditions, so it is not exactly rocket science. Nonetheless, you must be mindful of the basic principles and observe the highest standards of hygiene; remember to sterilize your utensils every time, otherwise the end result can be inconsistent and even dangerous. I must emphasize that the quality and purity of the raw materials are crucially important – so seek out free-range, organic meat whenever possible or, better still, use your own home-produced animals.

Dry-curing

Dry-curing simply entails rubbing good salt liberally and thoroughly onto meat or fish. For example, if you rub a handful of good salt into belly of pork every day for four to six days, you'll have bacon, which you can slice and fry or grill. Ideally you want to use 3 percent of the weight of the meat in salt (about ½oz for every pound). The salt can draw up to 26 percent of its weight in water from the meat.

Salt is essential for curing meat, but after you've mastered basic dry-curing, you may like to add some other flavor elements to your cure, e.g. herbs, spices and sugar, honey, or molasses. Gutsy herbs like bay, rosemary, and thyme and spices like peppercorns, juniper berries, cloves, and mace are delicious. Saltpeter gives cured meats a pinker color; otherwise they will remain an unappetizing gray.

How long do I cure?

There is no simple answer to how long you should dry-cure meat. You can have a light cure or a heavy cure, which will keep for longer. Prosciutto takes seven to 10 months to mature after it has been salted, but generally it depends on the thickness of the meat.

The longer you cure meat in salt, the saltier it will become and the longer it will keep. But don't worry if you err on the side of over-salting, excess salt can be removed by soaking a joint in cold water for a few hours or overnight, or by changing the cooking water several times.

Dry-cured ham

All you need to cure a ham is salt and time. You should also use ham from a free-range, organic pig, if available; otherwise it might not be worth the labor and anticipation. The flavor will vary depending on the breed and the feed of the pig, as well as the length of curing and hanging.

You can pack a whole leg of pork in salt in a large, deep plastic bowl. If you cover it and leave it in a cold place for three to four weeks, you will have a dry-cured ham that can be boiled. Alternatively, you can hang the dry-salted ham for a year or more to produce an air-cured ham that you can eat raw.

Hams you can eat raw include prosciutto, the generic name for Italian dry-cured and air-dried ham, and serrano ham, the generic name for Spanish dry-cured and air-dried ham.

Wet-curing

Wet-curing in a brine is quicker than dry-curing, particularly if you pierce the meat with needles or inject the brine into the meat with a syringe, which we sometimes do with hams.

Wet-curing is a method of soaking meat in a salted solution, most often salted water, with or without spices. You want a 20 percent salt solution, i.e. 7oz salt to 2½ cups. You can tell that your solution is salty enough when a fresh egg floats on its surface. Use fresh spring water, as tap water is sometimes treated with chemicals that will interfere with your brine.

When wet-curing, most of the meat's original moisture is replaced by the salty, seasoned liquid. Now the meat or fish will stay fresh longer and have a salty, sweet flavor. Wet-cured food is fully cooked before being eaten, such as boiled ham, baked glazed loin of bacon, and hot-smoked products.

Most commercial pork products are brined rather than dry-cured, because brining works much faster, and the joint of meat gains rather than loses weight. In commercial production, an apparatus called an injector that consists of many long needles containing brine is used to pump brine into the meat. There are little holes along the length of the needles at $\frac{1}{4}$in intervals, and the brine spurts out the whole length of the needle so that the meat is thoroughly brined.

Brining is also an option for home-curers. A small piece of bacon does not need to be injected with brine (just laid in it), but if you're going to brine a whole ham, you might want to invest in a small hand pump (available from butcher suppliers) that will inject brine deep enough into the ham so that the salt penetrates it completely.

It is important to ensure the salt or brine thoroughly penetrates the meat closest to the bone, as that is the first place to decay. Injecting a piece of meat with brine is therefore a safer way of curing meat than not injecting and it can also dramatically cut the brining time. If you inject a ham, it can be fully cured in as little as one to five days, but when you brine an equivalent ham without injecting it, it will take 20–25 days.

How do I know if the meat is cured?

Provided the proportion of salt is correct and you inject brine into large cuts, particularly around the bone, the ham should be fine. If in doubt, cut the ham open – the color of the meat should be consistent. Almost every part of the pig can be made into bacon; the back legs will be called ham.

Saltpeter (potassium nitrate)

Also known as nitrate of potash, saltpeter has been used in food preservation since the Middle Ages, and is still widely used today in commercial charcuterie and corned beef preparations. Saltpeter lends preserved meat its pink color, but concerns have arisen over the potentially carcinogenic implication of nitrates in food. We use saltpeter occasionally, but not very much. Saltpeter loses its toxicity after four weeks.

Which salt to use for curing

In curing, salt draws water out, inhibits the growth of dangerous bacteria, and permits beneficial bacteria to thrive.

Curing salt is made of rock or sea salt plus about 6 percent sodium nitrate or nitrite. In Ireland, curing salt is white, but in other countries, it is sometimes colored pink to differentiate it from normal salt. You can cure meat without nitrites, but it will be gray in color rather than the more appetizing pink color that we've become accustomed to.

SALT

There are two main types of salt: rock salt and sea salt. Rock salt, also known as sodium chloride (NaCl), is mined. Sea salt is made by evaporating seawater. Salts vary in saltiness, so be sure that you use the right kind. They also vary in texture from coarse granules and crystals to very fine.

HOW TO MAKE SALT

If you heat your house using a stove, just put some seawater in a pot on top of it. (Don't do this if you have an electric or gas stove, because it'll take a long time and a lot of energy for the water to boil down.) The next time you are by the ocean, bring home a bucket of seawater. Pour into one or two wide saucepans. Bring to a boil, uncovered. Eventually the water will evaporate and the particles of salt will crystallize on the base of the saucepan.

Simple dry-cure

This simple dry-cure mix can be used to rub into meat. (See below for other dry cures flavored with herbs or spices.)

2¼lb pork, loin or shoulder
2¼lb salt
1 teaspoon saltpeter (optional)
½ cup brown sugar
1 tablespoon freshly ground black
   pepper

AIR-DRIED HAM (PROSCIUTTO-STYLE)

I absolutely love prosciutto, but really good prosciutto is very expensive. When you buy a few paper-thin slices at the deli counter, unless they are eaten immediately they inevitably dry out in the fridge and often disappoint. If you make your own, however, you can slice it to order whenever you've got a few friends over. Each time you cure a ham it will be slightly different, and it keeps for 12–18 months so you can justify being generous with it.

1 whole, fresh leg of pork,
   preferably free-range and
   organic (the fresher the leg,
   the better)
22lb sea salt or pure vacuum dairy
   table salt

wooden wine box
a 20lb weight

Put the leg, skin-side down, on the worktop. Remove the aitchbone from the leg. Hold the trotter with your left hand and press firmly down along the center of the leg with the thumb of your right hand toward the ball of the joint. Continue to massage to remove all the blood that remained in the vein between the trotter and the ball and socket joint. Wipe with paper towels. Do this carefully! If any blood stays in the leg, the ham may start to deteriorate and decay.

Cover the entire base of the wine box with 1in of salt. Lay the ham on top (you will need to saw off the trotter if the leg is too long). Cover the leg completely with the rest of the salt, rubbing it into the leg well. Then put the lid or a secure cover on the box, and put a heavy weight (or stone) on top of the lid. This will speed up the moisture loss and salt penetration.

For every 2¼lb of pork, allow 2½ days for it to cure in the salt. So, if we assume the leg weighs 12lb, allow about 2 weeks in salt. When you remove the ham from the box, brush off the salt and hang it in a cool, dry place for a minimum of 8 months. Flies will not settle on the ham because of the high salt content. If you are concerned, cover the ham with muslin or cheesecloth. If there is any mold growing on the outside, don't panic – just cut off the moldy bit; the inside will be still delicious.

To serve, cut into wafer-thin slivers with a long, thin, sharp blade – and relish every morsel.

To make the most of your precious ham and eliminate waste, it's useful to learn the skill of cutting a cured ham. I like to watch the handsome boys cutting exquisite Spanish *pata negra* at the Brindisa stall at Borough Market in London. They sometimes give out diagrams, but you can always find one online.

GUANCIALE

You can use this Italian dry-cured meat like bacon or pancetta. You can cut it paper-thin like prosciutto, or use it in pasta sauces as you would pancetta.

½ cup pickling salt
½ cup sugar
1½ tablespoons coarsely cracked
   black peppercorns
4 sprigs of thyme
2lb fresh pork cheeks

Mix the salt with the sugar, cracked peppercorns, and thyme leaves and rub into the cheeks. Place into a plastic box or a stainless-steel bowl. Cover and refrigerate for 5–6 days.

Remove the cured meat, hang each piece from a butcher's hook or tie with kitchen string so they can be hung for 3 weeks (or more) in a cool, dry place. By then, the meat will have become quite firm and easy to slice.

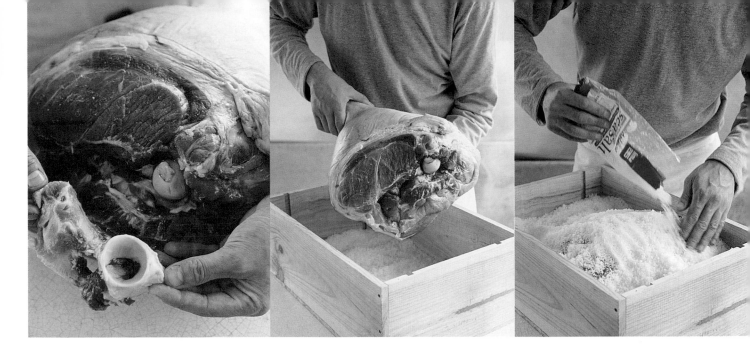

Above, left: *Remove the aitchbone from the leg.* **Above, middle:** *Cover the base of the wine box with salt and lay the ham on top.*
Above, right: *Cover the ham completely with the rest of the salt.* **Below, left:** *Hang the salted ham in a cool dry place for a minimun of eight months.* **Below, right:** *Cut into paper-thin slices with a very sharp knife.*

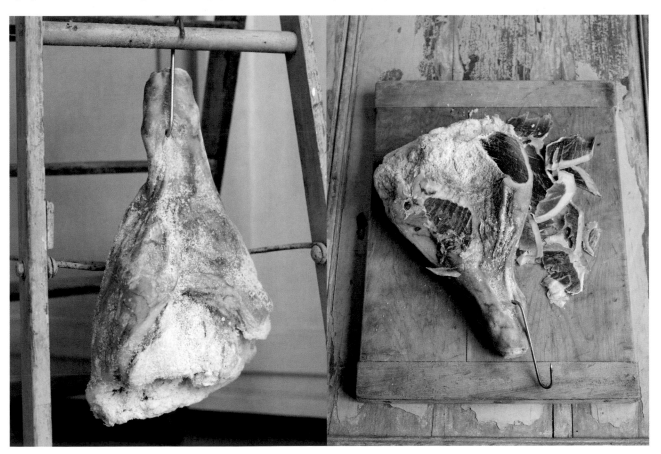

DRY-CURED BACON

A dry-cure can just be salt, or a combination of salt, sugar, and flavorings such as spices and herbs. In a dry-cure, the salt or salt and sugar dehydrate the meat or fish. The spices and herbs add flavor. Some dry-cured meats do not need to be cooked, like prosciutto, pancetta, and smoked salmon. On the other hand, others do, such as bacon or ham · **2¼LB BACON, SERVES 6**

pork (loin or shoulder):
  for every 2¼lb, use:
1 tablespoon pickling salt
1 teaspoon Demerara sugar
1 teaspoon ground coriander
1 teaspoon ground nutmeg
1 teaspoon finely chopped bay leaf
1 teaspoon chopped rosemary
1 teaspoon finely chopped thyme

Mix all the cure ingredients together. Remove the rind from the pork. (If you prefer, you can leave the rind on; it takes just a few hours longer to cure). Then rub the cure mixture thoroughly into the surface of the meat with your fingers.

Place the meat in a plastic box or a stainless-steel or enamel roasting pan. If you are doing more than one piece, you can layer the meat, making sure to rub both sides with the curing mixture. Transfer to a fridge or cold-room to cure. Place something under the container (like a towel or book) on one side so it is on an angle and the juices can run off. Take the meat out after curing and rinse it under cold tap water.

Hang the piece of bacon in a cold, airy spot to dry. If you are doing more than one piece, make sure they are not touching while drying. After that, the bacon is ready to be cooked. It keeps for weeks and sometimes months, depending on the quality and size.

Curing times
Pork cheeks – 1 day
Pork belly – 2 to 5 days to 2 weeks
    (depending on how long you
    want it to keep)
Pork loin – 3 days
Pork neck – 3 days

How much can I cure at one time?
If you are curing a few pieces of pork, you can pile them on top of one another. Just be sure to move the bottom piece to the top and top to the bottom halfway through the curing time.

How do I know if it's salty enough?
Taste. Cut a little and cook in the frying pan over medium heat. If it's not salty enough, cure it for 12 more hours, if it's too salty, soak the meat in water for 6 hours.

PADDY WARD'S WET-CURE FOR HAM OR BACON

This is a formula for wet-curing that can be increased by any factor to give additional brine. When wet-curing, inject 20 percent brine in proportion to the weight of the meat, so 2¼lb brine would be sufficient for 11lb of meat · **MAKES 2¼LB OF BRINE**

leg of organic pork

½ cup curing salt (see page 307), available from butcher's suppliers
¼ cup brown sugar
½ tablespoon mustard powder

Dissolve all the dry ingredients in 1lb 14oz of cold water to form a brine. Stir well to ensure that all the mustard is dissolved. Using a hand-held brine pump, inject the brine into a fresh leg of pork until the weight increases by 20 percent. Ensure that all parts of the leg receive an equal portion of brine.

The leg can now be stored in excess brine or vacuum sealed and stored in a fridge for up to 2 weeks. If you don't have a vacuum sealer, ask your local butcher to vacuum seal the pork leg for you.

For cooking, you can cut the leg into smaller portions, cover it in tin foil and dry-roast it or boil the whole ham in the usual way. There is no need to steep it in water.

PHILIP'S WET-CURE

This is a formula that can be easily multiplied by the quarts or gallons of water. It makes a milky brine that gives a lovely flavor. Thick cuts of meat need to be brined for longer. Brined pork loin or belly is called bacon · **MAKES ENOUGH TO BRINE ANY OF THE CUTS MENTIONED BELOW**

for 1 gallon of cold water:
1½ cups pickling salt
½ cup soft brown sugar
1 cup white wine
zest and juice of 4 organic lemons
4 garlic cloves, chopped
4 tablespoons chopped sage

Put the cold water in a deep stainless-steel or plastic container and add the salt, sugar, and white wine. Add the lemon zest and juice. Add the garlic and sage and mix the brine with your hands, a wooden spoon, or whisk. There is no need to heat or boil the brine, just be sure the dry ingredients are dissolved.

Place the meat into the container. Ensure that the meat is completely covered with brine. Put in a cool place, preferably in a fridge.

Brine for the following times:
• Pork belly – 1 day
• Pork loin, neck, or shoulder (boned) – 4 days
• Pork leg – 4 days for a boned leg and up to 8 days for a leg that still has the bones in it

Remove the meat from the brine and let it sit on a wire rack for another half-day or overnight to dry and to let the salt soak through. After that, the meat is ready to eat and will keep for 1 week. You can hot or cold smoke any of the pieces of meat after they have been drying for a half-day on a wire rack or hanging up (see page 472). It is important that the meat is dry; otherwise the smoke cannot penetrate.

JUNIPER BERRY BRINE

Every time you remove a joint from this brine, you remove salt as well. This doesn't matter with a couple of trotters, but if you remove a really large joint, the curing power of the brine may be seriously weakened, so a concentrated solution of salt and water can be *added. As with the other brines, you can use trotters, ham hocks, belly, loin, shoulder, ham – or a combination ·* MAKES ENOUGH TO BRINE ANY OF THE CUTS MENTIONED BELOW

3 **quarts of soft water or rainwater**
1¼ **cups sea salt**
1½ **cups granulated or brown sugar**
¼ **cup saltpeter (potassium nitrate)**
1 **level teaspoon juniper berries**
dash of nutmeg
1 **bay leaf**
3 **sprigs of thyme**
1 **teaspoon black peppercorns**
4 **cloves**

square of muslin or cheesecloth

Add the water, sea salt, sugar, and saltpeter to a large saucepan and bring it very slowly to a boil for a minute or two, stirring occasionally to dissolve the salt and the sugar.

Place the juniper berries, nutmeg, bay leaf, thyme, peppercorns, and cloves into the muslin or cheesecloth and tie securely.

Sterilize a large stockpot with boiling water and dry with a clean towel.

When the brine comes to a boil, skim off the froth and remove the saucepan from the heat. Add the bag of spices and herbs and allow the brine to cool completely. (The cooling down takes much longer than you might think. You can hurry it up by pouring a boiling brine straight into the stockpot through a cloth-lined strainer and adding the bag of seasonings then. It should be removed before adding the meat to the cold brine.) Strain the brine into the sterilized stockpot and add in the meat.

Weigh down the meat to keep it below the surface.

After 3 days, stir the contents of the pot with a sterilized wooden spoon. You can now remove small joints, which will be lightly brined. After 6 days, you can remove some of the thinner pieces – belly of pork or ham hocks. After 7 days, leg and shoulder of pork should be ready for immediate use.

PICKLED PORK

Usually we use belly of pork. It's lightly pickled, so it tastes sweet and mild and is particularly good with lentils, split peas, or cannellini beans · SERVES 10-12

whole boned or unboned pork loin or belly, about 4lb 8oz
½ **cup of pure dairy or sea salt**
½ **cup brown sugar**

Cure the pork in a deep-sided container just large enough to take it. Use enough water to cover the meat by 2–3in and brine for 24–48 hours in the salt-sugar-water mixture, depending on the thickness of the piece. Best kept in a cool pantry; otherwise, refrigerate, but note that the cold slows down the curing.

Ham

Strictly speaking, ham is the term for the detached, cooked, and cured back leg, but nowadays people use ham to refer to both raw and cooked ham.

A whole ham is a wonderful standby when you are entertaining or need to feed lots of people. It can be enjoyed hot as in the recipe below or cold in salads and sandwiches. Even the tiny scraps can be added to soups, stews, or gratins.

GLAZED HAM

I know this sounds a bit old hat, but of all of the glazes that I do, this is the one that I keep coming back to. Or you could just use marmalade. You'll know when a glazed ham is cooked when the rind comes off the fat easily ·
SERVES 12–15

1 (10lb) fresh or lightly smoked
   ham (be sure it has a nice
   layer of fat)
30 or more cloves, depending on
   the size of the diamonds
1½ cups brown sugar
a couple of tablespoons of
   pineapple juice from a small
   can of pineapple

If the ham is salty, soak it in cold water overnight and discard the water the next day. Cover the ham with fresh, cold water and bring it slowly to a boil. If the meat is still salty, there will be a white froth on top of the water. In this case it is preferable to discard this water, cover the ham with fresh cold water again, and repeat the process.

Finally, cover the ham with hot water, put the lid on the saucepan, and simmer until it is almost cooked. Allow 20 minutes of cooking time for every 1lb of ham (usually about 4 hours, but depends on the size of the ham). When the ham is fully cooked, the rind will peel off easily and the small bone at the base of the leg will feel loose.

To glaze the ham: preheat the oven to 500°F. While still warm, peel the rind from the cooked ham, cut the fat into a diamond pattern, and stud each diamond with a clove. Blend the brown sugar to a paste with a little pineapple juice. Be careful not to make it too liquid. Transfer the ham to a roasting pan just large enough to fit the joint.

Spread the thick glaze over the entire surface of the ham, but not underneath. Bake it in the oven for 20 minutes or until it has caramelized. While it is glazing, baste the ham regularly with the syrup and juices.

Serve hot or cold.

Variation

GLAZED LOIN OR BELLY
OF BACON
Both of these cuts are delicious glazed as above. The latter is inexpensive yet sweet and succulent.

ANOTHER GLAZE FOR HAM
OR BACON
Mix together 1 cup of apricot jam, 1 cup of sifted superfine sugar, 3 tablespoons of whole grain mustard with honey, and the juice of 1 orange. Spoon the glaze over the ham and cook as above, basting at regular intervals.

HAM COOKED IN HAY

If you can find organic hay, this is a traditional way to cook a ham that imbues it with an unusual but delicious flavor · **SERVES 16–20**

sweet-smelling organic hay

2 sprigs of thyme
1 teaspoon black peppercorns
1 teaspoon juniper berries
2 bay leaves
1 raw ham (unsmoked), about 10lb

1 large deep saucepan and lid

Make a bed of hay in the base of a deep saucepan. Sprinkle with the herbs and spices. Lay the ham on top. Tuck more hay around the sides and over the top. Cover with cold water. Bring to a boil, then reduce the heat. Cover tightly and simmer for 3½–4 hours; when it is cooked, a skewer should slide easily through the meat and the rind should lift easily from the fat.

Remove the covering of hay. Transfer the ham onto a carving dish. Serve in slices with cabbage or rutabaga, Parsley Sauce (see page 315), and Champ (see page 383).

Bacon

Smoking bacon was originally a way of further preserving the meat, but nowadays it's done simply for the smoky flavor it adds.

A thin slice of back or pork belly bacon is also called a rasher in Ireland, and the skin on it is called bacon rind. Back bacon has a higher ratio of lean meat to fat than bacon from the pork belly. You can also have shoulder, collar, or oyster-cut bacon. Lardons of bacon are ¼in slices cut into smaller strips.

When cooked in a hot pan, good bacon exudes some liquid fat, which helps it to crisp. When the bacon is from organic, free-range pigs, this fat is especially wonderful and should be saved for frying eggs, slices of cooked potato, or bread – decadent but delicious.

BACON AND EGG PIE

This is an old-fashioned lunch pie, and a traditional picnic food in our family. This pie is even better if Billy's Cream Pastry (see page 209), flaky pastry, or puff pastry is used for the top instead of shortcrust, although the shortcrust pastry is perfect for the base. If using pastries other than shortcrust, preheat the oven to 450°F and cook for 15 minutes before reducing to 350°F for another 30 minutes · **SERVES 8**

FOR THE SHORTCRUST PASTRY
1¾ **cups all-purpose flour**
4 **tablespoons diced butter**
4 **tablespoons lard (see page 316), diced (or use all butter)**
1 **organic egg, beaten**
a little water

FOR THE FILLING
8oz **cold cooked ham or crisp bacon or, better still, home-cured bacon**
English mustard
4 **organic eggs**
1 **tablespoon freshly chopped mixed herbs such as parsley, chives, and tarragon or thyme leaves**
sea salt and freshly ground black pepper
egg wash (see page 539)

1 x 9in Pyrex or ovenproof plate

First make the pastry. Sift the flour into a bowl and rub the butter and lard into the flour with the tips of your fingers. Toss in the beaten egg lightly with a fork, and add a little extra water if needed. Add it gradually, using just enough to make a firm pastry. Divide in half, flatten into two rounds, cover with plastic wrap or parchment paper and rest for 30 minutes in the refrigerator.

Preheat the oven to 350°F.

Roll one piece of pastry into a thin round large enough to cover the plate. Lay slices of ham or bacon on the rolled-out pastry on the plate. Spread a little mustard on each piece. Carefully break the eggs on top of the ham, keeping the yolks intact. Sprinkle with some freshly chopped herbs and season with a few flakes of sea salt and freshly ground pepper. Moisten the edges of the pastry with water or beaten egg, and carefully top with the second rolled-out round of pastry. Crimp the edges with a knife and

decorate with extra pieces of the pastry trimmings.

Brush the top of the pie with egg wash and bake for about 45 minutes, or until golden.

When cutting the pie, each slice should have half a yolk in it, i.e. cut through the center of the egg yolks. This may mean marking their positions, on the pastry on the outside of the pie. Serve with a good tomato salad or a green salad.

SWISS SALADE FRISÉE WITH BACON AND OEUFS MOLLET

I got this simple recipe, which serves eggs two ways, in a little café in Verbier, Switzerland. Oeufs mollet are boiled and peeled, but the yolk is still soft inside. The bitterness of the frisée cuts the fattiness of the bacon. It is surprisingly delicious after a long day on the slopes · **SERVES 4**

4 **handfuls of frisée lettuce**
1 **tablespoon sunflower oil**
6oz **lightly smoked pieces of bacon, cut into ¼in pieces**
4 **organic eggs**

FOR THE DRESSING
3 **tablespoons extra virgin olive oil**
1 **tablespoon red wine vinegar**
1 **small garlic clove, crushed**
(⅓ **teaspoon Dijon mustard**
salt and freshly ground black pepper

TO SERVE
2 **hard-boiled organic eggs**
1 **tablespoon chopped parsley**
1 **tablespoon chopped chives**

First, make the dressing. Whisk all the dressing ingredients together in a bowl. Wash and dry the frisée salad leaves.

Meanwhile, heat the sunflower oil in a frying pan over high heat. Add the pieces of bacon and cook until crisp and golden. Drain on paper towels. Just before serving, poach the eggs in barely simmering water for 4 minutes or until "mollet," i.e. still soft in the center.

In a deep bowl, toss the salad with the dressing and divide between 4 plates. Chop the hard-boiled eggs coarsely and scatter over each of the salads. Next, sprinkle the hot, crispy lardons of bacon over the top. Top each salad with a poached egg. Garnish with chopped parsley and chives and serve immediately.

TRADITIONAL IRISH BACON, CABBAGE, AND PARSLEY SAUCE

Ireland's national dish of bacon and cabbage is often a sorry disappointment nowadays, partly because it is so difficult to get good-quality bacon with a decent bit of fat on it. Traditionally, the cabbage was always cooked in the bacon water. People could only hang one pot over the fire at a time, so when the bacon was almost cooked, they added the cabbage for the last half hour or 45 minutes of cooking. The bacon water gives a salty, unforgettable flavor, which many people, including me, still hanker for. You will need to order the loin well in advance, especially with rind on · SERVES 12–15

about 5lb loin, collar thick-cut bacon
1 Savoy cabbages
4 tablespoons butter
freshly ground black pepper
Parsley Sauce (see below)

Cover the bacon in cold water in a large pot and bring slowly to a boil. If the bacon is very salty there will be a white froth on top of the water, in which case it is preferable to discard the water and start again. It may be necessary to change the water several times, depending on how salty the bacon is. Finally, cover with hot water and the lid of the pot and simmer until almost cooked, allowing 20 minutes for every 1lb.

Meanwhile, trim the outer leaves of the cabbage and cut it into quarters, removing the core. Discard the core and outer leaves. Slice the cabbage across the grain into thin shreds. If necessary, wash it quickly in cold water. About 20 minutes before the end of cooking the bacon, add the shredded cabbage to the water in which the bacon is boiling. Stir, cover, and continue to boil gently until both the cabbage and bacon are cooked – about 1³/₄ hours.

Take the bacon out. Strain the cabbage and discard the water (or, if it's not too salty, save it for soup). Add a lump of butter to the cabbage. Season with lots of ground pepper; it's unlikely to need more salt, but add some if necessary. Serve the bacon with the cabbage, parsley sauce, and floury potatoes.

PARSLEY SAUCE

2 cups whole milk
a few parsley stems
sprig of thyme
a few slices of carrot (optional)
a few slices of onion (optional)
salt and freshly ground black pepper
4 tablespoons Roux (see page 165)
about 4 tablespoons freshly chopped curly parsley

Add the cold milk to a saucepan and add the herbs and vegetables (if using). Bring the mixture to simmering point, season with salt and pepper, and simmer for 4–5 minutes. Strain the milk, bring it back to a boil, and whisk in the roux until the sauce is a light coating consistency. Season again with salt and pepper. Add the chopped parsley and simmer over very low heat for 4–5 minutes. Taste and adjust the seasoning if necessary.

Other good things to serve with bacon:
· Kale
· Rutabaga
· Tomato Fondue (see page 378)
· Wild Mushrooms à la Crème (see page 50)

Opposite: *Traditional Irish Bacon, Cabbage, and Parsley Sauce.*

Lard

Lard is made from pig fat rendered slowly in the oven. When making lard, make the effort to use a free-range pig, or better still, organic. The best lard is made from the back fat and also the flare fat from around the kidneys.

To render fat into lard, chop up pig fat and put it in an ovenproof dish or roasting pan. Roast in a preheated 225°F oven. The liquid fat will render out slowly and the length of time depends on the quantity you are rendering, but should take about 30 minutes to an hour (don't hurry it).

Store in a fridge or pantry in jars or a covered stainless-steel bowl until needed. The lard will keep for 3–4 months. Use for frying, roasting, or for pastry.

When we were children, fries were always cooked in lard. You could buy big blocks of lard, render it down, and put it in a deep fryer. It had a particular flavor that I loved.

SHORTCRUST PASTRY WITH LARD

Good-quality lard, just beginning to make an appearance again, makes wonderful pastry. Snatch it up if you come across it in a food shop or farmer's market. Alternatively, get some flare or back fat from a pork butcher and render your own · **MAKES ENOUGH TO LINE A 12IN TART PAN**

2¾ **cups all-purpose flour**
pinch of salt
6 **tablespoons cubed cold butter**
6 **tablespoons cubed chilled lard (see left)**
2–3 **tablespoons cold water**

Sift the flour and salt into a large bowl. Add the cubed butter and lard and toss them in the flour, then rub in until the mixture resembles coarse bread crumbs.

Use a fork to stir enough cold water to bind. The pastry should just come together but not stick to your hand. Flatten into a round, wrap and chill for 30 minutes. Use for savory tarts and pies.

BIZCOCHITOS

I love Mexico with a passion and have spent many happy Christmases and New Years there with Mexican friends. These New Year's biscuits, a perfect showcase for lard, are hopelessly addictive · **MAKES ABOUT 30**

1 **cup lard (see left)**
½ **cup superfine sugar**
1 **teaspoon anise seeds**
1 **organic egg**
¼ **teaspoon pure vanilla extract**
3 **tablespoons brandy or sherry**
2¾ **cups all-purpose flour**
1½ **teaspoons baking powder**
½ **teaspoon salt**

cinnamon sugar: 1 tablespoon superfine sugar mixed with 2 teaspoons cinnamon

Cream the lard in a bowl, add the sugar and anise seeds, and beat until light and fluffy. Add the egg, vanilla extract, and brandy or sherry. Mix well. Stir in the flour, baking powder, and salt and mix to a dough.

Divide in half and roll into two discs. Wrap in plastic wrap and chill until firm – about 30 minutes.

Preheat the oven to 350°F.

Slice the dough into ¼in rounds and dip in the cinnamon sugar. Cook on non-stick baking sheets for 10–12 minutes. Remove and cool on a wire rack.

Confit

Confiting is an ancient method of preserving food (for more on confiting, see the Eggs and Poultry chapter, page 234). By covering the meat with fat, air is excluded and so the food is protected from food spoilage organisms. To take meat out, you can just put the jar in a bowl of hot water so that the fat liquefies and the meat is easily extracted. Then, let the fat become solid again, covering the meat. The remaining meat needs to be completely covered in fat to continue being preserved.

CONFIT PORK BELLY

Living on an organic farm that raises pigs, we have a regular supply of pork with which to experiment. Some of our students are particularly interested in learning more about butchering and charcuterie. One day, past student J.C. Collery showed up to the kitchen door with a Kilner jar of pork belly confit. It was a case of the teacher being taught! Delicious · **SERVES 8**

one full-sized pork belly
a handful of best-quality sea salt
extra pork fat for rendering
  (ask your butcher)

Mason jars

Buy a full-sized belly from a good butcher. Ask for as much extra pork fat as you can get.

Score the rind with a sharp knife (see box on page 294). Put the scored belly onto a rack, salt it heavily and put it in the fridge overnight to draw out any excess water.

Meanwhile, render down the extra fat that you got from the butcher. Cut the fat into cubes the size of a thumbnail and place it into a roasting pan in preheated 225°F oven. Render down until all the fat has melted into liquid. Strain the liquid lard and save. Discard the crispy bits or sprinkle with salt and nibble.

Increase the oven temperature to 325°F. Remove the pork belly from the fridge, rub off any excess salt, and pat the meat dry. Cut the pork belly into portion-sized pieces, about the size of a credit card should be adequate as pork belly is so rich. Place the belly pieces into a deep roasting pan, leaving a small gap between each one. Pour the rendered fat around the pieces, just covering them. If you do not have enough rendered pork fat, you can use duck fat as well.

Place the pan in the oven, and cook for about 1¾ hours, or until the pork is meltingly tender when tested with a skewer.

Meanwhile, clean and dry some Mason jars thoroughly.

When the pork is cooked, carefully remove the roasting pan from the oven and leave it to cool for a couple of minutes. Remove one belly piece at a time and stack them into the Mason jars. When each jar is full, pour the melted lard around the belly pieces. Let the contents cool completely before you close the lid, otherwise the heat will create a vacuum and render your Mason jar un-openable. The fat will act to preserve the meat for months. I have used confit of our own organic pork belly up to almost a year after I first preserved it. Just be prudent as the keeping time depends on the quality of the pork that you start off with.

When you want to use the preserved meat, open your jar and remove the required portions with some of the surrounding fat. Place the pork in a preheated 350°F oven for 30–40 minutes, making sure you have enough fat to cover the meat. Once the pork is fully heated through, remove the pieces from the fat and place them directly under a preheated broiler. Wait for the rind to crisp, but not burn.

Serve with lentils in winter, or a fresh pea shoot salad in summer.

Blood Sausages

Making homemade blood sausages is not for the faint-hearted. Not everyone can stir a bucket of blood without retching, particularly these days when people have become more and more squeamish. But for those of us who can remember what these black and white puddings

(as they're called in the UK) used to taste like, the memory is an incentive to go beyond one's comfort zone.

Virtually all blood sausages in Ireland are made with freeze-dried imported blood, and the resulting sausages, no matter how good, have a much firmer texture. Sausages made from fresh blood have a lovely crumbly texture and ooze out from the ends of the casing when sliced and cooked. Undoubtedly, they are slightly more difficult to handle than the firmer-textured ones, but there is an incredible difference in flavor and succulence.

In the US and the UK, it's not against regulations for butchers to make their own blood sausage, but the regulations are so stringent and the cost of compliance so high that most butchers have opted out. In the UK, people had been making blood sausages in butcher shops for hundreds of years and the Food Safety Authority has confirmed that nobody in Ireland ever died from eating it! The efforts of the Artisan Food Forum (UK) encouraged the food safety authorities to source "vampire knives," an implement that allows for hygienic blood harvesting at the time of slaughter (see Resources, page 584). Sadly, this measure came too late – most small butchers had already given up and understandably, few of them are prepared to risk the hassle again. It's a real shame, because there was considerable regional variety in blood sausages, one of the real hallmarks of Europe's traditional food culture.

Where to find fresh blood

Not in your supermarket! But if this section moves you to try your hand at making blood sausage, then ask your butcher to contact you when they are going to kill a pig, preferably a free-range pig or one of the traditional breeds. Blood is a very perishable product, so you need to collect it immediately and have all the other ingredients ready to go. It needs to be stirred and salted, otherwise it will coagulate and oxidize. Blood is also a perfect medium for bacteria to grow, so all of the utensils need to be spotlessly clean. You also need to work fast and be cognizant of the fact that you are working with a product that deteriorates easily. If, for whatever reason, fresh blood is proving elusive, you can order freeze-dried blood from a butcher's supply website, but the texture of your pudding will be completely different than it would made with fresh.

Preparing fresh intestines to use as casings

For blood sausages and "white puddings" (made without blood), the fat must be detached from the intestines. Cut the fat off with scissors, removing the sweetbread first. Wash the intestines thoroughly under cold running water, then put them into plenty of saltwater until needed. Change the brine often, about four times a day. Rinse, drain, and fill. Cut up the fat from the intestines, wash it and put it into salt and water until needed. Change the water regularly as for the intestines to remove the blood. This fat is used for the blood sausage.

BLOOD SAUSAGE

I learned how to make blood sausage (black pudding) when I was only about eight or nine years old, from my Great-Aunt Lil in Ireland. It was a completely matter-of-fact activity, and seemed very normal to me – part of the natural cycle. I never felt squeamish about the blood. If you are going to make your own blood sausage, consider gathering older children to watch. This may sound rather gruesome, but it's a healthy thing for them to understand the reality of nature and traditional food production · **MAKES ROUGHLY 15½–17½LB**

About 4lb 8oz fat scraped from the intestines of one freshly slaughtered pig (see above)
2¾ quarts blood from a fresh, free-range pig (as soon as the blood is drawn, stir and add 1 tablespoon or more salt)
2oz ground allspice
1oz ground white pepper
salt to taste
1 nutmeg, freshly grated
2 teaspoons thyme leaves
dash of cayenne pepper
1 cup white bread crumbs
¾ cup wholewheat flour

natural casings

Boil the fat from the intestines in 2½ quarts of water or pork broth until it is cooked. Strain the fat and grind. Beat the blood and press it through a sieve. Place the cooking liquid into a basin of hot water. Add all the other ingredients. Increase the amount of bread crumbs and flour slightly if the mixture is not thick enough – it should be the consistency of sloppy porridge. Warm a frying pan, pour a tablespoon of the mixture into the pan, allow to cook over low heat for a minute or two, then taste and adjust the seasoning. Fill the casings with a funnel (do not fill too much as you need to allow for swelling) and prick with a sterilized darning needle so they don't burst. Place the filled casings into a saucepan of cold water, bring to a boil, and simmer very gently for about 1 hour.

Blood sausages can be stored in the fridge for up to 6 days. Traditionally, they were cut into thick slices and cooked gently on both sides in a little bacon fat or melted butter. Eat them with crispy bacon for breakfast or on their own with bread and butter.

"WHITE PUDDING" SAUSAGES

In making white puddings it was customary to use the large intestine, while "black puddings" (blood sausages) were made using the small intestine. Traditionally, the liver, lungs, and heart of the pig were used to make white pudding, which did not have blood in it. As with the blood sausage, this is also my Aunt Lil's recipe, and we'd eat it simply pan-fried, accompanied by bread and butter · **MAKES ROUGHLY 15½–17½LB**

the liver, lungs, and heart from a freshly slaughtered, free-range organic pig
about 4lb white bread crumbs

7–8lb pork belly
3lb wholewheat flour
2oz ground allspice
1 nutmeg, finely grated
3 teaspoons or more thyme
dash of cayenne pepper
about 1oz white pepper (to taste)
salt

large intestine casing
white butcher's twine

Boil the liver, lungs, and heart until tender. Boil the pork belly meat and any scraps left around when pig is cut up in about 1½ quarts of water. Remove and save the water for cooking the sausages.

Grind all the meat with the bread crumbs and flour and boil together with the herbs and spices. If you think the mixture is not dry enough, add more flour and bread crumbs.

Tie one end of the casing firmly with the twine. Fill with the mixture. Secure the other end with another length of twine. Connect the two ends, but allow enough extra twine so that when the sausages are suspended from a stick across the top of a saucepan to boil, the whole of the sausage will be submerged.

Fill a large saucepan with cold water. Add salt and put a plate in the base of the pot. Hang the loops from a stick placed across the top of the saucepan. Be sure that the sausages are submerged, and bring to a boil. Simmer very gently for about 45 minutes.

Remove sausages from the water and leave to cool, still suspended on the stick. Store in a cool place. The sausages may be eaten immediately or within a few days. Aunt Lil hung the white puddings from the rafters and they were eaten over a period of months.

Delicious Bits and Pieces

If you kill your own pig, you'll have all kinds of bits and pieces, and something delicious can be made with every single scrap.

All cultures have recipes that use every morsel of the pig. Interestingly, now there's been a tremendous revival in offal and charcuterie, led by top chefs who delight in serving alternative bits in sometimes a totally traditional and other times innovative ways. They find that it's a challenge they enjoy, making something delicious out of parts usually considered waste.

Because the population in general is so far removed from the reality of nature, people have become very squeamish. It is undoubtedly a learned reflex. Children are not born that way, they become that way if they only see a carcass for the first time as adults. You can nip this in the bud by exposing them to blood and guts early. One of our sons, who has two daughters, has a few weanling pigs. My granddaughters love feeding them every day with their friends, but it's always understood that the pigs will turn into food one day.

Trotters (crubeens)
Years ago, crubeens, especially the meatier front trotters, were the original "pub grub," an especially salty food that encouraged people to drink more. But crubeens became less popular as pub owners tired of cleaning greasy glasses and picking little bones up off the floor. Pigs' trotters have loads of gelatin in them. If you're using them fresh, they're wonderful thrown in a stockpot, as it gives the liquid extra body and a fuller mouthfeel. It's particularly good if you want to set the stock into a jelly, or make something like brawn. They aren't very fleshy and have got quite a bit of gristle but they're soft and sweet. Crubeens, while still available, are not as widespread as before – however three-star chefs love to bone them out and stuff them to embellish their menus.

Pigs' tails
Pigs' tails are like trotters –mostly skin and bones but also sweet and crunchy. They really are delicious and will certainly liven up a dinner-party menu. In Cork Co., Ireland, many of the butchers' workers were once paid part of their wage in offal, which they came to love, and Cork people still eat more offal than anywhere else in Ireland.

Only last year I inquired from a customer at a stalls in the English Market what she was going to do with the bag of pigs' tails she had just purchased. She replied without hesitation, "I've got 10 in the family, I'll split them in half and boil them up with turnips and then they'll go further." The group of Americans I was showing around the market couldn't believe their ears!

Above: *Brawn.*

Deep-fry the pork until golden brown and crispy, about 5 or 6 minutes, or cook in the preheated oven for 6–10 minutes. Remove and drain on paper towels. Season with salt and serve immediately.

BRAWN

Every time we kill a pig we make brawn. It's a good way of using up the head, which might otherwise go to waste. You don't need to keep your own pigs to make brawn. Have a talk with your pork butcher to source a pig head. The days are long gone when pigs' heads were piled high on the counter, so you may need to order one a week or two in advance. If it's fresh, you'll have to brine it first.

There are countless different recipes for brawn. Many use pig's head as a basis and some also include a couple of crubeens, ox, or lambs' tongues or a bit of shin of beef. Our grandparents would be amused to note that brawn is making a comeback and now appears regularly on the menus of trendy restaurants. I play around with this recipe, adding more or less herbs, sometimes a little lemon juice, and even some spices, such as coriander and crushed black and white peppercorns. The recipe makes lots, so you can give little pots to your more adventurous pals · **SERVES 20–30**

1 fresh pig head, quartered
  (including the tongue), or buy a
  brined head from your butcher
2 pig trotters
2 onions, peeled and quartered
2 carrots, peeled and quartered
1 celery rib
a large bouquet garni – including

PORK RINDS

Pork rinds, or chicharrones, are made, as the name suggests, from the rind, or skin, of the pig, a very inexpensive piece. It is, however, possibly the most delicious part of the pig, if you don't mind the occasional calorie. Pork rinds are a popular finger food all over the world.

Nowadays, when you go to buy pork, more often than not the skin and most of the fat (when the pig has any at all!) has already been removed, so unless you have your own pigs, you'll *have to go to a proper pork butcher and ask whether you can buy a sheet of pork rind (with a nice bit of fat attached) to make your own rinds* · **MAKES 3LB**

3lb pork rind
sea salt to taste

Cut the pork skin into pieces 2in long and ½in thick. Sprinkle lightly with sea salt. Cover and refrigerate for 1 hour.

Preheat a deep fryer to 400°F or preheat the oven to 475°F.

parsley stems, 2 bay leaves,
  2 sprigs of thyme, 2 sprigs of
  marjoram, 2 teaspoons each of
  freshly ground cloves, cilantro,
  black and white peppercorns
blade of mace, if available
1 tablespoon or more freshly
  cracked coriander seeds
a handful of chopped parsley
salt and freshly ground black
  pepper
juice of ½ lemon

FOR THE BRINE
2¼lb pickling salt
3 quarts water

If you are using a fresh pig head,
start 1 day ahead as you'll need to
brine it first.

Mix the pickling salt with the
water in a deep, stainless-steel
saucepan or a sterilized earthenware
pot. Cut the ears off the head and
give them a good scrub under
running water. Be sure to remove
the ear-wax! Then put the ears,
quartered head, and tongue in the
brine for 24 hours.

Place the quartered head and
head parts, trotters, onions, carrots,
celery, and bouquet garni in a large,
deep saucepan. Cover with cold
water and bring slowly to a boil.
Skim regularly, and cook uncovered
at a very gentle simmer for 4–4½
hours or until all the meat is
completely tender and falling away
from the bones. You may need to
top off the pan with water if the
level drops.

When everything is soft and
tender, lift the meat out onto a large
baking sheet and let sit until cool
enough to handle. Peel the skin off

the tongue and discard. Separate the
meat, skin, and fat from the bones (it
will come away easily) and discard
any bristly hairs. Coarsely chop up
all the bits of meat, including the fat,
skin, and tongue. Then dice the fat
and discard some of the really fat
cheek if you like – I usually use
everything. Transfer the lot to a
large bowl and add the cilantro and
chopped parsley. Season to taste
with a little salt, pepper, and include
lots of freshly squeezed lemon juice.
Mix well.

Strain the cooking liquid through
a fine sieve and boil until it is
reduced by about half. Add enough
of the liquid to the meat to make it
nice and juicy. Press the meat
mixture into 2 or 3 bowls,
earthenware terrines or loaf tins
lined with parchment paper. Pour a
little more of the reduced liquid
over the top – just enough to barely
cover it. Lay a plate and heavy
weight on top of each bowl to
compact the mixture, and transfer it
to the refrigerator to set.

Brawn can be served from the
terrine or turned out of its mold on
to a plate. Serve the brawn cold, cut
in thick slices with pickles and
gherkins and a good green salad, or
with hot, buttered toast. Brawn will
keep in the fridge for a couple of
weeks. It freezes well, but the salt
flavor intensifies when it is freezes.

PIG'S HEAD WITH RUTABAGA

*My grandchildren were appalled at the
unmentionable bits that they
occasionally glimpsed while I tested
recipes for this book; pig's head, pigs'*
*tails, tripe, drisheen ... such a lily-
livered lot, this generation ·*
SERVES 6–8

half a pig head (salted)
1 rutabaga, peeled and cut
  into 1in cubes
butter
salt and freshly ground black
  pepper
freshly chopped parsley

Remove the brain from the pig head
and discard. Wash the head well,
then put it in a large saucepan and
cover with cold water. Bring to a
boil, discard the water, cover with
more water, and continue to cook in
a covered saucepan for 3–4 hours or
until the meat is soft and tender and
almost lifting off the bones. About
an hour before the end of cooking,
add the rutabaga chunks to the pot,
cover, and continue to cook until
both the pig head and the rutabaga
are soft and tender.

Remove the pig head and set
aside. Drain and mash the rutabaga
with a generous lump of butter.
Season with lots of freshly ground
pepper. People who aren't
squeamish will simply plop the pig
head on the mashed rutabaga and
serve sprinkled with some freshly
chopped parsley, but for a less
spectacular presentation, you can
remove the bones and cut the pig
head into slices. Don't forget to give
everyone a piece of tongue and ear
(the ear is a particular favorite).

PIG'S EAR WITH RADISH AND CUCUMBER SALAD

In Spain, where I participated in a traditional matanza *in Andalucia, the snout and ears of the pigs were awarded to the slaughterman as a special prize. The charming image of Pedro going home through the woods with the ears slung over his shoulder in the most matter-of-fact way will always remain with me. There's not much flesh on the ears; in fact they're rather gristly and the white cartilage gives a crunchy texture, but what meat there is, is very sweet* · **SERVES 8**

8 pig ears; about 2lb, and snout
    if available
salt
2 small onions, quartered
1 celery rib, cut into chunks
2 carrots, cut into chunks
a few peppercorns
1 bay leaf
2 sprigs of thyme
flat parsley, coarsely chopped

TO SERVE
salsa verde
watercress and arugula leaves
20 radishes, thinly sliced
1 cucumber, diced

Wash the ears well. Make the brine (see brine for Brawn, page 320). Put the ears and snout into a non-reactive bowl, cover with brine, and leave overnight.

The next day, discard the brine, rinse the meat, place into a deep pot, add the quartered onions, chunks of celery and carrot, peppercorns, bay leaf, and thyme, and cover with cold water.

Bring the pot slowly to a boil, skim and simmer gently for 2–2½ hours until the meat on the ears is tender (the cartilage will always stay slightly crunchy). Leave the mixture to cool in the broth. When the ears and snout are cool enough to handle, slice the ears into thin strips, about ¼in thick and discard any tough bits. Chop the snout into ¼in cubes. Put all the meat into a Pyrex bowl. Add the coarsely snipped parsley and mix together gently. Then either leave the mixture in the bowl, or pack it into a couple of earthenware terrines. Pour the strained boiling liquid over the top, using just enough to cover the mixture. Lay a piece of parchment paper on top and invert the lid or put a saucer or side plate on top to weigh it down gently.

Cover and refrigerate the mixture. It can be eaten as soon as the jelly sets, but it's even better after a couple of days.

Serve with a herb, watercress, and arugula salad with slivered radishes and diced cucumber and a little salsa verde.

It doesn't cut easily into beautiful slices, so serve in coarse wedges or just scooped out with a spoon. It will taste delicious.

TRIPE AND TROTTERS WITH CHORIZO

There are loads of people who don't like tripe, but the Spanish influence of chorizo and tomatoes in this recipe lends the dish flavors that woo many tripe-haters · **SERVES 6–8**

2 fresh pig trotters
2¼lb honeycomb beef tripe, cut
    into thin strips
salt
2 tablespoons extra virgin olive oil
1 large onion, chopped
1 garlic clove, chopped
1 large red bell pepper, sliced
salt and freshly ground black
    pepper
2 tomatoes, peeled, seeded, and
    chopped
½ teaspoon chile powder
9oz cooked ham, chopped
9oz chorizo, sliced ¼in thick
4 tablespoons chopped parsley

Place the pig trotters into a deep saucepan. Cover with cold water and bring to a boil, then cover and simmer for 2½ hours. Drain. Put the trotters back into the saucepan with the tripe, barely cover with fresh water, add some salt, and cook for 1½–2 hours, or until tender and the meat is almost falling from the bones.

Remove the trotters. When cool enough to handle, remove the bones and discard. Chop the meat coarsely and add back to the tripe.

Heat the olive oil in a saucepan. Add the onion, cover, and cook for 4–5 minutes. Add the chopped garlic and pepper and season with salt and freshly ground pepper. Add the tomatoes and cook for 5–6 minutes, or until soft. Add the chile powder, ham, and chorizo. Stir well and cook for about 20 minutes. Add this mixture to the tripe and trotters. Taste, adjust the seasoning, add the chopped parsley, and serve.

Opposite: *Tripe and Trotters with Chorizo.*

ARBUTUS LODGE CRUBEENS

The much-missed Arbutus Lodge in Cork proudly served traditional Irish dishes on their menu for many years. Owner Declan Ryan explained to me how to cook crubeens · SERVES 6

6 crubeens (salted pig trotters)
1 large onion
1 large carrot
1 bay leaf
6 parsley stems
sprig of thyme
a few peppercorns

Place all the ingredients into a large pot, cover with plenty of cold water, bring to a boil, and skim. Boil gently for 2 –3 hours or until the meat is soft and tender and falling off the bone.

Eat either warm or cold, with a little mustard if you wish.

FRESH OR SMOKED HAM HOCKS

They are delicious with so many things – cabbage, lentils, a bean stew, shredded into a broth with diced vegetables, or in a split pea soup. We also love to add chunks of quartered cabbages to the cooking water about half an hour before the end of cooking · SERVES 4

4 fresh or smoked ham hocks
1 onion
4 garlic cloves
1 carrot, thickly sliced
2 celery ribs, chopped
1 bay leaf
1 teaspoon black peppercorns

Place the ham hocks into a deep saucepan, and add the vegetables and seasonings. Cover well with cold water, bring to a boil, and simmer for 2–2½ hours or until the meat is virtually falling off the bones. Serve with accompaniments of your choice and lots of mustard.

KIDNEYS AND CHORIZO IN FINO SHERRY

Kidneys in fino and chorizo in fino are both much-loved Spanish tapas. Here, we put the two together, with delicious results. Use this to tempt kidney-haters to have a go. Pig kidneys in fact are much milder than beef kidneys (although stronger than lamb kidneys), and have quite a firm texture · SERVES 6

3 pig kidneys or 6 lamb kidneys
4 tablespoons extra virgin olive oil
4oz chorizo, thinly sliced
1 medium onion, chopped
1 garlic clove, sliced thinly
sea salt and freshly ground black pepper
½ cup fino, dry oloroso, or amontillado sherry
flat parsley sprigs, for garnish

First, prepare the kidneys.

How to Prepare Kidneys
If the kidneys are still encased in their hard, white fat or suet, simply remove and peel off the thin membrane. For lamb's kidneys, slice in half lengthwise and with a pair of scissors snip out as much of the tough, white gristle as possible without cutting away any of the actual flesh. Cut into ¼in slices. Wash well,

place into a bowl, and cover with cold water. Sprinkle in 1 teaspoon of salt and allow it to steep for 10–15 minutes. Discard the water and wash again. Drain and dry on paper towels.

Heat the olive oil in a frying or sauté pan over a medium heat. Add the sliced chorizo and cook for a minute or two until the oil runs. Remove the chorizo. Add the onion, cover, and cook until golden and almost soft. Continue to cook until the onions start to caramelize slightly. Add the garlic and cook for 20 seconds, then add the kidneys. Season with salt and freshly ground pepper. Toss. When the kidneys are sealed on all sides, add the sherry and the chorizo, reduce the heat, and simmer for a minute or two to burn off the alcohol.

The kidneys should be tender and juicy and still a little pink in the middle when served. Taste and adjust the seasoning. Serve immediately with some fried crusty potatoes or bread.

CHINESE PIG'S KIDNEY SALAD

My favorite pork chop is the one from the center loin that has a little bit of pig kidney attached to it, but nowadays the kidneys are detached and it's not all that easy to buy them, because few people crave them as I do. This is a little gem of a recipe that was given to me by a Chinese chef friend named Deh-ta Hsiung · SERVES 2

2 fresh pig kidneys, about 8oz
2 fists of small salad leaves
2 slices fresh ginger, peeled and
   thinly shredded

FOR THE SAUCE
½ teaspoon salt
2 tablespoons rice wine or dry
   sherry
1 tablespoon sesame seed oil

GARNISH
2 scallions, sliced at an angle

Peel the membrane from the outside
of the kidneys. Split them in half
lengthwise and remove all the tough
white bits in the middle. Score the
outer surface of the kidneys
diagonally in a criss-cross pattern,
then cut each one into thin slices.

Bring 2 cups of water to a boil
over medium heat. Add the kidney
slices to the water. Be careful not to
overcook: just as soon as the water
starts to simmer again, remove and
drain the kidneys. Refresh them
under cold water for a few seconds.
Drain them again well.

Put the salad leaves on a serving
dish, top with the kidney, and
scatter the shredded ginger on top.
Mix the ingredients for the dressing
and spoon it over. Let marinate for
10–15 minutes, then garnish with
lots of scallions and serve.

SKIRTS AND KIDNEYS

*The skirt is a thin strip of meat from
the diaphragm of the pig; each pig has
two. Skirt is marvelously cheap and
has lots of flavor. The traditional way
to prepare skirt was, and still is, very
simple – and very tasty* · **SERVES 6**

2lb pork skirts
2 pig kidneys
seasoned flour
3 onions, sliced thickly

Remove the membrane from the
skirts and cut them into 2in pieces.
Split the kidney, remove the
"plumbing" and cut into 1in pieces.
Wash and clean as above, dry well,
and toss both the skirts and kidneys
in seasoned flour.

Place the meat and sliced
onions into a saucepan, cover with
water, bring to a boil, and simmer
for 1–1½ hours or until soft and
tender. Serve with mashed potatoes
and boiled rutabaga.

"FAGGOTS" (OFFAL MEATBALLS)

*It's difficult to be specific with a recipe
for faggots because they were made
using bits and pieces of pork scraps and
offal that would have otherwise gone to
waste. I love them – they're packed
with rich, gutsy flavor and the recipe
uses up lots of miscellaneous bits of
offal* · **MAKES 6**

1 pig heart
9oz pork scraps or fat pork belly
9oz fresh pig liver
5½oz bacon or ham
1 medium onion, chopped and
   cooked in butter
1 cup fresh white bread crumbs
2 teaspoons freshly chopped
   thyme leaves
1 tablespoon freshly chopped
   parsley
salt and freshly ground black
   pepper
¼ teaspoon freshly grated nutmeg

CAUL FAT

Caul fat is the fatty membrane from
around the stomach and intestines
of a pig. It comes in large, lacy
sheets and can be kept in cold
water or frozen in little pots for later
use. It is a light, sweet fat and
deserves to be more widely known
and used.

Caul fat is a great way to make
lean meat juicy. Wrap it around a
haunch of venison, for example,
and watch the light, lacy fat melt
and baste the joint as it roasts.

Homemade lamb burgers are
usually more crumbly than mass-
produced versions. We wrap these
loosely in caul fat, which makes
them much easier to turn, either in
a pan or on the grill. Caul fat is also
used to wrap traditional "faggots"
in Great Britain and is called *crépine*
in France, where it is used to
make *crépinettes*, caul-fat-wrapped
packages of sausage meat that are
pounded flat and fried.

pork caul fat (softened in cold water and drained) or 12 slices of bacon

Preheat the oven to 350°F.

Trim the heart, split it in half, and wash out any blood under cold, running water. Cut all the meat into smallish cubes and run through the coarse blade of a grinder into a bowl. Add the cooled cooked onions, bread crumbs, and freshly chopped herbs. Season well with salt, pepper, and freshly grated nutmeg. Mix together. Heat a frying pan and cook a spoonful. Taste and adjust the seasoning.

Divide the mixture into 6 parts and shape each into a balls. Wrap each ball in caul fat and place them side by side in an ovenproof dish. (Alternatively, wrap each one in thin bacon slices – you can stretch them with a rolling pin. You may need 2 bacon slices per meatball. Criss-cross them over the top to help keep the ball shape intact.)

Bake the faggots for 45 minutes to an hour, or until they are cooked through and nicely brown on top. Degrease the cooking dish for making gravy from the juices (see page 337). Serve the faggots hot with mashed potatoes. They will keep covered in the fridge for several days and can be reheated.

PORK RILLETTES

Making rillettes is a way of preserving meat, but they never last long around here anyway · SERVES 12-15

1lb 2oz pork shoulder
1lb 2oz fatty pork belly (rindless)
10½oz homemade lard
**   (see page 316)**
2 tablespoons juniper berries
2 teaspoons peppercorns
2 bay leaves
4 sprigs of thyme
salt, freshly ground black pepper,
**   and freshly grated nutmeg**
2 teaspoons thyme leaves

Preheat the oven to 250°F.

Cut the pork shoulder and pork belly into small pieces, about ½in wide. Add ½ cup water and the fat to a stockpot and add the meat. Tie the juniper berries, peppercorns, bay leaves, and thyme sprigs into a small, loose muslin bag and add it to the casserole.

Warm the pot gently for a few minutes over low heat. Don't let it boil, or the meat will stick and congeal. Cover the pot tightly and transfer to the preheated oven. Cook for about 4 hours, by which time the meat will be meltingly tender and slightly browned.

Let the meat cool for a few minutes, remove the muslin bag, and then pull the meat into shreds with two forks. Taste and season well, adding a little grated nutmeg and some thyme leaves.

When you are happy with the flavor, transfer the rillettes to an earthenware pot or pots. Pack it down well, cover with parchment paper and leave to mature for a day or two in the fridge.

Serve with warm crusty bread or toast and maybe a few crunchy cornichons or radishes on the side.

We also love to accompany them with Beet and Ginger Relish (see page 439).

Rillettes will keep in the refrigerator for up to 3–4 months, depending on the quality of the pork used.

DANISH PÂTÉ

My father-in-law, Ivan Allen, was a very progressive farmer in his day. He and Myrtle regularly visited farms in Denmark to learn from their farming methods. They were invited for a simple lunch on one of the farms. Myrtle loved the delicious pig-liver pâté and the farmer's wife was so flattered that she gave Myrtle the recipe and it has been made at Ballymaloe House every week since · SERVES ABOUT 20 (MAKES 2 LOAVES OF PÂTÉ)

1lb 2oz fresh pork liver, diced
1lb 2oz bacon fat, diced
2 onions, peeled and quartered
1 stick butter
1 cup wholewheat flour
1 teaspoon salt
2 cup whole milk
6 organic eggs, separated

2 (5 x 8in) loaf tins

Preheat the oven to 350°F.

Combine the liver, fat, and onions. Melt the butter, and stir in the flour, salt, and milk. Remove from the heat and add the egg yolks. Mix with the meat and liquidize. If no liquidizer is available, the meat should be put through a grinder 3 times. Beat the egg whites stiffly and fold in.

Cook a spoonful in a pan to taste for seasoning. More salt should be added if pork fat is used. Bake for about 1½ hours in a bain marie in the preheated oven.

This pâté keeps well, but the flavor is best when freshly cooked. It can also be cut in slices and fried.

Serve with crusty bread, a green salad, and maybe Beet and Ginger Relish (see page 439).

PIG LIVER PÂTÉ

This is a perfect way to utilize pig liver. Eating fresh livers pan-fried in butter may not be everyone's cup of tea, but putting pig livers into a pâté is a whole different story! This is a German recipe that was passed on to me by Philip Dennhardt. You can either store it in five jam jars or in sausage casings. When making this pâté, it is important to keep the temperature of the mixture at about 140°F. If the temperature is too low, the fat-meat-liver emulsion won't work. If the meat is too hot and you add the raw liver, the protein in the liver will coagulate and the emulsion will not work · SERVES 12

1½lb pork belly (50 percent lean, 50 percent fat)
9oz fresh pork liver
½ cup heavy cream
1 tablespoon salt
1 teaspoon vanilla sugar (see page 527)
dried thyme or marjoram (optional)

5 small Mason or jam jars or natural casings

Above: *Pig Liver Pâté.*

Cut the pork belly into 2in pieces. Place into a saucepan with hot water. Bring to a boil and simmer for about 20–25 minutes, until soft but not too soft. Transfer to a food processor with about 2 tablespoons of the cooking liquid and process for a few minutes until it reaches a very smooth texture. Transfer the mixture to a Pyrex bowl and place over a saucepan of hot water to keep warm.

Transfer the liver to a food processor and process to the same stage as the pork belly. Heat the cream to just under boiling point in a saucepan. Add the liver, heated cream, salt, and vanilla sugar to the hot bowl with the cooked pork belly. Mix everything together well and keep at 140°F. Fill into glass jars, cover, and cook for 2 hours. It keeps for 6 months.

If you fill the pâté into natural casings, you only need to cook it for about 45 minutes. These keep for 6–7 days after 4 hours' smoking.

PORK OSSO BUCCO

This recipe is also lovely made with lamb or rosé veal shanks. The leftover meat and juicy are delicious over pasta · SERVES 8

4 tablespoons extra virgin olive oil
3 medium onions, sliced
5 garlic cloves, chopped
2 red bell peppers, seeded and sliced
2 yellow bell peppers, seeded and sliced
2 bay leaves
1 sprig of thyme
1 x 14oz can of chopped tomatoes
salt and freshly ground black pepper
2 tablespoons sweet or smoked paprika
3 cups Chicken Stock (see page 262)
16 thick slices of pork shanks (you'll want 4 shanks for 8 people; ask the butcher to cut them into thick slices for you or do it yourself)
seasoned all-purpose flour
1½ cups dry white wine
1 cup sour cream
4 tablespoons Roux (see page 165)
lots of flat-leaf parsley

a cast-iron or heavy roasting pan

Preheat the oven to 325°F.

Heat 2 tablespoons of olive oil in a heavy pot, add the sliced onion and garlic, toss, cover, and cook over medium heat. Add the peppers and continue to cook until the onion and peppers are soft. Add the bay leaves, thyme, and chopped tomatoes with their juice. Add salt, freshly ground pepper, and paprika. Stir, then add the chicken stock, and bring to a boil.

Meanwhile, heat another 2 tablespoons of extra virgin olive oil in a frying pan. Toss the pork in seasoned flour. Sear the meat a few pieces at a time, and add to the tomato base. Deglaze the pan with white wine and bring to a boil. Dissolve the caramelized meat juices in the wine. Add to the pot. Cover and cook over low heat for 2–2½ hours.

When the meat is almost falling from the bones, remove the pork from the pot and set aside. Skim the fat off the cooking sauce, add the sour cream, bring to a boil and thicken lightly with roux. Taste and adjust the seasoning. Return the pork shanks and their juices to the sauce. Simmer over medium heat until the meat heats through. Taste and adjust the seasoning.

Transfer to a shallow serving dish. Scatter with lots of flat-leaf parsley sprigs and serve with noodles, rice, or mashed potatoes. Serve one small and one large piece of shank per person.

PIGS' TAILS WITH PUY LENTILS

In Ireland, pigs' tails traditionally would have been served with rutabaga or cabbage, but we love them served in the French way, with Puy lentils · SERVES 6

6 pigs' tails from organic pigs (salted)
8oz Puy lentils
1 carrot, cut in half
1 onion, stuck with 2 cloves
a little bouquet garni of fresh herbs – a few parsley stems, sprig of thyme, and marjoram
sea salt and freshly ground black pepper
butter or extra virgin olive oil
juice from 1 lemon, or to taste
2 tablespoons chopped fresh herbs e.g. fresh oregano, marjoram, and flat-leaf parsley

To Serve
watercress salad
Dijon mustard

Place the pigs' tails in a deep saucepan, cover with cold water, bring to a boil, then discard the water. Cover with fresh, cold water and bring to a boil again. Cover and simmer for 1 hour or more, until the meat is almost falling off the bones.

Meanwhile, wash the lentils and put them into a large saucepan. Fill with cold water and add the carrot, onion, and bouquet garni. Bring slowly to a boil, then reduce the heat and simmer very gently for 15–20 minutes, testing regularly. The lentils should be al dente, but not hard. Drain, remove, and discard the carrot, onion, and bouquet garni.

Season the lentils while they are warm, adding 2 tablespoons butter or some extra virgin olive oil, and lots of freshly squeezed lemon juice and some finely chopped herbs.

When the tails are cooked, remove them from the pot and keep to one side. Serve on top of the lentils, along with a watercress salad and some Dijon mustard.

Variation

CRISPY PIGS' TAILS
WITH AIOLI
Cook the pigs' tails as above. When cool, coat in seasoned flour, beaten egg, and fresh, white bread crumbs (see page 577). Deep-fry in hot oil at 350°F. Serve hot with aioli and a good green salad.

And Finally

Suckling pig, which is a baby pig up to the age of two months, is well worth preparing, especially for a dinner party. It's one of the world's great festive dishes and really causes a stir.

ROAST SUCKLING PIG WITH APPLE AND ROSEMARY JELLY

I have an ambiguous relationship with suckling pig; I love the flavor of it, but I'm sort of traumatized by its appearance on the dish. I go on and on about the importance of not being squeamish, but I have to confess that a suckling pig does really look like a cooked baby pig. That said, it's so delicious that all my misgivings evaporate as soon as I taste that lovely thin, crispy skin.

Just be sure your oven is big enough, because if you go through the trouble of preparing suckling pig for a party and find that it won't fit in your oven, you won't be happy about it!

· **SERVES 10-12**

sea salt and freshly ground black
    pepper
4 tablespoons freshly chopped
    rosemary or thyme leaves,
    optional
1 suckling pig
extra virgin olive oil
2 x Sage and Onion Stuffing
    recipe (see page 278)
rosemary and watercress sprigs
1¼ quarts Chicken Stock
    (see page 262)
Roux (see page 165), optional
Crabapple (or cooking apple) and
    Rosemary Jelly (see page 40)

Rub the salt, pepper, and herbs over the skin and into the cavity of the pig. Let marinate overnight in a cold place.

Next, make the stuffing and use it to fill the cavity loosely. Lay the pig on its back on the countertop. Sew with kitchen string to close the cavity. Turn it over, make an incision along the backbone with a sharp knife, then score the rind diagonally at 1in intervals from head to tail.

Preheat the oven to 350°F.

Transfer the suckling pig on its belly to a large roasting pan. Sprinkle sea salt over the pig and drizzle with extra virgin olive oil. Wrap the ears with tin foil to protect them from the direct heat as they scorch easily.

Roast for 2½–3½ hours, basting about every 30 minutes. A 10lb pig will be cooked in about 2½ hours. Allow 3 hours for a 13lb animal and 3½ hours for a 18lb pig, by which time the skin will have turned to crisp, golden crackling. If you have a meat thermometer, when the temperature of the thigh reaches 165°F, the pig is cooked. Alternatively, prick the thigh at the thickest part and examine the juices – they should be clear.

Remove the suckling pig to a hot serving plate, and let rest for 15–20 minutes so the juices can redistribute. Degrease the cooking juices from the pan. Add stock to the juices, return to the heat, and allow the caramelized meat juices to dissolve into the gravy. Season with salt, freshly ground pepper, and add some thyme. Taste and adjust seasoning. Whisk a very little roux into a boiling gravy to thicken slightly if you like. Serve the suckling pig with the gravy and apple and rosemary jelly.

Lamb

When I was little I would love to spend time "helping" our local farmers around the village. Now that I look back I'm sure that I was more of a hindrance than a help, but Bill Walsh and Paddy Delaney were unfailingly patient and cheerful. In spring, I loved to be allowed to see the pet lambs. These were orphan lambs that had to be bottle-fed twice a day. We warmed the milk, poured it into glass bottles, and put a stout black teat on top. The little lambs sucked eagerly, tails wagging as they drank. Sometimes a weak lamb would be brought into the kitchen for extra warmth. Many times a frostbitten lamb was coaxed back to life in the coolest oven of the Aga.

Lamb is probably, of all the meats, the purest. It is the most free-range and free of chemicals as it's simply not worth farmers putting fertilizer on the ground because they won't recoup their investment. In order to survive tough economic times, several enterprising sheep farmers have decided to butcher their own meat and sell it directly to private customers or at farmer's markets.

Unfortunately lamb, like beef, is often bred to favor exportability rather than flavor. Farmers rearing traditional breeds, unless they're selling to a speciality butcher, aren't getting paid any more for doing so. Yet there are many breeds – Blackface, Cheviot, Texel, to name a few – each with a distinct flavor, depending on the terrain as well as the breed. Mountain sheep tend to be leaner and thus marginally less tender, and benefit from being cooked slowly. And if you can manage to get lamb raised on salt marshes, they have a delicious salty tang that is sought after by gourmets.

Although some producers are now realizing the value in differentiating between breeds and highlighting locally produced meats, I long for all butchers and shops to identify different breeds for their customers. Increasingly, chefs also want to know the story behind what they serve, as more customers ask questions about what they are eating and where it comes from. Try to buy meat from a local butcher and don't be afraid to ask questions.

During the boom years butchers found it difficult to sell anything apart from rack of lamb, leg, or lamb cutlets and were often left with lots of shoulder, scrag end, and breast of lamb. People lost both the inclination and skill of thrifty cooking with the less-than-prime cuts, not realizing that the shoulder, lap, neck, scrag end, and shank are sweeter and more succulent. The cuts of the animal that have the most exercise are more muscular. These are the least expensive cuts and those that benefit from slower, gentler cooking. There is no such thing as an inferior cut of meat. Everything can be turned into something delicious with sympathetic cooking.

The art of using leftovers is another almost forgotten skill for several reasons, not least of which is that most meals are bought ready-made in portions carefully judged to suit the modern appetite. For example, people don't remember that a "proper" shepherd's pie used to be made with scraps from the Sunday roast. On Monday you would have had cold meat, on Tuesday you'd have croquettes, and on Wednesday maybe shepherd's pie.

The age of lamb is incredibly important from the cook's point of view but doesn't seem to be given much consideration these days – I've gone into more detail about this on page 335. However, sheep eaten at every age are popular all over the world, especially in Muslim and Jewish cultures at weddings, births, and festivals like Passover. In Christian cultures, lamb is especially prized at Easter. In India, I've enjoyed wonderful mutton stews (although when they say mutton, they often mean goat) that are just delicious. Sheep meat figures in Mediterranean cuisine, especially in the Basque country or wherever its sheep herders have emigrated, such as the western United States, Australia, and New Zealand.

Cuts of Lamb

1 Shank: from leg or shoulder.
(**a**) Foreshank: slow cook or braise and serve with a variety of garnishes.
(**b**) Hindshank: cook as the foreshank.

2 Leg: roast whole, bone, and roll or butterfly – marinate and roast or grill.
(**a**) *Fillet end:* roast whole or cut lamb steaks and grill.
(**b**) *Shank end:* roast.

3 Chump: roast whole or boned or cut into chump chops, grill or pan-fry.

4 Loin: roast whole on the bone, or bone, stuff, roll, and roast or divide into 2 joints:
(**a**) *Rack or best end:* roast whole on the bone or cut into cutlets and fry or pan-grill.
(**b**) *Center loin:* roast whole or cut into center loin chops and fry or pan-grill.
(**c**) *Lamb fillet:* roast or fry. The saddle comprises of both loin pieces attached at the backbone – you will need to order specially as the butcher normally splits the carcass in half lengthwise.

5 Lap or breast of lamb: bone, stuff, and roll with stuffing of choice.

The rib end can be cut into riblets, marinated and roasted. For epigrams, cut lap into 3in pieces. Flour, egg, crumb, and roast.

6 Shoulder: slow roast whole. Bone, roll, and slow roast. Use for stews or casseroles. Cut into thick chops – gigot or rack chops for stews and casseroles. Grind for lamb burgers.

7 Neck or scrag end: use for Irish stew or other stews.

8 Lamb cheeks: slow cook in a stew or braise.

Lamb definitions

Nowadays, it doesn't seem to matter what the actual age of a lamb is, as everything is labeled "lamb." There are, however, five main categories of lamb:

Suckling, milk-fed lambs are eaten in certain cultures and are available as fresh meat only in the spring. They can be anything from a week to several weeks old and are very mild in flavor and tender.

Spring lambs are born before Christmas and are ready for the Easter lamb market, so are young, sweet, and succulent.

Lamb served between Easter and the following Christmas is known just as lamb.

Hogget is what it's called after the second Christmas.

Mutton is lamb that is more than two years old.

I have a standing order with my butcher from one year to the next for spring lamb. For me, this is the quintessential taste of Easter. As Easter is a movable feast, spring lambs vary in age but are most delicious when they are about 12–14 weeks old and weigh about 20–22lb.

Spring lambs will have mainly been milk-fed, along with a little clover pasture. These days, however, they are often fed lamb nuts, a high-protein mix that is an effective feed but which also adversely affects the flavor of the lamb.

"Cuckoo" lambs are born in May but they often don't thrive very well. Their flavor isn't as sweet and their flesh is firmer in texture, so be careful not to confuse them with spring lamb.

Older lamb, served between Easter and Christmas, takes longer to cook than spring lamb and benefits from some additional herbs and spices, like little sprigs of rosemary and garlic inserted into the lamb, or freshly roasted coriander or cumin seeds rubbed into the scored surface with some sea salt.

From Christmas onwards, when the flavor of hogget gets progressively stronger, rather than roasting the meat we tend to braise the legs and make lots of bubbly lamb stews from the shoulders. By Easter, we find ourselves longing for the sweet, gentle flavor of roast spring lamb, so I make sure to order well ahead from our local butcher.

The demand for mutton steadily decreased as it was looked down on as something to eat in less affluent times. Those who love it found that it became increasingly difficult to get a hold of. Fortunately Prince Charles, who also has a penchant for mutton, started a campaign to bring it back and now it features proudly on trendy menus again and is more widely available. You may still need to order it ahead, however. Mutton has to be cooked slowly. Good old-fashioned boiled leg of mutton with caper sauce is something I look forward to with relish. I commission several hill farmers in Ireland to rear mutton for me every year and I look forward to eating it. It's a real treat – we ask friends over to enjoy it and we all swoon with nostalgia.

Roasting

There are few easier meals than popping a roast into the oven. You don't need to have all the trimmings either – a few roast potatoes or vegetables sprinkled with lots of fresh herbs and a good green salad make a delicious meal.

Preparing a leg of lamb for roasting

Trimming the shank end of a leg of lamb is done merely for appearance, while the removal of the pelvic bone is essential because it makes carving so much easier. Your butcher may do this for you, but it only takes a few minutes for you to do at home.

The pelvic bone is made up of the aitchbone and the hipbone. Because it is an irregular shaped bone at an angle to the leg bone, it makes carving difficult. It is attached by a ball and socket joint.

Place the leg of lamb on a cutting board, underside up. Trace the outline of the bone with a sharp knife and cut deeper around the pelvic bone, keeping the knife as close to the bone as possible. Free all the bones and then loosen and separate the ball and socket joint. Use this bone and the shank end to make a little stock for gravy.

To trim the shank end, saw through the bone just above the knuckle. Trim the meat off the end of the bone. Add to a stockpot and cook over medium heat for about 1½ hours. During cooking, the meat will shrink a little further up the shank bone and leave the end of the bone exposed. A paper frill may be slipped over the end of the bone when serving.

Butterflying a leg of lamb

Butterflying a leg of lamb helps the joint cook faster and the uneven texture means the meat cooks unevenly – some pieces will be slightly charred and well done, whereas the thicker pieces will be rosy pink or medium. If the leg has already been boned, simply cut it open from top to bottom and lay it flat. It will roughly resemble the shape of a butterfly. Alternatively, cut along the leg and shank bone on the underside and carefully remove.

Open out the lamb as above. You will need to make a few extra cuts to allow the leg to lie flat on the board. To then roast the leg of lamb, transfer it to a roasting pan. Season it well with freshly ground pepper and sprinkle with one or a mixture of freshly chopped rosemary, thyme, parsley, and chives. Drizzle with extra virgin olive oil, and let marinate for an hour or so if time allows. Just before cooking, season well with sea salt.

To prepare a rack of lamb or lamb cutlets

Chill the meat well first. If you like, remove the skin: lift a corner of the skin with a small knife, hold it firmly, and peel it off (use a cloth to get a good grip). However, I love the flavor so I prefer to leave the skin on. Chine if the butcher has not already done so; this means to saw carefully through the chine bone (or spine) just where it meets the rib bones. Be careful not to saw right through into the eye of the meat. Now remove the chine bone completely. Chop off the cutlet bones so that the length of the remaining bones is not more than twice the length of the eye of the meat. Remove the half-moon shaped piece of flexible cartilage found between the layers of fat and meat at the thicker end of the best end. This is the tip of the shoulder blade. It is simple to work out with a knife and your fingers.

If thin small cutlets are required, cut between each bone as evenly as possible, splitting the rack into six or seven small cutlets. If thicker cutlets are required, carefully ease out every other rib bone, then cut between the remaining bones into thick cutlets. Now trim the fat from the thick end of each cutlet, and scrape the rib bones free of any flesh or skin.

Noisettes of lamb

These are boneless cutlets, tied into a neat round shape with a string. They are made from the loin of best end. To prepare, first skin the meat: lift a corner of the skin with a small knife, holding it firmly (using a cloth to get a good grip), and pull it off or else trim off neatly with the knife. Now remove first the chine bone and then all the rib bones, easing them out with a short sharp knife.

Trim off most of the fat from the meat. Roll it up tightly, starting at the meaty thick side and working toward the thin flap. Tie the roll neatly with separate pieces of kitchen string tied at 1½in intervals. Trim the ragged ends of the roll to neaten them. Chill well, then cut the roll into slices, cutting accurately between each string. The average best end will give four good noisettes. Remove the string from each noisette after cooking. Noisettes are often served on a piece of fried bread or a potato galette.

Crown roast

Two racks (side loin) are needed. For a more impressive roast, use three. Each side loin is prepared in the same way as for roast rack of lamb but the bones are left slightly longer. It is skinned, chined, and the shoulder cartilage is removed. All fat needs to be removed and the top 1–2in of the bones are scraped in the same way.

Bend each best end into a semi-circle, with the fatty side of the ribs inside. To facilitate this it may be necessary to cut through the membrane about 1in, between each cutlet, from the thick end. Be careful not to cut into the fleshy part of the meat.

With kitchen string sew the end of the racks together to make a circle with the meaty part forming the base of the crown. Tie a piece of string around the waist of the crown. Traditionally crown roast is stuffed, but this can result in undercooked inside fat unless it is completely trimmed before cooking.

Guard of honor

Prepare two best end racks or side loins exactly as for the crown roast. Score the fat in a criss-cross pattern.

Hold the two best ends, one in each hand facing each other with the meaty part of the racks on the board, and the fatty sides on the outside. Adjust them so the rib bones interlock and cross at the top.

Tie with kitchen string in several places. Stuff the arch if required.

Serve with cutlet frills on top of each bone for extra posh or a retro look.

Resting meat before carving

When you're calculating the approximate cooking time for a joint of roast meat, you need to allow a minimum of 10 minutes resting time (this can be the time during which you make the gravy) so that the juices can redistribute themselves evenly in the meat. This is particularly important when you are carving a joint of meat that has been cooked rare. If you carve it immediately, it will be less tender and the bloody juices will run out of the meat rather than being distributed evenly throughout the joint. Add any extra juices to the gravy.

Making gravy

Gravy should to be made in the roasting pan because that is where the flavor is. Usually there is not a great deal of juice in the roasting pan – there will be some caramelized meat juices and lamb fat. These are precious because they form the basis of the gravy. Tilt the roasting pan so the fat collects in one corner. Spoon off as much fat as possible. Then pour icy cold stock into the roasting pan. This will cause the last few globules of fat to solidify so they can be quickly skimmed off the top with a slotted spoon. Then continue to make gravy as in the recipe.

Leftover gravy keeps for weeks, even months, in a glass jar in the fridge, provided it is covered with a layer of the relevant fat (like beef, lamb, and chicken).

TRADITIONAL LAMB PATTERNS

There was a lovely tradition in the Irish butcher shops with the Easter lamb where they would rub blood on the outside of the carcass and then cut a leaf pattern into the fat. Each butcher had a unique pattern and would hang it in the window. Now you'd probably be arrested for doing that with government regulations! Easter lamb was so lean that the butcher would give you some of the lamb caul fat to wrap around the roast.

A FORGOTTEN USE FOR LAMB FAT

When I came to Ballymaloe, in the winter when we were making marmalade, I was intrigued to see Myrtle Allen, my mother-in-law, rendering down pans of lamb caul fat, which she then used to pour over the tops of the big crocks of marmalade that we made during the Seville orange season. Lamb fat is flavorless, so it was perfect for the job. We poured about ¼in of lamb fat over the top of the marmalade. It would then set solid and protect the jam so that no mold could grow. When we wanted to get some jam, we just cracked the fat and took out whatever marmalade we needed, then rinsed the lamb fat, melted it and poured it over again.

Degreasing

No one enjoys a gravy or sauce swimming in fat, so it is important to degrease the cooking liquid. There are a variety of ways to degrease. You can use a slotted spoon to skim the fat off the top, but for a larger quantity we prefer to strain the juices into a glass jug or bowl.

If you have a degreasing cup it's an easy matter to degrease – the fat naturally rises to the top and you just pour the fat-free liquid through the spout.

LAMB À LA BOULANGÈRE AND BOULANGÈRE POTATOES

One of my favorite ways to cook a lamb supper is to slide a big dish of Boulangère potatoes into the oven and put a leg of lamb on a rack above. During cooking, the juices from the lamb drop into the potatoes to flavor and enrich the dish · SERVES 6–8

leg of lamb, about 6½ lb
salt and freshly ground black
    pepper
4lb potatoes, peeled and thinly
    sliced
4 tablespoons butter
1 large onion, thinly sliced
salt and freshly ground black
    pepper
2 cups Lamb Stock or Chicken
    Stock (see pages 341 and 262)

Preheat the oven to 350°F.

Season the leg of lamb with salt and freshly ground pepper. If it's a big leg and you suspect it might take more than an hour to cook, pop it on a rack in the preheated oven while you prepare the potatoes (have an oven rack not far beneath to catch the juices). While the lamb is cooking, butter a pie dish with 1–2 tablespoons of butter and arrange the potatoes in alternating layers with the sliced onion. Season each layer with salt and freshly ground pepper. Arrange the top layer of potatoes in overlapping slices, dot with the remaining butter, and pour in the hot stock. Place the pie dish into the oven right under the rack with the leg of lamb cooking on it, so the juices drop down. Bake for about an hour or until the potatoes are cooked and the top is golden brown.

BUTTERFLIED LEG OF LAMB WITH GARLIC AND MARJORAM

When you butterfly a leg of lamb, you can leave it completely plain or flavor it with lots of fresh herbs or one or a mixture of spices, giving it the flavor of the Mediterranean, the Caribbean, or the British Isles · SERVES 10–15

6 garlic cloves, cut into slivers
6 tablespoons marjoram or oregano
7–8 tablespoons extra virgin
    olive oil
leg of lamb, 6½ lb, boned
    and butterflied
freshly cracked pepper
sea salt

A few hours before cooking, scatter half the slivered garlic and half the chopped marjoram or oregano over the base of a large baking dish. Drizzle with some olive oil. Slash the skin side of the meat a few times and lay it on top of the garlic and herbs. Sprinkle the remaining herbs, garlic, and olive oil over the top. Season with lots of freshly cracked pepper. Cover and let marinate for a minimum of 2–3 hours or, better still, overnight.

Remove the meat from the marinade, season with sea salt and cook on a preheated griddle or grill. Grill for 30–40 minutes, turning once halfway through cooking time for medium rare. Let rest for 10 minutes and then carve into thin slices. Serve at once.

Alternatively, roast in a preheated 450°F oven for 30–40 minutes or until cooked to your liking. Serve with lots of crusty roast potatoes, and perhaps some apple and marjoram jelly.

ROAST SPRING LAMB WITH MINT SAUCE

The flesh of young spring lamb is sweet and succulent and needs virtually no embellishment, apart from a dusting of sea salt and freshly ground pepper and a little fresh mint sauce. You can cook older leg of lamb this way too, but allow a slightly longer roasting time · SERVES 6–8

1 leg of spring lamb, about 6lb
sea salt and freshly ground pepper

FOR THE GRAVY
2 cups Lamb Stock or Chicken
    Stock (see pages 341 and 262)
2 tablespoons Roux (see page 165)
salt and freshly ground black
    pepper

roasted potatoes
spring vegetables
Mint Sauce (see next recipe)

Preheat the oven to 350°F.

Remove the aitchbone from the top of the leg of lamb or ask your butcher to do it for you. This makes it so much easier to carve later. Then saw off the knuckle from the end of the leg. Season the skin with salt and freshly ground pepper and transfer the leg into a roasting pan.

Roast for about 1–1¼ hours (pink), 1¼–1½ hours (medium to well done), depending on size. When the lamb is cooked to your taste, remove the joint to a hot carving dish. Rest the lamb in a cool oven at 225°F for 10 minutes before carving.

Meanwhile, make the gravy. Degrease the meat juices in the roasting pan, then add the stock. Bring to a boil and whisk in just enough roux to thicken it slightly. Taste, and allow to bubble until the flavor is rich enough. Season to taste and serve hot with the lamb, roasted spring vegetables, lots of crusty roasted potatoes, and the mint sauce.

MINT SAUCE

Traditional mint sauce, made with tender young shoots of fresh mint, takes only minutes to make. For those who are expecting a bright green jelly, real mint sauce has a slightly dull color and watery texture · MAKES ABOUT ¾ CUP; SERVES ABOUT 6

1oz fresh mint, finely chopped
1 tablespoon sugar

½ cup boiling water
2 tablespoons white wine vinegar or freshly squeezed lemon juice

Put the freshly chopped mint and sugar into a sauce boat. Add a boiling water and vinegar or lemon juice. Allow to infuse for 5–10 minutes, before serving.

ROAST STUFFED LOIN OF LAMB WITH MUSHROOM AND MARJORAM

A roast stuffed loin of lamb is a terrific joint for a family meal or dinner party. As with the recipe above, you can stuff it with all kinds of things – herby bread stuffing, duxelle stuffing, or even dried fruit (apricots, prunes, dates) for a Moroccan-inspired flavor.

I'm such a fan of lamb's kidneys that sometimes I'll prepare a line of kidneys by sprinkling them with fresh marjoram before rolling them up · SERVES 10–12

whole loin of lamb, about 6½ lb; order untrimmed and with the bone still in
salt and freshly ground black pepper

FOR THE MUSHROOM STUFFING
1 stick plus 2 tablespoons butter
1½ cups chopped onions
1lb mushrooms, chopped
salt and freshly ground black pepper
4 tablespoons marjoram
4oz bread crumbs

FOR THE MARJORAM GRAVY
2 cups Lamb Stock (see page 341)
2 tablespoons Roux (see page 165)

1 tablespoon freshly chopped marjoram

kitchen string

Bone the loin of lamb (or ask your butcher to do it for you) and use the bones to make stock (see page 341). Lightly score the fat side and season it with salt. Turn over and trim off the excess flap (lap of lamb), and reserve it to make epigrams (see page 341). Sprinkle the inside of the joint with freshly ground pepper.

Then make the stuffing. Melt the butter in a heavy-bottomed saucepan over low heat and add the chopped onions. Continue cooking until soft, about 6–8 minutes. Increase the heat, add the chopped mushrooms, season with salt and pepper, and cook for 5–6 minutes. Add the marjoram and bread crumbs, taste, and check the seasoning. Let the mixture cool before stuffing the loin of lamb.

Spread the stuffing on the boned side, roll up, and tie with kitchen string.

Roast in a preheated 350°F oven, for about 1–1¼ hours. When the loin is cooked, remove from the roasting pan, place on a serving dish, and rest for 10 minutes.

To make the gravy, degrease the roasting pan and deglaze with the stock. Allow the stock to boil for a few minutes. Whisk in a little roux if a slightly thick gravy is preferred. Season with salt and freshly ground pepper. Add a sprinkling of freshly chopped marjoram.

ROAST STUFFED LOIN OF LAMB WITH ROAST PEPPERS, TAPENADE, AND BASIL

Irish lamb is still remarkably sweet and for the most part naturally reared. No lamb I've tasted on any of the starred restaurant menus in Europe could equal the flavor of the lamb I buy from my local butcher, who rears his animals on rich, old pastures full of wild flowers and herbs · SERVES 10–12

whole loin of lamb, about 6½ lb
salt and freshly ground black
    pepper
Tapenade (see next recipe)
6 red bell peppers (or fewer if
    they are large), roasted,
    peeled, and seeded
4 tablespoons chopped basil
sprigs of flowering rosemary,
    if available

kitchen string

Bone and prepare the loin of lamb as for the Roast Stuffed Loin of Lamb with Mushroom and Marjoram (see previous page).

Slather the tapenade on the boned side of the loin and lay the peppers on top. Sprinkle with chopped basil. Roll up each piece and tie with kitchen string.

Roast in a preheated 350°F oven for about 1½ hours. When the loin is cooked, remove from the roasting pan, place on a serving dish, and rest for 10 minutes. Garnish with sprigs of flowering rosemary, carve, and serve immediately.

Above: *Epigrams.*

TAPENADE

9oz black olives, pitted
3 large garlic cloves, peeled and
    chopped
3 anchovies
3 tablespoons extra virgin olive oil

Place the olives, garlic, anchovies, and olive oil into a food-processor and process for a few seconds, until the olives are coarsely chopped; it shouldn't be a purée.

RACK OF LAMB

An easy yet impressive way to carve a joint and serve for a dinner party · SERVES 2–3

1 rack of lamb

Prepare the rack of lamb as on page 336. Roast the rack of lamb in a preheated 425°F oven for 20–25 minutes. Turn off the heat and rest for 5–8 minutes while making the gravy.

GUARD OF HONOR

SERVES 6

2 racks of lamb, 6 cutlets each

Ensure the two racks are tied together. Roast in a preheated 400°F oven for 35–40 minutes, depending on size.

Turn off the oven when the meat is cooked to taste. Allow the meat to rest while making the gravy. If you want to go retro, you could put a cutlet frill on each bone tip. Serve on a hot carving platter.

Five good things to serve with rack of lamb:
• Fresh mint chutney
• Mint sauce, sauce soubise, red currant sauce, or sauce paloise
• Cucumber neapolitana
• Spiced eggplant
• Green bean casserole

EPIGRAMS

A simple way to turn a very cheap piece of meat into something delicious · **MAKES 12–16**

2lb lap of lamb or trimmings from the end of a rack of lamb
all-purpose flour, seasoned with salt and freshly ground black pepper
beaten organic egg
fresh white bread crumbs

Preheat the oven to 350°F.

Cut the lamb into pieces about 3in wide and 4in long (size isn't crucial here, but they shrink as they cook so don't cut them too small). Dip each piece in well-seasoned flour, then in beaten egg and finally into bread crumbs. Transfer to a roasting pan and cook in a single layer for 30–45 minutes, depending on size. They should be crisp and golden. Turn once or twice during cooking so they crisp evenly on each side.

Serve with sauce paloise (like a béarnaise, but made with mint), onion sauce, mint and apple, or red currant jelly.

BREAST OF LAMB WITH SEA SALT AND CORIANDER

Breast of lamb – also called flank, flap, or lap – is the sweet and delicious equivalent of pork belly, and is a very inexpensive cut of meat. Lean layers are interspersed with layers of fat, which renders out and gives the meat a sweet, succulent flavor. Freshly roasted and ground cumin is also delicious in this recipe, as is a mixture of coriander and cumin · **SERVES 6**

1 breast of lamb, about 2¼lb
1½ tablespoons coriander seeds
1½ tablespoons sea salt

Preheat the oven to 350°F.

Score the fat side of the breast of lamb with a sharp knife.

Roast the coriander seeds over medium heat for 3–4 minutes or until they begin to smell aromatic. Transfer the seeds to a mortar and pestle or a spice grinder and grind into a coarse powder.

Mix the coriander powder with the sea salt. Sprinkle and then rub it evenly over both sides of the lamb. Roast for about 45 minutes.

Serve with roast potatoes.

LAMB STOCK

This stock will keep for two to three days in the refrigerator. If you want to keep it for longer, boil it for 10 minutes and then chill again. It can also be frozen · **MAKES ABOUT 3½ QUARTS**

5–6lb lamb bones
2 large onions, coarsely chopped
2 large carrots, coarsely chopped
2 celery ribs, coarsely chopped
bouquet garni made up of a sprig of thyme, parsley stalks, and a small bay leaf
10 peppercorns

Preheat the oven to 450°F.

Place the bones into a roasting pan and roast for 30 minutes or until they are well browned.

Add the onions, carrots, and celery and return to the oven until the vegetables are also browned. Transfer the bones and vegetables to the stockpot with a metal spoon. Add the bouquet garni and peppercorns. Degrease the roasting pan and deglaze with some water, bring to a boil and pour over the bones and vegetables. Add more water to cover the bones and bring slowly to a boil. Skim the stock and simmer gently for 4–5 hours. Strain the stock and allow it to cool. Skim off the fat before use.

MOROCCAN LAMB RIBLETS

Lamb riblets are the part of the breast that has the bones in it and are good value – and this is a tasty way to use them. You can toss them in gutsy herbs, sweet chile sauce, or toasted sesame seeds, but in this case, we're using some Moroccan spices for a bolder flavor – they're irresistible · SERVES 6

1 tablespoon coriander seeds
1 tablespoon cumin seeds
3 garlic cloves, peeled and crushed
5 tablespoons extra virgin olive oil
3 tablespoons freshly squeezed lemon juice
1 tablespoon Harissa (see below)
2¼ lb fresh lamb ribs, cut into individual riblets
salt

Heat a non-stick pan over medium heat. Add the coriander seeds and stir-fry for 2 minutes, then add the cumin seeds and continue to stir for another minute or so. Transfer the seeds into a pestle and mortar or a spice grinder and grind fairly finely. Then transfer to a bowl and add the garlic, olive oil, lemon juice, and harissa. Toss the lamb riblets in the spicy mixture and allow to marinate for 30 minutes or more.

Preheat the oven to 400°F.

Sprinkle the lamb with salt and spread it in a single layer in a roasting pan or pans. Cook for 20–30 minutes, turning once or twice during cooking. The ribs may also be grilled.

Serve hot on a bed of salad leaves and watercress sprigs.

ROAST ROLLED SHOULDER OF LAMB WITH HARISSA

There are lots of good things you can stuff inside a rolled shoulder of lamb, but they need to have a strong, robust flavor. Some of our favorites are tapenade, wild garlic pesto and, in this version, harissa. The fiery flavor really enlivens the shoulder of lamb · SERVES 16-20

1 shoulder of lamb, 8lb with bones and 7lb without bones
2 tablespoons Harissa (see below)
2 tablespoons chopped rosemary
3 cups Lamb Stock (see page 341) or Chicken Stock (see page 262), for the gravy

Preheat the oven to 350°F.

Ask your butcher to bone the shoulder of lamb for you or do it yourself. Use the bones to make the stock for the gravy.

Score the fat of the lamb slightly, then put the meat skin-side down on your countertop. Remove surplus fat from the inside, spread the harissa over the lamb, sprinkle with chopped rosemary, and roll lengthwise, tying at regular intervals with kitchen string. Sprinkle lightly with salt and roast in the oven for about 1¼ hours. This will produce lamb with a faint pink tinge.

Transfer to a carving dish and allow to rest while you make the gravy in the usual way (see page 337). Carve at the table and serve with a little gravy, some chargrilled vegetables (eggplant, peppers, zucchini) and some Rustic Roast Potatoes (see page 383).

HARISSA

6 chiles, roasted, peeled, and seeded
6 tablespoons tomato paste
8 garlic cloves, crushed
3 teaspoons cumin seeds, roasted and ground
3 teaspoons coriander seeds, roasted and ground
6 tablespoons olive oil
1 teaspoon of red wine vinegar
3 tablespoons cilantro
salt, freshly ground black pepper, and sugar

Put the chiles, tomato paste, garlic, and ground spices in a food processor. Process until smooth. Drizzle in the olive oil and vinegar. Add the cilantro. Correct the seasoning and add a little more olive oil if necessary.

SHEPHERD'S PIE

The best shepherd's pie is made with ground cooked meat, not raw, and leftover gravy. A blob of garlic butter melting into the center of the potato really lifts the flavors. When you're making this, really think about getting the proportion of potato right – you shouldn't have to add potatoes separately; there should be enough on top · SERVES 6

2 tablespoons butter
¾ cup chopped onion
¼ cup flour
1½ cups stock and leftover gravy
2 teaspoons Grandpoppy's Mushroom Ketchup (see page 56), if available
2 teaspoons chopped parsley

1 teaspoon thyme leaves
salt and freshly ground black
  pepper
1lb cooked lamb, ground
1lb cooked potatoes, mashed
parsley, for garnish
Garlic Butter (see page 217)

1 quart pie dish or 6 individual
  pie dishes

In a heavy saucepan, melt the butter, add the onion, and cover with a round of buttered parchment paper. Cook over low heat for 5 minutes. Add the flour and cook until it begins to color. Gradually add the leftover gravy and stock, stirring all the time to avoid lumps, and bring to a boil. Skim. Add the mushroom ketchup (if available), parsley, thyme, salt, and freshly ground pepper. Simmer for 5 minutes.

Add the cooked meat to the sauce and bring to a boil for a few minutes. Transfer to a pie dish, cover with an even layer of mashed potatoes, and score with a fork. Reheat in a preheated 350°F oven for about 30 minutes. Garnish with parsley and serve with garlic butter.

SPICY LAMB BURGERS WITH MINT, YOGURT, AND ARUGULA

Lamb burgers are a tasty way of using cheaper cuts of lamb – shoulder, breast, etc. Here we use a mixture of fresh spices, but fresh herbs or lots of garlic or even a blob of harissa are other good alternatives · SERVES 6

FOR THE BURGERS
1 teaspoon ginger, freshly grated
2 garlic cloves, crushed
1 shallot or small onion, finely
  chopped
1 red chile (more or less depending
  on heat), seeded and chopped
½ teaspoon cumin, freshly roasted
  and ground
4 green cardamom, seeded and
  finely ground
¼ teaspoon coriander, freshly
  ground
pinch of allspice or paprika
2 tablespoons cilantro leaves,
  freshly chopped
1 beaten organic egg, or use egg
  white if available
1lb shoulder of lamb, ground
salt and freshly ground black
  pepper
extra virgin olive oil, for cooking

ACCOMPANIMENTS
½ cup natural yogurt
2 tablespoons mint or cilantro,
  freshly chopped
salt and freshly ground black
  pepper
arugula
ciabatta, grilled

Put all the lamb burger ingredients except the lamb and olive oil into a bowl and mix well. Add the ground lamb, season with salt and freshly ground pepper, and combine well. The burgers are best cooked immediately, but if making ahead do not add the salt until just before cooking and do not keep for more than 30 minutes in a fridge, or the raw onion will taint the mixture. Shape into 6 burgers. Heat a little extra virgin olive oil in a frying pan.

Cook over medium heat for 3–4 minutes carefully, then turn over and cook on the other side. Meanwhile, mix the freshly chopped herbs with the yogurt and season with salt and freshly ground pepper. Serve a dollop with each lamb burger, as well as fresh arugula and grilled ciabatta. Serve with Radish, Cucumber, and Mint Salad (see page 417).

SPICY GROUND LAMB WITH MARJORAM

An all-purpose mixture that can be used in all sorts of ways. Pile onto rice or pasta or even mashed potatoes · SERVES 6

2 tablespoons sunflower oil
6oz onions, chopped
2 garlic cloves, crushed
1lb freshly ground lamb
1 teaspoon freshly ground cumin
2 teaspoons chopped marjoram
1 fresh chile, seeded and chopped
good dash of soy sauce
salt, freshly ground black pepper,
  and a pinch of sugar

Heat the oil in a frying pan, add the chopped onion and garlic, and cook over medium heat until soft and slightly golden. Increase the heat, add the ground beef, and stir until brown. Add the cumin, marjoram, and chile. Then shake in the soy sauce and season well with salt, pepper, and sugar. Taste – this mixture needs a surprising amount of salt.

Slow Cooking

Despite the fast-food mania of recent years, slow-cooking methods are having a welcome revival. Once the secret gets out that slow cooking produces succulent results, and "takes time but not your time," people will adopt this method with enthusiasm.

I slow cook in my slow-cooker, but any oven will do the job as long as the temperature doesn't come above 250°F. The gentle heat over a long period of time allows the protein-breaking enzymes in the meat to tenderize the joint. Below that temperature, the moist surface dries out very slowly, resulting in less browning.

Slow-roasted meat results in minimum weight loss and tends to be uniformly done. It is best suited for tougher cuts of meat, but tender cuts may also be cooked in this way and remain moist.

Another great thing about slow cooking is that it can save you considerable cost. A shoulder of lamb costs than a leg or loin; the flavor, too, is so wonderfully sweet and juicy. It's trickier to carve but is worth the extra effort, particularly at home where perfect slices of meat are not obligatory.

BRAISED LAMB SHANKS WITH GARLIC, ROSEMARY, AND CANNELLINI BEANS

This is where the magic of slow cooking transforms something that, cooked over high heat, would be very tough, into something soft and tender
• SERVES 4

4 lamb shanks, about 2¼ lb
8 small sprigs of rosemary
8 garlic slivers
4 anchovy fillets, halved
salt and freshly ground black
    pepper

FOR BRAISING
2 tablespoons duck fat or olive oil
8oz bacon
2 carrots, coarsely chopped
2 celery ribs, coarsely chopped
1 leek, coarsely chopped
1 onion, coarsely chopped
1 garlic head, halved horizontally
1 cup good red wine
1 cup Lamb Stock (see page 341)
    or Chicken Stock (see page
    262)
sprig of thyme
2 sprigs of rosemary
2 bay leaves
2 strips of dried orange peel

ACCOMPANIMENT
1 x quantity Tomato Fondue
    (see page 378)
14-oz can cannellini beans, drained
    or 7oz dried cannellini beans,
    soaked overnight and then
    boiled rapidly for 30 minutes
2 cups Chicken Stock (see
    page 262) or Lamb Stock
    (see page 341)
2 sprigs of thyme
leaves from 2 sprigs of rosemary,
    chopped
sprigs of rosemary, for garnish

Preheat the oven to 300°F.

Remove most of the fat from each shank and then scrape the meat away from the bone to loosen it. Make two deep incisions in each joint and insert a sprig of rosemary and a sliver of garlic wrapped in half an anchovy fillet into each incision. Season the meat with salt and ground black pepper.

Heat the duck fat or olive oil in a heavy sauté pan or casserole and sauté the lamb until it is well browned on all sides. Remove the lamb shanks from the pan.

Next add the bacon and cook until crisp, then add the carrots, celery, leek, onion, and garlic and cook over high heat until slightly browned. Add the red wine to the pan and bring to a boil, stirring for a minute or two. Add the stock, herbs, and orange peel to the pan, then place the lamb shanks on top. Cover and cook in the oven for 2¼ hours.

Remove from the oven and add the tomato fondue, cannellini beans, herbs, and enough stock to half-cover the beans. Cover and simmer for another ¾ –1 hour.

When the lamb has finished cooking it should be falling off the bone. Remove the thyme, bay leaves, and orange peel. Taste and adjust the seasoning.

Serve the lamb shanks in a hot, deep dish with the beans and vegetables poured over and around. Garnish with sprigs of fresh rosemary and thyme.

Opposite: *Braised Lamb Shanks with Garlic, Rosemary, and Cannellini Beans.*

Left *Slow-roasted Shoulder of Lamb with Coriander Seeds.*

Preheat the oven to 300°F.

Score the fat side of the shoulder of lamb. Heat a little extra virgin olive oil in a wide, shallow pan, and add a few sprigs of thyme. Lay the shoulder fat-side down in the pan, and brown over low heat – don't rush this stage or the pan may burn.

Lift out the lamb, pour off and discard the excess fat. Deglaze the pan with dry white wine. Bring to a boil for 4–5 minutes. Then add the stock.

Add the unpeeled garlic heads, 2 or 3 sprigs of fresh thyme, and the lamb. Return to a boil. Cover tightly, transfer to the oven and cook for 2–2½ hours or until the meat is tender and succulent and almost falling off the bone. Transfer to a carving dish, and surround with the cooked garlic cloves.

Strain and degrease the cooking juices, return to the pan and cook uncovered over high heat to concentrate the flavor. Taste and adjust the seasoning. Serve these delicious juices with the lamb, cut in thick slices, and surrounded with the cooked garlic cloves, sprigs of fresh thyme, and flat parsley.

Mashed potatoes or Colcannon (see page 384) make a delicious accompaniment.

SLOW-BRAISED SHOULDER OF LAMB WITH GARLIC AND THYME

Like the neck, this is another part of the animal that gets quite a bit of exercise, so a slow-cooking method, be it roasting or braising, will transform the connective tissue into meltingly tender meat. You may cook this recipe on top of the stove rather than in the oven · **SERVES 6-8**

1 **shoulder of lamb, about 8–10lb**
3 **tablespoons extra virgin olive oil**
6 **fresh thyme sprigs**
1 **cup dry white wine**
1¼ **cups Chicken Stock (see page 262)**
6 **organic garlic heads**
salt and freshly ground black pepper

GARNISH
sprigs of fresh thyme
flat parsley

SLOW-ROASTED SHOULDER OF LAMB WITH CORIANDER SEEDS

I sometimes put this into a slow-cooker in the morning. By the evening, it is beautifully cooked – how easy is that! When I ask my butcher for a shoulder, he gives me a forequarter, so that's what this recipe is for · **SERVES 8-10**

2 tablespoons coriander seeds
whole shoulder of lamb, about
    8lb on the bone
sea salt and freshly ground black
    pepper
extra virgin olive oil

FOR THE CORIANDER GRAVY
2 cups Lamb Stock or Chicken
    Stock (see pages 341 and 262)
2 teaspoons freshly roasted ground
    coriander
2 tablespoons Roux (see page 165),
    optional

TO SERVE
crusty roast potatoes

Warm the coriander seeds slightly in a dry pan, then crush them in a pestle and mortar. Score the skin of the lamb in a diamond pattern with a sharp knife. Sprinkle the meat with sea salt, freshly ground pepper, and the crushed coriander seeds, and then drizzle with olive oil.

Roast in a preheated 275°F oven for 6–7 hours to give the meat a delicious, juicy succulent texture. Alternatively, cook, in a preheated 325°F oven for 2½–3 hours. The coriander seeds will impart a delicious flavor to the meat. Carve the meat into thick slices so that everybody gets some coriander.

To make the coriander gravy, spoon the fat off the roasting pan. Add the stock to the remaining cooking juice. Boil for a few minutes, stirring and scraping the pan well, to dissolve the caramelized meat juices (I find a small whisk ideal for this). Add the freshly ground coriander. Allow the gravy to thicken with a very little bit of roux if you like.

Taste and add salt and freshly ground pepper if necessary. Strain and serve the gravy separately in a gravy boat.

Serve with crusty roast potatoes.

Variation
SLOW-ROASTED LAMB WITH CUMIN
Try substituting freshly ground cumin seeds for the coriander seeds in the recipe above, or mix together a tablespoon each of roasted cumin and coriander seeds. Or use a leg of lamb in place of the shoulder.

MOROCCAN LAMB TAGINE WITH TOMATOES AND HONEY

I'm borrowing this slow-cooking technique from North Africa. A tagine is named after the conical earthenware pot in which it is cooked, but you can just use a wide, shallow, enamel pot or stainless-steel sauté pan. This tagine has a Moroccan flavor, and can be made with chicken instead of lamb · **SERVES 8-10**

3 tablespoons extra virgin olive oil
1 onion, diced
1 garlic clove, crushed
1 teaspoon cinnamon
1 teaspoon fresh ginger, peeled
    and grated
pinch of saffron
3lb very ripe tomatoes, skinned
    and chopped or 3 (14-oz) cans
    tomatoes
3lb lamb cubes cut from the
    shoulder
salt and freshly ground black
    pepper
2 tablespoons honey

GARNISH
4–5 tablespoons blanched almonds
1 tablespoon sesame seeds

Heat the olive oil in a wide casserole, and add the onion, garlic, and spices. Stir and cook for a minute or two, then add the tomatoes and lamb cubes. Season with salt and freshly ground pepper. Cover and cook gently, stirring occasionally, until the lamb is meltingly tender.

Remove the lamb and set it aside. Reduce the tomato sauce uncovered until it thickens. Stir the sauce regularly so the bottom does not stick or burn as the sugar in the tomatoes begins to caramelize. Add the honey and return the lamb to the casserole to heat it through.

Meanwhile, toast the almonds in a preheated 300°F oven until they are pale golden, or toss the sesame seeds in a dry pan for a minute or two until they start to pop.

Transfer the lamb to a hot serving dish and garnish with the toasted almonds and sesame seeds.

Stews

If you ask someone who knows nothing about Irish food to name one Irish dish, they will probably say Irish stew.

There is no quintessential Irish stew recipe, but generally people would agree that it is made with lamb. In Northern Ireland, Irish stew is a white version, with just lamb, potato, and onion, whereas further south, carrots are added. Others might throw in parsnips or, as in the Bantry Irish stew recipe below, rutabaga.

How do I use a casserole?

Manufacturers of cast-iron casseroles that are lined with enamel advise that they are never heated higher than medium heat. Consequently, we start the sautéing of all stews and braises in a hot frying pan and then transfer the contents to the casserole. This will prolong the life of your casserole for many years.

BALLYMALOE IRISH STEW

Stew is something we think of as a winter dish, but in reality, Irish stew is best in early summer, made with youngish lamb and the new season's sweet onions and carrots. In this recipe, the fact that the meat is cooked on the bone (we use shoulder and neck chops) greatly enhances the flavor · **SERVES 4–6**

3lb lamb chops (gigot or rack chops) not less than 1in thick
6 medium or 12 baby onions
6 medium or 12 baby carrots
salt and freshly ground black pepper
3 cups Lamb Stock or Chicken Stock (see pages 341 and 262) or hot water
12 russet potatoes
sprig of thyme
about 1 tablespoon Roux (see page 165), optional

GARNISH
2 tablespoons freshly chopped parsley
1 tablespoon freshly chopped chives

Preheat the oven to 350°F.

Cut the chops in 2oz pieces and trim off some of the excess fat. Set the pieces aside and render down the fat over low heat in a heavy frying pan (discard the rendered-down pieces).

Peel the onions and scrape or thinly peel the carrots (if they are young, leave some of the green stalks on the onions and carrots). Cut the carrots into large chunks, or if they are young, leave them whole. If the onions are large, quarter them; if they are small, they are best left whole.

Toss the meat in the hot fat until it is slightly brown. Transfer the meat into a casserole, then quickly toss the onions and carrots in the fat. Build the meat, carrots, and onions up in layers in the casserole. Season each layer generously with salt and pepper. Deglaze the frying pan with lamb or chicken stock and pour into the casserole.

Peel the potatoes and lay them on top of the casserole, so they steam while the stew cooks. Season the potatoes. Add a sprig of thyme and bring to a boil on top of the stove. Then cover and transfer to a warm oven or allow to simmer on top of the stove until the stew is cooked, about 1–2 hours, depending on whether the stew is being made with lamb or mutton.

When the stew is cooked, the meat should be almost falling off the bones. Pour off the cooking liquid, degrease, and reheat the liquid in a saucepan. If you like, slightly thicken the juices with a little roux. Check the seasoning, then add chopped parsley and chives and pour it back over the stew. Bring it back up to boiling point and serve from the pot or in a large serving dish.

Variation

IRISH STEW WITH PEARL BARLEY
Add 2 tablespoons of pearl barley to the stew with the vegetables and increase the liquid to 1 quart as the pearl barley absorbs a considerable amount of liquid.

EMER FITZGERALD'S BRAISED LAMB NECK MOUSSAKA

This joint of meat is unquestionably the sweetest and most succulent of all the lamb cuts and has the added bonus of being the least expensive. The potato makes it go further and the raisins add a tantalizing sweetness. We love this version of moussaka · **SERVES 8**

2 tablespoons olive oil
2 x lamb necks or scrag end (approximately 3½ lb total)
1lb onions
4 garlic cloves, chopped

2 x 14-oz cans chopped tomatoes
½ teaspoon ground cinnamon
¼ teaspoon ground nutmeg
1 tablespoon fresh marjoram leaves
    chopped
salt, freshly ground black pepper,
    and sugar
3 cups Lamb Stock (see page 341)
2 eggplants (1lb in total)
1lb potatoes, scrubbed well
⅓ cup raisins

FOR THE CHEESE SAUCE
4 tablespoons butter
½ cup all-purpose flour
2½ cups whole milk
1 bay leaf
salt and freshly ground black
    pepper
2 organic egg yolks
1 tablespoon heavy cream
4oz Gruyère cheese, grated

10 x 8½in earthenware dish

1 large casserole dish

Preheat the oven to 300°F. Heat the
olive oil in a large casserole dish.
Season the lamb necks. Brown the
meat on all sides in the oil. Remove
and place on a plate. Add the onions
and garlic to the casserole and cook
over medium heat for 3–4 minutes
until soft and beginning to brown.
Add the chopped tomatoes, ground
cinnamon, nutmeg, and chopped
marjoram. Season with salt and
pepper and sugar. Cook for 5
minutes. Add the lamb stock and
bring to a boil. Return the lamb
necks to the casserole. Cover the
casserole and place in the preheated
oven for 2–2½ hours or until tender.

The meat should be falling off the
bone.

Meanwhile, cook the potatoes
in boiling salted water until two-
thirds cooked. Peel and slice into
¼in slices.

Slice the eggplant into ½in slices.
Sprinkle with salt and allow to sweat
in a colander for half an hour. Pat
the eggplant dry and toss in olive
oil. Cook over medium heat until
golden on both sides. When the
lamb is cooked, remove from the
braising liquid. Coarsely shred the
lamb, removing any bones or sinew.
Strain the vegetables from the liquid
and add to the lamb. Moisten this
mixture with some of the braising
liquid (3–4 tablespoons) Season to
taste and add the raisins.

Lay the eggplant slices on the
base of the earthenware dish, top
with the lamb mixture, then cover
with slightly overlapping slices of
potato.

For the sauce, melt the butter in
a saucepan. Stir in the flour and
cook, stirring, for 1 minute. Add the
milk slowly, whisking out the lumps
as you go, then remove from the
heat. Add the bay leaf and season
with salt and freshly ground black
pepper. Return to the heat and
simmer for 2 minutes. Mix the egg
yolks and cream in a large bowl.
Pour the hot sauce into this mixture,
whisking all the time. Add half the
cheese and pour over the dish.
Sprinkle the rest of the cheese on
top and bake for 35–40 minutes
until completely reheated and
golden brown on the top.

HAYBOX

The haybox is a brilliant invention
that certainly dates back to
wartime and possibly long before.
The idea is to make an insulated
box. Start with a wooden box, or
a couple of wine boxes that can be
adapted. Add rope handles, so you
can carry your haybox for
a picnic. Layer the base and sides
with soft hay to a thickness of at
least 3in. When a casserole or
earthenware pot of bubbling stew
or tagine is almost cooked, tuck it
into the haybox, pack more hay in
around the sides and cover with
another thick layer of hay and then
the wooden lid. Your haybox can
then be transported in the trunk of
the car for a picnic later in the day.
I always get a great response when
I remove the lid and produce a
piping hot stew hours later! You can
either cook the stew to completion
before you put it in the box, or, if
you've got a distance to travel, get it
bubbling well and put it in the
haybox to finish cooking.

Offal

People either absolutely love or hate offal – there's no middle ground. There are those who find the idea of eating offal totally repulsive and couldn't imagine letting a piece of liver, kidney, or a juicy sweetbread pass their lips, even if they were starving. And then there are the rest of us, who can't get enough of it. I hope the following recipes will entice offal haters.

Sweetbreads

Sweetbreads, which come in pairs, is the name given to either the thymus or pancreatic glands of young, milk-fed calves and lambs. The pancreatic glands contain less fat and are more regularly shaped and thus easier to cook. When the animal's diet changes from milk to grass or grain, the sweetbreads tend to shrink, so they are best eaten before this transition.

We only ever see lamb's sweetbreads around Easter, when

spring lambs are being killed. The sweetbreads only keep fresh for 24 hours, so many come frozen, but it is worth seeking out fresh ones because they taste better. Not many people eat sweetbreads at all, so ask your butcher to save them for you. They are delicate, tender, delicious, and inexpensive. Choose sweetbreads that are white or pale pink in color, not bruised and compact in texture. They are extremely perishable when raw, so should be prepared and precooked immediately.

To prepare sweetbreads

Put the sweetbreads into a bowl, cover with cold water, and let them soak for 3 hours. Discard the water and cut away any discolored parts from the sweetbreads.

To Cook

Cover the sweetbreads in fresh cold water or chicken stock, bring to a boil, and simmer for 3 minutes (lamb) to 5 minutes (calf) and then drain.

Cool the sweetbreads and gently pull away any extra membrane or tissue, but be careful that the sweetbreads don't come apart. They now need to be pressed and chilled before being sliced for further cooking.

To Press

Press between 2 plates and top with a weight not more than 2lb or they will be squashed (see left).

Chill for a few hours or overnight and use as soon as possible in your chosen recipe.

SALAD OF WARM SWEETBREADS WITH POTATO CHIPS, ANCHOVIES, AND WILD GARLIC

Sweetbreads are definitely a forgotten treat. The salty tang of the anchovies in this recipe gives another dimension and adds lots of complementary flavor without compromising the sweetness of the sweetbreads. · **SERVES 4**

4 lamb or 2 veal sweetbreads
1 small carrot
1 onion
2 celery ribs
2 tablespoons butter
bouquet garni
**2 cups Chicken Stock (see
    page 262)**
**a selection of salad leaves (little
    gem, oakleaf, sorrel, watercress,
    and wild garlic leaves and
    flowers)**
**all-purpose flour, well seasoned
    with salt and freshly ground
    black pepper**
1 beaten organic egg
butter and oil for sautéing

FOR THE DRESSING
1 tablespoon white wine vinegar
3 tablespoons extra virgin olive oil
¼ teaspoon Dijon mustard
**salt and freshly ground black
    pepper**

TO SERVE
**Homemade Potato Chips (see
    page 387)**
4 anchovies
**wild garlic flowers (or chive
    flowers depending on the
    season)**

Prepare the sweetbreads as on page 350, but don't cook them yet.

Dice the carrot, onion, and celery and cook them in butter. Add the bouquet garni, then the chicken stock, and bring to a boil.

Poach the sweetbreads gently in the simmering stock for 3–5 minutes or until they feel firm to the touch. Cool, then remove the gelatinous membranes and any fatty bits carefully. Press the sweetbreads gently as on page 350.

Prepare the salad. Wash and dry the lettuces and salad leaves and whisk together the ingredients for the dressing.

Slice the sweetbreads into scallops, dip in well-seasoned flour, and then in beaten egg. Sauté over medium heat in a little foaming butter and oil in a heavy pan until golden on both sides.

Toss the salad leaves in the dressing, divide between 4 plates and lay the hot sweetbreads and then potato chips on top of the salad. Sprinkle with chopped anchovy and wild garlic flowers or chive flowers and serve immediately.

SWEETBREADS WITH PEA AND MINT PURÉE, CHORIZO, AND CARAMELIZED SHALLOTS

Sweetbreads are so delicate that many people just fry them with a little butter, scatter them with a few fresh herbs, and eat them on toasted bread with a mushroom sauce, but I love the freshness of the pea purée here, and the sweetness of the caramelized onions · SERVES 6

1½ lb lamb sweetbreads
butter
extra virgin olive oil
4oz chorizo, peeled and diced

FOR THE CARAMELIZED SHALLOTS
18 shallots
2 tablespoons butter

FOR THE PEA AND MINT PURÉE
1 teaspoon salt
1 teaspoon sugar
1lb freshly shelled peas or frozen peas
a lump of butter
2 tablespoons fresh mint, chopped
freshly ground pepper

GARNISH
pea shoots or the curly tendrils that extend beyond the pea shoot, at the tip, when in season

Several hours or a day ahead, cook, trim, and press the sweetbreads (see page 350).

Peel the shallots, melt a little butter in a small cast-iron saucepan, add the shallots, cover, and cook very gently until soft. Remove the lid and continue to cook, stirring regularly until the shallots caramelize on all sides.

Meanwhile, bring ½ cup water to a boil and add the salt, sugar, and peas. Cover, bring back to a boil, and continue to cook for 4 or 5 minutes or until the peas are just soft. Mash or put the mixture into the bowl of a food processor, adding the butter, mint, and a little cooking water. Process until smooth, taste, and adjust the seasoning. Keep warm.

Slice the cooked sweetbreads into ¼in thick slices. Melt a little butter in a frying pan, season the sweetbreads, cook on both sides until golden, and transfer to a plate. Add the olive oil to the pan, then add the chorizo. Cook over medium heat until the oil runs out and the chorizo become crisp.

Put a bed of pea purée on each plate, top with a few pieces of sweetbread, and scatter some caramelized onions and chorizo over the top. Drizzle with a little of the chorizo oil. Decorate with a few pea shoots when in season.

LAMB'S LIVER WITH CRISPY SAGE LEAVES

The robust flavor of sage is great with lamb or veal liver, so keep a sage plant in a pot near your kitchen door. Sage leaves crisped in olive oil make an irresistible garnish · SERVES 4

1lb very fresh spring lamb's liver, cut into ½in slices
all-purpose flour, seasoned with salt and freshly ground black pepper
4 tablespoons extra virgin olive oil
12 fresh sage leaves

Lamb's liver toughens very quickly once cooked and it really just needs to be flash fried in the pan, so wait until your guests are sitting around the table before you start to cook.

Toss the liver in well-seasoned flour and pat off the excess. Heat half the olive oil in a frying pan and add the slices of liver. Sauté gently for 2–3 minutes on each side. Remove the slices while they are still slightly pink in the center.

Put the remaining olive oil in the pan, add the sage leaves, and allow to sizzle for a few seconds until crisp. Pour the oil, juices, and sage leaves over the liver and serve immediately. Even if liver is perfectly cooked, it toughens very quickly if kept hot.

LAMB KIDNEYS IN THEIR OVERCOAT

When I take apart a lamb in demonstration, I show students how to butcher a lamb. They're surprised at how easy it is. Basically it divides into shoulder, loin, and leg with the kidney tucked inside the loin. I bake a lamb's kidney in its own suet fat. I go on about how good it is, but they find it hard to believe until they taste it. To make this dish, the oven needs to be very hot and the kidneys need lots of sea salt ·

SERVES 2

2 kidneys
sea salt

To Serve
boiled potatoes
green salad

Preheat the oven to 450°F.

If there is an excessive amount of suet on the kidneys, trim them a little. Generously sprinkle with sea salt. Cook in a roasting pan for 10–15 minutes, depending on size. The fat should be crispy on the outside and soft within. When the kidneys are almost cooked, allow them rest for a few minutes, then serve with boiled potatoes and a green salad.

Above: *Lamb Kidneys in their Overcoat.*

Mutton and Hogget

Although Prince Charles's efforts have made mutton easier to source in Britain, it is still rather difficult to find in the US (as is hogget). Try local Middle Eastern meat markets or you may have to order it online to ship from Britain. The following recipes can be made with lamb, but will have a less rich flavor. Cooking times will need to be reduced slightly.

HOGGET WITH GARDEN HERBS

Hogget, being a bit older than lamb and quite a bit older than spring lamb, is stronger and gamier in flavor. It's lovely roasted with winter herbs like this, but hogget is very amenable to braising too · SERVES 8–10

leg of hogget – an average weight for a leg or shoulder of hogget is 7½lb and will serve 8–10 people; allow about 6oz per person
sea salt

FOR THE HERB MARINADE
3 large garlic cloves
¾ cup extra virgin olive oil
2oz chopped herbs: parsley, thyme, mint, tarragon, chives, rosemary, and marjoram; or whatever fresh herbs you have
freshly ground black pepper

FOR THE GRAVY
2 cups Lamb Stock or Chicken Stock (see pages 341 and 262)
2 teaspoons freshly chopped herbs, as above
2 tablespoons Roux (see page 165)
salt and freshly ground black pepper

GARNISH
sprigs of fresh mint and parsley

First make the herb marinade. Peel the garlic cloves and make them into a paste. Place them with the olive oil and fresh herbs into a food processor and process them for about 1 minute or until you have a soft, green paste. Otherwise, just mix in a bowl.

If possible, remove the aitchbone from the top of the leg of hogget so that it will be easier to carve later, then trim the end of the leg. Score the fat lightly, transfer to the roasting pan, rub the herb mixture all over the surface of the lamb, and let marinate for several hours if possible.

Preheat the oven to 325°F. Sprinkle the hogget with sea salt. Roast for 1¾ hours (medium) or 2 hours (well-done). When the hogget is cooked to your taste, transfer the joint to a carving dish. Rest the lamb for 10 minutes before carving.

Degrease the juices in the roasting pan. Add stock, bring to a boil, and thicken with a little roux if desired. Just before serving, whisk in 1–2 tablespoons of butter to enrich the gravy, and add some freshly chopped herbs.

BOILED LEG OF MUTTON WITH CAPER SAUCE

Mutton has a complexity that comes with age, the way mature cheese also does. The flavor of this dish can be unforgettable, with a slightly wild, mountain flavor · SERVES 8–10

1 leg of mutton, about 8lb
5 quarts cold water
1 tablespoon salt
4 medium-sized carrots
2 turnips, cut into quarters
4 celery ribs, cut into 3 pieces
sprig of thyme

FOR THE CAPER SAUCE
4 tablespoons butter
½ cup all-purpose flour
2 cup whole milk
salt and freshly ground black pepper
2 tablespoons capers
2 teaspoons vinegar from caper jar
2 tablespoons chopped parsley

GARNISH
sprigs of flat-leaf parsley

Trim the knuckle from the shanks and end. Remove the aitchbones as you would if roasting lamb. Put the leg of mutton into a deep saucepan. Cover with cold water, add salt, bring slowly to a boil, and simmer for 5 minutes. Skim thoroughly.

Tuck the vegetables and the thyme around the edge of the saucepan. Continue to simmer for 1½–2 hours, depending on the size (as a rough guide weigh the mutton and allow 15 minutes per pound and 15 minutes extra).

Meanwhile, make the caper sauce. Melt the butter, add in the flour, and cook, stirring continuously for a minute or two. Remove from the heat. Whisk in the milk gradually and bring to a boil, stirring all the time. Season with salt and pepper. Add the capers, vinegar, and a few tablespoons of parsley. Let it bubble for a few minutes before serving.

When the meat is ready, a skewer should pierce it easily. Transfer the meat to a hot serving dish, surround with the vegetables, sprinkle with little sprigs of flat-leaf parsley, and serve with the caper sauce.

MUTTON BROTH

Mutton broth has kind of gone out of style – it's not the sort of thing most cookbook authors have been including in their books in the last 15 or 20 years – they're more into new tastes and clever twists. But this is light and homey and comforting, a tradition that deserves to be revived · SERVES 6-8

2lb neck of lamb or hogget, or
    bits of lean lap of lamb
2 quarts Lamb Stock (see page
    341), Mutton Broth (see page
    357), or hot water
3 tablespoons pearl barley
1½ cups chopped onions
1½ cups carrots, diced ½in thick
3 celery ribs, diced
1 small turnip, quartered
bouquet garni
salt and freshly ground black
    pepper

TO SERVE
lots of parsley, freshly chopped

Trim as much fat off the mutton as possible. Then dice the meat into small cubes about ¼in thick. Place them into a large saucepan with the bones and cover with cold stock or water. Add the pearl barley and about 1 teaspoon of salt. Bring slowly to a boil and simmer for 30 minutes.

Add the chopped onion, carrot, celery, turnip, and bouquet garni. Continue to cook for about 1–1½ hours, remove the bones, and the bouquet garni.

Taste and adjust the seasoning. Sprinkle with lots of freshly chopped parsley and serve.

Left: *Mutton Broth.*

The Doyenne of Mutton Pies

I was in Listowel, Ireland for the annual Food Fair and strayed into the legendary family pub founded by John B. Keane. Before long, Mary, wife of the late playwright, matriarch of the Keane dynasty, and doyenne of mutton pies herself (she being the winner of the Listowel mutton pie competition in 2007) strolled into the pub. Mary was taught how to make traditional pies by her mother-in-law, Hannah Purtill, and she passed on the skill to me. According to Mary, the tradition of pie making in Listowel came about because the women wanted to go to the horse races, so would make a "blast of pies" a few days before the races so as not to be deprived of their fun.

MARY KEANE'S LISTOWEL MUTTON PIES

The way Listowel mutton pies are eaten is unique. The pastry is quite robust because of the small proportion of shortening to flour, but not at all fragile. A big pot of mutton broth is made from the bones with maybe an onion or two added. On race day, the pies are slipped, a couple at a time, into the pot of strained broth. They simmer away and are then served into wide shallow soup bowls with a ladle full of hot broth on top · **SERVES 8**

1lb mutton or hogget, a mixture of neck, shank and scrag end (buy a bit more to allow for trimming)

salt and ground white pepper

FOR THE PASTRY
2lb all-purpose flour
1 stick margarine or butter
3½ cups buttermilk
½ teaspoon salt
egg wash (see page 539)

FOR THE MUTTON BROTH
mutton or hogget bones, about 6lb
3–4 large onions, peeled and quartered
a couple of carrots, celery ribs, parsley stalks, a couple of sprigs of thyme, or 2 stock cubes
salt and freshly ground black pepper

Prepare the lamb. Trim off the fat and any gristle or membrane. Cut into tiny pieces, roughly ⅛in, and put into a shallow bowl. Season well with salt and ground white pepper. Toss to ensure the meat is evenly coated.

Make the pastry. Put the flour and salt into a bowl. Add in the margarine or butter, followed by the buttermilk, and mix with your hand into a firm dough, similar to (though drier than) the texture of white soda bread. Knead the dough for 30 seconds to 1 minute to firm it up. Divide it into 2 pieces. On a floured board, roll the pastry out as thinly as possible, to about ¼in thick. Using a saucer as a template, cut out 2 circles at a time. Take 1 round and roll it out a little further to thin the pastry to about 2–3mm (⅛ in). Put a good half-fistful of seasoned mutton or hogget into the center. Brush the edge of the pastry with a little buttermilk and cover with another round that has also been rolled to a ⅛in thickness. Press the edges together with the tines of a fork, then prick the top several times. Brush the top of the pastry with egg wash.

Preheat the oven to 450°F. Meanwhile, continue to make the remainder of the pies. When the first 4 are ready, cook on a baking sheet for 20–30 minutes. Check the pies occasionally and turn the sheet if necessary. Continue to make pies until all the pastry and filling is used up. Leave the pies to cool on a wire rack. At this point, they can be kept wrapped for several days or frozen for later use.

Next, make a simple broth. Put the mutton or hogget bones into a deep saucepan, add the onions, cover with cold water, and bring to a boil. Mary adds a couple of stock cubes later, but if you'd rather not she suggested adding a few thickly sliced carrots, a few celery ribs, a sprig or two of thyme, and some parsley stalks. Simmer for 1–1½ hours, covered.

Strain the stock and taste, adding salt and pepper as necessary. The broth will keep in a fridge for several days or may be frozen. To serve the mutton pies, bring the broth to a boil in a deep saucepan, then drop a couple of meat pies into the broth. Simmer for 20 minutes. Remove with a slotted spoon. Transfer each pie into a wide, shallow soup bowl. Pour a ladle of mutton broth on top. Eat with a fork and spoon and extra pepper and salt, depending on your taste.

Vegetables, herbs, and salad

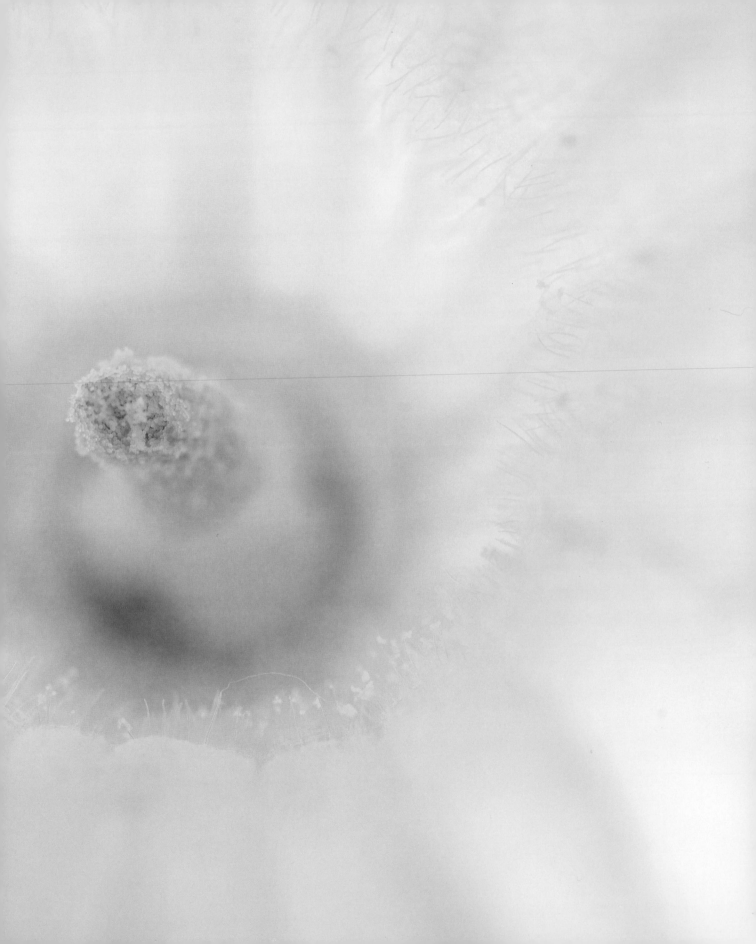

Everyone knows how passionate I am about keeping hens, but I am equally passionate about gardening. When I was growing up, the kitchen garden was an essential part of life. Most people assumed they would have one and planned their garden space accordingly. Herbs, salads, and vegetables were home-produced – and they had a fresh flavor quite unlike the tired, wilted, jet-lagged vegetables sometimes on sale in the supermarkets of today. If flavor is lacking in your vegetables to begin with, as a cook you have to work so much harder to spruce them up and compensate for that. When you've grown something yourself, however, you'll probably need no further embellishment than a little drizzle of extra virgin olive oil or a dab of good butter.

I am convinced that the reason most children won't eat vegetables is because they don't taste good to them. We've had some interesting experiences with children's reactions to vegetables. When occasionally some of our children's school pals came to supper, they would refuse to eat vegetables. Our children would persuade them to taste them, and when they did, the pals would polish off all of them. When their parents came to get them, they were amazed to see their children eating vegetables they wouldn't touch at home. So I've long suspected that fresh, organic vegetables taste very different from intensively produced vegetables.

Vegetables are by far the most important food group, and the decrease in nutrients since intensive production was ramped up in the 1950s is alarming. The dramatic loss of vitamins, minerals, and trace elements in vegetables and fruit since then has been confirmed by several pieces of peer-reviewed research, including the Widdowson and McCance study on the composition of foods. I'm also convinced that there's a link between flavor and nutrients, but it's difficult to get research done on something as esoteric as this – no doubt, however, it will be proven in the end. Freshness is also vitally important to nutrition; nutrients leach out of vegetables once they've been picked and as they age, and there's no better way to get something fresh than if you pick it yourself.

The convenience aspect is another great benefit of growing your own. Salads and herbs, for example, are difficult to buy in sensible quantities. You may suddenly find you need some fresh thyme leaves or a few sprigs of rosemary for a dish – but at the supermarket you can buy only larger amounts of these herbs; usually in plastic containers at an exorbitant price and after they have traveled a long way. Then, when you have used the sprig, what do you do with the rest? Often it ends up in the garbage. How much more convenient is it to go out to the garden or to the windowsill and simply snip off the sprig you need? You can plan your salad leaves to last throughout the seasons and have ready-to-eat salads and herbs right beside your kitchen door for a good part of the year. This is a forgotten convenience that you can reclaim, whatever the size of your growing space.

Whether you choose to grow in pots, a community garden, or your own garden, there will, of course, be some work involved at the start of the process, but it has a lot of satisfaction attached, not least of which is the pleasure of being linked to the rhythms of sowing, planting, and waiting for things to grow. It's the kind of work that slows down the system and is a good antidote to the fast pace of modern life.

I had an excruciatingly difficult time trying to decide which of the 100-plus vegetables to include in this book. There is such a huge variety to choose from as a gardener and as a cook that you really need to be led by your heart as well as your palate. I have also tried to stick with suggestions for vegetables that will give a good return on your investment of time and effort.

Growing Your Own

For those who haven't grown anything before, the whole idea can be quite intimidating. Even though this is not a gardening book, I wanted to sneak in a few tips to encourage you to get started and there are plenty of helpful books that cover every aspect of vegetable gardening in detail (see Resources, page 584).

What to grow

The amount of space you have is, of course, a major consideration. One of the best pieces of advice I can offer is not to be overambitious when you start growing vegetables. Choose a few favorites to experiment with and add to them over time as you become more familiar with what works within the space you have.

Consider what fresh produce you can buy locally – what's lacking? You might also think about expense: which vegetables are the costliest to buy? Why not grow these and buy the less expensive ones?

If you opt for salads and herbs, choose seasonal varieties and salad leaves that will provide you with fresh-cut greens throughout the year – some, for example, mache, will even survive in snow, while some only thrive in summer.

It's often difficult to gauge how much of a particular vegetable to grow. The UK *Gardener's World* TV host Sarah Raven gave me a terrific tip: every time you use a vegetable, make a note on the fridge door.

Over time, this will give you an idea of how much of each vegetable you eat. The reality is that there are often too many seeds in packages and it's soul-destroying to have 30 lettuces all ready at the same time. How about linking up with a few neighbors and friends – have a digging party and share seedlings, plants, and growing tips over an après-digging drink.

Where to grow

Until fairly recently, houses came with large yards, often about a third of an acre, to allow for this essential part of feeding a family. And, of course, there were also community gardens. Nowadays, many people have far less or no garden space to accommodate such needs, and the concept of a productive garden as a part of life virtually disappeared. Fortunately, the enthusiasm for growing your own is gathering momentum again. People are discovering that even with a tiny, concrete outdoor space, they can grow herbs, salads, and vegetables, and reclaim a sense of connection with the source of their food.

If you become more ambitious, you might explore the possibility of joining a community garden – they can be difficult to find but they are available in many larger cities. Some farmers on the outskirts of towns, instead of selling their land for development, are converting their fields into community gardens. Some city people with garden space have even offered to let others come and garden it. There are other initiatives, too, like Capital Growth in London, England, to use all green spaces, such as highway medians and abandoned railroad yards, to grow food. In Havana, Cuba, almost 80 percent of the food that's eaten is produced in the city, and not just vegetables, but poultry and pork as well.

There's something empowering and reassuring about a raised bed with a wooden edging – it's a finite size and feels manageable, even to the most tentative and reluctant gardener. Even though we have plenty of space here on our farm, we also have several raised beds and it's amazing how much food we produce in them. Our raised beds are two or three railroad ties high, so we don't even have to bend down to pick a vegetable – they are also a perfect height for wheelchair users. If you can't get your hands on recycled wood, you can build basic walls using concrete blocks or bricks covered over with plaster – don't forget to leave holes for drainage.

Just because you live in a high-rise apartment doesn't mean you can't grow food. You can grow on rooftops, in tin cans, up walls, down walls, in hanging baskets, tubs, pots, barrels – the sky's the limit. Neither do you need expensive containers to propagate seedlings. Egg cartons and used yogurt containers or even the cardboard interior of toilet paper rolls can be used. Where there's a will, there's most definitely a way – use whatever space you have to your best advantage.

Growing organic

It's really worth starting out with organic plants; don't waste your time on cheap, forced plants that keel

Above, left: *A few raised beds can provide enough fresh produce to nourish and delight a whole family.* **Above, right:** *A motley collection of containers growing zucchinis, strawberries, and peas.* **Below, left:** *Save egg cartons to propagate seedlings – they are also biodegradable.* **Below, right:** *Fortunate are those who have access to a community garden.*

Above: *Magic compost, the foundation of good garden produce.*

over almost before you arrive home – organic plants tend to be much more resilient and less susceptible to disease. Try to buy organic seed, too; in our experience they have more vitality.

The fundamental principle when growing organically is the need to feed, nourish, and enhance the soil. Our experience and the experience of many other home gardeners is that the quality of compost-grown vegetables surpasses that of vegetables grown in soil boosted by artificial fertilizers. A few years ago, we even compared vegetables grown in our own organic soil with vegetables grown in our compost-enriched organic soil. There was clearly a difference, both in appearance and flavor.

Pests

A major concern for organic gardeners is how to stop the dreaded slugs and other pests from chomping their precious plants. On a small scale, a small bowl of beer nestled in the ground lures slugs and snails, and they don't much like crawling over broken eggshells either. An upturned grapefruit half also makes a reasonably effective trap, but one of the best ways to get rid of slugs, unquestionably, is to go out with a flashlight at night and pick off the pests. I'll leave it to you to decide what to do with them. If you do this a few nights in a row, you'll get most of them. You can also buy organic slug pellets, which are moderately effective.

When you buy a plant you need to be extremely fussy and check that it doesn't have whitefly or greenfly or any other bug. If you're not vigilant, it's very easy to bring pests into your garden. So carefully examine underneath the leaves on the plant – the flies are tiny, but you'll see them. When a plant is stressed, as with humans, it's more prone to disease or infestation so remember to water and feed them.

In the Cookery School gardens, we use a variety of biological controls, like ladybugs, nemetoids, and little aphid predators, but this is more difficult to do at home. As mentioned in the Poultry chapter, a duck or two can be very effective in the vegetable garden for gobbling up slugs. Chickens, too, can clear the ground of a variety of pests and fertilize the soil during winter months (but keep them out of the garden during the growing season).

Composting

Composting is the traditional and holistic way to achieve the twin goals of feeding the soil and getting rid of household waste. Making compost is like making a cake – instead of tossing everything in, you need carefully balanced proportions – see the compost menu opposite, illustrated by my daughter, Lydia.

At least a quarter of everything you throw away or burn could be recycled to make your garden flourish – saving you money and helping you preserve the environment. So don't look on it as just a heap of garbage; do your bit to reduce pollution and landfill waste and nourish your own soil.

Making compost is all part of a holistic cycle. It uses natural processes, but speeds them up.

BALLYMALOE COOKERY SCHOOL

COMPOST MENU

To make good compost, you must lay on a feast for microorganisms – which means recycling all your valuable organic wastes.

Ingredients: grass clippings, leaves, prunings, weeds, wood ash, straw, shredded newspaper, sawdust, hair, flowers, feathers, manures, vegetable peelings, other kitchen waste, tea bags, water, and air.

Avoid: glass, plastic, glossy or colored paper, coal, charcoal and its ash, diseased plants, toxic chemicals, pet litter, and roots of perennial weeds. Cooked food and meat may encourage rats.

Compost is easily made in layers. Alternate a layer of strawy material, high in carbon, with a layer of juicy, wet ingredients, e.g., kitchen waste, grass cuttings, etc. Ensure the "strawy" material is not dry. All ingredients must be small in size, the smaller the pieces, the quicker it breaks down. The compost should be warm enough to bake a potato (about 150°F or thereabouts). Turn the heap occasionally to add air and speed up the composting process.

Organic waste from the house can be added to the compost that you can use to make your soil more fertile to grow nutritious herbs and vegetables for your family and friends. Feed the soil to feed the plants that feed you.

Green "waste" turns into dark, crumbly, sweet-smelling humus. By adding this to your soil, you're feeding the bacteria within it, which in turn release nutrients to make your garden grow.

Always site your heap perfectly onto the soil so that earthworms can complete the composting process. A container is essential to improve the quality and keep the heap neat and tidy. Whichever type you choose, aim for a size of about 3 x 3ft. A good container will provide insulation so that your compost doesn't dry out in the summer and stays warm in the winter. Insulate the top, too, and make it rainproof – a piece of old carpet or underlay is perfect for the job.

Too much dry or woody material in your heap will make it slow to break down: you might spot a "white mold" on strawy material if it's too dry. A dry heap should be turned, adding water and green matter or manure.

If it smells like ammonia, it means you've added too much green material, e.g., grass. Turn the heap, adding dry or woody material.

If making compost is not possible for you, you still need to feed your soil. You might consider using nettle or comfrey tea (see below). Also, rotating your crops is vital for success – every gardener worth his or her salt knows that if you grow a crop in the same spot every year it depletes the soil of a particular set of nutrients and eventually results in weak plants that are unable to resist disease. Again, find a trusty gardening book for more on this subject.

Comfrey or nettle tea for plants

Comfrey or nettles can be used to make a really potent plant food full of nutrients. This "tea" is energy-boosting tonic for plants, particularly good for fast-growing summer crops like tomatoes, corn, and cucumbers.

Fill a deep barrel or container to the top with young comfrey or nettle leaves. We use a 5-gallon drum, but a plastic bucket would do. Fill to the top with cold water, cover the container and leave to steep, preferably in a shady place, for about 2 weeks – it will stink to high heaven, so choose your site carefully. Strain and discard the leaves. Transfer to screw-top containers – we use recycled plastic milk bottles. To use, dilute 10 parts water to 1 part comfrey/nettle tea and use to feed your plants.

Storing fruit and vegetables

This is definitely a skill that was lost with the advent of home freezers. It's little known now that some produce, given optimum conditions, will keep in its fresh state for several months: apples, pears, onions, garlic, pumpkins, vegetable marrows, squash, and root vegetables, for instance. Use main crop varieties and store them from fall onward.

Above: *Comfrey.*

General storage guidelines:

• Handle both fruit and vegetables gently, so as not to bruise or damage them. Store only perfect fruit and vegetables because bruised or damaged produce will start to rot and may cause the rest to deteriorate. Use up slightly damaged produce as soon as possible.
• Rub off excess soil rather than washing. If necessary, wipe apples and pears gently.

Some vegetables, such as rutabaga, turnips, parsnips, carrots, and Jerusalem artichokes, can be left in the ground and dug up as you require. However, if your garden is prone to flooding, or if you are in a frost pocket, it may be better to harvest and store them in a cool place or in vegetable "pits."

Herbs

Fresh herbs add magic to your cooking, and my kind of cooking depends on having access to lots and lots of them. I've always had a little herb garden. The reward is immense and it will make such a difference to your cooking and garnishing. Dried herbs just aren't the same, although herbs you dry yourself (see page 460 in the Preserving chapter) will be far superior to most you can buy. They will also have a more concentrated flavor so use in smaller quantities. Some herbs freeze well and can be used in cooking, but I wouldn't use them as a substitute for fresh – for example, frozen basil works in peperonata or tomato fondue, but not in pesto. For more ideas for preserving herbs, including using them to flavor oils and vinegars, see the Preserving chapter.

If you are starting a herb garden, put it as close to the kitchen as possible. It can be as simple as a window box or a couple of herbs in a barrel, or as complex as the formal herb garden we have here at the Ballymaloe Cookery School. Even though I have an elaborate herb garden, it's the little patch outside my kitchen door that I nip out to most often. Practicality is very important. It's such a joy to snip a little mint to make a fresh tisane after dinner, or to pick a few herb flowers to sprinkle over salads.

When I first started my *Simply Delicious* book series, people kept asking me where they could find herbs. These days, they can be bought in virtually every corner store and supermarket, but often the package contains much more than you need, and there is lots of waste. Furthermore, they may have traveled from anywhere in the world, so there's yet another plastic tray to dispose of. I sometimes find that the flavor of bought herbs is stronger and more acrid, and the texture of herbs like mint and cilantro is certainly different – I wonder if this is due to the need for more robust varieties to withstand global transportation.

Herb garden

If you decide to grow herbs, start with the most common ones. Most herbs are perennial. The advantage of that is that if you plant them, they come back year after year. Others are annual or biannual – including mint, chives, chervil, and lemon balm. There are some very tender herbs, like basil, that are native to warmer climates, so you'll only have those in the summer. Hardy herbs that grow all year round include bay, rosemary, sage, thyme, and lemon verbena.

Your herbs need to be in a large enough pot so they actually have room to grow. Transplant the herbs out of the tiny pots you bought them in as soon as you get home.

If herbs are grown in a pot, they must be watered regularly – don't rely on the rain. No matter how large the container, after a time the herb will absorb all the available nutrients, so you will need to feed and replenish the soil. Try to buy an organic plant food.

Herbs are at their most aromatic and flavorful before they flower. Afterward, the flavor is more acrid and the texture becomes tougher. Strong herbs such as sage, thyme, rosemary, and bay leaf are best used in cooking. But fresh herbs such as chervil, flat parsley, mint, tarragon, dill, fennel sprigs, chives, basil, and marjoram work well in salads. You can also use mint, lemon verbena, sweet cicely, rose geranium, or lemon balm to garnish candies, desserts, and drinks, while herbs such as parsley, basil, or sage are delicious crisped in oil and nibbled or used as a garnish.

Angelica *(Angelica)*: a tall umbelliferous plant with thick hollow stems, angelica comes in a green or purple version. In April, we use the stems to make Candied Angelica (see page 458) to use as a garnish. Don't be surprised if it is not bright green like the store-bought version, most of which is dyed. In Niort, France, where angelica is used in large quantities for candying in the confectionery trade, they also make a liqueur called Angelique. Angelica is also an ingredient in Chartreuse. The celerylike flavor of the stalks gives them a natural affinity with fish. They make a wonderful addition to a court bouillon for poaching fish, and in Lapland and other northern places, fish is wrapped in angelica leaves, which are antimicrobial and act as a preservative, as well as flavoring the fish. Angelica stalks can be cooked with onions and greens such as spinach, or added to stewed tart fruits like rhubarb and plums to reduce some of the sugar.

Above: *Recycled tin cans make stylish containers for herb seedlings like basil.*

Basil *(Ocimum basilicum)*: there are many varieties of basil, including Genovese, opal, green, purple, lemon basil, large-leafed sweet basil, and Thai basil for Asian cooking. You can use basil to make pesto, and it also has a wonderful affinity with tomatoes, mozzarella, pasta sauces, vegetable stews, and salads. Add it at the end of cooking, since it's one of the few herbs that increases in flavor when cooked. Use it copiously before it flowers. You can flavor oil with it (see page 424) or preserve it by freezing, but use it directly from frozen because it becomes slimy when it defrosts. Basil is native to Italy and really needs the sun to thrive. If you don't have a greenhouse, put it on your sunniest windowsill, where it will also deter flies. Most basil plants fail because they're in too small a pot. If it threatens to go to flower, pinch out the flower heads right away. It ought to survive until the beginning of fall.

Bay *(Laurus nobilis)*: this perennial shrub can grow into a tree up to 35–40ft high. It has a strong, gutsy flavor that can predominate, so use cautiously. Use it in beef stock and in robust beef or venison stews and casseroles. Notable exceptions in which the flavor of bay is meant to dominate are Baked Bay Leaf Custard (see page 207) and sugar flavored with bay. Bay leaf can be used fresh (we always do) but dries well also; the fresh leaves are stronger in flavor than dried ones. You can put bay on the coals for a barbecue.

Borage *(Borago officinalis)*: this annual herb grows in profusion and tends to seed all over the place in summer. Borage has pretty purple flowers, which attract bees into the garden and feed them – an important consideration at a time when there's worldwide alarm at the decrease of the bee population. The little flowers can be used to decorate cupcakes or scatter over salads, or for garnishing in general. The flowers are pretty in ice cubes, too. The leaves are a bit off-putting because they're hairy, but if you have the courage to try them, they soften in your mouth and exude a lovely cucumber flavor. Cut them up finely in salads, add them to cream cheese, labneh, or yogurt. They work well as a garnish for cold soups, too.

Chervil *(Anthriscus cerefolium)*: a deliciously delicate little herb, both in fragrance and appearance, chervil deserves to be better known and more widely grown. It turns a purple color when touched by frost and is delicious added into sauces and salads. Herbalists value its medicinal uses as a digestive aid. Add chervil at the end of cooking to avoid loss of flavor.

Chives *(Allium schoenoprasum)* and **garlic chives** *(Allium tuberosum)*: ordinary chives have round stalks, whereas garlic chives have flat stalks and a distinct garlicky flavor. They are slightly hardier and have white, starlike flowers as opposed to the pretty purple flowers of common chives. Chives are seasonal. In mild climates, they reemerge from the ground around early spring, flower a few months later, and gradually get tougher as the season goes on. Treat them as a "cut-and-come" herb. Even if you're growing them in a pot, they will come back year after year. They have quite a strong, oniony flavor, so use them to enhance salads, chive butter, vegetables, soups and stews, omelets, scrambled eggs, and egg-salad sandwiches. We use the flowers a lot. We break up the pom-pomlike heads into individual flowers and sprinkle them over salads. Avoid the stems of chives that have flowered, though, since they'll be tough.

Coriander *(Coriandrum sativum)*: the most widely used herb in the world, much more so than parsley. It's incredibly versatile because every part of this herb can be used. The root is much prized in Asia and Thailand for Thai curry paste; the stalks can be chopped up and used in sauces and stews; and the fresh green leaves (cilantro) are

Above: *Chive flowers.*

an essential ingredient in Asian, Moroccan, South American, Mexican, and Caribbean cuisine. You can also use the pretty white flowers in salads, and the seed is the spice that we all know and love, with its slightly burnt-orange taste. All the parts of the plant (leaves, stalks, root, seeds) have distinctly different flavors. Coriander seeds have a wonderful affinity with cumin and are used in curries and garam masala. They can also be added to cakes, cookies, apple tarts, and marmalade.

Dill *(Anethum graveolens)*: dill looks very similar to fennel, and our students sometimes have difficulty telling the difference between the two. Dill is much stronger in flavor and more aromatic. It is good with fish, and little sprigs are lovely in salads, sauces, and soups. Add to white wine vinegar to make dill vinegar, which is wonderful with cucumber, gherkin, cauliflower, and

dill pickles. In many places, dill is underused, but in the Caribbean they add it to tomato sauces and in Greece, on the island of Agina, I've enjoyed liberal quantities of dill in green salads. Dill tea is a good remedy for stomach upsets, hiccups, and insomnia. It also increases milk flow in nursing mothers.

Fennel *(Foeniculum vulgare)*: fennel has tall, feathery leaves and umbelliferous flower heads. The herb has a slightly aniseedy, liquorice flavor that is particularly good with fish, pork, and marinades. Fennel tea is a traditional remedy for flatulence. You can use the flowers and the pollen, as well as the leaves, and when the flowers turn to seeds, you can use those, too. To dry fennel seed, just chop off the plant and hang it from a warm place in a paper bag with holes in it so that the seeds will collect in the bag. Fennel seeds are terrific with roast pork or in bread. To collect fennel pollen, cut the flowers on a dry day and shake the pollen onto silicone paper.

Fennel (the herb) is related to fennel (the vegetable), but in the vegetable the bulb swells more. Fennel also grows in the wild easily and is a perennial (including the bronze version). The vegetable is known as Florence fennel *(finocchio)* and is an annual. In Italy, they use dried fennel stalks as a kebab skewer (they call them *spiedini)*.

Lemon balm *(Melissa officinalis)*: this is a lemon-flavored herb, sometimes called Melissa, which is also delicious in salads, sauces, and to use for sweet or

savory garnishing. It is wonderful in cream cheese, yogurt, or sour cream, and we often use it to make lemon balm infusions. It can also be crystallized (see page 458) since it is one of the sweeter herbs.

Lemon verbena *(Aloysia triphylla)*: also a shrub, lemon verbena dries really well. Use for infusions or in fruit poaching liquids, ice creams and sorbets, lemonades, and cocktails. If you plant this, allow enough space, because it can grow up to 6ft tall. It's tender, so needs to be protected from winter frost – a severe frost will kill it.

Lovage *(Levisticum officinale)*: a leafy plant with a distinct celery flavor, we use lovage in stocks, soups, and stews and love it in a grape, grapefruit, and lovage cocktail. Use lovage judiciously, because of the strength of its flavor.

Above: *Fennel flowers look very similar to dill crowns but have a milder flavor.*

Above: *Parsley.*

Try snipping it sparingly into a green salad, where it creates an intriguing burst of flavor. Lovage is a tall plant, so it's good to keep cutting it down so that it produces fresh, green growth, although if you're planting it in a container, use a pot large enough to allow it to grow to 5ft tall.

Marjoram *(Origanum)*: if I could choose just one herb, this would be the one. Sweet, knotty, or annual marjoram are all names for the same herb, and there are others, too. It is wonderful with chicken, guinea fowl, lamb, or pork and I also use it raw in salads and in sauces, marinades, vegetable dishes, pizzas, and soups. Annual marjoram is the same as oregano. It also can be used in an infusion. Golden marjoram is a perennial that grows better out of direct sun; it has a distinctly different flavor and we use little sprigs of it in salads and as a garnish or in stuffings. We also use

marjoram in coarse pâtés and terrines. It dries well and then is known as oregano.

Mint *(Mentha)*: some people are concerned that mint will take over the garden because of its tendency to spread, but I think you can never have enough of it. There are lots of different varieties, of which spearmint is unquestionably the most versatile. You can make an infusion or tisane (herb tea) with any of the mints, but peppermint tea is deliciously light and refreshing, and a very effective remedy for colds and indigestion. Apple mint is good with fruit and there's also pineapple mint and ginger mint. Mint is almost more versatile than parsley, because you can use it in savory and sweet dishes, or as garnishing for both. Mint spreads like crazy, so in small gardens it might be prudent to contain it. If space is not a problem, let it romp away because there are so many good ways you can use an abundance of mint. For a treat, paint or dip fresh, dark spearmint leaves in melted chocolate and leave to chill on parchment paper. Serve as a nibble with a cup of espresso.

Parsley *(Petroselinum)*: this all-purpose herb is wonderfully versatile and goes with so many things. There is little difference in flavor between flat and curly parsley, but the curly parsley seems to have taken on a somewhat old-fashioned image. Flat parsley's fernlike leaves are somewhat prettier for garnishing. Parsley tea is good for cleansing the kidneys and it has lots of vitamin C. If parsley is

planted in a good spot and likes your soil, it will grow in abundance. One of my favorite suppers is a good parsley sauce with bacon and cabbage (page 315). Deep-fry sprigs of parsley for a garnish, or put some in your gin and tonic. There are lots of delicious ways to utilize a glut. Use it as the green in a green soup, make it the star of a salad, or make parsley pesto (follow the method on page 29, replacing wild garlic with parsley).

Rose geranium *(Pelargonium graveolens)*: this is not really a herb, but we often use it to flavor syrups, as garnishing, and it makes a delicious infusion. We also put the leaves under a sponge cake mixture, so the flavor seeps into it. Rose geranium has a particular affinity with blackberries. A rose geranium plant sits on the windowsill in every kitchen in the Cookery School and we regularly give rose geraniums to people as presents. Students who come to the school and taste it are grateful for the introduction. There's some confusion about the name, but if you ask for *Pelargonium graveolens* at a garden center, they should be able to help you out.

Rosemary *(Rosmarinus officinalis)*: this shrub is often planted in remembrance of someone or to mark a special occasion. There's a common belief that it only thrives in a house where the woman wears the pants! It goes particularly well with lamb or chicken and even fish, which surprises people. The wooden stems can be used as kebab skewers and dried sticks can be thrown on a fire in the winter for a delicious smell. As with sage and thyme, it is very good to add to bread dough. We also love rosemary and chocolate mousse, spinach and rosemary soups, stewed apples with rosemary, and rosemary in syrups for lemonade. Rosemary tea is worth knowing about, too, since it allegedly helps your memory. Rosemary is the first herb to flower in the spring, so we garnish all sorts of dishes with its pretty purple-blue flowers.

Sage (Salvia): this strong, robustly flavored herb is most commonly used in this part of the world in things like Sage and Onion Stuffing (see page 278). The leaves are delicious crisped up in oil or butter and sprinkled over risotto or pasta. Because of its robust flavor, sage must be used judiciously. A sage infusion has numerous medicinal uses and has astringent, antiseptic, and anti-irritant properties, as does sage jelly. Because of its digestive properties, it's good to cook it with rich and fatty meats like pork. Sage's pretty bluish-purple flowers are good to plant for bees and can be used as garnish as well. A bunch of sage (or basil) in a room discourages flies. Sage is antiseptic and kills off bugs in meat as it cooks. It is used in sausage because of its preservative properties. For a delicious little snack, pick fresh sage leaves and sandwich an anchovy between two leaves. Then beat a little egg white, just enough to break it up. Then dip the "sandwich" and cook in hot oil until crisp. Eat immediately – a bit fussy to make, but you won't be able to stop eating them!

Sweet cicely (Myrrhis odorata): this underused herb has a high sugar content and is in season in late spring and early summer. Its lovely fernlike leaves are wonderful for crystallizing and using as garnish. We use it in poaching liquids for fruits, too. In his book, *Wild Food*, Roger Phillips quotes a 16th-century text saying, it's "very good for old people that are dull and without courage; it rejoiceth and comforteth the heart and increases their lust and strength." So I must try that soon!

Tarragon (Artemisia dracunculus): another of the *fines herbes* (parsley, chervil, chives, and tarragon) that are used in French cooking, for example, omelettes and herb sauces. The two most common varieties of tarragon are French and Russian; French has a superior taste. You can't buy seeds for French tarragon; you have to buy plants, because they're propagated by root

Above: *Sage.*

Above: *Sweet cicely.*

cuttings. The flavor of tarragon is fragrant and perfumed, so it can be eaten cold in salads, but is also wonderful in sauces, soups, and fruit poaching syrups – and is an essential ingredient in Béarnaise Sauce (see page 173). Tarragon and chicken is a marriage made in heaven.

Thyme (Thymus): this is a huge family of plants and you could have a thyme garden of its own, but when you're starting off, try common thyme. Variegated lemon thyme is also worth considering for its distinct lemon flavor, which is good for stuffing, roasted vegetables, and fish. It's also useful in bouquet garni for stocks, soups, and stews. Thyme dries really well; just place it near a radiator. I dry thyme on the shelf over my stove. You can scatter the flowers over potato salad or green salad and use them to decorate little dishes of chicken liver pâté, which include thyme leaves. Thyme tea is good for hangovers; try it sometime!

Salads and Microgreens

Aside from herbs, one of the most worthwhile things to grow is salad leaves. At their simplest, these can be grown in a seed tray, even in a high-rise apartment. I know that it's very tempting and convenient to buy a little bag of mixed leaves at the supermarket, but you may be interested to know that they are often washed in a chlorine solution 18 times stronger than the solution used for swimming pools.

You can buy a package of mesclun or "salad easy" seeds, in which you get a mixture of little lettuces and salad leaves and sometimes tiny spring onions. These are based on a Provençal mixture (mesclun, in fact, means "mixture" in a local dialect) and might include arugula, dandelion, lamb's lettuce, purslane, chervil, mustard greens, and endive, and if you grow it yourself, you'll be amazed by how infinitely better it is than the gas-flushed bags of mesclun you can buy at the supermarket.

You can sprinkle the seed mixture onto a seed tray in potting compost. Within four or five days in the summer (a bit longer in winter) the little leaves will emerge and you can use them in the beginning as microgreens. Then, as they get bigger, cut them and they'll come again, and you'll get a less abundant second growth and a rather straggly third growth. After the third growth, throw them into the compost and start again. You can also grow lettuce plants in big, individual pots

Above: *Mixed salad leaves.*

on the windowsill and harvest individual leaves on the outside whenever you need them.

Organic salad leaves will keep very well in the fridge for four to five days, provided they're not bruised during washing. You can keep them in a damp kitchen towel, damp paper towel, or simply a plastic bag and put them in the vegetable crisper of the refrigerator.

We serve green salad with lunch and dinner, both in the Cookery School and at family meals – it's a vital and integral part of the way we eat. Ideally, a green salad should reflect the seasons; in the late spring and early summer, the more delicate leaves appear (and we add wild garlic and sorrel and pennywort); in the winter, we use robust leaves like kale, cabbage, or sprouting broccoli.

A plate of lettuces and salad leaves after a main course has the magical effect of making you feel less full, so you have room for dessert. People simply don't believe me when I say this, and very often when you ask someone if they'd like a green salad, they say "No, I'm too full." But when you feel too full, you ought to have a green salad because it has this effect.

Despite my best efforts of over 25 years of articles, television programs, and teaching thousands of cooks, it's still very difficult to get a good green salad in a restaurant. More often than not, when you ask for a green salad you get a mixed salad, loaded with cucumbers, peppers, and tomatoes or even kiwi, and this definitely won't make you feel less full.

Salad dressing

Many people seem to think that making a salad dressing is a lot more complicated than it is. All you need are really good-quality ingredients – three parts of a terrific, cold-pressed extra virgin olive oil to one part of a high-quality wine vinegar. Be just as finicky about your vinegar as you are with your olive oil, because a bad vinegar can ruin a beautiful olive oil. Then you just need a pinch of sea salt and freshly ground black pepper. Whisk it all together and anoint the leaves with it. If you like, you can add crushed garlic, chopped herbs, a little mustard, and some honey. Extra sweetness is particularly welcome in the winter when you may be adding kale and finely shredded cabbage to your salad.

On the next page are a few recipes for salad dressings, so you'll never have to use a store-bought version again. Dressings in the supermarket often use terrible oils and are very expensive. It's a welcome development that we can now buy good-quality bottles of extra virgin olive oil in the supermarket, but I'm sorry to say you're not likely to find the best quality there. As with vinegar, you use so little of it at a time that it's really worth getting the best one you can.

All salad dressings are best when freshly made. If you would like to keep them for a day or two, don't add the fresh herbs and garlic until just before use.

Edible flowers

Many people don't realize that the flowers of lots of plants are edible, too. We use them to add a little extra magic to our food. They make a pretty garnish, and we also scatter them into soups and salads, incorporate them into appetizers, add to ice creams, and freeze them inside ice cubes to serve with summer drinks.

Edible flowers from the garden include nasturtiums, carnations, fragrant roses, camomile, pansies, marigolds, and nigella.

You can eat the flowers of many vegetables such as zucchinis, fava beans, peas, fennel, and arugula.

Herb flowers such as chive, dill, borage, sage, thyme, sweet cicely, and many more are all decorative and delicious.

In fact, the nasturtium is a powerful antioxidant and is incredibly versatile, since all parts of the plant are edible, not just the flower. When capers were not so easily accessible, people pickled nasturtium seeds and used them as a substitute. Capers are widely available now, but it's still fun to pick nasturtium seeds to add to salads. You might also want to try nasturtium leaf sandwiches by laying nasturtium leaves, or flowers, or both, on buttered white, sliced bread or on bread with a little cream cheese.

You can also forage for edible wild flowers such as elderflowers, violets, and wild garlic flowers – see page 32 in the Foraging chapter.

Below: *Nasturtiums are one of the many edible flowers we use.*

SUMMER SALAD WITH A CLASSIC FRENCH DRESSING

In the summer, you might use a selection or combination of any of the following:

lettuces and **salad leaves**: butterhead, oak leaf, iceberg, mesclun, lollo rosso, frisée, mizuna, mibuna, red orach, arugula, edible chrysanthemum leaves, young nasturtium leaves, wild sorrel leaves, or French sorrel
flowers: wild garlic flowers, nasturtium flowers, marigold petals, chive flowers, borage flowers, violas, zucchini blossoms, fava bean flowers
herbs: herb leaves such as lemon balm, mint, and flat parsley; golden or annual marjoram; salad burnet; tiny sprigs of dill, tarragon, or mint
vegetable leaves: green pea shoots, fava bean tips, tiny chard, spinach, and beet leaves

For the French Dressing

MAKES 1 CUP

¼ **cup wine vinegar**
¾ **cup extra virgin olive oil or a mixture of olive and other oils, e.g., sunflower and peanut**
1 **level teaspoon mustard (Dijon or English)**
1 **large garlic clove**
1 **spring onion**
sprig of parsley
sprig of watercress
1 **level teaspoon salt**
few grinds of fresh pepper

Choose a mixture of leaves, herbs, and edible flowers in season. Carefully separate and detach the lettuce leaves from the head (rough handling will damage the leaves). Snip off any pieces of stalks and throw in the hen or compost bucket. Gently agitate the leaves in lots of cold water in a deep sink so that any soil or little bugs will drift down to the bottom. Dry in small quantities in a large salad spinner. Transfer to a deep salad bowl.

Make the dressing by putting all the ingredients into a blender and run at medium speed for about 1 minute.

Just before serving, add the edible flowers. Use just enough dressing to make the leaves glisten when tossed with salad tongs. The salad should not be tossed in dressing until just before eating; otherwise, the leaves will wilt and lose their fresh texture and flavor.

Left: *Wild arugula.*

WINTER SALAD WITH HERB AND HONEY DRESSING

In the winter, you might use a selection or combination of any of the following:

lamb's lettuce
kale, stemmed and torn into bite-sized pieces
shredded cabbage
broccoli greens
winter purslane
winter watercress
radicchio

For the Herb and Honey Dressing

MAKES 1 CUP

¾ **cup extra virgin olive oil**
¼ **cup cider vinegar**
1 **teaspoon honey**
1 **garlic clove, crushed**
2 **tablespoons mixed herbs, e.g., parsley, chives, mint, watercress, thyme, all freshly chopped**
salt and freshly ground black pepper

Put all the dressing ingredients into a screw-top jar, adding salt and freshly ground pepper to taste. Shake well to emulsify before use; otherwise, blend all the ingredients together in a food processor or blender for a few seconds. As a variation, you could use 4 tablespoons fresh lemon juice or wine vinegar instead of cider vinegar.

Tomatoes

Tomatoes grown at home are so much more delicious than store-bought ones. Even people in high-rise apartments can put a grow bag – a plastic bag filled with compost that you plant your tomatoes directly into – on a balcony, which will produce a fine crop. As they ripen on the vine, they'll gradually swell and color, and it's a real thrill picking them off after the tantalizing wait of watching them grow. Just make sure to remove the side shoots, otherwise the plant will produce lots of leaves instead of fruit.

It's well known that when tomatoes are allowed to ripen fully on the vine they have infinitely more flavor than when they ripen in a box in transit. However, not all vine tomatoes that one buys are worth the extra money, so I suspect that some producers now pick off the entire truss of tomatoes underripe and put them in boxes so they can charge extra. Do not be conned – only pay more if they actually taste better.

Be really fussy about the varieties you choose. Sun Gold and Gardener's Delight are tried and tested for the home gardener, and a lot of the cherry tomatoes have better flavor than larger ones. At the Cookery School, we grow between 20 and 40 varieties every year, including many heirloom varieties and old varieties no longer considered commercially viable.

If you grow tomatoes, you may notice a glut in late summer or early fall, but this is when they're at their most intensely flavored. When you grow your own tomatoes, each and every one is precious. There are myriad ways to preserve and concentrate those sunny flavors for winter use, but if you have the freezer space the best thing to do is to remove the calyx (green stem at the top) and freeze the tomatoes whole, then take them out as you need them. They tend to need a bit more sugar when they come out of the freezer, and are slightly more watery, but are perfectly suited to ratatouille, tomato fondue, peperonata, and soup (cook them with the lid off). When you take them out of the freezer, all you need to do is drop them, a few at a time, into cold water for a couple of seconds; the skin will rub off immediately when you take them out of the water.

Above: *Don't waste even one green tomato – there are lots of good things you can make with them.*

To peel fresh tomatoes

First prick them with the tip of a knife and put them into a deep bowl. Bring a kettle of water to a boil and cover the tomatoes completely with boiling water. Count to 10 slowly. Fish one out and try to peel it – the peel should come away easily. If so, drain the rest immediately and peel them. Be careful not to leave them in the boiling water for too long or they'll semicook and you'll lose a lot of the precious outer layer of the tomato.

Left: *Cherry tomatoes.*

Left: *Oven-roasted Tomatoes.*

of the year it will be worth it. Another use for a food mill is ricing potatoes ·
MAKES 1½ QUARTS

6lb very ripe tomatoes
1 medium onion, chopped
good pinch of salt
a few twists of black pepper
1 teaspoon sugar

Cut the tomatoes into quarters and put into a stainless-steel saucepan with the onion, salt, freshly ground pepper, and sugar. Cook on a gentle heat for 10–15 minutes, until the tomatoes are soft (no water is needed). Put through the fine blade of the food mill or a nylon sieve.

Allow to get cold and refrigerate or freeze. We freeze tomato paste in milk containers, but any containers of a volume that suits your lifestyle would be fine. Ensure that you allow room for expansion when the liquid freezes; otherwise, the container may burst.

HOMEMADE TOMATO SOUP

In this recipe, basil or mint may be added, and coconut milk can be substituted for Béchamel sauce with delicious results. Note that fresh milk cannot be added to the soup, since the acidity in the tomatoes will cause it to curdle. For tomato and basil soup or tomato mint soup, simply add 2 tablespoons of your chosen herb at the same time as you add the sugar ·
SERVES 8

OVEN-ROASTED TOMATOES

Only worth doing if you have a glut of superripe tomatoes. Use in salads, pasta, or sauces. It is possible to do them much faster at 300ºF for about 2 hours, but the result is not as good.

very large ripe tomatoes or
**   round cherry tomatoes**
salt and freshly ground black
**   pepper**
extra virgin olive oil
basil leaves (optional)

Preheat the oven to its lowest setting. Cut the tomatoes in half if large and sprinkle with a little salt and extra virgin olive oil. Place cut-side up on a flat baking pan. Roast in the oven for around 5–6 hours or until they look wizened – the roasting time will depend on the quality and size of tomatoes. Add extra virgin olive oil and basil leaves (if using), and a bit of ground pepper to serve. If not using immediately, store in sterilized jars in the refrigerator until needed.

TOMATO PASTE

Tomato paste is one of the best ways to preserve the flavor of ripe summer tomatoes for winter use in soups, stews, casseroles, and tagines. A food mill is really the only gadget that works for this. So buy one and even if it sits in the back of your cupboard for the rest

1 onion, finely chopped

2 tablespoons butter OR 4
    tablespoons extra virgin
    olive oil

5 cups homemade Tomato Paste
    (see previous recipe), made
    from very ripe tomatoes

1¼ cups Béchamel Sauce (see page
    116)

1¼ cups Chicken Stock (see page
    262) or Vegetable Stock (see
    page 390)

salt, freshly ground black pepper
    and sugar

½ cup heavy cream (optional)

Sweat the onion in the butter or oil on a gentle heat until soft but not colored. Add the tomato paste, Béchamel sauce, and stock. Season with salt, freshly ground pepper, and sugar. Bring to a boil and simmer for a few minutes.

Purée, taste, and dilute more, if necessary. Bring back to a boil, correct the seasoning, and serve with the addition of a little cream, if necessary.

Four good things to serve with tomato soup:
· Drizzle with Basil Oil (see page 424), Basil Pesto (see page 29), or Tapenade (see page 340)
· Gujerati spices – heat 4 tablespoons olive oil in a pan, add 4 chopped garlic cloves, 1 tablespoon black mustard seeds, and ½–1 chile. Sizzle and then spoon over the top of each bowl. Serve immediately.
· Serve a crispy pancetta slice with each helping
· Tapenade or pesto finger sandwiches

HEIRLOOM TOMATO SALAD WITH BASIL, OLIVE OIL, AND HONEY

The Ballymaloe Cookery School stall at the Midleton Farmers' Market has a unique selection of heirloom tomatoes in all shapes and sizes. Red, yellow, black, striped, round, pear shaped, and oval. They make a divine tomato salad and are wonderful with fresh buffalo mozzarella and lots of fresh basil ·

SERVES 4

8 very ripe heirloom tomatoes

salt and freshly ground black
    pepper

3 tablespoons extra virgin olive oil

1–2 tablespoons lemon juice

2 teaspoons honey

2 teaspoons fresh basil leaves, torn

Cut the tomatoes into ¼in thick slices. Sprinkle with salt and pepper. Mix the oil, lemon juice, and honey together. Add the basil leaves, pour the mixture over the tomatoes, and toss gently. Taste and correct the seasoning, if necessary. A little freshly squeezed lemon juice enhances the flavor in a very delicious way.

PAPPA AL POMODORO

This Tuscan bread soup may not seem like a soup as we know it. Made with sweet, ripe tomatoes, good bread, and extra virgin olive oil, it is the most sublime comfort food. It is also a delicious way to use up leftover bread, and although traditionally it is made with Italian country bread, white soda bread also works remarkably well ·

SERVES 5-6

extra virgin olive oil

2 garlic cloves, peeled and
    chopped

5lb very ripe sweet tomatoes,
    peeled, seeded, and chopped

2½ x 14oz cans organic plum
    tomatoes, chopped

⅓ cup extra virgin olive oil

sea salt, freshly ground black
    pepper, and a pinch of sugar

2 loaves stale sourdough bread or
    white soda bread

To Serve

lots of fresh basil leaves

¼ cup extra virgin olive oil

Heat about 5 tablespoons of olive oil in a heavy saucepan over medium heat. Add the garlic and cook gently for a few minutes. Just as the garlic begins to turn golden, add the tomatoes. Simmer for about 30 minutes, stirring occasionally, until the tomatoes become rich and concentrated. Season with salt, pepper, and sugar. Add 1¼ cups of water and bring to a boil.

Cut most of the crust off the loaves of bread. Break or cut the remainder into large chunks. Add the bread to the tomato mixture and stir until the bread absorbs the liquid, adding more boiling water if it is too thick. Remove from the heat and leave to cool slightly.

Stir torn basil leaves into the soup with ¼ cup of extra virgin olive oil. Leave to sit for 5–10 minutes before serving to allow the bread to absorb the flavor of the basil and olive oil. Drizzle a little more extra virgin olive oil over each bowl.

TOMATO FONDUE

Tomato fondue has a number of uses. We serve it as a vegetable, a sauce for pasta, filling for omelettes, and topping for pizza. It is vital for the success of this dish that the onions are completely soft before the tomatoes are added. In the winter, you can use canned or frozen tomatoes (see page 375), but they need to be cooked for longer · **SERVES ABOUT 6**

1 tablespoon extra virgin olive oil
4oz onions, sliced
1 garlic clove, crushed
2lb very ripe tomatoes, peeled
salt, freshly ground black pepper, and sugar to taste
2 tablespoons of any or a combination of the following: freshly chopped mint, thyme, parsley, lemon balm, marjoram, or torn basil
a few drops of balsamic vinegar (optional)

Heat the oil in a casserole dish or a stainless-steel saucepan. Add the onions and garlic and toss until coated. Cover and sweat on a gentle heat until the onions and garlic are soft but not colored. Slice the tomatoes and add with all the juice to the onions. Season with salt, freshly ground pepper, and sugar. Add a generous sprinkling of herbs.

Cook, uncovered, for about 10 minutes, or until the tomatoes soften.

A few drops of balsamic vinegar added at the end of cooking greatly enhance the flavor.

Variations

TOMATO AND CHILE FONDUE
Add 1–2 chopped fresh chiles to the onions when sweating.

PENNE WITH TOMATO FONDUE
Toss 1lb of cooked penne or spaghetti with the Tomato and Chile Fondue.

TOMATO, BEAN, AND ROSEMARY STEW
Add 1 x 14oz can of navy beans or black-eyed peas and 1 tablespoon of chopped rosemary to the main recipe.

TOMATO AND PECORINO TARTE TATIN

This uses a lot of tomatoes, so it's the thing to make when you have a glut of superripe tomatoes at the end of the crop, in September. We also may use Irish farmhouse cheeses as a substitute for pecorino (Desmond, Gabriel, or an aged Coolea). This recipe may be cooked ahead and reheated before serving · **SERVES 8**

savory Shortcrust Pastry (see page 250) made with 1⅓ cups flour
1lb ripe tomatoes
salt
4 tablespoons butter
12oz onion, chopped
½–1 red chile, chopped
2 garlic cloves, crushed
2lb very ripe tomatoes, peeled, seeded, and chopped
salt, freshly ground black pepper, and a little sugar
8 fresh basil leaves, torn
½ cup pecorino cheese, grated
9in ceramic pie pan
silicone parchment paper and a little melted butter

Preheat the oven to 375°F.

First, make the pastry, then flatten it into a round, wrap in plastic wrap, and leave to rest in the fridge for 15 minutes. Peel, seed, and slice the tomatoes. Sprinkle with salt and leave to drain in a nylon sieve for 10–15 minutes.

Melt the butter in a wide sauté pan, add the onion, chile, and garlic. Cook until soft and just beginning to caramelize. Add the sliced tomatoes and season well with salt, freshly ground pepper, and a little sugar. Simmer until reduced to a thickish paste. Add the torn basil leaves. Taste and correct the seasoning.

Line the base of a ceramic quiche or pie pan with a circle of silicone parchment paper. Brush generously with melted butter. Arrange the drained tomato slices in an overlapping pattern in concentric circles over the base of the pan. Spread the cooked filling evenly over the tomato slices. Scatter with the pecorino cheese. Top with a circle of savory shortcrust pastry.

Bake in the oven until the pastry is golden brown and cooked through. Remove and leave to cool a little before inverting the pie onto a hot plate and removing the pie pan and the silicone paper. Serve warm or at room temperature with a good green salad.

Potatoes

Ironic as it may seem, it is incredibly difficult to find a decent potato (by my standards) these days. That is, unless you grow your own or have access to a small grower or local gardener who has a passion for old varieties. All of the more modern varieties are bred for shelf life and ease of packaging rather than flavor and texture and many of their quirky attributes have been bred out of them. We don't grow a big acreage of potatoes, maybe six or seven varieties, depending on the year and the seed available. We are, however, fortunate to live in an area where several farmers still grow small quantities of potatoes, using very little or no nitrogen, for local markets. They cost more to produce, so the growers ought to be paid more so they can stay in business.

Above: *Even if you are a seasoned gardener, digging your own potatoes is still thrilling – these are an organic variety called Santa.*

One of the most exciting things of all is growing and digging your own potatoes, and I urge those who have never grown anything before to try planting a few potatoes. I love growing old varieties – I bring a few freshly dug potatoes into the kitchen, scrub them up, and drop them into a pot of well-salted boiling water or, better still, seawater. We are fortunate to have an old greenhouse, so we plant a crop in mid-December. The first new potatoes are ready by about the end of April. We dig well-rotted compost and seaweed into the soil before planting. The potatoes are then sown directly into the rich, fertile soil. We always grow organic and blight-resistant varieties, and in the past we have found this to give reasonably good results. (It has to be said that just because it's organic doesn't necessarily mean it will have a fantastic flavor and texture.) My favorite early varieties for our area are Home Guard, Sharpe's Express, and British Queens.

Our own greenhouse crop is usually finished by mid-May, after which we have a hungry gap until our neighbor Patrick Walsh's are ready to dig in mid-June. If you have even a simple tunnel you could grow a few short drills of early spuds, too. Other varieties worth growing are Russets, Red (Durangoes and Sangres), Yukon Golds, Kerr's Pinks, and Fingerlings.

Floury vs. waxy

As everybody knows, in Ireland we love our potatoes, especially the dry, floury kind, which my son-in-law says is because they're the best ones

to soak up plenty of Irish butter!

The texture of potatoes varies depending on the variety. Floury potatoes can be quite a challenge to cook since they tend to burst, sometimes well before they are fully cooked in the center. In recent years, many of the varieties developed for commercial production are more waxy in texture, and they can be boiled for hours without bursting.

Fingerling potatoes are waxy in texture and excellent for the home gardener because they are incredibly prolific. They're particularly fun to grow if you have children, because they grow into knobbly shapes. They're wonderful in potato salads, and also just boiled and eaten with sea salt and butter.

Potato storage

Potatoes should always be stored away from the light. Light turns them green and encourages them to sprout, which is only desirable if you want to plant them. Green potatoes are toxic, so compost or discard them.

Main crop varieties can be stored for months in a dark, vermin-free shed. Spread in a thin layer on the ground and check them regularly. They need to be covered with an old sack to exclude the light. Pick out and compost or discard any deteriorating tubers every few days.

You can also store potatoes in a pit, or potato "clamp," in your yard. Lay a thick layer of straw on the ground in a rectangular shape. Pick over the potatoes and remove any that show signs of deterioration. Heap them into a mound onto the

Left *Potatoes will happily grow in a large container – enough for a meal for the whole family in one pot.*

straw. Cover completely with a thick layer of more straw and pile a thick layer of soil on top. Use the dirt from around the clamp to create a drainage trench.

How to sprout or "chit" potatoes

In late winter or early spring, examine any remaining potatoes and place them in an old egg carton or seed tray with the maximum number of eyes facing upward. Put the trays in a cool, frost-free room. Keep them out of direct sunlight. After a few weeks, they will start to sprout and by about 5 or 6 weeks, the sprouts should be about ½in long. They should be strong and dark in appearance. If they are pale and spindly they have insufficient light and may also be too warm. If, on the other hand, the sprouts are tiny or slow to appear, the temperature may be too cold, so try increasing it to encourage stronger growth.

Urban gardening: growing potatoes

Early varieties such as Russet Norkotah, Dark Red Norland, Caribe, Irish Cobbler, Red Pontiac, Superior, Early Rose, and Frontier Russet are best for growing in containers. Choose a large bucket or tub or tank at least 14in across and 12in deep with good drainage holes. Even a plastic crate or empty compost bag may be used, but drainage holes in the base are essential. Find some bits of broken flowerpots, crockery, or sharp stones to put at the base of the container so the drainage holes don't get clogged with soil or compost.

Place a 5–6in layer of soil and compost mixed in the bottom of the container. Place one to three sprouted potatoes, depending on the variety, on top of the soil (if the potatoes are large, they can be divided in two as long as each piece has several sprouts). Cover the tubers with a further 6in of soil and compost (or all compost). Water until the soil is well moistened. The container should be in a bright, sheltered spot. Keep it weed-free and water it if necessary (this will depend on the rainfall).

When the shoots grow to about 6in tall, earth up the plant(s) with a further 5in of soil and compost. This will prevent the light from reaching the potatoes and stops them from turning green. Continue adding soil and compost in this way until you run out of depth in your container. After the plant flowers, you may need to water the potatoes to help them swell.

Another alternative is to get a few old tires and put them on top of each other and fill with soil and compost, as above, and plant the potatoes. As they begin to grow, add another tire and some more soil. Three or four tires will be sufficient.

POTATO SOUP

It is vital for the success of this and other soups based on the basic soup formula (see opposite) to season the potato and onion base well at the beginning. One can correct the seasoning at the end, but it's very difficult to get it right if no salt was added in the initial stage · SERVES 6

4 tablespoons butter
1¼lb potatoes, peeled and cut into ⅓in cubes
¾ cup diced onions, peeled and cut into ⅓in cubes
salt and freshly ground black pepper
5 cups Chicken Stock or Vegetable Stock (see pages 262 and 390)
½ cup whole milk
freshly chopped herbs and herb flowers (optional)

Melt the butter in a heavy saucepan. When it foams, add the potatoes and onions and toss them in the butter until well coated. Season with salt and a few grinds of pepper. Cover with a piece of parchment paper and the lid of the saucepan and sweat on a gentle heat for about 10 minutes.

Meanwhile, bring the stock to a boil. When the vegetables are tender but not colored, add the stock and continue to cook until the vegetables are soft. Purée the soup in a blender or food processor. Taste and adjust the seasoning. Thin with the milk to the required consistency.

Serve sprinkled with a few freshly chopped herbs and herb flowers, if available.

BAKED POTATOES

New potatoes don't bake well, but Yukon Golds and Kerr's Pinks are perfect for baking. Never put foil around baked potatoes, it's a ridiculous affectation that is counterproductive to the flavor and texture.

8 x 8oz baking potatoes, e.g. Yukon Golds or Kerr's Pinks
sea salt and butter

Preheat the oven to 400°F.

Scrub the skins of the potatoes very well. Prick each potato 3–4 times and bake for 1 hour or so, depending on the size. When cooked, serve immediately while the skins are still crisp and eat with lots of butter and sea salt.

Good things to serve with baked potatoes
• Melted Irish farmhouse cheeses such as Gubbeen or Ardrahan
• Sour cream, lime zest, and sweet chile sauce
• Smoked mackerel, horseradish cream, and dill
• Warm chorizo and sour cream

BASIC SOUP FORMULA

Many of the soups that we make at Ballymaloe are made on a simple formula that Myrtle Allen passed on to me: 1 part diced onion, 1 part diced potato, 3 parts vegetables of your choice, and 5 parts stock or a mixture of stock, water, and milk. We call it the 1:1:3:5 method. The base of sweated onion and potato flavors and thickens the soup, and then you can choose any vegetable in season, either one or a mixture of two or three.

If you choose one vegetable, like carrot, you can just make a straightforward carrot soup or use herbs, spices, or other flavors to ring the changes: carrot and mint, carrot and coriander, or carrot and orange, for example. Or you could make a root vegetable soup using carrot, parsnips, celeriac, and Jerusalem artichokes. Or you could use green vegetables: greens, salad leaves, or a mixture, anything from spinach to Brussels sprout tops to fava bean shoots to radish leaves to wild garlic or watercress. If you're making a green soup, add the greens at the end, so they don't overcook and cook, uncovered, for 3–4 minutes (depending on the tenderness of the vegetable).

We use a cup or a mug to measure each item (it doesn't matter what size you use as long as you use the same cup each time) but if you'd rather weigh, see opposite for a simple potato soup based on the formula.

You can play around with the proportion of potatoes and onions in the recipe; if you want it more oniony, just add more onions. Or you can drizzle Wild Garlic Pesto (see page 29), Arugula Pesto (see page 29), or Harissa (see page 342) over the top. Garnish with Croutons (see page 579), crispy chorizo or cabanossi sausage, or Guanciale (see page 308). One of our all-time favorites is homemade Potato Chips (see page 387), piled on top of the soup with sizzling garlic butter poured over them.

FROZEN SOUP

It's always worth making a bit more soup than you need and freezing the surplus in small containers – we use tubs large enough for two generous helpings. This size is really handy because it defrosts quickly in an emergency. You might also want to pour some into ice cube trays. Once frozen, put the cubes into a plastic bag and refreeze. They defrost in minutes. This is a great way of having portions on hand for feeding babies, but reduce the seasoning.

TRADITIONAL IRISH BOILED POTATOES

Here is the best way to cook most potato varieties, so they don't dissolve into a mush before they are fully cooked. It's not at all traditional, but a Chinese steamer (with well-salted water underneath) works really well, and the potatoes remain intact. Many people now peel potatoes before they boil them, but it's worth remembering that they have considerably more flavor if you keep the skins on. Plus, there's less waste, and most of the nutrients are just underneath the skin ·
SERVES 4

2lb potatoes such as Yukon Golds, Kerr's Pink, or Russets
salt

3 teaspoons of salt to every 5 cups water

Put the potatoes in a deep saucepan, cover with fresh, cold water, and add salt. Cover and bring to a boil and continue to cook over a medium heat about 15 minutes, until half-cooked. Pour off most of the water, leaving about 1in liquid in the saucepan. Reduce the heat, cover, and leave the potatoes to steam for the remainder of the cooking time, at least another 15 minutes, until a skewer goes through the center easily.

Serve in a hot serving dish with lots of good butter or a terrific olive oil and a sprinkle of sea salt.

CRISPY POTATO SKINS WITH DIPS

This is a way of using what Cork people, who eat their potatoes skin and all, would consider to be the best part of the potato · **SERVES 8**

8 large potatoes, e.g., Yukon Golds or Kerr's Pink
melted butter or extra virgin olive oil
salt and freshly ground black pepper

Preheat the oven to 400°F.

Prick the potatoes once or twice with the tip of a knife. Bake for 45–60 minutes, depending on size. When the potatoes are cooked, slice in half lengthwise and scoop the flesh into a bowl. Use for mashed potatoes, potato cakes, or fish cakes.

Increase the heat to 450°F. Cut the skins into 2 or 3 pieces, depending on size, and arrange in a single layer in a roasting pan. Brush well with melted butter or extra virgin olive oil, and season with salt and freshly ground pepper. Cook for 10–15 minutes or until crisp and delicious.

Serve while still warm with a selection of dips, such as Sweet Chile Sauce (see page 433); crab mayonnaise and cucumber; tomato, chile, and cilantro salsa; sour cream and lime juice; or melted Gubbeen, Ardrahan, or Vacherin du Mont d'Or cheese.

ROAST POTATOES

A big roasting pan of crusty roast potatoes always invokes a positive response. Everyone loves them. They are easy to achieve but I still get asked over and over for the secret of crunchy golden "roasties." So here are my top tips:

• Grow or seek out good-quality dry, floury potatoes such as Yukon Golds or Kerr's Pinks. New potatoes do not produce good roast potatoes.
• For best results, peel the potatoes just before roasting. Resist the temptation to soak them in water, or, understandably, they will be soggy, due to the water they absorb. This has become common practice when people want to prepare ahead, not just for roasting, but also before boiling.
• After peeling, dry the potatoes meticulously with a kitchen towel or paper towel. Otherwise, even when tossed in fat or oil, they will stick to the roasting pan. Consequently, when you turn them over, as you will need to do halfway through the cooking, the crispy part underneath will stick to the pan.
• If you wish to prepare potatoes ahead, there are two options. Peel and dry each potato carefully, toss in extra virgin olive oil or fat of your choice, put into a bowl, cover, and refrigerate. Alternatively, put into a plastic bag, twist the end, and refrigerate until needed. They will keep for 5 or 6 hours or overnight without discoloring.

Roast potatoes may be cooked in extra virgin olive oil, top-quality sunflower oil, duck fat, goose fat, pork fat (lard), or beef drippings. Each gives a delicious but different flavor.

Depending on the flavor and texture you like, choose from the following cooking methods:

1 Toss the potatoes in the chosen fat and cook.

2 If you prefer a crunchier crust, put the peeled potatoes into a deep saucepan, cover with cold water, bring to a boil, simmer for 2–4 minutes only, and drain. Dry each blanched potato and score the surface of each one with a fork. Then toss in the chosen oil or fat, season with salt, and cook in a single layer in a heavy roasting pan in a preheated oven at 450°F.

3 Drain the blanched potatoes, then put the saucepan with the potatoes inside over medium heat, and shake the pot to dry the potatoes and fluff the blanched surface. Toss in your chosen oil or fat, season with salt, and roast as above.

NOTE: some cooks, to create an even crunchier crust, like to toss the potatoes in a little flour seasoned with salt and freshly ground pepper, and maybe a pinch of cayenne pepper or smoked paprika.

Variation

RUSTIC ROAST POTATOES

For a more nutritious rustic roast potato, scrub the potato well, cut the unpeeled potatoes into wedges, toss in oil or fat, season with salt and freshly ground pepper. Cook until soft in the center and crusty on the outside, about 20–30 minutes.

ROAST POTATO SALAD

Here's a forgotten way of using up leftover roast potatoes · SERVES 8

2lb roast potatoes
extra virgin olive oil
1 tablespoon rosemary, freshly chopped
salt and freshly ground black pepper

FOR THE DRESSING
¼ cup homemade Mayonnaise (see page 252)
3 tablespoons parsley, freshly chopped
3 tablespoons scallions, chopped
4 tablespoons French Dressing (see page 374) or other French dressing

Preheat the oven to 475°F.

Cut the leftover potatoes into large cubes and toss in the olive oil and rosemary. Season with salt and freshly ground pepper.

Mix the mayonnaise with the chopped parsley, scallions, and crushed garlic. Thin with French dressing. Toss the potatoes in the dressing. Season with salt and freshly ground pepper. Taste and correct the seasoning if necessary.

TINY POTATOES DIPPED IN AIOLI

When you grow your own potatoes, you won't want to waste even one, so use this recipe for the smallest potatoes in your crop · SERVES 6-8

2lb small, waxy new potatoes
Aioli (see page 96)

Cook the potatoes in boiling, well-salted water. If they are a variety that is inclined to burst, pour off most of the water about halfway through, then cover, and steam until fully cooked.

To serve, thin out the aioli with a couple of tablespoons of warm water and put in a small bowl in the center of a plate. Surround the aioli with new potatoes on wooden toothpicks. Guests can then dip the warm potatoes in the aioli. Simple and delicious.

CHAMP

I've come across versions of champ that include sweated or boiled nettles, crispy onions (onions fried in butter, pork or beef fat), buttered leek, wild garlic, and watercress, and a particularly delicious summer version in the North of Ireland that includes fresh peas and parsley (this has become one of our favorites). Put out a little bowl of champ for the fairies on Halloween, preferably under a whitethorn or hawthorn tree. In Ireland, this was done in the past to keep away the mischievous fairies for the rest of the year · SERVES 6

6–8 unpeeled potatoes, e.g., Yukon Golds or Kerr's Pinks
1½ cups whole milk
1 cup scallions, chopped (use the bulb and green stem)
4 tablespoons butter, or more
salt and freshly ground black pepper

Scrub the potatoes and keep them unpeeled. Cover with cold milk and bring slowly to a boil. Simmer for about 3–4 minutes, turn off the heat, and leave to infuse.

Remove the potatoes and peel them. While they are still hot, mash them with the boiling milk and chopped onions. Beat in the butter. Season to taste with salt and freshly ground pepper.

Serve in 1 large or 6 individual bowls with a dab of butter melting in the center.

Champ may be left aside and reheated later in a moderate oven, at 350°F. Cover with aluminum foil while it reheats, so that it doesn't get a skin.

COLCANNON

Colcannon is another traditional mashed potato dish like champ, but with kale or cabbage instead of scallions. For another variation try mashed parsnips, a delightful addition · **SERVES ABOUT 8**

1lb Savoy, spring cabbage, or kale (kale is the most traditional)
3lb potatoes, e.g., Yukon Golds or Kerr's Pinks
about 1 cup milk
salt and freshly ground black pepper
4 tablespoons butter

Scrub the potatoes, put them in a saucepan of cold water, add a good pinch of salt, and bring to a boil. When the potatoes are half-cooked after about 15 minutes, strain off two-thirds of the water, replace the lid on the saucepan, and put over a low heat, leaving the potatoes to steam until they are cooked.

Meanwhile, if using cabbage, remove the dark outer leaves, wash the remainder, cut it into quarters, remove the core, and cut finely across the grain. Boil in a little boiling water or bacon cooking water until soft. Drain and season with salt, freshly ground pepper, and a little butter.

When the potatoes are just cooked, put the milk and the finely chopped shallots into a saucepan and bring to a boil. Pull the peel off the potatoes and discard. Mash the potatoes quickly, while they are still warm, and beat in enough boiling milk to make a fluffy purée. (If you have a large quantity, put the potatoes in the bowl of a food mixer and beat with the flat beater.) Then stir in the cooked cabbage and taste for seasoning. For perfection, serve immediately in a hot dish with a lump of butter melting in the center.

Colcannon may be prepared ahead up to this point and reheated later in a moderate oven (350°F) for 20–25 minutes. Cover while reheating so it doesn't get too crusty on top.

Variation

POTATO CAKES – BUBBLE AND SQUEAK

Leftover champ or colcannon can be made into potato cakes and fried in bacon fat or olive oil – it's then called Bubble and Squeak. Potato cakes are a terrific way to eke out an expensive ingredient – a little morsel of something delicious like smoked eel or caviar or a plump oyster makes them into a feast. They can be served as a base for finger food, as an appetizer, or as an accompaniment for a main dish.

Good things to serve atop potato cakes:

• Sour cream and a cube of smoked cod roe
• Salmon, mackerel, eel, or cod roe
• Strips of roasted red pepper, piquillo, or peppadew peppers with sour cream, a basil leaf, and a drizzle of pesto
• Tuna fish and a cube of celery or cucumber, or sardines with mayo, dill, or sour cream
• Crispy bacon, pancetta, chorizo, or cabanossi
• A few cooked shrimp tossed in garlic and parsley butter

GRATIN OF POTATO, CHEDDAR CHEESE, AND SEASONAL GREENS

There are two kinds of gratins: the very rich gratin dauphinois version, and a less rich one, such as this, that uses stock rather than cream. If you want, you can make this gratin more substantial by adding cubed Guanciale (see page 308), bacon, Chorizo (see page 305), Pancetta (see page 486), or any leftover cooked meat you have around · **SERVES 6 AS A MAIN COURSE OR 8 AS AN ACCOMPANIMENT**

4lb potatoes, e.g., Yukon Golds or Kerr's Pinks, peeled
1 bunch scallions, watercress, arugula, or other greens in season
2 tablespoons butter
1½ cups or more mature Cheddar cheese, grated, or a mixture of

leftover grated cheese (even a
little blue cheese would be
delicious)
salt and freshly ground black
pepper
1¾ cup Chicken Stock or Vegetable
Stock (see pages 262 and 390)

oval ovenproof gratin dish –
12 x 2in

Preheat the oven to 450°F.

Slice the potatoes thinly, then
blanch, and refresh. Trim the
scallions and chop both the green
and white parts into ¼in slices with
scissors or a knife.

Rub an ovenproof dish thickly
with half the butter. Scatter with
some of the scallions or greens, then
a layer of potatoes, and then some
grated cheese. Season well. Continue
to build up the layers, finishing with
an overlapping layer of potatoes.
Pour in boiling stock, scatter with
the remaining cheese, and dot with
the remaining butter.

Bake in the oven for 1–1¼ hours,
until the potatoes are tender and the
top is brown and crispy.

GRATIN DAUPHINOIS

*The classic gratin dauphinois doesn't
have any odds and ends added to it,
but I find it serves as a great vehicle
for leftover cooked shrimp, little bits of
smoked mackerel or salmon, chorizo,
bacon, duck confit, or little crispy bits
of pork. It's filthy rich, but wonderful
with dark meats, such as a haunch of
venison or rib of beef or steak ·*
SERVES 6

2lb equally sized potatoes
salt and freshly ground black
pepper
1 cup whole milk
1 cup heavy cream
small garlic clove, peeled and
crushed
freshly grated nutmeg

Peel the potatoes and slice them into
rounds ¼in thick. Do not wash them.
Dab them dry with a cloth. Spread
them out on the countertop and
season with salt and freshly ground
pepper, mixing it in with your
hands. Pour the milk into a
saucepan, add the potatoes, and
bring to a boil. Cover, reduce the
heat, and simmer gently for 10
minutes.

Preheat the oven to 400°F.

Add the cream, garlic, and a
generous grating of nutmeg. Simmer
for another 20 minutes, stirring
occasionally, so the potatoes do not
stick to the saucepan. As soon as the
potatoes are cooked, take them out
with a slotted spoon and put them
into 1 large or 6 small ovenproof
dishes. Pour the creamy liquid over
them. Heat in a double boiler in the
oven for 10–20 minutes, until they
are bubbly and golden on top.

Variations
GRATIN LYONNAIS
Sweat about 1½ cups of sliced onion
in a little butter until it begins to
brown. Put a layer of onions
between two layers of potato and
continue as above.

Above: *Pink Fir Apple fingerling
potatoes.*

GRATIN SAVOYARD
Sprinkle ½ cup of grated Gruyère
and Parmesan or a sharp, hard
farmhouse cheese over the top of
the gratin before baking.

BLUE CHEESE AND
ROSEMARY GRATIN
Omit the garlic in the recipe above
and instead sprinkle about ¾ cup of
crumbled blue cheese (Gorgonzola,
Roquefort, Stilton, etc.) between two
layers of potato. If you like, sprinkle
1 tablespoon of freshly chopped
rosemary over the cheese before
adding more potatoes.

POTATO AND SCALLION SALAD

The secret of a good potato salad is to use freshly cooked potatoes and then season and toss in French dressing while they are still warm. This simple trick makes a phenomenal difference to the flavor of the finished salad. I've had delicious results with both waxy and floury potatoes, although waxy potatoes are definitely easier to handle

· SERVES 4–6

3½lb raw potatoes
salt and freshly ground black
    pepper
3 tablespoons chopped chives or
    scallions
3 tablespoons chopped parsley
⅔ cup French Dressing (see
    page 374)
⅔ cup homemade Mayonnaise
    (see page 252), thinned with
    a little water

Boil the potatoes in their skins in a large amount of well-salted water. Peel and dice the potatoes while they are still hot and put into a large, wide dish. Season with salt and pepper. Sprinkle immediately with the chives or scallions and the parsley. Drizzle over the French dressing and mix well. Leave to cool and then add the mayonnaise. Taste and correct seasoning.

Variations

MASHED POTATO SALAD
We "discovered" this recipe when a whole pot of potatoes destined for the above potato salad overcooked into a mush. In the moment of crisis, with 50 people waiting for dinner in the dining room, we decided to drain the potatoes, pick out the peels, and mash them. Then we added the other ingredients as above. The end result was so delicious we've been making it ever since! It should be a soft consistency and can even be piped onto individual lettuce leaves or used to garnish appetizer salads or hors d'oeuvres.

HOT POTATO SALAD
Make as above, but omit the mayonnaise. Fold in 2 diced hard-boiled eggs and 2 tablespoons of chopped gherkins. Serve warm with sausages, boiled bacon, warm terrine, hot spiced beef, or Danish Pâté (see page 326).

POTATO AND MINT LEAF SALAD
For a light summer salad, add 4 tablespoons of freshly chopped spearmint leaves instead of the chives and parsley and omit the mayonnaise.

HAND-CUT POTATO FRIES

Sales of frozen and pre-prepared fries have skyrocketed in a relatively short time, so much so that I feel many people have forgotten how easy it is to make fries at home. When people do make their own fries, they often use poor-quality oil and are disappointed with the result, so if you're going to go to the trouble of cutting your own potatoes, I would urge you to consider rendering your own beef fat (see page 177) or pork lard (see page 316) for it. Contrary to popular belief, beef fat, particularly from organic animals, is not less healthy than the cheap vegetable fats usually used.

good-quality potatoes, such as
    Yukon Golds or Kerr's Pinks
best-quality oil, lard, or beef fat for
    frying
salt

Scrub the potatoes well and peel or leave unpeeled, according to taste. Cut into similar sized fries so they will cook evenly. Cut them whatever size you want, but it's worth noting that if they're on the bigger side (bigger than ½in), they benefit from being fried twice, as below. If you're making matchstick or straw potatoes, you can just fry them once at 375°F for 1–2 minutes.

Rinse the fries quickly in cold water, but do not soak them. Dry meticulously with a kitchen towel or paper towels before cooking; otherwise, the water will boil on contact with the oil in the deep fryer and may cause it to overflow.

For larger fries, fry twice in a deep fryer – once at 320°F for 4–10 minutes, depending on size, until they are soft and just beginning to brown. Drain, increase the heat to 375°F, and fry again for another 1–2 minutes, until crisp and golden. Do not overload the basket, otherwise the temperature of the oil will be lowered, and, consequently, the fries will be greasy rather than crisp. Shake the pan once or twice to separate the fries while cooking.

Drain well, toss onto paper towels, sprinkle with a little salt, turn onto a hot serving dish, and serve immediately.

Above: *Homemade Potato Chips or "Game Chips."*

HOMEMADE POTATO CHIPS OR "GAME CHIPS"

Making chips at home is definitely worthwhile – a few potatoes produce a ton of chips and nothing you buy in any store will be even half as delicious. A mandolin is well worth buying for making chips – but watch your fingers! When these are served with roast pheasant they are called game chips · **SERVES 4**

1lb large, even-sized potatoes
extra virgin olive oil or beef
dripping (see page 177) for
deep frying
salt

Wash and peel the potatoes. For even-sized chips, trim each potato with a swivel-top peeler until smooth. Slice them very finely, preferably with a mandolin. Soak in cold water to remove the excess starch (this will also prevent them from discoloring or sticking together). Drain off the water and dry well.

In a deep fryer, heat the oil or dripping to 350°F. Drop in the dry potato slices a few at a time and fry until golden and completely crisp. Drain on paper towels and sprinkle lightly with salt. Repeat until they are all cooked.

If they are not to be served immediately, they may be stored in a tin box and reheated in a low oven just before serving.

Left: *Our onion crop drying in the greenhouse.*

down through the stalk, and this ripens the onions and enables them to mature properly. We hang them in bunches of five or six from the wire in the greenhouse – they dry perfectly in those conditions. They look great and are up out of harm's way. As you sort through the onions, identify any that are slightly damaged. Damaged onions deteriorate faster, so ensure you use those first.

Another way to dry the stalks is to spread the onions out on plastic or wire crates so the air can circulate. In Ireland, traditionally, they were often spread on a galvanized or slate roof facing south or on the tops of stone walls until the stalks were totally dry. Once the stalks are dry, store the onions in a well-ventilated dry spot for winter use. Alternatively, make onion braids by braiding the dry stalks (see below) and using as needed.

How to make an onion braid

Lay six onions on the table with the dried stalks close to you. Lay one beside and slightly above the other, weaving the dried stalks as you go. Braid from the outside in, every second one. Tie the strands together with kitchen string at the end and hang in a dry, airy place. They must be stored in the light, otherwise they will start to sprout.

How to dye eggs with onion skins

It's fun to dye eggs for Easter. Once you've accumulated lots of onion

Onions

Considering that onions are so easy to buy, I find it difficult to convince people that onions are well worth growing yourself. Homegrown onions both taste and cook differently. They tend to be sweeter and hugely enhance the flavor of the hundreds of dishes of which they are a part. The added bonus is that you can use them at all the different stages of growth. During the growing season, we sometimes steal a shoot here and there from young onions to add to soups, potato salads, champ, or colcannon.

In late-July to mid-August, once the stalks topple over, we begin to harvest. Don't be tempted to trim the tops; if you do, the onions won't keep well. The natural sugars go skins, put them into a saucepan and cover them with cold water. Bring them to a boil and cook for about 10 minutes. Lower your eggs into the water gently and hard-boil the eggs for about 10 minutes, by which time the eggs should be a gorgeous dark brown color. If you want to make fancy patterns on the eggs, you can put tape or rubber bands around the eggs; when you take off the tape or rubber bands, the egg will be patterned.

MELTED SCALLIONS WITH MARJORAM OR THYME LEAVES

Onions become sweet and succulent when cooked slowly, so the technique of gentle cooking is worth mastering. We use onions as a vegetable dish in their own right, as a base for other dishes, and as a sauce for pasta · SERVES 4

1lb new season onions with green leaves
2 tablespoons butter or a mixture of butter and olive oil
salt and freshly ground black pepper
1 tablespoon thyme leaves or 2 tablespoons of annual marjoram, chopped

Peel the outer layer from the onion. Slice the green leaves and the bulb into rings. Melt the butter (or butter and olive oil) in a saucepan over medium heat. Add the onions, stir, and toss gently to coat. Season with salt and pepper. Add the thyme or marjoram and toss again.

Cover with the lid of the saucepan and cook gently for about 15 minutes. Remove the lid and cook for another 5 minutes. Serve with fish, meat, or pasta.

Variation
SHALLOTS WITH THYME LEAVES
Peel shallots and cook, whole, as above, until they're soft and tender – you can't imagine how delicious these are with roast chicken or duck.

FRENCH ONION SOUP

A classic French onion soup will taste even better with homegrown onions. The skill here is in the gentle and patient caramelizing of the onions before the stock is added · SERVES 6

4 tablespoons butter
3lb onions, peeled and thinly sliced
2 quarts Beef Stock (see page 159), Chicken Stock (see page 262), or Vegetable Stock (see page 390)
salt and freshly ground pepper

TO SERVE
6 slices of good baguette (French bread), ½in thick, toasted
⅔ cup grated Gruyère cheese

Melt the butter in a saucepan. Add the onion and cook over low heat for about 40–60 minutes with the lid off, stirring frequently. Keep your nerve – the onions must be very well caramelized; otherwise the soup will be too weak and sweet. They will reduce down to a fraction of the original volume and be dark in color.

Add the stock, season with salt and freshly ground pepper, bring to a boil, and cook for another 10 minutes. Ladle into deep soup bowls, and put a piece of toasted baguette covered with grated cheese on top of each one. Put under the broiler until the cheese melts and turns golden. Serve immediately, but beware – it will be very hot. Bon appetit!

ONION SAUCE

Served with roast lamb or pan-grilled lamb chops, onion sauce is a sort of "forgotten flavor" that makes a delicious change from the more usual mint jelly. If "onion sauce" sounds a bit dull, use its French name, sauce soubise. *I urge you not to gloss over this sauce; it really is worth making* · SERVES 8–10

4 tablespoons butter
3 onions, about 1lb in weight, thinly sliced or finely chopped
½ teaspoon salt
¼ teaspoon freshly ground black pepper
½ tablespoon all-purpose flour
1¼ cups whole milk or 1 cup milk and ¼ cup cream

Melt the butter over low heat, add the onions, and cook in a covered saucepan until very soft but not colored. Season with the salt and pepper. Stir in the flour, add the milk, and simmer gently for another 5 minutes.

This sauce keeps for 3–4 days covered in the fridge and may be reheated.

ROAST ONIONS

I'm always surprised that so few people cook onions in this ultra-simple way. This recipe is our great standby; we just throw the onions into a heated stove. Although we call them roast onions, I suppose, strictly speaking, they are baked. Either way, they are absolutely delicious, and my children adore them.

**small or medium-sized onions,
    unpeeled**
olive oil
sea salt

Preheat the oven to 400°F.

Roast the unpeeled onions until soft. This can take anywhere from 30 to 45 minutes, depending on size. Serve in their skins.

Serve with olive oil and sea salt. To eat, cut off the root end and, if small enough, squeeze out the onion. Larger onions are best split in half and served with a dab of fresh herb butter melting in the center. They're so exquisite that you won't want anything else for supper.

Variation
ROAST ONION HALVES
Cut the raw, unpeeled onions in half from top to bottom. Put in a roasting pan in a single layer. Drizzle with extra virgin olive oil and scatter over some freshly picked thyme leaves, if available. Season with salt and freshly ground pepper. Roast in a preheated oven at (450°F), for 20–40 minutes, depending on size. Turn once, halfway through cooking.

ONION RINGS

The mere mention of onion rings puts fear and dread into those watching their figures, but these involve only a little milk and seasoned flour, so they have a delicious crisp coating. Recently, my nephew Ivan Whelan gave me a great tip. He found that when he added a lightly whisked egg white to the milk it made the onion rings even crispier. The watch point here is not to cut the onion rings thicker than the recipe calls for, or else the coating will be overcooked, while the onions will still be raw. Onion rings are wonderful with beef, but we pile them up on salads and pan-fried venison, too. Paprika, Sichuan pepper, cumin, and coriander can all be added to the flour for a change of flavor · SERVES 6

1 organic egg white, optional
1½ cups whole milk
2 large onions, peeled
1¾ cups seasoned flour
**good-quality oil or beef dripping
    for deep-frying**

Whisk the egg white lightly and add it to the milk. Slice the onion into ¼ in rings around the middle. Separate the rings and cover with the milk mixture until needed. (The leftover milk may be boiled up, thickened with roux, and used for a white or parsley sauce).

Just before serving, heat the oil or beef dripping to 350°F. Toss the rings a few at a time in well-seasoned flour. Deep-fry for 2–3 minutes, or until golden in the hot oil. Drain on paper towels and serve hot.

VEGETABLE STOCK

This is just a rough guide. Basically, you can make a vegetable stock from whatever vegetables you have available, but try not to use too much of any one vegetable unless you want that flavor to predominate. Beets contribute a delicious sweet flavor but dye the stock pink, so use only if the stock is needed for beet soup. Potatoes soak up flavor and brassicas give an off-flavor, so avoid using those · MAKES ABOUT 1¾ QUARTS

1 small white turnip
**2 onions, peeled and roughly
    sliced**
green parts of 2–3 leeks
**3 celery ribs, washed and roughly
    chopped**
**3 large carrots, scrubbed and
    roughly chopped**
½ fennel bulb, roughly chopped
**4oz mushrooms or mushroom
    stalks**
4–6 parsley stalks
bouquet garni
a few peppercorns

Put all the ingredients into a large saucepan. Add 2½ quarts of cold water. Bring to a boil, reduce the heat, cover, and leave to simmer for 1–1½ hours. Strain through a sieve.

Vegetable stock keeps for a week in the fridge or may be frozen.

Opposite: *Roast Onion Halves.*

Beets

Like tomatoes, potatoes, and onions, beets are one of my top 10 vegetables. With beets, you can use all three parts of the plant: the greens, the stalks, and the root. If you plant them at the end of January or in early February you will be able to harvest some tiny beet greens to add to your salad in 10–12 weeks. When the beets swell to the size of a golf ball, you can cook them whole. Beets are wonderful both served hot as a vegetable or at room temperature in salads.

For most people, the only introduction to beets is through the mouth-puckeringly vinegary pickle that comes in jars. It is therefore no wonder that many people don't like beets. They have no idea that they can be eaten any other way. But there are so many other things to do with beets, and pickled beets can be delicious as well. We sell lots of our home-pickled beets at the Midleton Farmers' Market and convert a lot of ardent beet haters.

Fresh, young beet leaves and stalks are delicious cooked like spinach and slathered with butter or extra virgin olive oil. I just cut them into ¾in pieces and cook them in a little boiling salted water. Drain, then toss in a little chile oil with lots of freshly chopped parsley and maybe a couple of chopped anchovies.

Beets can be boiled, roasted, or baked. When sliced into thin rounds and fried in oil, the result is irresistible beet chips. A glut of beets can be pickled or stored in a simple pit (see page 379) for winter use. Pick them while they are still young and tender, rather than waiting for them to get old and woody.

How to cook beets

Leave 2in of stalks on top and the whole root intact. Wash off the mud under running water with the palms of your hands, so that you don't damage the skin (resist the temptation to attack it with a vegetable brush); otherwise, it will bleed during cooking. Cover with cold water and add a little salt and sugar. Cover the pot, bring to a boil, and simmer on the stovetop or in an oven for 1–2 hours, depending on size. Beets are usually cooked when the skin rubs off easily and when they dent if pressed with a finger. If in doubt, test with a skewer or the tip of a knife. They should feel tender the whole way through.

How to harvest and store beets

You can keep beets in the ground but they just become woodier and woodier, so it's best to harvest them at optimum size. When harvesting, be careful not to damage the root. Trim the leaves about 2in from the top (they can be added to the compost heap). Store beets in layers in damp sand, either in wooden boxes (such as wine boxes) or in a heap against an inside wall in a frost-free shed.

ROASTED BEETS

We are addicted to beets, so we grow the classic varieties – Bolthardy, a golden beet called Golden Detroit (or Detroit Red Beets), and Chioggia, a pink and white candy-striped beet that cooks faster, is more delicate in flavor, and is also delicious eaten raw ·
SERVES 4

12 baby beets, a mixture of red, golden, and Chioggia would work well
extra virgin olive oil
sea salt

Preheat the oven to 450°F.

Wrap the beets in aluminum foil and roast in the oven for 1 hour, depending on size, until soft and cooked through. You'll know when they're cooked if there's a bit of give when you press the foil, or unwrap a beet and see if the skin will rub off. Once the beets are cooked, rub off the skins, toss in extra virgin olive oil, and sprinkle with sea salt.

Above: *Chioggia beet.*

HOT BEETS WITH CREAM AND MARJORAM

This is a revelation to people who have only ever tasted beets from a jar and have no idea they can be served any other way. We particularly love this dish with duck and goose, or with goat cheese melting over the top ·
SERVES 6-8

1½lb beets, cooked
1 tablespoon butter
Sea salt and freshly ground black
    pepper
a sprinkling of sugar
½ cup cream, or more
1 tablespoon marjoram leaves

Peel the beets – use rubber gloves for this operation if you are vain! Chop the beet flesh into cubes. Melt the butter in a sauté pan. Add the beets and toss. Then add the cream and marjoram and leave to bubble for a few minutes. Season with sea salt and freshly ground pepper and sugar. Taste and add a squeeze of lemon juice if necessary. Serve immediately.

BEET TOPS

Young beet tops are full of flavor and are often unnecessarily discarded; but if you grow your own beets, remember to cook the stalks as well. When the leaves are tiny they make a really worthwhile addition to the salad bowl, both in terms of nutrition and flavor. This isn't worth doing unless you have lovely young leaves. When they become old and slightly wilted, feed them to the hens or add them to the compost ·
SERVES 4

1lb fresh beet tops
salt and freshly ground black
    pepper
butter or olive oil

Keeping them separate, cut the beet stalks and leaves into rough 2in pieces. First, cook the stalks in boiling salted water (use 1¾ quarts of water to 1½ teaspoons of salt) for 3–4 minutes, or until tender. Then add the leaves and cook for another 2–3 minutes. Drain, season, and toss in a little butter or olive oil. Serve immediately.

Right: *Beets: a three-in-one vegetable – leaves, stalks, and bulbs.*

Variation

BEET TOPS WITH CREAM
Substitute ¼–⅓ cup of cream for olive oil in the recipe above. A little freshly grated nutmeg is also delicious.

BEET CHIPS

You can make vegetable chips from a variety of different vegetables: parsley, celeriac, carrots, Jerusalem artichokes, and potatoes, of course. But you need to be careful with the ones that are very high in sugar, because they need to be cooked at a lower temperature, otherwise, they'll be dark and bitter ·
SERVES ABOUT 8

a few raw beets, small to medium-sized
oil in a deep fryer
salt

Use a vegetable peeler to peel the beets. Then slice on a mandolin into paper-thin slices. Leave them to dry out on paper towels (this may take several hours). You want them to be dry; otherwise, they'll end up being soggy when you cook them.

Heat the oil in a deepfryer to 275°F and cook slowly, a few at a time. Drain on paper towels and sprinkle with salt.

OVEN-ROASTED WINTER ROOT VEGETABLES WITH ROSEMARY OR THYME LEAVES

Because roast vegetables sound so easy, many cooks are lulled into complacency with this method, but it takes considerable skill to pull it off successfully. There's a big difference between the nasty acrid flavor of burned vegetables and vegetables that are nicely caramelized around the edges. All too often, roasted vegetables tend to be cooked hours ahead and, as a result, are served soggy. The secret is to sprinkle them with lots of freshly chopped herbs and get them straight to the table from the oven while they're still sizzling. Freshly roasted and ground cumin or coriander is also a delicious addition just before the end of cooking.

ABOUT EQUAL VOLUMES OF:

parsnips, peeled
rutabaga, peeled
beets, peeled
celeriac, peeled
carrot, peeled
onions, peeled and quartered
pumpkin (optional)
extra virgin olive oil
salt and freshly ground black pepper
2 tablespoons rosemary or thyme leaves, plus extra fresh winter herbs, for garnish
a few whole garlic cloves (optional)

Preheat the oven to 400°F.

Cut all the peeled vegetables into similar-sized pieces (1in cubes are a good size) and put them into a large bowl. Drizzle generously with olive oil and season well with salt and freshly ground pepper. Spread them in a single layer on one or several roasting pans and sprinkle with the chopped herbs. If using the whole garlic cloves, add them about halfway through cooking.

Roast, uncovered, stirring occasionally until they are fully cooked and just beginning to caramelize. Be careful – a little color makes them sweeter, but there is a fine line between caramelizing and burning. If they become too dark they will be bitter. Serve sprinkled with freshly chopped winter herbs, e.g., thyme, rosemary, chives, and parsley.

Spinach

Spinach is definitely a contender for the top 10 crops that are well worth growing. A line or two of spinach in your garden will keep you supplied throughout the year. Spinach is another vegetable that has lost a lot of nutrients since the 1950s, because of intensive production, so it's well worth growing at home.

There are two varieties: summer spinach and perpetual spinach. The former has small, tender leaves with a melting texture when cooked; however, the disadvantage is that it's an annual and runs to seed at the end of the summer. Perpetual spinach, also known as spinach beet, is a biannual and less likely to bolt and go to seed. The more you cut spinach, the more it comes. It's much hardier, the leaves are larger, and you'll get nice fleshy stalks. When preparing perpetual spinach, it's essential to cook and serve the stalks separately from the leaves; you get two vegetables for the price of one! Depending on size, this may need to be done with annual spinach, too.

How to string spinach

Fold a leaf in half with the stalk uppermost and pull the stalk downward, away from the leaf. Save the stalks, which make a tasty vegetable when chopped up and cooked in boiling salted water. You need about 8oz of spinach per person, because it really disappears when you cook it.

COOKED SPINACH

Here are three different basic methods for cooking spinach, all of which are a huge improvement over watery, frozen spinach · SERVES 4–6

2lb fresh spinach, stalks removed
salt, freshly ground black pepper
4 tablespoons butter, or more
freshly grated nutmeg

Method 1 (wilted method)

Wash the prepared spinach and drain. Melt a dab of butter in a wide frying pan, toss in as much spinach as will fit easily, and season with salt and freshly ground pepper. As soon as the spinach wilts and becomes tender, strain off all the liquid, increase the heat, and add some butter and freshly grated nutmeg. Serve immediately.

Method 2 (no-water method)

Wash the prepared spinach and drain. Put into a heavy saucepan over very low heat, season, and cover tightly. After a few minutes, stir, and then replace the lid. As soon as the spinach is cooked, in about 5–8 minutes, strain off the copious amount of liquid and press the spinach between two plates until almost dry. Chop, or blend in a food processor if you like a smooth texture. Increase the heat, add butter, correct the seasoning, and add a little freshly grated nutmeg to taste.

Method 3 (water method)

Cook the spinach, uncovered, in a large saucepan of boiling salted water until soft (about 4–5 minutes). Drain and press out all the water. Continue as in method 2. Method 3 produces a brighter colored spinach.

NOTE: spinach soaks up butter like nothing else, but those who can't eat dairy should substitute extra virgin olive oil to enhance the flavor.

Variations

CREAMED SPINACH

This is a delicious recipe, as well as a wonderful way of conserving a glut – make this recipe and freeze it. Cook spinach by method 2 or 3 and drain very well. Add ¾–1½ cups of cream to the spinach and bring to a boil. Stir well and thicken with a little roux if desired; otherwise, stir over the heat until the spinach has absorbed most of the cream. Season with salt, pepper, and freshly grated nutmeg to taste. Creamed spinach may be cooked ahead of time and reheated.

SPINACH STALKS

People usually throw out the stalks after they've strung perpetual spinach, but they're delicious and it's a pity to waste them after all the hard work of growing them. Chop the spinach stalks you have reserved into 1in pieces. Cook in boiling

Above: *Perpetual spinach – use both the stalks and leaves.*

salted water – use 1 teaspoon of salt for every 2 cups of water – until tender, about 3–4 minutes. Drain well. Toss in a little butter or extra virgin olive oil. I sometimes toss in a few chile flakes and freshly chopped herbs. If you feel like an Asian flavor, substitute soy sauce or oyster sauce for the butter or olive oil.

FRIED SPINACH LEAVES

Spinach leaves are delicious deep-fried. You can either fry the dry, fresh spinach leaves in the deep fryer for a few seconds, or they can be dipped first in a batter made from thin gram flour (dried chickpea flour, available at Asian or health-food stores). In India, they're often served on their own or with other fried vegetables and are called pakoras.

Chard

Plant chard (also known as Swiss chard) in late summer and you'll have green leaves and stalks in winter. It's two vegetables in one, since both the leaves and stalks can be eaten, and they take on other flavors really well. There are many different colors of chard, depending on the variety: the stalks can be white, like the original, but also red, yellow, pink, or slightly orange. With ruby chard, the leaf is wine-colored, similar to beet leaves.

Chard is wonderful added at the end of a freshly cooked Tomato Fondue (see page 378), or replace the spinach in the Hake with Tomatoes and Spinach Stalks (see page 89) with chard. Chard can be grown in big pots near your kitchen door and is worth growing just for its spectacular appearance.

SIMPLE COOKED CHARD

The chopped green leaf can be added a minute or two before the end of cooking if you want to serve both together, or you can cook and serve the leaves separately as you would spinach ·
SERVES 6–8

1lb Swiss chard
butter or extra virgin olive oil
freshly chopped herbs of your
   choice – marjoram, rosemary,
   or tarragon are good
salt and freshly ground black
   pepper

Pull the green leaves off the chard stalks and wash, drain, and chop. Cut the chard stalks into pieces

Above: *Beautiful ruby chard.*
Below right: *Melted Chard Stalks with Bacon and Hazelnuts.*

about 2in long. Cook in boiling salted water until they feel almost tender when pierced with the tip of a knife – about 3–4 minutes. Add the chopped greens, and toss for 2–3 minutes, until the leaves are soft and wilted. Drain well. Toss in a little butter or olive oil and the herbs; taste and correct the seasoning and serve immediately.

MELTED CHARD STALKS WITH BACON AND HAZELNUTS

There are several ways to cook chard stalks, aside from boiling it. The blanched stalks can be sprinkled with a bit of grated cheese and gratinated under a broiler, or coated in Mornay sauce. They are also delicious marinated in olive oil and lemon juice and chargrilled, or cooked in the following delicious combination ·
SERVES 4–6

2lb white or ruby chard stalks
1 tablespoon butter
2 tablespoons extra virgin
   olive oil
2oz streaky bacon, cut into
   fine pieces
⅔ cup onion, finely diced
salt, freshly ground black pepper
½ cup hazelnuts
1 tablespoon chopped fresh
   marjoram or ½ tablespoon sage

String the chard stalks with a swivel-top vegetable peeler and chop into 3in lengths. Melt the butter and olive oil in an oval casserole dish. Add the bacon and cook for 1–2 minutes. Add the onion and sweat for another 2–3 minutes. Add the chard stalks, toss, season, cover the casserole dish, and cook over low heat for 20–25 minutes.

Meanwhile, roast the hazelnuts in a moderate oven for 5–8 minutes, until the skins loosen. Rub off the skins, chop, add the marjoram or sage to the chard, and cook for a minute or two. Add the toasted hazelnuts, toss, and serve.

Peas

You get such good value from pea plants. It's virtually impossible to get really fresh peas in a supermarket, and peas taste best when you pluck them right off the plant. Be very picky about the variety (Kelvedon Wonder is a wonderful heirloom variety). You can use peas at all the different stages of growth. Young pea shoots can be used in salads and have a wonderful fresh pea flavor, while pea tendrils (wizard's whiskers) are a fun garnish for plates. Don't be too overenthusiastic about picking off the pea flowers – remember, they will eventually be peas. The tiny pods can be eaten raw or eaten like snap peas. When the little peas start to form, you can eat them like sugar snaps peas (pod and all), and when the peas actually swell in the pod, go and hide in the pea row and gorge yourself.

One of my favorite summer appetizers for a meal is to give each person a bowl of freshly picked peas to shell and eat, raw, maybe with a little sea salt. They have to have been picked right before dinner though, since they lose their sweetness and become mealy very quickly. You won't know what the magic is about if you don't pick them, shell them, and eat them within an hour. Afterward, don't throw out the peapods; make a peapod soup with them.

MUSHY PEAS WITH MINT

Real mushy peas are actually made from marrowfat peas, a variety grown especially for drying that one rarely sees around anymore. Today, we make this with fresh peas or, I have to confess, frozen ones · **SERVES 4**

1lb fresh or frozen peas
salt, freshly ground black pepper
4 tablespoons butter
1 teaspoon sugar
1–2 tablespoons chopped mint

Bring 1 cup of water to a fast, rolling boil. Add ½ teaspoon salt, toss in the peas, and stir.

Cover the saucepan, bring back to a boil on high heat. Uncover and cook for 4–5 minutes. Drain, but save some of the cooking liquid. Add butter, salt, and freshly ground pepper and a good pinch of sugar to the peas. Pulse in a food processor or mash with a potato masher, adding some of the cooking liquid, if necessary. Add freshly chopped mint. Taste and correct the seasoning. Serve with "fish and chips."

PEAPOD SOUP

This is a way of using up the peapods from shelled peas that would otherwise go to waste. They really must be fresh, though, or this soup isn't worth making · **SERVES 6**

1lb really fresh peapods
2 tablespoons butter
1 onion, finely chopped
5 cups Chicken Stock (see page 262), warmed
salt, freshly ground black pepper, and sugar, to taste
2 sprigs of mint
½ cup fresh or frozen peas (optional)

Slice the fresh peapods fairly finely. Melt the butter in a saucepan, add the onion, and sweat on a gentle heat until soft but not colored, about 5–6 minutes. Add the hot stock, bring to a boil, and add the peapods and, if you can spare them, the peas. Season well with salt and pepper and a good pinch of sugar. Cook for another 6–8 minutes. Add the mint, and then put through a food mill or blend in a food processor. Sieve to extract the strings. Taste and correct the seasoning. Swirl in a little cream if you like. Decorate with pea shoots, pea tendrils, and a few pea flowers, if available.

Above: *Pea plants with emerging wizard's whiskers.*

SUMMER GREEN PEA SOUP

This soup tastes of summer. If you use fresh peas, reserve the pods for a soup or to add to the vegetable stock that will serve as the base for this soup. Having said that, best-quality frozen peas also make a delicious soup. This soup may also be served chilled, but serve in smaller portions. Be careful not to overcook this soup or you will lose the fresh taste and bright-green color. Add a little extra stock if the soup is too thick · SERVES 6–8

1oz lean bacon
1 tablespoon butter
2 medium scallions, chopped
1½lb podded peas, fresh or frozen
outside leaves of a head of lettuce, shredded
a sprig of mint
5 cups Chicken Stock (see page 262) or hot water
salt, freshly ground black pepper, and sugar
2 tablespoons heavy cream

GARNISH
blanched fresh or frozen peas and pea shoots
whipped cream
freshly chopped mint

Cut the bacon into very fine pieces. Melt the butter and sweat the bacon for about 5 minutes, then add the scallions and cook for another 1–2 minutes. Add the peas, lettuce, mint, and the hot chicken stock or water. Season with salt, pepper, and sugar.

Bring to a boil with the lid off and cook for about 5 minutes, until the peas are just tender.

Puree and add a little cream to taste. To serve, put a few fresh peas and pea shoots into wide soup bowls. Put the soup in a pitcher – each guest pours soup into his or her own bowl.

If this soup is made ahead, reheat it, uncovered, and serve immediately. It will lose its fresh taste and bright, lively color if it sits in a double boiler or simmers at length in a pot.

WILTED PEA SHOOTS

Fresh pea shoots are a delicious addition to green salads and appetizer salads. If you are fortunate enough to have a surplus, this is a perfect way to cook them · SERVES 4

3 tablespoons extra virgin olive oil
2 garlic cloves, crushed
a good pinch of chile flakes
1lb pea shoots
sea salt and freshly ground black pepper
10–12 mint leaves

Heat the extra virgin olive oil in a wide sauté pan or wok. Add the garlic and chile flakes and leave to sizzle for a few seconds. Add the pea shoots, toss, and season with sea salt and freshly ground pepper. Add the mint leaves, taste, and serve immediately in a hot serving dish.

SUGAR PEAS, SNOW PEAS, OR SUGAR SNAP PEAS

These are the "mangetout" family of peas, whereby you eat the pod and all. Sugar peas are pods with barely discernible peas inside and are about 2in long. Snow peas are similar but twice the length, and sugar snap peas are about the same size as sugar peas but have more fully formed peas inside. Beware, the peas in this family go on cooking after they've been drained so err on the side of undercooking. Keep the lid off to retain the bright green color. Tiny fava bean pods, not longer than 3in may be treated in exactly the same way · SERVES 6

1lb sugar peas, sugar snap peas, or snow peas
3 teaspoons salt
freshly ground black pepper
2–4 tablespoons butter

String the sugar peas, if using. Bring 5 cups of water to a rolling boil, add the salt and the peas and continue to boil furiously with the lid off, until just cooked (about 3–4 minutes): they should still have a slight crunch. Drain immediately* and toss in a little melted butter. Taste and correct the seasoning. Serve immediately in a hot serving dish.

* As with many green vegetables, sugar peas, snow peas, or sugar snap peas can be refreshed in cold water at this point and reheated in boiling salted water just before serving.

Opposite: *Summer Green Pea Soup.*

Beans

I urge you to grow as many of the bean family as you have the space for. If I'm to choose the most forgotten or neglected of the beans, I'd say scarlet runners. Every garden should have a bamboo wigwam so you can admire the bright red flowers. I tell my grandchildren the Jack and the Beanstalk story, which intrigues them so they eat the beans!

You can eat scarlet runner beans at all different sizes. When they're 3in long, cook them whole. When they're bigger, about 7–8in, they should be soft and still pliable. If they snap when you bend them over, however, they have become too mature; they are too tough to eat

Above: *Flat and round pod French beans, some mature enough to shell.*

and the inside membrane has become fibrous. But all is not lost. They are now into a new category, which we call shell beans. The ones you miss you may want to leave on the plant and continue to grow until the beans form inside. Then you have two options: you can shell them and take out the beans and cook them as fresh shell beans, or you can let them get a little bit more mature and dry out in the pod and harvest them dry and use them as you would legumes. You can dry any bean, but the maximum flavor will come from varieties like flageolets or cranberry beans that are bred to be dried.

French beans can also be used at all the different sizes, and if they snap when you bend them they, too, are too mature. In that case, dry them on the vine and they become navy beans.

Runner beans are prepared in a different way from any other bean. The string needs to be removed before cooking (throw it into the hen's bucket or compost). You can buy a special bean slicer that you put the beans through and they come out in strips. It's sometimes attached to a swivel-top peeler, so keep an eye out for it. If you don't have one of these gadgets, simply cut the bean into thin strips at an angle and cook in boiling salted water.

When fava beans arrive at the market before ours are ready, I get unbearably tempted, but I once bought organic ones that had traveled all the way from France and they were no good. There's only one way to eat fava beans: right after

you pick them. Make it a party where everyone shells – it's such a tactile thing, and we love it. The grandchildren especially adore taking the fava beans out of their furry, snuggly pods and as a result of being connected to them like this, they eat them both raw and cooked.

Home gardeners should pinch out the fava bean tops to prevent blackfly, which is always attracted to fava bean plants, and you can chop the tops up and throw them in fresh pasta or risotto or salad. Summer savory is a good plant to grow alongside fava beans to prevent pests. When the fava beans are 2½–3in in length, you can pick them off, cook them in boiling salted water, and eat them whole. Or make fava bean pod soup (see page 402).

It's important to note that if you're just relying on beans bought in the supermarket, you won't be able to taste them at all their different stages and you will miss out on a variety of wonderful experiences – yet another reason to get out there with your shovel and trowel.

We are really picky about measuring our boiling salted water: it's the same for every green vegetable – for every 5 cups of water, use 3 heaping teaspoons of salt.

Sprouting seeds for beansprouts

Legumes and seeds for sprouting can be obtained in natural food stores and health-food stores. We particularly recommend using alfalfa seeds because of their delicate taste. But you can also use mung or soybeans.

Use about 2 tablespoons of seeds or 4 tablespoons of legumes, alfalfa, mung beans, or soybeans. Put the seeds in a quart jar. Cover them with warm water and soak for 8 hours. Drain off the liquid. Rinse the seeds and drain them well. Now lay the jar on its side. Rinse the sprouts two or three times a day and put the jar back on its side. Be careful not to let the sprouts sit too long in water or dry out, since this will cause them to spoil. Within three or four days the sprouts will have developed completely and they will be ready to eat and/or refrigerate.

It is best to keep the sprout jar in a dark place such as a cupboard for the first two or three days and bring it out in the light on the last day when the chlorophyll develops. This process generally produces nice, green sprouts.

FRENCH BEANS

French beans need a lot of salt in the cooking water to bring out the flavor. They don't benefit from being left standing, so if you need to cook them ahead, try the method I suggest below. The proportion of salt to water is vitally important for the flavor of the beans. French beans are a vegetable that you can buy all year round in the supermarket. They come trimmed, ready to be cooked, but I prefer to eat and enjoy them only when we have our own, in season · SERVES 8

Right: *Windowsill cooking – sprouting seeds.*

3 teaspoons sea salt
2lb French beans
2–4 tablespoons butter or extra virgin olive oil
salt, freshly ground black pepper

Trim the ends off the beans. If they are small and thin, leave them whole; if they are larger, cut them into 1–1½in pieces at an angle.

Bring 5 cups of water to a fast, rolling boil. Add the salt and then toss in the beans. Continue to boil very fast for 5–6 minutes, or until just cooked (they should still retain a little bite). Drain immediately.* Heat the butter or oil in the saucepan, toss the beans in it, taste and season with pepper and a little sea salt, if necessary.

* The beans may be refreshed under cold water at this point and kept aside for several hours. Just before serving, plunge them into boiling salted water for 30 seconds to 1 minute, drain, and toss in butter. Season and serve immediately.

Variations
FRENCH BEANS WITH FRESH CHILE
When the beans are cooked, drain well. Heat 2 tablespoons of olive oil in a wide sauté pan, add 1 chopped garlic clove and 1–2 chopped chiles. Toss, season well, and add 1 tablespoon coarsely chopped parsley. Toss, taste, and serve.

Above: *Fava beans.*

RUNNER BEANS
Trim and string the beans and cook as for French beans.

FRENCH BEANS WITH
TOMATO FONDUE
Cook the French beans as in the master recipe and drain. Mix with Tomato Fondue (see page 378). Heat through and serve.

FAVA BEAN-POD SOUP

This recipe is only worth doing when you grow you own fava beans and have really fresh pods · SERVES 8

2lb young fava bean pods
2 tablespoons butter
3 scallions, chopped
3–4 outside leaves of lettuce,
    roughly sliced
2–3 sprigs of summer savory, plus
    more to serve
3½ cups Chicken Stock (see page
    262)
salt, freshly ground black pepper
    and sugar
1¼ cups whole milk
a handful of cooked fava beans,
    for garnish
cream, for garnish

Trim the young fava bean pods and cut in half crosswise.

Melt a little butter in a saucepan. Add the scallions and cook over low heat. Add the pods to the saucepan with the lettuce, summer savory, and hot stock. Season with salt, pepper, and sugar. Cover and cook for 10–15 minutes, or until the pods are soft.

Strain off and blend in a food processor with a little milk and a tablespoon or two of chopped summer savory. Taste and correct the seasoning. Serve in a hot bowl with a little cream and some cooked fava beans on top.

SHELL BEANS

We leave the large, mature pods of the cranberry beans on the vine until the beans swell inside. The pods are too tough to eat at that stage, but we pod the beans, which we call shell beans, and cook them until they're tender. Then we dress them in our very best extra virgin olive oil and freshly chopped herbs · SERVES 6

1lb shell beans
sprig of thyme
1 onion, quartered
1 carrot, cut into chunks
salt, freshly ground black pepper
extra virgin olive oil
freshly chopped herbs like chervil,
    tarragon, or marjoram

Cover the shell beans with cold water, add the onion, thyme, and carrot. Bring to a boil and cook for 30–45 minutes, or until tender. Drain, add salt and freshly ground pepper. Drizzle generously with extra virgin olive oil and freshly chopped herbs. Serve with pickled pork, bacon, or Polish sausage.

FARRO WITH FAVA BEANS, PEAS, ASPARAGUS, AND ARUGULA

If you don't have farro, put this into a risotto. Otherwise, dress the leaves lightly and serve quickly, while the flavors are at their freshest ·
SERVES 8

1½ cups cooked farro
a handful of arugula leaves
⅓ cup cooked peas
⅓ cup fava beans (blanched and
    refreshed)
8 asparagus spears, quickly
    blanched
8 cherry tomatoes, cut in half
4 tablespoons extra virgin olive oil
juice of 1 lemon
salt and freshly ground black
    pepper

Put the farro, arugula leaves, peas, fava beans, asparagus, and tomato halves into a bowl. Dress with olive oil and lemon juice. Season with sea salt and pepper and toss together lightly with your fingers.

Zucchini, Squash, and Pumpkins

You really only need two or three plants of zucchini, because it's either feast or famine with them. They're very heavy feeders, so dig a nice, big hole and put in plenty of well-rotted manure. Most people eat zucchini when they're the size of a cucumber, but their optimum size is about 5in. Remember to harvest zucchini at this size because if you leave them on the plant they almost double overnight. The bigger they get, the less flavor they have and they stop the other ones from swelling. If one escapes and gets hidden underneath, take it off as soon as you see it and toss it into a tomato fondue or with lots of herbs and spices.

The other bonus of growing zucchini is the flower: the one that grows on the stalk is the male and the one attached to the vegetable is the female, so don't take the latter because it'll grow into a zucchini. Don't take all the male ones off either, or you won't get enough cross-pollination.

Today, most people think of vegetable marrows as overgrown zucchini, but the true vegetable marrow has a hard yellow skin and a distinct if undistinguished flavor. Having said that, one of my favorite winter meals is a roast marrow stuffed with a well-flavored meat ragu and a bubbly cheese sauce on top. Even writing it makes me lick my lips.

Above: *From left to right: Kabocha, Kuri, and spaghetti squash.*

Squash and pumpkins

Extensive cross-breeding has resulted in numerous mixes that blur the distinguishing characteristics of what defines a squash and pumpkin. Of all the families of fruit and vegetables, I've come to the conclusion that pumpkins and squashes must surely be the most confusing. Not only are there hundreds of varieties, but some go by a multitude of names.

Roughly, they seem to divide into summer squash and pumpkins and vegetable marrows and winter squash and pumpkins and edible gourds. Botanically speaking, they are all members of the *Cucurbitaceae* family, which also includes cucumbers, melons, and decorative gourds. The majority of summer squash are native to Central America and Mexico, while many of the winter squash originated in the Argentine Andes. Squash grows in both bush and vine form, both are easy to grow, and a few plants will provide you with enough squash to share with all your family and friends.

Pumpkins have been rediscovered in recent years by

cooks and chefs, and rightly so. For a long time they suffered from a slightly dull image, mostly because of the unadventurous way that they were cooked. But now we've woken up to the numerous possibilities they offer, realizing what a good vehicle pumpkins are for taking on other flavors. In fact, they're truly exotic – there are so many different varieties, peculiar shapes, colors, and flavors.

These vegetables were also an incredibly important crop to past generations. They were valued because of their hard skins, which meant they could be kept for months stacked up in the attic so one always had a fresh vegetable in winter. Today, we'd be more likely to display them around the house because they are so beautiful.

Pumpkins are good to grow with children, partly because the seeds are so big. They not only love planting them, but also adore carving scary faces for Halloween. Sow the seeds early spring and plant them out a couple of months later.

They are heavy feeders and will even grow on top of the compost heap. Harvest them in the fall and they will provide a great store of food through the winter and beyond.

If you have lots of space, you can go to town and grow many varieties. If constricted for space, choose more carefully. Early butternut has a wonderful flavor, as do Golden Hubbard and Red Kuri. The Japanese onion squash is also delicious, as is the Italian Zucca da Marmellata while of the white-skinned varieties, both Crown Prince and Queensland Blue, are worth considering.

It's also fun to grow a couple of spaghetti squash, which are so called because the interior has an uncanny resemblance to spaghetti. The flavor is delicate, but we love to serve them with a gutsy Bolognese sauce or ragu piled over the top with lots of freshly grated cheese or even a strong garlic butter. Cook the spaghetti squash whole in boiling salted water for anything from 15 to 45 minutes, depending on the size, until tender. Split it in half and it will look like spaghetti inside. Serve with Garlic Butter (see page 217), Tomato Fondue (see page 378), or, better still, both.

Even though Turk's Turban doesn't have such a great flavor, we grow it every year because it's so exotic looking and makes you want to pick up a camera or paintbrush.

Left: *Zucchini Salad with Olive Oil and Sea Salt.*

ZUCCHINI SALAD WITH OLIVE OIL AND SEA SALT

This simple salad is delicious served warm with nothing more than a sprinkling of extra virgin olive oil and a little sea salt · SERVES 4-6

8 small zucchini with flowers, if available (choose shiny, firm zucchini)
sea salt and freshly ground black pepper
extra virgin olive oil

Separate the flowers from the zucchini. Remove the stamens and little thorns from the base of the flowers.

Plunge the whole zucchini into boiling salted water and poach them until barely tender – 4–5 minutes. Remove from the pot and leave to cool slightly. While still warm, slice them at an angle to allow six slices to each zucchini.

Season the zucchini slices with sea salt and freshly ground pepper and then sprinkle with extra virgin oilve oil. Toss gently and serve immediately, surrounded by the torn zucchini flowers.

Hot crusty bread is the only accompaniment needed.

AJLOUK DE ZUCCHINI

Claudia Roden introduced me to this way of cooking zucchini. It's really just mashed zucchini with olive oil, but the end result is simply delicious · SERVES 8

1½lb zucchini – about 5in each
sea salt
juice of ½ lemon
2 tablespoons extra virgin olive oil
3 garlic cloves, crushed
1 teaspoon ground coriander

GARNISH
8 Kalamata olives

Cook the zucchini whole in salted boiling water, until soft. Drain and press gently to squeeze out the excess water, then chop and mash with a fork. Add the freshly squeezed lemon juice, crushed garlic, and coriander. Mix well. Taste. Add a few flakes of sea salt, if necessary.

Transfer to a serving dish and garnish with olives. Serve cold or at room temperature with crusty bread.

DEEP-FRIED ZUCCHINI FLOWERS

In Europe you can buy zucchini flowers at your local market. In the US, they're beginning to appear in farmers' markets, but more than likely you'll have to grow them yourself. We usually use the male flowers for this recipe, because taking the female flower means you'll deprive yourself of a zucchini. They're delicious just dipped in batter and deep-fried, but they're also a vehicle for lots of different stuffings · SERVES 6

12–16 zucchini flowers (allow 1–3 flowers per person)
Batter (see page 94 for fish and chip batter)
sunflower oil for deep frying

Above: *Zucchini flowers.*

First, make the batter. Then heat the oil in a deep fryer until it's very hot.

Remove the thorns from the base of the flowers and insert your fingers into the center and remove the stamens. Dip each flower in batter, shake off the excess and drop, one by one, into the hot oil. Fry on one side for about 2 minutes and then turn over. They will take about 4 minutes in total and should be crisp and golden. Drain on paper towels and serve immediately, as part of a fritto misto or as a nibble. They're delicious served with a fresh tomato sauce or sweet chile sauce.

Variations

Zucchini blossoms are also delicious stuffed. Some suggested fillings:
• Buffalo mozzarella with pesto, tapenade, or concentrated tomato fondue and a basil leaf
• Goat cheese, chopped chorizo, and flat parsley
• Chicken or scallop mousse

ROAST STUFFED VEGETABLE MARROW

This recipe is best when made with a good old-fashioned vegetable marrow, but if you can't get your hands on one then it's the perfect way to make an entire meal of and add lots of badly needed flavor to an overblown zucchini. You can dream up all sorts of stuffings, but they should be tasty and well-seasoned; otherwise the end result can be exceedingly dull · **SERVES 8-10**

1 vegetable marrow, about 5½lb
salt and freshly ground black
    pepper
a sprig or two of marjoram
    (optional)
2 cups Mornay Sauce (see page
    119)
⅓ cup grated Cheddar cheese
¼ cup buttered bread crumbs

FOR THE STUFFING
2 tablespoons extra virgin olive oil
4oz bacon, diced
¾ cup chopped onion
1–2 garlic cloves, crushed
    (optional)
4oz mushrooms, chopped
salt, freshly ground black pepper
1lb ground beef
1 tablespoon parsley
2 teaspoons thyme

2 teaspoons chopped chives, or
    2 tablespoons annual marjoram
14oz can of tomatoes
salt, freshly ground black pepper
    and sugar

TO SERVE
Garlic Butter (see page 217)

First, make the stuffing. Heat 1 tablespoon of the oil in a wide saucepan or sauté pan. Add the bacon and cook until crisp. Remove to a plate. Reduce the heat, add the onion and garlic, if using, and sweat for a few minutes. Add to the bacon. Increase the heat, add the mushrooms, season with salt and freshly ground pepper, toss for a minute or two, and add to the bacon mixture.

Add another tablespoon of olive oil to the pan. Toss the ground beef on high heat until it changes color, then add the bacon mixture. Add the fresh herbs – marjoram is delicious, but a mixture of parsley chives and thyme or even some rosemary would also be very good. Finally, add the tomatoes and season with salt, pepper, and a good pinch of sugar. Increase the heat and cook until the mixture is thick and concentrated, but still juicy.

Preheat the oven to 350°F.

Split the vegetable marrow in half lengthwise and scoop out the seeds from one half. Save the other half for another recipe, perhaps Vegetable Marrow in Cheese Sauce (see below), one of my favorite things in the whole world.

When the stuffing has reduced, taste and correct the seasoning; it should be intense and lively.

Season the cavity of the vegetable marrow with salt and freshly ground pepper and a sprig or two of marjoram, if you have it. Then fill it with the stuffing.

Coat with thick, well-seasoned Mornay sauce and sprinkle the top generously with a mixture of grated cheese and buttered bread crumbs. Bake for about 1 hour, until the marrow is very tender – it is cooked when a knife can pierce it without any resistance. Serve with garlic butter and a tasty green salad.

Variation
STUFFED VEGETABLE
MARROW FOR ONE
Cut a circular piece of vegetable marrow about 1½ in thick. Scoop out the center, fill with Tomato Fondue (see page 378), Peperonata (see page 87), or any filling of your choice. Coat with Mornay Sauce (see page 119) and sprinkle with a mixture of Buttered Crumbs (see page 577) and grated cheese. Bake in a moderate oven at 350°F for about 15–20 minutes. Serve with Garlic Butter (see page 217).

ZUCCHINI OR VEGETABLE MARROW IN CHEESE SAUCE

Most people who grow zucchini find it difficult to eat them fast enough; when they turn into vegetable marrows try this – it is unexpectedly good · **SERVES 4-6**

3lb large zucchini OR small
    vegetable marrows (should
    yield about 2lb prepared)
3 tablespoons butter
salt, freshly ground black pepper

¾ **cup grated Cheddar cheese, or a mixture of Parmesan and Gruyère**

1 cup whole milk

Roux (see page 165)

Peel and seed the zucchini or vegetable marrow and cut the flesh into 1in chunks. Melt the butter in a heavy casserole dish, toss in the zucchini or vegetable marrow, and season with salt and freshly ground pepper. Cover with a piece of parchment paper and the lid of the saucepan. Cook on low heat until soft and juicy, about 20 minutes.

Remove the marrow or zucchini with a slotted spoon to a serving dish. Add the milk to the juices in the casserole dish and bring to a boil. Whisk in enough roux to thicken the sauce. Add the cheese, taste, and correct the seasoning. Pour the sauce over the vegetable and serve sprinkled with chopped parsley.

Variations

• Sprinkle extra grated cheese or a mixture of grated cheese and buttered bread crumbs on top and flash under the broiler until crispy and golden.
• Put a layer of Shepherd's Pie (see page 342) mixture in the serving dish or dishes, then top with marrow and cheese sauce.
• A layer of Tomato Fondue (see page 378) with the above would also be delicious.

ZUCCHINI SOUP WITH CURRY SPICES

My brother Rory O'Connell has cooked me many memorable meals. He came up with this tasty recipe that is perfect for using up zucchini that have got away on you · **SERVES 12**

8 tablespoons butter
4 teaspoons curry powder
¾lb onions, chopped
8 large zucchini, chopped (about 2lb in weight)
salt and freshly ground pepper
2½ quarts Chicken Stock (see page 262)
chopped parsley and chives
heavy cream, to serve (optional)

Melt the butter over low heat. When it foams, add the curry powder and onions. Stir to coat the onions in the spiced butter. Cover with a piece of parchment paper and the lid of the saucepan. Sweat gently until the onions are tender, about 8–10 minutes.

Add the zucchini and season. Add the hot stock and bring back to a boil. Cook, uncovered, until the zucchini are just tender. Purée immediately, taste, and correct the seasoning. Thin with extra stock if necessary. Serve topped with chopped parsley and chives. Add a little cream if the soup needs it.

ROAST PUMPKIN

All pumpkin and squash benefit from roasting. Boiling does nothing for them, although having said that, the little gem squash is one of the exceptions to this rule. Roasting is one of the easiest ways to cook pumpkin and squash and intensifies the taste. It also allows you to add extra flavors in terms of herbs and spices · **SERVES 6-8**

Above: *A prolific zucchini plant.*

1 small pumpkin or butternut squash, seeds and cottony fibers removed
salt and freshly ground pepper
olive oil or beef dripping
fresh thyme, sage, or rosemary, chopped
soy sauce, mushroom soy sauce, or herb-flavored oil, to serve

Preheat the oven to 350°F.

Cut the pumpkin into chunks with a bit of skin on each piece. Transfer to a roasting pan or earthenware dish. Season with salt and pepper. Toss in olive oil or melted drippings. Sprinkle on the chopped herbs, if using, and toss again. Roast for 45 minutes to 1 hour, depending on size, turning occasionally during cooking.

To serve, drizzle over soy sauce, mushroom soy sauce, or herb-flavored oil.

Variation

Arrange the roasted pumpkin in a dish, scatter with grated Gruyère cheese, and flash under a broiler until the cheese becomes bubbly and brown. If you like, scatter it with crispy bacon and lots of chopped parsley; you'll have a supper dish, rather than just an accompanying vegetable.

THAI-SPICED SQUASH SOUP WITH NOODLES

There are many good pumpkin soup recipes – a simple formula is one cup of chopped onion, four cups of chopped pumpkin, five cups of chicken or vegetable stock, and plenty of seasoning. Notice I've omitted potato in the base because it tends to dull the flavor and the pumpkin itself has enough texture to thicken the soup.

Pumpkins also take on other flavors like chiles and spices really well. This delicious version, served at the Ballymaloe Shop Café, is my current favorite, and I am deeply grateful to chef Alison Henderson for sharing the recipe with me ·
SERVES 6–8

1½ tablespoons sunflower oil
1 tablespoon or more Thai red curry paste (**Mae ploy**)
2 teaspoons freshly ground coriander seeds
2 teaspoons green cardamoms, bruised
14fl oz can coconut milk

5 cups Chicken or VegetableStock (see pages 262 and 390))
1 butternut squash, peeled, seeded, and cut into 1¼in chunks
2 lemongrass stalks, finely chopped (remove coarse outer leaves)
1 kaffir lime leaf, sliced (or grated zest and juice of ½ lime)
2 leeks, finely sliced
2 celery ribs, finely sliced
salt and pepper
2 tablespoons fish sauce (**Nam pla**)
4oz Chinese fine dried egg noodles (optional)

GARNISH
1 red chile, seeded and finely diced
1½ scallions, finely sliced
2 tablespoons chopped cilantro

Warm the oil in a deep pot and add the curry paste, coriander, and cardamom. Stir-fry until fragrant, about 1 minute. Pour in the coconut milk and stock and bring to a boil. Add the butternut squash, lemongrass, lime leaf or zest, leeks, and celery. Simmer gently for about 15 minutes, until the squash is tender. Season to taste with salt and freshly ground pepper and add the fish sauce and lime juice, if using.

Cook the noodles in plenty of boiling salted water until just tender to the bite (see the package for timing). Drain, rinse in cold water, and drain again.

To serve, put some noodles into the bottom of a deep soup bowl. Ladle over the hot soup and sprinkle with garnish. A drizzle or rosemary or thyme oil over the top of each bowl of soup just before serving is one of our favorite touches.

SQUASH WITH BASIL OR MARJORAM

Patty pan squash are great to grow because they are so prolific and pretty – bright yellow with little scalloped edges. Don't let them get much bigger than 2½in in diameter because the flavor dilutes with every extra inch. They're also delicious cut into wedges, dipped in milk, and then a spicy seasoned flour – and deep-fried until crispy at the edges. Serve immediately with a wedge of lemon · **SERVES 6**

12–18 patty pan squash or a mixture of patty pan squash and small green zucchini
extra virgin olive oil
salt and freshly ground black pepper
2 tablespoons freshly chopped marjoram or torn basil leaves
a few drops of lemon juice, optional

Trim the squash and cut each into 6 or 8 pie-shaped pieces, depending on size. If using, cut the zucchini on the diagonal into ½in slices.

Heat a few tablespoons of olive oil in an iron pan or wok, add the squash and zucchini, if using. Season with salt and pepper, toss rapidly over the heat for 3–4 minutes and add the herbs. Toss for another minute or so.

Taste, and correct the seasoning. Add a few drops of lemon juice and serve immediately.

ROASTED PUMPKIN SEEDS

Roast pumpkin seeds with salt or sugar and add them to breakfast cereals, breads, or simply nibble to your heart's content. Alternatively, dry the seed and save for next year's crop.

pumpkin seeds
sea salt

Preheat the oven to 250°F.

Remove the seeds from the flesh and rinse under cold water. Lay a single layer on a baking sheet and sprinkle with a generous amount of sea salt.

Dry roast in the oven for 30–40 minutes, by which time the seeds should be nice and crunchy.

Cabbages

There is a perception, not totally without justification, that brassica plants are difficult to grow. If growing brassica plants from seed is more than you feel you can take on, just look out for a few organic cabbage, cauliflower, or Brussels sprout plants at your local garden center or farmers' market. It's easy to establish them in a vegetable garden, provided you don't have a pigeon problem; pigeons are notoriously fond of them.

Cabbages and other brassicas prefer poor-quality soil – in fact, if the soil is too rich they may suffer from club root. You may not think it's worth growing cabbage because it's so widely available, but when you taste one that's homegrown, you'll realize why the tradition of buying cabbage plants for the garden in January and February still lives on in Ireland.

The traditional way of cooking cabbage is to boil fairly finely shredded cabbage (stalks removed) in boiling salted water or, better still, bacon cooking water. The cooking time varies depending on the variety of cabbage, so keep a watchful eye and drain the cabbage just as soon as it is cooked. Add a nice lump of butter, season with lots of freshly ground pepper and a little more salt, if necessary.

BUTTERED CABBAGE

The flavor of this quickly cooked cabbage has been a revelation for many and has converted numerous determined cabbage haters back to Ireland's national vegetable ·
SERVES 6

1lb fresh Savoy cabbage
2 tablespoons butter (or more if you like)
salt and freshly ground pepper
a dab of butter

Remove the tough outer leaves and divide the cabbage into 4. Cut out the stalks and then cut each section into fine shreds across the grain.

Put 2 or 3 tablespoons of water into a wide saucepan with the butter and a pinch of salt. Bring to a boil, add the cabbage and toss constantly over high heat, then cover for a few minutes. Toss again and add some more salt, freshly ground pepper, and the dab of butter. Serve immediately.

Variations
CABBAGE WITH CARAWAY SEEDS
Add 1–2 tablespoons of caraway seeds to the cabbage and toss constantly as above.

CABBAGE WITH CRISPY BACON
Fry 2–3 srips of bacon in a little oil while the cabbage cooks, then cut into pieces and add to the cabbage at the end.

EMILY'S CABBAGE
Add 3 tablespoons or more of fresh thyme leaves.

SPICED CABBAGE SOUP

Follow the recipe for Curly Kale Soup on page 413, using chopped Savoy cabbage leaves instead of curly kale.

Heat a little vegetable oil in a large frying pan over medium heat. When hot, add 1 tablespoon whole black mustard seeds. As soon as they begin to pop, add 4 chopped garlic cloves and stir in. Add 1 chopped dried red chile and ½ teaspoon sugar and stir for a few seconds. Add this spice mix to the puréed soup and correct the seasoning.

Serve piping hot and top with a few cilantro leaves.

Brussels Sprouts

The allure of homegrown Brussels sprouts for me is that yet again it is a three-in-one vegetable. We eat the sprouts themselves, the Brussels sprout tops, and the shoots. The shoots, which sprout out from the bottom of the stalk at the end of the crop, were a new discovery last winter, and are some of the most delicious things I've ever tasted.

If you're hungry enough, there is also a fourth option – peel off the tough outer layer and then dice the stalk. Cook it in boiling salted water, then drain, and toss in a little butter or olive oil and marjoram or thyme leaves.

When we finally pull out the plants, we throw them to the pigs. They then crunch them up, so not a single scrap is wasted. How about that for a return on the price of a few Brussels sprout plants?

BRUSSELS SPROUTS

These days, Brussels sprouts are often served overcooked, but the traditional way to cook sprouts was to cut a cross in the stalk so they would cook more evenly. I discovered quite by accident when I was in a rush one day that if you cut the sprouts in half lengthwise they cook much faster and taste infinitely more delicious. If you prefer, use olive oil instead of butter · **SERVES 4–6**

1lb Brussels sprouts
1½ teaspoons salt
2 tablespoons butter (or more if
**   you like)**
salt, freshly ground black pepper

Choose even, medium-sized sprouts. Trim the outer leaves if necessary and cut them in half lengthwise. Salt 2 cups of water and bring it to a fast, rolling boil. Toss in the sprouts, cover the saucepan for a minute until the water returns to a boil, then uncover and continue to simmer for 5–6 minutes, or until the sprouts are cooked through but still have a slight bite. Drain very well.

Melt a little butter in the saucepan and roll the sprouts around gently. Season with lots of freshly ground pepper and salt. Taste and serve immediately in a hot serving dish.

If the sprouts are not to be served immediately, refresh them under cold water just as soon as they are cooked. Just before serving, drop them into boiling salted water for a few seconds to heat through. Drain and toss in the butter, season and serve. This way they will taste almost as good as if they were freshly cooked: certainly much more delicious than sprouts kept warm for half an hour in an oven.

SPICY BRUSSELS SPROUTS

People tend to cook Brussels sprouts the same way every time. Here is one way to perk them up – by shredding them and adding spices. They are delicious and ready in minutes · **SERVES 4–6**

1lb Brussels sprouts
2 tablespoons butter
2 tablespoons extra virgin olive oil
½ teaspoon freshly ground cumin
½ teaspoon freshly ground
**   coriander**
salt, freshly ground black pepper
splash of lime or lemon juice

Trim the outer leaves of the Brussels sprouts, if necessary, and cut in half or quarters lengthwise, depending on size. Shred the remainder. Melt the butter and olive oil in a sauté pan. Add the spices, stir, and cook for a minute. Add the sprouts. Season with salt and freshly ground pepper, and toss for 3–4 minutes. Add a little lemon or lime juice to perk up the flavor. Serve immediately in a warm serving dish.

BRUSSELS SPROUT TOPS

You won't find these in a supermarket, but they are a real bonus for home gardeners who grow Brussels sprouts. These come from the top of the plant and look like shot Brussels sprouts. You can cook them as you would kale, or slice them thinly and add to salads and soups. Chefs are also starting to discover them, so look out for them on restaurant menus · **SERVES 4–6**

1lb Brussels sprout tops
6 teaspoons salt
butter or extra virgin olive oil
freshly ground black pepper

Pick over the tops, trim any tough bits of stalk, and chop the leaves roughly. Pop the surplus into the compost or hens' bucket.

Bring a large, high-sided saucepan of 2½ quarts of cold water to a boil over high heat. Add the salt and the sprout tops and stir. Cover the saucepan. When the water comes back to a boil, remove the lid and continue to cook for 3–4

Right: *Purple sprouting broccoli.*

minutes, or until the sprout tops are tender. Drain well.

Melt a little butter or heat a few tablespoons of extra virgin olive oil in the saucepan, toss in the well-drained sprout tops. Season generously with freshly ground pepper. Taste, correct the seasoning, and serve as soon as possible.

Variations

BRUSSELS SPROUT SHOOTS

These are a great new discovery for me, but probably well-known to our grandparents' generation, who didn't waste a scrap of anything. The shoots grow from the Brussels sprouts at the base of the plant and are completely tender and delicious. Follow the recipe as above, but use 5–6in of each tender shoot.

Additions to tops and shoots

Chopped crispy bacon and good bacon fat may be added. A little diced chorizo is also delicious, as is a bit of diced anchovy, lots of chopped parsley, and sizzling butter.

Broccoli

We have an abundance of summer vegetables, but winter vegetables are scarcer, so they're extra special. Plant your seeds in midspring or, if you miss that deadline, look for little plants at the garden center in late spring and you'll be able to eat sprouting broccoli in the earlier months of the following year.

There are three types, all of which are terrific: green sprouting, white sprouting, and purple sprouting broccoli. It will continue to produce until the following spring, and the more you pick it, the more it comes. You pick off the main flower, and that encourages little sprouts to emerge from the stalks. Sprouting broccoli is cooked in a couple of minutes and, like all the Brassicas, is tremendously delicious. The leaves also make a great soup.

SPROUTING BROCCOLI

Even though there are lots of things you can do with sprouting broccoli, I find that it's so gorgeous that I just like to leave it alone. The secret to delicious green vegetables is freshness, coupled with well-salted cooking water ·
SERVES 4–6

1lb sprouting broccoli
3 teaspoons salt
freshly ground black pepper

Peel the broccoli stems with a knife or potato peeler, cut off the stalk close to the head and cut the stems into ½in pieces. If the heads are large, divide the florets into smaller clusters.

Add the salt to 5 cups of water and bring to a fast boil. Add the stalks, cook for 1 minute, and then add the florets. Cook, uncovered, at a rolling boil for 5–6 minutes. Drain while the broccoli still has a bite. Season with pepper.

Kale

Mummy grew curly kale every winter. She felt very strongly about the importance of it as a winter green for the health of the family, and kale, to me, remains a wonder food. It's the most nutritious of all the Brassicas, it's full of iron and other trace elements, and every time I eat kale I literally feel better immediately. Kale can be sliced very thinly and added into salads and soups as well as cooked.

Besides common curly kale, we grow several different varieties. Some of the leaves are serrated, others crinkly, others almost feathery. They come in shades ranging from greeny-gray to blue, green, deep purple, cream, and yellow. Red Russian Kale is one of our favorites; I can hardly bear to pick the deeply serrated leaves, since they look so beautiful in the winter garden when it is covered with frost. In the early morning, when the sun shines on the droplets of dew on the leaves, the tussle between the cook and gardener in me is at its most acute!

You can eat kale in all its different stages: raw when young, cooked when older, and it makes absolutely wonderful soups. A few nights of frost greatly enhance the sweetness of kale, which these days can be a bit of a dilemma, because entire winters may go by without a frost. Kale is tolerant of poor soil and generally resistant to club root and cabbage root fly. There's also a purple variety that's so beautiful, frilly, and decorative, that we plant it throughout the herbaceous border as well.

We also love the old variety known as cut-and-come (*Brassica oleracea)*, or cottier's kale, also known as "hungry gap" because it was once the only green available between the end of winter and the first of the early summer vegetables. This particular type of kale always seems to catch the botanist's eye when walking around my garden, because it's so rare. It's propagated only by slips, so you must know somebody who has some if you want to get some; in the olden days, it was passed from one cottage garden to another. My slip of kale came from the 18th-century walled garden at Glin Castle in Co. Limerick. They planted their kale

Left: *Curly kale and Red Russian – must-have winter greens.*

from a slip brought in by the cook, May Liston, from her cottage garden in Lower Athea, close by.

If you find someone who has it, ask them to pull off a piece with a "heel." If you just plant that into the ground, it'll take root and grow into your own plant. It's called cut-and-come because the more you cut it, the more it comes back. You can find sea kale, or strand cabbage (see page 72), another forgotten flavor, in old kitchen gardens and occasionally at the farmers' market. It, too, is really worth seeking out.

KALE

Like spinach, kale reduces significantly during cooking, so you'll need to start with a great big pot full. When kale is really young, you do not need to destalk it. If you would rather not have a smooth texture to your kale, roughly chop the leaves beforehand and skip the step where you purée the kale below · SERVES 4

3 teaspoons salt
1lb curly kale, destalked (about 10oz without stalks)
salt, freshly ground black pepper, and a little grated nutmeg (optional)
4 tablespoons butter
½ cup cream

Put 3½ quarts of water in a large saucepan, add the salt, and bring to a boil. Add the curly kale and boil, uncovered, on high heat until tender. This will take about 8–10 minutes.

Drain off the water and purée the kale in a food processor. Return

to the saucepan and season with salt, pepper, and a little nutmeg if you like. Add the butter and cream, bubble, and taste. Serve hot.

CURLY KALE WITH BACON AND CHESTNUTS

Kale is so good simply cooked, that I rarely add much else to it. Here, however, the chestnuts and bacon are a lovely twist on the basic recipe. This is a wonderful accompaniment to pheasant, partridge, or grouse · SERVES 8

2 tablespoons salt
2lb kale
9oz bacon
extra virgin olive oil
1 cup chestnuts, peeled and roughly chopped
dab of butter and olive oil
freshly ground black pepper

In a large saucepan, bring 3½ quarts of water to a boil, with the salt added. Meanwhile, destalk the kale and wash it quickly in cold water. Drain and cook the kale at a fast, rolling boil for 8–10 minutes, until tender.

Cut the bacon into ¼in pieces. Heat a couple of tablespoons of extra virgin olive oil in a frying pan, add the bacon, and cook until crisp and golden. Add the chopped chestnuts and cook for another minute or two.

Drain the kale well and add to the bacon and chestnuts. Add a dab of butter and drizzle generously with olive oil, toss, taste, and season with lots of freshly ground pepper. Serve immediately.

CURLY KALE SOUP

If you have curly kale, you usually have lots of it. One way to use it up is in this delicious soup. When I eat this, I feel like every mouthful is doing me good. Note that if this soup is to be reheated, just bring it to a boil and serve. Prolonged boiling spoils the color and flavor of green soups · SERVES 6

4 tablespoons butter
5oz potatoes, peeled and cut into ½in cubes
¾ cup onions, peeled and cut into ½in cubes
salt and freshly ground black pepper
5 cups Chicken Stock (see page 262) or Vegetable Stock (see page 390)
9oz curly kale leaves, stalks removed and chopped
¼–½ cup cream or whole milk

Melt the butter in a heavy saucepan. When it foams, add the potatoes and onions and turn them in the butter until well-coated. Sprinkle with salt and freshly ground pepper. Cover and sweat on a gentle heat for 10 minutes. Add the stock and boil gently, covered, until the potatoes are soft. Add the kale and cook with the lid off, until the kale is cooked.

Keep the lid off to retain the green color. Do not overcook or the vegetables will lose both their fresh flavor and color. Purée the soup in a blender or food processor. Taste, and adjust the seasoning. Add the cream or milk just before serving.

BRAISED CAVOLO NERO

Crinkled black kale is known as cavolo nero (black Tuscan cabbage). Serve it on its own, as a vegetable, or as a topping for polenta · SERVES 4–6

2¼ lb cavolo nero
sea salt and freshly ground black
    pepper
3 tablespoons extra virgin olive oil
2 garlic cloves, peeled and finely
    sliced
extra virgin olive oil

Remove the leaves from the cavolo nero stems. Blanch in a large pot of boiling, well-salted water for 5–15 minutes. Be careful not to overcook. Drain well.

    Heat the olive oil in a heavy-bottomed saucepan. Add the garlic and fry gently. When it begins to color, add the cavolo nero and

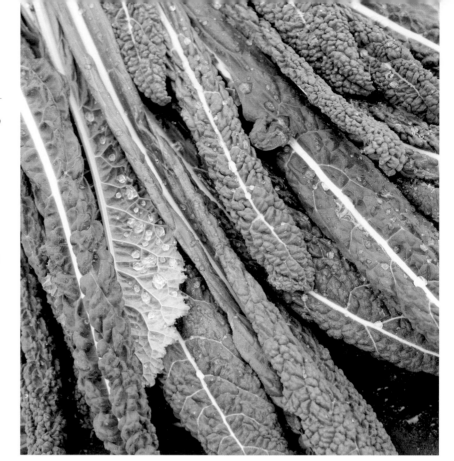

Above: *Cavolo Nero/black Tuscan kale.* **Opposite:** *Cavolo Nero Bruschetta.*

Above: *Cottier's kale, also known as hungry gap or cut-and-come.*

season generously with salt and pepper. Cook for about 5 minutes. Transfer to a bowl and drizzle generously with extra virgin olive oil.

CAVOLO NERO BRUSCHETTA
One of my favorite haunts in Florence, Osteria dei Benci, serves this mixture piled onto a slice of chargrilled sourdough bread.

COTTIER'S KALE, CUT-AND-COME, OR HUNGRY GAP

Cut-and-come kale, also known as cottier's kale or hungry gap, is very different from curly kale. The texture is melting, like spinach, but it has the flavor of kale · SERVES 6

3lb cottier's kale
3 teaspoons salt
salt and freshly ground black
    pepper
4 tablespoons butter

Strip the leaves from the stalks and wash the kale. In a saucepan, bring 1¾ quarts of water and the salt to a fast rolling boil. Add the kale and cook, uncovered, for about 25 minutes, or until tender. Drain off the water and season the kale well with salt and freshly ground pepper. Chop well (I use an egg slicer) and beat in a generous lump of butter. Taste, and add a bit more seasoning if you need to.

Radishes

Radishes are one of the easiest of all vegetables to grow. My granddaughter, Willow, is the "Radish Queen" and has been growing radishes every summer since she was three years old. During the summer growing season, they grow from seed to being ready to pick in just 14 days. Don't sow too many together or you won't be able to eat them fast enough.

Young radish leaves are delicious in green salads, and the slightly older leaves make a delicious soup (see the basic soup formula on page 380). Drizzle a little crème fraîche over the top and add a few paper-thin slivers of radish as garnish. If you can't quite keep up with the crop, here's a forgotten skill: sprinkle the radish flowers over salads or let them develop into seed pods, which are crunchy and delicious. They are not to be missed and certainly shouldn't be wasted. You may want to nibble them as a snack, but they are also good in salads.

RADISHES WITH BUTTER, SEA SALT, AND CRUSTY BREAD

When I was just 18, alone and frightened as a young au pair in Besançon, France, a French girl took pity on me and invited me to have lunch with her in a café. We had a plate of charcuterie and radishes. I watched, fascinated, as she buttered her radishes, dipped them in sea salt and ate them greedily. I followed suit and have never forgotten the flavor.

**fresh radishes, complete with
    leaves**
unsalted butter pats (see page 216)
good sea salt

Gently wash the radishes, trimming the tail and the top of the leaves if they are large. Cut a chunk of butter into ½in cubes. If you have butter bats, soak them in cold water and then use them to roll each cube into a butter ball. Drop into a bowl of iced water.

To serve, put 7 or 8 chilled radishes on each plate. Add 2 or 3 butter balls and a little mound of sea salt. Serve with fresh, crusty bread.

Right: *An old saucepan is given a new lease of life. Don't forget to use the tender leaves of baby radishes in salad or soup.*

RADISH LEAF SOUP

Here is a way of using up every precious scrap of the radish crop you've put the time and energy into growing. This uses the basic soup formula (see page 380). White turnip leaves also make a remarkably good soup and can also be cooked as greens · SERVES 4

3 tablespoons butter
5oz potatoes, peeled and chopped
¾ cup onion, peeled and chopped
salt and freshly ground black
    pepper
3 cups water or Chicken Stock (see
    page 262) or Vegetable Stock
    (see page 390)
1 cup whole milk
5oz radish leaves, chopped

Melt the butter in a heavy-bottomed saucepan. When it foams, add the potatoes and onions, and toss until well coated. Season with salt and pepper. Stir well, cover, and sweat on a gentle heat for 10 minutes.

When the vegetables are almost soft but not colored, add the stock and milk. Bring to a boil and simmer until the potatoes and onions are fully cooked. Add the radish leaves and boil with the lid off for 4–5 minutes, until the radish leaves are cooked. Do not overcook or the soup will lose its fresh green color. Purée in a blender. Taste, and adjust the seasoning.

RADISH, CUCUMBER, AND MINT SALAD

This is a delicious little salad as well as a wonderful way to use up a glut of radishes. Serve it alone or with pan-grilled lamb chops or a crispy-skinned organic chicken thigh · SERVES 6

1 fresh cucumber
18–24 radishes, trimmed and
    quartered
18 yellow cherry tomatoes, halved
a handful of fresh mint leaves
3 tablespoons extra virgin olive oil
1 tablespoon white wine vinegar
sea salt and freshly ground black
    pepper
½ teaspoon honey

Slit the cucumber lengthwise. Scoop out the seeds with a melon baller or a pointed teaspoon (we feed them to the hens). Cut each side lengthwise again, and then into ¼in slices at an angle. Add the radishes and tomatoes to the cucumber with the mint leaves. Whisk the oil and vinegar together with the honey and season with a few flakes of sea salt and freshly ground pepper. Drizzle over the vegetables and toss gently.

CUCUMBER, RADISH, FETA, PARSLEY, AND NIGELLA SEED SALAD

If you have a glut of radishes, this is a good way to let them shine - fresh, crunchy, and delicious · SERVES 6-8

1 cucumber
2 bunches radishes
8oz feta
salt, freshly ground black pepper
extra virgin olive oil
freshly squeezed lemon juice
lots of flat parsley sprigs and
    mint leaves
2 tablespoons nigella seeds (see
    page 460)

Cut the cucumber, radishes, and feta into ½in cubes and put in a bowl. Season, and drizzle with olive oil and lemon juice. Toss gently, and add the parsley and mint leaves. Taste, and correct the seasoning. Sprinkle with nigella seeds and serve.

Jerusalem Artichokes

These knotty roots are a wonderful vegetable because they remain in the ground all winter, like potatoes, and can be dug up as you need them. Jerusalem artichokes are a perennial, so once you plant them, they usually reemerge every year and can spread like crazy if you are not careful. They have the highest inulin content of any vegetable – this promotes good bacteria in your intestines, so is particularly important if you've been on a course of antibiotics, which kill the good as well as bad bacteria in your system.

From the point of view of the cook, Jerusalem artichokes are enormously versatile. As soon as you've dug them, scrub them under cold running water; then they can be boiled, roasted, peeled, or puréed, or made into a soup or gratin. They go particularly well with shellfish, especially scallops and mussels. I also love to pack them around pheasant when I'm casserole roasting, so they become imbued with the pheasant juices. There's only one slight little hitch. Their nickname "fartichokes" is well justified – but that's because they're so good for the digestive system.

ROAST JERUSALEM ARTICHOKES

It has to be said that roast Jerusalem artichokes don't look that appealing, but don't let that put you off. They are particularly good with goose, duck, or pheasant, animals that enjoy eating Jerusalem artichokes themselves – which may or may not be a coincidence! · SERVES 4-6

1lb Jerusalem artichokes, well-scrubbed
2 tablespoons sunflower or olive oil
salt and freshly ground black pepper
a few rosemary or thyme sprigs, optional

Preheat the oven to 400°F.

Leave the artichokes whole or, if they are large, cut them in half lengthwise. Toss them with the oil and season well with salt. Transfer to a shallow gratin dish or roasting pan and bake for 20–30 minutes. Test with the tip of a knife – they should be mostly tender but offer some resistance. Sprinkle with thyme or rosemary sprigs, season with pepper, and serve.

BRAISED JERUSALEM ARTICHOKES

The maddening thing about artichokes is that they cook unevenly, so it will be necessary to test them with a skewer at regular intervals. Cooking them in a covered casserole dish is a particularly good method, because you can turn off the heat after about 10 minutes – the artichokes will continue to cook in the heat of the casserole dish and will also hold their shape. Serve with pheasant or venison · SERVES 4

1½lb Jerusalem artichokes
2 tablespoons butter
salt and freshly ground black pepper
freshly chopped parsley

Peel the artichokes thinly and slice them ¼ in thick. Melt the butter in a cast-iron casserole dish, toss the artichokes, and season with salt and freshly ground pepper. Add 2 teaspoons of water and cover with a piece of parchment paper (to keep in the steam) and the casserole lid. Cook over low heat on the stovetop or put in a moderate oven at 350°F for about 15–20 minutes, until the artichokes are soft, but still keep their shape. Toss every now and then during cooking. Serve sprinkled with chopped parsley.

WARM SALAD OF JERUSALEM ARTICHOKES WITH HAZELNUT OIL DRESSING

White turnips and kohlrabi are also delicious cooked and served in this way. This recipe provides a perfect first course for a winter dinner party, and raises the Jerusalem artichoke to a more sophisticated level · SERVES 4

12oz Jerusalem artichokes, very carefully peeled to a smooth shape
½ tablespoon butter
salt and freshly ground black pepper

FOR THE HAZELNUT OIL DRESSING
3 tablespoons hazelnut oil
1½ tablespoons white wine vinegar
¼ teaspoon Dijon mustard
salt, freshly ground black pepper, and sugar to taste

TO SERVE
a few oakleaf lettuce leaves
¼ cup hazelnuts, toasted and sliced
sprigs of chervil, for garnish

Cut the artichokes into ½in slices. Bring ½ cup of water and the butter to a boil in a heavy saucepan and add the artichokes. Season. Cover, and cook gently until the artichokes are almost cooked. Turn off the heat and leave in the covered saucepan until they are almost tender. Test with a skewer at regular intervals; they usually take about 15 minutes from the point at which you turn off the heat.

While the artichokes are cooking, prepare the hazelnut dressing by mixing all the ingredients together.

When the artichokes are cooked, carefully remove from the saucepan, making sure not to break them up. Place them on a flat dish in a single layer. Spoon over some of the hazelnut dressing, and toss while still warm. Taste and correct the seasoning, if necessary.

To assemble the salad, divide the sliced artichokes between 4 plates. Put a little circle of lettuce around the vegetables and sprinkle some of the dressing over the lettuce. Garnish with the hazelnuts and chervil sprigs. Eat while the artichokes are still warm.

Globe Artichokes

These are spectacular perennial plants with gray-green textured leaves. They are very easy to grow and return effortlessly every year in early summer. There are several varieties – we have a particularly good one, which sadly doesn't have a name, since it's been handed down through the generations in my mother-in-law's family and moved from one kitchen garden to another. We start to eat them while they're still about the size of a closed fist and continue to enjoy them when they get much bigger. The ones we miss we allow to blossom into the beautiful purple-blue thistles.

When artichokes are ready to harvest, simply slice the stalk about 1in underneath the head. When you're ready to cook, score the stalk just underneath the head. Lay the artichoke on its side on the edge of a work surface so the stalk is hanging over the edge, then push the stalk down and pull it away from the head, bringing any tough fibers from the base of the heart with it.

GLOBE ARTICHOKES WITH MELTED BUTTER

Globe artichokes are one of the scariest things to land in front of you if you've never handled one. Don't worry, just follow my beginner's guide · SERVES 6

6 globe artichokes
lemon juice or vinegar
2 teaspoons white wine vinegar
2 teaspoons salt
1½ sticks butter
freshly squeezed juice of 3 lemons

Trim the base of the artichokes just before cooking, so they sit steadily on a plate, then rub the cut end with lemon juice or vinegar to prevent it from discoloring.

Have a large saucepan of about 1 quart of boiling water ready. Add 2 teaspoons of vinegar and 2 teaspoons of salt to every quart of water. Pop in the artichokes and bring the water back to a boil. Simmer steadily for about 25 minutes. After about 20 minutes, you could try testing to see if the artichokes are done. I do this by tugging off one of the larger leaves at the base; it should come away easily. If it doesn't, continue to cook for another 5–10 minutes. Remove, and drain upside down on a plate.

While they are cooking, melt the butter and add lemon juice to taste.

To serve, put each warm artichoke onto a hot plate, and serve the melted butter in a little bowl. Artichokes are eaten with your fingers, so provide a finger bowl. A spare plate to collect all the nibbled leaves and chokes is also useful.

To eat: starting with the big leaves at the base, pull off one at a time and dip it in the butter. There is a little morsel of flesh at the base of each leaf that you can bite onto and scrape off with your teeth. Work your way toward the center, until eventually you are rewarded for your patience when you come to the artichoke heart. Scrape off the bristly "choke" in the center with a knife or spoon, and discard. Then cut the heart into pieces, sprinkle with a little sea salt and dip into the sauce or melted butter. Hollandaise sauce or French dressing are also divine.

USES FOR LEFTOVER VEGETABLES

• The green part of leeks – use in soups.
• Cauliflower leaves – finely chop any that are not wilted, plus the stalk, and cook in very little boiling salted water. Put the florets on top to steam. Serve with a little Mornay Sauce (see page 119) or Parsley Sauce (see page 315) or add to Tomato Fondue (see page 378).
• Celery leaves – can be sliced and added to salad or deep-fried.
• Mushroom stalks – can be added to stock or sliced and added to any mushroom dish; they taste just as good.
• Lettuce – use in soups. It doesn't occur to most people to cook lettuce, but if you have a glut, this is one way to use it. Use the basic soup formula on page 380. The combination of lettuce, cucumber, and peas with fresh mint is one we particularly enjoy. Or try shredding lettuce thinly and tossing it quickly on high heat in extra virgin olive oil with some chile flakes and fresh herbs until it wilts. Enjoy immediately.

Preserving

Years ago, preserving skills were essential for survival through our long winter months. A glut in the garden provoked a frenzy of activity in order to harvest every bit of the precious crop. There was a great sense of urgency in the days before electricity because it was the only opportunity people had to lay down a store to get themselves through the fallow seasons. Preserving was acutely important in the rhythm of the year.

During my childhood, waste was not an option – food was too precious and scarce to be thrown away. Since the advent of electricity, most households have freezers and surplus food can easily be frozen, so the reasons for preserving have changed. Recently I've seen a huge revival of interest and creativity as people experiment, combining old and new techniques and flavors. Chefs who just a few years ago wouldn't have been seen dead jam making or regarded it merely the domain of homemakers are now proudly offering their own chutneys and pickles at their restaurants as an integral part of their food style.

I love the smell of chutneys and marmalades bubbling on the stove. You can't help feeling a glow of satisfaction every time you look into a well-stocked pantry and see your bottles and jam jars lined up on the shelf like good deeds. It also means you have a ready supply of terrific gifts to take along to a dinner party – much more welcome than a cheap bottle of wine. For a lot of people preserving can seem like a really big deal, and so I thought I might share a little anecdote that took the mystery out of jam making for me.

When I was little, Mummy had several big jam-making sessions throughout the year, particularly in the soft fruit season. When the gooseberries and black currants were ripe they needed to be picked and dealt with before the birds (and us kids) polished them all off. She'd decide on an appointed day and there would be a big build-up to the jam-making session. She'd stock up with lots of sugar, jam jars, and little packages of jam covers. When we arrived home from school in the evening the kitchen would be piled high with jars of jam, sticky pots and labels, and Mummy would be taking a tray of scones with sugary tops out of the oven for us to enjoy with the first of the freshly made jam and a blob of cream. So to me, jam making was always something I looked forward to, but was unquestionably a big deal that disrupted the normal daily routine and was not to be embarked upon lightly.

Years later, shortly after I had arrived at Ballymaloe House, I was in the kitchen with Myrtle Allen, then my boss, now my mother-in-law, who was doing her evening ritual of checking the fridges to see what needed to be incorporated into the lunch menu for the following day. Everybody else had gone home by then, and I suddenly heard her say from the depths of the cold-room, "Oh my goodness, there are some strawberries here, they should have been used up today – we should make them into jam." I couldn't believe my ears – it was about 11.30 at night; surely she couldn't be suggesting that we start to make jam at this hour? The idea of casually embarking on a jam-making session without all the preliminary build-up was inconceivable to me, but I was new and eager to impress, so instead of arguing, I offered to help. She called out the recipe across the kitchen as she continued checking the fridges – hull and weigh the berries, equal quantity of sugar, squeeze a lemon or two and so on. I followed her instructions and hey presto, the jam was made in a few minutes. I couldn't believe how easy it was, but the difference was that Mummy always made a huge quantity of jam at a time, whereas this small quantity was made in minutes. For me, that was a eureka moment that took the mystery out of jam making, and now I'll make jam spontaneously at any time with the smallest box of fruit. That's the secret, so for the most delicious results, use your freezer to save fruit and make jam little and often.

Flavored Oils and Vinegars

If you have an abundance of herbs, one the easiest ways to preserve them, apart from freezing or drying, is to immerse them in oil or vinegar. We've had success with mushrooms, garlic, horseradish, and thinly sliced orange and lemon zest – the latter produces a delicious citrus oil that's surprisingly versatile. When such ingredients are completely submerged in oil, the air is excluded and so the oil preserves them. Cheese can also be preserved in oil. Shepherds and cheesemakers have been doing this for centuries – see the Labne recipe (page 225) in the Dairy chapter.

Provided you store the oils in a cold place, they'll keep for months. Nonetheless, they will gradually deteriorate, so resist the temptation to make too much and use it up sooner rather than later. It is best to keep flavored oils in the fridge – if they get too warm, they'll go rancid.

Herbs are at their most aromatic just before they flower. So in June and July we make our stock of infused oils for the year. We started years ago with basil oil. When basil was rare and scarce, this was a way of preserving every last precious leaf. It led to experiments with other herbs, such as rosemary, annual marjoram, oregano, thyme leaves, and sage. In our experience, oils flavored with organic herbs have enhanced keeping qualities, so now I only make flavored oils with freshly picked organic herbs.

Some herbs, such as tarragon and dill, preserve better in vinegar, and we've also had success with elderflower vinegar. Fruit vinegars work well, but we make very little because in practice we used only very small quantities after the initial novelty had worn off.

We use herb oils and vinegars in abundance and find more uses for them all the time. Chile oil, roasted garlic oil, and dried mushroom oil have also become standard drizzles for everything from flavoring croutons to pasta, salads, soups, mashed potatoes, or just an addictive dip for crusty bread.

Which oil should I use?

In general we are not very scientific in the way we make our flavored oils. In most cases I use extra virgin olive oil, but a good-quality vegetable oil could also be used and would be less expensive. We simply pour out a little oil from the bottle and stuff the organic herbs down into the bottle, then fill the bottles with oil and replace the lid tightly. The quantity varies depending on whether you want a mild or strong flavor – so experiment to discover what works best for you.

Should I wash the herbs?

I'm sure it would be more correct to wash and carefully dry the herbs but I have to say that I rarely do because the organic herbs come straight into the kitchen from the garden or greenhouse.

I store basil oil in a fridge or cold-room, but the other oils sit on a shelf in the pantry and kitchens. They are best left to infuse for a few days and then used within a few weeks, though again I have to say many have been around for months and are still fine, though stronger and in some cases even better in flavor.

BASIL OIL

Basil may be used either to flavor the oil or the oil may be used to preserve the basil, depending on the quantity used. If using a large quantity of basil, you can preserve it in a jar with enough olive oil to completely cover it for up to three months. Basil oil may be used in salad dressings, vegetable stews, pasta sauces, or many other instances.

extra virgin olive oil
fresh organic basil leaves

Ensure the basil leaves are clean and dry. Pour a little of the olive oil from the bottle and stuff at least 8–10 basil leaves into the bottle, or more if you like. The basil must be covered by at least ½ in of oil. Seal and store in a cold place. We sometimes fill bottles three quarters full and then chill them. When the oil solidifies somewhat, we fill the space with another layer of oil. If the basil is not submerged in the oil, it will become moldy in a relatively short period of time.

Opposite: *Raspberry Vinegar, Rosemary Oil, and Basil Oil.*

CHILE OIL – OLIO PICCANTE

Pour a little oil out of the bottle, then drop 1–6 chiles into the bottle, fill with oil, and leave to infuse for a few days before using. Dried chiles may also be used, though the flavor will be more pungent.

Variations

CHILE OIL IN A HURRY
Put 1oz of chile flakes into a saucepan in 2 cups of olive oil. Gradually heat them together until hot but certainly not at smoking point, then turn off the heat immediately and leave to cool. This chile oil has instant zing and lasts almost indefinitely.

CHILE, HERB, AND PEPPER OIL
One of my favorite combinations is one or two chiles, a sprig or two of rosemary or annual marjoram, and a teaspoon of black peppercorns. This is particularly good for brushing over steaks, lamb chops, or chicken breasts for a barbecue.

ROASTED GARLIC OIL

Drizzle this garlic-flavored oil over croutons, crostini, salads, soups, vegetables, stews, mashed potatoes, and pasta. Make small quantities and use within a few weeks. You can make raw garlic oil as well but a word of warning: it can go alcoholic and become toxic. You need to use it up in three or four days. The roasted garlic method is much safer and actually more delicious · SERVES 4

4 medium heads of organic garlic
sprig of thyme
sprig of rosemary
salt and freshly ground black pepper
extra virgin olive oil
4 crostini cooked in olive oil

Preheat the oven to 300°F.

Put the heads of garlic into a small ovenproof dish or stainless-steel saucepan, and add the herbs. Season with salt and freshly ground pepper and cover with olive oil. Cover the dish or saucepan and bake in the oven for 1–1½ hours, depending on the size of the bulbs.

Either eat the roasted garlic straight away, or put into sterilized jars and cover with the oil it has been cooked in. If you decide to eat the garlic immediately, don't waste a drop of the delicious roasted garlic-flavored oil. Pour it into sterilized bottles, store in a cool place, and use as you like.

DRIED PORCINI OIL

This is almost double preserving – take your precious dried mushrooms (see page 462) and preserve them in oil – then you get a delicious mushroom flavored oil into the bargain. You can also preserve wild mushrooms in this way (see page 56).

extra virgin olive oil
dried porcini mushrooms

Half fill a sterilized jar with porcini and cover completely with olive oil. Seal the jar and leave the mixture to macerate for at least a week before using.

Vinegar

The word vinegar is derived from the French *vin-aigre,* meaning "sour wine." Because it comes from a natural process that has been around for as long as wine or ale, vinegar is one of the oldest ingredients used in cooking. In European cuisine it was used for thousands of years to add acidity, before lemon juice was available. When any liquid less than 18 percent alcohol is exposed to the air, the vinegar-producing bacteria, acetobactor, will attack it and gradually turn it to vinegar.

To make your own wine vinegar from red or white wine, champagne, or fortified wine such as sherry, simply leave leftover bottles of wine open to the air. The acetobactor in the air will feed on the wine, sour it, and make it into vinegar. Although it's a gamble, you can often get a better product than the cheap wine vinegars that are on the market, though remember that the better quality the wine, the better quality the vinegar. If you can get your hands on a vinegar mother – the starter used for vinegars – it will speed up the process and ensure that the end result is more consistent.

Vinegar enthusiasts pass vinegar mother from one person to the other, but if you can't get hold of one, you may well be able to grow one yourself. I've managed to get a vinegar mother accidentally by leaving a half-used bottle of bought red or white wine vinegar on a sunny windowsill in my kitchen. After a couple of months I discovered that a vinegar mother, which looks like a little jellyfish, had developed inside the bottle. This happens naturally if there's some residual non-fermented sugar or alcohol present. If mother of vinegar forms in your vinegar bottle, don't panic – it's completely harmless; you can look on it as a bonus and use it to start your own vinegar. If this idea doesn't appeal to you, you can simply fish it out and discard it, and go on using the rest of the vinegar.

In days gone by, most households would have had a vinegar crock in which to pour leftover ale or wine to make malt or wine vinegar and use it for preserving. Vinegar is an ideal medium to use for preserving because the acid in it is an anathema to most bacteria. You can preserve herbs and fruit in vinegar, which at the same time add flavor to the vinegar. Vinegar is also one of the preservatives in pickles, chutneys, and ketchups. Things that are preserved in vinegar tend to keep for longer than those in oils because of the acid conditions. Vinegar can be made from wine, ale, apple or pear cider, honey, or rice.

Flavored vinegar
Wine vinegars may be flavored with herbs, such as French tarragon, rosemary, basil, thyme, dill, or oregano, or fruit. We sometimes use chile and peppercorns, or even elderflowers (see page 34). Every year we make lots of flavored vinegars, but in reality, the one we make most is tarragon vinegar because we use it as a base for Béarnaise Sauce (see page 173). It's made in minutes and making your

own means you will have a better and less expensive version than what you can buy in the shops. The tarragon leaves in the vinegar bottle may also be used for recipes such as Béarnaise sauce.

TARRAGON OR OTHER HERB VINEGAR

To flavor vinegar, put a few sprigs of your chosen fresh herb into a bottle of good-quality wine vinegar. I usually use white wine vinegar as opposed to red, because it's milder. Simply stuff a few sprigs into each bottle – and, as with flavored oils, ensure the herbs are totally submerged in the vinegar; otherwise they will deteriorate. Cork or seal the bottle tightly and leave to stand for at least a week before using.

RASPBERRY VINEGAR

This recipe was given to me about 25 years ago by Mrs. Mackey of Ringduffrin in County Down, as she presided over a wonderful afternoon tea on the long mahogany table in her dining room. Mrs. Mackey diluted it with iced water for a refreshing summer drink, but it's also delicious added to sauces and gravies ·
MAKES 4 PINTS

2 cups white wine vinegar
6lb raspberries

Put the unblemished fruit into a crock or deep non-reactive container (plastic or stainless steel). Cover with the vinegar, and stir well. Allow to macerate for 3 days in the fridge, stirring occasionally.

Pour into a jelly bag or piece of cheesecloth and allow to drip for at least 6 hours or overnight.

Measure the juice and put in a stainless-steel saucepan. Add 2 cups of sugar to each 2 cups of juice. Put over low heat, and stir until the sugar dissolves. Bring to a boil and simmer for 8–10 minutes. Skim well to remove all the scum. Pour into sterilized bottles. This vinegar will keep indefinitely.

VIOLET VINEGAR

Don't bother to make this unless you can get your hands on the old-fashioned, highly scented violets (Viola violaceae) which flower in late winter/early spring (see page 32). Use this vinegar in salad dressings or to make violet Prosecco (see below) ·
MAKES 1¾ PINTS

3oz violet petals
4¼ cups white wine vinegar

Pick old-fashioned scented violets. Put the petals into a sterilized glass jar or wide-mouthed bottle. Cover with fine-quality white wine vinegar. Cork or seal the bottle and leave it to sit in the sun or in a warm spot in your kitchen for 2–3 weeks. Strain, rebottle, cork, and store in a dry, airy place.

Variation
VIOLET PROSECCO
For a delicious and unusual aperitif, put a teaspoon of violet vinegar into a glass, top with a few tablespoons of sugar syrup, and fill with prosecco or sparkling water.

Mustard

The antimicrobial qualities of mustard help to preserve food. You can, of course, buy a huge variety of mustards, but it's fun and easy to make your own. Real mustard aficionados will want to have a can of mustard powder handy; nothing hits the spot in quite the same way.

Mustard should only be added in the final stages of cooking as it loses its flavor when subjected to heat.

EMER'S WHOLEGRAIN MUSTARD

Emer Fitzgerald, who's been teaching at the Cookery School for many years, came up with this recipe. We have tried lots of mustard recipes and combinations, but this one has become a firm favorite · **MAKE 2 X 9OZ JARS**

⅔ **cup white wine vinegar**
6 **tablespoons black or brown mustard seeds**
¼ **cup yellow mustard seeds**
¼ **cup white wine vinegar**
2 **tablespoons honey**
2 **teaspoons salt**

Pour the white wine vinegar over the black or brown mustard seeds and leave to soak for 3–5 days (the longer you leave it, the hotter it seems to get).

When it is finished soaking, use a pestle and mortar to roughly grind the mixture of black or brown mustard seeds and vinegar. Then grind the yellow mustard seeds into a fine powder in a clean spice or

Opposite: *Mustard Fruits.*

coffee grinder. Mix the two mustards together with the remaining white wine vinegar, honey, and salt. Fill into small glass jars. Cover and store in a cool, dry place.

ENGLISH MUSTARD

English mustard is one of the best things in life. I'm not referring to ready-made mustard, but to the kind that comes in powder form in the classic mustard-yellow and red cans. Made by Colman's of Norwich, no house should be without a can.

To make 1 tablespoon of mustard, simply put 1 tablespoon of mustard powder into a small bowl and add 2–3 teaspoons of water to mix to a paste. Continue to add water until the mustard is a soft, flowing consistency. If there is some mustard left over after the meal, cover and use the next day. It is best made in small quantities.

HORSERADISH MUSTARD

This mustard is particularly good with roast beef or smoked fish · **MAKES 1 X 7FL OZ JAR**

5 **tablespoons white mustard seeds, ground to a coarse powder**
1 **tablespoon grated horseradish**
¼ **cup extra virgin olive oil**
½ **cup cider vinegar**
2 **teaspoons honey**
1 **teaspoon salt**
1 **garlic clove, peeled and quartered**
1 **teaspoon organic lemon zest**

Blend all the ingredients together and store in sterilized jars.

MUSTARD FRUITS

This crystallized fruit is delicious served as an accompaniment to bollito misto *or cold meats. You can buy verjuice from speciality food stores* · **MAKES 2 X 9OZ JARS**

2¼ **cups sugar**
a few strips of organic lemon zest
18oz **fruit e.g. pears, figs, peaches, apricots, peeled (one or a mixture), peeled**
¼ **cup honey**
½ **cup verjuice or white wine vinegar**
2 **tablespoons mustard seeds, lightly crushed**
1 **teaspoon fennel seeds**
1 **small cinnamon stick**
3–4 **cloves**

Put the sugar, 2¼ cups cold water, and the lemon zest into a stainless-steel saucepan over medium heat. Stir until the sugar dissolves, bring to a boil, and add the peeled fruit. Simmer until tender. Remove, drain, and add the honey, verjuice, mustard seeds, and spices to the mixture. Bring back to a boil and reduce to a thick syrup, being careful not to allow it to caramelize.

Meanwhile, lift the fruit out with a slotted spoon and pack it into sterilized jars. Cover with the hot syrup and close the jars immediately. Store in a cool place or the refrigerator for a few days before eating. Keeps for months.

Pickles – the Basics

I often use white wine or cider vinegar in pickles, whereas I use malt vinegar in chutneys (see page 437). I also use white granulated sugar and a mixture of spices, many of which have an antiseptic quality that helps to preserve the pickles.

Nathalie (my research assistant) and I had a wonderful afternoon with Helen Morgan, whose family lived at Ballymaloe House before the Allen family. Helen is well known among her friends for home preserves. All her life she's been honing her craft, and we spent an intriguing afternoon during which she very generously passed on many of her recipes, not all of which we were able to reproduce as beautifully as her. After a lifetime of preserving, she knows how to adapt to the ingredients in a way that's very finely tuned.

What kind of jars can I use?

For pickles, chutneys, jellies, or jams you can use recycled jars, but ensure they're spotlessly clean. It doesn't matter if you have a variety of sizes, but if you plan to sell them, you'll probably want uniform jars with screw-top lids. For chutneys and vinegars, the lids must have a non-reactive plastic coating inside (metal lids will be corroded by the vinegar).

How to sterilize jars

Jars must be washed and dried thoroughly. Remember to remove any previous label and any traces of glue, which can sometimes be tricky, but rubbing alcohol should do the job. Then put the jars in the oven at 350°F, for 10–15 minutes to ensure that they are completely sterilized. Reduce the heat until the jars are needed. Fill the jars while they are still hot.

How to fill the jars

We give prizes at the cookery school to students who manage to pot up their jam, pickle, or chutney without making a huge sticky mess of themselves, their teachers, and their workspace. Here's the secret: scoop some of the pickle or chutney into a Pyrex measuring jug with a handle that's connected to the jug at only one end, so you can hang it over the edge of the cooking pot while you're not using it. Insert a jam funnel (if you have one) into the neck of the hot jam jar and hold it with a dry kitchen towel over the edge of the saucepan. Then use the Pyrex measuring jug to pour the hot jam or chutney into the jar. Hold the measuring jug over the pot so that any drips will fall back in. Fill the jars to within 1½in of the rim, put each sterilized lid on immediately and screw tightly. Wipe the jars clean. You can hang the measuring jug by its handle on the side of the pot between filling the jars.

When we make a lot of jam or chutney, we fill the dishwasher tray with the sealed pots of jam and chutney and run a three-minute cycle that leaves them clean, dry and ready to be labeled. If you want to sell your jars at a farmers' market, you'll need to label them accurately and put on a tamper-proof label over the lid.

Labeling jars

While the preserve is cooling, write the labels with the name of the preserve and the date. My grandchildren love to help me with this; they draw little pictures and funny faces and write messages like "Granny keep off" or "Especially for Mom..."

HELEN MORGAN'S USA PICKLE

Helen got this recipe from an American friend, hence the name! Serve with cold meat or game or to perk up a sandwich · MAKES 22 X 7FL OZ JARS

12–14 cucumbers
6 medium onions, finely sliced
1 green bell pepper, quartered, seeded, and finely sliced
1 yellow bell pepper, quartered, seeded, and finely sliced
2 red bell peppers, quartered, seeded, and finely sliced
⅔ cup coarse salt
5 cups sugar
1¼ quarts malt (or cider) vinegar
1½ teaspoons allspice berries
2 tablespoons yellow mustard seeds
1½ teaspoons celery seeds
½ teaspoon ground cloves or a 1in cinnamon stick

Put the cucumbers standing upright into a deep saucepan. Cover the cucumbers with boiling water and leave for 2 minutes before pouring off the water. Refresh in cold water (this could also be done, say, in a sink).

Drain, slice the cucumbers as thinly as possible and put into a bowl with the sliced onions and bell peppers. Add the salt. Cover with a sterilized plate and weigh down the mixture. Put in a cold place for 12 hours. Drain off the accumulated liquid. Rinse the cucumber mixture with cold water until almost all the salt has been rinsed away. Dry and put the mixture into a large, deep stainless-steel saucepan.

Meanwhile, make the syrup by heating together the sugar, vinegar, and spices in a saucepan. Bring to a boil and pour over the vegetables in the other saucepan. Heat to boiling, boil for 2 minutes and then put into hot, sterilized Mason or jam jars. Cover and seal.

PICKLED WALNUTS

This is an old-fashioned country-house pickle. A walnut (Juglans niger) *is a beautiful tree to plant. It will grow to a height of 30–130 feet and takes a while to fruit, but then you will have an abundance of walnuts almost every year. This pickle is an acquired taste at first. Pick the walnuts in early summer, before the shells harden ·* **MAKES 4 JARS**

100 young walnuts
4lb dairy or sea salt in total

1¼ quarts wine vinegar
2 tablespoons fresh ginger, bruised
2 tablespoons allspice
1 blade mace
1 teaspoon mustard seeds

Prick the walnuts well with a fork. Put them into a sterilized crock or plastic bucket. In a separate container, make a brine by dissolving the salt in 8 pints of warm water. Leave the brine to get cold, pour enough over the pricked walnuts to cover and leave to soak for 9 days, reserving the rest of the brine. Use it when you change the brine, every 3 days. Drain, spread the walnuts out onto baking sheets and leave in a warm sunny spot for 3 days, in which time they will turn black.

Divide the walnuts between small, sterilized glass or Mason jars. Bring the vinegar to a boil with the bruised ginger and spices. After it has simmered for 10 minutes, pour it over the walnuts, which must be submerged in the vinegar. Cover the jars with tight-fitting lids (plastic lined if metal) and leave to mellow for 3–4 weeks before eating. They will keep for 2–3 years.

PICKLED BEETS

The memory of the flavor of jars of pickled beets is responsible for putting half of Ireland off beets in any form. This recipe will convert you, and it is very easy to make. Wine vinegar is a huge improvement on the rather fierce malt vinegar used in commercially pickled beets · **MAKES 4 X 13OZ JARS**

1lb cooked beets (see page 392)
1 cup sugar
1 cup white wine vinegar

Peel and slice the beets and put it into a bowl. Dissolve the sugar in a saucepan with 2 cups of water and bring to a boil. Simmer for 3–4 minutes. Add the vinegar and then pour the mixture over the beets. Leave to cool.

Keep the beets in a covered bowl in the fridge if you plan to eat it within a few days, otherwise use tongs to put it into sterilized jars. Cover tightly and seal. Beets will keep for several months when stored in a cool, dry place.

PICKLED PEARS

Pears are in season in fall, although you can make this pickle at other times of the year with store-bought pears. It is particularly delicious with smoked duck, watercress, and blue cheese salad, venison, or pigeon · **MAKES 6 X 1LB POTS**

4lb pears (Conference or Doyenne de Comice are perfect, but Bartlett pears will also suffice)
juice and zest of 1 organic lemon
2 cups white wine vinegar
2 tablespoons sherry vinegar (optional)
2¼ cups sugar
1in piece of fresh ginger, peeled and sliced
1 cinnamon stick
2 star anise
4 cloves

Peel, core, and quarter the pears and put them into a stainless-steel saucepan. Remove the lemon zest with a swivel-top peeler, squeeze the juice over the fruit, and toss well. Cover and cook on a gentle heat while you prepare the pickle.

Put the vinegars, sugar, spices, and lemon zest into a stainless-steel saucepan. Bring to a boil, stirring until all the sugar is dissolved.

Simmer for 5 minutes, then add the pears and continue to cook until the pears are completely soft, about 10–30 minutes, depending on the variety and degree of ripeness.

Fill the pears into sterilized jars, while continuing to cook the liquid. Pour a boiling liquid over the pears, making sure they are well covered. Seal and, if possible, leave for a couple of weeks to mellow before diving in!

PICKLED PEACHES

Sometimes in summer you'll find a tray of inexpensive peaches at the store. When you've eaten your fill, try making some pickled peaches, which go well with glazed ham, bacon, duck, or goose · **MAKES 6 X 13OZ JARS**

2 cups cold Stock Syrup
  (see page 468)
1 small cinnamon stick
1 chile, halved and seeded
1in piece of fresh ginger, sliced
6 cloves
2 slices of lemon
10 peaches or nectarines, peeled
  and sliced into segments

Preheat the oven to 350°F.

Put all the ingredients into an oven-proof saucepan. Bring to a boil, cover, and put in the oven for 20 minutes. Remove the chile, cinnamon stick, and lemon slices. Cool and store in the fridge, or fill into sterilized Mason jars, seal, and store in a cool place.

They will keep for a year but are best used within 2 or 3 months.

PICKLED BLOOD PLUMS

Blood plums are the dark, bitter-sweet plums that are in season in the fall and winter. It's rare nowadays to find really good ones, but even mediocre fruit is transformed by this recipe. Serve with duck, goose, venison, or coarse pâtés · **MAKES 3-4 SMALL JARS**

½ cup cider or wine vinegar
¾ cup superfine sugar
1 cinnamon stick
2 star anise
1lb blood plums, stoned and
  quartered

Put the vinegar and sugar in a stainless-steel saucepan with the cinnamon and star anise. Heat and stir until the sugar dissolves. Add the quartered and stoned plums and simmer gently for about 20 minutes or until the plums are tender and the liquid is syrupy. Pour into jars. Cover and keep in the fridge and use within a few weeks.

PICKLED CHERRIES

This pickle is delicious with game, cold meats, and particularly duck · **MAKES 10 X 7FL OZ JARS**

2lb cherries
1 quart white wine vinegar
1½ cups granulated sugar
4 cloves
6 peppercorns
1 allspice berry

Check the cherries carefully to ensure they are unblemished; otherwise the pickle won't keep. Put

the vinegar, sugar, cloves, peppercorns, and allspice into a stainless-steel saucepan. Bring to a boil for 3–4 minutes. Add the cherries, bring back to a boil, and simmer for a further 2 minutes.

Fill into sterilized jars, cover, and seal. Store in a cool, dark cupboard for at least a month before eating.

PICKLED KUMQUATS AND TANGERINE SLICES

This pickle looks divine in glass jars. It will keep for months, but seldom lasts that long. It is particularly delicious with glazed ham or pork. If you don't have tangerines, small oranges also work brilliantly · **MAKES ABOUT 2 X 13OZ JARS**

8oz kumquats
3 tangerines, or 4 if they are small
1¼ cups sugar
1 cup white wine vinegar
2in piece of cinnamon stick
8 whole cloves
2 blades mace

Try to find organic fruit, then scrub the tangerines well and rinse the kumquats. Cut a slice off the top and bottom of the tangerines, down as far as the flesh and discard those 2 pieces of peel. Cut the rest of the tangerines into slices and put them in a wide, stainless-steel saucepan with the kumquats. Cover generously with cold water.

Bring to a boil, cover, and simmer for about 15–20 minutes, until the tangerine slices are tender. The kumquats will probably be ready before the tangerine slices, so keep an eye on them and remove them if they show signs of collapsing.

Meanwhile, in a stainless-steel saucepan, dissolve the sugar in the white wine vinegar, and add the cinnamon, cloves, and mace. Stir until it comes to a boil.

Drain all the liquid off the tangerines and keep it aside in case you need it. Then put the kumquats and tangerines into the vinegar syrup. If necessary, use some of the cooking liquid to cover the fruit. Simmer for about 15 minutes, until the tangerine slices look transparent and slightly candied.

Arrange the fruit in a wide-mouthed sterilized glass jar. Pour a boiling syrup over, cover, and seal tightly (do not use a metal lid). Label and leave to mature for 3–4 weeks before use.

RORY O'CONNELL'S TOMATO KETCHUP

This recipe comes from my brother Rory, who teaches at the school and also gives private cooking classes. We found that when we used Cox's orange pippin apples, they produced exactly the same thick consistency as that well-known brand, so do try to find them. The flavor was also irresistibly delicious · MAKES 6 X 8FL OZ BOTTLES

3½lb tomatoes, peeled and
    chopped
1lb eating apples, peeled, cored
    and chopped (weigh after
    peeling and coring)
1lb onions, chopped
2¼ cups sugar

2 cups cider vinegar
1 level tablespoon sea salt
¼ teaspoon cayenne
6 black peppercorns
6 allspice/pimento berries
6 cloves

Place all the ingredients in a stainless-steel saucepan. Bring to a boil and simmer for about 1 hour, stirring regularly to avoid sticking, until it has the consistency of ketchup.

Leave to cool for 4–5 minutes, then blend to a smooth purée. If the consistency is a bit thin, return to the saucepan and cook to reduce further. Remember: it will thicken as it cools. Pour into sterilized glass bottles and store in a cool, dry place, for 3 months or more.

SWEET CHILE SAUCE

We grow about six or eight varieties of chile in the greenhouse. They vary enormously in heat, even on the same plant. For consistency, you're probably best to use Thai red chiles that are widely available in the stores.

3 large red chiles, finely chopped
    (seeds and all)
½ cup rice vinegar
1 teaspoon salt
¾ cup sugar
1 garlic clove, crushed

Put all the ingredients into a little saucepan over low heat and stir to dissolve the sugar. Bring to a boil and cook for 5–6 minutes, until the mixture thickens to a syrupy texture. Cool and fill into a sterilized jam jar

or bottle. Store in a cool, dry place. It will keep for a year or more, though you are unlikely to have it for that long.

HORSERADISH

Preserved horseradish can be used as a basis for horseradish sauce or added to mashed potatoes. When you find a nice, fat piece of horseradish this is a good way to preserve it for the day when you don't have access to the fresh product · MAKES 1 X 7FL OZ JAR

4oz or 8 tablespoons horseradish
    root, peeled and grated; this
    will require a 10oz piece of
    horseradish root prior to
    peeling and grating
½ teaspoon salt or more
1 teaspoon sugar
⅓–½ cup white wine or malt
    vinegar

Wash the horseradish root (you'll need a vegetable brush to remove the earth), then peel and grate on a microplane. Add the salt and sugar and mix well. Pack into a small jar so it is about two-thirds full. Fill to the top with vinegar (the amount used depends on how tightly the horseradish mixture is packed).

Cover with a non-corrosive lid and store in a cool, dry place. If you use malt vinegar, you will need to leave it to mellow for a week or two before using.

Bottling

Bottling refers to preserving food by heating – usually in a glass container. The heat kills food spoilage organisms and creates a partial vacuum that seals the jar or bottle and prevents recontamination. Most bacteria that cause food spoilage are destroyed at temperatures between 165°F and 212°F. This is easily achieved by heating bottled food, which can be either raw or cooked, in a simple water bath. Cooked food takes a shorter time to preserve.

To bottle, you'll need preserving jars – Mason jars are the most readily available nowadays – and a saucepan deep enough so the jars or bottles can be completely submerged in water.

The size of the bottle or jar, the temperature of the food when it goes into the container, and the level of acidity are all factors that affect the temperature and length of time needed to process the food.

Foods like fruits and tomatoes that are high in acid can be sterilized at 212°F, boiling point. Fortunately, these are the foods that most home-bottlers like to preserve. While there is no real need nowadays to bottle fruit, given the fact that you can just freeze it, those of us who enjoyed bottled fruit as children just long for the flavor.

Foods that are low in acidity, like fish and meat, have to be processed for longer, so bottling them is best avoided at home. If you would like to learn more about bottling and preserving these foods, there are specialized books you can find that explain the process in more detail.

To seal jars

Always wash jars and the seals thoroughly in hot soapy water and rinse well before using. Immerse the rubber rings in boiling water before use. Do not use the rubber seals more than once – always replace with new ones. Never fill the jar above the filling line. Seal and close the jar immediately, making sure the rubber ring is clean and dry. Arrange the jars upright in a deep saucepan. The jar must be completely covered by about 1¼in water. Follow the cooking times on the recipe faithfully. After boiling, allow the jar to cool slowly. Check that the jar is airtight and completely sealed – try to lift it up by the lid to check. If a jar hasn't properly sealed, refrigerate and eat the contents within a couple of days. Store in a cool, dark cupboard away from the light. Before you eat, inspect the jars again to make sure the seal hasn't broken – if it has broken, don't under any circumstances eat the contents or give to the hens.

BOTTLED STRAWBERRIES

This is the way strawberries were preserved in Kinoith, the house we now live in, by a Quaker lady called Lydia Strangman in the early 20th century – pre-electricity. Lydia passed on the technique to my mother-in-law, Myrtle Allen, who in turn taught me. There was a note on the original handwritten recipe saying: "This method keeps color better. Best to do small amounts at a time." Black currants, red currants, gooseberries, pears, plums, and damsons can all be bottled in this way. The juice, which is copious, is delicious over ice cream or as a base for homemade lemonade · MAKES 3 SMALL JARS OR 1 LARGE BOTTLE

1lb perfect strawberries, hulled
1 cup sugar

Put the jars into an oven at 325°F to sterilize.

Put the sugar and 1 cup of water into a stainless-steel saucepan over medium heat. Stir to dissolve the sugar, bring to a boil for 3 minutes. Add the strawberries and simmer slowly until the fruit softens. It will seem as though there isn't enough liquid, but when the fruit softens there will be lots. This will take about 10 minutes. Leave the pot on the heat while you fill the hot, sterilized jars with the strawberries and hot syrup. Seal immediately and store in a cool, dry place.

BOTTLED PEARS

6 pears
½ cup sugar
juice and thinly pared zest of 1 organic lemon

Preheat the oven to 200°F.

Peel the pears thinly and core carefully. Then halve or quarter them, keeping a good shape. Put them in a saucepan or baking dish that just fits them nicely. Add the sugar and the lemon zest and juice.

Cover with a tight-fitting lid and cook gently in the oven, for 2½–3 hours, until tender and translucent. Bottle immediately and store in a cool, dry place.

Above, left: *Soaking up gems of wisdom from Myrtle Allen, my mother-in-law.* **Above, right:** *First, hull the strawberries.*
Below, left: *Filling the strawberries into sterilized jars.* **Below, right:** *Store Bottled Strawberries in a cool, dark cupboard until you can no longer resist eating them – alone, or with homemade ice cream.*

Chutneys

For chutneys, you need vinegar, sugar, spices, and pickling salt – all of these are preservatives. When you start to make chutneys, follow the recipes faithfully, but later, you can start to play around with flavorings and spices. Always remember that you must have enough vinegar, sugar, and salt to actually preserve the vegetables and fruit; otherwise the chutney won't keep. Malt or wine vinegar may be used but if you use less expensive malt vinegar you will need to let the chutneys mellow for at least two weeks before using.

APPLE AND TOMATO CHUTNEY

There are a million recipes for tomato chutney. This is definitely one of the best and has the advantage of using up a glut of windfall apples as well ·
MAKES 12 X 1LB POTS

8lb ripe tomatoes, peeled and chopped
1lb onions, peeled and chopped
1lb eating apples, peeled and chopped
6 cups sugar
3 cups white malt vinegar
2 tablespoons salt
2 teaspoons ground ginger
3 teaspoons ground black pepper
3 teaspoons allspice
4 garlic cloves, crushed
1 level teaspoon cayenne pepper
1½ cups golden raisins

Opposite: *The makings of Ballymaloe Green Tomato Chutney.*

Prepare all the ingredients and put into a large, wide stainless-steel saucepan. Bring to a boil. Simmer steadily, uncovered, for about 1 hour, until reduced by one-third and slightly thick. Pot in sterilized jars, cover with non-reactive lids and store in a cool, dry place.

BALLYMALOE GREEN TOMATO CHUTNEY

When you grow your own tomatoes, you can't bear to waste a single one. This recipe will use up the end of the precious crop and add extra oomph to winter meals · **MAKES 12 X 7FL OZ JARS**

2¼ lb cooking apples, peeled and diced
1lb onions, chopped
2¼ lb green tomatoes, chopped (no need to peel)
1½ cups white sugar
1¾ cups turbinado sugar
1lb golden raisins
2 teaspoons ground ginger
2 teaspoons allspice
2 teaspoons freshly cracked black pepper
2 garlic cloves, coarsely crushed
1 tablespoon salt
3 cups white wine vinegar

Put the apples and onions into a wide, stainless-steel saucepan and add the remaining ingredients. Stir well, bring to a boil and simmer gently, uncovered, for about 45 minutes or until reduced by more than half. Stir regularly, particularly toward the end of cooking.

Pot into sterilized jars and cover immediately with non-reactive lids. Store in a dark, airy place and leave to mellow for at least 2 weeks before using.

VEGETABLE MARROW AND TOMATO CHUTNEY

It's good to have a few recipes for vegetable marrow up your sleeve. I love it served simply in a cheese sauce or stuffed with well-flavored ground beef, but jam and chutney also work well ·
MAKES 7 X 7FL OZ JARS

3lb vegetable marrow
1lb ripe tomatoes
1 large onion, about 8oz
3 garlic cloves
1 teaspoon black peppercorns
1 teaspoon whole allspice
1 tablespoon salt
1 teaspoon ground ginger
3 cups granulated sugar
2¼ cups malt or cider vinegar

Peel the marrow and remove the seeds. Cut into ½in dice. Peel and roughly chop the tomatoes. Peel and chop the onions and garlic.

Crush the peppercorns and allspice using a mortar and pestle. Place all the ingredients together in a preserving pan. Heat gently, stirring occasionally to dissolve the sugar. Bring to a boil and simmer steadily for about 50 minutes, until reduced by half. Cool slightly, pot in sterilized jars and cover with non-reactive lids. Keeps for 6 months.

APPLE AND GRAPE CHUTNEY

This chutney is great with a coarse pâté de campagne or cold meats. If you have a warm porch, a tunnel, or greenhouse, think about growing a grape vine. Muscat de Alexandia and Black Hamburg are two delicious varieties. This recipe is good for using a glut of slightly under-ripe grapes. The vine leaves may also be used for dolmades or for wrapping goat cheese or mozzarella to cook on a grill, or they can be laid underneath cheeses on a cheeseboard (see page 460) ·

MAKES ABOUT 2¼LB OR 5 X 13OZ JARS

Below: *Bramley's Seedling apples.*

5 **cooking apples (2½lb in weight, before peeling and coring)**
6oz **onion, finely chopped**
⅓ **cup balsamic vinegar (you don't need the finest balsamic)**
⅓ **cup white wine vinegar**
½ **cup brandy**
2¼lb **green seedless grapes**
¾ **cup granulated sugar**
salt
1 **teaspoon mixed spice**
1 **teaspoon ground cinnamon**
½ **teaspoon ground ginger**

Peel and dice the apples into ½in pieces. Add the chopped onion, the vinegars, and brandy. Simmer in a saucepan for 30 minutes. Stir in the grapes, sugar, salt, and spices and continue to simmer, uncovered, for 1–1½ hours over a low heat.

Stir occasionally when the mixture becomes thick and pulpy. Leave to cool, then fill into sterilized jars, cover with non-reactive lids, and store in a cool place.

RED PEPPER, TOMATO, AND LEMONGRASS CHUTNEY

This chutney is good with spiced beef, cold meats, or coarse pâtés and terrines · **MAKES 3–5 JARS, DEPENDING ON SIZE**

8oz **onion, finely chopped**
4 **tablespoons extra virgin olive oil**
1lb **very ripe red bell peppers, seeded and diced**
½ **teaspoon salt**
½ **teaspoon allspice**
½ **teaspoon mace**
½ **teaspoon nutmeg**
½ **teaspoon freshly grated ginger**
1 **stalk of lemongrass, finely chopped**
1lb **very ripe tomatoes, peeled and chopped**
½ **cup raisins**
1 **garlic clove, chopped**
1 **cup superfine sugar**
½ **cup white wine vinegar**

Sweat the onions in the olive oil in a stainless-steel saucepan. Add the peppers, salt, spices, grated ginger, and lemongrass. After 10 minutes, add the tomatoes, raisins, garlic, sugar, and vinegar. Bring to a boil and simmer very gently for about 1½ hours, until it looks thickish. Pour into sterilized glass jars, cover with non-reactive lids and store in a cool, dry place.

MEDJOOL DATE AND COCONUT CHUTNEY

Claudia Roden, whose books I love, introduced me to this Jewish recipe when she taught a class at the school in 2007. It's a gem – keep some in your fridge and you'll find yourself eating it with everything · **MAKES 3 X 7FL OZ JARS**

½ **cup desiccated coconut**
2oz **cilantro leaves**
juice of 2 limes or lemons
2 **garlic cloves, crushed**
10 **Medjool dates, stoned**
1 **tablespoon tamarind paste dissolved in 2 tablespoons boiling water**
½ **teaspoon salt**
¼ **teaspoon cayenne pepper**

Pour ½ cup of water over the desiccated coconut and let sit for about 15–20 minutes, until the water is absorbed. Chop the cilantro leaves in a food processor, then add the lime or lemon juice, crushed garlic, dates, and tamarind paste dissolved in 2 tablespoons boiling water. (NOTE: a 1oz block of tamarind soaked for 20 minutes in 2fl oz of boiling water makes 1 tablespoon of tamarind purée.)

Season with the sea salt and cayenne and blend to a paste. Add 1–2 tablespoons of water if necessary, to make a soft, creamy paste. Fill into small jars, cover with non-reactive lids and store in the refrigerator.

BEET CHUTNEY

We grow lots of beets and use the fresh stalks and leaves as well. This beet chutney is delicious with cold meats, game, and cheese · **MAKES 6 X 7FL OZ JARS**

2lb **raw beets, peeled and finely chopped**
1lb **onion, diced**
1lb **cooking apples, peeled and diced**
2 **tablespoons grated ginger**
1 **teaspoon salt**
2 **cups cider vinegar**
1½ **cups granulated sugar**

Put the beets into a stainless-steel saucepan with the onion and apples. Add the ginger, salt, and vinegar.

Cover and simmer about 1–1½ hours, until the beets are soft and the apples have cooked to a fluff. Then add the sugar and cook for a further 15–20 minutes, until the chutney is thick. Pot into sterilized jars, cover with non-reactive lids, and store in a dark, airy place.

BEET AND GINGER RELISH

This sweet-sour relish keeps for ages and is particularly good with cold meats, coarse country terrines, or goat cheese salads · **MAKES 4 JARS**

8oz **onion, chopped**
3 **tablespoons butter**
3 **tablespoons sugar**
salt and freshly ground pepper
1lb **raw beets, peeled and grated**
2 **teaspoons freshly grated ginger**
2 **tablespoons sherry vinegar**
½ **cup red wine**

Cook the onions slowly in butter until they are very soft. Add the sugar and seasoning, then add the rest of the ingredients and cook gently for 30 minutes. Serve cold.

SPICED FRUIT

This relish keeps for months and you'll find lots of ways to use it. It perks up oatmeal and rice pudding and is delicious with cold ham or bacon · **MAKES 18FL OZ OR 2 X 13OZ JAM JARS**

¼ **cup yellow raisins**
¼ **cup muscatel raisins**
¼ **cup currants, sliced**
¼ **cup apricots, sliced**
1oz **candied peel, chopped**
1 **cup sugar**
1 **cinnamon stick**
4 **cardamom pods**

Cover the dried fruit with warm water. Leave to soak for 3–4 hours. When the fruit has plumped up, put the sugar and 5fl oz of water into a saucepan and add the cinnamon and cracked cardamom pods. Bring to a boil and simmer for 4–5 minutes, until the syrup thickens. Drain the fruit, add to the syrup with the candied peel and bubble for 2–3 minutes. Pot into sterilized jars and store in a cool, dry place.

Jams

Until recently, there was a misguided belief that one should only use second-rate fruit for jam making. You can indeed make jam from less than perfect fruit, but the reality is that poor-quality fruit makes poor-quality jam. The secret to making really delicious jam is to make it in small quantities from gorgeous fresh fruit.

Before rural electrification, the soft fruit season was a pretty hectic time for those who wanted to have their shelves packed with jams and preserves for the winter. Now that fruit can be frozen at the peak of perfection, there is not such an urgency because you can make jam all year round. However, the best jam is still made from beautiful fresh fruit in season. If you don't want to spend your whole summer in the kitchen, the most practical approach is to freeze fruit in perfect condition in small, measured quantities, so that you can make jam as you need it throughout the year. Jam made from frozen fruit will taste infinitely fresher and more delicious than a six- or seven-month-old jam even if it is made in peak season. Slightly under-ripe fruit makes better jam, because it has a higher acidity. The faster jam is made, the fresher it'll taste, so for that reason, we always warm the sugar.

In Ireland, the tradition of making and selling jam at farmers' markets and local festivals is alive and well. Homemade jam is much sought after. If you decide to sell your jam, cost it properly, taking jars, covers, labels, and food costs, into consideration. A formula used by many is food cost x 3. This would cover all the other items mentioned. If you are producing jam for sale you may need to contact your local health authority and comply with their regulations.

Pectin

Pectin is a jelling substance that occurs naturally in many fruits. It is most concentrated in seeds, cores, and skin. The cell walls of under-ripe fruit contain pectose, an insoluble substance that changes into soluble pectin as the fruit ripens. Slightly under-ripe fruits are best for jellies and jams.

Some fruits are high in pectin, while others have very little. One can compensate for those by mixing low and high pectin fruits such as blackberry and apple.

High-pectin fruits

Crabapples, black currants, gooseberries, plums, red currants, cooking apples, cranberries, damsons, quince, oranges, lemons, and many plums.

Fruits with moderate pectin

Raspberries, loganberries, boysenberries, and apricots.

Low-pectin fruits

Blackberries, blueberries, strawberries, rhubarb, elderberries, peaches, sweet cherries, dessert apples, pears, figs, and vegetable marrow.

Do I need a preserving pan?

Great if you have one, but not essential. Alternatively, choose a low-sided, wide stainless-steel saucepan so that the jam cooks quickly. Avoid aluminum because the acid in the fruit will react with it and give a slightly metallic taste.

Should I use jam sugar?

Jam sugar contains added pectin. I don't use it because I don't like the solid texture of the jam that it makes. The only exception I might make is for strawberry jam, which is difficult to set. However, we usually use some red currant juice or lemon juice to bring up the acidity, but you could use a small proportion of jam sugar if you like. The end result may be more like bought jam than handmade jam, though. I use ordinary granulated sugar rather than superfine sugar for jam making.

How to heat the sugar

Heat the sugar in a stainless-steel bowl in a moderate oven for about 15 minutes. It should feel hot to the touch. Be careful not to leave it in too long or the sugar will begin to melt around the edges of the bowl and will eventually caramelize.

Why heat the sugar?

The faster jam is made, the fresher and more delicious it tastes. If you add cold sugar to jam, it will take longer to return to a boil and will taste less fresh.

When do I add sugar?

Citrus fruit peel, black currants, and gooseberries must be thoroughly softened before sugar is added, as sugar has a hardening effect on the fruit. If you add the sugar too early, no amount of boiling will soften the rind or skins. You can vary the amount of sugar you use to taste. For example, if the fruit is very sweet, use less sugar.

Should I skim the jam?
Don't skim the jam constantly while it's being cooked. Just skim it at the end, to reduce wastage.

Here's an old-fashioned tip that was passed on to me by my late next-door neighbor Peggy Walsh. If there's a bit of scum left after skimming, then drop a tiny lump of butter (about the size of a fingernail) into the jam. It will dissolve the remainder of the scum.

How do I know the jam has reached setting point?
If you want to take the guesswork out of it, buy a jam thermometer (quite an expensive piece of equipment); when the thermometer hits 220°F, the jam is set. But we rarely use a sugar thermometer, because I want students to be able to judge when jam is set without any fancy equipment.

Another way to tell when your jam will set is to put a plate in the fridge to chill. When the jam looks as though it's almost set, take a teaspoonful and put it onto the cold plate. Push the outer edge of the jam puddle into the center with your index finger. If the jam wrinkles even a little, it will set.

Covering jam jars
When the jam has reached setting point, pour it into sterilized jars (see page 430) and cover immediately. You can still buy packets of jam covers in most stores and supermarkets. These are made up of three elements, a silicone disk of paper, a large round of cellophane, and a rubber band. Cover each jar with a silicone disk (slippy side down onto the surface of the jam). Wet one side of the cellophane round, then stretch dry side over the jar, and secure with a rubber band. If the cellophane disk is not moistened, it will not become taut when the jam gets cold.

Alternatively, use screw-top lids, which should be sterilized in boiling water and dried before use. Later the jars can be covered with doilies, rounds of material, or colored paper. These covers can be secured with plain or colored rubber bands, narrow florist's ribbon tied into bows, or ordinary ribbon with perhaps little dried flowers or herbs.

What can go wrong?
1. Mold on the top
If mold starts to grow on top of jam, I just spoon it off, give it to the hens and continue to eat the rest. Keep the jam in the fridge from then on and use it as soon as possible. When we were little, Mummy would just tell us to stir in the mold and eat it because it was penicillin and good for us – I'm not sure about that, but I am alive to tell the tale! Having said that, eating moldy store-bought jam is a different matter and certainly not advisable. If you remove jam to a separate dish to serve it in, do not add it back to the main pot afterward or it will start to ferment. Mold grows on top of jam when:
(a) jars are not properly sterilized
(b) the fruit was picked while wet

2. Crystallization
Sugar crystals appear on top and sometimes through the jam. The jam is safe to eat but will taste very sweet and gritty. Crystallization is caused when:
(a) too much sugar is added
(b) the sugar is not properly dissolved
(c) the jam is over- or under-boiled

3. Fermentation
When fermentation occurs, the jam will start to bubble and can smell gassy when the lid is removed. Jam that has fermented should not be eaten. Fermentation can occur when:
(a) the jam is undercooked
(b) the fruit was wet when harvested
(c) the jars were not properly cleaned and sterilized

Storing jam
Normally, there is no need to store jams in a fridge. They should be stored in a cool, dry, airy place.

RED CURRANT JUICE

This juice can be frozen for use another time if necessary. Use it to bring up the acidity and pectin level when making jam · MAKES ½ PINT

1lb red currants

To obtain ¼ pint of juice, put 1lb of red currants (they can be fresh or frozen) into a stainless-steel saucepan with ¾ cup of water. Bring to a boil and simmer for about 20 minutes. Strain through a fine sieve.

RASPBERRY, BOYSENBERRY, OR LOGANBERRY JAM

If you've never made jam before, this is a good place to start. Raspberry jam is the easiest and quickest of all jams to make, and one of the most delicious. Loganberries or boysenberries may be used in this recipe, too. Because it uses equal amounts of sugar and fruit, you don't necessarily need as much as the recipe calls for. Sometimes when I'm trying to take the mystery out of jam making for students, I put some scones into the oven, then make jam, and by the time the scones are out of the oven, the jam is made. It's that easy! ·
MAKES 3 X 1LB POTS

2lb fresh or frozen berries
4 cups granulated sugar, warmed, see page 440 (use ½ cup less if the fruit is very sweet)

Wash, dry, and sterilize the jars in the oven for 15 minutes. Put the berries into a wide, stainless-steel saucepan. Mash them a little and cook for 3–4 minutes over medium heat until the juice begins to run, then add the warmed sugar and stir over low heat until the sugar is fully dissolved. Increase the heat, bring to a boil and cook steadily for about 5 minutes, stirring frequently (frozen berries will take 6 minutes).

Test for a set by putting about a teaspoon of jam on a cold plate and leaving it for a few minutes in a cool place. Press the jam with your index finger. If it wrinkles even slightly, it is set. Remove from the heat immediately. Skim and pour into sterilized jam jars. Cover immediately.

Keep the jam in a cool place or put on a shelf in your kitchen so you can feel great every time you look at it! Anyway, it will be so delicious it won't last long!

UNCOOKED RASPBERRY JAM

Great for using smaller quantities of raspberries, this is the best and freshest raspberry jam you'll ever taste. It keeps just as well as other jams.

equal amounts of fresh raspberries and granulated sugar
brandy

Preheat the oven to 350°F.

Put the raspberries into a wide, shallow dish or baking sheet and sprinkle with sugar. Cook for 20 minutes in the oven, until very hot but not boiling. Turn into a bowl and mix thoroughly with a wooden spoon. Pour into sterilized jars. Dip a round silicone paper in brandy and lay on top of each jar and seal immediately. Store in a cool, dry place. It will keep for a year, but the sooner it is eaten, the more delicious it will taste.

STRAWBERRY AND RED CURRANT JAM

Strawberries are low in pectin. Consequently, strawberry jam can be one of the trickiest jams to make. Choose beautiful, perfect berries. Cooks are often tempted to use jam sugar, which has added pectin, but I prefer to use lemon juice or, better still, red currant juice to bring up the acidity and pectin level. You could also use try the recipe for Mummy's Strawberry Jam on page 447 · **MAKES ABOUT 7LB**

½ cup red currant juice (see previous page) or, if unavailable, the juice of 2 lemons
4lb unblemished strawberries
7 cups granulated sugar, warmed (see page 440)

Preheat the oven to 325°F.

Prepare the fruit juice (see previous page). Put the strawberries into a wide, stainless-steel saucepan with the juice. Use a potato masher to crush the berries. Bring to a boil and cook the crushed strawberries in the juice for about 2–3 minutes.

Add the warmed sugar to the fruit. Stir over low heat, until the sugar is dissolved. Increase the heat and boil for about 10–15 minutes, stirring frequently. This jam sticks and burns very easily, so be careful. Skim, test, and pot the jam into sterilized jars. Cover and store in a cool, dry cupboard.

Opposite: *"Good deeds" on my pantry shelf – Raspberry and Black Currant Jam.*

Left: *Wild Blackberry, Apple, and Rose Geranium Jam.*

Preheat the oven to 300°F.

Remove the strings from the black currants and put the fruit into a greased preserving pan. Add 1¼ quarts of water and cook until the fruit begins to burst.

Meanwhile, put the sugar into a stainless-steel bowl and heat for almost 10 minutes in the oven. It is vital that the fruit is soft before the sugar is added; otherwise the black currants will taste hard and tough in the finished jam. Add the heated sugar and stir over a gentle heat until the sugar is completely dissolved. Boil briskly for about 20 minutes, stirring frequently. Skim, test, and pot into sterilized jars. Cover and store in a cool, dry place.

GREEN GOOSEBERRY AND ELDERFLOWER JAM

It takes a real act of faith to believe that small, mouth-puckeringly tart green gooseberries are ready to use in late spring. As soon as you spy the elderflower blossom in the hedgerows, gather up the courage and pick the small, hard berries off the prickly branches. They are best for pies, tarts, and sauces at this stage. The elderflower gives the gooseberry a haunting muscat flavor. This jam should be a fresh green color, so be careful not to overcook it · MAKES 6 X 1LB POTS

BLACK CURRANT JAM

The strings, or stalks, can be removed from fresh black currants with fingers or a fork. Frozen black currants may also be used, but the jam will take longer to cook. Black currants freeze well, but don't bother to remove the strings beforehand; when they are frozen, just shake the bag – the strings will detach and are easy to pick out · MAKES 11–12 X 13OZ POTS

4lb fresh or frozen black currants
10 cups granulated sugar

3½lb green gooseberries

5 or more (depending on size) elderflower heads, tied in muslin

7 cups granulated sugar, warmed (see page 440)

Wash the gooseberries, then top and tail them and put them into a wide, stainless-steel preserving pan with 2 cups of water and the elderflowers. Simmer for about 30 minutes, until the gooseberries are soft and the contents of the pan are reduced by one-third.

Remove the elderflowers and add the warmed sugar, stirring until it has completely dissolved. Boil rapidly for about 10 minutes, until setting point is reached, at 220°F on a jam thermometer. Pour into hot, clean jars. Cover and store in a dry, airy cupboard.

WILD BLACKBERRY, APPLE, AND ROSE GERANIUM JAM

Blackberries are famously low in pectin, so the tart apples help it to set and add extra flavor. Go foraging for blackberries in the early fall before they're over-ripe. Cultivated blackberries tend to be sweeter so you may need to reduce the sugar · MAKES ABOUT 10 X 1LB JARS

2lb cooking apples or crabapples

5lb blackberries

8 cups granulated sugar (decrease by 1 cup if the blackberries are very sweet), warmed (see page 440)

8 or more rose geranium leaves (*Pelargonium graveolens*)

Wash, peel, core, and slice the apples. Stew them until soft in 1 cup of water in a stainless-steel saucepan, then beat to a pulp.

Pick over the blackberries and put into a wide, stainless-steel saucepan or preserving pan and cook until soft, stirring occasionally. Add the apple pulp and the heated sugar. Destalk and chop the geranium leaves and add. Stir over a gentle heat until the sugar is dissolved. Then bring to a boil and cook steadily for about 15 minutes. Skim the jam, test it for a set, and pot into warm, spotlessly clean jars. Cover and store in a cool, dry place.

PLUM AND APPLE JAM

Plums and cooking apples are both in season at the same time, so try this combination. Not only is it really good with bread, but I also sometimes serve a dollop with cold meats, particularly pork or ham · MAKES 6 X 1LB JARS

2lb plums

1lb cooking apples

5 cups granulated sugar, warmed (see page 440)

Cut the plums in half and remove the seeds, then cut each half into 4. Peel and core the apples and cut them into chunks. Put the plums and apples into a wide, stainless-steel pan with ½ cup of water. Cook, covered, for 10–15 minutes, until the apples and plums are both soft. Meanwhile, heat the sugar in an oven. When the fruit is soft, add the warm sugar and cook, uncovered, for about 8–10 minutes, until the jam is set.

Pour into hot, clean jars. Cover and store in a dry, airy cupboard.

WILD DAMSON AND APPLE JAM

Wild damsons have a delicious bittersweet flavor and I personally prefer them to the much sweeter, cultivated varieties. Elderberries are also good with damsons and are in season at the same time · MAKES 7 X 13OZ JARS

2lb wild damsons

2lb cooking apples, peeled, cored, and chopped

6 cups granulated sugar

Put the damsons, chopped apples, and 1 cup of water into a greased, stainless-steel saucepan. Cook over medium heat for about 25–30 minutes, until the damsons are soft and the apples have broken down into a fluff. Meanwhile, heat the sugar in a low oven.

Add the sugar to the damsons and apples and stir until it is fully dissolved. Increase the heat and boil until setting point (425°F) is reached. As the fruit softens, the damson stones will rise to the surface. Skim off and remove as many as possible. (It's really tedious to remove every last stone so warn people that a few stones may remain.) Pour into hot, sterilized jars. Seal and store in a cool, dry place.

GREENGAGE JAM

Greengages are the green plums that appear in the shops in the height of summer. Even though I have several greengage trees in the fruit garden, they rarely produce more than a handful of fruit, so I usually end up buying them to make this jam – and greengage tarts and compotes. You may want to add more or less sugar depending on the sweetness of the fruit · MAKES 7 X 1LB JARS

4lb greengages
7 cups granulated sugar, warmed (see page 440)

Rinse the greengages. Cut and twist to separate the stones from the halves, then put them into a pot with 1½ cups of water. Bring to a boil and simmer until the fruit is soft and melting. Add the warmed sugar to the fruit. Stir to dissolve. Bring to a boil and cook until it reaches a set. Pot into jam jars, cover, and store as usual.

Variation

VICTORIA PLUM JAM
Make as above, with the following proportions: 4lb Victoria or other variety plums, 6–8 cups sugar (taste the plums if they are very sweet, then use the minimum), and 2 cups water.

BLUEBERRY AND LEMON VERBENA JAM

If lemon verbena is not available, include the zest of the lemons instead · MAKES 5 X 13OZ JARS

2½lb firm blueberries
juice of 2 lemons
a large handful (about 50) lemon verbena leaves, roughly chopped
3 cups granulated sugar, warmed (see page 440)

Pick over the blueberries and discard any that are bruised. Put the blueberries in a wide, low-sided saucepan or preserving pan. Add the lemon juice, lemon verbena, and 1 cup of water. Bring to a boil and cook for 10 minutes.

Add the warmed sugar and stir until the sugar dissolves. Boil until a setting point is reached (see page 441). Fill the jam into sterilized jars, cover, and store in a cool, dry place.

APPLE AND GINGER JAM

Try to find home-grown apples. They have quite a different flavor and texture from commercial varieties that have now been adapted to keep their shape in cooking rather than dissolving into a fluff as cooking apples once did · MAKES 10 X 7FL OZ JARS

4lb tart cooking apples
2 organic lemons
2 tablespoons fresh ginger, peeled and finely chopped
7 cups granulated sugar, warmed (see page 440)

Peel the apples and remove their cores. Put the peels and cores into a stainless-steel saucepan with 1½ cups of water. Cook over medium heat until soft.

Meanwhile, chop the apples and put them into a wide, stainless-steel saucepan. Add the finely grated zest and freshly squeezed juice from the 2 lemons, plus the ginger and 2 cups of water. Bring to a boil and cook until the apples dissolve into a purée.

As soon as the apple peels and cores are soft, strain though a nylon sieve into the other saucepan. Bring the mixture back to a boil, add the hot sugar, and stir to dissolve. Boil until the jam reaches a setting point (see page 441). Pot into sterilized jars and cover while still hot. Store in a cool, dry place.

CRANBERRY AND APPLE JAM

This is another dual-purpose jam that can be used as a sweet or savory accompaniment. Delicious on scones or with curd cheese, cold turkey, ham, pork, or venison · MAKES 7 X 1LB JARS

2lb cooking apples
2lb cranberries
7½ cups granulated sugar, warmed (see page 440)

Peel, core, and chop the apples. Put the chopped apple into a wide, stainless-steel saucepan and add the cranberries and 1 cup of water. Bring slowly to a boil and continue to cook over medium heat until the apples and cranberries dissolve into a pulp. Add the warmed sugar and stir to dissolve. Increase the heat and cook until it reaches a set. Bottle in sterilized jars and cover while still hot. Store in a cool, dry place.

PEACH OR NECTARINE AND ROSE GERANIUM JAM

MAKES 4 X 7FL OZ JARS

2lb sliced nectarines or peeled
    peaches
4 tablespoons water
1½ cups granulated sugar, warmed
    (see page 440)
freshly squeezed juice of 1 lemon
3 rose geranium leaves

Put the fruit and water into a
stainless-steel saucepan. Add the
lemon juice and the rose geranium
leaves. Simmer over medium heat.
Cook until the fruit is soft, about
10 minutes. Add the warmed sugar.
Bring to a boil and cook for 5
minutes, until set. Pour in sterilized
jars, cover and store in a cool, dry
place. Eat soon, although it will
keep for 4–5 months.

**The following jams need to
be started a day ahead.**

MUMMY'S STRAWBERRY JAM

*Mummy discovered by accident that
this jam is easier to set when left
overnight. This method also seems to
give you a fresher-tasting jam ·*
MAKES ABOUT 7 X 13OZ JARS

4lb unblemished strawberries
juice of 2 lemons
7 cups granulated sugar, warmed,
    see page 440 (**not superfine
    or jam sugar**)

Put the strawberries and lemon juice
in a stainless-steel saucepan and
cover with the sugar. Leave
overnight.

Next day, bring the strawberries
to a boil and stir until the sugar is
dissolved. Mash some of the berries
with a potato masher. Continue to
boil until it reaches a set – about
30 minutes. Pour into sterilized jars,
cover immediately, and store in a
cool, dry, and dark cupboard.

PLUM AND ELDERBERRY JAM

*I sometimes crack a few of the plum
stones to extract the kernels and add to
the jam while cooking. They add a
slightly bitter flavor ·* **MAKES ABOUT
7 X 13OZ JARS**

2¼lb elderberries, stalks removed
2lb blood plums
7 cups granulated sugar, warmed
    (see page 440)

Put the elderberries into a saucepan
with 1 cup of water and bring to a
boil. Cook for 5–8 minutes, or until
the elderberries have dissolved into
a pulp. Pour into a jelly bag or
cheesecloth and leave the juices to
drip into a bowl for a few hours or
overnight, whatever suits you best.

Next day, put the stoned plums
with ¾ cup of water into a
preserving pan. Bring to a boil
and cook until both the skins
and plums are soft. Then add
the elderberry juice (you should
have about 1 quart).

Add the warmed sugar and
stir until it is fully dissolved. Bring

to a boil and continue to cook until
the jam reaches a setting point. Pour
into sterilized jars, cover, and leave
to set. Store in a cool, dry place.

RHUBARB AND GINGER JAM

*This delicious jam should be made
when rhubarb is in full season and is
not yet thick and tough. I feel it's so
worth planting a few stools of rhubarb
– it's easy to grow and loves rich,
fertile soil and lots of farmyard
manure and will emerge every year for
ever and ever if you feed it well ·*
MAKES 8 X 1LB JARS

4lb rhubarb, trimmed
8 cups granulated sugar
grated zest and juice of 2 organic
    lemons
¼ cup fresh ginger, bruised and
    tied in cheesecloth
¼ cup chopped crystallized ginger
    or stem ginger preserved in
    syrup (optional)

Wipe the rhubarb and cut into 1in
pieces. Put it into a large, stainless-
steel or Pyrex bowl layered with the
sugar. Add the lemon zest and juice
and leave to stand overnight.

Next day, put the mixture into a
preserving pan, add the bruised
ginger. Bring to a boil until it is a
thick pulp, about 30–45 minutes,
and test for a set. Remove the bag of
ginger and then pour the jam into
hot, sterilized jars. Cover and store
in a cool, airy cupboard.

If you like, ¼ cup of chopped,
crystallized ginger or preserved stem
ginger can be added at the end.

RHUBARB AND RASPBERRY JAM

Rhubarb also freezes well. Cut into 1in lengths and freeze 2¼lb at a time in strong plastic bags · MAKES 3 X 1LB POTS

1lb rhubarb
3½ cups granulated sugar
11oz raspberries (use frozen when
   not in season)

Chop the rhubarb, put in a bowl, cover with sugar, and leave overnight to extract the juices.

Next day, heat the raspberries in a stainless-steel saucepan until they are juicy and boiling. Transfer the rhubarb mixture into another stainless-steel saucepan, place on the heat, and stir until the sugar has dissolved. Then add the raspberries. Bring to a quick boil and simmer for 8–10 minutes, until setting point is reached (see page 441). Fill into sterilized jars and cover with tightly fitting lids. Store in a cool, dark place.

FRESH APRICOT JAM

This is a lovely golden preserve that keeps well · MAKES 8 X 13OZ POTS

3½lb whole fresh apricots to yield
   3lb fresh apricots when stoned
6 cups granulated sugar
juice of 2 lemons

Halve the apricots and remove the stones, keeping a few kernels to add to the finished jam. In a large bowl, layer the apricots and sugar, finishing with a layer of sugar.

Leave in a cool place overnight.

Next day, put the lemon juice in a large saucepan and add the fruit and sugar mixture. (If the fruit is lacking in juice, you could add 1 cup of water to the lemon juice). Bring to a boil very slowly. Ensure the sugar has dissolved, then simmer for 30–40 minutes, stirring occasionally. Add blanched and halved kernels halfway through the simmering.

Test for a set (see page 441) and allow the jam to cool slightly before potting.

DRIED APRICOT JAM

This jam was regularly made in our house when I was a child because fresh apricots were an unheard-of luxury in our stores. It may sound less desirable than fresh apricot jam but it's very good, less expensive and well worth making · MAKES 8 X 7FL OZ JARS

1lb dried apricots
juice and zest of 1 organic lemon
8 cups granulated sugar, warmed
   (see page 440)
6 almonds, peeled and split
   (optional)

Chop the apricots into quarters and put into a bowl. Add the freshly grated lemon zest and juice and 1¾ quarts of warm water. Cover and soak overnight.

Next day, put the mixture into a greased preserving pan or a wide, stainless-steel saucepan. Add the warmed sugar and stir until all the sugar is dissolved. Increase the heat and boil rapidly for 20–30 minutes, until setting point is reached. If you wish, add about 5–6 split, peeled

almonds, a delicious and traditional addition, halfway through. Fill into sterilized pots, cover, and store in a cool, dry place.

VEGETABLE MARROW, LEMON, AND GINGER JAM

This old-fashioned jam is notoriously difficult to set. The syrup should be thick enough to spread on bread without running off the edge · MAKES 7 X 1LB JARS

4lb vegetable marrow, weight after
   peeling and seeding
2 tablespoons salt
8 cups granulated sugar
juice and zest of 4 organic lemons
2 tablespoons fresh ginger, crushed
   and tied in cheesecloth
2 tablespoons diced crystallized
   ginger (optional)

Halve the vegetable marrow, scoop out the seeds and fibers, and discard to the compost heap. Remove the peel, cut the marrow into cubes, and transfer to a bowl. Sprinkle with the salt and leave to draw out the excess liquid overnight (the texture will become firmer).

Next day, drain off the liquid, quickly run the marrow under a cold tap and drain again. Then put the marrow back into the bowl and cover with sugar. Toss to coat the marrow. Cover and leave for 3–4 hours.

Transfer the marrow and all the liquid into a preserving pan or wide, shallow saucepan. Add the lemon zest and juice and the ginger.

Bring the mixture slowly to a

boil, stirring gently from time to time to dissolve the sugar. Continue to boil for about 20 minutes, until the marrow is translucent and the syrup is thick. About 10 minutes before the end of cooking, add the diced crystallized ginger, if using. Remove the cheesecloth bag. Allow the jam to sit in the saucepan for 15–20 minutes before potting in sterilized jars. Cover and store in a cool, dry place.

Savory Jams

These jams are made from vegetables or a combination of vegetables and fruit and are usually served as a savory accompaniment. However, Janie's Green Tomato Jam is dual-purpose – it is just as good on scones as with goat cheese.

JANIE'S GREEN TOMATO JAM

This recipe, given to me by Janie Suthering, is delicious with cold meats or pâté. We use the green fruit for predictable things like fried green tomatoes and chutneys. When we make this for the farmers' market, people are always a bit wary initially – until they taste it. But the good thing is that you can use this jam for either sweet or savory dishes · **MAKES 2 SMALL JARS**

18oz green tomatoes
1¼ cups granulated sugar
finely grated zest and juice of
   1 organic lemon

Above: *Green tomatoes.*

Wash and slice the tomatoes (no need to peel), and put into a large pan with 1½ cups of water. Bring to a boil and simmer, covered, for 50–60 minutes, until tender. Add the remaining ingredients over low heat, stirring occasionally to dissolve the sugar. Once the sugar is dissolved, boil rapidly for 10–12 minutes, or until setting point is reached. Fill into sterilized jars, cover, and store in a cool, dry cupboard.

Above: *Tomato and Chile Jam.*

TOMATO AND CHILE JAM

This zingy jam is great with everything from fried eggs to cold meat. Try it on a piece of chicken breast or fish, or spread on bruschetta with goat cheese and arugula leaves · **MAKES 1 LARGE OR 2 SMALL POTS**

18oz very ripe tomatoes
2–4 red chiles, depending on the strength
4 garlic cloves, peeled
1in piece of fresh ginger, peeled and roughly chopped
2 tablespoons fish sauce (nam pla)
1¼ cups superfine sugar
½ cup red wine vinegar

Peel the tomatoes and chop into ½in dice. Purée the chiles, garlic, ginger, and fish sauce in a blender. Put the purée, superfine sugar, and vinegar into a stainless-steel saucepan, add the tomatoes and bring to a boil slowly, stirring occasionally. Cook gently for 30–40 minutes, stirring every now and then to prevent sticking.

When cooked, pour into warmed, sterilized glass jars. Leave to cool and store in a cool place. It will keep for months.

ONION JAM

Here is another little gem, and a great way to use up a glut of onions. Confiture d'oignons, as the French call this recipe, will keep for seven to eight months and is a brilliant standby to serve with coarse pâtes, lamb, beef, or goat cheese · **MAKES 16FL OZ**

1½lb onions
2 tablespoons butter
⅔ cup superfine sugar
1 teaspoon salt
½ teaspoon freshly ground black pepper
7 tablespoons sherry vinegar
1 cup plus 2 tablespons full-bodied red wine
2 tablespoons crème de cassis (optional)

Peel and slice the onions fairly thinly. Melt the butter in a frying pan and hold your nerve until it becomes a deep, nut-brown color, but be careful not to let it burn. This will give the onions a delicious, rich flavor. Toss in the onions and sugar, add the salt and freshly ground pepper, and stir well.

Cover the saucepan and cook for 30 minutes over a gentle heat, keeping an eye on the onions and stirring from time to time with a wooden spoon.

Add the sherry vinegar, red wine, and crème de cassis, if using. Cook for a further 30 minutes, uncovered, stirring regularly. Cook very gently, but don't let it reduce too much. Spoon into jars, cover, and store in a cool, dry place.

Jellies

Unlike jams, jellies are made from fruit juice only, so you get a lower yield. However, the leftover pulp can be used to make fruit butter and cheeses (see page 452). Jellies can be made from all kinds of fruits and berries – cooking apples or crabapples, red currants, black currants, blueberries, quince, medlars, japonica ... Jellies keep for up to a year, but needless to say, the sooner they are eaten the fresher and more delicious the flavor.

If you've never made a jelly before and are intimidated by the thought of jelly bags and juice dripping overnight, why not start with the red currant jelly below, which is made in minutes. Because this recipe uses no water, just pure juice, the intensity of flavor is superb. You'll never buy anything nearly as delicious in a store.

Most jelly recipes tell you to drip the fruit overnight, which can seem like a bit of an ordeal. But it's no big deal starting it one day and finishing the next. Also try the Crabapple or Cooking Apple Jelly in the Foraging chapter (see page 40). This is a marvelous master recipe that can be adapted for a myriad of sweet or savory jellies.

RED CURRANT OR WHITE CURRANT JELLY

Most jellies are dripped overnight, but this is a happy exception. It only takes eight minutes to reach setting point and you can use the pulp as well, so you get twice the return on your red currants. The leftover pulp can be used as a filling for a tart or as the basis of a red currant sauce. Just add a little water and perhaps a dash of kirsch or brandy. Then it can be served either with ice cream or lamb.

The jelly itself is a wonderfully versatile product and is a must-have in the pastry section of any restaurant kitchen as it is invaluable as a glaze for red fruit tarts. You'll also find it indispensable in your pantry. Serve as an accompaniment to roast lamb, bacon, and ham. It is also good with some rough pâtés and game and is the base of Cumberland sauce.

You can use frozen fruits for this recipe, and you can use white currants – which will be difficult to find unless you have your own bush. The white currant version is wonderful with cream cheese as a dessert or makes a perfect accompaniment to lamb or pork · **MAKES 6 X 8OZ JARS**

2lb red currants or white currants
4 cups granulated sugar

Remove the strings from the red currants either by hand or with a fork. Put the currants and sugar into a wide, stainless-steel saucepan. Heat and stir continuously until they come to a boil. Boil for exactly 8 minutes, stirring only if they appear to be sticking to the base. Skim carefully. Turn into a nylon sieve and leave to drip through – do not push the pulp through or the jelly will be cloudy. You can stir gently once or twice just to free the bottom of the sieve of pulp.

Pour the jelly into sterilized pots immediately. Cover and store in a cool, dry place. Red currants are very high in pectin, so the jelly will begin to set just as soon as it begins to cool.

MEDLAR JELLY

Medlars are a bizarre-looking fruit of the malus family. It doesn't matter if a few are soft and bletted (very over-ripe). Serve this jelly with game, pork, coarse patés, or Coeur à la Crème (see page 228) · **MAKES 7 X 13OZ POTS**

4lb medlars
granulated sugar (see below)
piece of cinnamon stick
2 cloves
2 strips of organic lemon zest

Cut the fruit into quarters and put into a stainless-steel saucepan. Cover with water, bring to a boil, and cook until soft. Pour into a jelly bag and leave to drip overnight. Don't squeeze the jelly through the bag or the juice will be cloudy.

Next day, measure the juice and allow 2 cups of sugar to every 2 cups of juice. Heat the sugar and add to the hot juice. Add the spices and lemon peel and boil until setting point is reached. Remove the spices and lemon peel. Then pour into hot sterilized jars, cover immediately, and store in a cool, dry place.

BLACK CURRANT JELLY

This jelly is made with the same technique as the Red Currant Jelly (see previous page), so does not need to be dripped overnight. I've made this intense and wonderful jelly with both fresh and frozen fruit. The leftover pulp may be used in sweet tart shells with lots of stiffly whipped cream on top · **MAKES 2LB**

2lb black currants
3 cups granulated sugar

Put the black currants into a large, stainless-steel pan with the sugar and ⅔ cup of water. Stir over medium heat until the sugar dissolves and the mixture comes to a boil. Skim off the scum as it rises, and boil fast for just 10 minutes. Pour into a nylon sieve placed over a bowl and let the juice run through. Press the fruit lightly with a wooden spoon. Pour the jelly while still warm into small glass jars and seal. Store in a cool place away from direct sunlight.

JAPONICA JELLY

Many people are unaware that the small, hard green fruit of the flowering japonica (Chaenomeles speciosa) makes a delicious jelly which is particularly good served with roast pheasant or guinea fowl · **MAKES 4 X 13OZ POTS**

2lb japonica fruit
1 organic lemon
granulated sugar (see below)
3 lemon verbena leaves (optional)

Wash the fruit, cut into quarters, and put into a stainless-steel saucepan with finely peeled lemon zest. Cover with water, bring to a boil, and continue to cook until soft.

Strain through a jelly bag or butter muslin.

Measure the juice and allow a scant 2 cups of sugar to every 2½ cups of juice. Return the juice to the clean saucepan. Add the sugar, squeezed juice of the lemon, and 3 lemon verbena leaves (if available).

Stir over medium heat to dissolve the sugar. Bring to a boil and continue to cook until the jelly reaches setting point, about 6–7 minutes.

Discard the lemon verbena leaves. Fill the jelly into sterilized jars, cover, label, and store in a cool, dry place.

Fruit Butters and Fruit Cheeses

Years ago, when people had more of a thrifty mindset, virtually nothing was wasted. These fruit butters and cheeses would originally have been made from the purée left over from making jellies when the juice had finished dripping. It's a happy coincidence that the fruits used for jellies tend also to be good for making fruit butters and cheeses. Nowadays, one usually makes the purée from scratch so the result will be more flavorsome.

Fruit butters and cheeses are thick fruit purées that are so-called because their texture resembles that of their dairy namesakes. Fruit butters are soft, spreadable, and delicious on bread or toast, while fruit cheeses, which are cooked to a purée stiff enough to be unmolded, can be sliced and served with cold meats, game, cheese, or as a dessert.

APPLE BUTTER

Here, I am starting from scratch to make apple butter, but you could use the purée leftover from an apple jelly and flavor it with spices which are important to supplement the flavor which has been leached out when the juice was dripped · **MAKES 8 X 7FL OZ JARS**

1 quart sweet cider
4lb 8oz sweet apples – Fuji or Gala
2¼ cups granulated sugar
1 teaspoon ground cinnamon
¼ teaspoon ground cloves
½ teaspoon ground ginger
¼ teaspoon ground nutmeg

Put the cider into a large stainless-steel saucepan. Bring to a boil and reduce by half. Core the apples and chop into ½ inch dice, and add to the pan. Bring back to a boil, cover, and simmer until the apples are completely soft (about 30 minutes). Purée through a food mill or push through a sieve. Put this purée back into the saucepan. Add the sugar, cinnamon, cloves, ginger, and nutmeg. Bring to a boil and simmer for 35–40 minutes, until thickened.

Pour into sterilized jars immediately and store in the fridge.

APPLE CHEESE

If you had a couple of quinces, you could add them to the apples ·

MAKES 5 X 7FL OZ JARS

2lb cooking apples
2 cups sugar
juice of 1 lemon
juice of 1 orange
¼ teaspoon ground cloves
½ teaspoon ground coriander seeds

Core the apples and quinces, if using. Chop coarsely and simmer in 2 tablespoons of water in a stainless-steel saucepan over low heat until very soft. Push the fruit through a food mill back into the saucepan.

Add the citrus juice and freshly ground spices and heat slowly, stirring until dissolved. Continue to cook over low heat, stirring very often to prevent sticking, until the mixture is thick. Pot in sterilized jars and store in a cool, dry place.

QUINCE CHEESE – MEMBRILLO

Making quince cheese takes a bit of time, but it's so worth it. The resulting paste will keep for over a year if you can manage to resist nibbling it. Serve it with cheese – it's particularly good with Manchego, Cheddar, goat, or blue cheese.

as many quinces as you can lay
**   your hands on**
¾ that weight of sugar

2 x 9in x 12in jelly roll pan

Preheat the oven to 225°F.

Use a cloth to rub the down off the skins of as many quinces as you can pack into a large earthernware jar. Do not add any water. Cover the pot and place in a low oven for about 4 hours until the fruit is easily pierced with a skewer. Quarter the fruit, remove the cores and any blemishes, and put the pieces through a food mill, using the biggest disk. (If you do not have one, buy one!)

Weigh the quince pulp and add 3 parts of sugar to every 4 parts of pulp. Cook the mixture in a preserving pan over medium heat, stirring continuously with a wooden spatula until the mixture becomes rich in color and stops running together again when the spatula is drawn through the mixture.

Line 2 jelly roll trays with parchment or silicone paper. Spread evenly with the paste and leave overnight to cool and solidify.

The following day, dry the trays of quince paste out in a low oven (225°F) for about 4 hours until it is quite firm. Check it is ready by lifting a corner of the paste: it should be solid all the way through. When the paste has cooled, cut into 4 strips, wrap in baking parchment, and store in an airtight container. It will keep for about 4 months, but is best eaten when freshly made. Cut into 1in squares as a sweetmeat.

STORING FRUIT

APPLES

We like to store cooking apples for winter and early spring use. The apples available in the shops do not appear to be the same as the old homegrown varieties and certainly cook quite differently. Depending on the variety, apples can last for several months. We love Egremont Russet, but Cox's Orange Pippin and well-ripened Golden Delicious also keep well.

Wrap the apples individually in squares of newspaper and store in cool, dark, humid conditions. Store in a single layer on slatted racks, on stackable plastic chilling trays, or you can use the light wooden stackable boxes that fruit comes in. They must not touch each other. We recycle molded cardboard and polyester from our local suppliers. Check the apples regularly and remove and use any that are beginning to rot.

PEARS

Conference and Doyenne de Comice are well worth growing. Pick them off in the fall while they are still quite hard and crisp. Store them in the same way as apples, but in less humid conditions. They can be kept unwrapped, but still must be kept in a single layer.

QUINCES

These keep very well for months; store as above.

Marmalade

Marmalades are made with either a specific variety or a mixture of citrus fruits. Traditional marmalade is made with bitter Seville or Malaga oranges which are in season for about five or six weeks after Christmas. It's very fortuitous that oranges are in season then, as there tends to be a lull after the holiday season when things aren't quite so frantic, so that's when we make our stock of marmalade for Ballymaloe. But if you can't get round to making marmalade at this time, just buy the oranges and pop them into the freezer whole, and make marmalade when you have more time.

In marmalade making, every part of the citrus fruit is used; the peel, juice, and pulp give texture, body, and flavor and the seeds and pith yield the pectin needed for a good set. Marmalades usually have chunky pieces of tender peel suspended in the preserve, but one can also make a translucent jelly marmalade by straining out the peel at the end. Many recipes call for the sliced peel to be soaked overnight, which helps to tenderize it and results in a melting consistency. The sugar should not be added until the peel is thoroughly soft, it will have a hardening effect if it is added too early and no amount of boiling will soften it later.

Many of us, including me, are very fragile in the morning and I certainly don't like any surprises at breakfast. Marmalade is a really personal thing – some people like a dark, bitter marmalade whereas others prefer a fresher taste. Using the recipes below, you can choose the end result. If you would like a fresher tasting marmalade, ensure the liquid has reduced to between one-third and one-half of the original volume before you add the sugar and then boil quickly to a set. Alternatively, for a darker, more bitter marmalade, cover the saucepan while you cook the peel. As soon as the peel is soft, add the hot sugar and continue to boil to a set. It will take much longer, during which the color will darken and the flavor will become more bitter.

SEVILLE WHOLE ORANGE MARMALADE

Most recipes require you to slice the orange peel first, but with this one you boil the oranges whole and then slice the cooked peel later. With any marmalade it is vital that the original liquid has reduced by half or, better still, two-thirds before the sugar is added; otherwise it takes ages to reach a set and both the flavor and color will be spoiled. A wide, low-sided stainless-steel saucepan is best for this recipe, about 14in deep and 16in in diameter. If you don't have one that big, then cook the marmalade in two batches · **MAKES ABOUT 13–15LB**

4½ lb Seville or Malaga oranges (organic if possible)
5 cups sugar, warmed (see page 440)

Wash the oranges and put them in a stainless-steel saucepan with 5¼ quarts of water. Put a plate on top of the oranges to keep them under the surface of the water. Cover the saucepan, then simmer gently until the oranges are soft, about 2 hours. Cool and drain, reserving the water. (If more convenient, leave overnight and continue next day.)

Put a cutting board onto a large baking tray with sides so you won't lose any juice. Then cut the oranges in half and scoop out the soft center. Slice the peel finely and put the seeds into a cheesecloth bag.

Put the escaped juice, sliced oranges, and the cheesecloth bag of seeds into a large, wide stainless-steel saucepan with the reserved cooking liquid. Bring to a boil, reduce by half or, better still, two-thirds. Add the warmed sugar and stir over a brisk heat until dissolved. Boil fast until setting point is reached. Pot in sterilized jars and cover immediately. Store in a dark, airy cupboard.

Variations

GINGER MARMALADE
Add 6–8oz of peeled, finely chopped fresh ginger to the recipe. You may also like to substitute turbinado sugar for a fuller flavor and darker color.

WHISKEY MARMALADE
You can vary the flavor of marmalade by adding spices, whiskey, or liqueurs. For whiskey marmalade, add 6 tablespoons of Irish whiskey or your favorite single malt to the hot marmalade just before potting.

Opposite: *Seville Whole Orange Marmalade.*

BITTER ORANGE MARMALADE

This is a dark marmalade for those who enjoy a more bitter-tasting preserve · MAKES 10LB

3lb Seville oranges (organic if possible)
juice of 2 lemons
9 cups white sugar, warmed, (see page 440)
1 cup packed brown sugar, warmed

Scrub the oranges and put them into a large preserving pan. Put a plate on top to weigh them down and add enough water to cover. Bring to a boil, cover, and cook until tender, about 2 hours. Remove the fruit with a slotted spoon, reserve the cooking liquid, and when the fruit is cool enough to handle, cut it in half. Put the seeds and fibrous bits from the center aside. Cut the peel into ¼in strips. Put the seeds and fibrous bits into a small pan with some of the reserved cooking liquid and boil for 10 minutes.

Strain the cooking liquid back into the preserving pan into the preserving pan. You should have about 1½ quarts of cooking liquid; add more water if necessary. Add the sliced orange peel and freshly squeezed lemon juice. Bring to boiling point. Add warmed white and brown sugar. Bring to a boil, stirring, and cook rapidly until setting point is reached, about 20 minutes. Skim and leave to cool for a further 20 minutes. Pot into hot, sterilized jars. Cover and store in a cool, dry place.

ORANGE, LEMON, AND GRAPEFRUIT MARMALADE

Homemade marmalade is always a welcome present, particularly at Christmas. Seville oranges don't arrive into the stores until the end of January, though, so make this tangy three-fruit marmalade in the meantime. It is made from oranges, lemons, and grapefruits, so may be made at any time of year · MAKES 10 X 1LB JARS

3–4 organic sweet oranges and 2 grapefruits weighing 3lb altogether
4 organic lemons
9 cups white sugar, warmed (see page 440)

Wash all the citrus fruits, cut them all in half, and squeeze out the juice. Remove the membranes with a sharp spoon and leave to one side. Cut the peel in quarters and then slice across rather than lengthwise. Put the juice, sliced peel, and 3½ quarts of water into a bowl.

Put the seeds and membrane in a cheesecloth bag and add to the bowl. Leave overnight. The following day, simmer the entire mixture in a covered stainless-steel saucepan for 1 hour. Remove the cover and simmer for a further 30 minutes to 1 hour, until the peel is really soft. The liquid should be reduced to about one-third its original volume.

Remove the cheesecloth bag and discard. Add the warmed sugar to the soft peel and stir until the sugar has dissolved. Boil until it reaches setting point, about 8–10 minutes,

then pour into sterilized jars and cover while still hot.

KUMQUAT MARMALADE

Kumquats are expensive and difficult to slice, but this is so worth making. I was given this recipe by an Australian friend named Kate Engel · MAKES 3 POTS

2¼lb kumquats
8 cups white sugar, warmed (see page 440)

Slice the kumquats thinly crosswise. Put the seeds into a small bowl with 1 cup of water and leave overnight. Put the kumquats in a larger bowl with 1½ quarts of water, cover, and also leave overnight.

Next day, strain the seeds and reserve the liquid (this now contains the precious pectin, which contributes to the setting of the jam). Discard the seeds.

Put the kumquat mixture into a large saucepan with the reserved liquid from the seeds. Bring to a boil, reduce the heat, and simmer, covered, for 30 minutes or until the kumquats are very tender. Remove the lid and reduce by about one third of the original volume.

Add the warmed sugar and stir until it is fully dissolved. Bring the mixture back to a boil and cook rapidly with the lid off for about 15 minutes. Remove the pan from the heat while testing for a set by putting a teaspoon of the mixture on a cold saucer (it should barely wrinkle when pressed with a finger). Pour into sterilized jars. Cover, seal, and store in a cool, dry place.

HELEN MORGAN'S LIME MARMALADE

This is another one of Helen's delicious recipes. The method seems peculiar, but the end result is tart and delicious ·
MAKES 10 X 7FL OZ JARS

juice and coarsley grated zest of 8 organic limes
9 cups white sugar, warmed (see page 440)

Put the lime zest and juice into a stainless-steel saucepan. Tie everything that remains into a cheesecloth bag and add to the saucepan with 3 quarts of water. Bring to a boil and simmer until reduced by two-thirds. Remove from the heat. When cool enough to handle, take the cheesecloth bag out.

Place the remaining mixture in a food processor and blend until smooth. Add back to the saucepan, bring to a boil, and add the warmed sugar. Stir to dissolve. Bring back to a boil and cook until set, about 10–15 minutes. Pour into sterilized jars and seal immediately. Store in a cool, dry place.

GREEN TOMATO MARMALADE

This delicious recipe provides another way to use up the green tomatoes at the end of the season when there is no longer enough sun to ripen the last of the crop. We're using poetic licence here by calling it marmalade, but it does have candied peel and the end result is very good. Serve with anything from goat cheese to scones · **MAKES 6 X 7FL OZ POTS**

3lb green tomatoes
finely grated zest and juice of 1 organic lemon
5 cups white sugar, warmed (see page 440)
1½ tablespoons crushed fresh ginger
1 whole chile
1oz Candied Peel (see page 458), chopped

Wash the tomatoes and cut into dice. Put into a bowl with the lemon zest and juice, and cover with the sugar. Leave to rest overnight.

Next day, transfer the mixture into a wide, stainless-steel saucepan or preserving pan. Tie the ginger and chile in a little cheesecloth bag and add to the pan. Stir over medium heat to dissolve the sugar, then bring to a boil and cook for another 45 minutes, or until the jam is set. Remove the cheesecloth bag and add the candied peel. Pot into sterilized jars, cover immediately, and store in a cool, dry place.

Below: *Be sure to scrape out every last bit of marmalade from the preserving pan.*

Candying and Crystallizing

Sugar is a wonderful preservative: microbes cannot survive in a pure sugar environment. It has very little in the way of nourishment, but it is brilliant for candying and crystallizing, a branch of preserving that I particularly enjoy, and one that also fascinates the grandchildren.

Candying is a very effective way of preserving citrus fruit, ginger, chestnuts, and angelica. Edible flowers like primroses, rose petals, or violets are pretty and delicious when crystallized with a coating of fine sugar. There are still several companies in Provence in the south of France that specialize in crystallizing flowers in the same time-honored way that has been used since the Middle Ages.

Always choose edible, fresh, organic flowers for crystallizing. The smaller the flowers, the more attractive they are when crystallized. Primroses, violets, violas, lavender, rose petals, and apple blossom all work well – follow the recipe on page 32. We also crystallize leaves – choose fairly strong textured leaves, for example mint, wild strawberry, lemon verbena, lemon balm, sweet cicely, salad burnet, and marguerite daisy leaves. It's nice to have a mixture of leaves and flowers so you can make attractive arrangements on top of a special cake.

CANDIED PEEL

The fruit used in this recipe should be organic if possible; otherwise scrub the peel very well. Use just one citrus fruit, or a mixture of all three.

5 organic unwaxed oranges
5 organic unwaxed lemons
5 organic unwaxed grapefruit
1 teaspoon salt
3lb sugar

Cut the fruits in half and squeeze out the juice. Reserve the juice for another use, such as homemade lemonade. Put the halves of fruit into a large bowl (not aluminum), add the salt, and cover with cold water. Leave to soak for 24 hours.

Next day, discard the soaking water, put the fruit in a saucepan, and cover with fresh cold water. Bring to a boil, cover, and simmer very gently until the peel is soft, about 3 hours. Remove the fruit and discard the water. Scrape out any remaining flesh and membranes from inside the cut fruit, leaving the white pith and rind intact. Slice the peel into long strips or leave whole if you prefer.

Dissolve the sugar in 1¼ quarts of water, bring to a boil, add the peel, and simmer gently for about 30–60 minutes, until it looks translucent and the syrup forms a thread when the last drop falls off a metal spoon. Remove the candied peel with a slotted spoon and fill into sterilized glass jars. Pour the syrup over the peel, cover, and store in a cold place or in a fridge. It should keep for 6–8 weeks, or longer under refrigeration.

Variations

IN SUPERFINE SUGAR
Spread the peel on a baking sheet and leave to sit for 30–60 minutes to cool and dry out. Then toss the peel in superfine sugar and store in covered glass jars until needed.

TO NIBBLE
Cut the candied peel into ¼–½in slices, roll in superfine sugar, and serve with coffee.

CHOCOLATE CANDIED ORANGE
Dip the strips of candied orange peel into melted dark chocolate. Arrange individually on a sheet of silicone paper and leave to set.

CANDIED ANGELICA

Homemade angelica will not be vibrant green like the commercial version you can buy in specialized stores, but is so delicious you may have to hide it! Use for cakes and decorating, or just for nibbling. We pick angelica stalks in April, while they are still young.

young angelica stalks
granulated sugar
superfine sugar

Cut the angelica stalks into 3–4in lengths. Put into a stainless-steel saucepan, cover with fresh cold water, and bring to a boil. Drain off the water and run the angelica under cold water. Then peel off the tough, outer stem and fibers; a potato peeler works well for this.

Return the angelica pieces to the saucepan. Cover with boiling water and continue to cook for 4–5 minutes, by which time it will have become a deeper green.

Drain the angelica again and pat dry with paper towels. Sprinkle a layer of granulated sugar in a lasagne dish and cover with the angelica. Repeat, using equal quantities of sugar to angelica. Finish with a layer of sugar and leave to rest for 2–3 days.

Transfer the angelica and sugar into a deep saucepan. Heat gently and continue to simmer until the angelica is translucent. Remove the angelica pieces from the syrup. Spread out on a wire rack and leave to cool and dry, about 30 minutes.

Toss the angelica in superfine sugar. Leave to dry completely before storing in an airtight box.

ROSEWATER

This is a way of capturing the fragrance of roses in water. Use it to flavor cream, fruit salads, ice creams, Turkish delight, or Middle Eastern dishes. Use an old variety of scented rose (e.g. Fantin-Latour, Madame Isaac Pereire, Souvenir de Saint Anne's). The rose petals must be freshly picked and have no pesticides or chemicals used on them. Pick the roses just after the morning dew has evaporated, about two or three hours after sunrise, and use only the petals, not the stems or leaves. Wash the petals quickly to remove any bugs or specks of dirt and use immediately.

1 firmly packed cup of fragrant organic rose petals
2 cups boiling water

Above: *"Albertine" is an old variety of rose whose gorgeous scent can be preserved.*

Put the rose petals in a sterilized Mason jar and cover with the boiling water. Leave to steep until the liquid is cool. Strain, squeeze the liquid from the petals, and pour the rose water into a sterilized bottle. Seal and refrigerate. Use within a month.

ROSE PETAL SYRUP

Pour a little of this rose petal syrup into a champagne glass and top up with Cava or Prosecco to make a gorgeous perfumed aperitif. Stir and float a rose petal on top · **MAKES 1⅓ QUARTS**

8oz fragrant rose petals from an old variety of unsprayed roses
1½lb granulated sugar, warmed (see page 440)
2 tablespoons lemon juice

Put the petals into a stainless-steel saucepan with cold water. Bring to a boil and simmer gently for 20–30 minutes. Strain the petals through a sieve, pressing to get out as much of the liquid as possible. Add the sugar and lemon juice. Bring back to a boil and simmer, uncovered, until thick and syrupy. Bottle and seal.

Drying

One of the oldest and simplest preserving methods of all, drying deprives microorganisms of the moisture they need to grow and so preserves food indefinitely. Drying is used as a means of preserving all over the world – think of Bombay Duck, sun-dried fish from the west coast of India, jerky in the US, and the dried fruit that is central to foods from the Middle East.

Even everyday items like dried pulses, pasta, and noodles owe their shelf life to drying. Originally, such products would have been dried in mountain breezes or intense tropical sun, but in areas like the British Isles where you can't depend on the weather, excellent results can be achieved using a fan oven or a simple drying box.

Fruit

It's fun to dry one's own fruit and infinitely easier nowadays when we don't have to depend solely on the sun. A fan-assisted oven dries fruit brilliantly. We've had success with apricots, peaches, nectarines, apples, and grapes. The biggest challenge is to find really good-quality fruit to start with. Always seek out organic if at all possible.

PEACHES AND NECTARINES: split the ripe fruit in half, remove the pip and sprinkle with lemon juice or ascorbic acid to prevent discoloration. Lay cut-side upward on a wire rack and put into a cool oven at 240°F, or 200°F for a fan oven. They will take about 12 hours to dry. They should be pliable and feel slightly leathery.

APRICOTS: make a slit in the top of the fruit and remove the loose kernel. Then lay cut-side up on a wire rack and sprinkle with lemon juice or ascorbic acid. Dry as above, but they will take less time.

APPLE RINGS: peel and core ripe apples and cut into ¼in rings. Thread them on a cotton string and leave them to dry in a dark, well-ventilated spot for 5 or 6 days. They will gradually dry but will still be pliable. Pack into jars, cellophane, or plastic bags.

CITRUS PEEL: peel a washed, organic orange thinly with a swivel-top peeler. Thread the strips onto a piece of cotton thread using a needle. Hang in a warm place in the kitchen. I hang mine over the stove. The peel usually dries in a couple of days. It can then be stored in a glass jar or left hanging in the kitchen and used as required. Use in lamb, beef, or pork stews or blend with some superfine sugar to give the sugar a delicious orange-citrus flavor.

Chiles

Dried chiles keep their flavor for a year or more, but it's best to use them sooner rather than later.

Using a needle and strong cotton thread, push the needle through the stem end of each chile, allowing a little space between each one. We loop the strings of chiles along shelves in the kitchen and the Cookery School. They gradually dry out and shrink and we use the chiles as we need them.

Herbs

We use fresh herbs pretty much all the time, but herbs you dry yourself can be quite good. Among the best ones are oregano, fennel, thyme, rosemary, marjoram, and savory. Others, like parsley, chervil, and chives, are not worth trying to dry in home conditions. When you're picking fresh herbs for drying, it's best to do so just before they flower because that is when they are at their most aromatic.

To dry herbs, tie them in loose bunches, not too many together. Hang them in a warm, dry place out of direct sunlight. I find the shelf

Above *Drying* Vitis coignetiae *leaves*.

over my oven is perfect for this. Or if you have a rafter below your ceiling, that would work too. After one to three days, the herbs will crumble to the touch.

Leaves

Leaves have been used for years to wrap food, particularly cheese and, in some instances, meat. In summer, we use vine leaves and fig leaves under the cheese on the cheese cart. In early fall, we sometimes use the beautiful leaves of Virginia creeper and Crimson glory vine (*Vitis coignetiae)* as they begin to color. Then as the leaves begin to fall from the tree I collect baskets of them for pressing and drying. For this purpose, the leaves of the London Plane are particularly good, as are Spanish chestnut.

To dry leaves, take a stack of old newspapers and lay a few leaves between the pages. Use a thickness of 3 or 4 pages between layers of leaves. Lay a heavy weight on top. Forget about them for several weeks, by which time they will be completely dry. They can then be stored in a box or even a covered basket for years if necessary.

Seeds

The wild poppy (*Papaver rhoeas)* grows between early summer and fall. It is easy to harvest your own poppy seeds; just wait until the seedpods are dry in early autumn and shake out the seeds from the series of little holes below the flat top. I sometimes cut the stalks, tie them in small bunches and then hang them from the ceiling inside a brown paper bag to collect the

Above: *Dried Citrus Peel.*

dry seeds. The seeds can be used in breads, cakes, scones, sweets, and pastries. The dried pods make an interesting addition to dried flower arrangements, too.

The seeds of the nigella plant

(*Nigella damascena),* also known as Love-in-a-Mist, are thought to strengthen the immune system and increase vitality. They are a nice addition scattered over breads, pastries, and salads. Harvest the seed

Above: *Dried wild mushrooms –
Chanterelles, Wood Blewits, and Horn
of Plenty.*

heads in early autumn, in the same
manner as poppy seeds.

When onions go to seed in early
autumn, their seeds may be dried
and harvested in the same way,
and used in breads, salads, and
vegetable dishes.

Mushrooms: I've had terrific
success drying mushrooms – and not
just wild mushrooms either.
Ordinary button or flat mushrooms
dry brilliantly and, better still, the
flavor seems to intensify. My first
experiment was to line them up on a
shelf over the stove and forget about
them for a few days; they gradually
become dry and wizened. They can
then be packed in glass jars or boxes
and stored in a cool cupboard away
from direct light.

Dried mushrooms can be
chopped into a powder in a food
processor. This can then be added to
soups or stews to greatly enhance
the flavor. Alternatively, reconstitute
the mushrooms by covering them in
tepid water; 10–15 minutes is usually
enough. Drain, but save the liquid to
add to soups, stews, or sauces. The
soaked mushrooms can be sliced or
chopped, then sautéed or stewed as
desired. We also use dried morels or
porcini to flavor oil (see page 424).
Dried mushrooms gradually lose
their potency so use up within a few
months if possible.

Tomatoes

Drying is a great way to use up
surplus tomatoes, but don't even
attempt this unless your tomatoes
are really ripe and bursting with
intense flavor. In recent times, sun-
and semi-dried tomatoes have

become indispensable to cooks, wherever they happen to live. But unless you can reliably predict several days of breezy weather with low humidity and daytime temperatures in excess of 90°F – which is roughly never in Ireland, you'll have to fall back on other options.

The chief methods are using a dehydrator, a low oven with the door ajar, or a homemade drying box. An ingenious alternative is to place a rack of tomatoes in the area under your car's rear window on a hot day.

FULLY DRIED TOMATOES: drying times will vary according to the size of your tomatoes, but as a rule of thumb, it will take about 15 hours in a very low oven or 30 hours in a drying box to get fully dried tomatoes. However, tomatoes in any given batch will not dry at exactly the same rate, so you need to remove them individually as they become ready. This is when they are firm, but no longer juicy.

Whichever method you decide to use, you can proceed in one of two ways. You can cut the tomatoes in half, lay them face up on a fine-meshed rack and sprinkle with a few grains of sea salt on the cut side. Or you can dry them intact on the vine. This involves laying the tomatoes on a fine-meshed rack, vine stalk down, before cutting a small cross in the top of each tomato and filling it with a pinch of salt.

Once dried, tomatoes can be stored at ambient temperatures in sealable containers for up to 6 months. Before using, they will need to be rehydrated by soaking in warm water for half an hour. They should always be cooked before they are eaten.

SEMI-DRIED TOMATOES: as the name suggests, semi-dried tomatoes are removed from the source of heat halfway through the drying process. They are then packed into sterilized pots that are filled with olive oil. These will keep in the fridge for up to 6 months. They are moist and more than good enough to incorporate into stews, sandwiches, and sauces without further fuss. We've achieved our best results using various varieties of cherry tomatoes.

"SUN-DRIED" TOMATOES: sun-dried and sun-blushed tomatoes have become a new basic in a few short years. They can be bought at considerable expense preserved in olive oil, but you can make your own quite easily. The riper the tomatoes, the more intense the flavor.

Cut the tomatoes in half crosswise and arrange in a single layer on a wire rack. Season with sea salt and sugar and drizzle with extra virgin olive oil. If you have a greenhouse, you can use it to dry the tomatoes over a period of several days, but despite global warming, for most of us roasting them in an oven is a more reliable alternative. I leave them in the coolest oven of my ancient 4-door stove, or in a fan oven at the minimum temperature until they are totally dried out and wizened, which takes about 8–12 hours, depending on size (after about 8 hours turn them upside down).

Store sun-dried tomatoes in sterilized jars covered with olive oil. A few basil leaves or a couple of sprigs of rosemary, thyme, or annual marjoram added to the oil make them especially delicious. Cover and keep in a cool, dry, and preferably dark place. Use in salads or with pasta.

For semi-roasted tomatoes, proceed as above but remove and use the tomatoes while they are still plump but have reduced in size by half.

SUN-DRIED TOMATO PESTO

Scatter this pesto over goat cheese or crostini, or drizzle over pasta, pan-grilled fish, or chicken breast. Each time you take some from the jar, wipe the rim and edge and cover the surface of the pesto with more extra virgin olive oil; otherwise it may go moldy ·
MAKES 1 POT

3oz sun-dried tomatoes
2 large garlic cloves, crushed
¼ cup fresh pine nuts
¼–½ teaspoon chile flakes
1–2 tablespoons balsamic vinegar
salt and freshly ground pepper
½ cup extra virgin olive oil

Blend all the ingredients, except the oil, together for a second or two in a food processor. Add the extra virgin olive oil. Store in a sterilized jar in the fridge.

Alcohol

There was a great rush to make beer and wine in the 1970s, but now that the initial craze has petered out, it's much more challenging to find a demijohn or airlock. However, I sense a revival of interest coming on, and it's well worth dabbling with making homemade wines. We've had lots of fun making homemade wine and cider, with some delicious and some horrendous results. Like everything else, practice makes reasonably perfect and every new batch will add to your knowledge of what works and what doesn't.

Homemade wines are completely different from the wines you buy in stores. They're often sweeter, so are better for sipping and enjoying in small glasses before or after dinner rather than drinking with your meal. I haven't actually made beer at home, but then again I don't need to because my son-in-law makes great beer from his home-grown organic hops and barley.

If making your own wine or cider seems too much like hard work, I urge you to try flavoring spirits with fruits. As well as flavoring the alcohol, such recipes also preserve the fruit since no bacteria can grow in pure alcohol. For this reason it's important to use the purest spirits. All you have to do is infuse a spirit like grappa, eau-de-vie, brandy, schnapps, gin, or vodka. It couldn't be easier and the results are terrific, provided you use good-quality alcohol. Start with something simple like limoncello, cherry brandy, or sloe or damson gin.

LIMONCELLO

Limoncello was one of my favorite presents to bring friends from a trip to Italy, but since an Italian friend gave me this recipe, we make our own ·
MAKES ABOUT 2 QUARTS

25 organic lemons, washed and dried
1 quart vodka
3 cups sugar

Use a swivel-top peeler to pare the zest off the lemons in strips, removing just the zest but not the pith. (Use the lemon juice for homemade lemonade or freeze it in ice cube trays for later use.) Put the zest into a sterilized glass jar and cover with vodka, so the zest is submerged. Cover the jar tightly (we use a Mason jar), and put into a cool, dark cupboard for 48 hours.

Meanwhile, put the sugar and 3½ cups of water into a saucepan over high heat. Stir to dissolve the sugar, then bring to a boil for 2 minutes to stabilize. Cool and store until the zest in vodka is ready.

Two days later, strain the zest from the vodka through a fine nylon sieve. Combine with the sugar mixture and stir well.

The limoncello can be used immediately or can be bottled, lightly sealed, and stored in a cool place. For optimum flavor use within 2–3 months. Serve chilled in small glasses.

Variation
Tangerines or mandarins can also be infused in this way.

CHERRY BRANDY

This is a very simple infusion. You can also experiment with other kinds of fruit using this technique.

cherries, preferably bitter
superfine sugar
brandy

Prick each cherry in 3 or 4 places with a sterilized darning needle, then fill the Mason jar almost to the top with the cherries. Add superfine sugar so it comes about one-third of the way up the jar. Fill to the top with brandy.

Seal well and store in a cool, dark place until Christmas or longer if you have the patience. Drink in small glasses.

Variation
ORANGE BRANDY
Put the finely peeled zest of 4 organic oranges into a deep Mason jar. Add superfine sugar and cover with brandy. Leave to infuse for several months. Drink chilled.

CRÈME DE CASSIS

It's such fun to make your own cassis, and easy too. It keeps well for a year ·
MAKES 9 X 8FL OZ BOTTLES

2¼lb fresh organic black currants, stringed
1 quart good red wine
6 cups superfine sugar
3½ cups gin or vodka

Put the black currants into a stainless-steel bowl. Cover with red wine and leave to macerate overnight.

Left: *Dandelion Wine (recipe overleaf).*

APRICOT OR PEACH RATAFIA

Jane Grigson got me started on this with her recipe in Good Things. *As with cherry brandy, there is no need to strain off and re-bottle the liqueur. Many people like to eat a piece of brandy-soaked fruit with this drink, which can also be used in fruit salads, mincemeat, or water ices* · **MAKES 700ML (1¼ PINTS)**

8 large apricots (about 18oz) or
    generous 1lb peaches
2½ cups good brandy
1 cup sugar
½ in cinnamon stick
4 cloves
¼ teaspoon ground mace

I peel the peaches first, but apricots don't need to be peeled, just quarter the fruit. Remove the stones and extract and bruise the kernels. If peaches are used, cut the pieces in half again. Add the kernels and the rest of the ingredients to the fruit. Mix well. Fill into sterilized Mason jars. Cover tightly and store for at least a month before using or, better still, 3 months. Drink in small glasses, it's truly delicious but has quite a kick in it so watch out because it slips down very easily.

The next day, liquidize the wine and currants and strain through a fine nylon sieve into a stainless-steel saucepan. Measure and add 4½ cups of superfine sugar to every quart of black currant liquid. Stir over medium heat until the sugar dissolves, then leave on low to moderate heat for about 2 hours, by which time the liquid will be slightly syrupy. Do not allow to boil or the flavor will be rather jammy.

Mix 1 part gin or vodka to 3 parts black currant syrup. Store in vodka or gin bottles, seal, and leave to mature for at least a week before using. Crème de cassis keeps well, but do use it before the new season's crop.

THE CIDER TRADITION

Dick Keating, who gave me the recipe to the right, tells me that the practice of making cider on farms in Ireland persisted in some places right up until the late 1940s. Originally, people would have gone to the distillery in Fethard and bought whiskey barrels which held 60–80 gallons to use to ferment their cider. What they didn't know was that the cider stripped the alcohol from the barrels, so the feisty brew that resulted ended up being about 20 percent proof. It earned the cider the name "Johnny Jump-up!" Dick also remembers a traveling cider press mounted on horse and cart that went from farm to farm making cider right up to the 1940s. Local people could go along to the farm with a jug and get a flagon of cider for threepence. Dick Keating is one of the few remaining people in this area to continue the tradition and he generously passes on the skill to anybody who would like to learn. He and his wife Ann make one of Ireland's best-known farmhouse cheeses, known as "Baylough."

DANDELION WINE

For the best results, pick the flowers in full sunshine at midday when they are fully open and make the wine immediately · **MAKES 1½ GALLONS**

1lb dandelion flowers
6 cups white sugar
4 oranges (organic if possible)
1 teaspoon dried yeast

Measure the yellow dandelion heads, discarding as much green leaf as possible (without being too pernickety). Meanwhile bring 1 gallon of water to a boil.

Pour the boiling water over the flowerheads and leave to steep for 2 days. Don't exceed the time or what can be a delicious table wine may be spoiled.

Bring the mixture to a boil, add the thinly pared slivers of the orange zest (no white pith), and continue to boil for 10 minutes. Strain through cheesecloth onto the sugar and stir the mixture to dissolve the sugar fully.

Leave to cool. Then add the yeast and juice from the oranges. Put the mixture into a fermentation jar and fit an airlock. Siphon off into clean bottles when the wine has cleared – about 2 months. It should be just right for drinking by Christmas.

DICK KEATING'S ORIGINAL TIPPERARY CIDER

I really urge you to try and get organic apples for making cider, or at least apples that haven't been heavily sprayed. We've made cider with Dick Keating several times. We bring it into the kitchen to ferment close to the warmth of the oven. I love to sit quietly listening to the calming sound of the occasional bubble as the cider ferments. In Dick's words, the skills required here are determination, innovation, and a warm environment! · **MAKES 4½ QUARTS**

11lb tart apples – windfalls are fine, but Granny Smiths are preferable (use whatever you have)
2¼ cups granulated white sugar
½ teaspoon dried yeast or preferably dried wine yeast

Your ability to recover the juice from apples will determine the amount of apples you require, as an apple is about 80 percent juice. We use a centrifuge. You should get about 3½ quarts of juice from the apples. (Note that fresh apple juice must not be left around too long, as it oxidizes when exposed to the air and goes brown.)

Put half the juice into a demijohn, and gently warm about 2 cups of juice in a stainless-steel pan.

Add half of the sugar to the warmed juice and dissolve. Raise the heat to about 122°F, or just enough to dissolve the sugar. Then add the warm mixture to the demijohn. Check the temperature of the juice in the demijohn. Temperature control is crucial here – it must not be more than 86°F, or the yeast will be killed.

Dissolve the remaining sugar in the remaining juice. The juice must not boil. When the temperature of the juice in the demijohn is between 68–86°F, add the yeast. If the temperature is more than 86°F, then leave it to cool before adding the yeast.

The demijohn at this stage is about seven-eighths full. Place an airlock on the jar and put in warm place at 77–86°C. When fermentation slows down, add more juice or warm water (not chlorinated) to fill the jar and leave it to ferment for about 3 weeks, or until it stops fermenting. When fermentation is over, leave it in a cool, dark place until the liquid clears.

APPLE CIDER

This is an old 19th-century recipe that is brilliantly easy to make, with no need to peel or press the apples ·
MAKES ABOUT 3 QUARTS

6½ lb cooking apples
4 cups sugar
¼ cup grated fresh ginger
3 cinnamon sticks

Grate the apples into an enamel or stainless-steel bucket and cover with 2 gallons of cold water. Stir with a sterilized wooden spoon every day for a week. Strain.

Stir the sugar into the juice. Then add the spices and leave to macerate for a day. Strain through clean cheesecloth. Pour into sterilized bottles and seal well with screw-top lids.

Store in a cold dry place until Christmas.

Above: *Dick Keating's Original Tipperary Cider.*

Syrups and Cordials

Of course these non-alcoholic drinks contain sugar, but they're nothing like the high-fructose-corn-syrup-laden, aspartame-filled, preservative-and-additive-stuffed fizzy drinks that many kids are constantly drinking.

Cordials are concentrated fruit syrups that can be diluted with water to make a refreshing drink. The sugary fruit-flavored drinks that weigh down the supermarket shelves today would have been inspired by these once upon a time, but sadly they have strayed quite a long way from the original. In some cases, they are completely synthetic and have never been in contact with a piece of fruit! For years, we've tried to replicate a black currant flavored drink at home, and I've had terrific success making cassis, too.

Homemade lemonades and cordials are made up in minutes and keep easily in the fridge, so the kids (and adults) can serve themselves.

Flavored ice cubes

We have lots of fun making fancy ice cubes to float in lemonade, drinking water, or cocktails. Simply pop a little herb or edible flower leaves, whatever your chosen flavoring, into an ice cube tray and fill with water and freeze. Here are some ideas for what to add: gorse flowers, hawthorn, borage, violas, mint leaves, violets, lemon verbena, or lemon balm. Or put marjoram or basil into them and float them in cold soups. Pomegranate seeds are lovely in ice cubes, particularly around Christmas, or try star anise.

JUNE'S FROZEN LEMON SLICES
A thrifty friend, June Bennett, gave me this tip for saving leftover lemon segments or slices. Tray-freeze first so they don't stick together and then just pop them into a plastic bag or chill box. Put back in the freezer and use to flavor and cool gin and tonic or other aperitifs.

BASIC STOCK SYRUP

Flavored syrups are such an obvious thing to do that I can't imagine why people don't have some in their pantry all the time. We make many different ones and use them not only for homemade lemonades but also for fruit salads and compotes. Sweet geranium, lemongrass, and lemon verbena syrups are particularly good for poaching fruits. They keep for months in a fridge, or a shorter time if unrefrigerated · MAKES ABOUT 2½ CUPS

2 cups sugar
2½ cups water

Dissolve the sugar in the water and bring to a boil. Boil for 2 minutes, then leave it to cool. Store in the fridge until needed.

Flavored syrups

You can add any of the following herbs or flowers to the cold water and sugar in the saucepan before bringing to a boil:

Rosemary syrup: 2–4 sprigs of fresh rosemary
Ginger syrup: ¼ cup sliced ginger
Rose geranium syrup: 6–8 rose geranium leaves
Lemon verbena syrup:
6–8 lemon verbena leaves
Elderflower syrup:
8 elderflower heads
Lavender syrup: 1–2 tablespoons dried lavender flowers
Mint syrup: 4–6 sprigs of fresh mint, preferably spearmint

HOMEMADE LEMONADE

Whereas homemade syrups can be kept for several weeks in the fridge, homemade lemonades are best drunk within a few hours of being made or certainly on the same day. If kept for longer, the lemonade will oxidize because there is no added citric acid, which tends to destroy many of the vitamins. For fizzy lemonade, use sparkling instead of still water · SERVES 6

freshly squeezed juice of 3 lemons
1 cup syrup of your choice
3 cups water, sparkling or still
ice cubes

Mix all the ingredients together in a large pitcher. Add ice cubes just before serving.

RASPBERRY LEMONADE

This is my daughter-in-law Rachel's recipe for summer lemonade, which children and grown-ups alike adore · SERVES 8

9oz raspberries
⅓–⅔ cup superfine sugar, depending on the sweetness of the fruit
zest and juice of 2 organic lemons

2 cups sparkling or still water
ice cubes

In a food processor or blender, blend the raspberries and sugar, then strain through a sieve into a glass pitcher to remove the seeds. Add the lemon juice, zest, and water. Add ice and serve.

BLACK CURRANT LEAF LEMONADE

Young black currant leaves are wonderfully fragrant in early summer before the currants form on the bushes. After that, the leaves start to lose their fragrance. We use the leaves to flavor granitas, syrups, and custards ·
SERVES ABOUT 6

2 large handfuls of young black currant leaves
1 cup granulated sugar
juice of 3 freshly squeezed lemons
3–4 cups still or sparkling water
ice cubes

Crush the black currant leaves tightly in your hand, then put them into a stainless-steel saucepan with 2⅓ cups of water and the sugar. Stir to dissolve the sugar and bring to a boil slowly. Simmer for 2–3 minutes, then leave to cool completely.

Add 3 cups of water, taste, and add more water if necessary. Serve chilled with lots of ice.

BLACK CURRANT CORDIAL

This concentrated black currant cordial, packed with vitamin C, is delicious diluted with sparkling or plain water or sparkling wine. It keeps for several months in a cool place.

2½lb organic black currants
about 11 cups sugar
1 cup white wine vinegar

Boil the black currants and 4 quarts of water together in a stainless-steel saucepan for 15 minutes. Strain and add 13 parts of sugar to every 15 cups of liquid. Add the white vinegar and boil for 3 minutes. Pour into sterilized bottles and seal well. Dilute with water to taste.

LOGANBERRY CORDIAL

You can also make this cordial with tayberries, boysenberries, or raspberries instead of loganberries – or a mixture.

1½lb loganberries
1½ cups superfine sugar
juice of ½ lemon or more

Put the fruit, sugar, and 1 quart water into a stainless-steel saucepan over medium heat. Add the freshly squeezed lemon juice.

Bring to a boil and simmer for 5–6 minutes or until the loganberries soften and disintegrate. Remove from the heat and cool.

Pour through a nylon sieve. Rub the pulp through and discard the pips. Pour into sterilized bottles, seal, and store in the fridge. Dilute

with still or sparkling water for loganberry fizz.

ELDERFLOWER CORDIAL

Pick the elderflowers early in the season. If refrigerated, elderflower cordial will keep for up to a year. To serve, dilute with water, wine, or sparkling wine, using about one part elderflower syrup to six parts water ·
MAKES ABOUT 3½ CUPS

10 elderflower heads
4 cups sugar
finely grated zest and juice of
 1 organic lemon
1¾oz citric acid

Pick the elderflowers while they are dry. Examine them and shake, in case there are any insects.

Bring 2½ cups of water to a boil in a stainless-steel saucepan. Add the sugar and stir to dissolve. Remove from the heat. Leave to cool for 10 minutes.

Add the elderflowers and stir. Add the lemon zest and juice – alternatively, you can slice the lemon thinly and add to the syrup. Add the citric acid. Cover and leave overnight.

Next day, pour the syrup through a sieve and again through a fine nylon sieve. Pour into clean screw-top glass or plastic bottles and store in the fridge or a cool place.

If you used lemon slices, save them to add to homemade lemonade or gin and tonic. Freeze in a single layer on silicone paper, then pack in plastic boxes. Divine.

Variation

ELDERFLOWER BELLINI

Put a little elderflower cordial into a Champagne flute and top up with Prosecco. Serve immediately.

ELDERFLOWER FIZZ

This magical recipe transforms perfectly ordinary ingredients into a delicious sparkling drink. The children make it religiously every year and then share the "bubbly" with their friends. It's supposed to be non-alcoholic, but given that it ferments, I suspect there might be a small amount of alcohol in it.

2 heads of elderflowers
zest and juice of 1 organic lemon
¾ cup sugar
2 tablespoons white wine vinegar

Pick the elderflowers in full bloom. Remove the zest from the lemon with a swivel-top peeler. Put into a bowl with the elderflower, lemon juice, sugar, vinegar, and 4¾ quarts of cold water. Leave for 24 hours, then strain into strong screw-top bottles. The bottles need to be strong and well sealed; otherwise the elderflower "champagne" will pop its cork.

Lay them on their sides in a cool place. After 2 weeks, the elderflower fizz should be sparkling and ready to drink.

Left: *Elderflower Cordial in the making.*

TED'S GINGER BEER

Ted Berner came to Ireland from Sweden in his early teens, fell in love with my niece, and never returned to live in Sweden. He makes the greatest ginger beer, so we were delighted when he generously shared the recipe with us. It's an exercise in patience, as it takes three weeks before it's ready to drink, but that's what makes it so delicious ·

MAKES 22 X 12FL OZ BOTTLES

FOR THE WILD YEAST CULTURE
8 golden raisins, preferably organic
juice and pulp of 2 organic lemons
7 x 4 heaped teaspoons sugar, preferably dark cane sugar or Muscovado
7 x 2 heaped teaspoons ground ginger, as fresh as possible

First start the wild yeast culture. Combine all the ingredients together with 1¾ cups of water into a sterilized jar and seal it. Feed it each day for 7 days by adding a further 2 heaped teaspoons of sugar and 2 heaped teaspoons of ginger. After a few days, it'll start to bubble. That's how you know its aliiiiive!

When the starter is ready, gather the following ingredients:

3½ cups dark cane sugar or Muscovado
1 cup freshly squeezed organic lemon juice
2 teaspoons sugar
2 teaspoons ginger

In a large pot, dissolve the sugar into 1 quart of water by bringing it to a boil. Turn off the heat and add the lemon juice and a further 7 quarts of cold water. Then add the wild yeast culture to the now-tepid pot.

Line a big strainer with double cheesecloth, hang the strainer over another big pot, and pour the liquid through. Don't press the liquid through the sieve, but stir it gently to encourage as much liquid as possible to seep through.

When all the liquid has dripped through, divide whatever residue is left in the sieve and split the contents between two sterilized jars. Add the 2 teaspoons of sugar, 2 teaspoons ginger, and a further 2 cups of water to each of the jars. Now you'll have two new babies; keep one and give one to a friend; they will be the base of another batch.

The jars will keep quite happy in the fridge for several weeks or even months, until you're ready to start another batch. Then take the jar out and feed it every day for a week, as above.

Pour the strained liquid into sterilized bottles; you can sometimes even find traditional old ceramic and-stone ginger beer bottles. Seal them tightly, because the liquid is live and will produce carbon dioxide. Leave in a cool room (about 60–62°F) for 3 days. Then refrigerate at no higher than 39°F. This is important; otherwise they will eventually explode. Leave them in the fridge for at least 2 weeks to mature before drinking. They continue to improve over time.

Smoking

We've noticed a growing interest in home smoking over the past few years as the movement toward self-sufficiency continues to gather momentum. It's a most useful skill in times when fish are abundant. But beware, smoking can become addictive! Like everything else I do, I try to take the mystery out of the subject and reduce it down to the basic elements. Once you understand the basic principles of smoking, you can start to experiment.

People must have been inadvertantly smoking food certainly since the Stone Age, when primitive man used fire to cook food and keep warm. The meat would probably have been hanging in the shelter or cave as the wood fire smoked and smoldered. No doubt, they soon noted that the food acquired a distinctive smoky taste and the keeping qualities were considerably enhanced. At that time, the ability to preserve surplus fish and meat for leaner times could spell the difference between survival or not. Smoking helps to inhibit the growth of molds, but it doesn't fully preserve food, so the ingredients need to be salted or brined first. Salt inhibits the growth of harmful bacteria and draws out the moisture in which they thrive.

In the days before refrigeration, food was very highly salted and cold-smoked for days or even weeks. Meat and fish then lasted almost indefinitely, even at warm temperatures. When mechanical refrigeration was introduced in the late 19th and early 20th century, the emphasis shifted away from smoking as a method of preservation to a means of enhancing the flavor. Demand for lightly salted (not more than 2–3 percent) and lightly smoked food increased.

It's impossible to know for sure when pre-salting or brining was adopted as an essential part of the process as it is today, but it's safe to say that our ancestors soon became aware that the higher the salt content in a product and the longer the smoking period, the better the keeping quality.

In these days of refrigeration, food is rarely smoked for maximum keeping qualities – the object is to add flavor and variety.

Smoking, like so many other skills, is trial and error, so it's hard to give the quintessential recipe. My best advice is to enjoy the experimentation process and to keep a record of your efforts. Sometimes your food will be over-smoked, sometimes under-smoked, but it's not going to harm you. Practice makes perfect!

At the Cookery School, we smoke food in all sorts of ways; in a metal box, a wok, a galvanized trash can, a barrel, an old fridge, a tackle box designed for fishermen to take out on the river. We even have quite a sophisticated purpose-built timber smokehouse made for us by Frank Krawczyk, a West Cork artisan. If you're not into Heath Robinson-type contraptions and prefer something a bit more scientific, you may find a purpose-built smoker in kitchen stores or garden centres or on the Internet.

The basic smoking process

During the smoking process, food becomes coated with tarry deposits of an antiseptic nature and these, together with the salt, inhibit the growth of food spoilage bacteria. Left to their own devices, these would cause the meat or fish to decay. Food loses moisture (and, consequently, weight) during the smoking process; the greater the loss of moisture, the greater the keeping qualities. The weight loss is directly linked to the humidity of the atmosphere at the time of smoking. In a traditional smoker or kiln, food will take longer to dry out under humid conditions than under dry conditions. These variations don't occur in modern mechanical smokers, where humidity is controlled automatically.

There are two methods of smoking; cold smoking and hot smoking.

Hot smoking: with this method smoke is generated inside the main smoking chamber and the fish cooks as it smokes. Hot smoking is carried out at a temperature not lower than 130°F. Depending on the item you are smoking the temperature may need to be increased to 180–200°F for fish like mackerel, and from 180–240°F for poultry and meat. Hence the food is partially or fully cooked as well as smoked. Both the flavor and texture are altered but it keeps for significantly less time than cold-smoked food because the smoke has not had a chance to penetrate deep inside the flesh.

Above: *You can cold-smoke all kinds of foods; salt, butter, cheese, garlic, nuts, oatmeal ...*
Enjoy the experimentation process and learn from your mistakes as well as your triumphs.

Cold smoking: with this method the smoke is usually generated outside the main chamber containing the fish and allowed to cool before passing over the fish and curing it slowly. Cold smoking does not cook the product. It is usually done between 50–85°F, ideally at 75–80°F. Don't even attempt to cold-smoke in hot weather; if the temperature is above 80°F, cold smoking is very difficult – there's a reason why smoking was traditionally done in the fall! Some cold-smoked products need a further period of cooking in the kitchen, but a piece of gorgeous cold-smoked haddock, if it was fresh and delicate when smoked, will be delicious thinly sliced and eaten without cooking. This method does not alter the texture of the flesh significantly.

The "gray zone"

Beware of what fish smokers call the gray zone, the temperature between 80–140°F. Bacteria can multiply rapidly in that temperature zone.

How do I know when the food is smoked?

This is another difficult question to answer emphatically, as it depends whether you are aiming for a light or rich smoke. As a general rule, though, it's when the surface of the food is a good, rich color and the texture is firm, but still pliable to the touch. Lightly smoked food should be eaten within a few days – a week at most. Heavily smoked food will keep for longer. Cold smoking naturally takes considerably longer than hot smoking.

Hot and Cold Smoking – the Principles

A smoker doesn't need to be elaborate or complicated to do the job. Big, wide chimneys in old houses often had recesses to hang a ham that was gradually smoked as the cool smoke wafted upward.

In its simplest form, all you need is an enclosed chamber in which a sawdust fire can smolder. It needs to be sufficiently large to hang or support a good-sized fish, such as salmon, a ham, or a flitch of bacon with room to spare. There needs to be an outlet for the smoke.

You'll need a metal plate or shallow metal bowl to hold the sawdust and preferably a piece of perforated metal or wood baffle a

Below: *An old electric burner is the heat source in our large smoker.*

few inches above to disperse the smoke evenly as it rises.

You could use a barrel, an old fridge, or even an aluminum trash can; a simple structure can be built with breeze blocks or untreated wood. Once you've grasped the basic principle, there are many ways to build a smoker or smoke house.

Smoke can be delivered into the chamber in one of two ways:

1. LIGHT A SMOLDERING FIRE INSIDE THE SMOKER: this method can be used for hot or cold smoking. But if you want to cold-smoke, the smoker needs to be reasonably large, otherwise the heat source will significantly increase the internal temperature.

2. PIPE IN THE SMOKE FROM A REMOTE CHAMBER: this is the method used for cold smoking. For this option, buy a length of flexible heat-resistant pipe, 4–6in in diameter and at least 6 feet long to channel cold smoke into the chamber. This can be kept above ground or buried below.

Heat source

If you have a smoker large enough to walk in to, you might consider lighting a little fire directly on the earth floor. When it becomes established and burns down to glowing red coals, cover it entirely with sawdust. In a short time, you'll have dense smoke. If large joints are being smoked, you'll need to top up with sawdust from time to time, depending on the length of smoking

period. It's not a big problem if the fire goes out for a while. Just relight and continue on.

Alternatively, use a thermostatically controlled electric coiled ring, gas burner, or even a camp stove or Hibachi as the heat source and put a roasting tray or old frying pan full of sawdust on top.

Do I need a thermometer?

A thermometer will enable you to monitor the temperature for hot or cold smoking. It certainly helps to give confidence to a beginner, so it may well be worth the small investment.

How about a hygrometer?

Not essential, but again very useful to measure humidity inside the smoking chamber.

What kind of wood?

Smokers argue about which timber is best – apple, cherry, oak, beech, birch, hazel, ash, walnut, maple – all have their devotees but everyone agrees that it must be hardwood. Hardwoods come from deciduous trees – the ones that lose their leaves during the winter. Conifers, the sort of trees that have needles rather than leaves, are not suitable because the wood produces an acrid, tarry smoke which taints the food with an antiseptic flavor. Having said that, the Scandinavians are partial to that flavor.

There is unquestionably a distinct difference in flavor between different woods, so find one you like, but also experiment from time to time if you can get a variety of hardwoods. Do not use treated or painted wood, as it may create toxic fumes when burned.

Apple wood, our particular favorite, produces a delicious dense smoke over a long period. We have an apple orchard and use the prunings to make sawdust for smoking. We oil a chainsaw with cooking oil and saw the branches into thin slices to create lots of sawdust. We lay a sheet of plastic underneath the sawing area to catch the precious sawdust as it falls. My preference is for sawdust from green wood.

Fresh sawdust smolders well – beware if the sawdust is very dry, it can burst into flame. A water mister might be useful. I have read in several books that corn husks are good, but I haven't tried them.

Where can I source sawdust?
(1) A variety of sawdust from different wood is available in fishing stores.
(2) Go along to a local sawmill or cabinet maker and ask for sawdust from untreated wood.
(3) Handy types who own a chain-saw can saw narrow rings from a branch of an apple tree. Collect the sawdust from underneath. Fresh sawdust smolders well provided it is not too damp.

Where to smoke
One can smoke indoors or outdoors, depending on the method of smoking – metal box, wok, or smoking box can be used on a gas jet in the kitchen. Larger smoking chambers are best used outdoors or in a large covered area, e.g. a open shed or garage.

Below: *Applewood from our orchard is cut into thin slices (left) to create sawdust (right).*

BUILDING A HOT SMOKER

A galvanized trash can or trash can incinerator can easily be adapted as a smoker and this is great way to get started with home smoking. All you need to do is to punch a few holes in the base of the can. Then drill a series of parallel holes at one or two levels in the side of the can to support two wire rods on each level (rather like the racks in your oven). These can be used either to hang the items of food or to support wire racks with the food placed on top. You will also need to place a drip tray on the lowest level to stop drips from causing flare-ups. The smoke will escape through the holes in the side, but if you are using a galvanized trash can incinerator (as opposed to a regular trash can) it will already have a chimney in the lid. This can be blocked off with a piece of wood if there is difficulty reaching the required temperature. If you are using a regular trash can, just pop the lid on top.

Stand the trash can on two sturdy cement blocks. Place two smaller bricks inside to support the metal plate, preferably perforated, that the sawdust will smolder on. Finally, you need a simple gas ring to light the sawdust and to maintain the temperature in the smoking chamber.

If using an aluminum trash can, it's a good idea to run smoke through it for 12 hours before smoking any food so the inside gets coated with tarry smoke. This will prevent tainting of the food.

To smoke, light the fire, and then pile sawdust over the hot coals or embers. If using a gas jet or electric burner, put a metal pan filled with sawdust on top.

Use a thermometer to monitor the temperature and turn down the gas if the temperature is getting too hot. Remember, hot air rises, so you may want to swap the racks around halfway through to ensure even smoking.

After you've experimented with this a couple of times, you'll probably want to build something more permanent in your garden or back yard.

BUILDING A COLD SMOKER

In the smoker opposite we've used an old stove as a heat source. The smoke cools as it travels through the piping into the smoking chamber (an old whisky barrel from our local distillery). You can buy a length of aluminum piping from a DIY store. Cut out a hole of the same diameter as the piping in the side of the barrel. You can use caulking to seal around it, but make sure it is foodsafe. During smoking, we cover the barrel with a round of wood, but a damp hessian sack is more traditional and also works very well. Drill small holes in the sides near the top and pass metal rods through them. These can be used either to hang the items of food or to support wire racks with the food placed on top.

BUILDING A MORE PERMANENT SMOKER

If you want a more permanent structure for hot or cold smoking, you can build a chest-shaped structure with cement blocks or untreated wood. An ideal size for domestic use would be about 5ft high by 3ft square. Decide whether you want a door or a lid – preferably hinged. Don't forget to install supports on the inside of the chamber about 18in from the ground to support the smoke diffuser (if using) and to hold 2–3 wire racks. If you're hot smoking, place a small gas or electric burner on the base and then put some sawdust in a metal plate and

place it on top of the burner. You'll need a perforated metal sheet above to disperse the smoke more evenly. For cold smoking, you'll need to pipe the smoke in from a remote chamber as above.

Finally, you will need to make some vent holes a couple of inches below the roof or top to draw the smoke upward and out of the smoking chamber.

Salting and Brining

Before smoking, the raw materials should be dry-salted or soaked in brine (also referred to as "curing"). This inhibits the growth of bacteria by drawing out excess moisture and also adds flavor. In hot countries where preservation of the catch is of the utmost importance, more salt and longer brining periods are advisable. Dry-salting is favored by many commercial fish smokers. It has a better shelf life but more weight loss, so some commercial smokers brine, adding dye and other flavorings to increase and maintain weight.

In general, it's best to salt- or dry-cure fish with a low fat content and brine-cure fish with a high fat content, like mackerel and herring. However, the methods are interchangeable and don't seem to be carved in stone. Many people have purely personal preferences and there are also regional variations.

When to brine and when to salt

In general, it's advisable to brine larger joints – hams, etc. Brining produces a quicker result, however it takes longer for the brine to penetrate a whole fish with a high fat content (e.g. sprats or herrings) than fish fillets. It will take about four to five hours in an 80 percent brine. If the fish are landed in the evening, it can cause a dilemma – you may not fancy having to get up in the middle of the night to remove them from the brine, so in that situation you can add more water to weaken the brine and leave the fish until morning. It's a little haphazard, but you soon get the feel for it. Alternatively you could just sprinkle salt lightly over the fresh fish fillets and refrigerate; this will stiffen the fish and halt bacterial growth.

For cold smoking, many fish smokers prefer to dry salt, rinse, dry, and smoke. Rinsing takes time, but is essential.

In the US particularly, where low salting is preferred, many smokers use 70 percent salt to 30 percent sugar, or even half and half. Sugar also preserves, helps to tenderize and draw out excess liquid.

NOTE: most recipes in this section are brined rather than salted – with the exception of smoked salmon and smoked mackerel – though these can also be brined.

How to salt

Sprinkle the item lightly with plain pickling salt. If it's a salmon, stop sprinkling 2–3in from the tail where the flesh is thinner. Prop it up slightly, so the tail is marginally lower than the head and the salt will make its way down to the tail end. Salting is a method of preserving in itself – see the Pig chapter for recipes.

How much salt do I need?

People's salt tolerance varies but its good to know that a salt content of 5 percent will check the growth of most food spoilage organisms in fish and meat. Even a smaller proportion will have a preservative effect.

How to brine

Use fresh, preferably unchlorinated water – spring or bottled water is fine. Plain cooking salt or pickling salt – pure vacuum salt is best to use.

The most widely used brine is an 80 percent solution, which is made by dissolving 2lb 9oz of salt in 4.5 quarts of water. You can simply add the salt to the cold water and stir to dissolve, but I find that a quicker method is to dissolve the salt in 1.8 quarts of hot water and then add another 3 quarts of cold water to cool the brine.

The brine should be so concentrated that an egg or a piece of peeled potato will float. If you have a salinometer it will register 80 percent.

Don't pack the food too closely in the vessel, otherwise the brine may not be able to fully penetrate. Ensure that the food is completely submerged in the brine. You may need to weigh it down with a well-scrubbed, heavy cutting board. I also find that a plastic box with a weight inside placed directly on top of the food works well. Keep it in a cool place, preferably a fridge or cold-room.

Do I need a salinometer?

A salinometer is a device for measuring the amount of dissolved salt in a solution. It is a useful piece of equipment, but certainly not essential.

What to brine in

Choose a vessel large enough to hold the food you want to smoke. Originally, wooden barrels or tubs, even cement-lined tanks were used, but nowadays, plastic trays or even a plastic trash can are ideal. Earthenware or stoneware may also be used, but metal should be avoided because it can taint the product and will be corroded by the brine.

Brine solutions

If you find an 80 percent solution too salty, you can try using a weaker brine. Here are some guidelines:

For an 80 percent solution, use: 2lb 9oz salt to 4.5 quarts of water

For a 70 percent solution, use: 2lb 3oz salt to every 4.5 quarts of water

For a 60 percent solution, use: 1lb 13oz salt to 4.5 quarts of water

Flavor additions for brine

Salt alone can toughen the meat or fish, so other ingredients such as herbs, spices, sugar, and alcohol may be added to enhance the flavor and tenderness of the finished product. Some herbs or spices, such as fennel, pepper, bay, juniper, and rosemary also have anti-bacterial and insect-repelling properties.

Home smokers are often notoriously secretive about the flavorings they add to their brine. Favored ingredients are brown sugar, molasses, wine, brandy, pepper, cloves, bay, spices – all add extra flavor, but the only essential ingredient is pure vacuum-dried salt which is very inexpensive.

Brining times

The length of time for brining depends on the size and type of raw material and is often a question of trial and error. But basically, the bigger the item, the longer you need to brine it for. Large items like hams may need up to 48 hours, whereas mussels only need a quick dip. If you leave something too long in brine the salt will start to toughen it. Herrings or mackerel fillets will only need 10–20 minutes depending on size.

Fish should be brined separately from meat otherwise the meat may taste fishy; however, there is no problem smoking both together in a home situation (this wouldn't be allowed in a commercial smoker).

If meat is being brined for several days, the brine will need to be stirred every day or so to ensure even distribution.

It's best to make a fresh brine for each batch because some salt-tolerant bacteria can breed in stale brine.

Dry after brining – you can't smoke wet food!

Remove the fish or meat from the brine and give it a quick rinse in cold water, so salt crystals don't form on the surface. Some of the protein constituents that are dissolved in the saltwater will form a glazed film which looks like a thin, shiny layer on the surface as it dries – this is called the pellicle. This takes on an attractive color during smoking and also helps to preserve the fish or meat. The fish or meat must be allowed to dry properly before smoking, otherwise the

Above: *Dry-salting fish.*

pellicle won't form properly and both the appearance and the flavor will be affected. A word of caution however: if the surface of the skin dries too much, the smoke will not be able to penetrate properly.

How and where do I dry the brined fish or meat?

The fish or meat can hang from or lie on a wire rack, skin-side down, at room temperature in a good draft to form the glossy pellicle. It can also be dried in the smoker. If you don't have a cool natural breeze, use a fan to keep the air moving. The process usually takes two–three hours, depending on the size of the fish.

If the food is not dry enough before smoking, a white liquid may ooze from the surface. This is a mixture of the protein substances that normally form the pellicle. It's slightly unsightly, but it is totally harmless and is, in fact, quite tasty.

HOW TO SMOKE MACKEREL, CHICKEN BREAST, OR DUCK BREAST IN A SIMPLE SMOKER

This is a simple Heath Robinson way to smoke small items of food. It may be frowned upon by serious smokers, but it is great for beginners because it gives such quick results. The fish, duck, or chicken can be smoked without having been brined, but even a short salting or brining will improve flavor – 15–20 minutes should do it. Leave to dry for approximately 30 minutes before smoking.

mackerel or duck breast or organic chicken breast
sawdust
1 shallow metal box with tight-fitting lid
1 wire cake rack to fit inside
pure salt or 80 percent brine

Place a sheet of tin foil in the base of the metal box and sprinkle 3 or 4 tablespoons of sawdust over it. Lay the fish or meat on the wire rack skin-side upward, then cover the box with the lid.

Place the box on a gas jet or other heat source on medium heat. The sawdust will start to smolder and produce warm smoke that in turn both cooks and smokes the food. Reduce the heat to low. Mackerel will take about 8–10 minutes. Duck or chicken breast will take 20–30 minutes, depending on

Left: *Try smoking duck breasts in a metal box smoker.*

the size. Leave to rest before eating warm or at room temperature.

Alternatively, you could buy a simple smoking box from a fishing store or hot-smoke in a tightly covered wok over a gas jet in your own kitchen.

MACKEREL FILLETS

Local artisan smoker Frank Hederman from Belvelly Smokehouse near Cobh in County Cork adds a variety of flavors to his smoked mackerel fillets – whole mustard, chile flakes, cracked black pepper, chopped chives – which he jokingly tells his customers is cannabis so they sell like hot cakes! A slather of harissa on the flesh side is also good.

Brine for 15–20 minutes in an 80 percent solution. Lay on a wire rack to dry. Hot-smoke for 7–8 minutes, depending on size.

HOT-SMOKED MACKEREL

One of the most memorable meals I have ever eaten was lovely fresh mackerel smoked there and then on the beach, with russet potatoes boiled in seawater, eaten with melted butter. First sprinkle the mackerel with sea salt and then smoke them. If you like to fish, take a small metal box to the sea or river with you, and smoke your catch on the bank or in a boat. Mackerel are a good fish to practice smoking on because they are inexpensive.

whole fresh mackerel (head and tail on)

Gut the mackerel, preferably as soon as they are caught. Wash out the line of blood along the back bone.

Brine in an 80 percent solution for at least 1 hour and up to 4 hours. Drain, and allow to dry.

Hot-smoke in a metal box or smoking box for about 8–12 minutes depending on size. Alternatively, cold-smoke at 75–80°F for 8 hours and then hot-smoke at 180–200°F for 45 minutes.

CUCUMBER AND DILL SAUCE

Delicious with smoked and cured fish
· SERVES 8–10

1 crisp cucumber, peeled and cut
    into ½in cubes
salt and freshly ground pepper
    and sugar
1–2 garlic cloves, crushed
dash of freshly squeezed lemon
    juice
1 heaping tablespoon freshly
    chopped dill
2 cups Greek yogurt or best-quality
    natural yogurt
4 tablespoons heavy cream

Put the cubed cucumber into a sieve, sprinkle with salt, and allow to drain for about 30 minutes. Dry the cucumber on paper towels, put into a bowl, and mix with garlic, lemon juice, yogurt, and cream. Stir in the dill and taste; it may need a little salt and freshly ground pepper, or even a pinch of sugar.

Right: *Hot-smoked Mackerel.*

WOK-SMOKED SALMON

Hot-smoked salmon is quite different from cold-smoked salmon. Hot smoking a piece of fish can take as little as 15 minutes in a wok and it will have a more pronounced smokiness. Hot-smoked salmon has the texture of roast fish, rather than the pliable slices you may be more familiar with, and this makes it great for flaking into salads and pasta dishes. You can use any covered box or a saucepan or wok with a rack – here we use a combination of sugar, salt, rice, and tea leaves, but fine sawdust works perfectly too, especially in a fisherman's smoking box.

1lb thick salmon fillet, cut into
    4 even chunks, pin bones
    removed
3 tablespoons turbinado sugar
2 tablespoons sea salt
1¼ cup uncooked rice
4oz untreated wood chips or tea
    leaves

To Serve
homemade Mayonnaise (see
    page 252)
tomato and green salad

The easiest way to hot-smoke is to use a wok or sauté pan with a tight-fitting lid. First, lay the salmon pieces in a shallow dish and mix 2 tablespoons of the sugar and the salt and sprinkle over the flesh side. Rub it in. Leave to rest at room temperature for 30 minutes.

Meanwhile, line the wok or sauté pan tightly with 2 layers of foil, overlapping each other at 90 degrees. Each piece should overlap the sides of the wok or pan by 12in on each side. Sprinkle in the rice and tea (or wood chips) and the other tablespoon of sugar. Choose a round cake rack that will fit neatly inside the wok or sauté pan, about 1½–2in from the base.

Use paper towels to wipe the excess salt and sugar from the fish. Place the wok or sauté pan on a high heat. When smoke starts to rise, lay the fish, skin-side down, on top of the wire rack. Cover with the lid and fold the foil "flaps" tightly over the lid to seal in the smoke.

After about 3–4 minutes, turn down the heat to medium and continue to smoke for another 7–12 minutes (the amount of time depends on the thickness of the fish). To test, turn the heat off, peel back the foil, and then carefully remove the lid. There will be lots of smoke, so ensure the kitchen is well ventilated if you are indoors.

Test by inserting a small knife into the thickest part of the fish. The flesh should be almost opaque, but still moist and pink. If it still looks raw, put the lid back on and smoke for another few minutes. If it's ready, remove the fish, transfer to a serving plate, and leave to cool. Serve with homemade mayonnaise and perhaps a tomato and green salad.

COLD-SMOKED SALMON

It's best to use very fresh fish, but many commercial fish smokers freeze the fish first, and you can too. The results are still excellent provided the fish is blast frozen at -22°F. Nitrogen freezing takes just seconds and causes minimum cellular destruction.

1 wild or organic salmon
pure sea salt or brine (if you are
    brining, use an 80 percent
    salt solution: 2¾lb salt to
    4.5 quarts water)

First, fillet the salmon (see page 79), but there is no need to remove the scales. Lay each fillet skin-side down on a cutting board, trim off the rib bones and tidy the belly if necessary. Run your fingers along the fillet to identify the pin bones and remove them with tweezers or a fish pincers. Wash if necessary and dry very well. Weigh each fillet and record the weight.

Lay the fillets on a stainless-steel or Delft platter at a slight angle, so the dish tilts down toward the tail.

If salting the fish, sprinkle each fillet with sea salt to form a scant ¼in layer, but stop 2–3in from the tail. Leave to stand for 1½ to 2 hours, depending on the size of the fillet. Rinse the fillet under cold water to remove excess salt and dry well.

If you prefer to brine, choose an oval-shaped container. You will need to weigh the fish down to prevent it from floating to the surface. Leave the fish in the brine for 1–3 hours, depending on size and fat content (farmed fish tend to be fattier than wild fish).

If the fish has been brined, don't rinse off the brine. Hang the fish in the inactive smoker for 12–24 hours to dry it. If the fish is not dry enough it will be too moist to smoke properly.

Lay the fish fillets on a wire rack or suspend by a hook from a pole.

The smoking time depends on

your personal taste, the ambient temperature, and the humidity. The colder and more muggy the weather, the longer the process – for a whole fish, it can take up to 24 hours for cold smoking. The fish should weigh 17–18 percent less when it is fully smoked. Cold-smoke at 82°F for 12–24 hours. Smoke it for longer if you want a smokier flavor.

Try to resist eating the salmon for another 12–24 hours to allow the smoky flavor on the skin to penetrate the flesh.

Wrap in wax paper and store in a fridge. Smoked salmon will keep for up to 10 days.

SMOKED HERRINGS – KIPPERS

Home-smoked kippers will look quite unlike the more familiar luminous orange ones that you buy. That's because they are simply smoked and haven't been immersed in liquid smoke which dyes them that scary color.

really fresh herrings
80 percent brine

Split the herrings down the back. Gut them and remove the gills. Flatten them with the palm of your hand. Rinse in cold water and brine in an 80 percent solution for 1–2 hours. Hang or lay the fish to dry, then cold-smoke at 75–80°F for 2–3 hours or even longer, depending on how smoky you like it.

Variation

SMOKED SPRATS

Sometimes in the week after Christmas, a shoal of sprats will come into Ballycotton – it's either feast or famine. If we have lots, we use them in every way we can think of and smoke the rest. We eat them whole, including the intestines – yummy.

Sprats don't need to be gutted, just immerse them in brine for 3½–4 hours – longer than you might expect because they are still intact. Drain, dry, and smoke as above for 6–8 hours.

SMOKED HADDOCK

This can be lightly or heavily smoked. Lightly smoked haddock is delicious served "raw" in thin slices drizzled with a little extra virgin olive oil or served with Mustard and Dill Mayonnaise (see page 105). You could also make fishcakes by combining lightly cooked flaked haddock with mashed potatoes, lots of parsley, and a little egg to bind. Fry in a pan in some sizzling butter and serve with Tartare Sauce (see page 94) or Saffron Aioli (see page 97).

1 whole haddock
pure pickling salt

First, fillet the haddock. Remove the pin bones. There is no need to remove the scales.

Lay the fillets on a stainless-steel or Delft platter at a slight angle, so the dish tilts down toward the tail. Sprinkle each fillet with salt to form a scant layer but stop 2–3in from the tail. Allow to stand for 1 hour.

Above: *Gorgeous cold-smoked wild Irish salmon.*

Remove the fish, rinse, and dry very well. If the fish is not dry enough it will not smoke properly. Cold smoke the fish at 82°F for 12–24 hours. If possible, allow to sit for 8 hours or so to allow the smoky flavor on the skin to penetrate the fish.

SMOKED SHRIMP

Smoked shrimp are delicious served simply with homemade Mayonnaise (see page 252), added to pasta sauces, scrambled egg, omelettes, or risotto.

First cook the shrimp in well-salted water (see page 109). Drain, and arrange the shrimp in a single layer on a wire rack. Hot-smoke for 30–40 minutes, depending on size. Shrimp can also be cold smoked for 4–5 hours. Allow to dry for about 30 minutes.

Above: *Smoked Shrimp.*
Right: *Smoked Mussels.*

SMOKED MUSSELS

These hot-smoked mussels are delicious served with homemade Mayonnaise (see page 252), in pasta sauces, or in salads.

Wash the mussels well. Steam them open in a wide sauté pan (not too many at a time) for about 3–4 minutes, depending on size.

Remove the meat from the mussels and discard the shells. The mussels we have access to are quite salty, so we don't brine them, but you could dip them in a 50 percent brine (8oz salt per quart of water or 3oz salt to 2½ cups water) for no more than 30 seconds. Lay them on a fine mesh wire rack in a single layer to dry for about half an hour in a cool, airy place.

We hot-smoke mussels for 15–20 minutes, depending on the size. If possible, turn them over halfway through to ensure even smoking. Store in olive oil or a light French dressing in the fridge. They will keep for 7–10 days.

SMOKED OYSTERS

Open the oysters (see page 118) and drain off the salty brine. Arrange on a fine wire rack. Alternatively, put the oysters into a very hot oven at 450°F for 4–5 minutes or until they pop open. Remove the semi-cooked oysters from the shells. Arrange on the wire rack. Raw oysters should be cold smoked for an hour or so. Semi-cooked oysters should be ready in 35–45 minutes. Serve on a salad or with hot buttered toast.

SMOKED COD ROE

I adore smoked cod roe, I know there are lots of fancy things you can do with it like proper taramasalata but I just love it slathered on hot toast.

1 or 2 fresh cod roe
1¼ cups salt
5 cups water

Mix to dissolve the salt in the water. This is a 70 percent solution. Gently lower the cod roe into the brine – they are fragile, so handle carefully. Brine for 1–1¼ hours. Drain and dry gently for about 2 hours. Lay on a fine wire rack in an inactive smoker. Then cold-smoke at a temperature between 80–85°F for about 24 hours. The skin will be a rich mahogany color and the roe will have firmed up and lost about 25 percent of its weight. It can be stored in a fridge for 2–3 weeks. It will also freeze for up to 6 months but will become more salty.

HOT-SMOKED CHICKEN BREAST

Delicious served warm or cold in salads. Use organic chicken breasts for this.

Sprinkle the chicken breast on both sides with pickling salt. Leave to cure in a fridge for about 30 minutes.

Put 2 tablespoons of sawdust on some tin foil in a metal box or hot smoker. Put it on high heat until it starts to smoke. Lay the chicken on a wire rack over the sawdust. Put the lid on the smoker (ensure it's a tight fit). Turn the heat down to low. Hot-smoke for about 15 minutes, depending on size. Allow to rest for at least 10–12 minutes before eating.

SMOKED EGGS

These are delicious in salads or sandwiches, or to eat with a blob of good herby homemade Mayonnaise (see page 252).

organic hen or duck eggs
salt and freshly ground pepper

Bring a small saucepan of water to a boil, lower the eggs gradually into the water one by one, bring the water back to a boil and cook for 8–10 minutes. Pour off the hot water and cover the eggs with cold water.

Peel the cooled hard-boiled eggs, sprinkle with salt and freshly cracked pepper. Then place on wire racks in a cold smoker. Smoke at about 80°F for about 12 hours, by which time they should have turned a rich amber color and have a mild smoky flavor.

Above: *Smoked Eggs.*

Above: *Smoked Sausages.*

SMOKED BELLY OF PORK – PANCETTA

I know this recipe sounds like a huge quantity of meat but it's so delicious and versatile, and keeps so well that it's worth doing. Friends will be hugely impressed if you can bear to part with a piece as a present.

whole fresh belly of free-range, preferably organic pork from a traditional breed, with rind attached
salt or equal quantities of salt and sugar

Cut the belly into pieces measuring about 6 x 12in.

Sprinkle a layer of cure into a plastic box or tray. Rub the cure all over the surface of the meat. Lay the pieces on top of the cure in a single layer. Cover with another layer of cure. Alternatively, you can stack the pieces on top of each other, in which case you will need to alternate the pieces every couple of days and drain off any excess liquid. Leave to cure in a cold place for a week. (If you want a heavier cure, add more salt and leave for another week.) Hang up, leave to dry, and use as is, or cold-smoke for 2–5 days.

Variation
SMOKED BACON
Smoked bacon needs to be cured and dried well for 24–48 hours, depending on humidity. Cold-smoke between 75–80°F for 2–5 days, depending on your preference. Slice and fry or cover with cold water and boil. Serve with cabbage and parsley sauce.

SMOKED SAUSAGES

This recipe makes a large batch that you should refrigerate immediately after smoking. If you have more than your needs, they will freeze well or you might like to preserve some cooked sausages covered in lard in a sterilized crock in the time-honored way – one of my favorite ways to preserve them ·

MAKES 80, DEPENDING ON SIZE

10lb ground shoulder belly of pork
  – it should be 20–25 percent
  pork fat, well chilled
3 tablespoons salt
3 teaspoons freshly ground pepper
1½ tablespoons chopped sage
1–1½ tablespoons chile pepper
  flakes, to taste

Spread the well-chilled pork in a thin layer on a baking tray. Sprinkle evenly with the seasoning and mix well. Fry off a morsel to check the seasoning. When you are happy, fill into the sausage casings, link, and hang in the smoker.

Cold-smoke for 2–3 days. Chill and then poach before eating. Serve with lots of mustard and mashed potatoes or crusty bread.

SMOKED HOGGET OR MUTTON HAM

Don't use spring lamb for this recipe. Older lamb, hogget, or mutton is best.

1 leg of hogget or mutton, about
  6½lb

FOR THE BRINE
2¼lb pickling salt
2 bay leaves

14 juniper berries, crushed
1 tablespoon coriander seeds
2 tablespoons black peppercorns
2 tablespoons white peppercorns

Put all the ingredients for the brine into a pot with 3 quarts of water. Bring to a boil, skim, and leave to get completely cold.

Put the meat into a scalded earthenware container or a deep plastic box. Pour the cold brine over it. Weigh it down with a sterilized timber board or a plastic box with a weight inside. Brine for 2½–3 weeks. Turn the meat in the brine once a week, using sterilized tongs or wooden spoons. Remove from the brine, hang from the shank end, and leave to dry in a cool, airy place for 24 hours.

Cold-smoke for 3 days (about 72 hours). Wrap in cheesecloth and hang in a cool and dry, airy place until required.

To cook, soak the leg overnight in cold water. Discard the water, cover with fresh, cold water, bring to a boil and skim. Change water a second time if necessary. Simmer for 1½–2 hours, or until tender. Serve with parsley and caper sauce or red currant or medlar jelly.

SMOKED HAUNCH OF VENISON FROM ROE OR FALLOW DEER

The brining time will depend on the breed of venison. Prick the haunch all over before brining to facilitate absorption. You'll need an 80 percent brine for this: 2¾lb salt to 4.5 quarts water.

- a haunch of roe deer needs
3 hours in brine
- a haunch of fallow deer needs
3 hours in brine
- a haunch of red deer needs
6 hours in brine

First make the brine and leave to cool completely. Ensure that the haunch is completely submerged in the brine.

After the required time, remove the venison from the brine and hang by the shank to dry.

Venison needs to be well smoked. Roe and fallow deer will need 7 days of cold smoking at a temperature of 60–75°F. Red deer will take up to 10 days at a similar temperature.

After smoking, seek out the femoral artery on the inside of the haunch. Press and squeeze toward the cut end of the haunch. A little greenish, not very pleasant liquid will squeeze out and should be wiped away with paper towel. By now, the surface of the venison will be quite hard, so anoint it gently with extra virgin olive oil.

Light a hot smoker. Lay the haunch of venison on a rack and hot-smoke the roe or fallow deer for 2 hours at 220°F. Red deer will require 3 hours. The eye of the loin of venison may also be smoked, but it will take a much shorter time.

Leave to rest and mature for 24 hours before carving into thin slices. Serve with horseradish, Cumberland, or red currant sauce.

A Few Recipes to Show Off Your Smoked Foods

Once you've gone to the trouble of smoking your own food you'll probably find the delicious flavor needs little embellishment. But here are a few great ideas for making them the main event in other dishes.

SMOKED FISH WITH HORSERADISH SAUCE AND SWEET DILL MAYONNAISE

Occasionally we serve just three different types of smoked fish, for example salmon, mussels, and trout on tiny rounds of Ballymaloe Brown Yeast Bread (see page 569), topped with a little frill of fresh lollo rosso. A little blob of cucumber pickle goes with the smoked salmon, while a blob of homemade mayonnaise is delicious with marinated smoked mussels, and a blob of horseradish cream and a sprig of watercress complements the pink smoked trout. These three delicious morsels make a perfect light starter.

SMOKED MACKEREL OMELETTE

This delicious omelette would also be very good made with smoked salmon ·
SERVES 2 AS A MAIN COURSE

4oz smoked mackerel
½ cup cream
4 organic eggs
salt and freshly ground pepper
4 tablespoons Parmesan cheese, grated
2 tablespoons butter
parsley, freshly snipped

10in omelette pan, preferably non-stick

Flake the smoked mackerel. Toss the mackerel with 2 tablespoons of the cream and leave to one side. Separate the eggs, beat the yolks with a tablespoon of the cream, and season with salt and freshly ground pepper. Whip the egg whites stiffly. Fold into the yolks with the smoked mackerel and add half the grated Parmesan cheese.

Melt the butter in the omelette pan. Pour the mixture in gently and cook over medium heat, until the base of the omelette is golden. Spoon the remaining cream over the top and sprinkle with the rest of the finely grated Parmesan cheese. Pop under a hot grill for a minute or so until the top is golden and bubbly. Slide onto a hot dish, sprinkle with snipped parsley, and serve immediately accompanied by a green salad.

ROSETTE OF SMOKED SALMON WITH SWEET CUCUMBER PICKLE

This is a pretty way to serve a little good smoked salmon. It includes an easy technique for cutting too ·
SERVES 4

piece of smoked salmon, cut from a whole side, about 10oz

FOR THE SWEET CUCUMBER PICKLE
½ cucumber, very thinly sliced
2oz onion, cut into fine rings
¼ cup superfine sugar
1¼ teaspoon salt
3 tablespoons wine vinegar or 2 tablespoons cider vinegar

GARNISH
sprigs of flat parsley, dill, fennel, or chervil

First make the sweet cucumber pickle. Mix the cucumber with the onion, sugar, salt, and wine vinegar. Leave to marinate for about 1 hour.

Cut the smoked salmon into about 20 x ⅛in thick slices, cutting straight down onto the skin. Wrap one slice around your finger and set it in the center of a large plate. Wrap 3 or 4 more slices around the center slice to form a rosette. Repeat the process to make 3 more rosettes.

To serve, drain the cucumber slices and arrange them in a circle around the smoked salmon rosettes. Garnish with the fresh herbs.

A SALAD OF SMOKED CHICKEN, GUINEA FOWL, OR PHEASANT WITH PARSNIP CHIPS AND SPICED CRANBERRY SAUCE

You could also substitute myrtle berries for the cranberry sauce in this recipe ·
SERVES 4

a selection of mixed salad leaves (oakleaf, little gem, arugula, lamb's lettuce, and finely sliced Savoy cabbage)

French Dressing (see page 374)
**1 smoked chicken or pan-grilled
    guinea fowl or pheasant breast**
extra virgin olive oil
salt and freshly ground pepper

<small>To Serve</small>
Parsnip Chips (see below)
**Spiced Cranberry Sauce (see page
    271)**

<small>Garnish</small>
chervil or flat parsley

Put the salad leaves into a bowl.
Sprinkle with a little dressing and
toss until the leaves are nicely
coated. Taste and divide the salad
between 4 large plates.

Slice the chicken breast thinly
and arrange upward around the
salad. Place a clump of warm
parsnip chips on top, put a few dots
of cranberry sauce around the edge.
Garnish with chervil or flat parsley
and serve immediately.

PARSNIP CHIPS

*We serve these delicious chips on warm
salads, as a garnish for roast pheasant
or guinea fowl or as a topping for
parsnip or root vegetable soup.
Delicious chips may be made from
other vegetables apart from the much-
loved potato. Celery root, beet, leek,
and even carrots are also good ·*
<small>SERVES 6–8</small>

1 large parsnip
sunflower or peanut oil
salt

Heat good-quality oil in a deep-fryer
to 300°F.

Scrub and peel the parsnips.
Either slice into wafer-thin rounds or
peel off long slivers lengthwise with
a swivel-top peeler. Leave to dry on
paper towels.

Drop a few of the parsnip rounds
or slivers at a time into the hot oil;
they color and crisp up very quickly.
Drain on paper towels and sprinkle
lightly with salt.

SMOKED EGG, CHORIZO, AND ARUGULA SALAD

*Hard-boiled eggs with softish centers
are also delicious in this recipe ·*
<small>SERVES 6</small>

**6 freshly smoked, hard-boiled
    organic eggs**
6 tiny or 3 medium beets, cooked
sugar and salt
extra virgin olive oil
7oz chorizo (see page 305), sliced
**a mixture of salad leaves, such as
    cos, little gem, purslane, and
    arugula**
**a piece of aged Coolea, Desmond,
    or Gabriel cheese**

<small>For the Vinaigrette</small>
3 tablespoons extra virgin olive oil
3 tablespoons red wine vinegar
a little Dijon mustard
sea salt and freshly ground pepper

<small>To Serve</small>
**homemade Mayonnaise (see
    page 252)**

Prepare the eggs either by smoking
them (see page 485) or hard-boiling
them.

To prepare the beets, leave 2in of
leaf stalks on top and the whole root
on the beets. Hold it under a
running tap and wash off the mud
with the palms of your hands, so
that you don't damage the skin;
otherwise the beets will bleed during
cooking. Put into a saucepan, cover
with cold water and add a little salt
and sugar. Cover the pot, bring to a
boil and simmer for 1–2 hours,
depending on size. Beets are usually
cooked when the skin rubs off easily
and if they dent when pressed with a
finger. If in doubt, also test with a
skewer or the tip of a knife.

Meanwhile, whisk the
ingredients for the vinaigrette
together in a bowl. Just before
serving, heat a little olive oil in a
pan over medium heat and cook the
slices of chorizo for a minute or two
until they warm through and the oil
begins to run. Toss the salad leaves
in a little vinaigrette and arrange on
the base of a serving plate. Cut the
eggs lengthwise – the centers should
still be slightly soft and will be best
if still warm. Arrange haphazardly
on top of the leaves. Tuck beet
quarters in between the leaves and
sprinkle the slices of chorizo over
the salad. Grate some hard cheese
over the top. Drizzle the salad with
the chorizo oil from the pan and
serve immediately with lots of crusty
sourdough bread and some
homemade mayonnaise.

Desserts

In our house when I was a child, no meal was complete without dessert, and at that time, most other people lived that way too. We had a "sweet" every day after our midday meal, which was the main meal of the day. More often than not, it was something as simple as stewed fruit from the garden, whatever was in season: apples, rhubarb, gooseberries, black currants, or plums served with icy cold cream or custard. These are still some of my favorite things in the world. We had lots of tarts and pies, too. And sometimes, for a special occasion, we'd have canned fruit! In the winter, we'd have steamed puddings, maybe once a week, while on other days of the week it might be rice pudding or semolina pudding or tapioca pudding – and some of these are forgotten for a very good reason.

Mummy was absolutely determined that we come home from school for lunch. She really believed in the importance of a good meal in the middle of the day. I can't quite understand why so many people nowadays think that having dessert is bad for you – I still love having something sweet at the end of my meal.

Everyone who has the space should plant an old-fashioned apple tree. Most years it will produce an abundant crop which will supply the household with cooking apples until early spring if stored well (see page 453). A few stools of rhubarb are invaluable and I wouldn't be without a couple of gooseberry and black currant bushes as well. Strawberries and raspberries are available year round in the stores these days, but loganberries, tayberries, and boysenberries are difficult to source unless you grow some yourself. Autumn raspberries are definitely worth considering – they're particularly trouble-free to grow, and crop abundantly over a four- or five-week period. Just mow down the foliage after they've fruited and they'll re-emerge and produce like magic the next year.

Above, left: *A tray of beautiful Victoria plums.* **Above, right:** *Young Crimson Bramley apples.*
Below, left: *Conference pears.* **Below, right:** *An early crop of raspberries.*

APPLE AND ROSE GERANIUM COMPOTE

During my childhood we often had stewed apples for dessert: just plain apples stewed with a little water, sugar, and maybe a couple of cloves. There are stewed apples and stewed apples, though – the type of apple really gave a compote its individual flavor: I remember Bramley's Seedling, Lane's Prince Albert, Grenadier, and Arthur Turner. But rose geranium, which I didn't discover until I came to Ballymaloe, gives this compote a haunting lemony flavor.

8 medium eating apples (e.g. Golden Delicious)
¾ cup superfine sugar
juice of 1½ lemons and 2–3 strips of the lemon rind
3–4 rose geranium leaves (Pelargonium graveolens)

Peel, quarter, and slice the apples into ¼in segments. Put them into a stainless-steel or enamel saucepan. Add the sugar, lemon juice and rind, and the rose geranium leaves.

Cover with a parchment paper lid and the lid of the saucepan and cook over a gentle heat until the apples are soft but not broken. Alternatively, they can be cooked in a moderate oven (350°F) if it's more convenient. Remove the geranium leaves and discard. This compote will keep in the fridge for 5–6 days and is also wonderful served in buttery puff pastry vol-au-vents with Calvados-laced pastry cream or with natural yogurt.

Variation
APPLE SNOW
Fold two stiffly beaten egg whites through the sieved or liquidized smooth apple purée. We enjoy the fluffy and light result with Shortbread Cookies (see page 548). You can make it with either sweet or cooking apples; just adjust the sugar accordingly.

RHUBARB COMPOTE

When I had stewed rhubarb as a child, we just put the rhubarb into a pan with a little water and sugar, and stewed it to a mush, but now I'm frightfully fussy about keeping the pieces of rhubarb whole. This recipe is the way to do that, because the fruit is just brought to a boil and then left to stew in the hot syrup. If it does turn to a mush though, just make it into a fool. Some people like orange with their rhubarb. I've never been tempted by that combination, but I can quite easily indulge in rhubarb and ginger ·
SERVES 4

1lb red rhubarb, e.g. Timperley early
1½ cups Stock Syrup (see page 468)

Cut the rhubarb into 1in pieces. Put the cold syrup into a stainless steel saucepan, add the rhubarb, cover, bring to a boil, and simmer for just 1 minute (no longer or it will dissolve). Turn off the heat and leave the rhubarb in the covered saucepan to finish cooking, and then cool.

Variation
RHUBARB AND STRAWBERRY OR RASPBERRY COMPOTE
A truly gorgeous combination. Hull and halve lengthwise ½–1lb fresh strawberries. When the rhubarb compote is almost cool, add the strawberries and stir gently. Alternatively, add ½lb whole raspberries at the same stage.

Jello

Big bowls of wobbly jello and cream … the stuff that many nostalgic childhood memories are made of. It was homemade all right but originated as a block of squares from a package. Lemon or greengage were my favorites, especially when Mummy put in some sliced banana. Occasionally, as a treat, we had milk jello; I loved that too because it separated into two layers with slightly different textures.

I still love jello and cream and now that I've discovered how easy it is to make them I'm not keen to indulge in the brightly colored bought jello of my childhood.

Basically, jello can be made from any sweet – or savory – liquid. Sometimes we make jello from scratch, but more often than not we use the delicious surplus juices from fruit compotes to make a few homemade jello. Summer fruit salad with rose geranium, pears with saffron, rhubarb and strawberry, apricot and lemon verbena, bananas in lime syrup … all are divine served with light cream or a fresh herb cream. We use 2½–3 teaspoons of powdered gelatin to 2 cups of fruit juice.

To make jello with the juice from stewed fruit or compote, just sponge the gelatin in a little water and follow the method given in the recipe below.

SUMMER FRUIT JELLO WITH ROSE GERANIUM CREAM

You can serve this jello with a simple whipped cream but I like to infuse the cream with rose geranium leaves to add an extra-special dimension to this childhood favorite · MAKES 9–10 RAMEKINS

1 cup sugar
4 rose geranium leaves
    (*Pelargonium graveolens*)
1 tablespoon freshly squeezed
    lemon juice
non-scented vegetable oil, for
    greasing
3 heaping teaspoons gelatin
1lb total summer fruit,
    e.g. 8oz fresh raspberries,
    4oz fraises des bois or
    tiny strawberries, and 4oz
    blueberries or black currants

ROSE GERANIUM CREAM
4–5 rose geranium leaves
1 tablespoon lemon juice
½ cup cream
sugar to taste, optional

9–10 ramekins

Put ¾ cup cold water, the sugar, and geranium leaves into a stainless-steel saucepan and bring slowly to a boil. Simmer for a few minutes, let cool, and add the lemon juice.

Brush the ramekins lightly with non-scented vegetable oil, or line them with plastic wrap.

Put 3 tablespoons water into a heatproof bowl or measuring glass, sprinkle the gelatin in and leave for 4–5 minutes by which time the gelatin will have soaked up the water and become spongy. (This is known as "sponging" the gelatin in cooking jargon.) Place the bowl or glass in a saucepan of simmering water until the gelatin is completely melted. The liquid should be completely clear with no trace of gelatin granules.

Remove the geranium leaves from the syrup and discard. Gradually pour the cold syrup onto the gelatin, stirring well. Pour into a large bowl, add the fruit and stir gently. Fill into the prepared molds. Put into the fridge and leave to set for 3–4 hours.

Meanwhile, make the rose geranium cream: crush the leaves in a pestle and mortar with the lemon juice, add the cream, and stir: the lemon juice will thicken the cream. If the cream becomes too thick add a little water. Taste – if it's too bitter add a little sugar, but the cream needs to be tart to balance the sweetness of the jello.

To assemble, spread a little rose geranium cream onto a white plate, turn out a jello, and place in the center. Place 3–5 tiny rose geranium leaves on the cream. Decorate with a few perfect raspberries, and serve chilled.

Variation

RASPBERRY JELLO WITH MINT
Substitute raspberries (or loganberries) for the mixture of summer fruit, add a teaspoon of framboise liqueur to the syrup if available. Use mint leaves instead of rose geranium in the syrup and cream.

LEMON VERBENA SORBET

We also use lemon balm, rose geranium, mint leaves, black currant leaves, peach leaves, or other sweet herb or fruit leaves. We sometimes serve a splash of champagne or sparkling wine and sometimes a few pomegranate seeds with the sorbet · SERVES ABOUT 8

1 cup sugar
2 cups cold water
2 large handfuls lemon verbena
    or other sweet herb leaves
freshly squeezed juice of 3 lemons
1 organic egg white (for method
    3 only)

Put the sugar, water, and verbena in a non-reactive saucepan. Bring slowly to a boil and simmer for 2–3 minutes. Allow to get quite cold. Add the freshly squeezed lemon juice. Strain and freeze in one of the following 3 ways:

Method 1. Pour into the drum of an ice-cream maker or sorbetière and freeze for 20–25 minutes. Scoop out and serve immediately or store in a covered bowl in the freezer until needed.

Method 2. Pour the juice into a stainless-steel or plastic container and put into the freezer. After about 4–5 hours remove the semi-frozen sorbet and whisk until granular. Return to the freezer. Repeat several times. Cover and store in the freezer until needed.

Method 3. If you have a food processor, simply freeze the sorbet completely in a covered stainless steel or plastic bowl, then break into large pieces and blend in the food processor for a few seconds. Add one slightly beaten egg white, blend again for another few seconds, then return to the bowl. Freeze again until needed. Serve in chilled glasses or chilled white china bowls decorated with verbena leaves.

STRAWBERRY POPSICLES

Homemade popsicles are all the rage in our house. You can use any ice cream or sorbet mixture to make popsicles – the lemon verbena sorbet mixture above makes delicious ones. When I was little and we'd just got our first freezer, we used to make popsicles with artificially-flavored orange and lemon drink mixes, which I can't quite believe now I thought were delicious – I have to say these new-age ones are a great improvement · **MAKES 18FL OZ OR 8 X 3FL OZ POPSICLES**

14oz strawberries
½ cup Stock Syrup (see page 468)
lemon juice, to taste

3fl oz popsicle molds

Clean and hull the strawberries, put in a blender, and blend. Strain, then add the stock syrup and lemon juice to taste.

Pour into the popsicle molds and freeze for 3–4 hours.

Variations
Other flavors you might enjoy – raspberry, peach and lemon verbena, black currant, blackberry and rose geranium, green gooseberry and elderflower, rhubarb and rosewater ... the possibilities are endless.

Fruit Fools

I'm amazed people don't eat fools more often. We enjoy them at home and guests at Ballymaloe House also love them. Fools fall into two categories. In the first, you first stew the fruit (black currants, gooseberries, or rhubarb, for example) then sieve it and add cream, or a combination of cream and yogurt, to cut the richness. In the second, you simply purée fresh fruit (summer berries, for example), and swirl them in with the cream.

How to eat fool!
Put it either on a plate or in a deep wide soup bowl with a Shortbread Cookie (see page 548) on top. Tap the cookie with the back of your spoon and then eat a little of the broken-up cookie with each mouthful of fool.

BLACK CURRANT FOOL

SERVES ABOUT 6

12oz fresh or frozen black currants
7fl oz Stock Syrup (see page 468)
2 cups very softly whipped cream

Cover the black currants with stock syrup. Bring to a boil and cook for about 4–5 minutes until the fruit bursts. Liquidize and sieve or purée the fruit and syrup and measure it. When the purée has cooled, add the softly whipped cream. Serve with shortbread biscuits.

An alternative presentation is to layer the purée and softly whipped cream in tall sundae glasses, ending with a drizzle of thin purée over the top.

NOTE: frozen black currants tend to be less sweet. Taste – you may need to add extra sugar. A little stiffly beaten egg white may be added to lighten the fool. The fool should not be very stiff, more like the texture of softly whipped cream. If it is too stiff, stir in a little milk rather than more cream.

Variation
BLACK CURRANT ICE CREAM Leftover fool may be frozen to make delicious ice cream. Serve with coulis made by thinning the black currant purée with a little more water or stock syrup.

RASPBERRY FOOL WITH SHORTBREAD COOKIES

My brother Rory O'Connell, who gave me this recipe, says that this is one of those recipes that somehow is much greater than the sum of its parts. Three simple ingredients produce a rich and luscious result. When in season I use fresh raspberries, but this fool is also excellent made with frozen berries – I haven't quite decided if it is actually better with the latter. Soft fruit becomes more bitter when frozen but the flavor of the berries seems to be accentuated when frozen ones are used. Any leftover fool can be frozen to make ice cream · **SERVES 8–10**

1lb raspberries, fresh or frozen
½–1 cup superfine sugar
2 cups whipped cream

Shortbread Cookies (see page 548)

Lay the raspberries in a single layer on a dish. Sprinkle on the sugar and allow to macerate for 1 hour. If you are using frozen berries this should be long enough for them to defrost. Purée the fruit in a blender then pass through a nylon sieve to remove the seeds. Gently fold in the whipped cream – go lightly if you want to create a "swirly" effect. The fool is now ready to be served or can be chilled for serving later. Serve with shortbread cookies.

Above: *Raspberry Fool with Shortbread Cookies.*

Above: *Roast Apples with Cinnamon Cream.*

ROAST APPLES WITH CINNAMON CREAM

I think my grandfather had either stewed or roast apple every night of his life, so this always reminds me of Grandpoppy. Mostly he just had them with softly whipped cream and soft brown sugar melting over the top, but if you want to jazz them up a bit, you can add a little cinnamon or liqueur to the cream. These are quite plain, but you can put a bunch of different stuffings inside: mincemeat after Christmas, or marzipan, or nuts · SERVES 4

4 large cooking apples
4 tablespoons butter
¼ cup superfine sugar
finely grated zest of 1 lemon
2 tablespoons golden raisins
½ cup whipping cream
1 teaspoon cinnamon
confectioners' sugar, for dusting

Preheat the oven to 350°F.

First core the apples and score the skin across the equator. Mix the butter with the sugar, lemon zest, and raisins. Spoon the butter mixture into the apples. Stand the apples in an ovenproof baking dish and pour in ¼ cup water.

Roast for 45–60 minutes depending on size. The apples should be beginning to burst – this is vital, so hold your nerve – they should look fat and squishy. Meanwhile, whip the cream and add cinnamon to taste. Serve the apples straight from the oven with the cinnamon cream and dust with confectioners' sugar.

Variations
Stuff the apples with Homemade Mincemeat (see page 512). We also like them peeled then stuffed with marzipan, then rolled in melted butter and cinnamon sugar before roasting.

ROAST APPLES UNADORNED
Proceed as in the recipe above, but omit the fruit and zest. Serve with freshly whipped cream and soft brown sugar. Divine!

APPLE FRITTERS

Funny how one sometimes forgets a recipe; we hadn't had these for ages, but I remembered them recently and they taste just as good as ever. As children we particularly loved fritters because they used to fry into funny shapes, which caused great hilarity.

These can also be shallow-fried in a pan. You can add a teaspoon of cinnamon to the sugar to toss the apples in for extra flavor · SERVES 6–8

1 cup all-purpose white flour
pinch of salt
1 organic egg
½ cup milk
good-quality vegetable oil, for frying
1lb cooking apples (about 4)
½ cup superfine sugar

Sift the flour and salt into a bowl. Make a well in the center and drop in the egg. Use a whisk to bring in the flour gradually from the edges, slowly adding in the milk at the same time. Leave the batter in a cool place for about 1 hour.

Heat the oil in a deep-fryer to 350°F. Peel and core the apples. Cut into rings, no thicker than ¼in. Dip the rings into the batter and lift out with a skewer, allowing the surplus batter to drain off, then drop into hot fat, a few at a time. Fry until golden brown, drain well on paper towels. Toss each fritter in superfine sugar. Serve immediately on hot plates with softly whipped cream.

OLD-FASHIONED RICE PUDDING

A creamy rice pudding is one of the greatest treats on a cold winter's day. You need to use short-grain rice, which plumps up as it cooks. This is definitely a forgotten dessert and it's unbelievable the reaction we get to it every time we make it at the Cookery School. It's always the absolute favorite dessert at my evening courses ·
SERVES 6-8

3½oz pearl rice (short-grain rice)
¼ cup sugar
small dab of butter
2 pints milk

1 x 2 pint capacity pie dish

Preheat the oven to 350°F. Put the rice, sugar, and butter into a pie dish. Bring the milk to a boil and pour over. Bake for 1–1½ hours. The skin should be golden, the rice underneath should be cooked through and have soaked up the milk, but still be soft and creamy. Time it so that it's ready just in time for dessert. If it has to wait in the oven for ages it will be dry and dull and you'll wonder why you bothered.

Three good things to serve with rice pudding:
· Softly whipped cream and soft brown sugar
· Compote of apricots and cardamom
· Compote of sweet apples and rose geranium (see page 494)

MUMMY'S COUNTRY RHUBARB CAKE

This traditional Irish recipe is particularly interesting because it uses sour or buttermilk. The resulting texture is soft – more cakey than other pastries. Even though it is referred to as rhubarb cake, it was always made in the shape of a pie or tart on a plate. Mummy made it throughout the year with whatever fruit was in season: rhubarb and green gooseberries were especially irresistible because all the bittersweet juices soaked into the pastry. According to season, she also used plums, apples, blackberries, and damsons. It's important that firm fruit (such as apples and rhubarb) is thinly sliced, otherwise it doesn't cook properly · **SERVES 8**

FOR THE PASTRY
3 cups all-purpose flour
¼ teaspoon salt
1½oz superfine sugar
½ teaspoon baking soda
1 stick butter
1 organic egg, beaten
4fl oz sour milk or buttermilk (see page 198)

1½lb rhubarb, thinly sliced
1 heaping cup granulated sugar
egg wash

TO SERVE
superfine sugar, for sprinkling
soft brown sugar and softly whipped cream

10in enamel or Pyrex plate

Preheat the oven to 350°F.

Sift the flour, salt, sugar, and baking soda into a bowl. Rub in the butter. Add the beaten egg and enough sour milk to mix to a stiff dough. Turn out onto a floured board. Divide in two. Roll both pieces into rounds large enough to fit your enamel or Pyrex plate and line the plate with one of the rounds. Put a good layer of thinly sliced rhubarb on the pastry, sprinkle the sugar over the top and cover with the other piece of dough. Pinch the edges together. Brush the top with egg wash. Bake in the oven for about 1 hour or until the pastry is golden and the rhubarb is soft and juicy.

Sprinkle with superfine sugar; serve warm with soft brown sugar and softly whipped cream.

GROUND CINNAMON

Ground cinnamon is often mixed with ground cassia, a related but less expensive spice. We grind cinnamon sticks in a coffee grinder specially reserved for grinding spices. The resulting cinnamon is pale and sweet as opposed to the slightly acrid flavor of adulterated ground spices. Cinnamon is known to help lower cholesterol.

IRISH APPLE CAKE

Apple cakes like this one, made from what's almost a scone dough, were very traditional in Ireland. The previous recipe uses baking soda; this one uses baking powder. The texture of the pastry is cakier than either of the two following recipes. Irish Apple Cake varies from house to house and the technique has been passed from mother to daughter in farmhouses all over the country for generations. It would originally have been baked in a bastible or pot beside an open fire and later in the oven or stove on tin or enamel plates. These traditional enamel plates are much better than ovenproof glass because the heat travels through and cooks the pastry base more readily, which is worth remembering, as a tart with a soggy base is not appealing! In Ireland all apple cakes are made with cooking apples. The dough should be soft which makes it difficult to handle but don't be tempted to use too much flour or it will change the texture of the pastry · **SERVES ABOUT 6**

2 cups all-purpose flour
½ teaspoon baking powder
1 stick butter
½ cup superfine sugar
1 organic egg
about ¼–½ cup whole milk
1–2 cooking apples
2–3 cloves, optional
egg wash

10in ovenproof plate

Preheat the oven to 350°F.

Sift the flour and baking powder into a bowl. Rub in the butter with your fingertips until it resembles the texture of bread crumbs then add ⅓ cup of the superfine sugar. Make a well in the center and mix to a soft dough with the beaten egg and enough milk to form a soft dough. Turn out onto a board divide in two. Put one half onto an ovenproof plate and press it out with floured fingers to cover the base.

Peel, core, and chop up the apples, place them on the dough and tuck in the cloves, if using. Sprinkle over some or all of the remaining sugar, depending on the sweetness of the apples. Roll out the second half of the pastry and fit it on top – easier said than done as this "pastry" is more like scone dough and as a result is very soft. Press the sides together, cut a slit through the lid, egg wash, and bake for about 40 minutes or until cooked through and nicely browned on top. Dredge with superfine sugar and serve warm with raw sugar and softly whipped cream.

MUMMY'S APPLE PIE

I was fortunate to have a mother who was a really good cook, and she was famous for many of her dishes: scones, trifle, plum pudding, and this apple pie. What's quirky and worth highlighting about this recipe is that the pastry is made by the creaming method, so it's salvation for people who are convinced that they suffer from the genetic challenge of "hot hands." We call this "break all the rules pastry" · **SERVES 8–12**

BREAK ALL THE RULES PASTRY
2 sticks plus 2 tablespoons butter
¼ cup superfine sugar
2 organic eggs
3 cups all-purpose flour

FILLING
1½lb cooking apples
⅔ cup sugar
2–3 cloves
egg wash – made with 1 beaten organic egg and a dash of milk
superfine sugar for sprinkling

TO SERVE
softly whipped cream
soft brown sugar

1 baking pan, about 7 x 12 x 1in

First make the pastry. Cream the butter and sugar together by hand or in a food mixer (no need to overcream). Add the eggs and beat for a minute or two. Reduce to the lowest speed (if using a mixer) and mix the flour in gently.

Turn out onto a piece of floured parchment paper, flatten into a round, wrap, and chill. This pastry needs to be chilled for at least 2 hours, otherwise it is difficult to handle. Meanwhile, preheat the oven to 350°F.

Remove the pastry from the fridge and roll out to a thickness of about ⅛in. You will need about two-thirds of it to line the tin. Peel, quarter, and dice the apples into the pie, sprinkle with sugar, and add the cloves. Re-roll the pastry trimmings to the same thickness and make a lid for the pie. Seal edges, decorate with pastry leaves, egg wash, and bake for about 45 minutes to 1 hour until the apples are tender.

When cooked, sprinkle lightly with superfine sugar, cut into squares, and serve with the whipped cream and soft brown sugar.

Alternative suggestions and quantities for tart fillings

- Rhubarb – 2lb rhubarb
- Rhubarb and Strawberry – 1½lb rhubarb and 8oz strawberry
- Apple and Black Currant – 1½lb apples and 8oz black currants.
- Apple and Mincemeat – 3–4 cooking apples and ½ jar homemade Mincemeat (see page 512)
- Apple and Fresh Ginger – 3–4 cooking apples and 2–3 teaspoons freshly grated ginger
- Apple and Raspberry – 3–4 cooking apples and 4oz raspberries
- Apple, Blackberry, and Rose Geranium – 3–4 cooking apples, 4oz blackberries, and 6 rose geranium leaves
- Apple and Mixed Spice – 3–4 apples, 1–2 teaspoons mixed spice
- Apple, Golden Raisins, and Cinnamon – 2oz golden raisins, 3–4 apples, and 2 teaspoons cinnamon
- Worcesterberry – 1½lb worcesterberries
- Plum – 1½lb plums
- Damson – 1½lb damsons
- Damson and Apple – 1lb damsons and 2 cooking apples
- Green Gooseberry and Elderflower – 1½lb gooseberries and 3 elderflower heads
- Apricots, Peaches, and Nectarines – 2 of each fruit
- Peach and Raspberry – 3 peaches and 8oz raspberries

BALLYMALOE GREEN GOOSEBERRY AND ELDERFLOWER TART

I've chosen to use green gooseberries and elderflower in this recipe, but the filling changes with the season. We always have a fruit tart of some kind on the dessert tray at Ballymaloe, and it reflects what is in season at that time. Sometimes we add some spices, fresh herbs, or wild flavors like the elderflowers in this recipe – whatever complements the fruit · SERVES 6-8

8oz Sweet Shortcrust Pastry (see page 542) for the base
8–10oz Billy's Cream Pastry (see page 209) for the lid
1½lb green gooseberries
¾ cup white or golden superfine sugar (or more, depending on the tartness of the gooseberries)
2 elderflower heads
1 organic egg for egg wash

10in Pyrex or enamel plate

Preheat the oven to 475°F.

Roll out the shortcrust pastry and line the plate. Trim the edges.

Top and tail the gooseberries and pile them up on the plate, leaving a border of 1in. Pick the elderflower heads off the heavy stem and lay them over the gooseberries. Sprinkle the sugar evenly on top.

Roll out the cream pastry a little thicker than the base, wet the border around the gooseberries with a little egg wash or water, and press the pastry lid down onto it. Trim the pastry to within ½in of the rim of the pie. Crimp up the edges with a sharp knife and then scallop them.

Make a hole in the center to allow steam to escape. Egg wash the surface. Roll out the trimmings and cut into leaves and decorate the top of the tart, egg wash again.

Bake for 15–20 minutes, then turn down the heat to 350°F for a further 40–45 minutes. Test the gooseberries are soft by inserting a skewer. Sprinkle with superfine sugar, serve with soft brown sugar and softly whipped cream.

EVE'S PUDDING

This recipe brings back nostalgic memories for many of us, and it is certainly one that has stood the test of time. I remember it as an important part of the dessert repertoire of my childhood, and so will my children and grandchildren. Here you use the basic Madeira mixture for the topping and add fruit – whatever you please, depending on the season: rhubarb, pears, damsons, raspberries, gooseberries. Black currants are also gorgeous, as is a mixture of blackberry and apples or rhubarb and strawberries · SERVES 4-6

1½lb **cooking apples**
⅓–½ **cup sugar**

FOR THE TOPPING
4 **tablespoons butter**
¼ **cup sugar**
1 **organic egg, beaten**
¾ **self-rising flour**
1–2 **tablespoons milk**

2 **pint pie dish**

Preheat the oven to 400°F.

Peel, core, and slice the apples and put them in a heavy-bottomed saucepan with 1 tablespoon water and the sugar. Cover the pan and stew the apples gently until just soft, then tip into a buttered pie dish.

Whip the butter until soft, add the sugar, and beat until light and fluffy. Add the beaten egg by degrees and beat well until completely incorporated. Sift the flour and fold into the butter and egg mixture. Add about 1 tablespoon milk or enough to bring the mixture to a dropping consistency. Spread this mixture gently over the apple.

Bake in the oven for about 25 minutes, or until the sponge topping is firm to the touch in the center. Sprinkle with superfine sugar. Serve warm with homemade custard or lightly whipped cream.

APPLE CHARLOTTE

This is a great way to use up bread and apples deliciously.

We make this sublime dessert from old varieties of eating apples – my favorites are Egremont, Russet, Charles Ross, Cox's Orange Pippin, or Pitmaston Pineapple. It's sinfully rich but gorgeous · SERVES 4-6

2¼lb **apples**
8oz **Clarified Butter (see page 216)**
¾ **cup superfine sugar, plus extra for dusting the pan**
2 **organic egg yolks**
good-quality White Yeast Bread (see page 572)

5 x 8in **loaf pan**

Preheat the oven to 400°F.

Peel and core the apples. Melt a little of the clarified butter in a stainless-steel saucepan, chop the apples into cubes, and add to the pan with a couple of tablespoons of water and the superfine sugar. Cover and cook over low heat until the apples break into a thick pulp. Beat in the egg yolks, one at a time – this helps to enrich and thicken the apple purée. Taste and add a little more sugar if necessary.

Melt the remaining clarified butter and use a little of this to brush the inside of the pan then dust it with superfine sugar. Cut the crusts off the bread and cut into strips about 1½in wide and 5in high and quickly brush them with the clarified butter. Line the sides of the pan with butter-soaked bread. Cut another strip to fit tightly into the base of the pan. Brush it on both sides with butter and tuck it in tightly. Fill the center with the apple pulp. Cut another strip of bread to fit the top. Brush with melted butter on both sides and fit it neatly to cover the purée.

Bake for 20 minutes then reduce the heat to 350°F for another 15 minutes or until the bread is crisp and a rich golden color.

Run a knife around the edges in case the bread has stuck to the pan. Invert the apple charlotte onto a warm oval serving plate. It won't look like a thing of beauty; it may collapse a bit, but it will taste wonderful. Serve with softly whipped cream.

Variation
Individual Eve's Pudding and Apple Charlotte can be made in robust teacups.

Opposite: *Eve's Pudding made with blackberries and apples.*

STICKY GINGERBREAD PUDDINGS

My friend Barny Haughton has a wonderful restaurant in Bristol called Bordeaux Quay. He's passionate about using local, organic ingredients and is very involved in supporting sustainable agriculture. He, like me, loves to make and serve these old-fashioned desserts, which people flock to the restaurant for · SERVES 8

3½oz preserved ginger
1½ cups self-rising flour
⅓ teaspoon ground cinnamon
⅓ teaspoon ground cloves
¼ teaspoon ground ginger
½ teaspoon baking powder
¾ teaspoon baking soda
2 organic eggs
6 tablespoons soft butter
½ cup dark muscovado sugar
1 tablespoon molasses
1 heaping teaspoon grated fresh ginger
6oz cooking apples, peeled, cored, and chopped small
¾ cup warm water

FOR THE BOOZY SAUCE
1 stick unsalted butter
¾ cup dark muscovado sugar
1 shot brandy

Preheat the oven to 350°F. Butter 8 dariole molds or ramekins.

Put the ginger pieces in the food processor and process briefly. Add the flour, spices, and rising agents. Then add the eggs, butter, sugar, molasses, and ginger and process until smooth. Fold in the apple (or briefly blend in the food processor for a smoother texture). Add the water and mix well. Divide the mixture between molds and bake for 35 minutes.

To make the sauce, melt the butter and sugar in a small pan then whisk in the brandy.

Serve the puddings warm with fresh cream and the sauce.

CLEMENTINE SYRUP CAKE

A sticky, citrusy dessert that really hits the spot in frosty weather. In place of clementines you can use other citrus fruit, such as mandarins, tangerines, or satsumas. This is another recipe from Barny Haughton, who generously allowed me to pass it on to you · MAKES 16 INDIVIDUAL PUDDINGS

FOR THE SPONGE
5 sticks butter
1¾ cups sugar
5 organic eggs
4 cups all-purpose flour
1 tablespoon baking powder
2 teaspoons clementine zest
¾ cup clementine juice
7oz candied orange peel, finely diced

FOR THE SYRUP
½ cup clementine juice
½ cup sugar
1 stick butter
zest of 1 clementine
1 tablespoon Grand Marnier

TO DECORATE
8 clementines, sliced then glazed with sugar using a blowtorch

Preheat the oven to 325°F. Butter and flour 16 dariole molds or ramekins.

Whip the butter and sugar. Add the eggs gradually, then the remaining ingredients. Divide the mixture between the molds and bake for about 20 minutes until golden and risen.

To make the syrup, put all ingredients in a pan, slowly dissolve the sugar, then bring to a boil. Pour the syrup over the cake and serve with whipped cream and the glazed clementines.

FLUFFY LEMON PUDDING

This old fashioned family dessert is sometimes referred to rather confusingly as a lemon soufflé. Its charm is that it separates into two distinct layers when it cooks: a fluffy top and a creamy base. SERVES 4–6

3½ tablespoons butter
1 cup plus 1 tablespoon superfine sugar
3 organic eggs, separated
¾ cup flour
zest and juice of 2 unwaxed lemons
½ pint whole milk
confectioners' sugar, for dredging

2 pint pie dish

Preheat the oven to 350°F. Whip the butter well. Add the sugar and beat well. Add the egg yolks, one by one, then stir in the flour. Add the lemon zest, the juice, and lastly the milk. Whisk the egg whites stiffly and fold gently into the mixture. Pour into the pie dish and bake for about 40 minutes. Dredge with confectioners' sugar. Serve immediately with softly whipped cream.

FIGGY TOFFEE PUDDING

Like everyone else, we love sticky toffee pudding, which we always made with dates. One day, we had no dates and used plump dried Turkish figs instead. Now, it's the version we prefer! ·

SERVES 8–10

8oz chopped dried figs
½ pint tea
1 stick unsalted butter
¾ cup superfine sugar
3 organic eggs
2 cups self-rising flour
1 teaspoon baking soda
1 teaspoon pure vanilla extract
1 teaspoon espresso coffee

FOR THE HOT TOFFEE SAUCE
1 stick butter
¾ cup raw sugar
½ cup granulated sugar
10oz corn syrup
1 cup heavy cream
½ teaspoon pure vanilla extract

8in springform pan or a cake pan
　with removable base

Preheat the oven to 350°F. Brush the cake pan with oil and base-line with oiled parchment paper. Soak the figs in hot tea for 15 minutes.

Whip the butter and sugar until light and fluffy. Beat in the eggs, one at a time, then fold in the sifted flour. Add the baking soda, vanilla extract, and coffee to the figs and tea and stir this into the mixture. Turn into the lined pan and cook for 1–1½ hours or until a wooden skewer comes out clean.

Right: *Figgy Toffee Pudding.*

To make the sauce, put the butter, sugars, and syrup into a heavy-bottomed saucepan and melt gently over low heat. Simmer for about 5 minutes, remove from the heat, and gradually stir in the cream and the vanilla extract. Return to the heat and stir for 2–3 minutes until the sauce is quite smooth.

Pour some hot sauce on to a plate. Put the figgy toffee pudding on top, pour lots more sauce over the top. Put the remainder into a bowl, and serve with the pudding, as well as softly whipped cream.

Variation
Little figgy puds can be made in muffin pans.

MUMMY'S TRADITIONAL IRISH SHERRY TRIFLE

There's a few things, like gravy and trifle, that are very personal – your yardstick is whatever your mammy or granny used to make. In earlier years, Mummy would have made this trifle with the trifle sponges that could be bought in Mrs. Freeman's shop in our village around Christmas; they looked like sponge rusks. Over the years, as these sponges became more difficult to source, we started making the sponge ourselves – we use the recipe for Great-grandmother's Layer Cake (see page 528). We actually used to have a layer of canned peaches in this trifle, but now I'm too snooty to put them in; the truth is I prefer the trifle without them. Even when my brothers were in their late 40s and 50s, they seemed to revert back to childhood and squabble over the trifle, finishing it off in the

WHAT TO DO IF CUSTARD CURDLES

If your custard curdles, take it immediately off the heat and plunge the base of the pan into a sink of cold water (if you're nervous, have it ready just in case). Then, transfer the liquid into a blender. Process for a few seconds. That should re-emulsify the mixture.

middle of the night when they came home from the pub on Christmas Eve. Mummy would have to go to great lengths to hide it on the top of a cupboard or even in her wardrobe, but somehow they always managed to find it! So, why is it better than any other trifle you're likely to taste? Surprise, surprise – it's the quality of the ingredients. Use homemade sponge cake, homemade raspberry jam, and homemade custard made with good organic eggs, lashings of Bristol cream sherry (don't waste your time with cooking sherry), and you cannot go wrong.

Choose a bowl (glass for preference) that's not too deep, otherwise the layers will become disproportionate – either too luscious or too dry. For a posher version, line the glass bowl with slices of jelly roll · **SERVES 8-10**

1lb homemade sponge cake (we use Great-grandmother's Layer Cake, see page 528) or trifle sponges
8oz homemade Raspberry Jam (see page 442)

FOR THE CUSTARD
5 organic eggs
1¼ tablespoons superfine sugar
½ teaspoon pure vanilla extract
1¼ pints whole milk

⅔–¾ cup best-quality sweet or medium sherry – don't spare the sherry

DECORATION
1 pint whipped cream
8 cherries or Crystallized Violets (see page 32)

8 diamonds of Candied Angelica (see page 458)
a few toasted flaked almonds

3 pint trifle bowl, preferably glass

Sandwich the cake layers together with raspberry jam. If you are using trifle sponges, sandwich them in pairs (you'll need 5–6 pairs).

Next make the egg custard. Whisk the eggs with the sugar and vanilla extract. Heat the milk to the "shivery" stage and pour it over the egg mixture, whisking all the time. Return the mixture in a heavy saucepan over low heat and stir with a straight-ended wooden spoon until the custard lightly coats the back of the spoon. Don't allow it to boil or it will curdle (see box).

Cut the cake into ¾in slices and use these to line the bottom of a 3 pint glass bowl, drizzling generously with the sherry as you go along. Spoon over a layer of the warm egg custard then add another layer of cake and drizzle with the remainder of the sherry. Spread the rest of the custard over the top. Cover and leave for 5–6 hours, or preferably overnight in a cold pantry or fridge for the flavors to mature.

To serve, spread softly whipped cream over the top, piping rosettes if you wish, and decorate with cherries or crystallized violets and large diamonds of angelica. Scatter with a few toasted flaked almonds.

BREAD AND BUTTER PUDDING

This is one of the older desserts that has enjoyed a terrific revival, but initially it was just a way of recycling old bread, made with just milk and a scattering of dried fruit. It was something that you ate, but didn't necessarily relish. But there's nothing frugal about this recipe – it's got lots of fruit in it and a generous proportion of cream to milk. When people taste it, they just go "Wow!" I know it has a lot of cream in it, but don't skimp – just don't eat it every day! We play around with this formula and continue to come up with more and more delicious combinations, depending on what's in season and what we have around; see below for some of them ·

SERVES 6–8

12 slices good-quality white bread, crusts removed
4 tablespoon butter, preferably unsalted
½ teaspoon freshly grated nutmeg, cinnamon, or mixed spice
1 cup plump raisins
2 cups heavy cream
1 cup milk
4 large organic eggs, lightly beaten
1 teaspoon pure vanilla extract
¾ cup sugar plus 1 tablespoon for sprinkling
pinch of salt

1 x 8in square pottery or china dish

Butter the bread and arrange 4 slices, buttered-side down, in one layer in the buttered dish. Sprinkle the bread with half the spice and half the raisins, then arrange another layer of bread, buttered-side down, over the raisins, and sprinkle the remaining nutmeg and raisins on top. Cover the raisins with the remaining bread, again, buttered-side down.

In a bowl, whisk together the cream, milk, eggs, vanilla extract, sugar, and the pinch of salt. Pour the mixture through a fine sieve over the bread. Sprinkle the tablespoonful of sugar over the top and let the mixture stand, loosely covered, at room temperature for at least 1 hour or chill overnight.

Preheat the oven to 350°F. Place the pudding in a double boiler and pour in enough water to come halfway up the sides of the baking dish. Bake the pudding in the middle of the oven for about 1 hour or until the top is crisp and golden. Serve the pudding warm with some softly whipped cream.

NOTE: this Bread and Butter Pudding reheats perfectly.

Delicious Bread and Butter Puddings can be made using:
• Barmbrack as a base – add mixed spice or cinnamon
• Pannettone – proceed as above
• Brioche – proceed as above or use apricot jam and lace with apricot brandy
• Rhubarb or gooseberry and elderflower compote, or spiced apple purée may also be used
• Prunes soaked in Armagnac
• Chocolate chip is also pretty mindblowing

RAREISH FRUITS

Black currants, gooseberries, and worcesterberries are almost forgotten summer fruits. You can buy strawberries and raspberries throughout the year, but you only get gooseberries in season. They are ideally suited to the climate in the British Isles as well as North America from late spring through summer. As soon as the elderflowers blossom in the hedgerows, we search under the prickly branches to find the tart green gooseberries. They are best for pies, tarts, jams, and fools when they are about the size of a marble.

To prepare gooseberries just pinch off the top and tail with your fingers. Some people prefer to use a tiny fruit knife but I don't find it necessary. Use fresh or freeze while still green and use within a year. The skin of frozen gooseberries tends to be tough, so use a potato masher to mash when cooking for fool or green gooseberry sauce.

A savory Bread and Butter Pudding can also be made with cheese. Among our favorites are:
• Bread pudding with asparagus and fontina
• Bacon and Cheddar strata (see page 579)

SUMMER PUDDING

This is another dessert, like Bread and Butter Pudding, that can be interpreted frugally or extravagantly. Either way though, you're still using leftover ingredients, so you can feel virtuous! It may have been wonderful with bread if the bread was of good quality, but nowadays, the majority of sliced bread is so truly appalling that in my opinion, it's a complete waste of time and precious fruit to make this pudding with it. For years, we've been using leftover sponge cake (that's why we sometimes call it Marie Antoinette summer pudding!) and it absolutely blows people's minds, particularly those who've been turned off by the gloopy sliced pan version. Remember to pour the fruit and syrup while boiling into the sponge-lined bowl, otherwise it won't soak through the sponge properly. This is a great recipe if you have guests coming, as you can make it ahead of time, and it keeps in the fridge for 5–6 days. My favorite version is when it's made just with black currants, and even frozen ones work perfectly, so you can make it at any time of year. Enjoy it with lots of softly whipped cream · **SERVES 12–16**

2 x 7in cake layers – Great-
    grandmother's Layer Cake
    (see page 528) or Mrs Lamb's
    Layer Cake (see page 526)

3 cups granulated sugar
4–5 rose geranium leaves
8oz black currants
8oz red currants
1lb raspberries or 8oz raspberries
    and 8oz strawberries

3 pint plastic pudding bowl

First make the cake layers.

Cut each cake layer in half horizontally. Line the bowl with the cake, crusty side inward. (It doesn't matter if it looks quite patched, it will blend later.)

Put the sugar and 1¼ pints water into a saucepan, add the rose geranium leaves, and boil for 2 minutes. Add the black currants and red currants and cook until the fruit bursts – about 3 or 4 minutes – then add the raspberries (and strawberries). Taste. Remove the rose geranium leaves and discard. Immediately, ladle some of the hot liquid and fruit into the sponge-lined bowl. When about half full, if you have any scraps of cake left over, put them in the center. Then fill to the top with fruit. Cover with a layer of cake. Put a plate on top and press down with a heavy weight. Allow to get cold. Store in the refrigerator for a minimum of 24 hours before serving, but it will keep for 5 or 6 days.

To serve, unmold onto a deep serving dish and pour any leftover fruit and syrup over the top and around the side. Serve with lots of softly whipped cream.

HOT CHOCOLATE SOUFFLÉ

This is a brilliant, simple little recipe. Provided the chocolate is good, it makes an impressive and delicious soufflé and is ideal for people who are scared to attempt what is often seen as an advanced cooking skill. It serves one so is perfect for a greedy treat · **SERVES 1**

1½oz bar of dark chocolate
melted butter
superfine sugar
1 large organic egg, separated
confectioners' sugar, for dredging

¼ pint soufflé dish

Preheat the oven to 400°F.

Break up the chocolate into squares. Put into a heatproof bowl over a saucepan of hot water – the base of the bowl should not touch the water. Bring the water to a boil, then turn off the heat and leave the bowl over the hot water for about 5 minutes until the chocolate melts.

Brush the insides of a soufflé dish with melted butter, dust with superfine sugar. Whisk the egg yolk into the chocolate. In a spotlessly clean bowl, whisk the egg white until stiff peaks form, and fold into the chocolate mixture. Pour into the soufflé dish and bake for 8–10 minutes in the oven until well risen but still slightly runny in the center. Dredge with confectioners' sugar and serve immediately on a hot plate with softly whipped cream or sour cream.

Opposite: *A bowl of freshly picked strawberries destined for Summer Pudding.*

Steamed Puddings

When we ran up the hill from school on cold winter days for lunch, we'd run twice as fast when we knew that Mummy was going to be making a steamed pudding. She had a huge repertoire of them and each of us nine children had our own favorite which we would plead with her to make. I don't have room to include all of them here but here are four of my favorites. There was also another close contender – a lemon steamed pudding, which she served with homemade lemon curd sauce and lots of softly whipped cream.

SPOTTED DICK

Also called golden raisin pudding or Valencia pudding, this is especially good made with Muscatel or California raisins. Be generous with the fruit. As children we loved this best when it was served with lots of yellow custard ·
SERVES 4-6

1 tablespoon melted butter
½ cup fat golden raisins or split stoned Lexia or Muscatel raisins
1 stick soft butter
½ cup superfine sugar
grated zest of ½ unwaxed and organic lemon
2 organic eggs, beaten
1½ cup all-purpose flour
½ teaspoon baking powder
1–2 tablespoons milk

FOR THE HOMEMADE CUSTARD
½ vanilla pod or a few drops pure vanilla extract
1 cup whole milk
2 organic egg yolks
1 tablespoon superfine sugar

5in diameter bowl

Brush the bowl with melted butter. Press some of the raisins around the sides. Cream the butter, add the sugar and lemon zest, and beat until light and fluffy. Gradually add the eggs, beating well after each addition. Stir in the flour and baking powder and enough milk to make the mixture a dropping consistency then add the rest of the fruit. Spoon into the glass bowl. Cover with a double sheet of pleated parchment paper or aluminum foil and tie down. (See opposite page for how to cover the bowl securely.) Fill a saucepan about halfway with water, bring to a boil, and lower in the bowl. Cover and steam for 2 hours.

Meanwhile, make the custard. Put the vanilla pod (if using) into the cold milk and bring slowly to a boil. Whisk the egg yolks with the sugar in a bowl. Remove the vanilla pod from the milk and pour the milk onto the yolks, whisking all the time (and add the vanilla extract if using). Return the mixture to the pan. Stir over low heat until the mixture thickens just enough to coat the back of a spoon but it must not boil. Pour into a cold bowl and stir occasionally to prevent a skin forming.

To serve, turn out the pudding and serve with the warm custard.

TREACLE PUDDING

The name is a bit misleading because we use corn syrup instead of treacle. It's sweet and sticky and lovely ·
SERVES 4-6

½ tablespoon soft butter
2 tablespoons corn syrup
juice of ½ lemon (about 2 tablespoons)
2 tablespoons white bread crumbs (see page 577)
1 stick butter
½ cup superfine sugar
2 organic eggs
1⅓ cups self-rising flour
grated zest of 1 organic lemon
2 tablespoons milk

FOR THE SAUCE
3 tablespoons corn syrup
3 tablespoons freshly squeezed lemon juice

1 pint glass bowl

Brush the bottom of the bowl with soft butter.

Mix the syrup with the lemon juice and bread crumbs. Spoon around the base of the bowl. Whip the butter, add the superfine sugar, and beat until light and fluffy. Add the eggs, one at a time, beating well between each addition. Stir in the flour and grated lemon zest, add enough milk to make a softish mixture. Spoon into the bowl. Cover and steam for 1¼ hours. After steaming, carefully remove from the pan and let sit for 5 minutes. Remove paper. Carefully turn it upside down onto a warm serving dish (the syrup will be scalding hot).

Serve with lightly whipped cream or Homemade Custard (see page 510).

To steam a pudding

Choose a deep saucepan with a tight-fitting lid. Fill about halfway with water and bring to a boil. Lower the pudding into the saucepan. Cover and boil gently for required time. Keep checking the water level regularly – it needs to remain at least halfway up the bowl.

To cover a pudding bowl

Take two layers of silicone or parchment paper or aluminum foil and pleat in the center to allow for expansion. Lay flat on top of the bowl – there should be enough to come down over the sides. Secure the ledge with kitchen string. Make a handle for ease of lifting.

CANARY PUDDING

This too is based on the same kind of Madeira sponge, only in this case, jam is added, so the pudding is also known as jam pudding · SERVES 4–6

1 stick butter, at room temperature
½ cup sugar
2 organic eggs, beaten
a few drops of pure vanilla extract
1½ cups flour
½ teaspoon baking powder (optional)
about 1 tablespoon milk
4–6 tablespoons raspberry jam

TO SERVE
½ pot raspberry jam, thinned with water and lemon juice
2 pint glass bowl

Put the butter and sugar in a bowl and beat until white and creamy using a wooden spoon or electric mixer.

Beat the eggs and vanilla extract and add gradually to the butter and sugar and beat well. If preferred, the eggs may be broken and beaten into the mixture one at a time. A little sifted flour may be added between each addition of egg.

Fold in the rest of the flour using a metal spoon, adding a little milk if necessary to make to a dropping consistency. Add the baking power mixed with the last addition of flour. (The baking powder is not required if using an electric mixer.) Spread jam all over the bottom and sides of the glass bowl. Spoon in the mixture, and cover with a double thickness of parchment paper. Steam for about 1½ hours.

Meanwhile, put the raspberry jam into a stainless-steel saucepan, add lemon juice and water to thin. The quantity needed will depend on the thickness of the jam.

Remove the paper from the bowl, turn out and serve on a hot dish with the warm raspberry jam sauce.

WINTER APPLE AND MINCEMEAT PUDDING

This is a terrific way to use up mincemeat but it's so good that it's almost worth making mincemeat especially to make this pudding alone · SERVES 8–10

8oz cooking apples
zest and juice of 1 organic lemon

1 stick butter
½ cup soft light brown sugar
2 organic eggs
pinch of salt
good pinch of mace
little pinch of cinnamon
1½ cups self-rising flour
zest of ½ organic orange
3 tablespoons Ballymaloe Mincemeat (see page 512)
2oz candied orange and lemon peel, chopped

2 pint bowl, preferably Delft

Peel and chop the apples into ⅛in chunks. Whip the butter. Add the sugar and beat until light and fluffy. Add the eggs, one at a time, and continue to beat until well incorporated. Add a pinch of salt and the ground spices to the flour and fold gently into the base. Add the grated orange and lemon zest, lemon juice, finely chopped apple, mincemeat, and candied peel.

Spoon the mixture into the greased bowl. Cover the bowl (see left), tie securely, and provide a handle for ease of lifting. Select a saucepan that will accommodate the bowl. Half fill with water and bring to a boil. Add the pudding. Cover the pan and steam the pudding for 1½ hours. Check the water level regularly to make sure it remains at least halfway up the bowl.

Uncover and carefully turn out the pudding onto a hot serving plate. Serve on hot pudding plates with plenty of softly whipped cream.

BALLYMALOE MINCEMEAT

MAKES 8–9 POTS

2 cooking apples
finely grated zest and juice of
    2 organic lemons
1lb beef suet
pinch of salt
4oz Candied Peel (page 458)
2 tablespoons Seville Orange
    Marmalade (see page 454)
1 cup currants
1lb golden raisins
2lb raw sugar
¼ cup Irish whiskey

Core the apples and bake in the oven at 350°F, for about 30 minutes until soft. Allow to cool then remove the skin and mash the flesh to pulp. Stir the lemon zest and juice into the pulp. One by one, add the other ingredients, mixing thoroughly. Put

DELFT BOWLS

When you're making suet or plum puddings, of course you can cook them in a plastic bowl, but it's actually really worth finding a thick, old-fashioned pudding bowl. They're steaming for hours, so it affords more protection from the direct heat.

the mincemeat into sterilized jars, cover, and leave to mature for 2 weeks before using. It will keep for a year in a cool, airy place.

Steamed Suet Puddings

Suet gives a different texture to steamed puddings. They're richer, but nothing else quite hits the spot in the same way on a winter's day. They're a great tradition in country houses; wonderful after a shoot lunch. To make your own beef suet see page 176.

MARMALADE PUDDING

This steamed marmalade pudding always reminds me of my much-loved father-in-law Ivan Allen, who looked forward to every meal. On cold days in January when the whole house smelled of marmalade as we made our store for the coming year, he knew that his favorite marmalade suet pudding would be on the menu within a day or two. We remember him with great fondness every time we eat it · **SERVES 6**

1 cup all-purpose flour
½ cup ground beef suet
½ cup white bread crumbs
    (see page 577)
½ cup sugar
1 teaspoons baking powder
1 organic egg, beaten
2 tablespoons Seville Orange
    Marmalade (see page 454)

FOR THE SAUCE
2 tablespoons water
8oz Seville Orange Marmalade
    (see page 454)
freshly squeezed juice of ½ lemon

1 pint glass bowl

Mix the dry ingredients together. Add the egg, marmalade, and a little milk to moisten if necessary (the mixture should have the consistency of plum pudding). Fill into the bowl. Cover with a double sheet of parchment paper with a pleat in the center. Tie firmly and steam in a covered saucepan for 2–3 hours. Check regularly and top up with hot water if necessary (the water level should remain at least half way up the bowl).

To make the sauce, put the water and marmalade into a saucepan. Warm gently then boil for 2–3 minutes. Add the lemon juice, taste, and add a little sugar if necessary.

When the pudding is fully cooked, turn out onto a hot plate. Spoon some sauce over and around the pudding. Serve on very hot plates with softly whipped cream.

QUEEN OF PUDDINGS

Another dessert that conjures up childhood memories. Interestingly, everybody seems to have a different opinion about what Queen of Puddings should both look and taste like. This recipe is a combination of several people's firmly held views. It's delicious, but as I've discovered, it's hard to please everyone! **SERVES 6**

2 cups milk
4 tablespoons butter
1 teaspoon pure vanilla extract
5oz white bread crumbs
   (see page 577)
grated zest of 1 lemon
¾ cup superfine sugar, plus
   2 teaspoons for sprinkling
3 organic eggs, separated
3 tablespoons Red Currant or
   Black Currant jelly (see page
   451)

1 x 2 pint pie dish

Preheat the oven to 350°F and
grease the pie dish.

   Put the milk and butter into a
saucepan, bring almost to boiling
point, add the vanilla extract. Mix
the bread crumbs with the lemon
zest and ⅛ cup sugar. Stir in the hot
milk, leave for about 10 minutes.
Whisk in the egg yolks one by one.
Pour into the pie dish and bake for
about 25 minutes or until just set.

   Remove from the oven. Whisk
the egg whites in a spotlessly clean,
grease-free bowl. When it is just
becoming fluffy, add ¼ cup sugar.
Continue to whisk until it holds a
stiff peak. Fold in another ¼ cup
sugar. Warm the jelly slightly.
Spread very gently over the surface
of the custard. Pile the meringue on
top in soft folds. Sprinkle the
remaining sugar over the top.
Return to the oven and cook for 15
minutes or until the meringue is pale
gold and crisp on top. Serve with
lots of softly whipped cream.

APPLE AND CURRANT ROLY-POLY

These seriously filling puddings were a great favorite in years gone by before all the hype about cholesterol and low-fat diets gathered momentum. They are beginning to find favor again among those who realize that a little of what you like every now and then doesn't do a bit of harm! · **SERVES ABOUT 6**

8oz apples
¼ **cup currants**
¼ **cup sugar**
½ **teaspoon (or more) nutmeg or**
   mixed spice
2oz **beef suet (see page 176)**
1½ **cups all-purpose flour**

pinch of salt
½ teaspoon baking powder

Peel, core, and chop the apples,
wash the currants, and mix with the
sugar and the spice. Chop or grind
the suet finely and put into a bowl
with the flour, salt, and baking
powder. Mix well, then add cold
water to make a stiff paste. Roll out
to a thickness of ⅓in, spread the
apple mixture on the suet pastry,
wet the edges and roll up neatly.
Tie in a cloth wrung out in boiling
water and floured and boil gently
in an oblong saucepan or casserole
for 1½ hours. Unwrap, serve on a
very hot plate with softly whipped
cream and soft brown sugar.

MUMMY'S PLUM PUDDING WITH MRS. HANRAHAN'S SAUCE

Nowadays, people don't understand why we get so excited about Christmas puddings, but when I was growing up we weren't constantly surrounded by little luxuries, so it was really special and we looked forward to it all year long. Mummy would wait until after we came home from school so that we could all take part in the process. She'd show me how to skin the almonds, stone the Muscatel raisins (used at that time), grate the lemon zest on the finest part of the grater, and wash the thick syrup off the crystallized cherries. I now realize this was a way of passing on skills. We'd all stir to make a wish; we'd close our eyes tightly and send messages to Santa; now, of course, I understand this was a plot to get the ingredients thoroughly mixed! The plum puddings would be packed into Delft bowls, covered in parchment paper and tied; I remember putting my finger into the knot to help to secure it tightly.

It was tradition in our house to eat one of the plum puddings on the night it was made – it was the first taste of Christmas. Mummy would make five or six, eat one on the spot, give some away, keep one for Christmas, and maybe save one for Easter.

I'm always amazed at how many people are intimidated by the thought of making a plum pudding, but it's really only a question of mixing ingredients together. This recipe, which came down through the generations in my mother's family, is unquestionably the best recipe for plum pudding that I've come across, and I've tried lots ·

MAKES 2 X 3 PINT OR 3 X 2 PINT PUDDINGS; THE LARGE SIZE WILL SERVE 10-12 PEOPLE, THE MEDIUM 6-8

1½ cups raisins
1½ cups golden raisins
1½ cups currants
1½ cups brown sugar
1½ cups white bread crumbs (see page 577)
1½ cups finely chopped suet
4oz candied peel (preferably homemade)
2 cooking apples, peeled and diced or grated
finely grated zest of 1 lemon
3 cloves, pounded
pinch of salt
6 organic eggs
¼ cup Jamaica rum
½ cup skinned almonds, chopped

whiskey or brandy, for flaming

Choose a large bowl. Mix all the ingredients together very thoroughly and leave overnight; don't forget, everyone in the family must stir and make a wish! The following day, stir again for good measure. Fill into pudding bowls, allowing about 1½in space at the top of the bowl; cover with a double sheet of pleated parchment paper, tie it tightly under the rim with kitchen string, and make a handle for ease of lifting.

Steam the puddings in a covered saucepan of boiling water for 6 hours. The water should come halfway up the side of the bowl: check every hour or so and top up with boiling water. After 6 hours, remove the puddings. Allow to become cold and cover with fresh

parchment paper. Store in a cool dry place until required.

On the day you wish to serve the plum pudding, steam for a further 2 hours. Turn the pudding onto a very hot serving plate, pour over some whiskey or brandy and ignite. Serve immediately on very hot plates with Mrs. Hanrahan's Sauce (see below) or brandy butter.

MRS. HANRAHAN'S SAUCE

The traditional accompaniment to plum pudding is brandy butter (see page 217). This recipe was given to me by my sister-in-law's mother, so it's become known as Mrs. Hanrahan's sauce. I've shared it through books and newspaper columns with a lot of people in Ireland and beyond, many of whom tell me they enjoy Mrs. Hanrahan's sauce with their plum pudding every year. This makes a lot of sauce, but you can make the base and use it for several weeks, adding whipped cream to taste when needed. Mrs. Hanrahan has now passed on, but we are fortunate that she generously shared her recipe for posterity · MAKES 1.5 LITRES (2½ PINTS)

1 stick butter
1 cup raw sugar
1 organic egg
¼ cup port
¼ cup medium sherry
2¼–2½ pints lightly whipped cream

Melt the butter, stir in the sugar, and allow to cool slightly. Whisk the egg and add to the butter and sugar with the port and sherry. Refrigerate. Pour a little into a bowl when needed and add the lightly whipped cream to taste. This sauce is also very good with mince pies and other tarts.

BREAK ALL THE RULES MERINGUE

This is a gem of a recipe – so called because we use confectioners' sugar instead of superfine sugar and mix it all in together instead of adding the sugar in stages. I hope this will take the mystery and the terror out of meringue making for those who are daunted by the prospect. We use this all-purpose recipe for birthdays, anniversaries, Valentine's Day, or simply for a special dessert. Making meringues by hand was seriously hard work for our mothers and grandmothers. These days we have the bonus of being able to use a stand-alone food mixer – a piece of kitchen equipment that definitely earns its keep in my kitchen. Alternatively, you may want to use a handheld electric whisk ·

MAKES ABOUT 12

2 **organic egg whites**
1 **cup confectioners' sugar, sifted**
1 **cup whipped cream**

Preheat the oven to 300°F. Line a baking sheet with silicone paper.

Check that the mixing bowl is dry, spotlessly clean, and free from grease. Put the confectioners' sugar and egg whites into the bowl, and whisk until the mixture forms stiff dry peaks. Using a teaspoon, spoon out blobs of the mixture onto a baking sheet with a flourish. Bake immediately in the oven for 45 minutes or until crisp. Turn off the oven and allow to cool. The meringues should peel easily off the silicone paper.

The meringues will keep for several weeks in a metal or plastic container.

Variations

MERINGUE CAKE

Mark two 7½in circles on silicone paper or a prepared baking sheet. Make the meringue mixture as above, divide between the two circles and spread evenly with a offset spatula. Bake as before and cool – if you chill them for an hour before serving they will be easier to cut. Peel off the paper and sandwich the two rounds together with softly whipped cream and fresh berries.

Below: *Meringues.*

PASTEL MERINGUES

When I was little my mother didn't make meringues but my friend's mother always made gorgeous pale pink, green, and snowy white ones for afternoon tea – I was always so envious! Just add a very few drops of natural food coloring to the meringue mixture and shape, bake, and sandwich with whipped cream as above.

MERINGUE ROULADE

Make the meringue mixture as above. Line a 12 x 8in jelly roll pan with silicone paper, and spread the meringue evenly over it. Cook in a moderate oven for 15–18 minutes. When cold, fill with whipped cream and homemade lemon curd or fresh berries and roll up carefully like a jelly roll.

A Few Old-fashioned Sweets

I just had to include a few little recipes for favorite sweets – seldom made nowadays but really worth the effort. Here are a few ideas to take you down memory lane.

BALLYMALOE FUDGE

Fudge is timeless and in a straw poll I would wager that it comes out as many people's number-one sweet. It even puts a grin on grown men's faces · **MAKES ABOUT 96 PIECES**

2 sticks butter
4 cups light brown sugar or superfine sugar
1⅓ cups canned evaporated milk
3 teaspoons pure vanilla extract

jelly roll pan 9 x 13in

Melt the butter in a heavy-bottomed saucepan over low heat. Add the milk, 1 cup water, the sugar, and vanilla extract and stir with a whisk until the sugar is dissolved. Turn up the heat to simmer, stir constantly until it reaches the soft-ball stage. To test, put some of the fudge in a bowl of cold water, pull off the heat, and stir until it thickens and reaches the required consistency with the saucepan over cold water. Pour into a jelly roll pan and smooth out with a spatula.

Allow to cool and then cut before completely cold.

TOFFEE

I always poke around in a mixed box of sweeties to find the buttery toffees – my favorite. If you can find treacle, use it instead of corn syrup for a more richly flavored sweet · **MAKES ABOUT 96**

2 sticks butter
1 cup granulated sugar
4 tablespoons corn syrup
14oz can of condensed milk

8 x 12in jelly roll pan, lined with silicone paper
cellophane

Melt the butter in a heavy-bottomed saucepan (about 8½in wide) over medium heat. Add the sugar and corn syrup. Stir until well mixed. Add the condensed milk and stir constantly until the toffee is a rich golden brown and reaches the hard crack stage (about 30 minutes). If you have a sugar thermometer, it should register 320°F. Otherwise, fill a bowl or measuring cup with ice water and drop a teaspoon of the toffee into the cold water. If it is ready it will harden immediately to the texture of toffee. Pour into the lined pan and allow to set for about 15 minutes. Mark into squares or rectangles with a lightly oiled knife.

When cold, break into individual toffees, wrap in pieces of cellophane, and twist the ends.

Variation

CHOCOLATE TOFFEES
Melt 8oz chocolate in a Pyrex bowl set over a pan of hot but not simmering water. Coat the cold toffees in melted chocolate, transfer to a sheet of silicone paper and allow to set. Wrap as before.

MARSHMALLOWS

Real homemade marshmallows are a forgotten flavor but are easy and great fun to make. Toast them over an open fire or drop one into hot chocolate and watch it slowly melt · **MAKES ABOUT 64**

vegetable oil
2 teaspoons confectioners' sugar, sifted
2 teaspoons cornstarch, sifted
1oz powdered gelatin
2 organic egg whites
2¼ cups granulated sugar

1 x 8in square pan

Brush the pan with a little vegetable oil and coat with confectioners' sugar and cornstarch. Sprinkle the gelatin to cover ½ cup water in a small bowl. Allow to sponge for 3–4 minutes. Put the bowl in a saucepan of simmering water and stir until dissolved. Remove from the heat.

Whisk the egg whites until they hold stiff peaks, preferably in the bowl of a mixer – this makes adding the sugar syrup to the egg whites much easier.

Put the sugar into a saucepan with 1⅛ cups water. Stir over low heat until all the sugar has dissolved. Increase the heat and continue to boil fiercely until it reaches 252°F (the hard-ball stage) on a sugar thermometer. Turn off the heat.

Pour the dissolved gelatin into the syrup and stir. Watch out – the syrup will bubble up a little.

Switch the food mixer on the lowest setting so the egg whites carry on whisking, then pour the syrup down the side of the bowl in a gentle trickle, whisking all the time. The mixture will change texture and become creamy. Continue to whisk until the mixture becomes really thick but is still pourable. Pour into the prepared pan and leave to set in a cool place – but not the fridge – for an hour or two.

Dust a clean cutting board with the rest of the cornstarch and confectioners' sugar mixture and coat a sharp knife with vegetable oil. Gently ease the marshmallow out of the pan. Make sure it is dusted all over with confectioners' sugar, then cut into squares. Oil and dust the knife again as often as necessary. Thread the marshmallows onto skewers or spear them with forks. They are delicous toasted over an open fire.

TURKISH DELIGHT

Ridiculously sweet but naughty and so nice now and then · **MAKES 80–100**

½ **cup water**
3 **cups granulated sugar**
finely grated zest and juice of
　2 **organic lemons**
¾ **cup cornflour**
1oz **or** 6 **teaspoons of powdered**
　gelatin

FLAVORING
1oz **mint leaves, crushed, or**
　4 **tablespoons rose blossom or**
　orange blossom water

TO COAT
½ **cup confectioners' sugar**
½ **cup cornstarch**

1 x 8in **square pan**

Put the 5fl oz water, the sugar, lemon zest and juice, and crushed mint leaves if using into a heavy stainless-steel saucepan. Bring slowly to a boil and continue to cook uncovered over medium heat until the syrup reaches the "thread" stage, 236°F.

Mix the cornstarch with a little water until smooth and stir into the syrup. "Sponge" the gelatin in 6 tablespoons of water. Add to the saucepan and continue to boil until clear. Strain through a metal sieve into the prepared pan. Allow to cool and set (do not refrigerate).

If using rose or orange blossom water instead of mint to flavor the Turkish delight, stir into the mixture before straining.

When cool and set, cut into squares, toss in a mixture of sifted confectioners' sugar and cornstarch.

NOUGAT

This is my take on Italian Torrone, firmer in texture than the softer French version. Nougat will keep in an airtight container for up to three weeks if you can resist it! You can add more or less nuts as you like · **MAKES 64 SQUARE OR MORE**

2 **cups sugar**
9oz **liquid glucose**
7oz **honey**
2 **organic egg whites**
1 **teaspoon vanilla extract**
½ **cup pistachios, peeled**
½ **cup blanched almonds, toasted**

3 **sheets confectioner's rice paper**

8 x 8in **cake pan**

Line the base of the cake pan with rice paper.

Put the sugar, glucose, and honey into a wide frying pan. Stir over low heat until the sugar dissolves. Increase the heat and cook until the syrup reaches 266°F (hard crack) on a sugar thermometer.

Whisk the egg whites in a spotlessly clean and dry bowl to a firm peak. Slowly pour in half the syrup and whisk preferably in a food processor to combine. Add the vanilla extract and continue to whisk at a low speed. Meanwhile put the remaining syrup back on the heat and cook until the mixture reaches 302°F on a sugar thermometer. Slowly pour onto the egg white mixture and whisk until thick and glossy – about 5 minutes. Fold in the pistachios and toasted almonds.

Pour the nougat mixture into the prepared pan. Smooth the top with the back of a spoon or a spatula. Cover with a sheet of rice paper and press down gently. Allow to cool, then cut into 1in square pieces with a sharp knife and serve. Store in an airtight container.

Cakes and Cookies

When I was little, there was always a cake or some cookies in a tin in anticipation of someone just dropping by for a cup of tea – a daily occurrence back then. Sadly this is less often the case nowadays, perhaps because we're reluctant to have cakes in the house in case we might be tempted to eat them! The craving for all things sweet and delicious certainly persists, yet when we indulge it's often accompanied by a disproportionate feeling of guilt rather than pure enjoyment. So rather than going for a quick fix of calorie-laden, trans-fatty shop cakes, use good ingredients to make a gorgeous cake and enjoy a slice (not the whole cake!) shared with family and friends. It won't do you a bit of harm.

Most of us come to cooking through baking little buns or cakes with our mums or grannies, and in my case my Auntie Florence too. Now I adore baking with my own grandchildren and am not sure which of us has the best fun – it's thrilling to see how quickly they learn.

The art of cake making is still thriving, and the guardians of the inherited wisdom tend to be our mothers and grandmothers, many of whom were members of the Women's Institute or Irish Countrywoman's Association. Years ago people would've known who made the best cakes and breads in every village – it was a way of expressing creativity within the domestic sphere and something that people justifiably took great pride in. Many women still take their cake-baking skills very seriously indeed. There is a long tradition of competing in country shows, which still continues now that these events are enjoying a distinct revival.

Cake making was an extremely laborious activity in the days when everything had to be beaten and whisked by hand, and now, thankfully, food mixers make it a complete snap. The secret of successful baking lies in following a tried-and-tested recipe in detail; it is a precise science, so for success one must measure accurately.

Cake types

Cakes basically fall into two categories: those made with fat, and those made without fat, with variations on both themes.

Cakes made without fat
These cakes are also known as whisked-up sponge cakes; the traditional way to make them is to put eggs and sugar into a bowl over a saucepan of simmering water, and whisk the mixture until light and fluffy, then take the bowl off the heat, and continue whisking until cooled. When heated, the eggs trap the air whisked into the mixture. The air acts as a rising agent, resulting in a feather-light sponge cake. These days the same result can be achieved with a food mixer.

Cakes made with fat
In these cakes, the eggs are not whisked, so an external rising agent is needed. The fat (whichever you choose: butter, margarine, lard, or oil) can be creamed with sugar, or melted, or rubbed in. The majority of cakes are made by the **creaming method;** these keep well and are richer, with a soft, tender, even crumb. Cakes made by **melting (molten) method,** and combined with molasses or corn syrup have a moist texture and keep well. Cakes made by the **rubbed-in method** are generally less rich and should be eaten fresh.

Genoise sponge
This is a whisked-up sponge cake with melted butter folded in at the end so it is a combination of the above two methods. The resulting cake has the lightness of the whisked-up sponge cake but the added bonus of the keeping qualities of a butter sponge cake.

Baking Ingredients

A basic understanding of how ingredients like fat, sugar, flour, eggs, and rising agents react to each other is very helpful. Choosing the correct size pan, oven position, and temperature are also vitally important factors.

Fats

As with everything else, the quality of the ingredients you use will affect the taste and texture of your finished cake. The fats used in cakes are butter, margarine, oil, lard, or dripping, and each has its own characteristics. Even though the butter and margarine produce a similar texture, butter is my preferred option by far. Good-quality pure lard is difficult to source unless you know someone who rears free-range organic pigs for rendering your own lard. Do seek it out, though, for the excellent texture it lends to pastries and pies. Olive oil, sunflower oil, or corn oil can also be used in cakes, but each will yield a different flavor, so they are not necessarily interchangeable, especially when you compare milder, non-scented oils with fruity, extra virgin olive oil.

Sugar

Superfine sugar is finer than granulated sugar and is best for cakes and baking. The thick crystals in granulated sugar, which don't dissolve as well, can leave brown specks and spots in cakes when they caramelize unevenly. Golden baker's sugar, a less-refined sugar, also gives a delicious result. Light brown sugar or a proportion of light brown sugar can be used to enrich fruitcakes and wedding cakes. Honey, corn syrup, and molasses are sweeteners used in other cakes, such as gingerbread. Confectioners' sugar is used for icings, buttercreams, and occasionally in pastries.

Flour

For cakes, flour should be all-purpose or self-rising. Self-rising flour takes the guesswork out of baking but is only effective when it is fresh and dry, so ideally you'll want to use up small bags within a few months before moisture gets to it. All-purpose flour keeps longer than self-rising flour, but it should be kept dry as well. Note that some all-purpose flours actually have a small amount of rising agent included, which most people don't realize. If you're using it in a pastry, for example, roll it out a little thinner than you otherwise might because it will rise a little in the oven.

For yeast bread or bun doughs, its best to use bread flour or baker's flour for its higher protein content.

There will be a sell-by date on the flour. Flour is best kept in a dry, airy cupboard. I've found that it doesn't always keep as long as the sell-by date suggests unless it is kept in optimum storage environment. If it is stored in a damp, humid atmosphere, it will deteriorate faster. For that reason, it's very important to be able to judge by the appearance of flour whether or not it's still fresh and whether it is infested with weevils (see opposite).

Many recipes, particularly those for cakes, cookies, and breads, call for the flour to be sifted. This will take a few extra seconds, but is definitely worthwhile as it can dramatically lighten the texture.

Eggs

The quality of the eggs you choose matters greatly and organic eggs unquestionably make a huge difference to the flavor and texture of the finished product. Eggs and whichever fat you use should be at room temperature.

Rising agents

Whichever rising agent you use, always measure it accurately. Be very careful – if too much rising agent is used, the cake will first rise and then collapse. The rising agents used when making cakes, buns, and cookies include:

- Air
- Baking soda
- Baking powder
- Cream of tartar
- Yeast

Some cakes, in particular whisked-up sponge cakes, are leavened by the air that is whisked in. Sifting the flour also helps to further aerate the mixture.

Baking soda is sodium bicarbonate, an alkali that is used in conjunction with acid ingredients such as buttermilk, natural yogurt, and lemon juice. When the rising agent comes into contact with the liquid, a chemical reaction occurs which creates little bubbles of carbon dioxide. These expand during the baking process. Gluten, a protein in flour, stretches to accommodate the gas and so the cake rises. In some cakes such as gingerbread, which are made by the molten method, the acid in the molasses reacts with the baking soda in order to raise the mixture.

Baking powder is not to be confused with baking soda. Baking powder is a combination of cream of tartar (an acidifying agent) and baking soda (an alkali), so it does not require an outside acid ingredient to produce the chemical reaction. It can be duplicated at home by combining two parts cream of tartar to one part baking soda and should be stored in a screw-top jar. If moisture gets in, the mixture will lose its potency.

There are two types of baking powder – single-acting and double-acting. Single-acting baking powder is activated by moisture, so it is important to get the mixture into the oven immediately. Double-acting baking powder is most widely used in the baking industry and in the US. It reacts in two stages. When it comes into contact with the moisture of the mixture at room temperature some gas is released, but the majority is released when the temperature increases in the oven.

Baking pans

Nowadays, most cake pans are made of very light aluminum. Consequently, there is very little protection from the intense heat of the oven. Lining the pan provides insulation and keeps the outside from overcooking before the center is fully baked.

If you ever get the chance to get your hands on ancient, heavy black cake pans, snap them up. They'll be three or four times the gauge of most modern-day offerings, will probably cost next to nothing, and will be well worth it! Keep an ear to the ground for country-house auctions, where on occasion you might be lucky enough to find some.

CHECKING FOR WEEVILS IN FLOUR

Years ago, when I was in hotel school in Cathal Brugh Street in Dublin, our lecturer told us we would need to know how to tell whether there were weevils in flour. Needless to say, we all rolled our eyes doubting that we would ever be in a situation where we would need this information. But in reality it's very useful, particularly for people who don't bake very often, so I'll pass on this forgotten skill to you.

Take a spoon and fill it with flour, smooth the surface with a knife. Leave the spoon sitting for a few minutes and then check. Weevils cannot be seen by the naked eye, so if the surface is even slightly broken, that means there are weevils in the flour. Cooking weevil-infested flour will kill the weevils, but will result in a heavy texture. Give it to the hens instead. Wholewheat flour that is infested with weevils is even more obvious; when you look into the package it'll look dusty and brown on top.

Weevils can infest any grains, including nuts, seeds, rice, oats, and breakfast cereals. Bags of rice with really dusty bottoms are one clue, as are strings like cobwebs. If you store flour in a container, wash out and dry the container meticulously well between batches of flour to avoid weevils passing from one batch of flour to another.

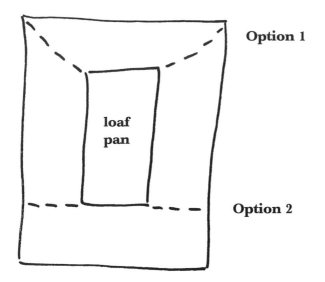

Option 1

**loaf
pan**

Option 2

Above: *Lining a loaf pan.*

TO LINE A SQUARE OR ROUND PAN

Put a folded sheet of parchment paper onto the counter. Lay the pan on top. With a pencil, draw around the base of the pan. Remove the pan and with a kitchen scissors, cut INSIDE the line so you have two pieces to fit inside the pan. Keep aside. Fold another sheet of parchment paper in two lengthwise, fold the base over, and crease well. With scissors, cut into the crease at a slight angle (see diagram). Line the sides of the cake pan with this piece (you may need to do a second piece if you need to overlap on a large pan). Drop the two bases into the pan and press down onto the base of the pan to secure them.

For a rich fruitcake, tie a double band of aluminum foil onto the outside of the pan for extra protection and lay a sheet of aluminum foil on the top as well.

HOW TO LINE A JELLY ROLL PAN WITH A PASTRY BASE

Make the pastry in the usual way but stop while it's still loose and crumby. Scatter it into a jelly roll pan. Lay a sheet of plastic wrap over the top. Use a rolling pin to roll the crumbs until they coalesce into an even layer. Peel off the plastic wrap and continue with the recipe.

PAN SIZE – DOES IT MATTER?

The pan must be the correct size for the mixture. If you don't have a pan of a particular size, check your saucepans or sauté pans. Provided they have metal, rather than plastic handles, you could just use these instead. For some cakes, particularly fruitcakes, I find that heavy stainless-steel saucepans or sauté pans work brilliantly and give extra protection to the cake.

LINING A CAKE PAN

It didn't occur to me that this was a forgotten skill until I saw cake liners for sale in a kitchen shop. I then realized that many cake recipes just nonchalantly say "line the cake pan" but don't give instructions.

The reason for lining the cake pan or loaf pan is to provide extra protection for sides particularly for cakes that will be in the oven for an hour or more. It also makes it easier to remove the cake from the pan.

TO LINE A LOAF PAN

Take a rectangular piece of parchment paper about one-and-a-half times the size of the pan. Lay the loaf pan in the center. With scissors cut into the corner as per the diagram (use either option). Lift off the pan and overlap the sides of the paper to fit neatly into the pan. The paper should come 1½–2½in above the top.

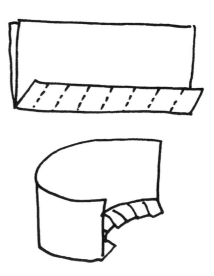

Above: *Lining a round pan.*

Cake Troubleshooting

The great thing when you're cooking is to know how to get out of a pickle, so here, for what it's worth, are my observations of things that can go wrong, and why, when baking a cake.

If the crust of the cake is too dark, perhaps:
• the oven was too hot
• the batter had too much sugar in it

If the cake is too small, perhaps:
• the batter didn't have enough rising agent
• the batter was too warm
• the ingredients were measured incorrectly
• the baking powder was too old
• the formula was unbalanced
• the oven was too hot
• the wrong kind of flour was used

If your cake has dark specks, perhaps:
• the sugar was too coarse, for example granulated rather than superfine sugar
• you didn't add enough liquid

If your cake shrinks, perhaps:
• it was not properly mixed
• it was overcooked

If your cake sinks during baking, perhaps:
• you didn't add enough flour
• it was underbaked
• the oven door was opened before the batter was fully set

If the cake cracks on top, perhaps:
• it wasn't properly mixed
• the batter was too stiff
• the oven was too hot
• an incorrect type of flour was used
• there was too much flour

If the crust is too thick, perhaps:
• the heat was too low

If the crumb is coarse or irregular, perhaps:
• the batter was not properly mixed
• it was too stiff
• too much rising agent was added
• the oven temperature was too hot or too cool
• the batter needed more eggs
• the recipe was incorrect

If the crumb is too dense, perhaps:
• there may not have been enough rising agent
• the batter was too thin
• the wrong kind of flour was used
• the recipe was incorrect

If the cake's flavor is poor, perhaps:
• too much rising agent was added
• the recipe was incorrect

If the cake is tough, perhaps:
• not enough sugar was added
• the wrong kind of flour was used
• there was too much flour
• there wasn't enough shortening (fat) or liquid added
• the recipe was incorrect

If the cake lacks body, perhaps:
• the batter was not properly mixed
• too much rising agent was added
• the oven wasn't hot enough
• there wasn't enough sugar or eggs in the mixture

If the fruit sinks, perhaps:
• too much rising agent was added
• the batter was too thin
• the wrong kind of flour was used
• the soaked fruit wasn't drained thoroughly
• the recipe was incorrect
• the oven door was opened before the batter was fully set

If the cake doesn't keep well, perhaps:
• the oven may have been too hot
• not enough eggs, sugar, or fat was used
• the wrong kind of flour was used
• the recipe was incorrect

Cakes Made Without Fat

MRS. LAMB'S LAYER CAKE

This type of feather-light layer cake induces waves of nostalgia in many people. The recipe came to me via Myrtle Allen. She was given it by a Quaker lady called Mrs. Lamb, who came to her rescue when, as a young bride, she confided that she couldn't seem to make a light, fluffy layer cake to equal those on the afternoon tea tables of her neighbors and friends. It was during the war and Myrtle felt guilty that she'd wasted so many precious eggs in vain. This recipe makes the tenderest of layers and is divine filled with sugared strawberries and softly whipped cream.

For the record, because it has baking powder and water in it, this is not a classic layer cake. It also has disproportionate amounts of eggs, sugar, and flour in it (a classic layer cake has equal quantities of each). Mrs. Lamb obviously wasn't leaving anything to chance, and decided to include a little baking powder to ensure that the cake rose enough to impress the neighbors! · SERVES 8–10

3 organic eggs
1 cup plus 2 tablespoons superfine sugar
¼ cup water
1⅓ cups all-purpose flour
1 teaspoon baking powder

FOR THE FILLING
sliced fresh strawberries, raspberries, blackberries, or kumquats
Green Gooseberry and Elderflower Compote (see page 35) or homemade jam
softly whipped cream

2 x 8in round cake pans

Preheat the oven to 375°F.

Separate the egg yolks from the whites. In a food mixer, whisk the yolks with the superfine sugar for 2 minutes and then add in the water. Whisk until light and fluffy, this will take about 10 minutes – or even more. The mixture will have greatly increased in volume and should hold a figure eight for a few seconds.

Sift the flour and baking powder together and gently fold into the mousse in batches. Then whisk the egg whites until they hold a stiff peak. Fold them in very gently.

Divide the mixture between two greased and floured cake pans and bake for 20 minutes.

Remove from the pans and cool on a wire rack.

When cool, sandwich the two together with the filling of your choice and whipped cream.

Sprinkle a little superfine sugar or confectioners' sugar over the top before serving. Serve on a pretty plate with a doily.

JELLY ROLL

This recipe is a basic jelly roll, with equal quantities of flour, eggs, and sugar. If you wish, you could bake it in 2 x 6in greased and floured pans to make a filled cake. If you choose to make a jelly roll, it may be rolled lengthwise or widthwise depending on the thickness required. It must be rolled while it is still warm and pliable. The forgotten skill here is rolling it up – one always holds one's breath! · SERVES 8

1 cup all-purpose flour
4 organic eggs
½ cup superfine sugar
2 tablespoons warm water
½ teaspoon vanilla extract
6 tablespoons warmed homemade Raspberry Jam (see recipe page 442)

10 x 15in jelly roll pan

Preheat the oven to 375°F.

Line the jelly roll pan with paper cut to fit the base of the pan exactly. Brush the paper and sides of the pan with melted butter and dust with flour.

Whisk the eggs and superfine sugar in a food mixer until much paler in color and three or four times the original size. You'll know the mixture is whisked well enough when a figure eight trailed on top holds its shape for about 30 seconds.

Gently stir in the water and vanilla extract. Sift about one-third of the flour at a time and fold it into the whisked mixture using a large metal spoon. Pour gently into the pan, tilting it so the mixture flows evenly into the corners.

Bake for 12–15 minutes. It is cooked when it feels firm to the touch in the center. The edges will have shrunk slightly from the sides of the pan.

Lay a damp kitchen towel on the countertop, put a sheet of parchment paper on top and sprinkle it lightly but evenly with superfine sugar. Decide whether you want a long, thin jelly roll from which you can get more slices, or a shorter, fatter one. For the former, turn out the jelly roll horizontally on top of the sugared parchment paper; for the latter, turn it out facing vertically. Remove the parchment paper from the base of the cake. The sheet of cake must be rolled into shape while warm and pliable. If anything other than jam will be part of the filling, you must wait until the cake has cooled to fill it, otherwise the filling is liable to melt. In that case, roll the parchment paper into the cake so that the cake doesn't stick to itself. When the cake has cooled, you can unroll it, add the filling and re-roll it without the paper. If you do the initial rolling while the cake is warm and pliable, it won't crack when you re-roll it with the filling.

If, however, you are just using jam, spread it sparingly over the warm cake. Then, with a knife, score the sheet of cake about ¾ in away from the edge closest to you. This will make it easier to begin the roll and ensure that it's tight. With both hands, catch the edge of the paper closest to you and roll the jelly roll away from you, using the paper to keep the roll tight. When you have finished rolling, wrap the parchment paper and then the damp kitchen towel around the jelly roll and leave to cool. To serve, trim both ends. Ensure there are children around to eat the trimmings.

GENOISE SPONGE

This type of cake is usually used as a base for gateaux and can be filled and iced with a variety of simple or luscious flavors · **SERVES 4**

4 organic eggs
½ cup superfine sugar
1 cup all-purpose flour
4 tablespoons clarified butter (see page 216), melted

9in round genoise pan, greased and lined with parchment paper

Preheat the oven to 350°F.

Whisk the eggs with the superfine sugar until light and fluffy. Sift the flour into the mixture in three batches, folding each batch as lightly as possible with a wooden spatula or wooden spoon. Just after the last batch, pour the cooled, clarified butter around the side of the bowl and fold in gently and quickly (because the whisked mixture quickly loses volume after the butter is added.)

Pour the mixture into the prepared pan and bake in the oven for 35–40 minutes. Turn out onto a rack to cool. Fill and ice as you fancy.

HOW TO MAKE HOMEMADE PURE VANILLA EXTRACT

Pure vanilla extract is gorgeous but enormously expensive. You can make your own superb extract quite easily. The flavor of the vanilla is extracted by the alcohol, which in turn becomes more mellow. The vanilla pods can later be used to flavor custards, creams, and mousses.

Split 3 or 4 vanilla pods lengthwise, put into a 1 pint bottle of vodka or brandy, seal tightly, and leave to infuse for at least 3 days, but better still for up to 4–6 weeks before using. Shake occasionally. Before use, strain the liquid through a fine sieve. Store in small airtight bottles. It keeps almost indefinitely.

VANILLA SUGAR

Good vanilla pods are expensive, so store them in a tall Mason jar of superfine sugar. They will flavor it and you can use it as vanilla sugar.

Fill a large mouthed jar with superfine sugar. Bury dry vanilla pods in the sugar and store; the more vanilla pods you use, the stronger the flavor will be. Use for cookies, cakes, custard, ice creams, etc.

LEMON/ORANGE SUGAR

We also flavor sugar with strips of lemon or orange zest.

Creaming or Whipping Method

When using this method, just ensure that the butter is nice and soft – at least at room temperature – before you start. If eggs are added to the whipped butter and sugar too quickly, the mixture will curdle and the cake will be heavier as a result. It's also worth emphasizing that if you're using your own eggs, they will vary in size, which is another reason to add them bit by bit (i.e. one at a time, or whisked together and then added little by little).

GREAT-GRANDMOTHER'S LAYER CAKE

A buttery layer cake was standard fare to serve with afternoon tea at my grandmother's house. When it was taken out of the Aga it was cooled on a wire rack by the window in the back kitchen. Thick yellow cream spooned off the top of the milk in the dairy was whipped and, as soon as the cake was cool, it was sandwiched together with homemade jam made from the raspberries picked at the top of the haggard. This is the best layer cake you'll ever taste. And it keeps incredibly well.

When we make a layer to use in the Marie Antoinette summer pudding (see page 509), we choose this one over Mrs. Lamb's because it has more body

· **SERVES ABOUT 8**

9 tablespoons butter
¾ cup plus 2 tablespoons superfine sugar
3 organic eggs
1½ cups all-purpose flour
1 teaspoon baking powder
1 tablespoon milk
superfine sugar, to sprinkle

FOR THE FILLING
1 cup homemade Raspberry Jam or Lemon Curd (see pages 442 and 224)
½ pint whipped cream

2 x 7in sponge cake pans

Preheat the oven to 375°F.

Grease the pan with melted butter, dust with flour, and line the base of each with a round of parchment paper.

Whip the butter and gradually add the superfine sugar, whisking until soft and light and quite pale in color. Add the eggs one at a time and whisk well between each addition. Sift the flour and baking powder together and stir in gradually. Mix together lightly and add the milk to moisten.

Divide the mixture evenly between the prepared pans, hollowing it slightly in the center. Bake for 20–25 minutes. The cake will shrink in slightly from the edge of the pans when cooked and the center should feel the same texture as the edge. Alternatively, a wooden skewer should come out clean when put into the center of the cake. Turn out onto a wire rack; leave to cool.

Sandwich together with homemade raspberry jam or lemon curd and whipped cream.

Sprinkle with sifted superfine sugar and serve on an old fashioned plate with a paper doily.

AUNT FLORENCE'S ORANGE CAKE

When my Aunt Florence brings a present of this delicious cake in a pan, lots of people suddenly emerge out of the woodwork pleading for a slice. It was chosen to celebrate the anniversary of the European parliament ·
SERVES ABOUT 8–10

1 cup butter
1 cup superfine sugar
finely grated zest of 1 organic orange
4 organic eggs
2 cups all-purpose flour
1 teaspoon baking powder
1 tablespoon freshly squeezed orange juice
1 or 2 pieces orange Candied Peel (see page 458), optional

FOR THE ORANGE BUTTERCREAM
8 tablespoons butter
1¾ cups confectioners' sugar
finely grated zest of 1 organic orange
1 tablespoon freshly squeezed orange juice

FOR THE ORANGE GLACÉ ICING
juice of 1 orange
2½ cups confectioners' sugar

2 x 8in round cake pans OR 1 x round cake pan 11in diameter and 2in deep

Preheat the oven to 350°F.

Grease and flour the cake pan or pans. Line the base of each with parchment paper.

Whip the butter and gradually add the superfine sugar. Whisk until soft and light and quite pale. Add the orange zest. Add the eggs one at a time, whisking well between each addition.

Sift the flour and baking powder together and stir in gradually. Mix lightly, then stir in the orange juice.

Divide the mixture evenly if using two pans, hollowing it slightly in the center. Bake for 35 minutes or until it is cooked. Turn out on to a wire rack and leave to cool.

Meanwhile, make the orange cream. Cream the butter; add the sifted confectioners' sugar and orange zest. Whisk in the orange juice bit by bit.

To make the icing, simply add enough orange juice to the confectioners' sugar to make a spreadable icing.

When the cakes are cold, split each one in two halves and spread with a little filling, then sandwich the two bases together. Spread the icing over the top and sides and decorate the top, if you like, with little diamonds of candied peel.

Variation

SINGLE ORANGE CAKES
We sometimes just ice the top and sides of each layer with orange buttercream and decorate the sides with toasted flaked almonds and the top with candied peel – two cakes for the price of one.

Above: *Great-grandmother's Layer Cake.*

MADEIRA CAKE

This is a delicious cake, provided it is made with good eggs, fine butter, and pure vanilla extract. It was originally made to be nibbled by the ladies as they sipped their Madeira or port wine and is also the base for many other cakes, e.g. Caraway Seed Cake or Cherry Cake (see Variations). Occasionally it might be presented with a piece of candied citron on top · **SERVES ABOUT 8**

¾ **cup soft butter**
¾ **cup superfine sugar**
3 **organic eggs**
½ **teaspoon pure vanilla extract**
2 **cups all-purpose flour**
½ **teaspoon baking powder**
about 1 tablespoon milk or water

**round cake pan 7in wide x
    3in deep**

Preheat the oven to 350°F.

Line the base and side of the cake pan with parchment paper (see page 524).

Whip the butter in a mixing bowl with a wooden spoon, add the sugar, and whisk until light and fluffy. This will give you a lighter, smoother cake than just dumping the sugar in with the butter at the beginning. Better still, cream the butter and sugar with your hand in the time-honored, old-fashioned way; it will cream faster from the heat of your hand and produce a lighter cake.

Whisk the eggs and vanilla extract together and gradually add to the whipped butter and sugar. Whisk well. If preferred, the eggs may be whisked into the mixture one at a time, and a little sifted flour may be added between each addition of egg. Fold in the remainder of the flour, adding the baking powder mixed in with the last addition of the flour. Add a little water or milk if necessary, to make a dropping consistency. Fill into the prepared cake pan.

Bake for about 50–60 minutes, remove from the oven and leave to cool in the pan.

Variations

CARAWAY SEED CAKE
I have a feeling that I hated seed cake as a child and now it's one of my great favorites – it must be an adult taste. My father had a passion for it so it was always an option when we went to visit our relatives in Tipperary on Sunday afternoons. Just add 1 tablespoon fresh caraway seeds to the Madeira cake mixture.

POPPY SEED CAKE
Add ⅓ cup poppy seeds (see Preserving chapter, page 461) to the Madeira cake mixture.

CHERRY CAKE
Prepare the Madeira mixture and after folding in the flour add 4oz of washed, dried, and halved glacé cherries – or better still candied sour cherries. Bake as above.

CHAPEL WINDOW CAKE

Mummy made this cake with us before Christmas every single year when we were little. We loved watching her assemble it. We all gathered round the kitchen table like little birds in a nest, waiting for tidbits and trimmings. It's called a chapel window cake because the different colors in the cake look like stained glass. It's a sticky job and a bit complicated but it was once a real Christmas tradition. As far as I'm concerned, the end result is worth the effort · **SERVES 10–12**

¾ **cup butter**
¾ **cup superfine sugar**
4 **organic eggs**
2 **cups all-purpose flour**
½ **teaspoon baking powder**
zest of ½ organic lemon
¼ **teaspoon pink food coloring and
    a drop of pure almond extract**
¼ **cup cocoa**
tiny bit of milk (optional)
8oz Almond Paste (see page 536)
¾ **pot homemade Raspberry Jam
    (see page 442)**
superfine sugar

**three 7½ x 4½ in pans, lined on
    the base and sides with
    parchment paper**

Preheat the oven to 350°F.

Whip the butter well, add the superfine sugar, and whisk until light and fluffy. Add the eggs one by one, whisking well between each addition. Then stir in the sifted flour and baking powder.

Divide the cake mixture into 3 equal parts. Flavor one part with the lemon zest, the next with almond extract and pink coloring. Stir the cocoa into the last portion and add a few drops of milk if it becomes too thick.

Spoon into the prepared pans and bake for 15–20 minutes. Turn out and leave to cool on a wire rack.

Remove the paper.

Meanwhile, make the almond paste and wrap in parchment paper until needed.

To assemble, trim the edges of the cakes and cut each one lengthwise into three equal strips. Spread a little jam over all of the sides of each strip. Assemble the strips into a 3 x 3 block so that the colors are mixed up. Press all the pieces firmly together and trim the edges if necessary to ensure a uniform shape.

Sprinkle a little sugar on the countertop. Roll out the almond paste to a thickness of a scant ¼in. Brush the base of the cake with a little more jam. Lay it on top of the almond paste. Brush the sides of the cake with a little more jam. Wrap the paste around the cake. Press the edges together to seal. Smooth the surface with a palette knife if necessary. Score the top into a diamond pattern, pinch the edges, and dredge with sugar.

NOTE: if you follow the instructions above, the two ends of the cake are left un-iced, so you can see the "chapel window." However, if you want to seal the cake entirely so it will keep for longer, roll out thinly an extra 4oz of almond paste and seal the ends. If you can resist, it keeps perfectly for 4–5 weeks.

COFFEE CAKE

This is a splendid recipe for an old-fashioned coffee cake – the sort Mummy made – and we still make it regularly. Everyone loves it. I'm a real purist about using extract rather than essence in the case of vanilla, but in this cake,

I prefer coffee essence (which is actually mostly chicory) to real coffee ·
SERVES 10–12

1 cup soft butter
1 cup plus 2 tablespoons superfine sugar
4 organic eggs
2 cups all-purpose flour, preferably unbleached
1 teaspoon baking powder
scant 2 tablespoons Irel or Camp coffee essence

FOR THE COFFEE BUTTERCREAM
4 tablespoons butter
1 cup confectioners' sugar, sifted
1–2 teaspoons Irel or Camp coffee essence

FOR THE COFFEE ICING
1lb confectioners' sugar
scant 2 tablespoons Irel or Camp coffee essence
about 4 tablespoons boiling water

TO DECORATE
toasted hazelnuts or chocolate-covered coffee beans

2 x 8in round cake pans

Preheat the oven to 350°F.

Line the base of the pans with circles of parchment paper. Brush the bottom and sides with melted butter and dust lightly with flour.

Beat the soft butter with a wooden spoon, add the sugar, and whisk until pale in color and light in texture. Whisk the eggs. Add to the mixture, bit by bit, whisking well between each addition.

Sift the flour with the baking powder and stir gently into the cake mixture. Finally, add in the coffee essence and mix thoroughly.

Divide the mixture evenly between the prepared cake pans and bake for 30 minutes. When the cakes are cooked, the center will be firm and springy and the edges will have shrunk from the sides of the pans. Leave to rest in the pans for a few minutes before turning out onto a wire rack. Remove the parchment paper from the base, then flip over so the top of the cakes don't get marked by the wire rack. Leave the cakes to cool on the wire rack.

To make the coffee buttercream, whisk the butter with the sifted confectioners' sugar and add the coffee essence. Continue to whisk until light and fluffy.

To make the coffee icing, sift the confectioners' sugar and put into a bowl. Add coffee essence and enough boiling water to make it the consistency of a thick cream.

When cold, sandwich together the bases of the cakes with the coffee buttercream and ice the top with the coffee icing. Decorate with the toasted hazelnuts or chocolate-covered coffee beans.

Variations
COFFEE BUTTERCREAM ICING
If you would prefer to ice the cake with Coffee Butter Cream, use 1 cup butter, 1lb confectioners' sugar and 1–2 tablespoons of Irel or Camp coffee essence and make as above.

TWO CAKES IN ONE
Ice and decorate each layer separately with coffee buttercream. Then decorate the sides with toasted flaked almonds or toasted coconut. This will result in smaller slices – less guilt!

LEMON CORNMEAL CAKE WITH LEMON CURD AND SOUR CREAM

This is a delicious moist and fresh-tasting cake that keeps really well. It is Californian in origin and is great served with afternoon tea or as a dessert served with a few fresh summer berries and a blob of sour cream. If you want to turn this into a gluten-free cake, simply use gluten-free baking powder · **SERVES 8-10**

1 cup butter, softened
1 cup plus 2 tablespoons superfine sugar
1½ cups ground almonds
1 teaspoon pure vanilla extract
3 organic eggs
grated zest of 2 unwaxed, washed lemons, and juice of 1 lemon
1 cup fine cornmeal or polenta
1 teaspoon baking powder
pinch of salt
½–1 pot homemade Lemon Curd (see page 224)
softly whipped cream or crème fraîche, to serve

1 x 9in spring form cake pan

Preheat the oven to 325°F.

Brush the cake pan with a little melted butter and flour the pan with rice flour. Put a round of parchment paper into the base of the pan.

In a large mixing bowl, whip the butter until pale and soft. Add the sugar and beat until light and creamy. Stir in the ground almonds and vanilla extract. Add the eggs, a little at a time, whisking thoroughly each time.

Fold in the lemon zest and lemon juice, cornmeal, baking powder, and salt.

Pour the mixture into the prepared cake pan and bake for about 50 minutes, until deep golden in color and when a skewer comes out clean. Leave to cool on a wire rack.

Meanwhile, make the lemon curd filling.

Split the cake in half with a sharp serrated knife, spread with a little lemon curd and sandwich the cake together. Spread a little more on top or dredge with confectioners' sugar.

Serve cut into slices with a blob of softly whipped cream or sour cream.

Cupcakes

Even people who don't do much in the way of baking can often be tempted to make a few little cupcakes, also known as fairy cakes or queen cakes. From one simple recipe there is a myriad of variations.

BASIC MIXTURE FOR CUPCAKES

Once you've made your cupcakes you can have fun icing and decorating, and putting twiddles and bows and whatever else on top! People used to make these laboriously, using the creaming method, but I now shoot the whole lot into a food processor, process it for 4–5 seconds, and bake in the usual way. It may not be a forgotten skill, but I don't see any virtue in getting blisters on your hands from creaming when this gives a very good result · **MAKES 12 BUNS**

8 tablespoons soft butter
½ cup superfine sugar
2 organic eggs
½ teaspoon pure vanilla extract or other chosen flavoring
1⅓ cups all-purpose flour
1 teaspoon baking powder
1 tablespoon milk or water
¼ cup golden raisins, cherries, or chocolate chips (optional)

1 muffin tray with paper liners

Preheat the oven to 425°F.

Whip the butter until really soft. Add the sugar and use a wooden spoon to beat until pale and creamy. Whisk the eggs with the vanilla extract or other flavoring and add the mixture, little by little, to the butter and sugar, beating well between each addition. Stir in the sifted flour and baking powder, adding a little milk or water if necessary, until you have a mixture that drops off the spoon easily. If adding golden raisins, cherries, or chocolate chips, now is the time.

Put into greased and floured bun trays or liners and bake for about 10 minutes. As soon as they begin to rise, reduce the temperature to 375°F. Bake for another 10 minutes or until golden. Leave to cool on a wire rack and decorate as desired.

Variations for cupcakes once baked:

There are many other possibilities, all one needs is a little imagination and some restraint!

BUTTERFLY CUPCAKES

Once they are baked, cut the rounded top off the cupcakes. Cut this piece in half and keep aside. Meanwhile, put a little homemade Raspberry Jam (see page 442) and a blob of cream onto the bottom part of the cupcake. Replace the two pieces, arranging them like little wings. Dredge with confectioners' sugar and serve immediately.

COCONUT CUPCAKES

Paint the top of the cupcakes with redcurrant jelly or Raspberry Jam (see page 442) and then dip into desiccated coconut.

ICED CUPCAKES

Make a little water icing or lemon, orange, or chocolate icing (see below) or Coffee Icing (see page 531) and ice the cupcakes. Decorate appropriately – for example, use half-cherries or crystallized primroses, violet or rose petals (see page 32) and leaves of angelica on white icing. If you don't have your own crystallized violets or rose petals, you can always use shop-bought ones instead. Or try a

shelled walnut half on chocolate or coffee icing, and so on. Silver dragees, sprinkles, jelly beans, and M&Ms can also be used for decoration.

GLACÉ ICING

This is the simplest way to make sparkling white glacé icing, also known as water icing.

2 cups confectioners' sugar

Sift the confectioners' sugar into a bowl and add 3 tablespoons of boiling water. Mix together until smooth.

LEMON GLACÉ ICING

The lemon juice and zest cut the sweetness and result in an off-white icing.

2 cups confectioners' sugar
finely grated zest of 1 organic lemon
about 3 tablespoons freshly squeezed lemon juice

Sift the confectioners' sugar into a mixing bowl. Grate the lemon zest over it. Add the strained lemon juice and stir to combine. Use to ice the cupcakes and decorate with crystallized lemon peel.

Variation

ORANGE GLACÉ ICING

As above, but substitute orange zest and juice for lemon. Decorate with candied orange peel.

HOW TO TELL WHEN A CAKE IS DONE

When the cooking time is nearly up, press down gently on the cake near the edge with your index finger. Note the texture. Then press in the center: both should feel the same. Insert a wooden skewer into the center of the cake: if it comes out clean the cake is ready. If it is even a little sticky the cake needs to cook for longer. When the cake is fully cooked you'll notice it will have shrunk a little from the edges of the pan.

DARK CHOCOLATE ICING

Glossy and delicious: great for éclairs.

1½ cups confectioners' sugar
½ cup unsweetened cocoa powder
6 tablespoons butter
½ cup superfine sugar

Sift the confectioners' sugar, and cocoa into a mixing bowl. Put the butter, sugar, and ¼ cup of water into a saucepan. Stir over a low heat until the sugar has dissolved and the butter melted. Bring just to a boil, then draw off the heat and pour at once into the dry ingredients. Beat with a wooden spoon until smooth and glossy; it will thicken as it cools.

Molten Method

Cakes made by the molten method involve melting fat and combining this with liquid such as molasses or corn syrup. Before it is cooked, the consistency of the cake is similar to a thick batter. Because the fat is melted in them and syrup or treacle is a main ingredient, these cakes have a dense and tacky texture.

GINGERBREAD

In Ireland, we make gingerbread into a loaf, like bread, and cut it into thick slices that we butter. This one is particularly good when it's fresh, so eat it quickly! Alternatively, you can bake in a square pan for less time, about 40–45 minutes, and serve cut into squares with a blob of cold apple sauce and cream or with crystallized ginger cream · **MAKES 1 LOAF**

2 **cups all-purpose flour**
¼ **teaspoon salt**
¾ **teaspoon ground ginger**
1 **teaspoon baking powder**
¼ **teaspoon baking soda**
½ **cup packed brown sugar**
6 **tablespoons butter, cut into cubes**
½ **cup molasses**
½ **cup milk**
½ **large or 1 very small organic egg**
¼ **cup golden raisins**
2 **tablespoons chopped crystallized ginger (optional)**

Opposite: *Tea party in the garden.*

9 x 5 x 2in loaf pan, lined with parchment paper (see page 524) OR 9in square pan, 3in deep

Preheat the oven to 350°F.

Sift the flour, salt, ginger, baking powder, and baking soda together in a large bowl.

Gently warm the brown sugar with the cubed butter and molasses. Add the milk. Leave to cool a little and stir into the dry ingredients, ensuring there are no little lumps of flour left (I use a whisk for this). Add the whisked egg, golden raisins and crystallized ginger, if using. Mix very thoroughly and bake for about 1 hour or until a wooden skewer inserted into the center comes out clean, then leave to cool in the pan.

ANGELICA AND MACAROON CAKE

If you make your own candied angelica (see page 458), which I urge you to do, this gives you an opportunity to use it up in this unusual fruitcake. I sometimes use the same macaroon topping on a Madeira Cake (see page 530) · **SERVES 8–10**

8 **tablespoons butter**
½ **cup superfine sugar**
1 **organic egg yolk (use the white for the topping) plus 2 organic eggs**
1⅓ **cups all-purpose flour**
¼ **cup ground almonds**
½ **cup candied angelica**
½ **cup golden raisins**
¼ **cup raisins**
¼ **cup currants**
⅓ **cup slivered almonds**

1 **organic egg white**
⅔ **cup superfine sugar**
½ **cup ground almonds**
a few drops of pure almond extract

7in round pan, lined with parchment paper (see page 524)

Whip the butter, add the sugar, and beat until light and fluffy before adding the egg yolk and then the eggs, one at a time. Beat well between each addition. Stir in the flour and ground almonds, add the chopped angelica, raisins, and currants and mix well. Turn into the lined pan and smooth the top.

Preheat the oven to 350°F.

Prepare the macaroon topping. Whisk the egg white until just fluffy, then fold in the sugar, ground almonds, and a couple of drops of almond extract. Spread evenly over the top of the cake. Sprinkle with the flaked almonds. Cover with a sheet of aluminum foil and bake for 1½ hours. Then remove the foil and continue to cook for a further 20–30 minutes.

DARINA ALLEN'S ICED CHRISTMAS CAKE

This makes a moist cake which keeps very well. It can either be made months ahead or, if you are frenetically busy then it will still be delish even if made just a few days before Christmas – believe me I know! · SERVES ABOUT 40

½ **cup real glacé cherries**
¼ **cup whole almonds**
1½ **cups best-quality golden raisins**
1½ **cups best-quality currants**
1½ **cups best-quality raisins**
4oz **homemade Candied Peel**
    (see page 458)
⅓ **cup ground almonds**
zest of 1 organic unwaxed lemon
zest of 1 organic unwaxed orange
⅓ **cup Irish whiskey**
1 **cup butter**
1 **cup packed brown sugar**
    or golden baker's sugar
6 **organic eggs**
2⅔ **cups all-purpose flour**
1 **teaspoon mixed spice**
1 **large or 2 small cooking apples,**
    grated

Line the base and sides of a 9in round, or 8in square pan with a double thickness of parchment paper. Then tie a double layer of aluminum foil around the outside of the pan. Have a sheet of aluminum foil or parchment paper to lay on top of the pan during cooking.

Wash the cherries and dry them gently. Cut in two or four as desired. Blanch the almonds in boiling water for 1–2 minutes, then rub off the skins and chop them finely. Mix the dried fruit, nuts, ground almonds,

and grated orange and lemon zest. Add about half of the whiskey and leave for 1 hour to macerate.

Preheat the oven to 325°F.

Whip the butter until very soft. Add the sugar and beat until light and fluffy. Whisk the eggs and add in bit by bit, beating well between each addition so that the mixture doesn't curdle. Mix the mixed spice with the flour and stir gently into the butter mixture. Add the grated cooking apple to the plumped up fruit and stir into the butter mixture gently but thoroughly (don't beat the mixture again or you will toughen the cake).

Put the mixture into the prepared cake pan. Make a slight hollow in the center, dip your hand in water, and pat it over the surface of the cake: this will ensure that the top is smooth when cooked.

Now lay a double sheet of aluminum foil on top of the cake to protect the surface from the direct heat. Bake for 1 hour. Then reduce the heat to 300°F and bake for a further 2½ hours, until cooked; test in the center with a wooden skewer – it should come out completely clean. Pour the remainder of the whiskey over the cake and leave it to cool in the pan.

Next day, remove the cake from the pan. Do not remove the lining paper but wrap the cake in some extra parchment paper and aluminum foil until required.

Store in a cool, dry place; the longer the cake is stored the more mature it will be.

ALMOND PASTE AND CAKE ICING

I ice the Christmas cake above with almond icing and decorate it with heart shapes made from the almond paste. Then I brush it with whisked egg yolk and pop it in the oven – simply delicious! · SERVES ABOUT 40

1lb **golden baker's sugar**
1lb **ground almonds**
2 **small organic eggs**
2 **tablespoons Irish whiskey**
a drop of pure almond extract

FOR BRUSHING ON THE CAKE
1 **organic egg white, lightly**
    whisked, or sieved apricot jam
    (see page 448)

FOR THE FONDANT ICING
1 **packet fondant (1lb)**

Sift the sugar and mix with the ground almonds. Whisk the eggs, add the whiskey and 1 drop of almond extract, then add to the other ingredients and mix to a stiff paste. (You may not need all of the egg).

Sprinkle the countertop with confectioners' sugar, turn out the almond paste, and work lightly until smooth.

Remove the paper from the cake. To make life easier for yourself, put a sheet of parchment paper onto the countertop and dust with some confectioners' sugar. Take about half the almond paste and roll it out on the paper: it should be a little less than ½in thick.

Paint the top of the cake with the egg white or apricot jam and put the cake, sticky-side down, onto the almond paste. Give the cake a thump to ensure it sticks and then cut around the edge. If the cake is a little round-shouldered, cut the almond paste a little larger; pull away the extra bits and keep for later to make hearts or holly leaves. Use an offset spatula to press the extra almond paste in against the top of the cake and fill any gaps. Then slide a knife underneath the cake or, better still, underneath the paper and turn the cake the right way up. Peel off the parchment paper.

Then roll out 2 long strips of almond paste: trim an edge to the height of the cake with a offset spatula. Paint both the cake and the almond paste lightly with egg white or apricot jam. Then press the strip against the sides of the cake: do not overlap or there will be a bulge with the uneven edge upwards. Trim the excess almond paste with a long-bladed knife and keep for decoration and to make almond cookies. Use a straight-sided water glass to even the edges and smooth the join. Then rub the cake well with your hand to ensure a nice flat surface.

Leave in a cool, dry place for a few days to allow the almond paste to dry out; otherwise the oil in the almonds will seep through the fondant icing.

To fondant ice: sprinkle a little confectioners' sugar onto the countertop. Roll out the sheet of fondant to a thickness of a scant ¼in. Paint the cake with egg white or apricot jam, then gently lift the sheet of icing and lay it over the top of the cake so it drapes evenly over the sides.

Press out any air bubbles with your hands, then trim the base. Decorate as you wish. We use a little posy of winter leaves and berries including crab apples, elderberries, rosemary, old man's beard, and viburnum.

That's just one option. You could also add simple shapes stamped out of the remaining fondant icing – stars, holly leaves, Santas – to produce an impressive result. If you are really creative, the fondant may be colored using edible food coloring and then you and all the family can really have fun!

Variation

TOASTED ALMOND CHRISTMAS CAKE

If you'd rather not have fondant icing, the almond paste can be toasted and will keep just as well and be irresistible to nibble. Roll out the remainder of the almond paste to about ¼in thick. Stamp out star shapes, paint the whole surface of the cake with whisked egg yolk and stick the star shapes at intervals around the sides of the cake and on top. Brush these with egg yolk also.

Preheat the oven to 425°F.

Carefully lift the cake onto a baking tray and bake for 15–20 minutes or until just slightly toasted. Remove from the oven, leave to cool, and then transfer onto a cake stand.

Decorate with sprigs of holly and a dusting of confectioners' sugar, or you may feel that holly leaves and berries made of almond paste would be more appropriate for Christmas!

IRISH PORTER CAKE

The porter, be it Guinness or Murphy, plumps up the fruit and gives it a very distinctive taste. If you can manage to hide it away, this cake keeps really well

· **SERVES ABOUT 20**

1 cup butter
1 cup plus 2 tablespoons golden bakers' sugar
1 cup stout (**Guinness or Murphy**)
zest of 1 orange
1 cup golden raisins
1 cup raisins
½ cup mixed peel
1lb all-purpose flour
1 teaspoon baking soda
2 teaspoons mixed spice
½ cup cherries, halved
3 organic eggs

9in round pan, lined with parchment paper (see page 524)

Preheat the oven to 350°F.

Melt the butter, sugar, and stout in a saucepan. Add the orange zest and the fruit and peel (except the cherries). Bring the mixture to a boil for 3–4 minutes, stirring frequently. Remove from the heat and leave to cool until it is lukewarm.

Sift the flour, baking soda, and mixed spice into a mixing bowl. Add the fruit mixture to the flour and add the cherries. Whisk the eggs; add them gradually, mixing evenly through the mixture.

Bake in the oven for about 1 hour and 10 minutes. If you wish, when the cake is cooked, you can pour 4 tablespoons of stout over it. Keep for 2–3 days before cutting.

BOILED FRUITCAKE

Like the Barmbrack that follows, this requires no egg. It's an old Irish recipe made by a very unorthodox method: boiling the fruit. Doing this plumps it up. This fruitcake keeps well in an airtight container · SERVES 8–10

½ cup golden raisins
¼ cup raisins
2 tablespoons currants
1oz Candied Peel (see page 458)
6 tablespoons butter
½ cup superfine sugar
2 cups all-purpose flour
¼ teaspoon salt
2 teaspoons baking powder
½ teaspoon or more mixed spice
1 teaspoon baking soda

6½ x 3in cake pan, lined with
    parchment paper (see
    page 524)

Preheat the oven to 350°F.

Put the dried fruit, candied peel, butter, and sugar into a saucepan with ½ cup water. Bring to a boil and simmer for 10 minutes over gentle heat, stirring occasionally. Leave to cool.

Sift the flour, salt, baking powder, and mixed spice into a bowl. Dissolve the baking soda in 1 tablespoon of water. Stir the baking soda into the fruit mixture and then combine the wet and dry mixtures. Stir well but don't beat it or you'll toughen the cake.

Pour into the lined cake pan and bake for about 1¼ hours. Leave to cool in the pan.

IRISH TEA BARMBRACK

This is a more modern version of barmbrack, now commonly called a tea brack because the dried fruit is soaked in tea overnight to plump it up (rather than boiled as in the recipe at left). This little gem of a recipe is much easier to make at home than the Halloween Barmbrack (see page 547). Even though it is a very rich bread, in Ireland it is traditionally served sliced and buttered · YIELDS ABOUT 12 SLICES (EAT THE CRUSTS, TOO!)

½ cup golden raisins
½ cup raisins
½ cup currants
¼ cup natural glacé cherries,
    halved or quartered
1 cup hot tea
1 organic egg, whisked
1 cup packed brown sugar
2 cups self-rising flour
1 teaspoon mixed spice
2oz homemade Candied Peel
    (see page 458)

1lb loaf pan – 5 x 8in
    OR 3 small loaf pans 6 x 3in

Put the dried fruit and cherries into a bowl. Cover with the hot tea and leave to plump up overnight.

Next day, line the loaf pan with parchment paper (see page 524).

Preheat the oven to 350°F.

Add the whisked egg, sugar, flour, and mixed spice to the fruit and tea mixture. Stir well. Put the mixture into the prepared loaf pan. Cook for about 1½ hours or until a wooden skewer comes out clean.

Leave to cool on a wire rack. Keeps well in an airtight container.

Rubbing-in Method

The following recipes are all made by the rubbing-in method, which means that you rub the butter into the flour with your fingertips – giving you a different texture. Cakes made this way don't keep as long as cakes made using the creaming method, but they are delicious anyway.

MUMMY'S SWEET WHITE SCONES

My mother gave me this recipe for the scones that delighted and comforted me as a child. I have evocative memories of a big baking pan of golden scones coming out of the oven as we raced in from school. My brothers and I argued over the sugary tops – nothing's changed – they're still my favorite. This recipe was in my first Simply Delicious *book as well as some of my other books, and every year zillions of people tell me they make them regularly* · MAKES 18–20 SCONES (USING A 3IN CUTTER)

2lb all-purpose flour
pinch of salt
3 heaping teaspoons baking
    powder
¼ cup superfine sugar
¾ cup butter
3 organic eggs
about 1½ cups whole milk, to mix

FOR THE EGG WASH
1 organic egg
2 teaspoons whole milk

FOR THE CRUNCHY TOPS
¼ cup granulated sugar

TO SERVE
homemade Raspberry Jam (see page 442)
whipped or clotted cream

Preheat the oven to 475°F.

Sift the flour into a large wide bowl, add the salt, baking powder, and sugar. Mix these dry ingredients thoroughly with your hands, lifting up to incorporate air.

Cut the butter into cubes, toss well in the flour mixture, and then use the tips of your fingers to rub in the butter until it resembles large flakes. Make a well in the center. Whisk the eggs with the milk and pour all at once into the center of the mixture. With the fingers of your dominant hand outstretched and stiff, mix in a full circular movement from the center to the outside of the bowl. This takes just seconds and, hey presto, the scone dough is made.

Sprinkle some flour onto the countertop. Turn out the dough onto the floured board. Scrape the dough off your fingers, then wash and dry your hands. Tidy around the edges of the dough, flip it over, and roll or pat it gently into a round about 1in thick. Then stamp into scones with a cutter or knife.

TO MAKE EGG WASH: whisk 1 organic egg thoroughly with 2 teaspoons of milk. This is brushed over the scones to help them brown in the oven.

Brush the tops with the egg wash and dip only the tops in granulated sugar. Put onto a baking pan. Gently gather the extra pieces of dough together, flatten, and repeat as above.

Bake for 10–12 minutes or until golden brown on top. Leave to cool on a wire rack. Split in half and serve with homemade raspberry jam and a blob of whipped or clotted cream. Scones are best served freshly baked.

PRACTICAL TIPS: scone mixture may be prepared in advance – even the day before. Butter may be rubbed in but do not add the rising agent or liquid until just before baking.

Leftover scones may be frozen or made into scone bread crumbs to add into sweet dishes and some cakes.

Variation
Instead of cutting the dough into scones, roll it into a rectangle ¾ in thick and then slather it with orange butter cream (see page 528), Seville Orange Marmalade (see page 454), chocolate-hazelnut spread, or Christmas Mincemeat (see page 512). Then roll it up and cut it into 1in pieces. They take about the same amount of time to bake as the scones but spread out much more, so allow plenty of space on your baking pan.

DRIPPING CAKE

In an old handwritten cookbook of my grandmother's, this cake is described as a well-keeping cake suitable for lunch or country teas. It's a very good old-fashioned fruitcake ·
SERVES ABOUT 12

1lb all-purpose flour
pinch of salt
1½ cups diced beef dripping (see page 177)
¼ teaspoon freshly grated nutmeg
¾ cup plus 2 tablespoons superfine sugar
2oz Candied Peel (see page 458), chopped
½ cup raisins
½ cup golden raisins
grated zest of 1 organic lemon or orange
2 organic eggs
1 cup whole milk
1 tablespoon molasses
1 teaspoon baking soda

8in round cake pan, lined

Preheat the oven to 325°F.

Sift the flour and salt into a bowl. Add the dripping and rub in until the mixture resembles fine bread crumbs. Add the nutmeg, sugar, candied peel, dried fruit, and lemon or orange zest. Whisk the eggs with ¾ cup of the milk. Add to the dry ingredients to make a stiffish mixture. Warm the rest of the milk, add the molasses and baking soda, add to the bowl, and mix well.

Turn the mixture into a lined cake pan. Bake for 1¾ hours. Leave to cool and then wrap in parchment paper and aluminum foil.

SEVILLE ORANGE
MARMALADE CAKE

*I love marmalade and am always
looking for ways to sneak it into other
things, like scones, muffins, tarts, and
bread and butter pudding, ice cream...
Here's just one example of that. When
fresh out of the oven, this cake makes a
gorgeous dessert with a blob of sour
cream, but it also keeps well ·*
SERVES 8–10

3 cups self-rising flour
pinch of salt
⅔ cup butter
¾ cup superfine sugar
4 tablespoons Seville Orange
 Marmalade (see page 454), the
 peel chopped; plus 2–3 extra
 tablespoons for the topping
2 organic eggs, lightly beaten
5 tablespoons whole milk
confectioners' sugar, for dusting

6½ x 3in cake pan, lined with
 parchment paper (see
 page 524)

Preheat the oven to 350°F.

Sift the flour and salt into a bowl,
rub in the butter, and add the sugar.
Make a well in the center, add the
4 tablespoons marmalade and the
eggs, and mix to a softish
consistency with the milk.

Put into the cake pan and bake
for about 1¼ hours. Then remove
from the oven and leave to cool on
a wire tray. Generously paint the top
with marmalade and dust with
confectioners' sugar. Serve with a
blob of sour cream or as it is with a
cup of tea or coffee.

RASPBERRY BUNS

*Raspberry buns just have to be
included in this collection. As far as
I can remember, they were the very first
thing I helped my Auntie Florence to
bake. My grandchildren love filling the
holes with jam, just as I did ·*
MAKES ABOUT 10

1½ cups self-rising flour and
 ¼ cup ground rice
 OR 2 cups self-rising flour
⅓ cup superfine sugar
6 tablespoons butter, diced
1 organic egg
1 tablespoon whole milk
homemade Raspberry Jam (see
 page 442)
egg wash
superfine sugar, to sprinkle

Preheat the oven to 425°F.

Put the flour and ground rice,
if using, into a bowl and add the
sugar. Add the diced butter to the
bowl and toss it in the flour. Then
rub it into the dry ingredients with
the tips of your fingers until the
mixture resembles fine bread
crumbs.

Whisk the egg with the milk
and then use a fork to mix it with
the dry ingredients until you have a
softish dough.

Divide the mixture in two, roll
each half into a thick rope and then
divide each into 5 pieces. Form each
piece into a round, dip your thumb
in flour and make an indentation in
the center of each bun.

Drop a little spoonful of
raspberry jam into the hole, then
pinch the edges of dough together
to cover the jam.

Transfer to a baking tray, brush
the top of each raspberry bun with
egg wash, and bake for 10–12
minutes. Transfer to a wire rack,
sprinkle with sugar, and eat while
nice and fresh.

FAT RASCALS

*This recipe was given to me by a
Yorkshire lady who remembers enjoying
these as a child. The name is intriguing,
but I have no idea where it comes from
– neither does she ·* **MAKES 10**

2 cups all-purpose flour
8 tablespoons butter
⅛ cup packed brown sugar
¼ cup currants
1 teaspoon baking powder
pinch of salt
whole milk, to mix
granulated sugar, to coat

Preheat the oven to 400°F.

Put the flour in a bowl. Rub in
the butter. Add the brown sugar,
currants, baking powder, and a
pinch of salt. Then bind with
enough milk to make a firm dough.

Dust the countertop with flour.
Roll out the dough to a ½in
thickness or stamp into rounds with
the top of a glass or a 2in cookie
cutter. Dip the tops in granulated
sugar. Bake for 20 minutes and
eat fresh.

Opposite: *Seville Orange
Marmalade Cake.*

PASTRY SHELLS

When we were little, several times a year Mummy would get an invitation to bring us all to afternoon tea. This was an occasion of great excitement and something we looked forward to. One of our favorite treats was to be invited to Granny Nicholson's, a friend of the family. Her grandchildren were our age. We'd all be dressed up for the occasion: I'd wear my best smocked dress and a little angora bolero, and the boys would be all washed and brushed. About five or six of us would be piled into the old Ford Zodiac car. On the way, Mummy would entreat us to behave and be polite.

These afternoon teas were very formal occasions with a strict protocol. We were to be seen and not heard. When we arrived we would shake hands and then run out to play with Granny Nicholson's grandchildren while the grown-ups chatted. When we were called in to tea – we had been warned, no matter how hungry we were, not to dash into the house – we had to walk in decorously. The long mahogany table in the dining room would be laid for tea, covered with a starched white linen cloth, laden with china cups and lots of silverware. You waited until you were offered something and first passed plates to other guests. We started with bread and butter and moved on to dainty finger sandwiches. Then came little cakes and pastries and meringues and, finally, we got to have a slice of coffee or chocolate cake. But of all the delicious things, and there were many, our absolute favorites were Granny Nicholson's pastry shells. Over the years I've made many attempts to find the recipe, but by the time I started my search, Granny Nicholson had passed on and nobody knew exactly how she'd made them. It wasn't until recently, when I went through my mother's and grandmother's handwritten cookbooks, that I came across this recipe for pastry shells. The secret behind its fine texture seems to be that it is made with lard ·

MAKES ABOUT 30

2 cups all-purpose flour
½ teaspoon salt
⅔ cup lard (see page 316), chopped
pinch of baking powder

TO SERVE
homemade Raspberry Jam (see page 442)
softly whipped cream

deep-based round muffin pan and 3in cutter

Preheat the oven to 425°F.

Put the flour and salt into a bowl. Rub in the chopped lard until the mixture resembles fine bread crumbs. Add the baking powder and mix to a very stiff dough with about ⅓ cup of cold water.

Roll out to ⅛ in thick and cut into rounds with the cutter. Place the rounds in a muffin pan and prick them all over. Place a small piece of parchment paper on top of the pastry and fill it with baking beans or rice. Bake blind for 10–12 minutes. Remove the beans and paper and bake for another few minutes until the pastry is fully baked. The baking beans can be used time after time.

Leave to cool on a wire rack and fill as desired. I put a small spoonful of raspberry jam and a blob of cream onto each one just before serving.

Variation
The original recipe says you can fill the pastry shells with jam, jelly, or a savory mixture if preferred.

SWEET SHORTCRUST PASTRY

Almost the most versatile of all the pastries and used in several recipes in this book. Use at least 1 part butter to 2 parts flour. The higher the proportion of butter, the more delicious the pastry, but the more difficult it will be to handle ·

MAKES ENOUGH PASTRY TO LINE A 9IN FLAN RING

1½ cups all-purpose flour
6 tablespoons butter
3 tablespoons superfine sugar
1 large organic egg, whisked

Dice the butter and leave to soften at room temperature for 30 minutes.

Sift the flour onto a countertop and rub in the butter. Add the sugar.

Make a well in the center and break in the egg, adding a little water if necessary. Use your fingertips to rub in, pulling in more flour mixture from the outside as you work. Knead with the heel of your hand, making three turns. You should end up with a silky smooth ball of dough. Wrap in plastic wrap and leave in the fridge for at least 1 hour before using. It will keep for a week in the fridge and also freezes well.

JAM TARTS AND STARLETS

You can make jam tarts from start to finish, but I usually make these with the trimmings when I'm making other pies and tarts, I can't bear to waste any scraps. If there are children around, get them involved, they love making jam tarts · **MAKES ABOUT 36**

Sweet Shortcrust Pastry (see previous recipe) OR Break all the Rules Shortcrust Pastry (see page 250) OR Shortbread Cookie mixture (see page 548)

homemade jam of your choice or Lemon Curd (see page 224)

1–2 shallow non-stick muffin pans

2½ in round or 3½ in star-shaped cutter

Make the pastry as directed in the recipe. Cover and chill for at least 1 hour; or better still make the pastry the day before.

Preheat the oven to 350°F.

Roll the pastry out thinly to about ⅛ in and stamp into rounds or star shapes. Use to line the muffin pans.

Put a small teaspoon of jam or lemon curd into the tartlets and bake for 14–18 minutes, until the pastry is a pale golden color.

Alternatively, bake the empty tartlets (no need to use beans). Leave them to cool. Fill the centers with a teaspoonful of jam or lemon curd.

BASIC YEAST BUN DOUGH

Many people in Ireland would associate sticky buns with a small chain of Quaker cafés called Bewley's. Originally they were operated on an honor system – a plate of buns was put out on the table and people ate to their heart's content and then (hopefully) paid for everything they'd eaten. The recipe below makes a basic bun dough that can be used to make many variations: doughnuts, bath buns, Chelsea buns, hot-cross buns, and so on.

Baker's or strong flour is higher in gluten than all-purpose flour so it is more suitable for yeast breads and puff and choux pastry.

2 tablespoons active dry yeast
2lb baker's or bread flour
⅓ cup superfine sugar
pinch of salt
¾ cup butter
2 organic eggs, whisked
1–1½ cups lukewarm water

Dissolve the yeast in a little of the tepid water. Sift the flour, sugar, and salt into a bowl. Rub in the butter and then add the whisked eggs. Add the yeast mixture and enough additional water to make a fairly soft dough. Cover and leave to rest for 10 minutes.

Turn out onto a floured cutting board. Knead well, about 5–10 minutes, until the dough becomes firm and springy. It should bounce back when pressed with a finger.

Put into a deep Pyrex bowl, cover with plastic wrap and leave to rise until it doubles in size. Punch down to knock out the air and redistribute the yeast back in contact with the dough. Knead well for 2–3 minutes. Leave to rest for a further 5 minutes, then use and shape as desired.

Bun wash

Put 2 cups water and 1lb sugar into a pan and boil for 2 minutes. Brush over the buns as soon as they come out of the oven to give them a sweet, sticky glaze. This makes a large quantity of bun wash but it keeps very well.

DOUGHNUTS

Homemade doughnuts don't look quite as perfect as the ones you buy in the shops, but they are much more delicious. I can't say they're not as detrimental to the hips, so you shouldn't live on them, but boy they're good from time to time.

Divide the basic yeast bun dough into 16 equal pieces. Shape each piece into a ball and poke a floured forefinger through the center. Spin your finger around in a circle to widen the hole to about ¾ in in diameter. Arrange the rings on a floured kitchen towel or tray, cover with oiled plastic wrap and leave to rise until doubled in size. Heat some good-quality sunflower oil in a deep-fryer to 375°F. Gently slip a few risen doughnuts into the oil. Cook for about a minute on each side, turning them with a slotted spoon until they are evenly brown. Remove and drain on paper towels. Leave to cool slightly.

Mix 1 cup superfine sugar and 3 teaspoons of cinnamon in a wide, shallow bowl. Toss the doughnuts in the cinnamon sugar.

Right: *Chelsea Buns.*

JAM DOUGHNUTS

Another method is to roll the bun dough out to ¼in thick (far easier said than done, it keeps springing back!), cut with a cookie cutter into 3in rounds, and pop a blob of jam in the center. Then, take another 3in round and press the two rounds together, pinching the edges with your fingers so that the jam is trapped inside. Leave to rest. Deep-fry and toss in superfine sugar.

ICED WHIRLS

Divide 1lb of bun dough into 8 equal pieces. Form each piece into a roll and then pull to about 10in long. Roll up from one end and seal with egg wash. Place cut-side upwards on a greased baking pan and leave to rise again until doubled in size. Egg wash and bake for about 15 minutes. Brush the top with bun wash and then ice with Glacé Icing (see page 533).

GLACÉ ICED BUNS

Mix confectioners' sugar with a little boiling water to make a fairly thick icing that can be brushed onto buns.

CHELSEA BUNS

This is a basic recipe for rolled-up buns; once you've mastered this technique, you can vary the fillings according to your fancy · MAKES 16

2½ **lb Basic Yeast Bun Dough**
  (see page 543)
4 **tablespoons melted butter**
½ **cup golden raisins**
4oz **Candied Peel (see page 458)**

¼–⅜ **cup packed brown sugar**
grated zest of 1 organic lemon
1 **teaspoon mixed spice**
  or cinnamon
egg wash
Bun Wash (see page 543)
confectioners' or superfine sugar
  for dusting

Roll the bun dough into a rectangle measuring about 10 x 16in. Brush with half of the cooled, melted butter. Combine the golden raisins, candied peel, brown sugar, lemon zest, and mixed spice or cinnamon in a bowl and mix.

Sprinkle the buttered dough evenly with the fruit mixture. Roll lengthwise into a fairly tight cylinder. Then brush with the remaining melted butter and divide into 12–16 pieces (as many as will fit into whatever size pan you have). Place them cut-side down on a lightly greased 1in deep pan, fairly close together. Egg wash the tops and leave to rise in a warm place until doubled in size. All the buns will be touching each other.

Bake at 425°F for about 15 minutes. Remove from the oven and while still hot, brush with bun wash, and dust with confectioners' or superfine sugar.

BATH BUNS

Bath buns are probably the best known and best loved of all the sticky buns ·
MAKES 16 BUNS

2½ lb Basic Yeast Bun Dough
   (see page 543)
½ cup golden raisins
2oz Candied Peel (see page 458),
   chopped
grated zest of 1 organic lemon
1 organic egg for egg wash
¼ cup sugar nibs or raw sugar
Bun Wash (see page 543)

Knead the golden raisins, candied peel, and lemon zest into the bun dough. Roll into a thick cylinder and break off into 16 equal pieces. Shape each into a round roll and arrange on a lined baking tray. Flatten slightly and brush the tops with egg wash. Dip the tops with nibbed sugar and leave to rise until doubled in size.

Bake at 450°F for 10 minutes.
Brush the tops with bun wash. Leave to cool on a wire rack.

CHERRY BUNS

These are also gorgeous made with sour cherries · **MAKES 16 BUNS**

2½ lb Basic Yeast Bun Dough
   (see page 543)
½ cup or more washed and dried
   natural glacé cherries, halved
   or quartered
Lemon Glacé Icing or plain Glacé
   Icing (see page 533)

Preheat the oven to 450°F.

Line a baking pan with a sheet of parchment paper.

Knead the cherries into the bun dough. Roll into a thick cylinder and break off into 16 equal pieces. Knead each into a round roll and place on the prepared baking tray. Flatten each one slightly and bake for 10 minutes. Leave to cool on a wire rack. When cool, ice with lemon glacé or plain glacé icing.

EASTER TEA RING

Use the Chelsea bun recipe and technique to make this irresistible Easter ring · **SERVES 8-10**

1 quantity Basic Yeast Bun Dough
   (see page 543)
4 tablespoons butter
½ cup superfine sugar
¼ cup raisins
¼ cup golden raisins
¼ cup mixed peel
1 teaspoon ground cinnamon
   (optional)

FOR THE DECORATION
6 tablespoons confectioners' sugar
   for glacé icing
⅓ cup slivered almonds
¼ cup cherries
¼ cup angelica, cut into
   diamonds

Make the bun dough and filling as for Chelsea Buns (see previous page) and roll as directed in the recipe. But instead of cutting the buns, curl the dough around into a ring. Pinch the ends tightly together. Lift carefully onto a lined baking pan.

Cut two-thirds of the way through the ring at 1in intervals with scissors or knife. Twist each cut slightly to expose more filling. Cover with a kitchen towel and leave to rise for 15–20 minutes.

Preheat the oven to 400°F. Then bake until golden brown, for about 25 minutes. Transfer to a wire rack.

Meanwhile, make the glacé icing: mix the confectioners' sugar with enough boiling water (about 2 tablespoons) to make a thickish icing and spread over the top of the Easter ring while it is still warm. Decorate with the nuts, cherries, and diamonds of angelica. Serve while still warm.

STALE CAKE

As with bread, there are plenty of traditions for using up bits of stale cake. We make a summer pudding that uses cake instead of stale sliced bread, and call it Marie Antoinette Summer Pudding (see page 509), which references her famous remark during the French Revolution, "Let them eat cake." Some cakes would have included cake crumbs in the mixture. And you can make a cookie cake out of leftover cookies and melted chocolate (or dried fruit perhaps), mixed together, poured into a cake pan, and cooled.

WALNUT OR PECAN STICKY BUNS

This recipe uses the same kind of technique as the Chelsea buns and should definitely have a government health warning on it. They are totally irresistible · MAKES 9

1 tablespoon dry active yeast
    and ½ cup warm water
1¾lb bread flour
1 tablespoon salt
1⅛ cups warm water
8 tablespoons unsalted butter,
    softened
⅔ cup dark brown sugar
¾ cup pecan nuts or walnuts,
    coarsely chopped
⅓ cup granulated sugar
1 teaspoon ground cinnamon
4 tablespoons unsalted butter,
    softened

9in square cake pan

In a small bowl, dissolve the yeast in warm water and leave for about 5 minutes. In a large, wide bowl mix the flour and salt together. Make a well in the center and pour the yeast into the flour; mix together well to form a dough.

Turn out onto a lightly floured countertop and knead for about 5 minutes. The dough should be quite soft. Cover with a large mixing bowl and leave on the countertop for about 20 minutes to rest.

When rested, gently knead the dough for a further 5 minutes, until it is smooth and shiny. Put the dough into a lightly oiled, large mixing bowl, turning the dough over in the bowl to coat with the oil.

Cover with plastic wrap and leave to rise for about 1½–2 hours or until it has doubled in size.

Meanwhile, melt the 8 tablespoons butter over a low heat and add the brown sugar.

Stir to mix and then take off the heat. Pour this caramel mixture into the cake pan. Tilt the pan a little so the mixture spreads evenly over the base. Sprinkle chopped pecan nuts over the caramel and press them down slightly. Put the pan in a fridge to chill.

Meanwhile, mix the granulated sugar and cinnamon together in a bowl. Set aside.

When the dough has doubled in size, knock it back. Then roll it into a 13 x 10in rectangle. Spread the remaining 4 tablespoons of soft butter evenly over the dough, leaving the top ½in of the dough unbuttered.

Sprinkle the cinnamon sugar evenly over the butter, again leaving the top ½in bare. Starting at the bottom, roll up the dough like a jelly roll. With a metal dough-cutter or knife, divide the roll into 9 equal-sized pieces. Arrange them cut-edge down in the pan. Cover and leave to rise for 1–1½ hours or until it is peeping over the top.

Preheat the oven to 375°F.

Bake for 30–40 minutes or until the buns are golden brown and crusty. Leave to stand in the pan for 5 minutes, then turn out onto a large serving plate. The delicious sticky pecan caramel will spread down over the sides. Scrape out any of the precious remaining caramel from the pan and spoon over the top.

HOT CROSS BUNS

These buns take about three hours to make from start to finish. It may sound like a lengthy process, but much of the time is in the kneading and rising. The end result is so satisfying and delicious it is certainly worth it · MAKES 14

1 tablespoon dry active yeast
¾–1 cup tepid milk
½ cup superfine sugar
1lb bread or baker's flour
6 tablespoons butter
¼ teaspoon cinnamon
¼ teaspoon nutmeg
2–3 teaspoons mixed spice,
    depending how fresh it is
pinch of salt
2 organic eggs
½ cup currants
¼ cup golden raisins
1oz Candied Peel, chopped (see
    page 458)
egg wash made with milk, sugar,
    and 1 organic egg yolk,
    whisked together
Shortcrust Pastry (see page 250)
    OR Liquid Cross (see below)

FOR THE LIQUID CROSS
½ cup all-purpose flour
1 tablespoon melted butter
4–5 tablespoons cold water

Bun Wash (see page 543)

2 heavy baking pans

Dissolve the yeast with 1 tablespoon of the sugar in about ⅛ cup of the tepid milk.

Put the flour into a bowl, rub in the butter, add the cinnamon, nutmeg, mixed spice, a pinch of salt, and the remainder of the sugar. Mix well. Whisk the eggs and add to the remaining milk. Make a well in the center of the flour add the yeast and most of the liquid. Mix to a soft dough, adding a little more milk if necessary.

Cover and leave to rest for 2 or 3 minutes, then knead by hand or in a food mixer, until smooth. Add the currants, golden raisins, and candied peel and continue to knead until the dough is shiny. Cover the bowl and let the dough rise in a warm place until it doubles in size.

Knock back by kneading for 3 or 4 minutes, then rest for a few minutes. Divide the mixture into 14 equal balls. Knead each slightly and shape into buns. Place on a lightly floured pan. Egg wash and leave to rise.

If using shortcrust, arrange a cross of pastry on each one. Leave to rise until double in size. Then egg wash a second time carefully.

We tend to decorate with what we call a "liquid cross." To make this, mix the flour, melted butter, and water together to form a thick liquid. Fill into a paper piping bag and pipe a liquid cross on top on each bun.

Preheat the oven to 425°F.

Bake for 5 minutes, then reduce the heat to 400°F and bake for another 10 minutes or until golden. Brush again with bun wash. Leave to cool on a wire rack. Split into two and serve with butter.

HALLOWEEN BARMBRACK

Everyone in Ireland loves a barmbrack, perhaps because it brings back lots of memories of excitement and games at Halloween. When the barmbrack was cut, everyone waited in anticipation to see what they'd find in their slice: a stick, a pea, a ring, and what it meant for their future. Now they're available in every Irish bakery, but here's a great recipe you can use to make one at home. It keeps for up to a week. If this recipe feels like too much work, make the teabrack (Irish Barmbrack, see page 538), which, after you've plumped up the fruit, takes mere minutes to mix ·

SERVES ABOUT 20

1lb bread or baker's flour
½ teaspoon ground cinnamon
½ teaspoon mixed spice
¼ teaspoon nutmeg
pinch of salt
2 tablespoons butter
1 tablespoon dry active yeast +
  1 teaspoon sugar + 1 teaspoon
  tepid milk
⅓ cup superfine sugar
1 cup tepid milk
1 organic egg, whisked
1 cup golden raisins
½ cup currants
2oz Candied Peel (see page 458),
  chopped

two 5 x 8in loaf pans

Bun Wash (see page 543)

FOR HALLOWEEN
ring, stick, pea, piece of cloth, all
  wrapped in parchment paper

It's a help if all utensils are warm before starting to make barmbrack. Sift the flour, cinnamon, mixed spice, nutmeg, and salt into a bowl. Rub in the butter.

Mix the yeast with 1 teaspoon of sugar and 1 teaspoon of tepid milk and leave for 4–5 minutes, until it becomes creamy and slightly bubbly.

Add the sugar to the flour mixture and mix well. Pour the tepid milk and the egg into the yeast mixture, then add to the flour. Knead well either by hand or in the warmed bowl of an electric mixer at high speed for 5 minutes. The dough should be stiff, but elastic. Fold in the dried fruit and peel, cover with a cloth and leave in a warm place until the dough has doubled in size.

Knock back again for 2–3 minutes. Grease the loaf pans and divide the dough between them. Add the ring, stick, pea, and piece of cloth, tucking them well in and ensure they are hidden by the dough. Cover again and leave to rise for about 30–45 minutes until well puffed up.

Preheat the oven to 350°F.

Bake for about 1 hour or until golden and fully cooked.

Glaze the top with bun wash, put back into the oven for about 2 or 3 minutes. Turn out to cool on a wire tray. When cool, serve cut into thick slices with butter.

Barmbrack keeps well, but if it gets a little stale, try it toasted or in a Bread and Butter Pudding (see page 507).

BALLOONS (NO YEAST)

I'm cheating a little by putting balloons into the yeast buns section – their texture is quite similar to doughnuts but they are much easier to make because no yeast is required. My mother-in-law, Myrtle Allen, made these for her children, and has passed on the recipe to her grandchildren and great-grandchildren. They've also been a favorite of guest children at our daily children's tea at Ballymaloe for over 40 years. They cook into funny little shapes, uneven in texture, which is a lot of fun – use your imagination to decide what they look like! · **MAKES ABOUT 10 BALLOONS**

1¼ **cups all-purpose flour**
2 **teaspoons superfine sugar**
pinch of salt
1 **teaspoon baking powder**
scant 1 cup whole milk
extra superfine sugar, to coat

Sift the dry ingredients into a bowl. Mix to a thick batter (dropping consistency) with milk.

Preheat a deep-fryer to 385°F.

Take a heaping teaspoonful of the mixture and push it gently off with your finger so that it drops in a round ball into the fat. Fry until puffed and golden. Remove and drain. Repeat the process until you have used up all the batter.

Roll the balloons in superfine sugar and serve at once.

Delicious with sweet apple sauce flavored with a little cinnamon, and a bowl of pastry cream for dipping.

Cookies

Cookies are a great way to get kids involved with cooking – they probably won't be quite as enthusiastic about making an Irish stew but little buns or cookies are guaranteed to interest them, especially if they can get involved with the icing and decorating. A little plastic bag of homemade cookies makes the sweetest gift, too, and are so much more personal than flowers (unless you have snipped a bunch in your garden!)

SHORTBREAD COOKIES

If I had to choose one cookie in the book, this would be it – it's probably the most versatile of all, and there are only three ingredients. You can stamp them out into any shape you like, they can be thick or thin, you can vary the cooking time and they're delicious when they're fresh, but they also keep well in a tin for a week or more. They taste like different cookies depending on whether you use salted or unsalted butter (then they taste French). They can accompany either coffee or dessert or you can sandwich them together with a little sweetened cream and summer berries for a three-star dessert.

Watch these cookies really carefully in the oven. Because of the high sugar content, they burn easily. They should be a pale golden color – any darker and they will be more bitter. If they are too pale, however, they will be undercooked and doughy · **MAKES 25**

1⅓ **cups all-purpose flour**
¼ **cup plus 2 tablespoons superfine sugar**

8 **tablespoons butter**
2½**in round, heart- or star-shaped cookie cutter**

Preheat the oven to 350°F.

Put the flour and sugar into a bowl and rub in the butter as for Shortcrust Pastry (see page 250). Gather the mixture together and knead lightly.

Roll out to ¼in thickness. Cut into rounds, heart, or star shapes with a cookie cutter. Bake until pale brown, about 8–15 minutes depending on the thickness of the cookies. Remove and leave to cool on a rack.

GINGER NUTS

Ginger has been popular ever since it was first imported to these islands, and ginger nuts still account for a good chunk of cookie sales. These homemade ones knock the socks off packaged cookies. They'll keep for ages in a tin · **MAKES ABOUT 55**

2¾ **cups all-purpose flour**
¾ **cup granulated sugar**
2 **teaspoons ground ginger**
2 **teaspoons baking soda**
1 **cup corn syrup**
⅔ **cup butter**

Preheat the oven to 350°F.

Sift the dry ingredients together into a bowl. Meanwhile, warm the corn syrup gently. Rub the butter into the dry ingredients. Add the warm syrup and mix well. Roll the mixture into walnut-sized balls and arrange well apart on a baking tray lined with parchment paper. Bake for 15–20 minutes.

Leave on the pan for 2–3 minutes, then lift off with an egg slice and cool on a wire rack.

LANA'S COFFEE AND WALNUT COOKIES

Lana Pringle lives at the other side of our village in an enchanting cottage with a huge open fireplace. She makes all her cakes by hand – each and every bite is truly memorable · **MAKES 8**

1½ **cups all-purpose flour**
6 **tablespoons butter**
¼ **cup superfine sugar**
1 **organic egg, whisked**
8 **fresh walnut halves, to decorate**

FOR THE COFFEE FILLING
2 **tablespoons butter**
½ **cup confectioners' sugar, sifted**
1 **teaspoon coffee essence, preferably Irel**

FOR THE COFFEE ICING
1 **cup confectioners' sugar, sifted**
scant ½ **tablespoon coffee essence, preferably Irel**
about 1 tablespoon boiling water

3½ **in round cutter**

Preheat the oven to 350°.

Sift the flour into a bowl. Rub in the butter, add the superfine sugar, and mix well. Mix the dry ingredients to a stiff dough with the whisked egg.

Turn onto a floured board and roll out to a ⅛ in thickness. Cut into 3½ in rounds.

Bake until golden brown, about 8 minutes. Transfer to a wire rack and leave to cool.

Meanwhile, make the coffee filling and icing. Whip the butter, then add the confectioners' sugar and coffee essence. Continue to whisk until light and fluffy.

To make the icing, put the sifted confectioners' sugar into a bowl. Add coffee essence and enough boiling water to make it the consistency of a very thick cream. Whisk until smooth and glossy.

Sandwich the cookies together with coffee filling and spread a little coffee icing on top. Then decorate each cookie with a walnut half.

DIGESTIVE COOKIES

Homemade digestives keep for ages in a tin, and are a favorite of young and old. These are great with Cheddar cheese · **MAKES ABOUT 45**

1lb **butter**
1 **cup plus 2 tablespoons superfine sugar**
2 **cups all-purpose flour**
¼ **teaspoon baking soda**
1¼lb **organic rolled oats**
extra rolled oats, to roll

egg wash and granulated sugar

3in **round cookie cutter**

Preheat the oven to 350°F.

Whip the butter and sugar until light and fluffy. Sift the flour and baking soda together and gradually add into the butter mixture with the oats.

Turn onto a board sprinkled with oatmeal and roll out to a thickness of ½ in. Cut into 3in rounds with a sharp cutter. Glaze with egg wash and sprinkle with granulated sugar.

Bake until pale and golden, about 20–25 minutes. Leave to cool on a wire rack, then store in a cookie tin or Mason jar.

OATCAKES

These are particularly delicious to eat with Irish farmhouse cheeses and keep well in a cookie tin · **MAKES ABOUT 18**

1½ **cups stoneground oatmeal (we use Macroom)**
½ **cup all-purpose flour**
pinch of baking powder
½ **teaspoon salt**
2 **tablespoons melted lard (see page 316), beef dripping (see page 177) or butter**
boiling water

Preheat the oven to 350°F.

Put the oatmeal, flour, baking powder, and salt into a bowl and mix well. Add the melted fat and enough boiling water to make a firm dough. Sprinkle a little flour and oatmeal onto the countertop. Roll the dough out as thinly as possible. Cut into squares or triangles and arrange on a baking pan or pans.

Bake for 25–30 minutes or until crisp and slightly golden. Alternatively, cook on a griddle over medium heat. Leave to cool on a wire rack.

Tray Bakes

I hate the term "tray bake" with a passion but the following are baked in a tray so I suppose there's no getting away from it. Large and medium-sized jelly roll pans are an essential bit of kitchen kit for baking. These recipes are terrific because you get a whole pan full of cookies that you can share with all and sundry – or squirrel away in a cupboard and eat yourself.

CLASSIC SHORTBREAD

Shortbread must be made with butter. This old family recipe is the classic version, and people always remark on the appealing grittiness of the texture · **MAKES 24–32, DEPENDING ON SIZE**

2¾ **cups all-purpose flour**
½ **cup superfine sugar**
¾ **cup ground rice**
good pinch of salt
scant ¼ **teaspoon baking powder**
1¼ **cups butter, cut into cubes**
Vanilla Sugar (see page 527) or
     superfine sugar for sprinkling

10 x 15in jelly roll pan

Preheat the oven to 350°F.

Sift the dry ingredients into a bowl. Rub in the butter until the whole mixture comes together. (Alternatively, process in a food processor until everything starts to combine.) Spread evenly into the pan and roll the surface flat.

Bake for 20–30 minutes, until pale golden and fully cooked through. Cut into squares or fingers while still hot. If you do this when it's cool, it will crack. Sprinkle with superfine or vanilla sugar and leave to cool in the pan.

FLAPJACKS

These nutritious oatmeal cookies keep very well in a tin. Children love to munch them with a banana. Don't compromise – make them with butter, because the flavor is immeasurably better. This is the recipe that I use when I want to prove to people who swear they can't boil water that they can cook. We often drizzle them with melted chocolate as an extra treat · **MAKES ABOUT 24**

1½ **cups butter**
1 **tablespoon corn syrup**
1 **teaspoon pure vanilla extract**
1 **cup superfine sugar**
1lb **rolled oats**

10 x 15in jelly roll pan

Preheat the oven to 350°F.

Melt the butter, add the corn syrup and vanilla extract, stir in the sugar and oatmeal, and mix well. Spread evenly into the jelly roll pan.

Bake until golden and slightly caramelized, about 30 minutes. Cut into squares while still warm – they will crisp up as they cool.

Variation
OATMEAL AND COCOUT FLAPJACKS
Substitute ½ cup desiccated coconut for ½ cup oatmeal in the above recipe.

RASPBERRY AND COCONUT SLICE

The following three recipes are made on this very simple spongy base, which you can then flavor and ice with whatever you fancy. It's definitely our most versatile "tray bake" (how I hate that phrase) at the school · **MAKES 24**

FOR THE BASE
¾ **cup soft butter**
¾ **cup plus 2 tablespoons superfine**
     sugar
2 **organic eggs**
1½ **cups self-rising flour**

FOR THE ICING
homemade Raspberry Jam (see
     page 442)
unsweetened desiccated coconut

10 x 7in jelly roll pan, well greased

Preheat the oven to 350°F.

Put the butter, sugar, eggs, and flour into a food processor and process for a few seconds to amalgamate. Spread evenly over the base of the pan.

Bake for about 20–25 minutes, until golden brown and well-risen. Leave to cool.

Spread the surface with raspberry jam and sprinkle with desiccated or shaved coconut. Cut into squares. If keeping for a few days, remove the cookies from the pan, unless the pan is coated with teflon. Store in an airtight container, interleaved with parchment paper.

Opposite: *Raspberry and Coconut Slice.*

SPICED ORANGE SQUARES

We use a variety of herb- and spice-flavored syrups to spoon over Madeira cakes and tray bakes with delicious results – a forgotten way of keeping cakes moist while enhancing the flavor · MAKES ABOUT 24

Base from Raspberry and Coconut Slice (see page 550)

FOR THE SPICE SYRUP
juice of 1 orange
juice of half a lemon
¾ cup sugar
2 cloves
1 cinnamon stick

Make the base as per the Raspberry and Coconut Slice on page 550.

While the base is baking, put all the ingredients for the syrup into a little stainless-steel saucepan and bring gently to a boil, stirring until the sugar has dissolved completely. Simmer for 3 minutes.

When the base has cooked but is still warm, spoon half the syrup over it. Leave to cool. If you have excess syrup, use it in cocktails or save it for another time. When cooled, cut into squares and serve with tea or as a dessert with a blob of sour cream.

SUE'S COFFEE AND PECAN SQUARES

One of our teachers, Sue Cullinane, introduced us to this variation on the same sort of theme. It's become a firm favorite and an inspiration for even more variations. The skill here is taking the basic recipe and thinking about how to vary it, given what you find in your pantry. Fresh walnuts or hazelnuts can be substituted for the pecans · MAKES 20

8 tablespoons butter, softened
1 cup muscovado sugar
1⅓ cups self-rising flour
1 teaspoon baking powder
2 organic eggs
1 tablespoon milk
1 tablespoon Irel coffee essence
¼ cup pecans, chopped

FOR THE ICING
4 tablespoons butter
1⅓ cups confectioners' sugar, sifted
1 teaspoon milk
1 teaspoon Irel coffee essence

toasted pecans, coarsely chopped

10 x 7in jelly roll pan, well greased

Preheat the oven 350°F.

Put all the ingredients into a food processor and process for 1–2 minutes to amalgamate. Spread the cake mixture evenly in the pan and smooth the top with an offset spatula. Bake for about 20–25 minutes, until well-risen. Leave to cool in the pan.

Meanwhile, make the icing. Whip the butter, whisk in the sifted confectioners' sugar, add the milk and coffee essence.

As soon as the cake mixture has cooled, spread the icing evenly over the top using an offset spatula.

Sprinkle chopped toasted pecans over the top. Cut into squares and serve.

TOFFEE AND WALNUT SQUARES

This takes a little bit more effort, but you can cook the pastry base ahead. Chopped pecans or slivered almonds are also yummy for a change · MAKES 24

1½ cups all-purpose flour
2 tablespoons superfine sugar
8 tablespoons butter
drop of vanilla extract
1 organic egg yolk or half a whole organic egg, whisked

FOR THE TOPPING
6 tablespoons butter
¼ cup light brown sugar
2 tablespoons honey
¼ cup walnuts
1 tablespoon cream

8 x 12in greased pan

Preheat the oven to 350°F.

Put the flour and sugar into a bowl, rub in the butter, add the vanilla extract, and bind with the egg yolk or enough whisked egg to make a pastry.

Press into a greased pan and roll evenly. Then prick the pastry and bake for 10–15 minutes or until golden.

To make the topping, put the butter, sugar, and honey into a medium saucepan over medium heat. When the butter melts, add the walnuts and continue to cook on a low heat until they are a pale-straw color. Stir in the cream and cook for a few more seconds. Spread this topping over the cooked base and bake until topping is a deep golden-brown color.

Cut into squares when almost cold. This can take anything from 8–20 minutes. depending how well the base is cooked and the length of time the topping ingredients were cooked for.

ALMOND AND APRICOT FINGERS

This is another "tray bake" that involves cooking a pastry base and then adding a couple of extra layers on top. This one has a layer of apricot jam hidden under the fluffy meringue and almond topping · MAKES 24

1½ **cups all-purpose flour**
6 **tablespoons butter**
¼ **cup superfine sugar**
¼ **teaspoon baking powder**
1 **organic egg**
¼ **cup milk**
½ **pot Apricot Jam (see page 448)**
¾ **cup confectioners' sugar**
⅛ **cup almonds, chopped or flaked**

Preheat the oven to 350°F.

Sift the flour into a bowl. Rub in the butter, add the sugar and baking powder, and mix well.

Separate the egg, whisk the egg yolk and save the white for the topping. Add the whisked yolk and milk to the butter mixture and mix to a stiff dough.

Turn out onto a floured board, knead lightly, roll out to a ¼ in thickness. Line a greased baking pan with the pastry. Spread the jam evenly on top.

Whisk the white of the egg stiffly in a large bowl and fold the confectioners' sugar through it. Spread over the jam and sprinkle

on chopped or flaked almonds.

Bake for about 30 minutes, then cut into fingers and cool on a wire tray.

MILLIONAIRE'S SQUARES

These much-loved cookies are complicated to make, so get the maximum flavor for your effort by making them with butter and best-quality chocolate · MAKES ABOUT 24

FOR THE PASTRY BASE
3 **cups self-rising flour**
1 **cup butter**
½ **cup superfine sugar**

FOR THE TOFFEE FILLING
1 **cup butter**
1 **cup plus 2 tablespoons granulated sugar (can be reduced to ¾ cup)**
4 **tablespoons corn syrup**
1 **x 14oz can condensed sweetened milk**

FOR THE CHOCOLATE TOP
8oz **fine dark chocolate such as Valrhona**

1 **large jelly roll pan (10 x 15in)**

Preheat the oven to 350°F.

Make the pastry base by mixing the flour with the sugar, rubbing in the butter, and working until the mixture comes together. Alternatively, blend the three ingredients in a food processor. Roll the mixture evenly into the jelly roll pan and prick the base with a fork. Cook for 15–20 minutes, until golden in color and fully cooked.

Next make the filling. Melt the butter over a low heat in a heavy-bottomed saucepan. Add the sugar, corn syrup, and lastly the condensed milk, stirring after each addition. Continue to stir over a low heat for the next 20 minutes. (The toffee burns very easily so don't stop stirring.)

When the toffee is golden brown, test by dropping a little blob into a bowl of cold water. A firm ball of toffee indicates a firm toffee, so if it's still a little soft continue to cook for a few more minutes; but be careful – if it gets too hard it will pull your teeth out later! When it reaches the correct stage, pour it evenly over the shortbread base. Leave to cool.

Melt the chocolate over gentle heat, preferably in a Pyrex bowl over hot, but not simmering, water and spread evenly over the toffee. Decorate immediately with a fork to give a wavy pattern.

Cut into small squares or fingers when the chocolate is set.

Variation
GROWN-UP CHOCOLATE AND SALTED TOFFEE SQUARES
Sprinkle Maldon, Halen Mon, or other best-quality sea salt over the top of the chocolate – surprising and delicious.

Bread

Everyone should experience the thrill of making a loaf of bread. I've been baking all my adult life and most of my childhood and yet every time I take a crusty loaf of bread out of the oven (and that's almost every day) I get a "whoops" in my tummy. Some breads are so easy you could bake them with your eyes closed. I learned how to bake from hanging on to my mother's apron strings when I was scarcely more than a toddler. Mummy baked soda bread virtually every day of her life, and she would give me a piece of dough to make my own little *cistin* (which means "little cake" in Gaelic). It would then bake alongside Mummy's loaf in the old Esse cooker (like an Aga). My early attempts were hard and chewy from overhandling, but everyone would lie through their teeth and tell me how delicious it was just to encourage me. Soon, baking bread became second nature to me and, of course, this is the way people used to learn – the skill was effortlessly passed from one generation to another.

Sadly, for the past two or three generations we have allowed our children and grandchildren to go out into the world with few, if any, essential life skills. The tradition in these islands over the last few hundred years is of breads that have been leavened, with lots of crumb and very little crust (particularly since ovens have become commonplace in people's houses). However, before that in Ireland, and still today in many other countries, there was a real tradition of making flatbreads cooked over an open fire, or on griddles, in *comals,* or over *kahdis* that look like upturned woks. It's really worth having a few good recipes for flatbreads in your repertoire because you can make them anywhere – in a studio apartment, on a picnic, in a high-rise flat, as well as in a luxury kitchen.

Bread was considered sacred in every ancient culture and wasting bread was deemed downright sinful or at the very best "unlucky"; consequently, every country has a myriad of tasty ways to use up leftover bread. In Mexico, leftover tortillas are used in soup and *chilaquiles*. In Italy, stale bread is used for *panzanella*, bruschetta, and *pan grattato*; in the Middle East, *fattoush*; in France, croutons and *pain perdu*. In Ireland and Great Britain, bread crumbs are used in stuffings, dumplings, to bulk out cakes, to sprinkle over gratins, in bread sauce and, of course, there's bread and butter pudding.

Bread is such an important staple that it *must* be wholesome, nourishing, and delicious. There's no difficulty in finding bread nowadays – it's available at every corner shop and gas station, so for many people there isn't much of an incentive to bake it themselves. However, the quality has changed out of all recognition since the 1950s. We are fortunate to have one of a growing number of artisan bakeries close by, but there is nothing quite like the loaf of bread you make yourself.

I hope the recipes that follow will encourage everybody to have a go. If you're a complete novice I suggest starting with soda breads, which are literally made in minutes, and once you've caught the bug I'm sure you'll want to go on to yeast breads and before long you'll be making your own sourdough. Remember, baking is an exact science and you need to use the proper ingredients and measure accurately. Don't be tempted, for example, to add more baking soda than a recipe calls for. If you use too much, despite what you may think, your loaf of bread won't rise more but will taste and smell strongly of soda. The bread may have a greeny, yellow tinge or dark brown streaks which indicate that the baking soda was not adequately mixed through the flour. To ensure success, always use recipes that suit your ingredients and then measure accurately. Before long, you'll be boring others at dinner parties with your new favorite topic of conversation!

What's Happened to Our Daily Bread?

Since the 1950s farmers and food producers have been encouraged to produce the maximum amount of food for minimum cost. Bakers have been no exception, for they, too, have been under pressure to produce a cheaper, more long-lasting loaf. The result has been disastrous both in health and socio-economic terms.

Up to the end of 1960, bakers made bread in the traditional way. The turning point came in 1961, when the British Baking Industries Research Association at Chorleywood in Herefordshire invented a bread-making method using low-protein wheat, a mesmerizing assortment of additives and high-speed mixing. From the time the flour went in at one end of the machine until the baked loaf emerged from the oven, it took less than two hours – as opposed to the five hours or more it took to make in the traditional way. This new method was enthusiastically embraced by industrial bakers.

More than 80 percent of the bread we buy in Britain and Ireland is now made by the Chorleywood Bread Process (CBP) method – or a similar process called ADD, which stands for Activated Dough Development. In the US, industrial bakers tend to use the Do-maker Process, which achieves similar results. The fast production methods tick all the boxes for efficiency and cheapness. They produce impressively light voluminous bread, soft and squishy with a long shelf life – in fact, a scarily long shelf life. I once came across a sliced bread that was still soft, spongy, and fresh after five weeks; how spooky is that – a technological marvel.

During the last 50 years the sales of bread have plummeted and the number of people with wheat allergies and full-blown celiac disease has skyrocketed. Once the CBP was universally adopted all research was dedicated to producing varieties of short-stem wheat, strains of yeast and additives to facilitate this fast production method. Nourishment just simply wasn't a factor. Advances in functional properties of wheat have come at the expense of nutritional quality. Several research projects have shown that modern wheat varieties have less than half the mineral and trace element content of traditional wheat varieties.

The enzymes or "processing aids" that are added in the bread-making process are the modern baking industry's big secret – a major cause for concern and mostly unidentified on the label. I do not have space in this book to tackle this issue – I'm just trying to make a case for making your own bread, but if it's a subject that concerns you, then you may want to seek out Andrew Whitley's excellent book *Bread Matters*.

Choosing the right flour

When baking bread, it is vital to use the appropriate type of flour to suit the bread you are making.

Soda bread
For soda bread, you need a soft flour that is low in gluten. Wholewheat flour, either stone-ground or roller-milled, is used for brown soda bread. For white soda bread, you will need all-purpose flour, preferably unbleached. This flour, along with self-rising flour (which includes leavening) is used for tender baked goods such as cakes and cookies.

Wholewheat flours may have a high or low gluten content, so choose fine, medium, coarse, or wholewheat flour depending on your taste or dietary needs. You can also balance quantities of white and brown flour. We normally use coarse or medium wholewheat flour and mix white and brown flour for brown soda bread.

Yeast bread
For yeast breads, you need what's called bread flour – either brown or white. This flour has a high gluten content, which is developed by kneading. It creates an elastic web of fibers that provides the structure for the bread to rise. This flour is also good for making puff pastry, flaky pastry, and choux pastry. For a very hearty loaf, substitute ¾ cup wholewheat flour, and 2 tablespoons each rye flakes and rye flour for every cup of wholewheat.

Sourdough
For sourdough breads, a bread flour is usually used, though you could use all-purpose flour, as well as other types of flours such as rye or kamut, or a mixture.

Other flour types

Spelt: this ancient type of wheat has not been manipulated and hybridized by plant breeders in the same way as more modern wheat varieties. Many people who have an intolerance to standard wheat seem to be able to tolerate spelt without ill effects, but it is not suitable for celiacs. It looks like a fine wholewheat and can be substituted for wheat flour in almost all recipes. However, it has a slightly weaker gluten content and in my experience doesn't absorb as much liquid. We also use it as a base for a sourdough starter. Its healthy population of natural yeasts and bacteria produce a lively vigorous sourdough culture in a short time. Emmer and Einkorn are two types of spelt that are also causing a stir, particularly in Germany. There is some anecdotal evidence that Einkorn is not harmful to celiacs but the jury is still out. All spelt flours contain more nutrients than modern hybrid wheat varieties.

Kamut: this flour is also worth knowing about. It is the trademarked name for a cereal derived from 36 grains which some say were grown by the pharaohs of Egypt. Kamut is an organic grain believed to be relative of durum wheat (the hard wheat used in some types of pasta). It is usually higher in protein than other wheats but with poorer-quality gluten. People who have a sensitivity to modern wheat can sometimes tolerate kamut, which can be used for yeast or sourdough breads.

Rye flour: this dark flour is known to help lower blood cholesterol. It is low in gluten and doesn't have much flavor of its own so is best combined with other flours or used with a sourdough starter.

Rising agents for baking

There are two basic types of rising agent: biological ones (such as yeast) and chemical ones (like baking soda and baking powder).

Yeast is a living organism that requires certain conditions to grow (namely warmth, moisture, and nourishment). The carbon dioxide bubbles that result puff up the dough, making it light and aerated. Yeast can be bought in three forms – fresh, dried, and fast-acting. For more on yeast and yeast breads, see pages 567–573.

Above: *Clockwise from top left: kamut, spelt, and wholewheat flour.*

Baking soda, bread soda, and bicarbonate of soda are all names for sodium bicarbonate, an alkali that is used in conjunction with acid ingredients such as sour milk, buttermilk, and natural yogurt to make soda bread. When the baking soda comes into contact with the acid, an immediate chemical reaction produces bubbles of carbon dioxide. These expand in the heat of the oven, thus rising the dough. It is important to put the dough into a preheated oven, to trap the action.

Sourdough was likely the first form of leavening used by bakers. It is made by using a small amount of starter dough which harnesses wild yeast from the air. The resulting bread has a delicious tangy taste.

Many ancient breads don't use any rising agent at all and I've included a few simple griddle breads and flatbreads to whet your appetite.

Soda Bread

The making of soda bread developed in Ireland because of the availability of ingredients. Traditional Irish soda breads use a technique which is particularly suited to the soft, low-gluten wheat that thrives in our climate. In the days before refrigeration, milk would have soured more quickly, so soda breads were a way of making use of it, although nowadays it is more common to use commercially produced buttermilk. Baking soda is the rising agent in soda breads. This was introduced during the first half of the 19th century, enabling cooks to develop the wide range of soda breads for which Ireland is now famous.

The great thing about soda bread is that it is made in minutes – you wouldn't have found your car keys and got down to the village shop in the time it takes to put the dough in the oven and take out a fresh loaf. Years ago soda bread would have been baked in the pot oven, or bastible, over the open fire – and you can recreate the resulting tender crust in a covered casserole in your oven. Or you can make the mixture a little softer and cook it on a griddle – so you can even make soda bread when you're camping. This sort of skill has been passed on from mother to daughter for generations.

Soda breads are best eaten on the day they are made, but are still good for a day or so more. Soda bread also makes great toast.

A note about buttermilk

In Ireland, shop-bought buttermilk tends to be very thin and low in fat, so Mummy often added a little sour cream or a scraping of butter from a butter wrapper to enrich the bread. This results in a more crumbly texture. Often, buttermilk is thicker and much more like the consistency of yogurt. If using this kind of buttermilk, you'll need to use more of it than specified in these recipes. If the dough is too dry, the bread will be heavy and close-textured.

The right balance of rising agent and acid is of vital importance. If you don't have sour milk or buttermilk to hand, add 2 tablespoons freshly squeezed lemon juice to 2 cups of milk in order to provide the acidity. Or you can make yogurt bread, replacing the buttermilk in the recipe with up to 2 cups of yogurt (you'll need more as yogurt tends to be thicker) and perhaps 1 tablespoon of lemon juice to increase the acidity.

For those who can't find buttermilk easily, it's worth noting that it freezes well and in my experience keeps for a week to 10 days beyond the best-before date on the carton. Experiment with what works as brands may vary.

Using other types of milk

Sour cow's milk makes the best soda bread, but you can use other types of milk. One variation we call "goaty bread" is made with sour goat's milk and we have also used rice milk successfully – just add the juice of half a lemon to provide the acidity.

MUMMY'S BROWN SODA BREAD

See page 199 in Dairy chapter.

BEGINNER'S BROWN SODA BREAD

Even though this is a modern rather than traditional version of soda bread, I've decided to put it first because it couldn't be simpler. Just mix all the ingredients together and pour into a well-greased pan. It's important to put all the milk in – the dough may seem too wet but it's meant to be that way for this particular bread. It will keep well for several days and is also great when toasted. Most modern soda bread recipes include far too much baking soda, which makes the bread very dark and taste strongly of soda · **MAKES 1 LARGE OR 3 SMALL LOAVES**

3⅓ cups stone-ground wholewheat flour
⅔ cup all-purpose flour, preferably unbleached
1 teaspoon salt
1 teaspoon baking soda, sifted
1 organic egg
1 tablespoon sunflower oil
1 teaspoon honey, molasses, or dark brown sugar
1⅔ cups buttermilk or sour milk
sunflower or sesame seeds (optional)

one loaf pan (9 x 5 x 2¾ in) OR three loaf pans (5½ x 3 x 2in)

Preheat the oven to 400°F. Brush the inside of the loaf pan or pans with vegetable oil.

Put all the dry ingredients including the sifted baking soda into a large bowl and mix well. Whisk the egg, adding to it the oil, honey, and the buttermilk or sour milk. Make a well in the center of the dry ingredients and pour in all the liquid. Mix well, adding more buttermilk if necessary (the mixture should be soft and slightly sloppy). Pour into the oiled pan or pans. If desired, sprinkle some sunflower or sesame seeds on top.

Bake for about 1 hour or until the bread is nice and crusty and sounds hollow when tapped. Leave to cool on a wire rack.

Variation

MULTISEED SODA BREAD
Add 1 tablespoon of sunflower seeds, 1 tablespoon of sesame seeds, 1 tablespoon of pumpkin seeds, and 1 tablespoon of kibbled wheat to the dry ingredients. Also scatter a mixture of the seeds over the top.

WHITE SODA BREAD

Years ago, white soda bread was referred to as "cake bread" and was considered to be more of a luxury than everyday wholewheat bread. This bread takes only a few minutes to make and about 45 minutes to bake. It can be plain or you can add sweet or savory bits to it · **MAKES 1 MEDIUM LOAF**

1lb all-purpose flour, preferably unbleached
1 teaspoon salt
1 teaspoon baking soda

1¾ cups low-fat or wholefat buttermilk, or sour milk, depending on consistency

Preheat the oven to 450°F.

Sift the dry ingredients into a large, wide bowl. Make a well in the center and pour most of the buttermilk or sour milk in at once. Grip the bowl with one hand and use the other hand to mix in the flour from the sides of the bowl, adding more milk if necessary. The dough should be softish and not too wet and sticky. When it all comes together, turn it out onto a well-floured work surface. Wash and dry your hands so the dough is easier to handle.

Tidy up the dough and flip it over gently. Then pat it into a round about 1in thick and cut a deep cross on it which is done according to Irish folklore in order to let the fairies out! Let the cuts go over the sides of the bread to make sure of this. Bake for 15 minutes, then turn down the oven to 400°F for 30 minutes or until cooked. If in doubt, tap the bottom of the bread: if it is cooked it will sound hollow.

Variations

Add 2 tablespoons of freshly chopped herbs, 2 tablespoons of chopped olives, 2 tablespoons of sundried tomatoes, ½ cup raisins or 1–2 teaspoons of curry powder and maybe some golden raisins, 2 tablespoons of caraway or other seeds – the possibilities are endless!

Above: *White Soda Scones.*

WHITE SODA SCONES
Make the dough as above, and flatten it into a round about 1in deep. Cut into scones. Cook for about 20 minutes in a hot oven. The tops can be egg washed and dipped in grated Cheddar cheese or a mixture of seeds and grains – sesame, pumpkin, sunflower, kibbled wheat, oat flakes.

KERRY TREACLE BREAD
This recipe was described to me by Mrs. McGillycuddy from Glencar in County Kerry, who still makes it occasionally. Follow the recipe for white soda bread, but whisk 2 tablespoons of treacle (molasses) into the buttermilk before adding it to the flour mixture.

SPOTTED DOG – RAILWAY CAKE

During my childhood, many people in the country were poor, and their daily staple would have been wholewheat bread. White flour was more expensive than brown so white soda bread was considered to be more luxurious – a treat for special occasions.

At times of the year when work was harder, such as at harvest or threshing, or maybe on a Sunday when visitors were expected, the woman of the house would add a bit of sugar and a fistful of dried fruit and an egg to the white bread to make it a bit more special. Nowadays, this does not seem such a big deal but back then any money that the woman of the house got from selling her eggs was considered to be her "pin money", used for little luxuries such as hatpins. Putting an egg into the bread was one egg less that she could sell, so it actually represented much more than it would for us today.

This bread was called spotted dog or railway cake, and when it was still warm, she'd wrap it in a kitchen towel and bring it out to the fields with hot sweetened tea in whiskey bottles wrapped in newspaper or cloth to insulate them. The farm workers would put down their tools and sit with their backs to the haystacks. She'd cut the bread into thick slices and slather on yellow country butter. My cherished memories of sitting down with them are still really vivid.

Opposite: *Spotted Dog.*

We sometimes make "spotted puppies" which are the same bread, shaped into 6 tiny round loaves and baked for 20 minutes · MAKES 1 LOAF

3½ **cups all-purpose flour, preferably unbleached**
1 **teaspoon baking soda**
1 **teaspoon salt**
2 **teaspoons sugar**
⅔ **cup golden or seedless raisins (or more if you'd like)**
1 **organic egg**
1⅓ **cups buttermilk**

Preheat the oven to 425°F.

Into a large mixing bowl, sift the flour and baking soda; then add the salt, sugar, and raisins. Mix well by lifting the flour and fruit up in to your hands and then letting them fall back into the bowl through your fingers. This adds more air and therefore more lightness to your finished bread. Now make a well in the center of the flour mixture.

Break the egg into the base of a measuring glass and add the buttermilk to the 1½ cups line (the egg is part of the liquid measurement) and mix together. Pour most of this milk and egg mixture into the flour. Using one hand with the fingers open and stiff, mix in a full circle drawing in the flour mixture from the sides of the bowl, adding more milk if necessary. The dough should be softish, but not too wet and sticky.

The trick with Spotted Dog, like all soda breads, is not to overmix the dough. Mix it as quickly and gently as possible, thus keeping it light and airy. When the dough all comes together, turn it out onto a well-floured work surface. Wash and dry your hands.

With floured fingers, roll the dough lightly for a few seconds – just enough to tidy it up. Then pat the dough into a round about 2in thick. Transfer to a baking sheet dusted lightly with flour. Use a sharp knife to cut a deep cross on it, letting the cuts go over the sides of the bread. Prick with a knife in the four triangles.

Put into the oven and immediately reduce the temperature to 400°F. Cook for 35–40 minutes. If you are in doubt about the bread being cooked, tap the bottom: if it is cooked it will sound hollow. This bread is cooked at a lower temperature than soda bread because the egg browns faster at a higher heat.

Serve freshly baked, cut into thick slices and smeared with butter and jam. Spotted Dog is also really good eaten with Cheddar cheese.

Variation

AMERICAN SODA BREAD
Caraway seeds and raisins were added to soda bread in Ireland long ago, but the tradition went by the wayside. Not so in America, where soda bread often has caraway seeds and raisins in it. Usually when I go to the US, I take Irish recipes there, but I was delighted to bring this one back to Ireland! Simply add 2 teaspoons of caraway seeds to the Spotted Dog recipe above.

The Bastible

A bastible is an iron pot, usually with three little legs underneath and a slightly domed lid, that was used as a pot oven to cook over an open fire. In small cottages and farmhouses, people didn't have actual ovens up until the 1950s, so they would've cooked simply but skillfully over an open fire. The bastible had two little ears and you could hook it up to a crane that hung over the fire. The lid also had a handle to enable the cook to lift it up to check on what was cooking inside. The cook would have taken hot embers from the turf fire and placed them on the lid so there was heat coming both from underneath and on top.

Everything from breads and tarts to stews and even a goose was cooked in a bastible. It was a very skilful way of cooking because people had to gauge the heat and guess what was going on in the pot without seeing inside. One of the skills was lifting the top without dropping ashes into the pot. Bread and tarts that were cooked in a bastible always had more tender crusts because the steam was trapped inside the pot, softening the crust. You can recreate a similar and tender crust effect by cooking the soda bread in a covered casserole in the oven.

BASTIBLE BREAD

I learned to cook over an open fire from my great-aunt in Tipperary on summer holidays throughout the 1950s. All of the cooking was done in the big, open fireplace. I still from time to time cook over the open fire for pure pleasure and the nostalgia it evokes. Perhaps it's my imagination, but things seem to taste better! Few people cook over an open fire nowadays, but you can more or less reproduce bastible bread by cooking the dough in a heavy iron casserole in the oven · MAKES 1 MEDIUM LOAF

1¾ **cups all-purpose flour, preferably unbleached**
1¾ **cups wholewheat flour**
1 **teaspoon salt**
¼ **teaspoon baking soda, sifted**
2 **cups buttermilk**

10in heavy casserole with lid

Preheat the oven to 450°F.

Line the base of the casserole with parchment paper. Heat the lined casserole in the oven.

Mix the flours in a large bowl, add the salt and sifted baking soda. Lift the flour mixture with your fingers to distribute the salt and baking soda.

Make a well in the center and pour in all the buttermilk. With your fingers stiff and outstretched, stir in a circular movement from the center to the outside of the bowl in ever-increasing concentric circles. When you reach the outside of the bowl seconds later, the dough should be complete.

Sprinkle a little flour on the countertop. Turn the dough out onto the flour. Wash and dry your hands to make the dough easier to handle. (Fill the bowl with cold water so it will be easy to wash later.) Sprinkle a little flour on your hands. Gently tidy the dough around the edges and flip onto the flour. Tuck the edges underneath with the inner edge of your hands and gently pat the dough with your fingers into a loaf about 1½in thick and just large enough to fit the casserole.

Cut a deep cross into the loaf and then prick in the center of the four sections to "let the fairies out."

Transfer to the hot casserole and cover with the lid. Bake for 40–50 minutes. Remove from the casserole and cool on a wire rack. The crust will be soft and tender and the bread will be almost spongy in texture.

Griddle Breads

Up until the early 1950s, many less affluent houses wouldn't have had an oven, so breads would have been cooked on a flat-iron griddle over an open fire. The entire *batterie de cuisine* would have consisted of a bastible, a griddle, a frying pan, and a three-legged pot.

The following recipes, some of which date back hundreds of years, would, of course, have been made on the griddle, but nowadays we make them in a heavy frying pan on a stove top.

GRIDDLE BREAD

This recipe is especially worth noting for students or those whose kitchens don't have an oven, because all you need is a griddle or frying pan and a single gas ring. I've made this bread successfully in a campervan in New Zealand and on a riverbank in Spain. Serve warm, cut into pie-shaped pieces, with butter and jam, cheese, crispy bacon, or cured meats · SERVES 4–8

1¾ cups all-purpose flour,
   preferably unbleached
½ teaspoon salt
½ teaspoon baking soda
¾ cup buttermilk

non-stick griddle or iron frying
   pan, 10in diameter

Preheat the griddle or a non-stick pan on a low heat.

Sift the dry ingredients and make a well in the center. Pour in most of the buttermilk. Using one hand mix in the flour from the sides of the bowl, adding more buttermilk if necessary. The dough should be softish, and not too wet and sticky. When it all comes together, turn it out onto a floured board and knead lightly for a second, just enough to tidy it up.

Roll the bread into a round about 1in thick. Put onto a hot griddle and cook over medium-low heat for about 15 minutes on one side. When it has a nice firm crust, turn it over and continue to cook on the other side for another 15 minutes, until nicely browned and cooked through.

BROWN GRIDDLE SCONES

This is another traditional recipe that deserves to be better known. These scones are best eaten warm and are also good with cold ham, bacon, or poached salmon. We sometimes make them over a campfire at picnics · MAKES 12–14

1¾ cups wholewheat flour
6 tablespoons all-purpose flour,
   preferably unbleached
¼ cup old-fashioned oatmeal
½ teaspoon salt
1 teaspoon baking soda
about 1¾ cups buttermilk
Clarified Butter (see page 216)

cast-iron griddle or a heavy iron
   pan

Mix the flour, oatmeal, and salt in a bowl. Measure the baking soda into the palm of your hand, cover with your other palm and rub out any lumps in the time-honored way. Add it to the dry ingredients in the bowl and mix together thoroughly. Pour in the buttermilk and mix with a wooden spoon to the consistency of a thick batter.

Heat the griddle or iron pan over medium heat and grease with a little clarified butter. Drop about 2 teaspoons of batter onto the griddle and cook for 5–6 minutes on each side; they should be well risen and golden.

Wrap the scones in a clean napkin or kitchen towel and serve warm with butter and marmalade or homemade jam.

TURKISH FLATBREAD

You can make this flatbread, known as yufka, in just a couple of minutes. Even though the recipe says to let the dough rest, and it does benefit from that, I've often disregarded that suggestion and had fine results anyway. It's a terrific standby recipe if you're out of bread. I teach this to young people who live in apartments that might only have hot plates as you can make this without an oven · MAKES 12

1 cup bread flour
1 cup all-purpose flour, preferably
   unbleached
6 tablespoons wholewheat flour
½ teaspoon salt
a scant 1 cup warm water

cast-iron griddle or a heavy iron
   or non-stick pan

Mix the flours with the salt in a bowl. Add the water and mix into a dough. Knead well for a few minutes. Shape into a roll and divide in 12 equal-sized pieces, cover and let stand for 20–30 minutes. (However, I sometimes cook it straight away.)

Roll each piece of dough into a thin round, no more than ⅛in thick.

Heat a griddle or large iron or non-stick frying pan. Cook the flatbread quickly on both sides until just spotted, about 2–3 minutes. Eat immediately with cheese or butter and honey or roll around a filling of roasted vegetables, cured meat, and salads. They are then called *dirim* meaning "roll."

Left: *Kerry Yellowmeal Griddle Bread.*

POTATO BREAD

This recipe comes from Northern Ireland where it is known as fadge. It can be cooked on a griddle, in a frying pan, or in the oven · SERVES 8

2lb baking potatoes, e.g. Burbanks
    or Russets
1 organic egg, beaten
2 tablespoons butter
2 tablespoons all-purpose flour,
    preferably unbleached
salt and freshly ground black
    pepper
whole milk
seasoned flour
oil, bacon fat, or butter for frying

Boil the potatoes, pull off the skin, and mash straight away. Add the egg, butter, and flour. Season with lots of salt and pepper, adding a few drops of milk if the mixture is altogether too stiff. Taste and correct the seasoning.

Shape into a 1in thick round or a square and then cut into quarters or eighths. Dip into the seasoned flour. Cook in oil on a griddle over an open fire or fry in bacon fat or melted butter over gentle heat. Cook the fadge until crusty and golden on one side, then flip over and cook on the other side, about 4–5 minutes each side.

Serve with an eggs and sausages or on its own on hot plates with a blob of butter melting on top.

KERRY CORNMEAL GRIDDLE BREAD

Cornmeal was sent to Ireland during the famine to alleviate hunger, so even still in folk memory it's connected to times of starvation and hardship. In parts of Ireland you can still buy "yellameal" in some of the village shops, and sometimes people throw a handful into their soda bread.

Mrs. McGillycuddy of Caragh Lake in Kerry described this griddle bread to me. It dates back to the middle of the 19th century and is very good served with crispy bacon for breakfast or supper. Alternatively, cook tablespoons full of batter for individual cornmeal cakes · SERVES 4

1 cup cornmeal or polenta
a good pinch of salt
¼ teaspoon baking soda, sifted
¾ cup buttermilk

griddle or 10in non-stick pan

Put the cornmeal, salt, and baking soda into a bowl. Lift up the mixture with your hands to distribute evenly. Add the buttermilk and beat well to a thick batter.

Heat a griddle or pan over medium heat. Pour the batter onto it and cook until crisp and golden underneath, about 4–5 minutes. Turn over carefully and cook on the other side. Cut into four and serve warm with butter.

Yeast Breads

In this era of instant gratification it can be difficult to persuade people that making their own yeast bread is a worthwhile activity. The mere mention conjures up daunting images of bouts of strenuous kneading interspersed with long waits for the bread to rise not just once, but twice. But one of the things that has kept me fired up about teaching through the 25-plus years of the Cookery School has been the look of delight on students' faces when they take their first loaf of bread out of the oven. It's almost more exciting than catching your first fish and I know that I've passed on an often forgotten skill that will touch their everyday lives for ever.

For those who are apprehensive about working with yeast, Ballymaloe Brown Yeast Bread is a great introduction to yeast bread because it requires no kneading and involves only one rising. It takes about 1½ hours to make from start to finish but most of that time is in the rising and baking – in real terms, it takes only about five minutes of your time. A wet dough ferments faster than a dry one.

Unlike the brown yeast bread, white yeast bread *does* involve kneading and double rising and knocking back. Much of that time is in the rising and baking, so you can get on with other chores. The satisfaction and end result are immense and more than worth the effort.

Brown Yeast Bread

A few notes about the three main ingredients:

The yeast
When making brown yeast bread, remember that yeast is a living organism. In order to grow, it requires warmth, moisture, and nourishment. The yeast feeds on sugar and produces bubbles of carbon dioxide that expand in the oven and rise the bread. Actually, there's no need to be scared of yeast, it's pretty good humored and, like many of us, it has a sweet tooth and likes to be warm, so be nice to it. The average warmth of a kitchen provides a suitable environment in which yeast can grow, but a temperature of more than 122°F will kill it, so ensure the water isn't too hot.

You can use dried yeast instead of fresh compressed yeast. Simply follow the same method, but use only half the weight given for fresh yeast. Leave it longer to rise. Fast-acting yeast may also be used; just follow the instructions on the packet. Note that the dough rises more rapidly with 1oz yeast than with ¾oz yeast.

Much of the fresh yeast now available is genetically modified, so ask questions before you buy.

The flour
For brown yeast bread, we use a strong, stone-ground wholewheat flour. Different flours produce breads of different textures and flavors. The amount of natural moisture in the flour varies according to atmospheric conditions, so the quantity of water added should be altered accordingly. The dough should be just too wet to knead (it does not require kneading).

The treacle (molasses)
At Ballymaloe we use treacle (molasses), but one can also use honey, golden syrup, white or brown sugar, or Barbados sugar (soft, dark brown sugar). Each will give a slightly different flavor to the bread.

USING OLD DOUGH

Old yeast dough adds extra flavor and interest to a batch of bread. Sometimes when I'm making brown yeast bread, I hold back a quarter of the dough and put it in a tall glass jar (if it's white yeast dough, I use a covered bowl). Then I can save it for a few weeks and use it as a base for the next batch. The dough gets more sour and the brown bread takes on a deeper flavor, almost like pumpernickel.

BALLYMALOE BROWN YEAST BREAD

This bread has been made by hand every day at Ballymaloe House for more than 60 years – originally for the family, and then for the guests. The recipe is based on one for a nutritious loaf that Doris Grant developed at the request of the British government in the 1940s. I can't really stress enough what a favor you'll be doing your family by baking this bread. The main ingredients – wholewheat flour, molasses, and yeast – are all highly nutritious. The ingredients and equipment should be at room temperature · **MAKES 1 LOAF**

3½ **cups stone-ground wholewheat flour OR 3 cups stone-ground wholewheat flour plus ½ cup bread flour**
1 **teaspoon salt**
1 **teaspoon molasses**
1⅔ **cups lukewarm water**
¾ **oz or more fresh compressed yeast**
sesame seeds (optional)
sunflower oil

loaf pan (5 x 8in)

Preheat the oven to 450°F.

Mix the flour with the salt in a mixing bowl. In a small bowl, mix the treacle with some of the water – (½ cup) – and crumble in the yeast. Let stand for a few minutes in a warm place to allow the yeast to start to work. Meanwhile, grease the bread pan with sunflower oil. Check to see if the yeast is rising. After about 4–5 minutes, it will have a creamy and slightly frothy appearance on top.

When ready, stir and pour it, with all the remaining water (1 cup), into the flour to make a loose, wet dough. (Don't mix it until all the water is in; otherwise it tends to go lumpy.) The mixture should be too wet to knead. Put the mixture directly into the greased pan. Sprinkle the top of the loaf with sesame seeds, if you like. Cover the pan with a kitchen towel to prevent a skin from forming and let the bread rise. This will take anything from 10–20 minutes, depending on the temperature of your kitchen.

When the dough has almost come to the top of the pan, remove the towel and pop the loaves into the oven. The bread will rise a little more in the oven; this is called "oven spring." If the bread rises to the top of the pan before you put it into the oven, it will continue to rise and will flow over the edges. Cook for 20 minutes, then reduce the temperature to 400°F and cook for another 40–50 minutes, until your bread looks nicely browned and sounds hollow when tapped.

We usually remove the loaves from the pan/pans about 10 minutes before the end of cooking and put them back into the oven to crisp the exterior, but if you like a softer crust there is no need for this.

Variation

BROWN MUFFINS
We sometimes bake this mixture in muffin pans, perfect for parties or school lunches. They take about 20 minutes in the oven.

To make more loaves:
Ballymaloe brown yeast bread is easy to make in large quantities. See the ingredients list below if you wish to make four large or five smaller loaves. We regularly mix enough dough by hand for 15 loaves at Ballymaloe House in a wide, shallow mixing bowl. Don't be tempted to use a machine to mix it – it will alter the texture of the finished bread and not for the better.

14 **cups stone-ground wholewheat flour OR 12 cups strong stone-ground wholewheat flour plus 2 cups bread flour**
up to about 6½ cups lukewarm water (use 1 cup of the lukewarm water to mix with the yeast)
1 **tablespoon salt**
2 **or more teaspoons molasses**
3oz **fresh compressed yeast**
sesame seeds (optional)

4 **or 5 x loaf pans about 5 x 8in**

Left: *Ballymaloe Brown Yeast Bread.*

White Yeast Bread

Unlike brown yeast bread, white yeast bread does involve kneading, double rising, and punching down. It takes time, but not your time, as much of it is in the rising and baking. It's very tempting to use a food mixer to knead bread, but I always encourage people to knead by hand to begin with. It can seem a chore but in fact it can be enormously therapeutic and relaxing when you enter into the spirit and just enjoy the process. With each loaf you make, you will continue to perfect your technique and will become more observant of the changes in the dough, depending on the flour, atmosphere, and even your humor.

If you do want to use a food mixer, however, use the dough hook and knead for 5–6 minutes rather than 10.

Why knead?
The process of kneading develops the elasticity of the dough. When the yeast feeds on the sugar and creates little bubbles of carbon dioxide, the strong stretchy web will facilitate the rising process.

What is gluten?
Gluten is the protein in the flour. When it is wet it becomes elastic, so flour with a higher gluten content will expand considerably as it rises and is therefore desirable for white yeast bread.

How do I knead?
There are several different styles of hand kneading, all equally effective, so choose the style that you feel most comfortable with. It doesn't matter which style or combination you settle for, but it's important to remember that you need to work and stretch the dough in order to develop the gluten structure, so don't just play with it. Kneading needs energy and has the added bonus of providing you with a physical workout which surely can only be desirable.

To start, scrape the dough out of the mixing bowl onto the countertop. Begin to stretch and fold. It usually takes about 10 minutes to get the dough to the correct consistency, but the length of time will depend on your technique. Here are my three suggestions:

Hand kneading: method 1
Stand upright with one foot slightly ahead of the other in front of the countertop. Sprinkle a little flour on the countertop and dust your hands, too. Tidy the dough into a manageable round. Now, with your right hand, stretch the top right-hand side of the dough and then fold it back towards you. With your left hand turn the dough anticlockwise and continue stretching and folding as you knead a different part of the dough, all the time, over and over.

Hand kneading: method 2
The second effective method is to stretch the top of the dough away from you while holding onto the end closest to you. Then roll the top edge of the dough inwards towards you and press away again with the heel of your hand. Again roll towards you, another stretch and a final roll which should bring all the dough as far as the bottom edge. Now you'll have what looks like a roulade cake in front of you. Turn it 90° and start the kneading process again from the narrow end. Continue until the dough is fully kneaded.

Hand kneading: method 3
This third method is effective, but very noisy. It's the best method for getting rid of frustration by far, but only attempt it if you are on your own! Knead the dough until it becomes a coherent mass, then form into a longish piece. Grip by the bottom end with your right hand. Lift up the dough, flick your wrist forward and bang the dough onto the countertop, flicking your wrist to the right in the same movement, then pick up the other end of the dough and repeat the action over and over again – you'll soon feel better and the dough will benefit from the workout, too!

How do I know the dough is kneaded enough?
You will be aware of the dough changing texture as you knead. At first, if you lift up the dough and pull it apart it will break into two distinct pieces but as you continue to knead you will be able to stretch it into a longer and longer piece without it breaking. It will also become much firmer and spring back without sticking when you

press it with your fingertip.

When kneaded enough, it will stretch into a long roll without breaking – so you'll be able to see the long strand of gluten you've developed with your hard work.

Is it possible to overknead?

You can, but it's unlikely to happen when you are hand kneading. A dough can be overkneaded in a machine. The telltale signs are when the texture of the dough changes from silky and elastic to a coarse, sticky dough that is slightly curdled in appearance.

Where can the bread rise?

Bread will rise almost anywhere (within reason) and 80°F is considered the optimum temperature, but remember that cold doesn't kill yeast; so if your kitchen is a bit colder than mine, the bread may take a little longer to rise, but will still be fine. Keep it out of drafts, but you don't need to put it in a cupboard or on top of a radiator – and no matter how much of a hurry you're in, don't be tempted to put it into a warming drawer or a low oven. Remember, heat over 122°F kills yeast – and breads that rise slowly have a much better flavor and are more nutritious and digestible than those that rise quickly.

What is happening when the dough is rising?

There is lots of enzyme action going on, but basically the yeast is feeding on the natural sugar in the flour and creating bubbles of carbon dioxide gas. The yeast builds up flavor from the acids and other by-products of fermentation – even a short period of rising greatly enhances the flavor of your bread.

Above: *Hand kneading using method 2. Tidy the dough into a manageable round on a floured board, stretch it away from you while holding on to the end closest to you, then roll the top edge of the dough inwards towards you. Continue as per instructions on page 570.*

SEASONING PANS

When you buy new cake or loaf pans that are not non-stick, greasing them will not be enough to stop them from sticking; you'll need to do what's referred to as "seasoning" the pans. You do this by brushing them with oil or butter and putting them in the oven for 10–15 minutes at a time. Let them cool down and repeat 3–4 times. Just to be on the safe side, put a bit of greased parchment paper at the base of the pan the first few times you fill it with dough, just to ensure it doesn't stick. I far prefer this method to using non-stick pans which generally lose their coating over time and can even be dangerous.

BALLYMALOE WHITE YEAST BREAD

The bread that was made in my home was always soda bread, so it wasn't until I went to school in Cathal Brugha Street in Dublin that I learned the skill of making white yeast bread. Later I brought it to Ballymaloe House and they've been making it there ever since. This dough can be used to make rolls, loaves, breadsticks, and all manner of bread shapes ·

MAKES 2 X 1LB LOAVES

1⅔ **cups lukewarm water**
¾**oz fresh compressed yeast**
5½ **cups bread flour, plus extra for dusting**
2 **teaspoons salt**
2½**teaspoons sugar**
2 **tablespoons butter**
egg wash and poppy or sesame seeds for topping (optional)

2 x **loaf pans (5 x 8in)**

Put ½ cup of lukewarm water into a small bowl. Crumble in the yeast and let stand in a warm place for about 2–3 minutes. Sift together the flour, salt, and sugar into a large, wide mixing bowl. Then rub in the butter and make a well in the center. Pour in the yeast mixture and most of the remaining lukewarm water. Mix to a loose dough, adding the remaining water or a little extra flour as needed.

Turn the dough onto a lightly floured work surface, cover, and leave to relax for about 5 minutes. Then knead for about 10 minutes or until smooth, springy, and elastic (if kneading in a food mixer with a dough hook, 5 minutes is usually long enough). Put the dough into a large bowl and cover the top tightly with plastic wrap. Yeast dough rises best in a warm moist atmosphere; 80°F is optimum, but a slower rising is preferable to one that is too fast.

After about 1½–2 hours, when the dough has more than doubled in size, knead it again for about 2–3 minutes to redistribute the yeast in contact with the dough so it will have a more even crumb. Cover and

let relax for another 10 minutes.

Shape the bread into loaves, braids (see below) or rolls, then transfer to a baking tray and cover with a kitchen towel. Let rise again in a warm place, until the shaped dough has again doubled in size (about 20–30 minutes).

Preheat the oven to 450°F.

The bread is ready for baking when a small dent remains if the dough is pressed lightly with the finger. Brush with water and dust with flour for a rustic looking loaf or brush with egg wash and sprinkle with poppy or sesame seeds for a more golden crust.

The bread will rise a little more when it goes into the oven – this is called "oven-spring." Bake for 25–35 minutes, depending on size. When baked, the bread should sound hollow if tapped underneath. Let cool on a wire rack.

Variations

OLIVE-OIL BREAD
Substitute 2 tablespoons of olive oil for butter in the above recipe and proceed as above.

BRAIDED BREAD
Take half the quantity of white yeast dough after it has been "punched down" and divide it into 3 equal pieces. Use both hands to roll each one into a rope – the thickness depends on how fat you want the braid to be. It will shrink at first so re-roll each piece a second time. Then pinch the 3 ends together at the top, bring each outside strand into the center alternatively to form a braid, pinch the ends, and tuck in neatly. Transfer onto a baking sheet,

cover, and let stand until doubled in size. Egg wash or mist the surface with water and dredge with flour before baking.

BEAN-CAN BREAD
Originally, this might have been done when people were short of loaf pans or cake pans, but it's a great way of using what you have to bake bread. Plus, it makes round slices! Choose bean cans that don't have a deep lip on top and open with a can opener that takes off the top of the can. Follow the white yeast dough recipe, then bake the dough in the well-greased cans. Fill the cans only about half full to allow for rising. Cans work best if they've been seasoned in the oven a few times before the dough is inserted (see box opposite); but if in doubt, line your cans with parchment paper.

FLOWERPOT BREAD
For an interesting shape, bake the white yeast dough in well-seasoned (see box opposite) terracotta flowerpots. Oil them well before using.

Above: *Bean-can Bread.*

BROTHERLY LOVE

Reneé Hague, the son-in-law of the renowned typographer Eric Gill, was virtually our next-door neighbor for many years. In his latter years, he loved to bake and particularly enjoyed making yeast doughs. We loved to be invited to tea, as one of his specialities was this traditional Suffolk bread called "Brotherly Love." Do not attempt to make this unless you have fine lard from a reliable butcher ·
SERVES 8

1lb White Yeast Bread dough (see page 572)
6 tablespoons soft pork lard (see page 316)
¼ cup sugar

Preheat the oven to 425°F.

Roll the dough into a 16 x 10in rectangular strip. Spread or dab lard over it, then sprinkle generously with most of the sugar. Roll up and let rise for 30–40 minutes.

Brush with water, and sprinkle with the remaining sugar. Bake for 10 minutes, then reduce the heat to 400°F and bake for 20 minutes or until fully baked and golden brown.

Let cool on a wire rack. Serve freshly baked and still warm, cut into slices and buttered.

Sourdough Bread

Sourdough, for me, is like magic. You don't need any baker's yeast to make it, as you're just harnessing the ambient yeast in the air. You can begin your starter with the natural yeast from grapes, potato, or flour, as we've done here. Unless you have your own well or a guaranteed source of non-chlorinated water, it's important to use bottled spring water or your sourdough won't be so active. This treasured leavening will provide you with a lifetime of amazing bread. Beware, this can become an absorbing passion!

Our sourdough bread recipe is a three-stage process: you make the starter, then the sponge and then the bread itself.

You can use either bread flour or spelt to make the starter, but we prefer the latter because it gives a more active starter.

BALLYMALOE SOURDOUGH STARTER

Some starter recipes suggest mixing the full amount of flour with water and leaving it for six days. However, we have found that we get a much more active starter when we feed it (i.e. add more water and flour) every day. You will need to allow at least six days for your sourdough starter to fully develop

Day 1: choose a large airtight jar that will hold at least 2 quarts – a glass jar is fine. Put ¼ cup of barely tepid (not hot) pure spring water and ¼ cup of spelt or bread flour into the jar. Stir well, close the jar, and leave at room temperature for 24 hours.

Day 2: add ¼ cup water and ¼ cup flour. Mix well, close the jar, and leave for 24 hours at room temperature

Day 3: add ¼ cup water and ¼ cup flour. Mix well, close the jar, and leave for 24 hours at room temperature.

Day 4: add ¼ cup water and ¼ cup flour. Mix well, close the jar, and leave for 24 hours at room temperature.

Day 5: add ¼ cup water and ¼ cup flour. Mix well, close the jar, and leave for 24 hours at room temperature.

Day 6: your sourdough starter is now ready for use. You should have at least 2 cups of lively starter, enough to make the sourdough bread recipe below.

Do I need to use the starter straight away?

It's good to use it immediately, but it can be stored in an airtight jar in the fridge indefinitely. It will need to be fed to reactivate it before use.

Once you've established the sourdough starter, making a loaf of sourdough bread from start to finish will take anywhere from 24 to 36 hours, depending on how lively the starter is.

Starter tips

• Your starter should smell distinctively beery, slightly yeasty, and fermented. It may have a layer of gray liquid on top, but that's fine – just give it a stir.
• Starter must not be allowed to get too warm.
• Starter grows best at comfortable room temperature.

• If the starter is too thick to beat easily, add a little more water. The flavor will grow more complex with use and age.

BALLYMALOE COOKERY SCHOOL SOURDOUGH BREAD

*Considering you can buy a loaf of bread in any shop, supermarket, or many drugstores, you could be forgiven for deciding that life is far too short to get involved in making sourdough bread, but still I urge you to have a go. Once you establish the starter, it's only a question of mixing the other ingredients and having patience. It does take time, but most of that time the bread is quietly rising or baking. Every loaf is an adventure, each will be slightly different and every time you make a loaf you will learn more about the process – enjoy experimenting!
Note: Making this bread is a two-day process* · **MAKES 1 LARGE LOAF**

To make the sponge

about 2 cups Ballymaloe Sourdough Starter (see above)
2 cups lukewarm spring water
4 cups bread flour

2-quart bowl

The night before: transfer the starter into the bowl. Add 1 cup of the tepid water, stir, add 2 cups of the flour, and mix well. Cover tightly with plastic wrap and leave to stand overnight at room temperature.

Opposite: *A loaf of Sourdough Bread.*

AN IDEAL MIXING BOWL

The size of mixing bowl really matters for all bread-making – if it is too small, you will feel constricted and won't be able to mix comfortably, hence the bread will be coarse-crumbed and heavy. We use large, wide, plastic bowls, not at all glamorous but a perfect shape.

HOW TO CUT BREAD

The trick is to saw, not squash, so you will need a serrated bread knife. If you are right-handed, grip the loaf gently with your left hand, or vice-versa if you are left-handed. Then, using very little downward pressure, saw backwards and forwards to cut off a slice of even thickness. Easy does it! If you press down on the bread you will compact the slice and the texture of the crumb will be spoiled.

Next morning, it will look puffy and very much alive – this is known as the "sponge" – the active yeast. Add the remaining 1 cup of lukewarm water and the remaining 2 cups of flour. Cover tightly and let stand for 5–6 hours at room temperature. It will have increased in size and be light and bubbly in appearance.

Take out 2 cups of this sponge and put back in the airtight jar. Cover and save it as the base for the next batch of bread. Refrigerate until needed.

Put the remainder of the sponge (about 4 cups) into a large mixing bowl. This is the base for your sourdough loaf.

To make the loaf

Add the following ingredients to your sponge and mix well:

⅔–¾ **cup water (depending on consistency of dough) at room temperature**
5½ **cups bread flour**
1 **tablespoon wheat germ**
1 **tablespoon rye flour**

Cover the bowl with plastic wrap or a damp cloth and let stand at room temperature for 20 minutes. Sprinkle with 2½ teaspoons salt. Knead the dough by machine for 6 minutes or by hand for 15 minutes. Check the consistency – the dough should stretch easily and be slightly sticky. If necessary, continue to knead for another 5 minutes or so.

Cover the bowl with plastic wrap or a towel and leave to rise until light and puffy (this can take 6–8

hours at room temperature).

Punch down the dough by kneading it for a few seconds. Then shape into 2 round loaves. Dust generously with flour and put into traditional bannetons or napkin-lined baskets. Cover or slip each basket into a large plastic bag and refrigerate overnight.

Next morning, the dough should have more or less doubled in size. The longer the rising time, the better quality bread in terms of both flavor and structure. Remove from the fridge and let return to room temperature, about 1–1½ hours.

Meanwhile, preheat the oven to 450°F.

Dust a heavy baking sheet with flour and gently turn the loaves onto it. Sprinkle or mist the top of the loaves with water and dust with flour. Slash the top with a sharp blade and bake for about 40 minutes or until the loaves sound hollow when tapped on the base. Let cool on a wire rack. Enjoy every morsel!

Forgotten ways of using up stale bread

If a loaf is just slightly stale, simply pop it back into a hot oven at 400°F for about 5 minutes. If it is several days old, however, dip it quickly in cold water, shake and then bake in a hot oven at 400°F for 8–10 minutes or until the bread is crusty and delicious. Eat immediately.

Fried bread

We used to eat fried bread quite a lot when we were children – usually Mummy's brown soda bread, fried in bacon fat. We'd have that with bacon slices, an egg, and maybe a fried tomato.

Things to do with stale bread

Other great ways included in this book to use stale bread are Bread and Butter Pudding (see page 507), Strata (see page 579), Apple Charlotte (see page 502), and Brown Bread Ice Cream (see page 208).

Otherwise, make bread crumbs and use them to coat fish, meat, and croquettes, and scatter them over gratins.

Bread crumbs

I've just been to the shops and seen bread crumbs for sale for more than the price of a loaf of bread for a container, so let me share the secret of how to make your own.

Before the days of blenders and food processors, we made bread crumbs by grating squares of stale bread on the coarsest part of a box grater. The bread crumbs were not as uniform as those made in a food processor but were absolutely fine. This doesn't work with modern sliced bread, which tends to be more rubbery. Bread crumbs are normally made with crusty bread but soda bread crumbs are also delicious.

Save all leftover white bread. For white bread crumbs, cut off the crusts and tear each slice into three or four pieces. Drop them into a blender or food processor, process for 30 seconds to a minute and hey presto – bread crumbs. Use

immediately or freeze in conveniently sized bags for use another time.

As a matter of fact, any time you have stale bread, get into the habit of processing it in the food processor, putting the bread crumbs in a bag and popping it into the freezer. They don't freeze solid, so you can get to them at any time, and there's something psychological about having them ready which will make you more likely to use them.

Brown bread crumbs

For brown bread crumbs, do as above, but include the crusts. They will be flecked with lots of crust but are good to use for stuffings, for example, see page 260, or any other dish where the crumbs do not need to be white.

Dried bread crumbs

To make dried bread crumbs, cut the crusts off the bread slices and spread out on a baking tray. Bake in a low oven (220°F) for 2–3 hours. Let cool, then pulverize the dry crusts a few at a time into fine bread crumbs in a blender. Sift and store in a jar or plastic container until needed. They will keep for months. Use for any recipe that requires dried bread crumbs.

Uses for bread crumbs

Stuffings, coating fish, plum puddings, meat, croquettes, fish cakes, bread sauce, Buttered Crumbs (see right). We keep a box of the latter in the fridge to sprinkle over Gratins (see page 385). They are even better when mixed with grated Cheddar cheese.

Above: *Pan Grattato.*

BUTTERED CRUMBS

Sprinkle over the top of creamy gratins. These will keep in an airtight container in the fridge for a week.

4 tablespoons butter
2 cups soft white bread crumbs

Melt the butter in a pan and stir in the bread crumbs. Remove from the heat and let cool.

Variation
PAN GRATTATO
Pan grattato is the Italian name for buttered crumbs, which uses extra virgin olive oil instead of butter and sprinkles in a handful of herbs as well. This Italian version of buttered crumbs is delicious sprinkled over all sorts of things from pasta to roast chicken.

FRENCH TOAST

French toast is fantastic, economical, and best of all, uses bread that you'd otherwise throw out – hence the French name, pain perdu, *or "lost bread."* Pain perdu, *French toast, Poor Knights of Windsor, and eggy bread are all pretty much the same thing. Not only is it a delicious way of using up leftover bread, it can be sweet or savory, and it's been a great way for many a crafty mother to get eggs into their toddlers.*

According to Margaret Costa, the Spaniards have another version where they dip the bread in a mixture of egg yolks and sweet sherry, fry it in hot oil, and serve it dusted with confectioners' sugar and cinnamon. I love it piled high with berries or slathered with butter, marmalade and a blob of vanilla ice cream or sour cream. It'd hardly be a sacrifice to eat stale bread prepared in that way! · SERVES 4

3 organic eggs
2 tablespoons whole milk or light
   cream
pinch of salt
4 slices good bread or brioche
4 tablespoons Clarified Butter (see
   page 216)

Whisk the eggs, milk, and salt together until well blended. Strain the mixture through a sieve into a shallow bowl in which you can easily dip a slice of bread. Dip both sides of each slice of bread in the batter.

Melt 2 tablespoons of the butter in a frying pan big enough to hold 2 slices at once. Fry the bread over medium heat until pale golden,

turning once. Keep warm in a low oven while frying the other pieces in the remaining butter.

Serve warm, sprinkled with confectioners' sugar.

MELBA TOAST

Melba toast is reminiscent of grand hotels – but now so retro and simply delicious to nibble on · MAKES 16 TRIANGLES

4 slices white bread, not too thinly
   sliced, ¼in thick

Preheat the broiler to its maximum heat. Slide an oven rack under the grill as close to the element as possible. Toast the bread on both sides, then lower the oven rack so it is about 5in from the element, giving the toast room to curl up – this should take less than a minute. Work quickly and while the toast is still hot, cut off the crusts and split the bread in half horizontally.

Scrape off any excess dough with a serrated knife or a teaspoon, then cut each slice into 2 or 4 triangles. Replace the toast under the grill on the rack or oven tray. It will probably curl up within seconds, but be careful not to let it burn.

The second stage may also be done in a low oven, at 300°F.

Melba toast will keep in an airtight container for a day or two but is best served immediately.

PARMESAN TOASTS

In many upscale delis, day-old bread is sliced thinly, sprinkled with finely grated cheese, baked, and sold for four times the price. Yet who could complain? It's delicious!

day old yeast or sourdough bread
   or good-quality baguette, cut
   into ⅛in thick slices (if using
   baguette, cut it at a long angle)
extra virgin olive oil
Parmesan cheese, finely grated

Preheat the oven to 300°F.

Brush one side of the thinly sliced bread with extra virgin olive oil and sprinkle with the freshly grated Parmesan cheese. Arrange in a single layer on a baking sheet and bake slowly until golden brown and crisp, about 30 minutes. Serve warm.

BRUSCHETTA

Originally this recipe was just a way of using up day-old bread. Nowadays, people pile all kinds of things on top of it, sometimes to delicious effect, but if you've got well-made bread and beautiful new season's olive oil, it's perfect in and of itself. When I first ate it at a Tuscan family lunch, where we had the original, it was divine.

In Catalonia, they rub tomato on the surface of the bread and call it pa amb tomàquet. *You can top bruschetta with arugula, tapenade, tomatoes and basil, roasted peppers, arugula, and shavings of Parmesan, blue cheese, and honey, or any number of other things* · SERVES 4

4 slices of crusty country white
    bread, ½in thick
1 garlic clove
extra virgin olive oil

Toast the bread on both sides in a
broiler or hot grill. Rub immediately
with a cut clove of garlic.

Drizzle with extra virgin olive oil
and serve.

CROUTONS

*Croutons can be made several hours or
even a day ahead with oil flavored by
sprigs of rosemary, thyme, or onion.
Cut into cubes or stamp out into
various shapes – hearts, stars, clubs,
diamonds, or whatever else takes your
fancy – and sprinkle over salads or
serve with soups* · SERVES 4

2 slices of slightly stale white
    bread, ¼in thick
sunflower or olive oil

First cut the crusts off the bread,
then cut into ¼in strips and finally
exact cubes.

Heat the oil in a frying pan. It
should be at least ¾in deep and
almost smoking. Put a heatproof
sieve over a heatproof bowl.

Add the croutons to the hot oil.
Stir once or twice; they will color
almost immediately. When the
croutons are golden brown in color,
pour the oil and croutons into the
sieve, then drain on paper towels.
Reheat the oil to cook another batch
or use for another purpose.

BACON AND CHEDDAR CHEESE STRATA

*A strata is like a savory bread and
butter pudding. If available, use top-
quality thickly sliced bacon for extra
deliciousness. This, like fried bread, is
a great way to use up day-old white
bread* · SERVES 4-6

4 slices day-old white bread, crusts
    removed
6 slices of bacon, cut into strips
6 large organic eggs
1½ cups milk
¼ teaspoon salt
freshly ground black pepper
¼–½ teaspoon Tabasco sauce
1 cup grated Cheddar, Colby, or
    Gruyère cheese
2 tablespoons chopped parsley
1 tablespoons chopped chives

8 x 11in lasagne dish, greased

Arrange two slices of bread so they
are slightly overlapping in the
lasagne dish. Heat a little extra
virgin olive oil in a frying pan, crisp
up the bacon, then scatter them,
along with half of the cheese, over
the top. Then add two more slices
of bread.

Whisk together the eggs and
milk, season with salt and pepper,
and add Tabasco to taste. Fold in
half of the grated cheese and the
parsley and chives. Pour the egg
mixture over the bread and sprinkle
with the remaining cheese. Cover
and refrigerate for several hours, or
overnight if possible.

Preheat the oven to 350°F.

Put the dish in a water bath.
Bake the strata, uncovered, until set,
about 45–50 minutes. Let cook for
10 minutes, then cut into squares
and serve.

PANZANELLA (TUSCAN BREAD SALAD

*A delicious way to use up slightly stale
sourdough bread* · SERVES 8

2–3 cloves garlic, thinly sliced
½ cup extra virgin olive oil
1lb crusty sourdough bread,
    cut into 1in cubes
1 red onion, roughly chopped
½ cup pitted Kalamata olives
24 large basil leaves, torn into
    pieces
8 ripe tomatoes, cut into 1in pieces
2 tablespoons balsamic vinegar
1 tablespoon white wine vinegar
½ cup extra virgin olive oil
salt and freshly ground black
    pepper

Preheat the oven to 350°F.

Put the garlic and olive oil in a
large bowl. Add the bread cubes and
toss to coat evenly. Spread on a
baking sheet and bake until golden,
5–6 minutes.

Return the croutons to the bowl
with the onion, olives, basil, and
tomatoes. Whisk the vinegars, olive
oil, salt, and pepper together, and
toss with the salad. Taste and adjust
the seasoning. Serve immediately.

Crêpes

For family cooking you always need to have a few things up your sleeve that can be thrown together quickly in an emergency. Crêpes have always been one of my great standbys. If you arrive home late and everyone is starving you can whizz up some batter and within a few minutes, the speckled crêpes will be coming off the pan.

CRÊPE BATTER

If you need to keep up with demand and you have the pans, it is perfectly possible to keep three or four going in rotation, but this is only necessary if you need to feed the multitudes! ·
MAKES 12 CRÊPES

1⅔ **cups all-purpose flour,**
    preferably unbleached
a good pinch of salt
3 **organic eggs, lightly beaten**
1½ **cups whole milk, or for very**
    crisp, light delicate crêpes, milk
    and water mixed
1–2 **tablespoons melted butter**

11in **frying pan**

Sift the flour and salt into a bowl, make a well in the center and drop in the eggs. Starting in the center, use a whisk or wooden spoon to mix the egg and, using a continuous circular movement, gradually bring in the flour. Add the liquid slowly and when it is all added, beat until the batter is covered with bubbles.

Let the batter stand in a cool place for an hour or so if possible (longer will do no harm). Just before you cook the crêpes, stir in 1–2 tablespoons of melted butter. This will make all the difference to the flavor and texture of the crêpes and will enable you to cook them without greasing the pan each time.

To cook, heat the pan on a high heat, pour in just enough batter to cover the base of the pan thinly (a small ladle can also be very useful for this). With a heatproof spatula, loosen the crêpe around the edge, flip it over and cook for a second or two on the other side. Slide the crêpe onto a plate; the crêpes may be stacked on top of each other and peeled apart later.

They will keep in the fridge for several days and also freeze perfectly. If freezing, it's probably a good idea to put a disc of waxed paper between each for extra safety.

Variations

· Serve the crêpes with sour cream or cream cheese and top with smoked salmon, roasted peppers, or Wild Garlic Pesto (see page 29).
· Add 2 tablespoons of freshly chopped herbs, e.g. parsley, thyme, and chives to the batter.
· For sweet crêpes, simply add a tablespoon of sugar to the batter recipe above.
· Add ½–2 teaspoons of apple pie spice to the savory or sweet batter, depending on taste.
· Slather the sweet crêpes with chocolate sauce and roll up.
· Spread any homemade jam over the sweet crêpes.
· Top the sweet crêpes with butterscotch or toffee sauce and mashed banana.
· Add crushed blueberries, a sprinkling of sugar and sour cream to the sweet crêpes.
· Add marmalade and clotted cream to the sweet crêpes.
· Serve the sweet crêpes with orange butter.
· Top sweet crêpes with Nutella, toasted hazelnuts, and thick cream.

FLORENCE BOWE'S "CRUMPETS"

My eccentric Auntie Florence is famous for these, as well as many other things. They go back as long as I can remember. If we were making tea, Florence would put a pan on the stove, make a batch of crumpet batter and we'd have them hot off the pan, spread with butter and with sugar sprinkled on top. I'm so grateful for this recipe because it's lovely to teach children and grandchildren, and is the best standby. Florence has now discovered the food processor and achieves great results by throwing all the batter ingedients in and just processing for a few seconds ·
MAKES ABOUT 15

1¾ **cups all-purpose flour,**
    preferably unbleached
¼ **cup superfine sugar**
¼ **teaspoon salt**
½ **teaspoon baking soda**
1 **teaspoon cream of tartar**
2 **tablespoons butter**
2 **organic eggs**
1 **cup milk**

TO SERVE
homemade jam, apple jelly, or
    lemon juice and sugar

Sift the dry ingredients into a bowl and rub in the butter. Drop the eggs

Left: *Florence Bowe's "Crumpets."*

RACHEL'S DROP SCONES

This recipe, given to me by my daughter-in-law Rachel, is even simpler than the crumpet one (you use baking powder, not cream of tartar). My grandsons, Joshua and Lucca, are champion drop-scone makers · **MAKES 12**

¾ **cup plus 1 tablespoon self-rising flour**
1 teaspoon baking powder
2 tablespoons superfine sugar
pinch of salt
1 organic egg
½ **cup milk**
drop of sunflower oil, for greasing

Sift the flour and baking powder into a bowl, add the sugar and salt, and stir to mix. Make a well in the center, crack in the egg and whisk, gradually drawing in the flour from the edge. Add the milk gradually, whisking all the time, to form a smooth batter.

Lightly grease a frying pan and warm it over moderate heat. Drop 3 tablespoons of the batter into the pan, keeping them well apart so they don't stick together. Cook for about 2 minutes, until bubbles appear on the surface and begin to burst and the drop scones are golden underneath (and not before). Then flip them over and cook on the other side for a minute or so, until golden on this side as well.

Remove from the pan and serve warm with butter and jam, apple jelly, Lemon Curd (see page 224), or chocolate spread.

into the center, add a little of the milk and whisk rapidly, allowing the flour to drop gradually in from the sides. When half the milk is added, beat the mixture until air bubbles rise. Add the remainder of the milk, cover and let stand for 1 hour.

Drop about 2 teaspoons of batter into a hot pan and cook until bubbles appear on the top. (It usually takes a bit of trial and error to get the temperature right.) Flip over and cook until golden on the other side.

Serve immediately with butter and homemade jam or apple jelly. Alternatively, crumpets can be served with lemon juice and sprinkled with sugar.

Variation

RACHEL'S CHOCOLATE CRUMPETS
My daughter-in-law Rachel makes great chocolate crumpets by adding 2oz or more chopped chocolate to the mixture.

Natural Cleaning Agents

The paranoia about germs and bacteria continues to grow, whipped up by media frenzy and expensive ad campaigns that terrorize the public into high alert about the hazards that lurk in every corner and under every ledge. For many of us, there is a growing concern about the misuse and overzealous use of sterilizing agents. I myself am shocked to see chefs and caterers spraying work surfaces with sanitizers and then putting food directly onto the surface. All these substances are completely banned from my home and Cookery School. I prefer the use of pure soap and water, a good, strong scrubbing brush, and plenty of elbow grease. We use lots of old-fashioned cleaning agents. Some of the most effective are basic kitchen ingredients such as salt, baking soda, vinegar, and lemon juice.

Lemons

Lemon juice is a natural bleach. To clean copper or silver, sprinkle salt onto the item and rub it with the cut surface of a lemon, which will lift the tarnish. Wash, rinse well, dry, and polish.

Right: *Lemons and baking soda are natural and effective cleaning agents.*

Lemon spray

Put a mixture of 1 part lemon juice and 3 parts water into a spray bottle. This is great for cleaning kitchen and bathroom surfaces. In the unlikely event that you have a surplus of lemons, add ½ cup to the

rinse cycle in the washing machine to brighten up your whites.

Baking soda

Also known as bread soda, baking soda is brilliant for removing tea or coffee stains from cups. It also

absorbs odors in a fridge. When mixed with vinegar or lemon juice it gets rid of soap scum. The paste can also be applied to sinks, tiles, or the shower door to clean grime. Rinse away and dry.

Vinegar

Plain white malt vinegar is most effective as a household cleanser. Use 1 part vinegar to 4 parts water to clean windows and mirrors, and use newspapers to buff them up to a shine. Use 1 part vinegar to 1 part water to lift lime scale from the toilet: pour it in last thing at night, brush and flush through in the morning.

To descale water faucets

White vinegar has natural anti-fungal and disinfectant properties and attacks all alkalines including lime scale. Pour a little vinegar into a bottle cap. Secure it around the mouth of the faucet with tape. Leave to soak for several hours, then remove and run water through to rinse. Do not do this on lacquered faucets.

Pet accidents

If your pet pees on the carpet, dab on some vinegar. It will evaporate the smell and discourage the animal from targeting that spot again.

Salt

We use dairy or cooking salt with no anti-caking agents. Salt is a natural antiseptic. Sprinkle a little on wooden cutting boards and scrub with a coarse scrubbing brush. Rinse well with hot water and leave to stand on its side to dry, preferably in the sun with the air circulating around.

To clean silver cutlery

Dissolve salt and baking soda with hot water in a non-metallic container (Pyrex or plastic is fine). Immerse the silver cutlery in the solution, which will remove the tarnish. Rinse well and polish with a soft cloth.

To clean the oven

Make a paste of baking soda, salt, and hot water, paint onto the oven, leave for 15 minutes, remove, and rinse well.

To clean a copper bowl

Copper bowls need to be cleaned just before using. Sprinkle a little sea salt into the bowl and add a couple of tablespoons of vinegar. Rub vigorously – the bowl will be clean in seconds. Rinse and dry well. Alternatively use half a lemon instead of the vinegar.

A Few Natural Remedies

Indigestion

Some time ago I was gobsmacked to discover that a local shop offered 11 different remedies for indigestion. For a natural remedy, simply mix a scant ¼ teaspoon of baking soda with 2–3 tablespoons of water. Drink it all at once – it'll do the trick!

Earache

Today every supermarket sells a selection of olive oil, but when I was a child the only time we ever used olive oil was when someone had an earache or a crick in their neck, and these remedies are as effective as ever. If you have an earache, one of the best remedies is to warm some olive oil gently (be careful it's not too hot) and get somebody to put a little into your ear with a teaspoon. Then block it with a piece of cotton. If this doesn't cure your earache, go to the doctor!

Neck pain

If you've got a crick in your neck, dip a sock in some warm olive oil and wrap it around your neck. It should be cured the following day.

Bee stings

Dab the affected area with vinegar for virtually instant relief.

Wasp stings

Cut an onion in half and rub over the affected area as soon as possible – it will soothe the sting almost immediately.

Nettle stings

Find a dock leaf, which always grow close to nettles. Rub the leaf over the affected area and the stinging will ease in a matter of minutes.

Burns

Immediately run the affected area under cold water and continue until the burning sensation ceases. Aloe vera is also a treasure to have on your window sill because, as our mothers and grandmothers knew, it's an effective cure for burns. Just pull off a leaf, cut it and squeeze the sap directly onto the affected area.

Resources

Bread

Bread Matters, by Andrew Whitley (Andrews McMeel, 2009), is a guide to why and how to make your own bread at home.
Dough, by Richard Bertinet (Kyle Books, 2006), shows how to make simple contemporary bread.

Dairy

New England Cheesemaking Supplies, www.cheesemaking.com, are suppliers of cheesemaking kits, equipment, advice, and support for home cheesemakers.

Fish

The Marine Conservation Society (MCS), www.fishonline.org, helps consumers to identify fish from well-managed sources or caught using sustainable methods.

The Marine Stewardship Council (MSC), www.msc.org, issues seafood ecolabels and certifies fisheries to promote sustainable fishing.

Monterey Bay Aquarium Seafood Watch, www.montereybayaquarium.org, uses pocket guides, Twitter and text messages to advise consumers on which seafoods to buy.

Foraging

Mushroom Feast, by Jane Grigson (Grub Street, 2008)
Mushrooms and Other Fungi of Great Britain and Europe, by Roger Phillips (Pan Books, 1981)
The Forager's Harvest, by Samuel Thayer (Forager's Harvest Press, 2006)
A Field Guide to Mushrooms: North America (Peterson Field Guide Series), by Kent H. McKnight and Vera B. McKnight (Houghton Mifflin, 1987)

Food Safety Authority of Ireland, http://fsai.ie/home.html, helps to ensure food sold in Ireland meets the highest standards of food safety and hygiene available.

Natural Resources Conservation Services, http://plants.usda.gov, provides a database of plants found in the US.

The Organic Center, www.theorganiccenter.com, communicates the benefits of organic farming and products.

Plants for a Future, www.pfaf.org/database/plants, is a database of edible, medicinal, and useful plants.

Rogers Mushrooms, www.rogersmushrooms.com, is a site based on Roger Phillips' book *Mushrooms and Other Fungi of Great Britain and Europe.*

Game

U.S. Fish and Wildlife Service, www.fws.com/hunting, provides information on hunting seasons for wild birds.

Gardening

Compost, by Kenneth Thompson (DK, 2007), explores the natural way to make food for your garden.
Going Organic, by Bob Flowerdew (Kyle Cathie, 2007), is a guide to organic gardening.
Grow Your Own, Eat Your Own, by Bob Flowerdew (Kyle Books, 2009), tells you how to make the most of your garden produce.
21st-century Smallholder, by Paul Waddington (Transworld, 2008), gives tips on how to make the most of your space to grow your own.
Jekka's Complete Herb Book, by Jekka McVicar (Kyle Cathie, 2009), is published in association with the Royal Horticultural Society, giving advice on planting herb gardens.

Grow your Own Fruit, by Carol Klein (Royal Horticultural Society, 2009), is an illustrated guide to buying and growing fruit.

Grow Vegetables, by Alan Buckingham (DK, 2007), is a reference book for gardeners.

Rodale's Ultimate Encyclopedia of Organic Gardening by Fern Marshall Bradley (Rodale, 2009), gives practical information for organic gardeners.

Sarah Raven's Kitchen and Garden, www.sarahraven.com, is a mail order company selling seeds, bulbs, books and things for the kitchen and garden.

Grow it Yourself Ireland, www.giyireland.com, is a national not-for-profit organization which is trying to inspire and teach people to grow their own food.

Hens

Order your own chicken house at Eglu, www.omlet.co.uk

For incubators and wall-mounted humane dispatcher or cone tripod poultry dispatcher, see Ascott Smallholding Supplies, www.ascott.biz

There are several magazines for people interested in smallholding, like *Country Smallholding* and *The Smallholder*. It is worth getting a subscription, not just for the articles but also the ads at the back – a mine of information about where to find the gadgets to make your life easier.

Keeping A Few Hens in Your Garden, by Francine Raymond and Melanie Clitheroe, (Kitchen Garden Press, 1998), offers advice on keeping a few hens in your garden.

British Poultry Standards, 6th edition (Wiley-Blackwell, 2008), is the official reference guide for all the recognized breeds in Great Britain.

Meat

Fresh blood for blood puddings can be purchased from a Butcher's supply website like Scobies, www.scobiesdirect.com

Natural casings are available from Harvest Essentials, www.harvestessentials.com, tel: 877-759-3758 OR The Sausage Maker, www.sausagemaker.com

If you're serious about charcuterie, look up these books, which reveal the science behind the process and explore the subject in greater depth:
Cooking by Hand by Paul Bertolli (Clarkson Potter, 2003)
Charcuterie by Michael Ruhlman (W.W. Norton, 2005)
Charcuterie and French Pork Cooking by Jane Grigson (Grub Street, 2001)
The River Cottage Meat Book by Hugh Fearnley-Whittingstall (Ten Speed Press, 2007)

Suppliers of vampire knives: Haarslev Limited, www.haarslev.com

General

Find your local farmers' market: www.farmersmarkets.net or www.localharvest.org

The Slow Food Movement, www.slowfood.org.uk, works to counteract fast food and the disappearance of local food traditions, and promotes sustainable agriculture.

Farm to Table, www.earthpledge.org/f2t, promotes planet-friendly food and farming through education, campaigns, and community programs.

The Irish Countywomen's Association, www.ica.ie, the largest women's organization in Ireland, provides a wide range of activities and courses.

Courses

The School of Artisan Food, www.schoolofartisanfood.org

The Ballymaloe Cookery School, 12-week Certificate and over 30 short courses, including Forgotten Skills Courses; tel: + 353 21 4646785; www.cookingisfun.ie

A

Aioli, 96–97
crispy pig's tails with aioli, 329
garlic and saffron aioli, 97
tiny potatoes dipped in aioli, 383
Alcohol, making, 464–467
Alexander, 70
alexander fritters, 70
cooked alexanders, 70
Alison Henderson's baked
cheesecake, 229
Almonds
almond and apricot squares, 553
almond paste, 536–537
toasted almond Christmas cake, 537
Anchovies
butter, 217
roast loin of rosé veal with
anchoïde, 180–181
salad of warm sweetbreads with
potato crisps, anchovies, and
wild garlic, 350, 352
Angelica, 367
angelica and macaroon cake, 535
candied angelica, 458–459
Apples
apple and currant roly–poly, 513
apple and ginger jam, 446
apple and grape chutney, 438
apple and rose geranium compote,
494
apple and rose geranium sauce,
222
apple and tomato chutney, 437
apple butter, 452
apple charlotte, 502
apple cheese, 453
apple cider, 467
apple fritters, 498
apple jelly, 40
apple sauce, 298
apple snow, 494
blackberry and apple muesli, 37
cranberry and apple jam, 446
damson and apple sauce, 41
drying, 460
Eve's pudding, 502
Irish apple cake, 500
Mummy's apple pie, 500–501
plum and apple jam, 445
pork and apple burgers, 296
roast apples with cinnamon cream,
498
storing, 453
tarte tatin with sour cream
shortcrust pastry, 210–211
wild blackberry, apple, and rose
geranium jam, 445
wild damson and apple jam, 445

winter apple and mincemeat
pudding, 511
Apricots
almond and apricot squares, 553
apricot ratafia, 465
dried apricot jam, 448
drying, 460
fresh apricot jam, 448
Arugula
arugula pesto, 29
carpaccio with arugula and
Parmesan, 175
farro with fava beans, peas,
asparagus, and arugula, 402
smoked egg, chorizo, and arugula
salad, 489
spiced beef with arugula leaves
and guacamole, 188
spicy lamb burgers with mint,
yogurt, and arugula, 343
Asparagus
farro with fava beans, peas,
asparagus, and arugula, 402
salad with duck eggs, Parmesan,
roast red pepper and asparagus, 254
Avocado
salad of quail eggs with smoked
venison and avocado, 255
spiced beef with arugula leaves
and guacamole, 188

B

Bacon
bacon and cheddar cheese strata,
579
bacon and egg pie, 313
bairneachs with bacon, 61
cabbage with crispy bacon, 409
crispy eggs with bacon and tomato
fondue, 246
curly kale with bacon and
chestnuts, 413
Danish pâté, 326
dry-cured, 310
eggs Benedict, 248
juniper berry brine, 311
melted chard stalks with bacon
and hazelnuts, 396
Paddy Ward's wet-cure, 310
pheasant with chorizo, bacon, and
tomatoes, 131
pheasant, bacon, and wild mushroom
casserole with scallion champ, 133
Philip's wet-cure, 310–311
smoked, 486
Swiss salade frisée with bacon and
oeufs mollet, 313, 315
traditional Irish bacon, cabbage,
and parsley sauce, 315
Ballymaloe brown yeast bread, 569
Ballymaloe chicken liver pâté with
Melba toast, 268
Ballymaloe Cookery School sourdough
bread, 574, 576

Ballymaloe fudge, 516
Ballymaloe green gooseberry and
elderflower tart, 501
Ballymaloe green tomato chutney,
437
Ballymaloe homemade sausages, 298
Ballymaloe Irish stew, 348
Ballymaloe mincemeat, 512
Ballymaloe praline ice cream, 208
Ballymaloe sourdough starter, 574
Ballymaloe spiced beef, 187–188
Ballymaloe vanilla ice cream, 207
Ballymaloe white yeast bread, 572
Basil, 368
basil oil, 424
basil pesto, 29
Bay, 368
Beans, 400
braised lamb shanks with garlic,
rosemary, and cannellini beans, 344
farro with fava beans, peas,
asparagus, and arugula, 402
fava bean-pod soup, 402
French beans, 401
French beans with fresh chile, 401
French beans with tomato fondue,
402
runner beans, 402
shell beans, 402
tomato, bean, and rosemary stew,
378
Beansprouts, 400–401
Beef, 151–155
aged meat, 155
American braised short ribs, 165
Ballymaloe spiced beef, 187–188
basic beef burgers, 171
beef cheeks with mustard fruits, 166
beef cheeks with parsnip champ, 166
beef consommé, 160
beef shin and oxtail stew, 162
beef stock, 159
beef stroganoff, 174–175
beef tea, 160
biltong, 185
bresaola, 188
brining, 186–188
carpaccio with arugula and
Parmesan, 175
consommé en geleé, 160
corned beef, 186
corned beef and cabbage, 186
cottage pie with garlic butter, 171
cuts, 154
demi-glace, 159, 262
dried meat jerky, 185
dripping, 177
dripping on toast, 177
glace de viande, 159
ground beef, 171–172
Julija's Lithuanian beef goulash, 168
leftover oxtail stew, 163
marrow bones with fresh herb salad, 165
meatballs with fresh tomato
sauce, 172

Michael Cuddigan's pickled ox tongue, 187
oxtail with grainy mustard sauce, 163
pan-grilled steak with Béarnaise sauce and frites, 173–174
pastrami, 186–187
red wine sauce for beef and steaks, 174
roast fillet of beef, 158
roast round of beef with horseradish sauce, gravy, and Yorkshire pudding, 156
roasting, 156, 158
scalloped potato with steak and kidney, 167
spiced beef with arugula leaves and guacamole, 188
steak and kidney pie, 170
steak and kidney pudding, 176–177
steak and oyster pie, 168
steaks, cutting, 172–173
stewing and braising, 162–170
stuffed beef heart, 158
suet, 176–177
terms, 155
traditional roast beef with horseradish sauce, gravy, and Yorkshire pudding, 156
tripe, 184
winter beef stew, 163
Beet, 392
beet and ginger relish, 439
beet chutney, 439
beet chips, 394
beet gravlax, 106
beet tops with cream, 394
beet tops, 393
beet tzatziki, 223
hot beets with cream and marjoram, 393
pickled beets, 431
roasted beets, 392
Bilberries, 38
bilberry jelly with fresh mint cream, 38–39
Biltong, 185
Black puddings, 318
Blackberries, 36
blackberry and apple muesli, 37
blackberry and rose geranium cordial, 37
blackberry and rose geranium sorbet, 37
blackberry ice cubes, 37
crab apple and blackberry tart, 41
sloe and blackberry cheese, 45
wild blackberry, apple, and rose geranium jam, 445
Black currants
black currant cordial, 469
black currant coulis, 228
black currant fool, 496
black currant ice cream, 496
black currant jam, 444
black currant jelly, 452

black currant leaf lemonade, 469
black currant swirl ice cream, 207
Blood puddings, 317–318
Blueberries
blueberry and lemon verbena jam, 446
crushed fraughans, 38
Emer Fitzgerald's fraughan scones, 38
wild, 38
Borage, 368
Bottling, 434
Boysenberry jam, 442
Brandy butter, 217
Brawn, 320–321
Bread, 556–558
American soda bread, 563
bacon and cheddar cheese strata, 579
Ballymaloe brown yeast bread, 569
Ballymaloe Cookery School sourdough bread, 574, 576
Ballymaloe sourdough starter, 574
Ballymaloe white yeast bread, 572
bastible bread, 564
bean can bread, 572
beginner's brown soda bread, 560–561
braided bread, 572
brotherly love, 573
brown bread ice cream, 208
brown griddle scones, 565
brown muffins, 569
brown yeast bread, 567, 569
bruschetta, 578–579
croutons, 579
cutting, 576
dillisk bread, 68
flours, 558–559
French toast, 578
griddle breads, 564–566
Kerry treacle bread, 561
Kerry cornmeal griddle bread, 566
Melba toast, 578
multiseed soda bread, 561
Mummy's brown soda bread, 199
olive oil bread, 572
panzanella, 579
pappa al pomodoro, 377
Parmesan toasts, 578
potato bread, 566
rising agents, 559
soda bread, 560–564
sourdough bread, 574, 576
spotted dog, 563
stale, using up, 576–579
toast with clotted cream and marmalade, 211
Turkish flatbread, 565
white soda bread, 561
white soda scones, 561
white yeast bread, 570–573
yeast breads, 567–573
Bread and butter pudding, 507
Bread sauce, 271

Bread crumbs, 577
buttered crumbs, 577
haddock with peperonata and buttered crumbs, 87
mackerel with almond migas, 84–85
pan grattato, 577
Bresaola, 188
Broccoli, 411
sprouting broccoli, 411
Brownies
hazelnut chocolate brownies, 46–47
Brussels sprouts, 410
Brussels sprout shoots, 411
Brussels sprout tops, 410–411
spicy Brussels sprouts, 410
Burdock, 21
Butter, 213
balls or pats, 216
brandy butter, 217
butter cookies, 218
clarified, 216
dill or fennel butter, 217
fresh herb butter, 216
garlic butter, 217
ghee, 216
maître d'hôtel, 216
making, 214
mint butter, 216
mustard and parsley butter, 217
nasturtium butter, 217
nut and butter cookies, 218
orange butter cookies, 218
rosemary butter, 216
rum butter, 217
salted, 214
spiced butter cookies, 218
spreadable, 214
traditional country butter, 218
watercress butter, 216
wild garlic butter, 216
Butter stamps, 213
Buttermilk, 198–199
buttermilk chocolate cake, 201
buttermilk onion rings, 200
buttermilk panna cotta, 200
homemade, 199
Mummy's brown soda bread, 199
Russian fluffy pancakes, 200

C

Cabbages, 409
buttered cabbage, 409
cabbage with caraway seeds, 409
cabbage with crispy bacon, 409
colcannon, 384
corned beef and cabbage, 186
Emily's cabbage, 409
red cabbage, 134
sautéed pheasant breasts with Savoy cabbage, 130–131
spiced cabbage soup, 409
traditional Irish bacon, cabbage, and parsley sauce, 315

Cakes, 520
  angelica and macaroon cake, 535
  Aunt Florence's orange cake,
    528–529
  baking ingredients, 522–523
  balloons, 548
  boiled fruitcake, 538
  buns. See Buns
  butterfly buns, 533
  buttermilk chocolate cake, 201
  caraway seed cake, 530
  chapel window cake, 530–531
  cherry cake, 530
  clementine syrup cake, 504
  coconut buns, 533
  coffee cake, 531
  creaming or whipping method, 528–532
  Darina Allen's iced Christmas
    cake, 536
  dripping cake, 539
  duck-egg sponge, 255
  Easter tea ring, 545
  fairy cakes, 532–533
  fat rascals, 540
  faults, 525
  Genoise sponge, 521, 527
  gingerbread, 535
  Great-grandmother's layer cake, 528
  Halloween barmbrack, 547
  iced buns, 533
  icing. See Icing
  Irish porter cake, 537
  Irish tea barmbrack, 538
  lemon cornmeal cake with lemon
    curd and sour cream, 532
  lining a cake pan, 524
  Lydia's lemon cake with
    crystallized violets and
    angelica, 33
  made without fat, 521, 526–527
  Madeira cake, 530
  molten method, 535–538
  Mrs. Lamb's layer cake, 526
  poppy seed cake, 530
  raspberry buns, 540
  rubbing-in method, 538–540
  Seville orange marmalade cake, 540
  stale, using, 545
  tins, 523–534
  toasted almond Christmas cake, 537
  types of, 520
  whisked-up jelly roll, 526–527
  wild strawberry cake, 44
Canary pudding, 511
Candied peel, 458
Candying, 458–459
Capers
  boiled leg of mutton with caper
    sauce, 354–355
Casseroles and stews
  Ballymaloe Irish stew, 348
  casserole, using, 348
  Emer Fitzgerald's braised lamb
    neck moussaka, 348–349
  hay box, in, 349

  Irish stew with pearl barley, 348
  Julija's Lithuanian beef goulash, 168
  Mummy's rabbit stew, 141
  pheasant, bacon, and wild mushroom
    casserole with scallion champ, 133
  shin of beef and oxtail stew, 162
  tomato, bean and rosemary stew,
    378
  venison stew with chestnuts, 146
  winter beef stew, 163
Cassoulet, 285–286
Caul fat, 325
Cavolo nero
  braised cavolo nero, 415
  cavolo nero bruschetta, 415
Celeriac and mashed parsnip, 134
Champ, 383
Chard, 396
  melted chard stalks with bacon
    and hazelnuts, 396
  simple cooked chard, 396
Cheese, 226
  bacon and cheddar cheese strata,
    579
  blue cheese and rosemary gratin, 385
  carpaccio with arugula and Parmesan,
    175
  cheddar cheese soufflé with chives, 252
  cheese soufflé omelette, 249
  cheese straws, 219
  coeur à la crème with summer
    berries, 228
  cottage cheese with nasturtium
    flowers, 227
  Doune McKenzie's cheese crisps,
    233
  gratin of potato, cheddar cheese,
    and seasonal greens, 384–385
  gratin Savoyard, 385
  homemade cottage cheese with
    fresh herbs and oatcakes, 227
  cottage cheese, 227
  homemade crackers for, 231
  homemade cream cheese, 228
  labne, 225
  making, 226
  marinated labne, 225
  mascarpone, 230
  paneer, 232
  Parmesan toasts, 578
  pheasant breast with paprika and
    Parmesan, 133
  rennet, 227
  salad with duck eggs, Parmesan,
    roasted red pepper, and asparagus, 254
  semi-hard, 232–233
  soft goat, 231
  soft yogurt cheese, 225
  starter, 230
  tiramisu, 230
  zucchini or vegetable marrow in
    cheese sauce, 406–407
Cheesecake
  Alison Henderson's baked
    cheesecake, 229

Cherries
  cherry brandy, 464
  cherry buns, 545
  cherry cake, 530
  pickled cherries, 432
Chervil, 368
Chestnuts
  chestnut stuffing, 270–271
  curly kale with bacon and
    chestnuts, 413
  venison stew with chestnuts, 146
Chicken
  breast, smoking, 480, 485
  chicken breasts with mushrooms
    and ginger, 198
  chicken broth for the soul,
    263
  chicken stock, 262
  chicken wings with sweet chile sauce,
    269
  chicken with morels, 54, 55
  confit of chicken legs, 280
  coq au vin, 267
  crispy chicken skin with plum or
    sweet chile sauce, 269
  gutting, 257–258
  hot-smoked chicken breast, 485
  jointing, 258
  killing, 256
  old hen with parsley sauce, 265, 267
  pasta with roast chicken,
    raisins, pine nuts, and parsley,
    265
  poulet a l'estragon, 263
  roast chicken supper in a dish, 264
  salad of smoked chicken with
    parsnip crisps and cranberry
    sauce, 488–489
  terrine of chicken, 268–269
  traditional roast stuffed
    chicken, 260
Chicken livers
  Ballymaloe chicken liver pâté
    with Melba toast, 268
  chicken liver pâté with
    caramelized onions, 268
  chicken liver pâté with
    mushrooms, 268
  crispy chicken livers with lime, 268
  terrine of chicken, 268–269
Chickweed, 21
Chile oil, 426
Chiles
  drying, 460
  sweet chile sauce, 433
  tomato and chile jam, 450
Chives, 368
Chocolate
  buttermilk chocolate cake, 201
  chocolate candied orange, 458
  chocolate crème Anglaise, 204
  chocolate toffees, 516
  dark chocolate icing, 533
  grown-up chocolate and salted toffee
    squares, 553

hazelnut chocolate brownies, 46–47
hot chocolate soufflés, 509
mendiants, 46
Rachel's chocolate crumpets, 581
tiramisu, 230
Chorizo, 305
chargrilled squid with chile and
parsley oil and chorizo, 99
kidneys and chorizo in fine
sherry, 324
pheasant with chorizo, bacon, and
tomatoes, 131
sweetbreads with pea and mint
puree, chorizo, and caramelized
shallots, 352
tripe and trotters with chorizo, 322
Chutneys
apple and grape chutney, 438
apple and tomato chutney, 437
Ballymaloe green tomato chutney,
437
beet chutney, 439
Medjool date and coconut chutney,
439
red pepper, tomato, and lemongrass
chutney, 438
vegetable marrow and tomato
chutney, 437
Cider, 466–467
Cinnamon
ground, 499
roast apples with cinnamon cream,
498
Cleaning agents, natural, 582–583
Coastal plants, 70–73
Cockles, 58
cleaning, 58
cockles India-style, 58
cockles provençale, 59
Coconut
coconut buns, 533
Medjool date and coconut chutney,
439
raspberry and coconut slice, 550
Cod
brandade de morue with piquillo
pepper and arugula leaves, 106
salt cod, 106
salt cod croquettes with garlic and
saffron aioli, 107
Cod roe
poached cod roe with anchovy
butter, 101
poached cod roe with herb
butter, 101
smoked cod roe, 484
taramasalata, 101
Coeur à la crème with summer berries,
228
Coffee
coffee buttercream icing, 531
coffee buttercream, 531
coffee cake, 531
coffee icing, 531
Lana's coffee and walnut cookies, 549

tiramisu, 230
Colcannon, 384
Comfrey, 22, 366
comfrey fritters, 22–23
comfrey or nettle tea, 366
Compost, 364–365
Cookies
almond and apricot squares, 553
bizcochitos, 316
butter cookies, 218
classic shortbread, 550
digestive cookies, 549
Doune McKenzie's cheese crisps,
233
ginger nuts, 548
grown-up chocolate and salted toffee
squares, 553
homemade crackers, 231
Lana's coffee and walnut
cookies, 549
millionaire's squares, 553
nut and butter cookies, 218
oatcakes, 549
orange butter cookies, 218
raspberry and coconut slice, 550
shortbread cookies, 548
spiced butter cookies, 218
spiced orange squares, 552
Sue's orange and pecan squares,
552
toffee and walnut squares, 552
tray bakes, 550–553
Coriander, 368, 369
Cowslip, 32
cowslip fritters, 32
Crab, 114
Ballymaloe crab soup, 116
buying, 114
claws, 114
cooking, 115
crab and wild garlic tarts, 31
crab cakes, 115
crab mayo, 115
meat, extracting, 115
old-fashioned hot dressed crab,
118
potted crab with Melba toast, 116
spider crabs, cooking, 115
Crabapples, 39
crabapple and blackberry tart, 41
crabapple and elderberry jelly, 40
crabapple and rose geranium jelly, 40
crabapple and rosemary jelly, 40
crabapple and rowanberry jelly, 40
crabapple and sage jelly, 40
crabapple and sloe jelly, 40
crabapple jelly, 40
pickled crabapples, 39
rose petal and crabapple jelly, 40
Cranberries
cranberry and apple jam, 446
spiced cranberry sauce, 271
Crayfish
humane cooking of, 113
potted crayfish, 110

Cream
Billy's cream pastry, 209
chocolate crème Anglaise, 204
clotted cream, 211
cooking with, 203
crème Anglaise, 204
milk, separating from, 202
skimming, 202
sour cream shortcrust pastry, 210
sour cream, 210–211
traditional cream dressing, 209
types of, 202
whipping, 203
Crème brûlée
classic, 204
crème brûlée ice cream, 205
crème brûlée with praline
topping, 205
lavender crème brûlée, 205
peach leaf crème brûlée, 205
Crème de cassis, 464–465
Crêpes
beestings pancakes, 197
Florence Bowe's "crumpets,"
580–581
Rachel's chocolate crumpets, 581
Rachel's drop scones, 581
Russian fluffy pancakes, 200
savory crêpe batter, 580
Crubeens, 319
Arbutus Lodge crubeens, 324
Crystallizing, 458–459
Cucumber
cucumber and dill sauce, 481
cucumber, radish, feta, parsley,
and nigella seed salad, 417
pig's ear with radish and
cucumber salad, 322
pomegranate and cucumber raita,
223
radish, cucumber, and mint salad, 417
rosette of smoked salmon with
sweet cucumber pickle, 488
Cupcakes
Bath buns, 545
bun wash, 543
butterfly cupcakes, 533
Chelsea buns, 544
cherry buns, 545
coconut cupcakes, 533
fairy cakes, 532–533
glacé iced buns, 544
hot cross buns, 546–547
iced cupcakes, 533
iced whirls, 544
raspberry buns, 540
walnut or pecan sticky buns, 546
Custard
homemade, 506, 510
baked bay leaf custard, 207

D

Damsons, 41
compote of damsons, 43

damson and apple sauce, 41
damson fool, 43
damson or plum sauce, 41
damson gin, 45
damson sauce, 41
damson vodka, 45
wild damson and apple jam, 445
Dandelion, 22
Dandelion wine, 466
Darina Allen's iced Christmas cake, 536

Dates
Medjool date and coconut chutney, 439
Desserts, 492
Dick Keating's original Tipperary cider, 466–467
Dill, 369
dill butter, 217
Doughnuts, 543
jam doughnuts, 544
Doune McKenzie's cheese crisps, 233
Dover sole
grilled Dover sole on the bone, 84
skinning, 85
Drinks
apple cider, 467
apricot or peach ratafia, 465
blackberry and rose geranium cordial, 37
black currant cordial, 469
black currant leaf lemonade, 469
cherry brandy, 464
crème de cassis, 464–465
damson gin, 45
damson vodka, 45
dandelion wine, 466
Dick Keating's original Tipperary cider, 466–467
elderflower bellini, 471
elderflower cordial, 469
elderflower fizz, 471
hawthorn brandy, gin or vodka, 23
homemade lemonade, 468
limoncello, 464
loganberry cordial, 469
orange brandy, 464
raspberry lemonade, 468
Roger Phillips' gorse wine, 35
Roger's nettle beer, 25
sloe gin, 45
sloe vodka, 45
Ted's ginger beer, 471
Drying, 460–463
Duck, 138, 274–277
breast, smoking, 480
confit de canard, 280
confit of duck legs with Puy lentils, roast parsnips, and roast potatoes, 280–281
cured duck hams, 281
duck confit quiche, 281
duck, ginger, and noodle broth, 279
duck gizzards cooked in duck fat, 283

duck hams with white beans, 283
duck liver pâté with Melba toast, 268
duck rillettes, 278
duck stock, 262
duck with Seville orange marmalade sauce, 278
eggs. See Eggs
fat, 276–277
jointing, 276
pan-grilling, 277
ragout of duck wings, 278–279
roast duck with potato stuffing, 285
roast pintail, 139
roast shoveler, 139
roast teal, 139
roast widgeon, 139
roast wild mallard stuffed with Jerusalem artichokes, 139
roast wild mallard with potato and parsnip stuffing, 139
roast wild mallard, 138–139
salade de gésiers, 283
traditional roast duck with sage and onion stuffing and apple sauce, 278

E
Eel
fresh fried eel, 95
kelp and smoked seafood salad, 69
smoked eel with lemon and horseradish cream, 103
Eggs, 233–237
bacon and egg pie, 313
buttered eggs, 250
crispy deep-fried eggs, 247
crispy eggs with bacon and tomato fondue, 246
duck-egg sponge cake, 255
duck eggs, 254–255, 274
dyeing with onion skins, 388–389
eggs Benedict, 248
egg wash, 539
free-range, 244
freshness, testing, 244–245
hard-boiled, 246
leftover whites and yolks, using, 253
omelettes. See Omelettes
organic, 244
perfect poached eggs on toast, 247
pickled eggs, 253
quail eggs, 255
quiche Lorraine, 250
salad of quail eggs with smoked venison and avocado, 255
salad with duck eggs, Parmesan, roasted red pepper, and asparagus, 254
salmonella, 242
scrambled eggs, 246
sea urchins with scrambled egg, 65

smoked egg, chorizo, and arugula salad, 489
smoked eggs, 485
soft-boiled eggs with soda bread "soldiers," 245
storing, 245
Swiss salade frisée with bacon and oeufs mollet, 313, 315
watercress salad with duck eggs and olives, 28
whites, whisking, 252
Elder, 34
Elderberries, 43
crabapple and elderberry jelly, 40
elderberry syrup, 43
frozen elderberries, 43
partridge wrapped in vine leaves with elderberries, 135
plum and elderberry jam, 447
Elderflowers, 34
Ballymaloe green gooseberry and elderflower tart, 501
elderflower bellini, 471
elderflower cordial, 469
elderflower fizz, 471
elderflower fritters, 35
elderflower vinegar, 34–35
Glenny's elderflower and lemon ice cream, 209
green gooseberry and elderflower compote, 35
green gooseberry and elderflower jam, 444–445
Elephants' ears, 219
Emer Fitzgerald's braised lamb neck moussaka, 348–349
Emer's wholegrain mustard, 429
Endive
partridge with braised endive, 136
Eve's pudding, 502

F
Faggots, 325–326
Farro with fava beans, peas, asparagus, and arugula, 402
Fat hen, 26
Fennel, 369
fennel butter, 217
salsiccia e finocchio, 300–301
slow-roasted pork chump with braised fennel, 296
Figs
figgy toffee pudding, 505
Fish. See also Salmon, etc.
Asian ceviche, 80
baked flat fish with herb butter, 85
baked on the bone, 85–89
basic fish stock, 80–81
classic fish pie, 90
fish and chips, 94
fish baked in a salt crust, 86
fish cooked in fig leaves with fresh herb butter, 89
flat, filleting, 79

fish fingers, 95
fresh and smoked seafood chowder, 81
fresh, buying, 78
frying, 94–97
grilled whole round fish on the bone, 84
gutting, 78
household fish stock, 81
pan-grilled fish with flavored butter, 82
pan-grilling, 82–85
poaching, 91–93
preparation, 78
preserving, 104–107
roe, 100–103
round, filleting, 79
salt, 107
scaling, 78
seasoning, 79
skinning, 79
smoked fish with horseradish sauce and sweet dill mayonnaise, 488
soused sprats, herrings, or mackerel with tomatoes and mustard seed, 107
smoked, 103
tickling, 89
Flapjacks, 550
Florence Bowe's "crumpets," 580–581
Flour, weevils in, 523
Flowers, edible, 373
Forager's salad, 18
Forager's soup, 18
Foraging, 8, 16–17
forager's salad, 18
forager's soup, 18
foraging year, 20–31
Fraughans, 38
crushed fraughans, 38
Emer Fitzgerald's fraughan scones, 38
French dressing, 374
French wafers, 219
Fruit. See also Apples, etc.
coeur à la crème with summer berries, 228
drying, 460
fools, 43, 496–497
Mummy's plum pudding with Mrs. Hanrahan's sauce, 514
mustard fruits, 429
spiced fruit, 439
storing, 366, 453
summer pudding, 509
wild, 36–45
Fruit butters, 452
Fruit cheeses, 452–453
Fudge, 516

G

Game
age, determining, 124
barding and larding, 126

birds, 126–139. See also Grouse, etc.
deterioration, 124
examination of, 124
freezing, 125–126
game stock, 149
game terrine, 149
hanging, 124–125
hare, 140–143. See also Hare
hunting seasons, 123
rabbit, 140–142. See also Rabbit
revival, 122
venison, 144–148. See also Venison
young bird fallacy, 124
Garlic. See also Wild garlic 217
garlic butter, 217
roasted garlic oil, 426
Ginger
apple and ginger jam, 446
beet and ginger relish, 439
chicken breasts with mushrooms and ginger, 198
duck, ginger, and noodle broth, 279
ginger marmalade, 454
ginger nuts, 548
ginger syrup, 468
vegetable marrow, lemon, and ginger jam, 448–449
rhubarb and ginger jam, 447
Ted's ginger beer, 471
Gingerbread, 535
sticky gingerbread puddings, 504
Glenny's elderflower and lemon ice cream, 209
Globe artichokes, 419
globe artichokes with melted butter, 419
Goose, 284
cassoulet, 285–286
fat, uses for, 284
goose liver pâté, 286
goose, pomegranate, and pecan salad, 285
goose stock, 262
roast goose with quince, 285
stuffed goose neck, 286
traditional roast goose with potato stuffing and apple and rose geranium sauce, 284
whole, using, 287
wing, making, 287
Gooseberries
Ballymaloe green gooseberry and elderflower tart, 501
green gooseberry and elderflower compote, 35
green gooseberry and elderflower jam, 444–445
Gorse, 35
Roger Phillips' gorse wine, 35
Grapefruit
candied peel, 458
orange, lemon and grapefruit marmalade, 456
Grapes
apple and grape chutney, 438

Gravlax
beet gravlax, 106
gravlax with mustard and dill mayonnaise, 105
Gravy
beef, 156
browning for, 159
lamb, 337
Grey mullet
fish baked in a salt crust, 86
Ground-elder, 21
Grouse, 137
roast grouse, 137
Guinea hens, 272
guinea hen stock, 262
pan-roasted guinea hens with parsley sauce, 272
salad of smoked guinea hen with parsnip crisps and cranberry sauce, 488–489

H

Haddock
haddock with peperonata and buttered crumbs, 87
smoked, 483
Hake with tomatoes and swiss chard, 89
Ham
air-dried ham, 308
curing, 306–308
eggs Benedict, 248
fresh or smoked ham hocks, 324
glazed ham, 312
ham cooked in hay, 312
juniper berry brine, 311
Paddy Ward's wet-cure, 310
Philip's wet-cure, 310–311
Hamburgers, 172
Hare, 140
fillet of hare with mushrooms and cream, 143
gutting, 141
jointing, 141
skinning, 140
Tuscan pasta with hare sauce, 143
Harissa, 342
roast rolled shoulder of lamb with harissa, 342
Hawthorn, 23
hawthorn brandy, gin or vodka, 23
Haybox, 349
Hazelnuts, 46
hazelnut brittle, 47
hazelnut chocolate brownies, 46–47
melted chard stalks with bacon and hazelnuts, 396
mendiants, 46
yogurt with honey and toasted hazelnuts, 47
Heart
stuffed beef heart, 158

Helen Morgan's lime marmalade, 457
Helen Morgan's USA pickle, 430–431
Herbs, 367. See also Basil, etc.
  drying, 460
  fresh herb butter, 216
  herb and honey dressing, 374
  herb vinegar, 427
  hogget with garden herbs, 354
  homemade cottage cheese with
    fresh herbs and oatcakes, 227
  marrow bones with fresh herb
    salad, 165
  pork, sorrel, and fresh herb
    terrine, 20–21
Herrings
  pickled herring, 104
  rollmops with cucumber pickle and
    mustard and dill mayonnaise, 104
  soft herring roe pâté, 101
  soused sprats, herrings, or mackerel with
    tomatoes and mustard seed, 107
Hogget, 354
  ham, smoked, 487
  hogget with garden herbs, 354
  slow braised shoulder of hogget
    with garlic and thyme, 346
Hollandaise sauce, 248
Horse parsley, 70
Horseradish, 24
  horseradish mustard, 429
  horseradish sauce, 24
  preserved, 433
  smoked eel with lemon and
    horseradish cream, 103

I

Ice cream
  Ballymaloe praline ice cream, 208
  Ballymaloe vanilla ice cream, 207
  black currant ice cream, 496
  black currant swirl ice cream, 207
  brown bread ice cream, 208
  crème brûlée ice cream, 205
  Glenny's elderflower and lemon
    ice cream, 209
  rum and raisin, 208
  Seville orange marmalade ice cream, 208
  strawberry popsicles, 496
  vanilla bean ice cream, 209
  yogurt ice cream, 225
Ice cubes, flavored, 468
Icing
  Christmas cake icing, 536–537
  coffee buttercream icing, 531
  coffee icing, 531
  dark chocolate icing, 533
  glacé icing, 533
  lemon glacé icing, 533
  orange buttercream, 528
  orange glacé icing, 533
Irish apple cake, 500
Irish stew with pearl barley, 348

J

Jams and jellies, 440–441, 451
  apple and ginger jam, 446
  black currant jam, 444
  black currant jelly, 452
  blueberry and lemon verbena jam,
    446
  crabapple jelly or cooking apple jelly,
    40
  crabapple and elderberry jelly, 40
  crabapple and rowanberry jelly, 40
  crabapple and rosemary jelly, 40
  crabapple and sage jelly, 40
  crabapple and sloe jelly, 40
  cranberry and apple jam, 446
  dried apricot jam, 448
  fresh apricot jam, 448
  green gooseberry and elderflower
    jam, 444–445
  greengage jam, 446
  Janie's green tomato jam, 449
  japonica jelly, 452
  marmalade, 454–457. See also
    Marmalade
  medlar jelly, 451
  Mummy's strawberry jam, 447
  onion jam, 450
  peach or nectarine and sweet
    geranium jam, 447
  plum and apple jam, 445
  plum and elderberry jam, 447
  raspberry, boysenberry, or loganberry
    jam, 442
  red currant or white currant jelly,
    451
  rhubarb and ginger jam, 447
  rhubarb and raspberry jam, 448
  rose hip jelly, 44
  rose petal and crabapple jelly, 40
  savory, 449–450
  setting point, 441
  sterilizing jars, 430
  strawberry and red currant jam,
    442
  tomato and chile jam, 450
  uncooked raspberry jam, 442
  vegetable marrow, lemon, and ginger
    jam, 448–449
  Victoria plum jam, 446
  wild blackberry, apple, and rose
    geranium jam, 445
  wild damson and apple jam, 445
  wild strawberry jam, 44
Janie's green tomato jam, 449
Japonica jelly, 452
Jello, 494. See also Jams and
    jellies
  bilberry jelly with fresh mint
    cream, 38–39
  crabapple jelly, 40
  raspberry jello with mint, 495
  summer fruit jello with rose
    geranium cream, 495
Jerky, 185

Jerusalem artichokes, 417
  braised Jerusalem artichokes, 418
  roast Jerusalem artichokes, 418
  roast wild mallard stuffed with
    Jerusalem artichokes, 139
  warm salad of Jerusalem
    artichokes with hazelnut oil
    dressing, 418
Julija's Lithuanian beef goulash,
    168
Junket, 231

K

Kale, 412–413
  braised cavolo nero, 415
  cavolo nero bruschetta, 415
  cottiers kale, 415
  curly kale soup, 413
  curly kale with bacon and
    chestnuts, 413
  cut-and-come, 415
  hungry gap, 415
  kale pesto, 29
Kidneys
  Chinese pig kidney salad, 325
  kidneys and chorizo in fine
    sherry, 324
  lamb's kidneys in their overcoat, 353
  preparing, 324
  skirts and kidneys, 325
Kippers
  proper breakfast kippers, 103
  smoking, 483
Kumquats
  pickled kumquats and tangerine
    slices, 432–433
  kumquat marmalade, 456

L

Lamb, 332–333
  Ballymaloe Irish stew, 348
  braised lamb shanks with garlic,
    rosemary, and cannellini beans, 344
  breast of lamb with sea salt and
    coriander, 341
  butterflied leg of lamb with
    garlic and marjoram, 338
  cuts of, 334
  definitions, 335
  Emer Fitzgerald's braised lamb
    neck moussaka, 348–349
  epigrams, 341
  fat, 337
  gravy, 337
  guard of honor, 337, 341
  Irish stew with pearl barley, 348
  lamb à la boulangère and
    boulangère potatoes, 338
  lamb stock, 341
  lamb's kidneys in their overcoat,
    353
  lamb's liver with crispy sage
    leaves, 352

Moroccan lamb riblets, 342
Moroccan lamb tagine with
  tomatoes and honey, 347
offal, 350–353
rack of lamb, 336, 340
roast rolled shoulder of lamb
  with harissa, 342
roast spring lamb with mint
  sauce, 338–339
roast stuffed loin of lamb with
  mushroom and marjoram, 339
roast stuffed loin of lamb with
  roast peppers, tapenade, and
  basil, 340
roasting, 336–338
shepherd's pie, 342–343
slow-braised shoulder of lamb with
  garlic and thyme, 346
slow cooking, 344–347
slow roasted shoulder of lamb
  with coriander seeds, 347
slow roasted shoulder of lamb
  with cumin, 347
spicy lamb burgers with mint,
  yogurt, and arugula, 343
spicy ground lamb with marjoram, 343
stews, 348–349
sweetbreads. See Sweetbreads
traditional patterns, 337
Lana's coffee and walnut cookies,
  549
Lard, 316
Lemon
candied peel, 458
fluffy lemon pudding, 504
Glenny's elderflower and lemon
  ice cream, 209
lemon cornmeal cake with lemon
  curd and sour cream, 532
lemon curd, 224
lemon glacé icing, 533
lemon mayonnaise, 62
lemon sugar, 527
Lydia's lemon cake with
  crystallized violets and
  angelica, 33
orange, lemon and grapefruit
  marmalade, 456
vegetable marrow, lemon, and ginger
  jam, 448–449
yogurt cake with lemon curd and
  sour cream, 224
Lemon balm, 369
Lemon verbena, 369
blueberry and lemon verbena jam,
  446
lemon verbena sorbet, 495–496
Lemonade
black currant leaf lemonade, 469
homemade, 468
raspberry lemonade, 468
Lentils
confit of duck legs with Puy
  lentils, roast parsnips, and
  roast potatoes, 280–281

pigs' tails with Puy lentils,
  328–329
Limes
Helen Morgan's lime marmalade,
  457
Limoncello, 464
Limpets, 59, 61
bairneachs with bacon, 61
Liver
calves' livers with caramelized
  onion, 183
chicken. See Chicken livers
Danish pâté, 326
lamb's liver with crispy sage
  leaves, 352
pig liver pâté, 327–328
venison, 144
venison liver with bubble and
  squeak, 148
Lobster, 112
buying, 112
handling, 112
hot buttered lobster, 113
humane cooking of, 113
lobster bisque, 112
lobster cooked in seawater, 113
lobster on brown bread with
  mayonnaise, 113
meat, extracting, 112–113
potted lobster, 110
Loganberries
loganberry cordial, 469
loganberry jam, 442
Lovage, 369–370
Lydia's lemon cake with
  crystallized violets and
  angelica, 33

M

Mackerel, 95
Alicia's soused mackerel, 104–105
crispy deep-fried mackerel with
  tartare sauce, 95
hot-smoked mackerel, 481
mackerel with almond migas, 84–85
marinated mackerel, 105
rollmops with cucumber pickle and
  mustard and dill mayonnaise, 104
smoked mackerel omelette, 488
smoking, 480–481
soused sprats, herrings, or mackerel with
  tomatoes and mustard seed, 107
warm poached mackerel with sauce
  de Quimper, 93
Marjoram, 370
Marmalade, 454
bitter orange marmalade, 456
duck with Seville orange
  marmalade sauce, 278
ginger marmalade, 454
green tomato marmalade, 457
Helen Morgan's lime marmalade,
  457
kumquat marmalade, 456

marmalade pudding, 512
orange, lemon, and grapefruit
  marmalade, 456
Seville orange marmalade cake,
  540
Seville orange marmalade ice
  cream, 208
Seville whole orange marmalade,
  454
whiskey marmalade, 454
Marsh samphire, 72–73
marsh samphire with melted
  butter, 73
pickled samphire, 73
Marshmallows, 516–517
Mary Keane's Listowel mutton pies,
  357
Mayonnaise, 252–253
Medlar jelly, 451
Membrillo, 453
Mendiants, 46
Meringue
break all the rules meringue,
  515
meringue cake, 515
meringue roulade, 515
pastel meringues, 515
Michael Cuddigan's pickled ox
  tongue, 187
Micro greens, 373
Milk, 192–193
beestings, 197
beestings curd, 197
beestings pancakes, 197
buttermilk. See Buttermilk
cooking in, 197–198
cream separating from, 202
fat content, 196
goat's, 196
homogenized, 196
organic, 196
pasteurized, 194
pork cooked in milk, 197
sleepy milk, 201
sour milk, 198–199
storing, 196
unpasteurized, 194
warming or heating, 196
Mincemeat
Ballymaloe mincemeat, 512
winter apple and mincemeat
  pudding, 511
Minnows, fried, 96
Mint, 370
bilberry jelly with fresh mint
  cream, 38–39
mint butter, 216
mint sauce, 339
mushy peas with mint, 397
potato and mint leaf salad, 386
radish, cucumber, and mint salad,
  417
raspberry jelly with mint, 495
spicy lamb burgers with mint,
  yogurt, and arugula, 343

sweetbreads with pea and mint puree, chorizo, and caramelized shallots, 352
Mrs. Hanrahan's sauce, 514
Mrs. Lamb's layer cake, 526
Muesli
  blackberry and apple muesli, 37
Mushrooms
  baked plaice with chanterelles, 54
  ceps, 54
  chanterelles à la crème, 53, 54
  chanterelles on buttered toast, 53
  chanterelles, 53
  chicken breasts with field mushrooms and ginger, 198
  chicken with morels, 54, 55
  crispy puffball, 55
  dried porcini oil, 426
  drying, 462
  field mushrooms, 48
  fillet of hare with mushrooms and cream, 143
  flat mushrooms, 48
  foraging for, 17
  Grandpoppy's mushroom ketchup, 56
  horse mushroom, 53
  morels, 54
  pavement mushrooms, 55
  pheasant, bacon, and wild mushroom casserole with scallion champ, 133
  pickled mushrooms, 56
  pigeon breasts with field mushrooms and tarragon, 129
  porcini, 54
  preserving, 56
  puffball, 55
  roast rosé veal with morels, 179
  roast stuffed loin of lamb with mushroom and marjoram, 339
  wild, 48–55
  wild mushrooms à la crème, 50
  wild mushroom and potato gratin, 50, 51
  wild mushroom soup, 48, 50
  wild mushroom vol au vents, 50
  wild mushrooms in oil, 56
  wild or flat mushroom frittata, 51
  wood blewit, 53
Mussels, 62
  cleaning, 62
  cooking, 62
  freshness, checking for, 62
  moules provençale, 64
  mussels with homemade mayonnaise, 62
  smoked, 484
Mustard
  Emer's wholegrain mustard, 429
  English mustard, 429
  horseradish mustard, 429
  mustard and parsley butter, 217
  mustard fruits, 429
Mutton, 354
  boiled leg of mutton with caper sauce, 354–355

ham, smoked, 487
Mary Keane's Listowel mutton pies, 357
mutton broth, 355

N

Nasturtiums
  cottage cheese with nasturtium flowers, 227
  nasturtium butter, 217
Natural remedies, 583
Navelwort, 26
Nectarines
  drying, 460
  nectarine and rose geranium jam, 447
Nettles, 24
  Irish nettle soup, 25
  nettle champ, 25
  nettle tea, 366
  Roger's nettle beer, 25
Noreen Conroy's homemade sausages, 300
Nougat, 517
Nuts. See also Hazelnuts, etc.
  nut and butter cookies, 218
  srikhand, 223
  wild, 46–47

O

Oils
  basil oil, 424
  chile oil, 426
  dried porcini oil, 426
  flavored, 424
  roasted garlic oil, 426
Olives
  tapenade, 340
Omelettes
  cheese soufflé omelette, 249
  classic French omelette, 248–249
  omelette fines herbes, 249
  tansy omelette, 27
  wild or flat mushroom frittata, 51
Onions, 388
  buttermilk onion rings, 200
  calves' livers with caramelized onion, 183
  champ, 383–384
  chicken liver pâté with caramelized onions, 268
  eggs, dyeing, 388–389
  French onion soup, 389
  gratin Lyonnais, 385
  melted scallions with marjoram or thyme leaves, 389
  onion jam, 450
  onion rings, 390
  onion sauce, 389
  pheasant, bacon, and wild mushroom casserole with scallion champ, 133
  potato and scallion salad, 386

roast onion halves, 390
roast onions, 390
Oranges
  Aunt Florence's orange cake, 528–529
  candied peel, 458
  chocolate candied orange, 458
  clementine syrup cake, 504
  marmalade, 454–457. See also Marmalade
  orange brandy, 464
  orange butter cookies, 218
  orange butter filling, 528–529
  orange glacé icing, 528–529, 533
  orange sugar, 527
  peel, drying, 461
  pickled kumquats and tangerine slices, 432–433
  spiced orange squares, 552
  Sue's orange and pecan squares, 552
Oxtail
  leftover oxtail stew, 163
  oxtail with grainy mustard sauce, 163
  shin of beef and oxtail stew, 162
Oysters, 118
  hot buttered oysters in the shell or on toast, 118–119
  opening, 118
  oysters au naturel, 118
  steak and oyster pie, 168

P

Palmiers, 219
Palourdes provençale, 59
Pancetta, 486
Paneer, 232
Panna cotta
  buttermilk panna cotta, 200
Parsley, 370
  mustard and parsley butter, 217
  parsley sauce, 272
  parsley sauce, 315
  traditional Irish bacon, cabbage, and parsley sauce, 315
Parsnips
  celeriac and mashed parsnip, 134
  parsnip chips, 489
  roast wild mallard with potato and parsnip stuffing, 139
Partridge, 135
  partridge with braised endive, 136
  partridge wrapped in vine leaves with elderberries, 135
  roast partridge, 135
Pasta
  pasta with roast chicken, raisins, pine nuts, and parsley, 265
  penne with tomato fondue, 378
  spaghetti with wild garlic and herbs, 30–31
  Tuscan pasta with hare sauce, 143

Pastrami, 186–187
Pastry
  basic shortcrust pastry, 250
  Billy's cream pastry, 209
  cheese straws, 219
  covering pie dish with, 147, 170
  elephants' ears, 219
  French wafers, 219
  pastry shells, 542
  puff pastry, 218–219
  shortcrust pastry made with lard, 316
  sour cream shortcrust pastry, 210
  suet pastry, 176
  sweet shortcrust pastry, 542
Pâtés and terrines
  Ballymaloe chicken liver pâté with Melba toast, 268
  chicken liver pâté with caramelized onions, 268
  chicken liver pâté with mushrooms, 268
  Danish pâté, 326
  duck, turkey, or pheasant liver pâté with Melba toast, 268
  game terrine, 149
  goose liver pâté, 286
  luting paste, 269
  pig liver pâté, 327–328
  soft herring roe pâté, 101
  terrine of chicken, 268–269
Peaches
  drying, 460
  peach and rose geranium jam, 447
  peach ratafia, 465
  pickled peaches, 432
Pears
  bottled pears, 434
  pickled pears, 431–432
  storing, 453
Peas, 397
  farro with fava beans, peas, asparagus, and arugula, 402
  mushy peas with mint, 397
  peapod soup, 397
  snow peas, 399
  sugar peas, 399
  sugar snaps, 399
  summer green pea soup, 399
  sweetbreads with pea and mint puree, chorizo, and caramelized shallots, 352
  wilted pea shoots, 399
Pecans
  goose, pomegranate and pecan salad, 285
  pecan sticky buns, 546
  Sue's orange and pecan squares, 552
Pennywort, 26
Peppers
  peperonata, 87
  red pepper, tomato and lemongrass chutney, 438
  salad with duck eggs, Parmesan, roasted red pepper, and asparagus, 254

Periwinkles, 61
  cleaning, 61
  periwinkles with homemade lemon mayonnaise, 62
Pesto
  arugula pesto, 29
  basil pesto, 29
  kale pesto, 29
  sun dried tomato pesto, 463
  wild garlic pesto, 29
Pheasant, 130
  pheasant, bacon, and wild mushroom casserole with scallion champ, 133
  pheasant braised with Cork gin, 133
  pheasant breast with paprika and Parmesan, 134
  pheasant liver pâté with Melba toast, 268
  pheasant stock, 262
  pheasant with chorizo, bacon, and tomatoes, 131
  salad of smoked pheasant with parsnip crisps and cranberry sauce, 488–489
  sautéed pheasant breasts with Savoy cabbage, 130–131
  traditional roast pheasant with all the trimmings, 130
Philip Dennhardt's homemade frankfurters, 301
Pickles
  Helen Morgan's USA pickle, 430–431
  jars, 430
  pickled beets, 431
  pickled blood plums, 432
  pickled cherries, 432
  pickled kumquats and tangerine slices, 432–433
  pickled peaches, 432
  pickled pears, 431–432
  pickled walnuts, 431
Pies
  bacon and egg pie, 313
  classic fish pie, 90
  Irish apple cake, 500
  Mary Keane's Listowel mutton pies, 357
  Mummy's apple pie, 500–501
  Mummy's country rhubarb cake, 499
  pastry, covering dish with, 147, 170
  shepherd's pie, 342–343
  steak and kidney pie, 170
  steak and oyster pie, 168
  venison and potato pie, 148
  venison pie, 147
  venison shepherd's pie, 145–146
  wood pigeon pie, 129
Pig's ear with radish and cucumber salad, 321
Pig's head with rutabaga, 321
Pigs' tails, 319
  crispy pig's tails with aioli, 329

pigs' tails with Puy lentils, 328–329
Pigs, 290–293
Plaice
  baked plaice with chanterelles, 54
Plums
  greengage jam, 446
  pickled blood plums, 432
  plum and apple jam, 445
  plum and elderberry jam, 447
  plum sauce, 41
  Victoria plum jam, 446
Pollock baked in cream and bay leaves, 86
Pomegranate
  goose, pomegranate, and pecan salad, 285
  pomegranate and cucumber raita, 223
Pork
  confit pork belly, 316–317
  crackling, 294
  curing, 306–308
  guanciale, 308
  juniper berry brine, 311
  meaning, 293
  pickled pork, 311
  pig liver pâté, 327–328
  pork and apple burgers, 296
  pork cooked in milk, 197
  pork osso bucco, 328
  pork, sorrel, and fresh herb terrine, 20–21
  pot-roasted pork steak, 294, 296
  roast pork with crackling and rhubarb sauce, 294
  skirts and kidneys, 325
  slow-roasted pork chump with braised fennel, 296
  smoked belly of pork, 486
  suckling pig with apple and rosemary jelly, 329
Pork rillettes, 326
Pork rinds, 320
Potatoes, 379
  baked potatoes, 381
  blue cheese and rosemary gratin, 385
  bubble and squeak, 384
  champ, 383–384
  colcannon, 384
  crispy potato skins with dips, 382
  dillisk champ, 68
  duchesse potatoes, 90
  game chips, 387
  gratin Dauphinous, 385
  gratin Lyonnais, 385
  gratin of potato, cheddar cheese, and seasonal greens, 384–385
  gratin Savoyard, 385
  growing, 380
  hand-cut potato fries, 386
  homemade potato chips, 387
  hot potato salad, 386
  lamb à la boulangère and boulangère potatoes, 338

mashed potato salad, 386
nettle champ, 25
pheasant, bacon, and wild mushroom
  casserole with scallion champ, 133
potato and mint leaf salad, 386
potato and scallion salad, 386
potato and wild garlic soup, 30
potato bread, 566
potato cakes, 384
potato soup, 380
potato stuffing, 284
roast potato salad, 383
roast potatoes, 382–383
roast wild mallard with potato
  and parsnip stuffing, 139
rustic roast potatoes, 383
scalloped potato with steak and
  kidney, 167
sprouting or chitting, 380
storage, 379
tiny potatoes dipped in aioli, 383
traditional Irish boiled
  potatoes, 382
venison and potato pie, 148
wild mushroom and potato gratin,
  50–51
Poultry, 256–259. See also Chicken, etc.
  bantams, 243
  basting, 264
  boning, 259
  breeds, 243
  carving, 260
  casserole roasting, 263–265
  chicken, day in the life of, 242–243
  giblets, 258
  gutting, 257–258
  hens, keeping, 238–242
  hybrids, 243
  plucking, 256
  singeing, 257
  terms, 243
  trussing, 258
Praline
  Ballymaloe praline ice cream, 208
  crème brûlée with praline
    topping, 205
Prawns, 108–112
  cooking, 108
  deep-fried prawns with tartare sauce, 110
  Dublin Bay, preparing, 109
  meat, extracting, 109
  potted prawns, 110
  prawn bisque, 112
  prawns on brown bread with
    mayonnaise, 110
  whole Ballycotton prawns in the
    shell, 109
Preserving, 422–423
Pumpkin, 403–404
  roast pumpkin, 407–408
  roasted pumpkin seeds, 409

Q

Quail, 272

eggs, 255
spatchcocked quail, 273
Queen of puddings, 512–513
Quiche Lorraine, 250
Quince
  membrillo, 453
  quince cheese, 453
  quince compote, 145
  roast goose with quince, 285
  storing, 453

R

Rabbit, 140
  gutting, 141
  jointing, 141
  Mummy's rabbit stew, 141
  rabbit stew with chorizo or cabanossi,
    141
  saddle of rabbit with cream,
    basil, and caramelized shallots,
    142
  skinning, 140
Rachel's chocolate crumpets, 581
Rachel's drop scones, 581
Radishes, 416
  cucumber, radish, feta, parsley,
    and nigella seed salad, 417
  pig's ear with radish and
    cucumber salad, 322
  radish, cucumber, and mint salad,
    417
  radish leaf soup, 417
  radishes with butter, sea salt,
    and crusty bread, 416
Raspberries
  raspberry and coconut slice, 550
  raspberry buns, 540
  raspberry coulis, 228
  raspberry fool with shortbread
    cookies, 497
  raspberry jam, 442
  raspberry jelly with mint, 495
  raspberry lemonade, 468
  raspberry vinegar, 427
  rhubarb and raspberry compote,
    494
  rhubarb and raspberry jam, 448
  uncooked raspberry jam, 442
Ray, 100
  warm ray wing with wild garlic
    and black olive pesto, 100
Razor clams, 64
  cleaning, 64
  pan-grilled razor clams with
    garlic butter, 64
  razor clam risotto, 64
Red currants
  red currant jelly, 451
  red currant juice, 441
  strawberry and red currant jam,
    442
Relish
  beet and ginger relish, 439
  spiced fruit, 439

Rhubarb
  carrageen moss pudding with
    rhubarb and sweet cicely
    compote, 66, 68
  Mummy's country rhubarb cake, 499
  rhubarb and ginger jam, 447
  rhubarb and raspberry jam, 448
  rhubarb and strawberry and
    raspberry compote, 494
  rhubarb compote, 494
Rice
  old-fashioned rice pudding, 499
  razor clam risotto, 64
  rice pilaf, 131
Rock samphire, 72–73
  pickled samphire, 73
  rock samphire with melted butter,
    73
Rollmops with cucumber pickle and
  mustard and dill mayonnaise, 104
Rory O'Connell's tomato ketchup, 433
Rose geranium, 370
  blackberry and rose geranium
    cordial, 37
  apple and rose geranium compote,
    494
  blackberry and rose geranium
    sorbet, 37
  crabapple and rose geranium jelly,
    40
  peach or nectarine and rose
    geranium jam, 447
  rose geranium syrup, 468
  summer fruit jelly with rose
    geranium cream, 495
  wild blackberry, apple, and rose
    geranium jam, 445
Rose hip, 44
  rose hip jelly, 44
  rose hip syrup, 44
Rose petal and crabapple jelly, 40
Rose petal syrup, 459
Rosemary, 370–371
  crabapple and rosemary jelly, 40
  rosemary butter, 216
  rosemary syrup, 468
Rosewater, 459
Roux, 165
Rowanberries
  crabapple and rowanberry jelly, 40
Rum and raisin ice cream, 208
Rum butter, 217
Rutabaga
  pig's head with rutabaga, 321

S

Sage, 371
  crabapple and sage jelly, 40
Salad dressing, 373
  French dressing, 374
  herb and honey dressing, 374
  traditional cream dressing, 209
Salads, 360–361, 372–373
  Chinese pig kidney salad, 325

forager's salad, 18
French dressing, 374
goose, pomegranate and pecan
     salad, 285
growing your own, 362–366
heirloom tomato salad with basil,
     olive oil, and honey, 377
hot potato salad, 386
kelp and smoked seafood salad, 69
marrow bones with fresh herb
     salad, 165
mashed potato salad, 386
old-fashioned salad with traditional
     cream dressing, 209
pig's ear with radish and
     cucumber salad, 322
potato and mint leaf salad, 386
potato and scallion salad, 386
radish, cucumber, and mint salad,
     417
roast potato salad, 383
rosette of smoked salmon with
     sweet cucumber pickle, 488
salad of quail eggs with smoked
     venison and avocado, 255
salad of smoked chicken, guinea
     fowl of pheasant with parsnip
     crisps and spiced cranberry sauce,
     488–489
salad of warm sweetbreads with
     potato chips, anchovies, and
     wild garlic, 350, 352
salad with duck eggs, Parmesan,
     roasted red pepper, and asparagus, 254
salade de gésiers, 283
smoked egg, chorizo, and arugula
     salad, 489
summer salad with a classic
     French dressing, 374
Swiss salade frisée with lardons
     and oeufs mollet, 313, 315
warm salad of Jerusalem
     artichokes with hazelnut oil
     dressing, 418
watercress salad with duck eggs
     and olives, 28
winter salad with herb and honey
     dressing, 374
zucchini salad with olive oil
     and sea salt, 405
Salami, 303
     casings, 304
     cultures, using, 304
     hanging, 304
     homemade, 304
     pork and beef salami, 305
Salmon
     beet gravlax, 106
     cold-smoked salmon, 482–483
     gravlax with mustard and dill
          mayonnaise, 105
     kelp and smoked seafood salad, 69
     piece, poached, 91
     rosette of smoked salmon with
          sweet cucumber pickle, 488

salmon cooked in newspaper, 88
whole fish baked in foil, 91–93
whole poached salmon, 92
wild salmon carpaccio, 80
wok-smoked salmon, 482
Salt, 307
Salting and brining, 478–481
Sauces
     aioli, 96–97
     anchoïde, 180
     apple and rose geranium sauce, 222
     apple sauce, 298
     Béarnaise sauce, 173–174
     Béchamel, 116
     bread sauce, 271
     caper sauce, 354–355
     cucumber and dill sauce, 481
     damson and apple sauce, 41
     damson sauce, 41
     garlic and saffron aioli, 97
     Grandpoppy's mushroom ketchup, 56
     Hollandaise sauce, 248
     horseradish sauce, 24
     lemon mayonnaise, 62
     mayonnaise, 252–253
     mint sauce, 339
     mornay, 119
     Mrs. Hanrahan's sauce, 514
     mustard and dill mayonnaise, 105
     onion sauce, 389
     parsley sauce, 272
     parsley sauce, 315
     plum sauce, 41
     red wine sauce for beef and
          steaks, 174
     Rory O'Connell's tomato ketchup, 433
     sauce de Quimper, 93
     spiced cranberry sauce, 271
     sweet chile sauce, 433
     tansy sauce, 27
     tartare sauce, 94
     traditional Irish bacon, cabbage,
          and parsley sauce, 315
Sausages, 297
     Ballymaloe homemade sausages,
          298
     bratwurst, 303
     casings, 297
     Cumberland sausages, 298, 300
     garlic and parsley sausages, 300
     Noreen Conroy's homemade
          sausages, 300
     paprika sausages, 301
     Philip Dennhardt's homemade
          frankfurters, 301
     rosé veal sausages, 181
     sage sausages, 300
     salsiccia e finocchio, 300–301
     saucissons de Toulouse, 300
     smoked, 487
Scallops, 119
     de-shelling, 119
     scallops mornay, 119
Scones
     brown griddle scones, 565

Emer Fitzgerald's fraughan
     scones, 38
Mummy's sweet fruit scones,
     538–539
Rachel's drop scones, 581
scones with clotted cream and
     jam, 211
white soda scones, 561
Sea beet, 70
Sea kale, 72
     sea kale with chervil hollandaise
          sauce, 72
Sea purslane, 72
Sea spinach, 70
     baked sea or rainbow trout with
          sea spinach butter sauce, 71
     sea spinach soup, 71
Sea urchin, 64, 65
     sea urchins with homemade
          mayonnaise, 65
     sea urchins with scrambled egg, 65
Seaweed, 65
     carrageen moss pudding with
          rhubarb and sweet cicely
          compote, 66, 68
     carrageen moss syrup, 68
     carrageen moss, 66
     dillisk bread, 68
     dillisk champ, 68
     dillisk sandwiches, 68
     dulse, 68
     Irish moss, 66
     kelp and smoked seafood salad, 69
     kelp, 68
     oarweed, 68
Seeds, drying, 460
Shallots
     caramelized shallots, 142–143
     shallots with thyme leaves, 389
     sweetbreads with pea and mint
          puree, chorizo, and caramelized
          shallots, 352
Shellfish. See also Mussels, etc.
     shellfish stock, 81
Shells, 59
Shepherd's pie, 342–343
Shortbread, classic, 550
Shrimp, 108–112
     cooking, 109
     meat, extracting, 109
     potted shrimp, 110
     shrimp on brown bread with
          mayonnaise, 110
     smoked, 484
Skate, 100
     skate with black butter, 100
Sloes, 45
     crabapple and sloe jelly, 40
     sloe and blackberry cheese, 45
     sloe gin, 45
     sloe vodka, 45
Smoking, home, 472–489
     basic process, 472
     cold smoking, 473–477, 479
     hot smoking, 472–478

Snipe, 136
  roast snipe, 136–137
Snowbell, 28–29
Sorbet
  blackberry and rose geranium
    sorbet, 37
  lemon verbena sorbet, 495–496
Sorrel, 20
  pork, sorrel, and fresh herb
    terrine, 20–21
Soup
  Ballymaloe crab soup, 116
  basic formula, 381
  beef consommé, 160
  consommé en geleé, 160
  curly kale soup, 413
  duck, ginger, and noodle broth,
    279
  fava bean-pod soup, 402
  forager's soup, 18
  freezing, 381
  French onion soup, 389
  fresh and smoked seafood chowder,
    81
  homemade tomato soup, 376–377
  Irish nettle soup, 25
  lobster bisque, 112
  mutton broth, 355
  pappa al pomodoro, 377
  peapod soup, 397
  potato and wild garlic soup, 30
  potato soup, 380
  prawn bisque, 112
  radish leaf soup, 417
  sea spinach soup, 71
  spiced cabbage soup, 409
  summer green pea soup, 399
  Thai-spiced squash soup with
    noodles, 408
  watercress salad with duck eggs
    and olives, 28
  watercress soup, 28
  wild mushroom soup, 48, 50
  zucchini soup with curry spices,
    407
Spinach, 394
  cooking methods, 395
  creamed spinach, 395
  fried spinach leaves, 395
  hake with tomatoes and Swiss chard
  spinach stalks, 395
  stringing, 395
  wilted, 395
Spotted dick, 510
Sprats, 96
  deep-fried sprats with aioli,
    96–97
  deep-fried sprats with garlic and
    saffron aioli, 97
  smoked, 483
  soused sprats, herrings, or mackerel with
    tomatoes and mustard seed, 107
Squash, 403–404
  squash with basil or marjoram,
    408

Thai-spiced squash soup with
  noodles, 408
Squid, 98
  chargrilled squid with chile and
    parsley oil and chorizo, 99
  deep-fried squid, 98–99
  squid provençale, 99
Srikhand, 223
Steamed puddings, 510–514
Stews. See Casseroles and stews
Stock
  basic fish stock, 80–81
  beef stock, 159
  brown veal stock, 182
  calves' foot, 182
  chicken stock, 262
  demi-glace, 159, 262
  demi-glace de poisson, 81
  game stock, 149
  giblet stock, 262
  glace de poisson, 81
  glace de viande, 159
  goose or duck stock, 262
  household fish stock, 81
  lamb stock, 341
  pheasant or guinea hen stock, 262
  safe, determining, 159
  shellfish stock, 81
  turkey stock, 262
  veal stock, 182
  vegetable stock, 390
Stock syrup, 468
Strawberries
  bottled strawberries, 434
  fresh strawberry coulis, 228
  Mummy's strawberry jam, 447
  rhubarb and strawberry compote,
    494
  strawberry and red currant jam,
    442
  strawberry popsicles, 496
  wild, 44
  wild strawberry jam, 44
  wild strawberry cake, 44
Suet, 176
  herb dumplings, 176
  steak and kidney pudding, 176–177
  steamed suet puddings, 512–514
  suet pastry, 176
Summer pudding, 509
Sweet cicely, 371
  carrageen moss pudding with
    rhubarb and sweet cicely
    compote, 66, 68
Sweetbreads, 350
  preparing, 350
  salad of warm sweetbreads with
    potato chips, anchovies, and
    wild garlic, 350, 352
  sweetbreads with pea and mint
    puree, chorizo, and caramelized
    shallots, 352
Syrups and cordials, 468–471

T

Tansy, 26
  tansy omelette, 27
  tansy sauce, 27
Tapenade, 340
Taramasalata, 101
Tarragon, 371
  pigeon breasts with field
    mushrooms and tarragon, 129
  poulet a l'estragon, 263
  tarragon vinegar, 427
Tartare sauce, 94
Tarts
  Ballymaloe green gooseberry and
    elderflower tart, 501
  crab and wild garlic tarts, 31
  crabapple and blackberry tart, 41
  duck confit quiche, 281
  jam tarts and tartlets, 543
  quiche Lorraine, 250
  tarte tatin with sour cream
    shortcrust pastry, 210–211
Tayberry jam, 442
Ted's ginger beer, 471
Thrifty cooking, 11–12
Thyme, 371
Tiramisu, 230
Tomatoes, 375
  apple and tomato chutney, 437
  Ballymaloe green tomato chutney,
    437
  crispy eggs with bacon and tomato
    fondue, 246
  drying, 462–463
  French beans with tomato fondue, 402
  green tomato marmalade, 457
  hake with tomatoes and swiss chard, 89
  heirloom tomato salad with basil,
    olive oil, and honey, 377
  homemade tomato soup, 376–377
  Janie's green tomato jam, 449
  meatballs with fresh tomato
    sauce, 172
  Moroccan lamb tagine with
    tomatoes and honey, 347
  oven-roasted tomatoes, 376
  pappa al pomodoro, 377
  penne with tomato fondue, 378
  peperonata, 87
  pheasant with chorizo, bacon, and
    tomatoes, 131
  red pepper, tomato, and lemongrass
    chutney, 438
  Rory O'Connell's tomato ketchup,
    433
  semi-dried, 463
  sun dried tomato pesto, 463
  sun-dried, 463
  tomato and chile fondue, 378
  tomato and chile jam, 450
  tomato, bean, and rosemary stew,
    378
  tomato fondue, 378
  tomato paste, 376
  tripe with tomatoes, 184

vegetable marrow and tomato
chutney, 437
Tongue
Michael Cuddigan's pickled ox
tongue, 187
Treacle pudding, 510
Treacle toffees, 516
Trifle
Mummy's traditional Irish sherry
trifle, 506
Tripe, 184
tripe and trotters with chorizo, 322
tripe with onions, 184
tripe with tomatoes, 184
Trotters, 319
Arbutus Lodge crubeens, 324
tripe and trotters with chorizo, 322
Trout
baked sea or rainbow trout with
sea spinach butter sauce, 71
whole fish baked in foil, 91–93
Turkey, 270
brining, 270
old-fashioned roast turkey with
chestnut stuffing and bread
sauce, 270–271
turkey liver pâté with Melba toast,
268
turkey stock, 262
Turkish delight, 517

V

Vanilla
Ballymaloe vanilla ice cream, 207
homemade extract, 527
vanilla bean ice cream, 209
vanilla sugar, 527
Veal, 179
brown veal stock, 182
calves' foot, 182
calves' livers with caramelized
onion, 183
classic blanquette of veal, 180
osso bucco alla Milanese, 181–182
roast loin of rosé veal with
anchoïde, 180–181
roast rosé veal with morels, 179
rosé veal chop with sage leaves, 179
rosé veal sausages, 181
veal stock, 182
Wiener schnitzel, 181
Vegetable marrow, 403
vegetable marrow and tomato
chutney, 437
vegetable marrow in cheese sauce,
406–407
vegetable marrow, lemon, and ginger
jam, 448–449
roast stuffed vegetable marrow, 406
stuffed vegetable marrow for one, 406
Vegetables, 360–361. See also
Onions, etc.
growing your own, 362–366
leftover, uses for, 419

oven-roasted winter root
vegetables with rosemary and
thyme leaves, 394
storing, 366
vegetable stock, 390
Venison, 144
carcass, examining, 144
cooking with, 144
liver, 144
potted venison with juniper
berries, 148
roast haunch of venison with
quince and rosemary gravy, 145
salad of quail eggs with smoked
venison and avocado, 255
smoked haunch of, 487
venison and potato pie, 148
venison burgers, 148
venison liver with bubble and
squeak, 148
venison pie, 147
venison shepherd's pie, 145–146
venison stew with chestnuts, 146
Vinegar
elderflower vinegar, 34–35
flavored, 424, 427
herb vinegar, 427
meaning, 426–427
raspberry vinegar, 427
tarragon vinegar, 427
violet vinegar, 427
Violet, 32
crystallized violets, 32–33
Lydia's lemon cake with
crystallized violets and
angelica, 33
violet prosecco, 427
violet vinegar, 427

W

Walnuts
Lana's coffee and walnut
cookies, 549
pickled walnuts, 431
toffee and walnut squares, 552
walnut sticky buns, 546
Watercress, 27
watercress butter, 216
watercress pesto, 29
watercress soup, 28
White puddings, 318–319
Whitebait, 96
deep-fried whitebait with aioli,
96–97
deep-fried whitebait with garlic
and saffron aioli, 97
whitebait fritters with a lemon
wedge, 96
White currant jelly, 451
Wild flowers, 32–35
Wild garlic, 28–29
crab and wild garlic tarts, 31
potato and wild garlic soup, 30
salad of warm sweetbreads with

potato crisps, anchovies, and
wild garlic, 350, 352
spaghetti with wild garlic and
herbs, 30–31
wild garlic butter, 216
wild garlic pesto, 29
Wood pigeon, 128
marinating, 128
pigeon breasts with field
mushrooms and tarragon, 129
skinning, 128
wood pigeon pie, 129
Woodcock, 136
roast woodcock, 136–137

Y

Yeast bun dough, 543
Yogurt, 220
beet tzatziki, 223
bhapa doi, 224
flavored, 222
labne bil zeyt, 225
labne, 225
making, 220, 222
marinated labne, 225
pomegranate and cucumber raita,
223
soft yogurt cheese, 225
spicy lamb burgers with mint,
yogurt, and arugula, 343
srikhand, 223
steamed sweetened yogurt, 224
uses for, 223
yogurt cake with lemon curd and
sour cream, 224
yogurt ice cream, 225
yogurt with honey and toasted
hazelnuts, 47
Yorkshire pudding, 156

Z

Zucchini, 403
ajlouk de zucchini, 405
deep-fried zucchini flowers, 405
zucchini in cheese sauce,
406–407
zucchini salad with olive oil
and sea salt, 405
zucchini soup with curry spices,
407

Acknowledgements

I once heard my publisher introducing me as, "my author who doesn't start to write the book in earnest until the deadline has passed." Oops. So I have to begin by thanking Kyle Cathie for her patience and endurance, closely followed by my long-suffering editor Jenny Wheatley, plus Susan Rossi-Crean and Stephanie Evans who were drafted in to check my copy.

Many others egged me on and helped in myriad ways. Nathalie Jordi struggled to interpret my scrawls and typed late into the night for months on end. Ide Ní Laoghaire was also very helpful in the early stages. At the Ballymaloe Cookery School, Sharon Hogan, Adrienne Forbes, and Susan McKeown did their best to help me out on top of their already heavy workload. Emer Fitzgerald tested and retested recipes until we were happy with the result. Mamie Hayes baked cookies and cakes. Philip Dennhardt cured and smoked. Eileen O'Donovan, Haulie Welsh, and all our gardeners and farmers provided wonderful produce for the recipes.

Many artisan producers were especially generous with their information – Dick and Anne Keating shared their knowledge of cider and cheese making, Sally Barnes gave wise advice on smoking, and Dr. Prannie Rhatigan shared her knowledge of seaweed. Helen Morgan contributed her secret jam and pickle recipes. Tom Duane, George Gossip, and Peter Lawton were generous with their knowledge of game and country living.

Eddie O'Neill and Sarah McSweeney at Moorepark Dairy Research Station were ever ready to clarify my queries as was Paddy Ward of Ashtown Food Research.

I can't remember exactly when I started this book. I've had conversations and encouragement from hundreds of people, so to all of them and the entire team at the Cookery School and my ever-supportive family, a huge thank you.

Last, but certainly not least, a very special mention to Peter Cassidy for the stunning photographs that bring the book to life. Thanks also to Linda Tubby, who makes my food look beautiful, and to Lucy Gowans and Carl Hodson for the inspired design. My daughter Lydia drew the spirited illustrations.

Thanks also to:
Myrtle Allen, Rory O'Connell, Roger Goodwillie, Veronica Steele, Michael Cuddigan, Frank Murphy, Michael Woulfe, Mary Taafe, Gerry Moynihan, Alison Henderson, Annie Dawes, Claire Ptak, Carmel Somers, Tim Cogan, Giana Ferguson, Sophie Miall, Susan Turner, and Harry Eastwood.

I am enormously grateful to everyone who generously shared their knowledge with me and hope I will be forgiven for any omissions.